Using 1-2-3®
Release 3

Developed by
Que® Corporation

CORPORATION
LEADING COMPUTER KNOWLEDGE

Using 1-2-3®
Release 3

Library of Congress Catalog No.: 89-60845
ISBN No.: 0-88022-440-1

92 91 90 89   8 7 6 5 4 3 2 1

Interpretation of the printing code: the rightmost double-digit number is the year of the book's printing; the rightmost single-digit number, the number of the book's printing. For example, a printing code of 89-1 shows that the first printing of the book occurred in 1989.

Appendix B.
Copyright © 1989 Lotus Development Corporation.
Used with permission.

Using 1-2-3 Release 3 is based on Release 3 of 1-2-3.

ABOUT THE AUTHORS

The team of authors who worked on this title is nearly as large and diverse as the book itself.

Ron Person is the author or coauthor of more than 10 books for Que Corporation, including *Using Excel: IBM Version* and *Using Microsoft Windows*. His firm, Ron Person & Co., based in San Francisco, trains and supports corporations nationwide in Excel and strategic Windows and OS/2 Presentation Manager applications.

Bill Weil works extensively with 1-2-3 and Symphony, and contributed also to Que's *1-2-3 Tips, Tricks, and Traps*, 2nd Edition. Weil, who has 20 years of experience with computers of all sizes, formed Pacific Micro Group in 1987 to provide consulting services to large businesses.

Stephen L. Nelson, C.P.A., consults in creating and using computer-based financial models. He is also a contributing editor for *Lotus Magazine* and the architect of Microsoft's Business and Personal Finance templates. He received his M.B.A. in finance from the University of Washington.

Peter C. Nelson, assistant professor at the University of Illinois at Chicago, teaches computer science courses in artificial intelligence and data structures and consults in the design of 1-2-3-based engineering models and applications. He received his Ph.D. in computer science from Northwestern University.

Peter G. Aitken is a member of the faculty at Duke University. He has written extensively for computer magazines and does consulting for government and private industry. Aitken is also the author of the book *QuickBasic Advanced Techniques*, to be published soon by Que Corporation.

Timothy S. Stanley has worked for Que Corporation since 1985 as a technical editor. In addition to technical editing a number of Que's books, he has contributed to *Absolute Reference: The Journal for 1-2-3 and Symphony Users*.

David P. Ewing is Publishing Director for Que Corporation. He is the author of Que's *1-2-3 Macro Library*, *Using 1-2-3 Workbook and Disk*, and *Using 1-2-3 Workbook Instructor's Guide*; coauthor of Que's *Using Symphony*, *Using Q&A*, *Using Javelin*, and *1-2-3 Macro Workbook*; and contributing author to *Using 1-2-3*, Special Edition, *1-2-3 QuickStart*, and *Upgrading to 1-2-3 Release 3*. Over the past five years, in addition to authoring and coauthoring a number of Que titles, Ewing has served as Product Development Director for many of Que's application software and DOS titles. He has directed the development of such Que series as the Que workbooks and instructor's guides, QueCards, and QuickStart books.

Publishing Director

David P. Ewing

Acquisitions Editor

Terrie Lynn Solomon

Product Directors

Ron Person
David P. Ewing

Developmental Editor

Kathie-Jo Arnoff

Editors

Mary Bednarek
Ann Campbell Holcombe
Lisa Hunt
Virginia Noble
Shelley O'Hara

Technical Editors

Bob Breedlove
Larry D. Lynch
William Coy Hatfield
David A. Knispel
David Maguiness

Book Design and Production

Dan Armstrong
Brad Chinn
Gail Francis
David Kline
Lori Lyons
Jennifer Matthews
Jon Ogle
Joe Ramon
Dennis Sheehan
Mae Louise Shinault

Indexed by

Sharon Hilgenberg

Composed in Garamond and Excellent No. 47
by Que Corporation

CONTENTS AT A GLANCE

Part I   Building the 1-2-3 Worksheet

Chapter 1   An Overview of 1-2-3 Release 3................... 11
Chapter 2   Getting Started.................................. 33
Chapter 3   Learning Worksheet Basics 57
Chapter 4   Using Fundamental 1-2-3 Commands.............. 89
Chapter 5   Formatting Cell Contents.......................153
Chapter 6   Using Functions in the Worksheet..............185
Chapter 7   Managing Files.................................261

Part II   Creating 1-2-3 Reports and Graphs

Chapter 8   Printing Reports...............................295
Chapter 9   Creating and Printing Graphs 347

Part III   Customizing 1-2-3

Chapter 10   Managing Data................................411
Chapter 11   Using Macros.................................513
Chapter 12   Introducing the Advanced Macro Commands 537

Part IV   Quick Reference Guide to 1-2-3

Troubleshooting 595
1-2-3 Command Reference 659

Appendix A   Installing 1-2-3 Release 3.......................823
Appendix B   Compose Sequences for the Lotus Multibyte
                 Character Set 845
Appendix C   Summary of Release 3 Features...................853
Index. 863

TABLE OF CONTENTS

Introduction 1

   The Authoring Team of *Using 1-2-3 Release 3* 2
   Who Should Read This Book? 3
   The Details of This Book 3
   Other Titles To Enhance Your Personal Computing 5
   Learning More about 1-2-3 6
   Summary 7

I   Building the 1-2-3 Worksheet

1   An Overview of 1-2-3 Release 3 11

   What Is 1-2-3 Release 3? 12
   The 1-2-3 "Electronic" Accountant's Pad 13
   Creating Formulas 17
   Playing "What If" 17
   Release 3 Functions 18
      Mathematical Functions 18
      Statistical Functions 18
      Financial Functions 19
      Logical Functions 19
      Special Functions 19
      Date and Time Functions 19
      String Functions 20
   Using the 1-2-3 Release 3 Command Menu 20
      Using Worksheet Commands 21
      Using Range Commands 21
      Copying and Moving Cell Entries 22
   1-2-3 File Management 22
   File and Worksheet Protection 23
   1-2-3 Graphics 23
   1-2-3 Database Management 24
      Database Commands and Functions 24
         Using the /Data Table Command 26
         Multiple Regression and Simultaneous Equations 26
         Using the /Data External Command 26
   Printing Reports and Graphs 27
   Keyboard Macros and Advanced Macro Commands 28
   1-2-3 Hardware Requirements and Options 29
      The Release 3 Operating System and Hardware
      Requirements 29

	Which Video Display Does Release 3 Support?	31
	Which Printers Does Release 3 Support?	31
	Chapter Summary	32

2   **Getting Started**   **33**

	Starting 1-2-3 from the Operating System	34
	Starting 1-2-3	34
	Exiting 1-2-3	35
	Using the 1-2-3 Access System	36
	Starting and Exiting 1-2-3 from the 1-2-3 Access System	38
	Using the Install Program	39
	Using the Translate Program	39
	Learning the 1-2-3 Keyboard	40
	The Alphanumeric Keyboard	42
	The Numeric Keypad and the Cursor-Movement Keys	43
	The Function Keys	43
	The Special Keys	45
	Learning the 1-2-3 Screen Display	46
	The Control Panel	47
	The Mode Indicators	48
	The Status Indicators	50
	The File and Clock Indicator	52
	The Error Messages Area	52
	Using the 1-2-3 Help Features	52
	Finding On-Screen Help	53
	Taking the 1-2-3 Tutorial	54
	Chapter Summary	55

3   **Learning Worksheet Basics**   **57**

	Introducing Worksheets and Files	58
	Introducing Multiple Worksheets	59
	Linking Files	60
	Using the Workspace	61
	Understanding the Display with Multiple Worksheets	61
	Moving Around the Worksheet	62
	Using the Basic Movement Keys	64
	Using the Scroll Lock Key	65
	Using the End Key	65
	Using the GoTo Key To Jump Directly to a Cell	68
	Entering Data into the Worksheet	68
	Entering Labels	69
	Entering Numbers	71
	Entering Formulas	73
	Using Operators in Numeric Formulas	74
	Using Operators in String Formulas	75
	Using Operators in Logical Functions	76
	Pointing to Cell References	77

Correcting Errors in Formulas 77
Addressing Cells 78
Changing Cell Formats 79
Adding Notes to a Cell 79
Editing Data in the Worksheet 79
Using the Undo Feature 80
Using Multiple Worksheets 82
Moving Around Multiple Worksheets 83
Entering Formulas with Multiple-Worksheet Files 86
Entering Formulas that Link Files 86
Choosing Between Multiple-Worksheet Files and
Linked Files 88
Chapter Summary 88

4   Using Fundamental 1-2-3 Commands **89**
Selecting Commands from Command Menus 90
Saving Your Files 94
Using Ranges 95
Typing the Addresses of the Range 96
Specifying a Range in POINT mode 96
Highlighting a Range 97
Dealing with Remembered Ranges 101
Specifying a Range with Range Names 102
Creating Range Names 104
Adding Notes about Ranges 105
Listing All Range Names and Notes 105
Using Ranges in Files with Multiple Worksheets 106
Setting Column Widths 108
Erasing and Deleting Rows, Columns, and Worksheets 109
Erasing Ranges 110
Deleting Rows and Columns 110
Using GROUP Mode To Change All the Worksheets
in a File 111
Deleting Worksheets and Files 112
Clearing the Entire Workspace 113
Inserting Rows, Columns, and Worksheets 114
Using Window Options 115
Changing the Display Format 115
Splitting the Screen 116
Zooming and Moving between Windows 118
Displaying a Graph in a Worksheet 119
Freezing Titles on the Screen 119
Protecting and Hiding Worksheet Data 122
Protecting Cells from Change 123
Using /Range Input 124
Hiding Data 125
Sealing a File To Prevent Tampering 128

Saving a File with a Password To Prevent Access......... 129
Controlling Recalculation 129
   Understanding Recalculation Methods................... 129
   Using Iteration To Solve Circular References............. 130
Moving the Contents of Cells............................. 132
   Moving the Contents of a Single Cell 133
   Moving the Contents of a Range 133
Copying the Contents of Cells............................ 137
   Copying the Contents of a Single Cell.................. 137
   Copying a Formula with Relative Addressing............. 138
   Copying a Formula with Absolute Addressing 139
   Copying One Cell's Contents a Number of Times 140
   Copying One Cell's Contents to a Range of Cells......... 140
   Copying the Contents of a Range....................... 142
   Copying with Mixed Addressing........................ 143
   Using Range Names with /Copy 145
   Using /Range Value To Convert Formulas to Values....... 145
   Using /Range Transpose 148
Finding and Replacing Data 148
Accessing the Operating System 151
Chapter Summary.. 151

5 Formatting Cell Contents **153**
Setting Worksheet Global Defaults 154
Setting Range and Worksheet Global Formats.............. 156
   The Available Formats 157
   The Contents versus the Format of a Cell 158
Using the Format Commands............................. 158
   General Format 162
   Fixed Format 163
   Comma Format 163
   Currency Format.................................... 164
   Percent Format 165
   Scientific Format 166
   The +/− Format 166
   Date and Time Formats 167
      Date Formats................................... 167
      Time Formats 170
   Text Format 172
   Hidden Format..................................... 173
   Label Format....................................... 174
   Automatic Format 174
   Parentheses Format................................. 176
   Color Format 177
   International Formats 177
Changing Label Prefixes 178
Justifying Text... 179

Suppressing the Display of Zeros. 182
Chapter Summary. 182

6   **Using Functions in the Worksheet** **185**

How To Enter a 1-2-3 Function. 186
Mathematical Functions. 188
    General Mathematical Functions. 188
        @ABS—Computing Absolute Value. 189
        @INT—Computing the Integer 189
        @MOD—Finding the Modulus or Remainder. 190
        @ROUND—Rounding Numbers 190
        @RAND—Producing Random Numbers. 191
        @SQRT—Calculating the Square Root 192
    Logarithmic Functions 192
        @LOG—Computing Logarithms 193
        @EXP—Finding Powers of e 193
        @LN—Computing Natural Logarithms. 193
    Trigonometric Functions 194
        @PI—Computing Pi. 194
        @COS, @SIN, and @TAN—Computing Trigonometric
            Functions. 195
        @ACOS, @ASIN, @ATAN, and @ATAN2—Computing
            Inverse Trigonometric Functions 195
    Statistical Functions 197
        @AVG—Computing the Arithmetic Mean. 198
        @COUNT—Counting Cell Entries. 198
        @MAX and @MIN—Finding Maximum and
            Minimum Values. 199
        @STD and @STDS—Calculating the Standard
            Deviation 200
        @SUM—Totaling Values 201
        @SUMPRODUCT—Using Matrix Algebra. 202
        @VAR and @VARS—Calculating the Variance 202
    Financial and Accounting Functions 203
        @IRR—Internal Rate of Return. 205
        @RATE—Compound Growth Rate 207
        @PMT—Loan Payment Amounts. 208
        @NPV—Net Present Value. 209
        @PV—Present Value of an Annuity 211
        @FV—Future Value. 211
        @TERM—Term of an Investment. 212
        @CTERM—Compound Term of an Investment 213
        @SLN—Straight-Line Depreciation 214
        @DDB—Double-Declining Balance Depreciation. 215
        @SYD—Sum-of-the-Years'-Digits Depreciation 215
        @VDB—Variable-Declining Balance Depreciation 216
    Logical Functions 217

@IF—Creating Conditional Tests 218
@ISERR and @ISNA—Trapping Errors in
  Conditional Tests................................ 221
@TRUE and @FALSE—Checking for Errors 222
@ISRANGE—Checking for a Range Name............ 222
@ISSTRING and @ISNUMBER—Checking the Cell's
  Aspect... 223
Special Functions 225
@@—Referencing Cells Indirectly................... 226
@CELL and @CELLPOINTER—Checking Cell
  Attributes..................................... 227
@COORD—Creating a Cell Address................. 229
@CHOOSE—Selecting an Item from a List 229
@COLS, @ROWS, and @SHEETS—Finding the
  Dimensions of Ranges 230
@ERR and @NA—Trapping Errors.................. 231
@HLOOKUP and @VLOOKUP—Looking Up Entries
  in a Table 232
@INDEX—Retrieving Data from Specified Locations.... 234
@INFO—Getting Current Session System Information .. 235
Date and Time Functions 237
@D360—Dealing with 360-Day Years 238
@DATE—Converting Date Values to Serial Numbers ... 238
@DATEVALUE—Changing Date Strings to Serial
  Numbers 239
@DAY, @MONTH, and @YEAR—Converting Serial
  Numbers to Dates 240
@NOW and @TODAY—Finding the Current Date
  and Time...................................... 241
@TIME—Converting Time Values to Serial Numbers ... 242
@TIMEVALUE—Converting Time Strings to Serial
  Values... 243
@SECOND, @MINUTE, and @HOUR—Converting
  Serial Numbers to Time Values 244
String Functions 245
@FIND—Locating One String within Another 247
@MID—Extracting One String from Another 248
@LEFT and @RIGHT—Extracting Strings from
  Left and Right................................. 250
@REPLACE—Replacing a String within a String........ 250
@LENGTH—Computing the Length of a String 251
@EXACT—Comparing Strings 251
@LOWER, @UPPER, and @PROPER—Converting
  the Case of Strings............................. 253
@REPEAT—Repeating Strings within a Cell 253
@TRIM—Removing Blank Spaces from a String....... 254
@N and @S—Testing for Strings and Values 255

@STRING—Converting Values to Strings 256
@VALUE—Converting Strings to Values 256
@CLEAN—Removing Nonprintable Characters
from Strings..................................... 257
Functions Used with LMBCS......................... 258
@CHAR—Displaying LMBCS Characters 258
@CODE—Computing the LMBCS Code............... 259
Chapter Summary.................................. 260

7   Managing Files...................................... **261**
Managing Active Files in Memory 262
Naming Files 263
Changing Directories................................ 265
Saving Files 265
Retrieving Files from Disk........................... 268
Using Wild Cards for File Retrieval 269
Retrieving Files from Subdirectories 269
Retrieving a File Automatically.................... 270
Opening a New File in Memory..................... 270
Extracting and Combining Data....................... 271
Extracting Information 271
Extracting Formulas........................... 274
Extracting Values 276
Combining Information from Other Files 276
Using /File Combine Copy....................... 277
Using /File Combine Add and /File Combine Subtract 280
Protecting Files with Passwords...................... 282
Erasing Files....................................... 284
Creating Lists and Tables of Files 284
Transferring Files 286
Transferring Files with /File Import 286
Importing Unstructured Text Files 286
Importing Delimited Files...................... 287
Transferring Files with the Translate Utility 288
Using Earlier 1-2-3 and Symphony Files in Release 3 289
Using External Databases 290
Using 1-2-3 in a Multiuser Environment................. 290
Chapter Summary.................................. 292

II   Creating 1-2-3 Reports and Graphs

8   Printing Reports.................................... **295**
Getting Started from the /Print Menu (/Print [P,F,E]) 297
Understanding the Default Print Settings 300
Current Printer Settings 300

Global Default Hardware-Specific Options 301
Default Page-Layout Options 302
Other Default Options: Wait, Setup, and Name 303
Printing Your Reports 305
Printing One Screenful of Data (PrtSc) 305
Printing a Report of One Page or Less 308
Printing a Multiple-Page Report 309
Horizontal Page Breaks 311
Vertical Page Breaks 313
Printing Multiple Ranges 316
Hiding Segments within the Designated Print Range 318
Excluding Rows 318
Excluding Columns 319
Hiding Ranges 320
Designing Your Reports 321
Creating Headers and Footers 321
Formatted or Unformatted Output 323
Blank-Header 323
Printing a Listing of Cell Contents 323
Printing Borders 325
Column and Row Borders 325
Frame Borders 328
Setting Page Layout: Margins and Page Length 328
Enhancing Your Reports 329
Improving the Layout 329
Changing the Pitch 330
Changing Line Spacing 332
Choosing Orientation 332
Selecting Fonts 333
Using Setup Strings 335
Selecting Color 338
Printing a Graph with Text (Image) 339
Naming and Saving the Current Print Settings 339
Controlling Your Printer 340
Choosing the Printer 340
Controlling the Movement of the Paper 340
Setting Your Printing Priorities 341
Holding a Print Job (Hold) 342
Pausing the Printer (Suspend and Wait) 342
Stopping the Printer (Cancel and Quit) 343
Clearing the Print Options 343
Preparing Output for Acceptance by Other Programs 344
Chapter Summary 345

9   Creating and Printing Graphs 347
Basic Hardware and Software Requirements for Creating
Graphs 348

Understanding Graphs 348
Creating Simple Graphs 350
  Selecting a Graph Type 352
  Specifying Data Ranges 353
    Specifying Data Ranges Manually 353
    Specifying Data Ranges Automatically 354
      Automatic Graphs 355
      /Graph Group 357
  Constructing the Default Line Graph 358
Enhancing the Appearance of a Basic Graph 359
  Adding Descriptive Labels and Numbers 360
    Using the Titles Option 360
    Entering Data Labels within a Graph 362
    Entering Labels Below the X-Axis 364
    Using the Legend Option 365
  Altering the Default Graph Display 366
    Selecting the Format for Data in Graphs 366
    Setting a Background Grid 367
  Modifying the Graph Axes 368
    Minimum and Maximum Axis Values 369
    Axis Number Format 370
    Axis Scale Indicator 371
    Axis Type 371
    Scale Number Exponent 372
    Scale Number Width 374
  Adding a Second Y Scale 374
  Using Other Features Menu Options 376
  Using Advanced Graph Options 378
    Colors 378
    Hatches 380
    Text 381
Viewing Graphs 383
  Viewing Graphs from the Worksheet 383
  Viewing Graphs in a Screen Window 384
  Viewing Graphs in Color 384
Saving Graphs and Graph Settings 385
  Saving Graphs on Disk 385
  Saving Graph Settings 386
Resetting the Current Graph 387
Developing Alternative Graph Types 387
  Selecting an Appropriate Graph Type 388
  Building All Graph Types 388
    Line Graphs 389
    Bar Graphs 389
    Stack-Bar Graphs 391
    Mixed Graphs 393
    Pie Graphs 393

XY Graphs 396
HLCO Graphs 399
Printing Graphs. 400
Basic Graph Printing. 400
Changing the Appearance of Printed Graphs 402
Image-Sz. 402
Rotate. 403
Density 403
Printing a Graph with Default Settings 404
Printing a Graph with Customized Print Settings 404
Saving Graph Print Settings 404
Including Graphs in Reports 405
Chapter Summary. 408

III   Customizing 1-2-3

10   Managing Data 411

What Is a Database? 412
What Can You Do with a 1-2-3 Database? 413
Creating a Database 415
Determining Required Output 415
Entering Data 416
Modifying a Database. 418
Sorting Database Records 420
The One-Key Sort 420
The Two-Key Sort. 422
The Extra-Key Sort 423
Determining the Sort Order 424
Restoring the Presort Order 426
Searching for Records 427
Using Minimum Search Requirements 428
Determining the Input Range. 429
Entering the Criteria Range 429
Using the Find Command 430
Listing All Specified Records 432
Defining the Output Range. 432
Executing the Extract Command. 433
Modifying Records 435
Handling More Complicated Criteria Ranges 437
Wild Cards in Criteria Ranges 438
Formulas in Criteria Ranges 438
AND Conditions 440
OR Conditions 442
String Searches 444

Special Operators.. 445
Performing Other Types of Searches..................... 446
Extracting Unique Records........................... 446
Deleting Specified Records.......................... 447
Joining Multiple Databases................................. 448
Creating Data Tables.. 451
General Terms and Concepts........................... 452
The Four Types of Data Tables....................... 453
Creating a Type 1 Data Table......................... 453
Creating a Cross-Tabulated Table with /Data Table 1...... 454
Creating a Type 2 Data Table......................... 456
Creating a Cross-Tabulated Table with /Data Table 2...... 457
Creating a Type 3 Data Table......................... 458
Creating a Three-Dimensional Cross-Tabulated Table...... 463
Creating a Labeled Data Table........................ 466
Positioning the Results Area.................... 468
Formatting the Results Area..................... 470
Creating a Sample Labeled Data Table............ 471
Using More Than Three Variables................ 476
Creating a Cross-Tabulated Table with /Data Table
Labeled.. 477
Using Database Functions................................... 479
Filling Ranges.. 484
Filling Ranges with Numbers........................... 484
Using Formulas and Functions To Fill Ranges........... 486
Filling Ranges with Dates or Times................... 486
Creating Frequency Distributions........................... 488
Using the /Data Regression Command........................ 489
Using the /Data Matrix Command............................. 494
Loading Data from Other Programs.......................... 495
Using the /Data Parse Command........................ 495
Using Caution with /Data Parse....................... 499
Working with External Databases........................... 499
Understanding External Database Terms................. 501
Using an Existing External Table..................... 501
Listing External Tables.............................. 503
Creating a New External Table........................ 504
Duplicating an Existing Structure.............. 505
Creating a New Structure....................... 506
Deleting an External Table........................... 507
Using Other /Data External Commands.................. 508
/Data External Other Refresh................... 508
/Data External Other Control................... 509
/Data External Other Translate................. 510
Disconnecting 1-2-3 and the External Table........... 511
Chapter Summary.. 511

11 **Using Macros**. **513**

What Is a Macro? 514
Writing Your First Macros 514
    Writing a Macro that Enters Text. 515
    Writing a Simple Command Macro 516
Using Keywords 517
Naming and Running Macros. 519
    Alt-Letter Macros that Work with a Key Press. 520
    Macros with Descriptive Names 521
    Automatic Macros that Work When Loaded. 522
Planning the Layout of a Macro. 524
Building a Simple Macro Library 525
    A Macro To Define Printer Setup Strings 525
    A Macro To Print a Report 526
    A Macro To Set Worksheet Recalculation. 526
    A Macro To Add a New Worksheet. 527
Recording and Testing Macros. 527
    Creating Macros with Record 528
    Using Playback To Repeat Keystrokes 531
    Using Record To Test Macros. 531
    Watching for Common Macro Errors. 533
Documenting Your Macros. 534
    Using Descriptive Names 534
    Using the /Range Name Note Feature 535
    Including Comments in Your Worksheet 535
    Keeping External Design Notes 535
Moving Up to the Advanced Macro Commands 536
Chapter Summary. 536

12 **Introducing the Advanced Macro Commands**. . **537**

Why Use the Advanced Macro Commands?. 538
What Are the Advanced Macro Commands? 539
The Elements of Advanced Macro Command Programs 541
Advanced Macro Command Syntax. 541
Creating, Using, and Debugging Advanced Macro Command
    Programs 542
The Advanced Macro Commands 543
    Commands for Accepting Input 544
        The ? Command. 544
        The GET Command. 545
        The GETLABEL Command 546
        The GETNUMBER Command. 547
        The LOOK Command 548
        The FORM Command 550
    Commands for Program Control. 551
        The BRANCH Command. 552

The MENUBRANCH Command 554
The MENUCALL Command. 556
The RETURN Command 557
The QUIT Command. 558
The ONERROR Command 558
The BREAKOFF Command 560
The BREAKON Command. 561
The WAIT Command. 562
The DISPATCH Command 562
The DEFINE Command. 563
The RESTART Command. 565
The SYSTEM Command. 566
Decision-Making Commands 567
The IF Command 567
The FOR and FORBREAK Commands. 569
Data Manipulation Commands. 570
The LET Command 570
The PUT Command 572
The CONTENTS Command 572
The BLANK Command 574
The APPENDBELOW Command 575
The APPENDRIGHT Command 576
Program Enhancement Commands. 577
The BEEP Command 577
The PANELOFF Command 578
The PANELON Command. 578
The WINDOWSOFF Command 579
The WINDOWSON Command. 580
The FRAMEOFF Command. 580
The FRAMEON Command 580
The GRAPHON Command 581
The GRAPHOFF Command. 582
The INDICATE Command. 582
he RECALC and RECALCCOL Commands 583
File Manipulation Commands 584
The OPEN Command 584
The CLOSE Command. 587
The READ Command. 588
The READLN Command 588
The WRITE Command. 589
The WRITELN Command 590
The SETPOS Command 590
The GETPOS Command 591
The FILESIZE Command 591
Chapter Summary. 591

IV   Quick Reference Guide to 1-2-3

Troubleshooting **595**

   Troubleshooting Installation 597
   Troubleshooting the 1-2-3 Worksheet 599
      Problems with Data Entry 599
      Problems with Circular References 600
      Problems that Result in ERR 604
      Problems with Memory Management 609
   Troubleshooting 1-2-3 Commands 611
      Problems with Range Names 611
      Problems with Relative and Absolute Addressing 613
      Problems with Recalculation 614
      Miscellaneous Problems 615
   Troubleshooting Functions 620
   Troubleshooting File Operations 624
   Troubleshooting Printing 628
   Troubleshooting Graphing 635
   Troubleshooting Data Management 645
   Troubleshooting Macros 652

1-2-3 Command Reference **659**

   Worksheet Commands (/W) 659
      Worksheet Global Format (/WGF) 661
      Worksheet Global Label (/WGL) 664
      Worksheet Global Col-Width (/WGC) 667
      Worksheet Global Prot (/WGP) 667
      Worksheet Global Zero (/WGZ) 668
      Worksheet Global Recalc (/WGR) 669
      Worksheet Global Default (/WGD) 671
      Worksheet Global Group (/WGG) 674
      Worksheet Insert [Column, Row, Sheet]
        (/WIC, /WIR, or /WIS) 674
      Worksheet Delete [Column, Row, Sheet, File]
        (/WDC, /WDR, /WDS, or /WDF) 676
      Worksheet Column [Set-Width, Reset-Width, Hide,
        Display, Column-Range] (/WCS, /WCR, /WCH,
        /WCD, or /WCC) 677
      Worksheet Erase (/WE) 679
      Worksheet Titles (/WT) 680
      Worksheet Window (/WW) 681
      Worksheet Status (/WS) 683
      Worksheet Page (/WP) 684
      Worksheet Hide (/WH) 685
   Range Commands (/R) 686
      Range Format (/RF) 686

Range Label (/RL) 689
Range Erase (/RE) 692
Range Name (/RN) 693
Range Justify (/RJ) 697
Range Prot and Range Unprot (/RP and /RU) 699
Range Input (/RI) 700
Range Value (/RV) 701
Range Trans (/RT) 702
Range Search (/RS) 704
Copy and Move Commands (/C and /M) 706
Copy (/C) 706
Move (/M) 708
File Commands (/F) 710
File Retrieve (/FR) 710
File Save (/FS) 712
File Combine (/FC) 714
File Xtract (/FX) 716
File Erase (/FE) 718
File List (/FL) 719
File Import (/FI) 720
File Dir (/FD) 722
File New (/FN) 723
File Open (/FO) 723
File Admin Reservation (/FAR) 724
File Admin Table (/FAT) 725
File Admin Seal (/FAS) 727
File Admin Link-Refresh (/FAL) 728
Print Commands (/P) 729
Print Printer (/PP) 730
Print File (/PF) 731
Print Encoded (/PE) 733
Print Suspend (/PS) 735
Print Resume (/PR) 735
Print Cancel (/PC) 736
Print [Printer, File, Encoded] Range
  (/PPR, /PFR, or /PER) 736
Print [Printer, File, Encoded] Line
  (/PPL, /PFL, or /PEL) 738
Print [Printer, File, Encoded] Page
  (/PPP, /PFP, or /PEP) 738
Print [Printer, File, Encoded] Options Header
  (/PPOH, /PFOH, or /PEOH) 739
Print [Printer, File, Encoded] Options Footer
  (/PPOF, /PFOF, or /PEOF) 741
Print [Printer, File, Encoded] Options Margins
  (/PPOM, /PFOM, or /PEOM) 741
Print [Printer, File, Encoded] Options Borders
  (/PPOB, /PFOB, or /PEOB) 743

Print [Printer, Encoded] Options Setup
(/PPOS or /PEOS) 744
Print [Printer, File, Encoded] Options Pg-Length
(/PPOP, /PFOP, or /PEOP) 746
Print [Printer, File, Encoded] Options Other
(/PPOO, /PFOO, or /PEOO) 746
Print [Printer, File, Encoded] Options Name
(/PPON, /PFON, or /PEON) 748
Print [Printer, File, Encoded] Options Advanced
(/PPOA, /PFOA, or /PEOA) 750
Print [Printer, File, Encoded] Clear
(/PPC, /PFC, or /PEC) 754
Print [Printer, File, Encoded] Go
(/PPG, /PFG, or /PEG) 755
Print [Printer, File, Encoded] Align
(/PPA, /PFA, or /PEA) 755
Print [Printer, Encoded] Image (/PPI or /PEI) 756
Print Printer Sample (/PPS) 757
Print [Printer, File, Encoded] Hold
(/PPH, /PFH, or /PEH) 758
Print [Printer, File, Encoded] Quit
(/PPQ, /PFQ, or /PEQ) 759
Graph Commands (/G) 760
Graph Type (/GT) 760
Graph X A B C D E F (/GX, /GA through /GF) 764
Graph Reset (/GR) 766
Graph View (/GV) 767
Graph Save (/GS) 768
Graph Options Legend (/GOL) 769
Graph Options Format (/GOF) 771
Graph Options Titles (/GOT) 773
Graph Options Grid (/GOG) 774
Graph Options Scale (/GOS) 775
Graph Options Color/B&W (/GOC or /GOB) 777
Graph Options Data-Labels (/GOD) 778
Graph Options Advanced Colors (/GOAC) 780
Graph Options Advanced Text and Text
[First, Second, Third] [Color, Font, Size] (/GOAT,
/GOATFC, /GOATSC, /GOATTC,
/GOATFF, /GOATSF, /GOATTF, /GOATFS,
/GOATSS, or /GOATTS) 781
Graph Options Advanced Hatches (/GOAH) 782
Graph Name (/GN) 783
Graph Group (/GG) 785
Data Commands (/D) 786
Data Fill (/DF) 786
Data Table 1 (/DT1) 789

Data Table 2 (/DT2) 791
Data Table 3 (/DT3) 792
Data Table Labeled (/DTL) 794
Data Sort (/DS) 797
Data Query Input (/DQI) 799
Data Query Criteria (/DQC) 799
Data Query Output (/DQO) 801
Data Query Find (/DQF) 802
Data Query Extract (/DQE) 803
Data Query Unique (/DQU) 805
Data Query Del (/DQD) 806
Data Query Modify (/DQM) 807
Data Distribution (/DD) 808
Data Matrix (/DM) 810
Data Regression (/DR) 811
Data Parse (/DP) 813
Data External Use (/DEU) 815
Data External List (/DEL) 815
Data External Create (/DEC) 816
Data External [Delete, Reset] (/DED or /DER) 818
Data External Other (/DEO) 819
System and Quit Commands (/S and /Q) 821
System (/S) 821
Quit (/Q) 821

A   Installing 1-2-3 Release 3 823
Checking DOS Configuration 823
Using the Install Program 824
Starting the Install Program 824
Registering Your Original Disks 825
Selecting Your Operating System 826
Choosing Files To Copy 826
Creating a Directory for the 1-2-3 Files 827
Copying Files 828
Configuring 1-2-3 for Your Computer 829
Changing 1-2-3's Configuration 835
Installing 1-2-3 for Two Display Drivers 840
Changing the Selected Country 841
Choosing Another DCF 843
Summary 843

B   Compose Sequences for the Lotus Multibyte
     Character Set 845

C   Summary of Release 3 Features 853

     Index 863

ACKNOWLEDGMENTS

Using 1-2-3 Release 3 is the result of the immense efforts of many dedicated people. Que Corporation thanks the following individuals for their contributions to the development of this book:

Kathie-Jo Arnoff, for her direction and coordination of the many editors working on this project, for providing developmental direction on many of the chapters, and for being determined to make *Using 1-2-3 Release 3* the best Release 3 title available.

Mary Bednarek and Ginny Noble, for their developmental direction on many of the chapters and dedication to ensuring high quality in the chapters they edited.

Terrie Lynn Solomon, for her incredible organizational skills and for masterminding and managing the flow of materials between authors and editors. Thanks also to Terrie for helping many of us "keep cool" when pushing to finish this book.

Chuck Stewart, for providing valuable developmental recommendations on chapters early in the project.

Lisa Hunt, Shelley O'Hara, and Ann Holcombe, for their versatility and outstanding editing skills that enabled them to "pinch hit" when needed on this project.

Jennifer Matthews, Dennis Sheehan, Dan Armstrong, Jon Ogle, Joe Ramon, Brad Chinn, Gail Francis, and Louise Shinault, for making this project a top priority for the Que typesetting and paste-up department and for being dedicated to producing the quality final pages for this book.

Lori Lyons and David Kline, for the excellent proofing they did on all chapters.

Sharon Hilgenberg, for the very complete index she developed for *Using 1-2-3 Release 3*.

David A. Knispel and Jeff Booher, for their willingness to create, recreate, and correct hundreds of figures used in this book.

Bill Hatfield and Dave Maguiness, for their review of the technical content and check of examples and figures.

Stacey Beheler and Joanetta Hendel, for handling the flow of materials between authors, editors, and production staff and for providing editorial assistance on the manuscript.

Last but not least, Que thanks Lotus Development Corporation for the tremendous support provided during the development of *Using 1-2-3 Release 3*:

Scott Tucker, Senior Product Design Manager, for his interest and time in providing Que with up-to-date information on the development of Release 3.

MaryBeth Rettger, Beta Test Administrator, and Ellen Keeffe, Design Verification Engineer, for providing technical assistance throughout the development of *Using 1-2-3 Release 3*.

Alexandria Trevelyan, Public Relations Specialist, for her assistance in answering questions and solving problems as they arose while authors and editors were developing *Using 1-2-3 Release 3*.

TRADEMARK ACKNOWLEDGMENTS

Que Corporation has made every attempt to supply trademark information about company names, products, and services mentioned in this book. Trademarks indicated below were derived from various sources. Que Corporation cannot attest to the accuracy of this information.

Apple and LaserWriter are registered trademarks of Apple Computer, Inc.

dBASE III Plus and dBASE IV are trademarks, and dBASE, dBASE II, and dBASE III are registered trademarks of Ashton-Tate Corporation.

DESQview is a trademark of Quarterdeck Office Systems.

DisplayWrite and ProPrinter are trademarks, and IBM, OS/2, and IBM Quietwriter are registered trademarks of International Business Machines Corporation.

Epson FX Series and Epson MX-80 are trademarks of EPSON America, Inc., and EPSON is a registered trademark of Epson Corporation.

Hercules Graphics Card is a trademark, and Hercules Monochrome Graphics Card is a registered trademark of Hercules Computer Technology.

HP DeskJet and HP LaserJet are trademarks, and HP and HP ThinkJet are registered trademarks of Hewlett-Packard Co.

Lotus Manuscript is a trademark, and 1-2-3, DIF, Freelance, Magellan, Symphony, and VisiCalc are registered trademarks of Lotus Development Corporation.

MS-DOS, Microsoft Multiplan, and Microsoft Windows are registered trademarks of Microsoft Corporation.

NEC is a registered trademark of NEC Information Systems.

OKIDATA and Microline are registered trademarks of Oki America, Inc.

PostScript is a registered trademark of Adobe Systems Incorporated.

SideKick and SideKick Plus are registered trademarks of Borland International, Inc.

WordStar is a registered trademark of MicroPro International Corporation.

CONVENTIONS USED IN THIS BOOK

A number of conventions are used in *Using 1-2-3 Release 3* to help you learn the program. One example is provided for each convention to help you distinguish among the different elements in 1-2-3.

References to keys are as they appear on the keyboard of the IBM Personal Computer. Direct quotations of words that appear on the screen are spelled as they appear on the screen and are printed in a special typeface. Information you are asked to type is printed in **boldface**.

The first letter of each command from 1-2-3's menu system appears in **boldface**: **/R**ange **F**ormat **C**urrency. Abbreviated commands appear as in the following example: /rfc. **/R**ange **F**ormat **C**urrency indicates that you type /rfc to select this command if you are entering it manually. The first letter of menu choices also appears in boldface: **C**opy.

Words printed in uppercase include range names (SALES), functions (@PMT), modes (READY), and cell references (A1..G5).

Conventions that pertain to macros deserve special mention here:

1. Macro names (Alt-character combinations) appear with the backslash (\ ) and single-character name in lowercase: \a. In this example, the \ indicates that you press the Alt key and hold it down while you also press the A key.

2. All /x macro commands, such as /xm or /xn, appear in lowercase, but 1-2-3's advanced macro commands appear within braces in uppercase: {WAIT}.

3. 1-2-3 menu keystrokes in a macro line appear in lowercase: /rnc.

4. Range names within macros appear in uppercase: /rncTEST.

5. In macros, representations of cursor-movement keys, such as {DOWN}; function keys, such as {CALC}; and editing keys, such as {DEL}, appear in uppercase letters and are surrounded by braces.

6. Enter is represented by the tilde (˜). (Note that throughout the text, Enter is used instead of Return.)

The function keys, F1 through F10, are used for special situations in 1-2-3. In the text, the function key name is usually followed by the number in parentheses: Graph (F10).

Ctrl-Break indicates that you press the Ctrl key and hold it down while you press also the Break key. Other hyphenated key combinations, such as Alt-F10, are performed in the same manner.

Introduction

Since 1983, Que has helped more than two million spreadsheet users learn the commands, features, and functions of Lotus 1-2-3. *Using 1-2-3*—through three editions—has become the standard guide to 1-2-3 for both new and experienced 1-2-3 users worldwide. Now, with the publication of *Using 1-2-3 Release 3*, Que builds on those six years of experience to bring you the most comprehensive tutorial and reference available for new Release 3.

Que's unprecedented experience with 1-2-3—and 1-2-3 users—has resulted in this high quality, highly informative book. But a book like *Using 1-2-3 Release 3* does not develop overnight. This book is the result of long hours of work from a team of expert authors and dedicated editors.

The development of *Using 1-2-3 Release 3* began immediately after Lotus announced that a new version of 1-2-3 was being planned. Even before the software was developed, Que's product development editors began searching for the best team of 1-2-3 experts available. This team of authors had to be able to cover the complex, powerful new program comprehensively, accurately, and clearly.

In March of 1989, Que's team of authors traveled to Lotus Development Corporation in Boston for a preview of Release 3. They met with the Release 3 development team and discussed the new product in depth. On seeing Release 3 demonstrated, the authors prepared to begin detailed use of the product, ready to discover the incredible capabilities provided by the program's new features.

While in Boston, the team outlined the strategies needed to produce the best book on Release 3. They reviewed comments from users, critiqued competing products, and analyzed the traits that made previous editions of *Using 1-2-3* the most popular 1-2-3 books on the market. The result is a comprehensive tutorial and reference, written in the easy-to-follow style expected from Que books.

As a result of this effort, *Using 1-2-3 Release 3* is the best available guide to 1-2-3 Release 3. Whether you are using 1-2-3 for inventory control, statistical analysis, or portfolio management, this book is designed for you. Like all previous editions of this title, *Using 1-2-3 Release 3* leads you step-by-step from spreadsheet basics to the advanced features of Release 3. Whether you are a new user or an experienced user upgrading to Release 3, this book will occupy a prominent place next to your computer, as a tried and valued reference to your most-used spreadsheet program.

The Authoring Team of *Using 1-2-3 Release 3*

The experts who developed *Using 1-2-3 Release 3* are experienced with many of the ways 1-2-3 is used everyday. As consultants, trainers, and 1-2-3 users, the authors of *Using 1-2-3 Release 3* have used 1-2-3 and have taught others how to use 1-2-3 to build many types of applications—from accounting and general business applications to scientific applications. This experience, combined with the expertise of the world's leading 1-2-3 publisher, brings you outstanding tutorial and reference information.

The authoring team of *Using 1-2-3 Release 3* is composed of Bill Weil, Stephen Nelson, Peter Nelson, Peter Aitken, Ron Person, Tim Stanley, and Dave Ewing. Bill Weil, who wrote Chapters 2, 3, 4, 5, 7, and the Troubleshooting reference, is a computer consultant who provides 1-2-3 consulting services to large businesses. Bill is also the author of the Troubleshooting reference in Que's *Using 1-2-3 Special Edition* and is a contributing author to Que's *1-2-3 Tips, Tricks, and Traps*, 2nd Edition.

Stephen Nelson and Peter Nelson together wrote Chapters 6, 11, and 12. Steve, who consults in the development and use of computer-based financial models, is a contributing editor for *Lotus Magazine*, and author of Que's *Using DacEasy*. Peter is an assistant professor at the University of Illinois at Chicago, teaching computer science courses.

Peter Aitken, the author of Chapters 8, 9, and 10, is a member of the faculty at Duke University. Peter consults with the government and private industry and has written articles for *Lotus Magazine* and *Absolute Reference: The Journal for 1-2-3 and Symphony Users*.

Ron Person brings many years of 1-2-3 consulting and training experience to his development of the Command Reference. Ron is also the author of Que's *1-2-3 Business Formula Handbook* and contributing author for *1-2-3 QueCards*.

Tim Stanley, who wrote Appendixes A and C, is the technical support coordinator for Que Corporation.

Dave Ewing, who wrote this introduction and Chapter 1, is the Publishing Director for Que Corporation and has authored and coauthored many Que titles, including *Using Symphony*, *1-2-3 Macro Library*, and *Using 1-2-3 Workbook and Disk*.

Who Should Read This Book?

Using 1-2-3 Release 3 is written and organized to meet the needs of a wide range of readers, from those for whom 1-2-3 Release 3 is their first spreadsheet product to experienced 1-2-3 Release 2.01 users who have upgraded to Release 3.

If Release 3 is your first 1-2-3 package, then this book will help you learn all the basics so that you can quickly begin using 1-2-3 for your needs. The first five chapters in particular teach you basic concepts for understanding 1-2-3—commands, special uses of the keyboard, features of the 1-2-3 screen, and methods for creating and modifying 1-2-3 worksheets.

If you are an experienced 1-2-3 Release 2.01 user and have upgraded to Release 3, this book describes all the new features in Release 3 and how to apply them as you develop worksheet applications, create graphs, and print reports and graphs. The special Release 3 icon in the margin marks those places in the text where a Release 3 feature is described.

Whether you are new to Release 3 or have upgraded, *Using 1-2-3 Release 3* provides tips and techniques to help experienced users get the most from 1-2-3. As you continue to use 1-2-3 Release 3, you'll find the 1-2-3 Command Reference with its easy-to-use format a frequently used guide, reminding you of the steps, tips, and cautions for using Release 3 commands.

The Details of This Book

If you flip quickly through this book, you can get a better sense of its organization and layout. The book is organized to follow the natural flow of learning and using 1-2-3.

Part I—Building the 1-2-3 Worksheet

Chapter 1, "An Overview of 1-2-3 Release 3," presents an overview of 1-2-3 Release 3, including the uses, features, and commands in Release 3 that are the same or similar to those in earlier versions as well as uses, features, and commands specific to Release 3. Also, this chapter introduces the general concepts for understanding 1-2-3 as a spreadsheet program and introduces the program's major uses—creating worksheets, databases, graphics, and macros.

Chapter 2, "Getting Started," helps you begin using 1-2-3 Release 3 for the first time, including starting and exiting from the program, learning special uses of the keyboard with 1-2-3, understanding features of the 1-2-3 screen display, getting on-screen help, and using the 1-2-3 tutorial.

Chapter 3, "Learning Worksheet Basics," introduces the concepts of worksheets and files, teaches you how to move the cell pointer around the worksheet, enter and edit data, and use Undo. You will also learn how to build multiple-worksheet files with Release 3 and create formulas that link cells among different files.

Chapter 4, "Using Fundamental 1-2-3 Commands," teaches you how to use the 1-2-3 Release 3 command menus and the most fundamental commands for building worksheets. You'll also learn how to save your worksheet files and leave 1-2-3 temporarily to return to the operating system.

Chapter 5, "Formatting Cell Contents," shows you how to change the way data appears on your screen, including the way values, formulas, and text are displayed. You will also learn how to suppress the display of zeros.

Chapter 6, "Using Functions in the Worksheet," covers the following functions available in Release 3: mathematical, trigonometric, statistical, financial, accounting, logical, special, date, time, and string functions.

Chapter 7, "Managing Files," covers those commands related to saving, erasing, and listing files as well as commands for combining data from several files, extracting data from one file to another, and opening more than one file in memory at a time. In addition to introducing you to these commands for using and changing 1-2-3 files, Chapter 7 teaches you how to transfer files between different programs and how to use 1-2-3 in a multiuser environment.

Part II—Creating 1-2-3 Reports and Graphs

Chapter 8, "Printing Reports," shows you how to print a report immediately, create a file for delayed printing, or create a file to be read by another program. You'll learn how to print a basic report by using only a few commands as well as enhance a report by using other commands that change page layout, type size, and character and line spacing, and let you add such elements as headers and footers.

Chapter 9, "Creating and Printing Graphs," teaches you how to create graphs from worksheet data manually and automatically. This chapter also covers all the options available to change the type of graph, label and title a graph, enhance a graph with a background grid, change the scaling of a graph, and view a graph in full- or partial-screen mode. Release 3 lets you print graphs directly from the /Print menu, and the process is somewhat less complex than printing graphs in prior releases. This chapter covers the commands in the /Print menu and steps for printing graphs in Release 3.

Part III—Customizing 1-2-3

Chapter 10, "Managing Data," introduces the advantages and limitations of 1-2-3's database and shows you how to create, modify, and maintain data records, including sorting, locating, and extracting data. Chapter 10 also covers the special commands and features of 1-2-3 data management, such as database statistical functions, parsing data to use in the worksheet, regression analysis, and accessing and manipulating data in a table in an external database.

Chapter 11, "Using Macros," is an introduction to the powerful macro capability in Release 3. This chapter teaches you how to create, name, and run macros and build a macro library. Also, the chapter covers macro features special to Release 3, such as creating a macro by automatically recording keystrokes, naming macros with descriptive names, and invoking macros from a menu.

Chapter 12, "Introducing the Advanced Macro Commands," explains the powerful advanced macro commands in Release 3 and includes a complete reference of all advanced macro commands with numerous examples of their use.

Part IV—Quick Reference Guide to 1-2-3

"Troubleshooting" is an easy-to-use problem-solving section that can help everyone from the novice user to the most advanced "power user." You can use the section both as a reference when you have problems and as a source of practical advice and tips during "browsing sessions."

"1-2-3 Command Reference" is a quick, easy-to-use, and comprehensive guide to the procedures for using almost every command on the command menus. This section also gives numerous Reminders, Important Cues, and Cautions that will greatly simplify and expedite your day-to-day use of 1-2-3.

Appendixes

Appendix A of this book shows you how to install 1-2-3 Release 3 for your hardware and operating system.

Appendix B presents a table of the Lotus Multibyte Character Set—characters not on your keyboard that can appear on your monitor and print with your printer. Your specific equipment determines which characters in this list you can display and print.

The final appendix in the book, Appendix C, provides a summary of the features specific to Release 3.

Other Titles To Enhance Your Personal Computing

Although *Using 1-2-3 Release 3* is a comprehensive guide to Release 3, no single book can fill all your 1-2-3 and personal computing needs. Que Corporation publishes a full line of microcomputer books that complement this best-seller.

Several Que books can help you learn and master your operating systems. *Using PC DOS*, 3rd Edition, is an excellent guide to the IBM-specific PC DOS operating system. Its counterpart—written for all DOS users—is *MS-DOS User's Guide*, 3rd Edition. Both books provide the same type of strong tutorial and complete Command Reference found in *Using 1-2-3 Release 3*. If you prefer to get up and running with DOS fundamentals in a quick and easy manner, try Que's *MS-DOS QuickStart*. This graphics-based tutorial helps you teach yourself the fundamentals of DOS. If you plan to run 1-2-3 Release 3 under OS/2, you will want the information and suggestions in *Using OS/2*.

You are probably using 1-2-3 on a personal computer equipped with a hard disk drive. The key to efficient computer use is effective hard disk management. Que's *Managing Your Hard Disk*, 2nd Edition, shows you how to get the most from your hard disk by streamlining your use of directories, creating batch files, and more. This well-written text will be an invaluable addition to your library of personal computer books.

As you are aware, 1-2-3 Release 3 requires the use of powerful equipment to run quickly and efficiently. If you find your current computer hardware not quite up to the task, examine Que's *Upgrading and Repairing PCs*. This informative text shows you how to get the most from your current hardware, and how to upgrade your system to handle the new breed of high-powered software—such as 1-2-3 Release 3. Mark Brownstein of *InfoWorld* called this book "one of the best books about the workings of personal computers I've ever seen; it will be a useful, easy-to-read, and interesting addition to most anyone's library."

Learning More about 1-2-3

If *Using 1-2-3 Release 3* whets your appetite for more information about 1-2-3, you're in good company. Close to one million *Using 1-2-3* readers have gone on to purchase one or more additional Que books about 1-2-3.

1-2-3 Release 3 Business Applications is a book and disk set that provides you with a series of business models in ready-to-run form. New Release 3 features are widely used, including 3D spreadsheets and enhanced graphics. This book is a real time-saver for the dedicated 1-2-3 user.

1-2-3 Database Techniques contains concepts and techniques to help you create complex 1-2-3 database applications. With an emphasis on Release 3 features, this book introduces database fundamentals, compares 1-2-3 with traditional database programs, offers numerous application tips, and discusses add-in programs.

1-2-3 Release 3 Quick Reference is an affordable, compact reference to the most commonly used Release 3 commands and functions. It's a great book to keep near your computer when you need to find quickly the function of a command and the steps for using it.

1-2-3 Tips, Tricks, and Traps, 3rd Edition, covers all releases of 1-2-3—including Release 3—and presents hundreds of tips and techniques to help you get the most from the program. This book covers Release 3's 3D spreadsheet capability, new graphics features, and enhancements to the database and Command Language.

In addition to these books, Que publishes several books for new Release 3 users: *1-2-3 Release 3 QuickStart* and *1-2-3 Release 3 Workbook and Disk. Upgrading to 1-2-3 Release 3* focuses on those features that are special to Release 3 and is written to help the upgrade user get started quickly using 1-2-3 Release 3. Keep in mind that Que also publishes a complete line of books for 1-2-3 Release 2 users.

Also from Que is a book on Lotus's newest program, Magellan. *Using Lotus Magellan* guides you through the operations and applications of Magellan, an advanced file management program of particular value to 1-2-3 users.

Finally, *Absolute Reference* is Que's monthly journal for 1-2-3 and Symphony power users. Now in its sixth year of publication, *Absolute Reference* is read by thousands of users eager to get new 1-2-3 information, applications, and tips every month.

All these books can be found in better bookstores worldwide. In the United States, you can call Que at 1-800-428-5331 to order books or obtain further information.

Summary

Using 1-2-3 Release 3 follows the Que tradition of providing quality text that is targeted appropriately for the 1-2-3 user. Because of the dedication to this goal, Que ultimately has only one way of getting better: by hearing from you. Let Que know how you feel about this book or any other Que title. Que wants to keep improving its books, and you are the best source of information.

Part I

Building the
1-2-3 Worksheet

Includes

An Overview of 1-2-3 Release 3

Getting Started

Learning Worksheet Basics

Using Fundamental 1-2-3 Commands

Formatting Cell Contents

Using Functions in the Worksheet

Managing Files

1

An Overview of
1-2-3 Release 3

For more than five years, 1-2-3 has been the dominant spreadsheet software product used in businesses worldwide. Today, 1-2-3 is used by four million people and continues to be the standard.

When first introduced in 1983, 1-2-3 revolutionized microcomputing by replacing the dominant spreadsheet product at the time, VisiCalc, and soon became the program identified with the IBM PC as the established tool for financial analysis. With the introduction of Release 3 of 1-2-3 in 1989, 1-2-3 remains the leader in microcomputer spreadsheet software by maintaining the overall functionality, command structure, and screen and keyboard features of its earlier versions. At the same time, however, through Release 3, Lotus Development Corporation has responded to the growing needs of users and the capabilities available in state-of-the-art microcomputers today.

Why is 1-2-3 so popular? 1-2-3 provides users with three fundamental applications integrated in one program. Without having to learn three separate kinds of software, users can perform financial analysis with the 1-2-3 worksheet, create database applications, and create graphics. Commands enabling users to develop all three types of applications are combined in one main menu. Commands are easily accessed by pressing the slash (/) key and then typing the first letter of the command or by highlighting the command and pressing Enter. When a command is selected, prompts guide users through each step needed to perform a task.

This chapter presents an overview of 1-2-3 Release 3, including the uses, features, and commands in Release 3 that are the same or similar to those in earlier versions of 1-2-3. This chapter also points out what's new in Release 3. If you are upgrading from an earlier release of 1-2-3, this chapter gives you a general introduction to the differences between earlier releases and Release 3 and identifies many of the features and commands that are unique to Release 3. Specifically in this chapter you'll learn about the following topics:

- The general capabilities of 1-2-3 (presented especially for those readers who are new to 1-2-3 as well as Release 3)

- An overview of the features that are special to Release 3 (developed for those readers who are planning to or have just upgraded from Release 2.01 to Release 3)

- Features that identify 1-2-3 as a spreadsheet program, including creating formulas in 1-2-3 and using functions

- An introduction to the commands available for creating, modifying, and using 1-2-3 worksheets

- 1-2-3 file management and worksheet and file protection

- 1-2-3 graphics, including an introduction to those enhancements in Release 3 graphics not available in earlier releases

- Database management with 1-2-3

- Keyboard macros and advanced macro commands

- The hardware and operating system requirements for running 1-2-3 Release 3

What Is 1-2-3 Release 3?

If you have used a previous version of 1-2-3, you will find the program unchanged in its primary functions. You can still use 1-2-3 for simple to complex financial applications, for organizing, sorting, extracting, and finding information, and for creating graphs from which you can analyze data or use in presentations. What makes Release 3 different from other versions? The major enhancements to Release 3 over Release 1, 1A, and 2.01 include the following:

- The capability to have up to 256 worksheets in one file and multiple files in memory at a time

- Enhancements that make Release 3 easier to use than earlier versions, such as the capabilities to cancel printing from the /Print menu, create graphs automatically, and enter dates in many different formats

- Enhancements that improve the quality of printed reports and on-screen and printed graphics

- Enhancements to 1-2-3's database capability, including the capability to access external databases

Probably the most significant change between Release 3 and prior versions of 1-2-3 is its multiple worksheet and multiple file capabilities. Previous releases of

1-2-3 limit you to one worksheet per file; only one file can be open at a time. Release 3 breaks this barrier, taking advantage of advances in hardware and operating system technology by providing up to 256 worksheets in a single file and multiple files in memory at one time. How many worksheets per file and files you can have in memory at one time, of course, depends on your hardware (see the section "Release 3 Operating System and Hardware Requirements" later in the chapter). When you create multiple worksheets, 1-2-3 lets you easily page through the stack of worksheets or display three consecutive worksheets onscreen at the same time.

What are the advantages to multiple worksheet and file capability? First of all, it's ideal for consolidations—consolidations of regional sales, consolidations of department budgets, consolidations of product forecasts, and so on. You can easily create formulas that reference cells in other worksheets and other files and are immediately updated when changes are made.

Besides consolidation applications, Release 3's multiple worksheet and file capability has many other uses. Rather than scattering separate applications and macros over one large worksheet, you can reserve a separate worksheet for each application—spreadsheet on one, database on another, and a macro library on a third. Using separate worksheets helps you avoid accidentally deleting or overwriting data when you delete a column or row or move and copy data from one part of the worksheet to another. Another valuable use for multiple worksheets is for "what if" applications. If you want to play out different business scenarios by changing a few assumptions within an original worksheet, you can copy a single worksheet to many other worksheets, change assumptions on each, and create graphs to show the results of each change.

The 1-2-3 "Electronic" Accountant's Pad

1-2-3 Release 3, as well as earlier versions, can be described as an electronic accountant's pad or electronic spreadsheet. When you start 1-2-3 Release 3, your computer screen displays a column/row area into which you can enter text, numbers, or formulas as an accountant would on one sheet of a columnar pad (and with the help of a calculator). The multiple worksheet and file capability of Release 3 extends this analogy further. Although Release 1, 1A, and 2.01 each can be thought of as a single, large spreadsheet, Release 3 provides you with multiple sheets and multiple pads with data accessible instantly (see fig. 1.1).

Fig. 1.1.
The new multiple worksheet capability offered in 1-2-3 Release 3.

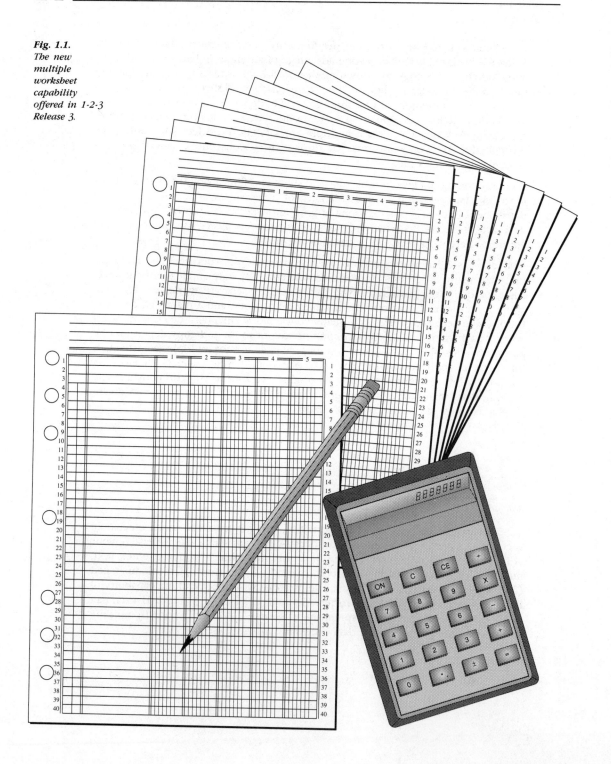

Release 3 frees you from the limitations and inconveniences of the single worksheet available with previous versions of 1-2-3. Release 2.01 gives users a single 256-column by 8,192-row grid on which to work. Of course, only a small part of this worksheet can be seen at any one time. Organizing applications on such a large grid can be very cumbersome. When you create multiple worksheets in Release 3, one behind another, you can easily page through, using special combinations of the keys on your keyboard, and view three consecutive worksheets on-screen at one time. Depending on the amount of memory in your machine, you can add up to 255 worksheets behind (or in front of) the original worksheet that appears on-screen when you first start 1-2-3.

With Release 3, as with earlier versions of 1-2-3, the worksheet is the basis for the whole product. Whether you are working with a database application or creating graphs, both are done within the structure of the worksheet. All commands are initiated from the main menu that appears above the border containing row numbers at the top of your screen (see fig. 1.2). Graphs are created from data entered in the worksheet; database operations are performed on data organized into the worksheet's column/row format, and macro programs are stored down a column of the worksheet.

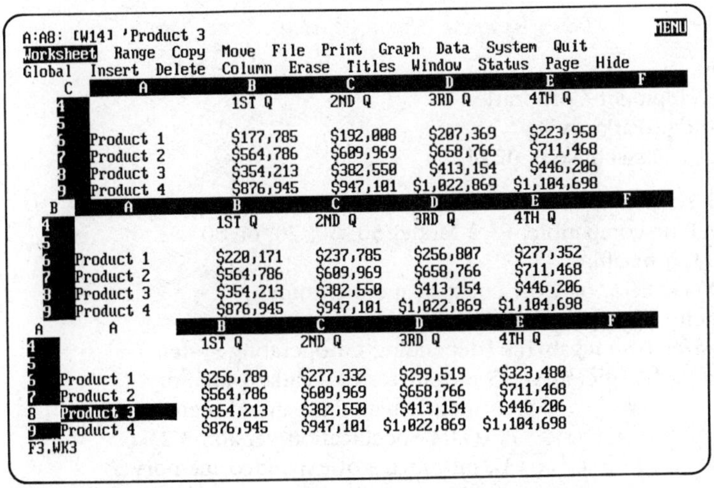

```
A:A8: [W14] 'Product 3                                              MENU
Worksheet Range Copy  Move  File  Print  Graph  Data  System  Quit
Global  Insert Delete Column Erase Titles Window Status Page Hide
    C        A              B          C          D          E          F
4                        1ST Q      2ND Q      3RD Q      4TH Q
5
6          Product 1     $177,785   $192,008   $207,369   $223,958
7          Product 2     $564,786   $609,969   $658,766   $711,468
8          Product 3     $354,213   $382,558   $413,154   $446,286
9          Product 4     $876,945   $947,101 $1,022,869 $1,104,698
    B        A              B          C          D          E          F
4                        1ST Q      2ND Q      3RD Q      4TH Q
5
6          Product 1     $220,171   $237,785   $256,807   $277,352
7          Product 2     $564,786   $609,969   $658,766   $711,468
8          Product 3     $354,213   $382,558   $413,154   $446,286
9          Product 4     $876,945   $947,101 $1,022,869 $1,104,698
    A        A              B          C          D          E          F
4                        1ST Q      2ND Q      3RD Q      4TH Q
5
6          Product 1     $256,789   $277,332   $299,519   $323,480
7          Product 2     $564,786   $609,969   $658,766   $711,468
8          Product 3     $354,213   $382,558   $413,154   $446,286
9          Product 4     $876,945   $947,101 $1,022,869 $1,104,698
F3.WK3
```

Fig. 1.2.
The main 1-2-3 command menu at the top of the screen.

All data—text, numbers, or formulas—are stored in individual cells in the worksheet. 1-2-3 sets aside a rectangular area, its location indicated by the intersection of a particular column and row on the worksheet. If you type a number in the cell two rows down from the top border and three columns to the left of the lefthand border, you are entering the number in cell C2 (see fig. 1.3). Columns in the worksheet are marked by letters from A to IV; rows are marked by numbers from 1 to 8,192. If you decide to open two or more worksheets, a cell is further identified by a letter prefix indicating which worksheet the cell is on. A is the first worksheet in the stack, B the second, C the third, and so on.

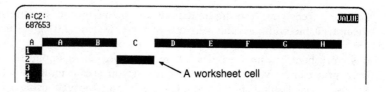

Fig. 1.3.
A 1-2-3
worksheet cell.

As you are working in the worksheet, 1-2-3 indicates in which cell you can enter data by highlighting the cell; this highlighting is referred to as the *cell pointer*. You change the highlight or move the cell pointer by using the cursor keys on your computer's keyboard (see Chapter 3 for more information on moving the cell pointer). Potentially, you could fill more than 2,000,000 cells in a single worksheet and 256 worksheets in a file. Most likely, few users will need or have computer equipment to handle this much data. At the minimum, though, Release 3 requires one megabyte of memory in your computer and requires that you have a computer with an 80286 or 80386 microprocessor. See table 1.1 for a complete list of 1-2-3 Release 3 specifications.

Table 1.1
1-2-3 Release 3 at a Glance

Published by:
    Lotus Development Corporation
    55 Cambridge Parkway
    Cambridge, Massachusetts 02142

System Requirement:
    IBM PC AT or compatible, PS/2 Model 50, 60, 70, or 80
    80286/80386 machine
    Display: VGA, EGA, or CGA color or monochrome
    Disk capacity: 5 megabytes
    Memory size: 1-3 megabytes (depending on operating system)
    Maximum usable memory: 15 megabytes of standard memory
                            8 megabytes of expanded memory
                                (LIM Specification version 3.2)
                            32 megabytes of expanded memory
                                (LIM Specification version 4.0)
    Operating System: DOS 3.0 or later or OS/2 1.0 or 1.1
    Other hardware: color/graphics adapter, printer, plotter,
                            expanded   memory,   80287   or   80387
                            math
                            microprocessor, hard disk

Price: $495

Creating Formulas

Because the primary use of 1-2-3 is financial applications, 1-2-3's capability to develop formulas is one of its most sophisticated and yet easy to use features. You can create a formula that is as simple as adding the values in two cells on the same worksheet:

    +A1+B1

This formula entered in another cell, such as C1, indicates that the value stored in cell A1 will be added to the value stored in B1. The formula does not depend on the specific values contained in A1 and B1, but adds whatever values are entered. If A1 originally contains the value 4 and B1 the value 3, the formula computes to 7. If you change the value in A1 to 5, the formula automatically recalculates to 8.

You can create formulas with *operators*—addition (+), subtraction (−), multiplication (*), and division (/). The capability of 1-2-3 Release 3 formulas, however, is best illustrated by linking data across worksheets and across files. By referencing cells in other worksheets and other files, formulas can calculate results from numerous, separate worksheet applications. When you create a formula linking data across worksheets, you first indicate what worksheet the data is located in (indicated by a letter A through IV); then you follow this letter with a colon (:) and enter the cell. The following example shows a formula linking data across three worksheets:

    +A:B3+B:C6+D:B4

If the formula links data across files, the file name is entered in the formula. The following formula is an example:

    +A:C6+<<SALES1.WK3>>A:C5

See Chapter 3 for more information on creating formulas that link data across files.

Playing "What If"

Because 1-2-3 remembers the relationships between cells and does not simply calculate values, you can change a value in a cell and see what happens when your formulas automatically recalculate. This "what if" capability makes 1-2-3 an incredibly powerful tool for many types of analysis. You can, for example, analyze the effect of an expected increase in cost of goods and determine what kind of product price increases may be needed to maintain your current profit margins.

With Release 3's multiple worksheet capability, you can play "what if" by creating a series of worksheets and accompanying graphs showing the effects of certain changes from one worksheet to another. One worksheet, for example, might show the effect of an increase of cost of goods without an accompanying increase in product price. Another worksheet might show the expected effect of special advertising or product promotion. You can easily create such a series of "what if" worksheets by simply copying the data on one worksheet to others and then changing each worksheet as needed to test various assumptions.

Release 3 Functions

Without the capabilities to calculate complex mathematical, statistical, logical, financial, and other types of formulas, building applications in 1-2-3 would be quite difficult. 1-2-3 Release 3, however, provides 108 functions that let you create complex formulas for a wide range of applications, including business, scientific, and engineering applications. Instead of entering complicated formulas containing numerous operators and parentheses, you can use functions as a shortcut to creating such formulas. All functions in 1-2-3 begin with the @ sign followed by the name of the function—for example, @SUM, @RAND, @ROUND. Many functions require that you enter an *argument*, the specifications the function needs to calculate the formula, after the function name.

Release 3 includes seven categories of functions: (1) mathematical and trigonometric, (2) statistical, (3) financial and accounting, (4) logical, (5) special, (6) date and time, and (7) string.

Mathematical Functions

The mathematical functions, which include logarithmic and trigonometric functions, provide convenient tools that let you easily perform a variety of standard arithmetical operations such as adding and rounding values or calculating square roots. For engineering and scientific applications, 1-2-3 includes all standard trigonometric functions, such as those to calculate sine @SIN, cosine @COS, and tangent @TAN.

Statistical Functions

1-2-3 Release 3 includes a set of 10 statistical and 11 database statistical functions that allow you to perform all the standard statistical calculations on your worksheet data or in a 1-2-3 database. You can find minimum and maximum values (@MIN and @MAX), calculate averages (@AVG), and compute standard deviations and variances (@STD and @VAR). Database statistical functions are specialized versions of the statistical functions that apply only to 1-2-3 databases.

Financial Functions

One of the most used categories of functions is financial functions. These functions allow you to perform a series of discounted cash flow, depreciation, and compound-interest calculations that ease considerably the burden and tediousness of investment analysis and accounting or budgeting for depreciable assets. Specifically, the 1-2-3 Release 3 functions include two that calculate returns on investments—@IRR and @RATE; one function that calculates loan investments—@PMT; two functions for calculating present values—@NPV and @PV; one function that calculates future values—@FV; two functions that perform compound-growth calculations—@TERM and @CTERM; and four functions that calculate asset depreciation—@SLN, @DDB, @SYD, and @VDB.

Logical Functions

The logical functions let you add standard Boolean logic to your worksheet and use the logic either alone or as part of other worksheet formulas. Essentially, each of the logical functions allows you to test whether a condition—either one you've defined or one of 1-2-3's predefined conditions—is true or false. The @IF function, for example, tests a condition and returns one result if the condition is true and another if the condition is false.

Special Functions

Special functions are tools for dealing with the worksheet itself. For example, one special function returns information about specific cells. Others count the number of row, columns, or worksheets in a range. For example, @CELL and @CELLPOINTER can return up to nine different characteristics of a cell, including the type of address and prefix, format, and width of a cell. @COORD specifies a cell address as absolute, relative, or mixed. @INFO lets you retrieve system-related information. The Special functions are often used in macro programs.

Date and Time Functions

The date and time functions allow you to convert dates, such as June 7, 1989, and times, such as 11:00 a.m., to serial numbers and then use these serial numbers to perform date and time arithmetic. These functions are a valuable aid when dates and times affect worksheet calculations and logic. Date and time functions are also useful for documenting your worksheets and printed reports. For example, you can enter at the beginning of your worksheet date and time functions that display the current date and time. If you include the cells containing these functions in your print range when you print a report, the report will show the exact date and time you prepared the report for printing.

String Functions

String functions help you manipulate text. You can use string functions to repeat text characters, to convert letters in a string to upper- or lowercase, and to change strings to numbers and numbers to strings. You can also use string functions to locate or extract characters and replace characters.

Using the 1-2-3 Release 3 Command Menu

The worksheet is the basis for all applications you create, modify, and print in 1-2-3. Into your worksheet cells, you enter data in the form of text, numbers, and formulas; one single main command menu lets you format, copy, move, print, create a graph from, and perform database operations on this data. In addition to the activities accessed by the main command menu, 1-2-3 provides menu commands that allow you to save and retrieve your worksheet as a file on disk, manage and change these files, and read files in formats different from a 1-2-3 worksheet file format. Still another command on the main 1-2-3 menu lets you temporarily leave a worksheet, return to the operating system, and then return to your original worksheet location.

The commands in the main menu lead to many sublevels of commands, in total approximately 800 commands. Some commands you will use frequently whenever you create or modify a worksheet application. Other commands, such as specialized database commands, you may rarely or never use. The following sections briefly introduce the commands you will probably use most frequently—those commands related to creating and modifying worksheet applications.

Understanding the 1-2-3 worksheet structure and the effect of certain commands on the worksheet is the first step in using 1-2-3 successfully for your applications. When you begin to investigate the 1-2-3 command menu, you will find that some commands affect a whole, single worksheet. And if you have multiple worksheets and want these commands to affect not just one but all, you need to use a special command, /Worksheet Global Group, before using the other command. If you want, for example, to widen all columns on one worksheet, you use the /Worksheet Global Col-Width command. If you want to widen all columns on every worksheet in your file, you first use /Worksheet Global Group and then use /Worksheet Global Col-Width.

Other commands in the 1-2-3 main menu affect only a portion or block of cells in your worksheet, referred to as a *range*. This range can be as small as a single cell or as large as thousands of cells, all contained on the same worksheet or spanning an area that stretches across multiple worksheets. Multiple cell ranges are always a contiguous block of cells, either square or rectangular in shape. One of the commands in the main 1-2-3 menu, the /Range command, affects only a designated cell or rectangular block of cells in your worksheet. As a beginning 1-2-3 user, you'll need to keep in mind whether you want a command to affect a single worksheet, all worksheets at once, or just a specific range.

Using Worksheet Commands

/Worksheet, the first command on the main 1-2-3 command menu, leads to those options that affect either the whole worksheet or columns and rows on the worksheet. With /Worksheet commands, you can change the way numbers and formulas appear on a single worksheet or multiple worksheets—in percentage format, in currency format, in comma format, and so on. Other commands that affect the overall worksheet include those for inserting and deleting columns, rows, or individual worksheets in a file containing multiple worksheets. The /Worksheet menu provides a command that lets you clear the current file from your screen and computer memory, and replaces the screen with a new, clean worksheet. You can also hide a worksheet or worksheets to keep data confidential or from printing on a report.

Some /Worksheet commands let you change the way data and graphs appear on-screen. You can, for example, freeze certain columns or rows so that they remain on-screen even though you move the cell pointer to other areas of the worksheet. You can also split your screen and display two areas of the worksheet at one time or split the screen so that worksheet data is displayed on the left side and a graph on the right. Finally, /Worksheet also gives you a status report displaying such information as how much memory is available for you to use and what settings are in effect for the worksheet.

Using Range Commands

Apart from the commands for copying and moving data from one area of the worksheet to another or from one worksheet to another, one other command, /Range, on the main 1-2-3 command menu affects single cells or a square/rectangular block of cells. Some /Range commands control the way data in one cell or block of cells appears on-screen and prints. You can, for example, change the way numbers and formulas are displayed, indicate whether you want text to be aligned to the left, right, or center of the cell, and justify the right margin of a block of text that spans down many rows of the worksheet. You can also change data from displaying in column format to row format and vice versa. /Range lets you protect certain areas of your worksheet so that you or other users do not accidentally change, erase, or overwrite data. If you want to erase data in one cell or block of cells, use /Range Erase.

One of the most useful /Range commands is a command that lets you attach a name to a single cell or block of cells. By naming a column of numbers, for example, you can create a formula that will total these numbers by simply entering the function @SUM followed in parentheses by its *range name*

—@SUM(QTR1). Range names are also useful for printing. Rather than having to define the exact cell boundaries for an area you want to print, you can give that area a name and enter the name when you are asked to indicate the part of the worksheet you want to print. Other uses for range names include naming parts of a single worksheet or naming parts of many worksheets so that you can easily move the cell pointer from one area to another. These are only a few of the many uses for range names. As you become accustomed to using range names, you'll find many occasions when they will simplify and save time as you create and use worksheet applications.

Copying and Moving Cell Entries

As indicated in the previous sections, /Worksheet and /Range are two of the most frequently used commands on the main 1-2-3 menu. Two other commands, however, are also commonly used for creating and modifying worksheet applications. These commands, /Copy and /Move, allow you, as their names indicate, to copy and move data from one cell or a block of cells to another on the same worksheet or from one cell or a block of cells to another worksheet.

The /Copy command will save you hours of time by letting you duplicate text, numbers, divider and formatting lines, and formulas. Copying formulas is one of the most important functions of this command. You can create a few key formulas and then copy these formulas to other parts of the worksheet where they will calculate values different from those that the original formula calculates.

When you use /Move, you can move not only the contents of one cell to another but the contents of a large block of cells to another area of the worksheet or another worksheet. Moving a large block is simply done by issuing the /Move command and then highlighting the cells you want to move and indicating the top left cell where you want the data to be located.

1-2-3 File Management

The type of file you will create most often when using 1-2-3 Release 3 is a worksheet file. This type of file saves all the data, formulas, and text you've entered into a worksheet and also saves such things as the format of cells, the alignment of text, names of ranges, and settings for ranges that are protected. Saved as Release 3 files, these files are stored with a .WK3 extension. Worksheet files can also have a .BAK extension, indicating that a backup file is saved on disk. A .WK1 extension indicates that the file is a Release 2 or 2.01 worksheet. Four other types of files may be created in 1-2-3 Release 3: text files denoted by a .PRN extension, encoded print-image files denoted by an .ENC extension, graph-image files denoted by a .PIC extension, and files in graphic metafile graph-image format denoted by a .CGM extension.

One of the commands on the main 1-2-3 command menu lets you perform most of the file operations you need when creating and using worksheet applications. The /File command provides a wide range of file management, modifications, and protection capabilities. Some of these commands are similar to your operating system commands, such as those that enable you to erase or list files. Other commands relate to specific 1-2-3 tasks and applications. You can, for example, combine data from several files, extract data from one file to another file, and open more than one file in memory at a time. You can also "reserve" a file so that only one user is permitted to write information to and update the file. This /File command is particularly important for those who are using 1-2-3 Release 3 on a network.

In addition to the options for managing, modifying, and protecting files available in the main 1-2-3 command menu, the Translate utility lets you "translate" several file formats that differ from the 1-2-3 worksheet file format. You can, for example, convert files from the following programs and read them into 1-2-3 Release 3: dBASE II, III, and III Plus; DisplayWrite, Manuscript, Multiplan, and files in DIF format. You can also convert Release 3 files to formats that can be read by 1-2-3 Release 1A, 2, and 2.01; dBASE II, III, and III Plus, DisplayWrite, Manuscript, Multiplan, and programs that use the DIF format. You do not need to use the Translate utility to read worksheet files created by 1-2-3 Release 1A, 2, and 2.01 and Symphony 1, 1.01, 1.1, 1.2, and 2.

File and Worksheet Protection

In addition to Release 3's command that lets you assign "reservation" status to a file, 1-2-3 Release 3 allows you to assign a password to a file so that file retrieval is restricted to only those with that password. You may, however, want to give other users access to a file but restrict their ability to make changes or delete, intentionally or unintentionally, data in the application. The /Worksheet Global Prot and /Range Prot commands allow you to "lock" areas of your worksheet from any change. See Chapter 4 for more information on /Worksheet Global Prot and /Range Prot.

1-2-3 Graphics

When 1-2-3 was first introduced, business users quickly recognized the advantages of being able to analyze worksheet data as instant graphs produced by the same worksheet program. 1-2-3 Release 3 lets you create seven types of graphs: line, bar, XY, stacked-bar, pie, high-low-close-open, and mixed (a bar graph overlaid with a line graph) graphs. Depending on how data is organized in your worksheet, 1-2-3 can create a graph automatically. If you position the cell pointer within the matrix of data in consecutive columns and rows, 1-2-3 will create a graph automatically from the data when you press the Graph (F10) key. You can also create a graph automatically by using the /Graph Group command and high-lighting a range of data.

Beyond creating a simple graph, 1-2-3 /Graph commands let you enhance and customize graphs for your needs. You can, for example, add titles and notes, label data points, change the format of values displayed on a graph, create a grid, and change the scaling along the x- or y-axes. By naming the settings you have entered to create a graph and saving this name, you can redisplay the graph whenever you access the file in the future. You can also use graph names to print graphs from the 1-2-3 /Print menu.

Although earlier 1-2-3 releases provided the necessary tools for analyzing data in graph form, these previous versions were primitive in their capability to produce high quality graphs on-screen and in printed form. Release 3 greatly improves on the screen and printed quality of graphs by supporting the most advanced moni-tor adapters as well as supporting high quality printers. Depending on your moni-tor, you can now view graphs either in full screen view or in combination with the 1-2-3 worksheet. The quality of Release 3 graphs is also improved through new options that let users change type font and size, color, and hatch patterns. Printing graphs in Release 3 is done through the /Print menu, the menu you also use to print worksheet data. Unlike Release 2.01, Release 3 does not require that you use a separate PrintGraph program.

1-2-3 Database Management

The column-row structure used to store data in the 1-2-3 worksheet is similar to the structure of a relational database. 1-2-3 provides true database management commands and functions so that you can sort, query, extract, and perform statis-tical analysis on data, and even access and manipulate data from an external database. One important advantage of 1-2-3's database manager over independent database programs is that its commands are similar to the other commands used in the 1-2-3 program. The user can, therefore, learn how to use the 1-2-3 database manager along with the rest of the 1-2-3 program.

Database Commands and Functions

After a database has been built in 1-2-3 (which is no different from building any other worksheet application), you can perform a variety of functions on the database. Some of these tasks can be accomplished with standard 1-2-3 com-mands. For example, records can be added to a database with the /wir (/Work-sheet Insert Row) command. Fields can be added with the /wic (/Worksheet Insert Column) command. Editing the contents of a database cell is as easy as editing any other cell; you simply move the cursor to that location, press Edit (F2) to call up the editor, and start typing.

Data can also be sorted. Sorts can be done on 1, 2, or up to 255 keys, in ascending or descending order, using alphabetic or numeric keys. In addition, various kinds of mathematical analyses can be performed on a field of data over a specified range of records. For example, you can count the number of items in a database that match a set of criteria; compute a mean, variance, or standard deviation; and find the maximum or minimum value in the range. The capacity to perform statistical analysis on a database is an advanced feature for database management systems on any microcomputer.

Other database operations require database commands, such as /dqu (/Data Query Unique) and /dqf (/Data Query Find). A 1-2-3 database can be queried in several ways. After specifying the criteria on which you are basing your search, you can ask the program to point to each selected record in turn, or to extract the selected records to a separate area of the worksheet. You can also ask the program to delete records that fit your specified criteria.

Several commands help the user make inquiries and clean the data of duplications. All of these commands are subcommands of the /dq (/Data Query) command. These commands require that the user specify one or more criteria for searching the database. The criteria refer to a field in the database and set the conditions that data must meet in order to be selected.

1-2-3 allows a great deal of latitude in defining criteria. As many as 256 cells across, each containing multiple criteria, can be included in the criteria range. Criteria can include complex formulas as well as simple numbers and text entries. Two or more criteria in the same row are considered to be joined with an *and*. Criteria in different rows are assumed to be combined with an *or*. Criteria can also include "wild-card" characters that stand for other characters.

1-2-3 also has a special set of statistical functions that operate only on information stored in the database. Like the query commands, the statistical functions use criteria to determine on which records they will operate.

The following database functions are supported: @DCOUNT, @DGET, @DSUM, @DAVG, @DSTD, @DSTDS, @DMAX, @DMIN, @DQUERY, @DVAR, and @DVARS. These functions perform essentially the same tasks as their spreadsheet counterparts. For example, @DMIN finds the minimum number in a given range. @DCOUNT counts all the nonzero entries in a range. @DSTD computes the standard deviation of the items in the range. @DQUERY selects a record from an external database.

The combination of these functions and 1-2-3's database commands makes this program a capable data manager. 1-2-3's data management capabilities, however, do not put the program in competition with more sophisticated database languages such as dBASE III Plus, dBASE IV, or R:BASE. These programs use a database language to translate the user's requests to the computer. By comparison, 1-2-3's data management is fairly simple. (1-2-3's data management capabilities are covered in detail in Chapter 10.)

Using the /Data Table Command

One of the most useful, but most misunderstood, commands in 1-2-3's menu of /Data commands is /Data Table. A data table is simply a way to look at all the outcomes of a set of conditions without having to enter each set into the equation manually. The command simply allows you to build a table that defines the formula you want to evaluate and contains all the values you want to test. A data table is similar to the X-Y decision grids you probably built as a math student in high school.

You can use the /Data Table command to structure a variety of "what if" problems. It can also be combined with 1-2-3's database and statistical functions to solve far more complex problems. (Chapter 10 explains in detail the /Data Table command and gives examples that will help you master this powerful tool.)

Multiple Regression and Simultaneous Equations

1-2-3's multiple regression command significantly expands the program's capabilities for statistical analysis. If you use regression analysis, the regression command could save you the cost of a stand-alone statistical package. For business applications, the /Data Regression command probably will meet all your regression analysis needs.

A /Data Matrix command can be used to solve systems of simultaneous equations. This capability, although likely to be of greater interest to scientific and engineering users, is available to all.

Using the /Data External Command

One of the most significant single commands in Release 3 is the /Data External command. With this command, Lotus introduces many exciting possibilities that make accessing data from many types of external databases a simple process. When you use the options available after selecting /Data External, you can access tables located in an external database—a file created and maintained by a database program such as dBASE III. Using the /Data External command and accessing data from an external table is only possible if a special driver file exists, making the transference between the database and 1-2-3 possible. At the time Release 3 began shipping, one driver file for dBASE III was available and is included on your 1-2-3 software disks.

If the right driver file exists and a connection or link is established between 1-2-3 and an external database, you can perform the several tasks. First, you can find and manipulate data in the external database and then work with that data in your worksheet. Second, you can use formulas and database functions to perform calculations based on data in the external database. And third, you can create a new external database that contains data from your worksheet or from an existing external database. (See Chapter 10 for more information on the /Data External command.)

Printing Reports and Graphs

By using 1-2-3's /Print command, you can access several levels of print options that let you print worksheet data and graphs for either draft review or more formal presentation. With the /Print command, you can send data and graphs directly from 1-2-3 to the printer or save worksheet data in a text file so that the data can be incorporated in another program, such as a word processing program. You can also save data and graphs to a file format that retains your selected report enhancements (such as boldface type, underlining, and italic) so that you can print later with an operating system command.

Release 3 provides much more flexibility in printing reports. Unlike Release 2.01, Release 3 does not limit you to entering one type of print range—a contiguous block of cells on one worksheet. With Release 3, you can enter a single worksheet range to print, but you can also enter

- A range that spans multiple worksheets or files
- A series of noncontiguous ranges from the same worksheet or from different worksheets or files
- A range of worksheet data and a graph name so that the data and graph print together

The /Print menu in 1-2-3 gives you considerable control over the design of printed output—from simple one-page reports to longer reports that incorporate data from many worksheets and include graphs. Three types of commands are available from the /Print menu that affect how your report and graph will look when printed. One type of command in the /Print menu provides options for developing page-layout features—setting margins, indicating text for headers and footers, telling 1-2-3 to print certain column or row data on every page, setting the length of the page, or telling 1-2-3 whether you want data printed as displayed on-screen or printed in formula notation. A second type of /Print command lets you enhance your report by changing type size, character and line spacing, or printing in color. The third set of commands is used specifically for printing graphs, including commands for rotating the position of the graph on the page, changing the graph size, and printing in draft or final quality.

Besides the commands that affect how your report and graph look when printed, other commands give you greater control over the printing process and operation of your printer. If you want to reuse settings that you have entered to print a report, you can name these settings, save them with the file, and then recall them at a later time. You can also easily clear settings—all or only certain settings—and reenter new ones in their place. Release 3 lets you temporarily stop the process of entering print settings, return to the worksheet to make a change, and then turn back to enter settings again, all without losing the initial settings.

For greater printer control, 1-2-3 Release 3 lets you stop your printer to change paper, ribbon, or toner cartridge, for example, and then resume printing at the point where it stopped. Also, unlike prior releases of 1-2-3, Release 3 lets you cancel printing from the main /**P**rint menu. One of the major benefits of printing with Release 3 over printing with earlier releases of 1-2-3 is that as you start printing, you can return to work within the worksheet while the printing job runs in the background.

Keyboard Macros and Advanced Macro Commands

One of 1-2-3's most exciting features is its macro capability, which allows you to automate and customize 1-2-3 for your special applications. 1-2-3's macro and advanced macro command capability allow you to create, inside the 1-2-3 worksheet, user-defined programs that can be used for a variety of purposes. At the simplest level, these programs are typing alternative programs that reduce, from many to two, the number of keystrokes for a 1-2-3 operation. At a more complex level, 1-2-3's advanced macro commands give the user a full-featured programming capability.

Release 3 makes creating macros much easier than creating macros in Release 2.01. With Release 3, you can use a record mode to record automatically a series of keystrokes. These keystrokes can then be copied to the worksheet as macros. In addition to naming a macro with the backslash (\) and a single letter as in Release 2.10, Release 3 lets you name a macro with a name consisting of up to 15 characters.

Whether you use 1-2-3's programming capability as a typing alternative or as a programming language, you'll find that it can simplify and automate many of your 1-2-3 applications. When you create typing-alternative macros, you group together and name a series of normal 1-2-3 commands, text, or numbers. After you have named a macro or advanced macro command program, you can activate its series of commands and input data by pressing two keys—the Alt key and a letter key—or by accessing a menu to select the macro name.

The implications for such typing-alternative macros are limited only by 1-2-3's capabilities. For example, typing the names of months as column headings is a task frequently performed in budget building. This task can be easily turned into a 1-2-3 macro, thereby reducing multiple keystrokes. A macro program in 1-2-3 can be structured to make decisions when the program is executed. These decisions can be based either on values found in the worksheet or on input from the user at the time the sequence is executed. By combining the typing-alternative features of 1-2-3's macro capability with the advanced macro commands, you can cause the program to pause and wait for user input.

When you begin to use 1-2-3's sophisticated advanced macro commands, you'll discover the power available for your special applications of 1-2-3. For the application developer, the advanced macro commands are much like a programming language (such as BASIC), but the programming process is simplified significantly by all the powerful features of 1-2-3's spreadsheet, database, and graphics commands. Whether you want to use 1-2-3 to create typing alternative macros or to program, Chapters 11 and 12 give you the information you need to get started.

1-2-3 Hardware Requirements and Options

Because Release 3 is a total rewrite of the 1-2-3 program and contains many features not included in prior versions, Release 3 places more demands on computer hardware than any versions of 1-2-3 previously written. In determining whether your system can (or what type of system you need to) run Release 3, five factors should be considered:

1. The type of architecture used by the computer

2. The type of microprocessor used by the computer

3. The amount of random access memory (RAM) in your computer

4. The amount of available memory on the computer's hard disk

5. The type of operating system under which you plan to run Release 3

The following sections explain the specific requirements for each of these five items needed to run Release 3.

Release 3 Operating System and Hardware Requirements

Because of the required system architecture by Release 3, many users will find their current systems unable to run Release 3. Also, much more memory is required than is required for previous versions. Simply stated, the basic hardware requirements for running Release 3 are virtually the same as those for running OS/2. In fact, OS/2 allows Release 3 to run most efficiently and with the highest performance. Many users, however, will hesitate changing operating systems from DOS to OS/2. With this in mind, Lotus provides Release 3 with a DOS-extender program that enables you to run Release 3 under conventional DOS and eliminates the requirement of OS/2 as the operating system.

The specific hardware requirements to run Release 3 are the same if you plan to run the program under OS/2 or DOS. At minimum, you need an AT-type system (a computer with an 80286 microprocessor). The amount of memory your machine needs to run Release 3, however, differs slightly depending on whether you are running the program under OS/2 or DOS.

The minimum requirements for running Release 3 under OS/2 include the following:

> System with AT-type architecture (80286)
> 1.5 to 2.5M of memory (all memory must be conventional or
>   extended)
>   1.5 to 2.0M for OS/2 version 1.0
>   2.0 to 2.5M for OS/2 version 1.1
> 10 to 13M of free disk space
>   5M for OS/2 V1.0 or 8M for OS/2 V1.1
>   5M for 1-2-3 Release 3

The minimum requirements for running Release 3 under DOS include the following:

> System with AT-type architecture
> DOS V3.0 or higher
> 1.5M of memory or more (all memory must be conventional
>   or extended)
>   Total memory limits spreadsheet size
> 5M of free disk space

Release 3 will not run on a PC or XT-type system. Only four types of systems will run Release 3:

> Industry Standard Architecture (ISA) AT-type Bus
>   80286 CPU
>   80386 CPU
>
> PS/2 Micro Channel Architecture (MCA) Bus
>   80286 CPU (16-bit MCA)
>   80386 CPU (32-bit MCA)

Note that at the time this book was first printed, another type of architecture was announced—the Enhanced Industry Standard Architecture or EISA. Machines developed with this architecture are expected to run Release 3; however, as of the date of this first printing, no actual systems with this architecture exist.

Release 3 runs exactly the same on a system with an 80286 or an 80386 processor. The program makes no real distinction about which processor your system has, and no additional features are enabled for those who use the 80386 chip. The only advantages for 386-based systems include increased processing speed derived from the higher clock rates of the 80386 as well as greater efficiency in switching modes with the DOS-extender program.

A few PC or XT-type systems actually have an 80286 or 80386 processor for increased performance. These systems usually have one or more 8-bit slots of the same system bus design featured on the original IBM PC. This type of machine will not run OS/2 or any software designed to run OS/2 such as 1-2-3 Release 3. This type of system will also not run 1-2-3 Release 3 under DOS because this system cannot run in the protected mode of 80286 or higher, a requirement of running Release 3 with the DOS-extender.

Which Video Display Does Release 3 Support?

Release 3 supports all of the existing display systems available on the market today. These systems include the following:

    Monochrome Display Adapter (MDA)
    Color Graphics Adapter (CGA)
    Multicolor Graphics Array (MCGA)
    Enhanced Graphics Adapter (EGA)
    Video Graphics Array (VGA)

In addition, Release 3 supports the following other graphics products:

    Hercules Graphics Card
    Hercules Mono Graphics display Adapter Plus with Ram-Font
    Hercules InColor Card

Although Release 3 runs on a Monochrome Display Adapter (MDA), you cannot display graphics with such a system. What color display, though, is best for Release 3? Because a Video Graphics Array (VGA) system provides the best graphics resolution of the color adapters in the preceding list, it is the best choice for Release 3. Also, because VGA can display 25, 34, or 60 lines on-screen at one time, you can take advantage of Release 3's capability to toggle between different display modes. If you install 1-2-3 for two different modes, you can use a command to switch between, for example, the 25-line mode when needing large characters and overall clarity, and 60-line mode when you want to see a much larger area of your worksheet on-screen.

Which Printers Does Release 3 Support?

In the past, 1-2-3 did not provide much support for laser printers. With Release 3, however, you can use a laser printer to more of an advantage.

The following are some of the printers you can install in Release 3:

    Apple LaserWriter
    EPSON FX Series, MX-80
    Epson LQ, LQ 800/1000, LQ 1500, LQ 2500
    HP Deskjet

HP ThinkJet
HP LaserJet
HP LaserJet +, 500 +
HP LaserJet II
HP PaintJet
IBM Graphics Printer
IBM ProPrinter
IBM ProPrinter II/XL
IBM ProPrinter X24/XL24
IBM Quietwriter I, II, or III
NEC Pinwriter P5
OKIDATA Microline 84, 92, 93, 294
Toshiba 351 Series

Release 3 also supports other printer that are compatible with the preceding list. Simply select the compatible printer during installation.

Chapter Summary

1-2-3 Release 3 is the impressive successor in the line of releases of 1-2-3 that revolutionized computing during the 1980's. With its tremendous power and capability, 1-2-3 Release 3 will spawn a new revolution of computer users—businesses where the capabilities of 1-2-3 Release 3 will replace outdated software and machines, providing what many business until now depended on from mini and mainframe computers. With the ability to create and manipulate data across many worksheets, link data among files, and produce high quality graphics and printing, Release 3 will become the new standard of the 1990's.

This chapter has described in general terms the capabilities that make 1-2-3 Release 3 an impressive program. Turn now to the remaining chapters of the book and learn how to use Release 3 features quickly, easily, and productively.

Getting Started

This chapter helps you get started using 1-2-3 for the first time. If you are new to computers and are using DOS or OS/2 for the first time, several books published by Que Corporation can give you a basic introduction to your operating system. If you are using 1-2-3 with DOS, the *MS-DOS QuickStart* provides a visually oriented approach to learning MS-DOS. Other Que titles that can serve as a reference when learning DOS include *Using PC DOS*, 3rd Edition, and *MS-DOS User's Guide*, 3rd Edition, both by Chris DeVoney. If you are using 1-2-3 with the OS/2 operating system, refer to *Using OS/2* by Caroline Halliday, David Gobel, and Mark Minasi.

If you are familiar with 1-2-3 but new to Release 3, you may find the introductory material too basic. If you want to begin using the 1-2-3 worksheet immediately, first read through the tables in this chapter, and then skip to Chapter 3. The tables include important reference information new with Release 3.

This chapter covers the following topics:

- Starting and exiting 1-2-3
- Using the 1-2-3 Access System
- How 1-2-3 uses the computer keyboard
- How 1-2-3 uses the screen display
- Finding on-screen help
- Using the 1-2-3 Tutorial

The last section in this chapter presents information on the 1-2-3 Tutorial. Many first-time users find the Tutorial a helpful introduction to 1-2-3. If you are new to 1-2-3, you can use the Tutorial as you read through this book for the first time. If you have worked with 1-2-3, but are new to Release 3, parts of the Tutorial will be useful for you as well.

Before you begin, be sure that 1-2-3 is installed on your computer system. Follow the instructions in Appendix A to complete the installation for your system.

Starting 1-2-3 from the Operating System

Two different methods of starting 1-2-3 are available. You can start from within the 1-2-3 Access System or directly from the operating system: DOS or OS/2. Most users start directly from the operating system because this method is easier, faster, and uses less memory. Starting from the operating system is covered in the following sections. Starting from the 1-2-3 Access System is covered later in the chapter.

Starting 1-2-3

If you have installed 1-2-3 according to the directions in Appendix A, the 1-2-3 program will be in a subdirectory named \123R3.

To start 1-2-3 directly from the operating system, use the following steps:

1. Change to the drive on which you installed 1-2-3. In most systems, this is drive C, but you may have installed 1-2-3 on drive D, E, or another drive. If 1-2-3 is installed on drive C and drive C is not the current drive, type **C:** and press Enter.

2. Type **CD \123R3** and press Enter to change to the \123R3 directory.

3. Type **123** and press Enter to start 1-2-3.

To simplify this process, you can create a start-up batch file or add 1-2-3 to a start-up menu. You can use a text editor or word processor to create an unformatted or text file if you are creating a batch file. The specific instructions depend on the program and operating system you use. If you are using OS/2, follow the instructions in the documentation or in *Using OS/2* for adding a program to the Start Programs window.

The following steps illustrate one way to create a start-up batch file by using the DOS COPY command. In most systems, batch files are kept in a directory called \BATCH, \BIN, or \UTILITY. In some systems, the batch files are in the \DOS or the root directory. The following example uses the \BATCH directory.

1. Change to the directory in which you keep your batch files. Type **CD \BATCH** and press Enter.

2. Type **COPY CON 123R3.BAT** and press Enter.

3. Type **C:** (or the name of the drive on which you have installed 1-2-3), and then press Enter.

4. Type **CD \123R3** and press Enter.

5. Type **123** and press Enter.

6. Type **CD** and press Enter.

7. Press Ctrl-Z (hold down the Ctrl key and press Z).

After creating this batch file, you need only to type **123R3** and press Enter to start 1-2-3.

After you start 1-2-3, the registration screen appears for a few seconds while the program loads. Then a blank worksheet appears, and you are ready to start using 1-2-3.

Exiting 1-2-3

To exit 1-2-3, you must use the 1-2-3 command menu. 1-2-3 commands and their menus are explained extensively throughout the book. At this point, however, you need to know only how to access the main menu and to use one easy command.

To access the 1-2-3 command menu, press the slash (/) key. A menu containing 10 options appears across the top of the worksheet (see fig. 2.1). The **/Quit** option exits the worksheet and returns you to the operating system.

Cue:
Press the slash key (/) to access the command menu at the top of the screen.

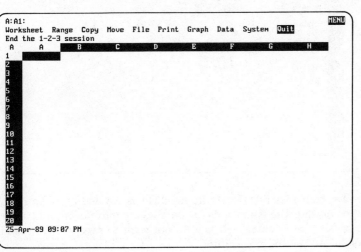

Fig. 2.1.
The 1-2-3 main command menu.

To select **/Quit**, use the right- and left-arrow keys to move the menu pointer or highlighter to **Quit**, and then press Enter. You must verify your choice before you exit 1-2-3. Unless you have saved them, all worksheet files and temporary settings are lost when you **/Quit** 1-2-3. To verify that you want to exit, move the highlighter to **Yes** and press Enter (see fig. 2.2). If you made changes to any worksheets and did not save them, 1-2-3 prompts you a second time to verify this choice before you exit (see fig. 2.3).

Caution:
Save your work before you /Quit the worksheet.

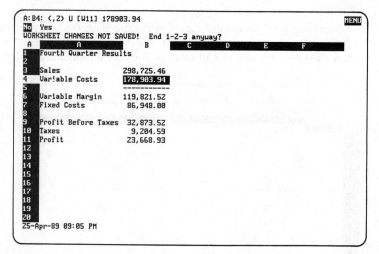

Fig. 2.2.
The
confirmation
prompt to quit
1-2-3.

Fig. 2.3.
The second
confirmation
prompt to quit
1-2-3.

If you want to save your files first, leave the highlight at No and press Enter to cancel the Quit command. The commands to save files are introduced in Chapter 4 and covered in detail in Chapter 7. If you do not want to save your files and want to quit, highlight Yes and press Enter.

Using the 1-2-3 Access System

The 1-2-3 Access System is a way to use menus to access not only the 1-2-3 worksheet but also to access the Install and Translate programs (see fig. 2.4).

Use the Install program to change any installation settings, such as the type of printer and display. (See Appendix A for a complete discussion of the Install program.) You use the Translate program to transfer files between 1-2-3 and other programs, such as dBASE II, III, and III Plus; Lotus Manuscript; programs that can read and write to the DIF format; and previous versions of 1-2-3 and Symphony. (See Chapter 7 for more information on the Translate program.)

Cue:
Appendix A
contains complete
installation
instructions.

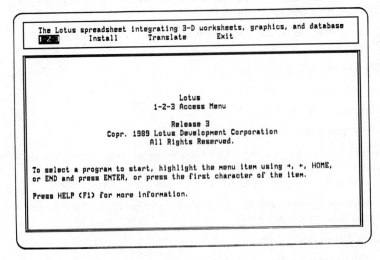

Fig. 2.4.
The 1-2-3
Access System
menu.

If you have installed 1-2-3 according to the directions in Appendix A, the 1-2-3 Access System will be in a subdirectory named \123R3.

Use the following steps to start the 1-2-3 Access System:

1. Change to the drive on which you installed 1-2-3. In most systems, this is drive C, but you may have installed 1-2-3 on drive D, E, or another drive. If 1-2-3 is installed on drive C and drive C is not the current drive, type **C:** and press Enter.

2. Type **CD \123R3** and press Enter to change to the \123R3 directory.

3. Type **LOTUS** and press Enter to start 1-2-3.

Notice that you type **LOTUS**, not **123**, even though the 1-2-3 Access System provides access only to 1-2-3, not to other Lotus products. (Originally, when Lotus sold only one product, this feature was called the Lotus Access System.)

Reminder:
*Type **LOTUS** to*
start the 1-2-3
Access System.

To simplify this process, you can create a start-up batch file or add 1-2-3 to a start-up menu. You can use a text editor or word processor to create an unformatted or text file if you are creating a batch file. The specific instructions depend on the program and operating system you use. If you are using OS/2, follow the instructions in the documentation or in *Using OS/2* for adding a program to the Start Programs window.

The following steps illustrate one way to create a start-up batch file by using the DOS COPY command. In most systems, batch files are kept in a directory called

\BATCH, \BIN, or \UTILITY. In some systems, the batch files are in the \DOS or the root directory. The following example uses the \BATCH directory.

1. Change to the directory in which you keep your batch files. Type **CD \BATCH** and press Enter.

2. Type **COPY CON LOTUS.BAT** and press Enter to name the batch file LOTUS.BAT. If you want to name the batch file ACCESS.BAT, type **COPY CON ACCESS.BAT** and press Enter.

3. Type **C:** (or the name of the drive on which you installed 1-2-3) and press Enter.

4. Type **CD \123R3** and press Enter.

5. Type **LOTUS** and press Enter.

6. Type **CD** and press Enter.

7. Press Ctrl-Z (hold down the Ctrl key and press Z).

After creating this batch file, you type **LOTUS** and press Enter from the DOS level to start the 1-2-3 Access System. If you have changed the batch-file name to **ACCESS.BAT** in Step 2, you type **ACCESS** to start the 1-2-3 Access System.

The 1-2-3 Access System command menu appears (see fig. 2.4). The command menu includes the following four options:

    1-2-3   Install   Translate   Exit

To select any of these options, highlight the menu entry and press Enter, or type the first letter of the menu entry.

Starting and Exiting 1-2-3 from the 1-2-3 Access System

The first option in the 1-2-3 Access System menu, **1-2-3**, starts 1-2-3. When the menu appears, the highlighter is on this option. To select the option, press Enter. If you have moved the highlighter to another option, use the right- and left-arrow keys to return to the first option, and then press Enter. After you start 1-2-3, the registration screen appears for a few seconds while the program loads. A blank worksheet appears, and you are ready to start using 1-2-3.

To exit the 1-2-3 program, press the slash (/) key to access the 1-2-3 main command menu. Use the right- and left-arrow keys to move the highlighter to the /Quit option, and then press Enter. You must verify this choice before you exit 1-2-3; when you /Quit 1-2-3, all worksheet files and temporary settings are lost unless you have saved them. To verify that you want to exit, move the highlighter to **Yes** and press Enter. If you made changes to any worksheets and did not save them, 1-2-3 prompts you a second time to verify this choice before you exit. To verify that you want to exit, move the highlighter to **Yes** again and press Enter.

If you have started 1-2-3 from the Access System, you return to the 1-2-3 Access System menu (see fig. 2.4) when you choose **Quit**. To exit the 1-2-3 Access System and return to the operating system, choose **Exit**.

Using the Install Program

Choose **Install** from the 1-2-3 Access Menu to access the Install program, which you can use to change the options you set during the initial installation. Complete installation instructions are found in Appendix A. You can run Install to prepare 1-2-3 for a different display or printer.

You can access up to two displays and up to 16 printers and plotters from within 1-2-3, but you must first use Install to tell 1-2-3 that these devices are available.

When you choose the **Install** option, you may be asked to place one or more of the driver or font disks into drive A to continue. Follow the prompts and insert any disks requested; then press Enter to continue the Install process.

You can go directly from the operating system to Install without using the 1-2-3 Access System. To start Install directly from the operating system, follow these steps:

1. Change to the drive on which you installed 1-2-3. In most systems, this is drive C, but you may have installed 1-2-3 on drive D, E, or another drive. If 1-2-3 is installed on drive C and drive C is not the current drive, type **C:** and press Enter.

2. Type **CD \123R3** and press Enter.

3. Type **INSTALL** and press Enter.

Cue:
*Type **INSTALL** to start the Install program directly from the operating system.*

Using the Translate Program

Choose **Translate** from the 1-2-3 Access Menu to access the Translate program. The Translate utility provides a method to convert files so that they can be read by a different program. To execute Translate, you must copy the Translate file onto your hard disk by using the Install program. (See Appendix A for details.)

Cue:
Use Translate to exchange data among many different programs.

You can convert files *to* 1-2-3 Release 3 from the following programs:

dBASE II, III, and III Plus
DisplayWrite and Manuscript using the RFT/DCA format
Multiplan
Products that use the DIF format

You do not have to convert files from previous releases of 1-2-3 or Symphony. Release 3 can retrieve these files directly. See Chapter 7 for information about translating and accessing files from previous versions of 1-2-3 and Symphony.

You can convert files *from* 1-2-3 Release 3 to the following programs:

1-2-3 Release 1A, 2, and 2.01
Symphony Release 1, 1.01, 1.1, 1.2, 2
dBASE II, III, and III Plus
DisplayWrite and Manuscript using the RFT/DCA format
Products that use the DIF format

Warning:
When you translate data from one program to another, you can lose some information.

When you convert 1-2-3 Release 3 files to previous releases of 1-2-3 or Symphony, you lose some information if you use any features unique to Release 3, such as multiple-worksheet files or new functions such as @SUMPRODUCT. If you do not use features unique to Release 3, you do not need to translate the files. Just save the files with a .WK1 extension (see Chapter 7 for details). These files can be read directly into previous releases of 1-2-3 and Symphony.

You can go directly from the operating system to the Translate program without using the 1-2-3 Access System.

Cue:
*Type **TRANS** to start the Translate program directly from the operating system.*

To start Translate directly from the operating system, follow these steps:

1. Change to the drive on which you installed 1-2-3. In most systems, this is drive C, but you may have installed 1-2-3 on drive D, E, or another drive. If 1-2-3 is installed on drive C and drive C is not the current drive, type **C:** and press Enter.

2. Type **CD \123R3** and press Enter.

3. Type **TRANS** and press Enter.

Learning the 1-2-3 Keyboard

The most common configurations for keyboards on IBM and IBM-compatible personal computers are shown in figures 2.5, 2.6, and 2.7. The Enhanced Keyboard, shown in figure 2.7, is now the standard keyboard on all new IBM personal computers and most compatibles. Some compatibles, especially laptops, have different keyboards.

The keyboards are divided into four or five sections: the alphanumeric keys in the center, the numeric keypad on the right, and the function keys on the left or across the top. The special keys are found in various locations. The cursor-movement keys are found in a separate section on the Enhanced Keyboard only.

Most keys in the alphanumeric section match the keys on a typewriter, and most maintain their normal functions in 1-2-3. Several keys, however, take on new and unique functions or are not found on typewriter keyboards.

You use the keys on the numeric keypad (on the right side of the keyboard) to enter numbers or to move the cell pointer around the screen.

The function keys provide special actions. For example, they can be used to access 1-2-3's editing functions, to display graphs, and to call up help messages.

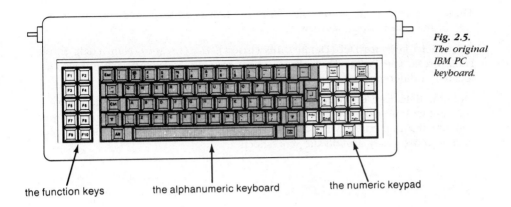

Fig. 2.5.
The original
IBM PC
keyboard.

the function keys   the alphanumeric keyboard   the numeric keypad

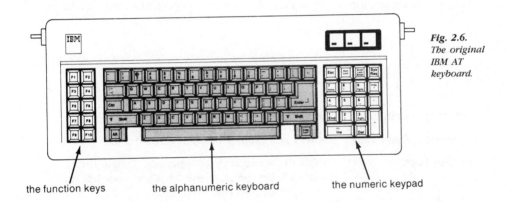

Fig. 2.6.
The original
IBM AT
keyboard.

the function keys   the alphanumeric keyboard   the numeric keypad

the function keys

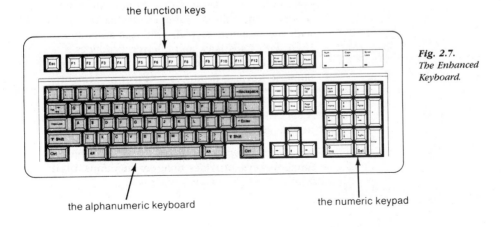

Fig. 2.7.
The Enhanced
Keyboard.

the alphanumeric keyboard   the numeric keypad

These keys are located across the top of the Enhanced Keyboard and on the left side of the other two keyboards.

The special keys are Del (Delete), Ins (Insert), Esc (Escape), Num Lock, Scroll Lock, Break, and Pause. These keys, which provide certain special actions, are located in different places on different keyboards.

Reminder:
With the Enhanced Keyboard, you can use the numeric keypad to enter numbers and the separate arrow keys to move around the worksheet.

Only the Enhanced Keyboard has a separate section for cursor-movement keys—the keys with up, down, left, and right arrows. With the Enhanced Keyboard, you can use the numeric keypad to enter numbers and use the cursor-movement keys to move easily around the worksheet.

The Alphanumeric Keyboard

Although most of the alphanumeric keys shown in figures 2.5, 2.6, and 2.7 have the same functions as on a typewriter, several keys have special functions in 1-2-3. These keys and their functions are listed in table 2.1. The meaning of these keys will become more clear as they are used and explained in later chapters.

Table 2.1
Alphanumeric Key Operation

Key	Function
⟶| (Tab)	Moves cell pointer one screen to the right
|⟵ (Shift-Tab)	Moves cell pointer one screen to the left
Caps Lock	Shifts the letter keys to uppercase. Unlike the shift-lock key on a typewriter, Caps Lock has no effect on numbers and symbols.
↑ (Shift)	Used with another key, shifts the character produced. Used with a letter, produces an uppercase letter. Used with a number or symbol, produces the shifted character on that key. Used with the numeric keypad, produces a number. Used with Caps Lock and a letter, produces a lowercase letter. Used with Num Lock and the numeric keypad, produces a cursor-movement key.
Ctrl	A special type of shift key. Used with several keys to change their functions.
Alt	An alternate type of shift key. Used with the function keys, provides different functions. Used with letter keys, invokes macros.

Key	Function
Backspace	During cell definition or editing, erases the preceding character. Cancels a range during some prompts that display the old range. Displays the previous help screen while using Help.
/ (slash)	Starts a command from READY mode. Used as the division sign while entering data or editing a formula in a cell.
< (less than sign)	Used as an alternate to the slash (/) to start a command from READY mode
. (period)	When used in a range address, separates the address of the cell at the beginning of the range from the address of the cell at the end of the range. In POINT mode, moves the anchor cell to another corner of the range.

The Numeric Keypad and the Cursor-Movement Keys

The keys in the numeric keypad on the right side of the IBM PC- and AT-style keyboards are used mainly for cursor movement (see figs. 2.5 and 2.6). With Num Lock off, these keys are used as movement keys. With Num Lock on, these keys serve as number keys. You can reverse the setting of Num Lock by holding down a Shift key before you press one of the numeric keys. The Enhanced Keyboard has separate keys for cursor movement (see fig. 2.7). The functions of the cursor-movement keys are explained in Chapter 3; the other special keys on the numeric keypad are discussed later in this chapter.

If you do not have an Enhanced Keyboard, you can use a macro to move the cell pointer every time you press Enter. You can then keep Num Lock on and use the numeric keypad to enter numbers. You can use different macros to move the cell pointer in different directions.

Cue:
Macros can solve numeric-keypad problems.

The Function Keys

The 10 function keys, F1 through F10 (see figs. 2.5, 2.6, and 2.7), are used for special actions in 1-2-3. These keys are located across the top of the Enhanced Keyboard and on the left side on the other two keyboards. The Enhanced Keyboard has 12 function keys, but 1-2-3 uses only the first 10. These keys may be used alone or with the Alt key. Table 2.2 lists the function keys and an explanation of each key's action.

Table 2.2
Function Key Operation

Key	Function
F1 (Help)	Accesses the on-line help facility
F2 (Edit)	Puts 1-2-3 into EDIT mode to change the current cell
F3 (Name)	Displays a list of names any time a command or formula can accept a range name or a file name. After @ is typed in a formula, displays a list of functions. After a left brace ({) is typed in a label, displays a list of macro names and advanced macro command keywords. Whenever a list of names is on the third line of the control panel, produces a full-screen display of all available names.
F4 (Abs)	Changes a cell or range address from relative to absolute to mixed
F5 (GoTo)	Moves the cell pointer to a cell address or range name
F6 (Window)	Moves the cell pointer to another window or worksheet when the screen is split
F7 (Query)	In READY mode, repeats the last /Data Query command. During a /Data Query Find, switches between FIND and READY mode.
F8 (Table)	Repeats the last /Data Table command
F9 (Calc)	In READY mode, recalculates all worksheets in memory. If entering or editing a formula, converts the formula to its current value.
F10 (Graph)	Displays the current graph if one exists. If no current graph exists, displays the data around the cell pointer.
Alt-F1 (Compose)	Creates international characters that cannot be typed directly using the keyboard
Alt-F2 (Record)	Allows you to save up to the last 512 keystrokes in a cell or to repeat a series of commands
Alt-F3 (Run)	Runs a macro
Alt-F4 (Undo)	Reverses the last action
Alt-F6 (Zoom)	Enlarges a split window to full size
Alt-F7 (App1)	Starts an LDE (Lotus Development Environment) application assigned to this key

Key	Function
Alt-F8 (App2)	Starts an LDE application assigned to this key
Alt-F9 (App3)	Starts an LDE application assigned to this key
Alt-F10 (Addin)	Accesses LDE applications

The Special Keys

The special keys provide some important 1-2-3 functions. For example, certain special keys cancel an action. Both Esc and Break cancel a menu. Also, Esc cancels an entry, and Break cancels a macro. The Del key deletes a character while editing a cell.

Some special keys change the actions of other keys. When you edit data in a cell, you can use the Ins key to change the mode from insert to overtype. Num Lock changes the meaning of the keys on the numeric keypad from movement keys to number keys. Scroll Lock changes how the arrow keys move the display. The functions and locations of the special keys on the different keyboards are listed in table 2.3.

Table 2.3
Special Key Operation

Key	Function
Break	Cancels a macro or cancels menu choices and returns to READY mode
	On the PC and AT keyboards, Break is Ctrl-Scroll Lock. On the Enhanced Keyboard, Break is Ctrl-Pause.
Del	While editing a cell, deletes one character at the cursor. In the Install program, reverses the selection of the highlighted display or printer choice.
Esc	When accessing the command menus, cancels the current menu and backs up to the previous menu. If at the main menu, returns to READY mode. When entering or editing data in a cell, clears the edit line. Cancels a range during some prompts that display the old range. Returns from the on-line help facility.
	On the original PC (see fig. 2.5), Esc is to the left of the 1 key in the alphanumeric section. On the AT style (see fig. 2.6), Esc is at the upper left of the numeric keypad. On the Enhanced Keyboard (see fig. 2.7), Esc is to the left of the F1 key.

Table 2.3—*Continued*

Key	Function
Ins	While editing a cell, changes mode to overtype. Any keystrokes replace whatever is at that cursor position in the cell. You toggle Ins to return to insert mode, and any keystrokes are inserted at the cursor position.
Num Lock	Shifts the actions of the numeric keypad from cursor-movement keys to numbers. On the PC and AT keyboards, Ctrl-Num Lock serves as the Pause key.
	On the original PC, Num Lock is at the upper left of the numeric keypad. On the AT style, Num Lock is next to Esc on the numeric keypad. On the Enhanced Keyboard, Num Lock is at the upper left of the numeric keypad.
Pause	Pauses a macro, a recalculation, and some commands until you press any key
	On the PC and AT keyboards, Pause is Ctrl-Num Lock. On the Enhanced Keyboard, Pause is a separate key to the right of Scroll Lock.
Scroll Lock	Scrolls the entire window when you use the arrow keys. On the PC and AT keyboards, Ctrl-Scroll Lock serves as the Break key.
	On the PC and AT keyboards, Scroll Lock is to the right of Num Lock on the numeric keypad. On the Enhanced Keyboard, Scroll Lock is to the right of the function keys.

Learning the 1-2-3 Screen Display

The main 1-2-3 display is divided into three parts: the control panel at the top of the screen, the worksheet area itself, and the status line at the bottom of the screen (see fig. 2.8). The reverse-video border marks the worksheet area. This border contains the letters and numbers that mark columns and rows.

The *cell pointer* marks the location of the current cell in the worksheet area. This is the intersection of a column and a row. When you enter data into the worksheet, the data goes into the location marked by the cell pointer.

A *file* is made up of 1 to 256 separate worksheets. More than one file can be in memory at one time. You can change the display to show multiple worksheets in two or three windows. These subjects are covered in later chapters. For now, the chapter looks at the display with one file and one worksheet in memory and one window.

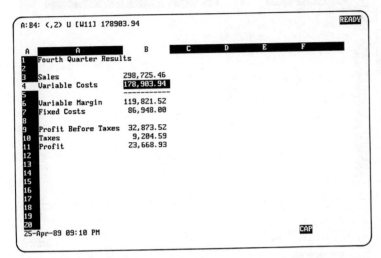

Fig. 2.8.
The control panel at the top of the display and the status line at the bottom.

The Control Panel

The three-line control panel is the area above the reverse-video border. The first line contains information about the current cell (see fig. 2.8). This information can include the address of the cell, the cell's contents, and the protection status (U if unprotected or PR if protected). The format and column width are included if different from the default; these attributes are explained in later chapters.

The cell's address is the worksheet, the column, and the row in the form A:B4 for worksheet A, column B, row 4 (see fig. 2.8). If the file contains only one worksheet, the worksheet is always A.

When you use the command menus, the second line displays the menu choices, and the third line contains explanations of the current command menu item or the next hierarchical menu (see fig. 2.9). As you move the pointer from one item to the next in a command menu, the explanation on the third line of the control panel changes. Compare the third line in figure 2.9 with the Worksheet command highlighted, and figure 2.1 with the Quit command highlighted.

When a command prompts you for information, the second line displays the prompt (see fig. 2.10). When a command prompts you for a file name, a range name, a graph name, or a print settings name, the third line displays the beginning of this list of names.

When you enter or edit data in a cell, the second line contains the data being entered or edited. When you enter or edit data that is too long to display on one line, the control panel area enlarges to accommodate the largest possible cell

Cue:
The third line of the command menu displays an explanation of the highlighted command or a preview of the next menu.

RELEASE 3

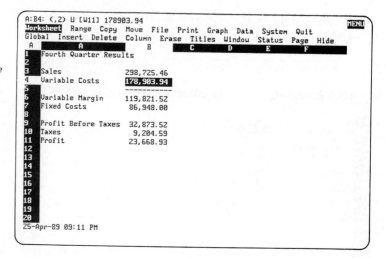

Fig. 2.9
The main menu with the Worksheet menu option highlighted.

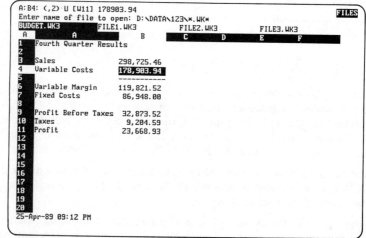

Fig. 2.10.
The display showing command prompts on the second line and lists of files or names on the third line.

entry, which is 512 characters. The worksheet area is pushed down to make room for the expanded control panel area (see fig. 2.11).

The Mode Indicators

The *mode indicator* is located in the upper-right corner of the control panel. This indicator tells you what mode 1-2-3 is in and what you can do next. When 1-2-3 is waiting for your next action, the mode indicator is READY (see fig. 2.12). Table 2.4 lists the mode indicators and their meanings.

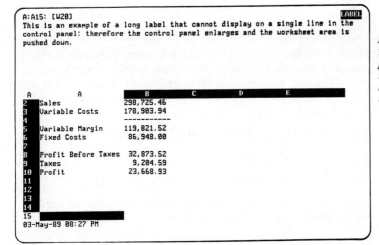

Fig. 2.11.
The control panel enlarged to accommodate the display of a long label.

Table 2.4
Mode Indicators

Mode	Description
EDIT	You are editing a cell entry.
ERROR	1-2-3 encountered an error, or you used Break to cancel a macro. Press Enter or Esc to clear the error message (located in the lower-left corner of the screen) and return to READY mode.
FILES	1-2-3 prompted you to select a file name from a list of files. Either type a file name or point to an existing file and press Enter.
FIND	1-2-3 is in the middle of a /Data Query Find operation.
HELP	You are in the Help facility. Press Esc to return to the worksheet.
LABEL	You are entering a label into a cell.
MENU	You are selecting command options from one of the command menus.
NAMES	1-2-3 prompted you to select a range name, graph name, print setting, database driver, external database, or an external table name, and then displayed a list of names. Either type an appropriate name or point to an existing name and press Enter.

RELEASE 3

Table 2.4—*Continued*

Mode	Description
POINT	Either 1-2-3 prompted you to select a range, or you used the cursor-movement keys to specify a range while entering a formula. Either type the cell coordinates or the name of the range, or highlight the range using the cursor-movement keys; then press Enter.
READY	1-2-3 is waiting for your next entry or command.
STAT	1-2-3 is displaying a status screen.
VALUE	You are entering a number or a formula into a cell.
WAIT	1-2-3 is in the middle of some activity. Do not proceed until the activity finishes and the WAIT indicator disappears.

Fig. 2.12. Several status indicators on the bottom line of the 1-2-3 display.

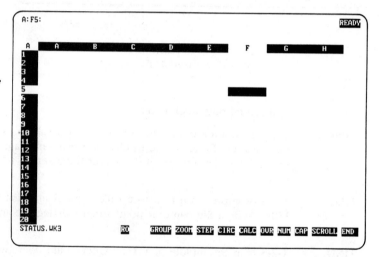

The Status Indicators

1-2-3 displays the *status indicators* in the middle and right side of the status line at the bottom of the display. These indicators give you various information about the state of the system. Each indicator displays in reverse video in a specific area (see fig. 2.12). These indicators and their meanings are listed in table 2.5.

Table 2.5
Status Indicators

Indicator	Description
CALC	If the CALC indicator is in white and is not flashing, the file is set to manual recalculation, and there has been a change since the last recalculation. Warns you that parts of the file may not be current. Press Calc (F9) to force a recalculation and clear this indicator.
	If the CALC indicator is in red on color monitors or is flashing on monochrome monitors, the file is set to automatic recalculation and is in the middle of a background recalculation. You can continue to work, but the values of some formulas may change during the recalculation.
CAP	You pressed Caps Lock. All letters are entered as uppercase. Press Caps Lock again to turn off the indicator.
CIRC	There is a circular reference in the worksheet. Use the /Worksheet Status command to find one of the cell addresses in the circular reference.
CMD	You are running a macro that has paused for input.
END	You pressed the End key with an arrow key to move across the worksheet.
FILE	You pressed Ctrl-End, the File key. When combined with an arrow key, the File key moves across multiple files in memory.
GROUP	You selected /Worksheet Global Group Enable to modify multiple worksheets in a file together.
MEM	You have less than 4,096 characters of memory left.
NUM	You pressed Num Lock. The keys on the numeric keypad now act as numbers, not cursor-movement keys. To use them as cursor-movement keys, press Num Lock again or hold down the Shift key.
OVR	You pressed Ins while editing a cell to change to overtype mode. Any keystrokes replace whatever is at that cursor position in the cell. Press Ins again to return to insert mode. Keystrokes are then inserted at the cursor position.
RO	The current file is read-only. The file can only be saved with a different name. Applies to files used on a network or multiuser system. Sometimes occurs if you run out of memory while reading a file.

Table 2.5—*Continued*

Indicator	Description
SCROLL	You pressed Scroll Lock. Whenever you use an arrow key, the entire window moves in the direction of the arrow. To use the arrow keys to move the cursor from cell-to-cell, press Scroll Lock again.
SST	You are executing a macro in single-step mode.
STEP	You turned on single-step mode for macros, but you are not currently running a macro. When you start a macro, this indicator changes to SST.
ZOOM	You used /Worksheet Window to split the screen into multiple windows, and then pressed Alt-F6 to enlarge the current window to fill the entire screen. To return the display to multiple windows, press Alt-F6 again.

The File and Clock Indicator

The lower-left corner of the screen shows the file name of the current file (see fig. 2.12). If you have just built the worksheet and you have never saved it, this area displays the date and time (see fig. 2.9).

The Error Messages Area

Cue:
If the mode indicator changes to ERROR, look at the lower-left corner of the screen for an error message.

When 1-2-3 encounters an error, the mode indicator changes to ERROR and an error message replaces the file or clock message in the lower-left corner of the screen (see fig. 2.13). Errors can be caused by many different situations. For example, you may have specified an invalid cell address or range name in response to a prompt or tried to retrieve a file that does not exist. Press Esc or Enter to clear the error and return to READY mode.

Using the 1-2-3 Help Features

1-2-3 includes features that provide help to users: the keyboard help facility and the 1-2-3 Tutorial.

1-2-3 provides on-line help at the touch of a key. You can be in the middle of any operation and press the Help (F1) key at any time to get one or more screens of explanations and advice on what to do next.

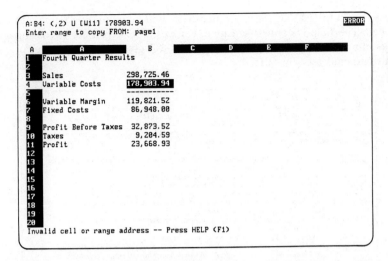

Fig. 2.13.
An error message displayed in the lower-left corner of the screen.

Lotus also includes in its documentation a printed Tutorial to help you learn 1-2-3. This self-paced instructional manual leads you through a series of actual 1-2-3 worksheets that use important features of the program.

Finding On-Screen Help

Press Help (F1) at any time to get to the on-line help facility. If you press Help while in READY mode, the Help Index appears (see fig. 2.14). Choose any of the topics in the Help Index to get to the other help screens.

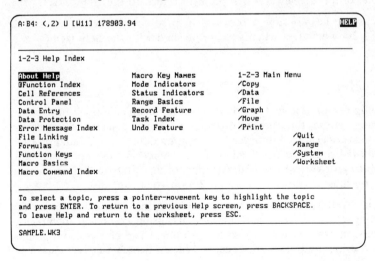

Fig. 2.14.
The Help Index screen.

Reminder:
The Help (F1) key
is context-
sensitive.

You can press the Help (F1) key at any time, even while executing a command or editing a cell. The help is context-sensitive. For example, if you are executing a particular command when you press Help (F1), 1-2-3 gives you a screenful of help on that command (see fig. 2.15).

Fig. 2.15.
A context-
sensitive help
screen that
explains the
/Worksheet
commands.

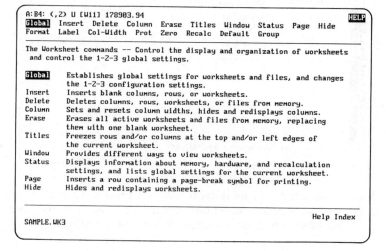

```
A:B4: (,2) U [W11] 178903.94                                          HELP
Global Insert Delete Column Erase Titles Window Status Page Hide
Format Label Col-Width Prot Zero Recalc Default Group

The Worksheet commands -- Control the display and organization of worksheets
 and control the 1-2-3 global settings.

Global      Establishes global settings for worksheets and files, and changes
            the 1-2-3 configuration settings.
Insert      Inserts blank columns, rows, or worksheets.
Delete      Deletes columns, rows, worksheets, or files from memory.
Column      Sets and resets column widths, hides and redisplays columns.
Erase       Erases all active worksheets and files from memory, replacing
            them with one blank worksheet.
Titles      Freezes rows and/or columns at the top and/or left edges of
            the current worksheet.
Window      Provides different ways to view worksheets.
Status      Displays information about memory, hardware, and recalculation
            settings, and lists global settings for the current worksheet.
Page        Inserts a row containing a page-break symbol for printing.
Hide        Hides and redisplays worksheets.


SAMPLE.WK3                                                    Help Index
```

Certain parts of the help screen identify additional help topics. These topics are displayed in boldface on a monochrome monitor or in green on a color monitor. To get more information about a topic, move the highlighter to that topic and press Enter. One or more additional topics are always located at the bottom of the screen. One of these is always the option to return to the Help Index.

Press the Backspace key to view a previous help screen. Press the Esc key to return to the 1-2-3 worksheet when you are finished with the help facility.

Taking the 1-2-3 Tutorial

Another learning resource from Lotus is the Tutorial manual, a book that comes with the documentation; the Tutorial provides a self-paced series of lessons on 1-2-3. The lessons are arranged in order of increasing difficulty and build on each other. The Tutorial does not cover all of 1-2-3's functions and commands but covers enough to give you a basic understanding of the program. Before you use the Tutorial, you must successfully install 1-2-3 on your hard disk.

The Tutorial is divided into 5 chapters with 17 lessons. Chapter 1 covers the basics of starting 1-2-3; entering and editing data; using command menus, formulas, functions, and ranges; formatting; and printing. Chapter 2 is about graphs. Chapter 3 is on using multiple worksheets and files. Chapter 4 covers databases, and Chapter 5 is about macros.

If you are new to 1-2-3, the best approach is to do one or two lessons at a time until you complete Chapter 1. After each lesson, work with 1-2-3 for a while before you tackle the more advanced topics. Only after you feel comfortable with all the material in Chapter 1 of the Tutorial should you try the other chapters. You can learn about the more specialized topics, such as the database or macros, without going through all the preceding lessons. If you are familiar with 1-2-3, but are new to Release 3, you should read through the entire Tutorial and try out the new features.

For further details on 1-2-3 functions and commands, you can refer to the Command Reference section or other appropriate sections of this book or to the 1-2-3 documentation.

Chapter Summary

This chapter presents the information you need to use 1-2-3 for the first time. You learned how to start and exit 1-2-3 from either the operating system or the 1-2-3 Access System and how to implement the Install and Translate programs. The features provided in the 1-2-3 display and how 1-2-3 uses the keyboard are also presented. You also learned how to use the on-line help facility and the Tutorial.

This chapter sets the stage so that you can begin to use 1-2-3 for useful work. The next chapter presents information on entering and editing data and moving around worksheets and files. Chapter 3 also introduces a feature new with Release 3—multiple worksheets.

3

Learning Worksheet Basics

This chapter presents the skills needed to use 1-2-3, the powerful electronic spreadsheet. If this is your first experience with spreadsheet software, you will learn how to use a spreadsheet for data analysis. If you are familiar with electronic spreadsheets but are new to 1-2-3 or to Release 3, you will find information in this chapter to help you understand the conventions and features of the program.

1-2-3 refers to its spreadsheet as a *worksheet*. To access the power of the 1-2-3 worksheet, the first step is being comfortable with moving around the worksheet. This chapter shows you how to move around the worksheet easily so that you can perform any needed actions.

Most of the actions you perform on a worksheet change it in some way. Several of these actions, such as entering and editing data, are covered in this chapter. The chapter also introduces the Undo feature, which enables you to reverse any changes made in error.

You use 1-2-3 to do data analysis—to manipulate and analyze data, numbers, and formulas. Because the worksheet is also used to report the results of your analysis, you need a method to organize the material. This chapter shows you how to use titles, headings, names, comments, descriptions, and a variety of other entries, called *labels*, that can make the final worksheet understandable to you and others.

A worksheet, a two-dimensional grid of columns and rows, can be expanded to a three-dimensional array with multiple-worksheet files. In this chapter and later chapters, you learn how to build multiple-worksheet files. Using multiple worksheets makes it easier for you to consolidate information.

For example, you can link files by writing formulas in one file that refer to cells in another file. If you need to work with large amounts of data or data from different sources, you can work with a number of files in the computer's memory at the same time.

This chapter begins by introducing the basic skills of using a single worksheet. These skills are then expanded to cover using multiple-worksheet files, linked files, and multiple files in memory.

In this chapter, you learn how to do the following:

- Work with worksheets and files
- Move the cell pointer around the worksheet
- Enter data
- Edit data
- Use the Undo feature
- Use multiple worksheets
- Use the linking features

Introducing Worksheets and Files

Reminder:
A file can be made up of one or more worksheets.

When you first start 1-2-3, you start with a blank worksheet file and build a worksheet in the computer's memory. To keep your worksheet, you save it in a file on disk with a file name. (Chapter 7 covers files in detail.) In 1-2-3, a file can be one worksheet (the simplest type of file), or a file can be made up of multiple worksheets. A multiple-worksheet file can contain up to 256 worksheets. Each worksheet in the file has a worksheet letter. The first worksheet is called A; the second, B; the 27th, AA; and so on to IV, the 256th worksheet in the file.

Whenever you enter data into the worksheet, the entry goes into the cell at the location of the cell pointer. This is called the *current cell*. To move around the worksheet, you move the cell pointer. By moving the cell pointer, you control where you put data in the worksheet. In figure 3.1, for example, any data you type goes into cell C6 until you move the cell pointer.

The name of the current file may be displayed in the lower-left corner of the screen once you've saved the worksheet. In figure 3.1, the current file is PROFIT.WK3. The current worksheet itself is displayed on-screen. If you use the

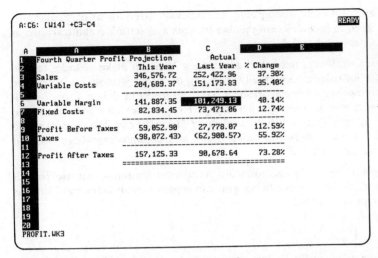

Fig. 3.1.
A sample worksheet with numbers, labels, and formulas.

window options to display more than one worksheet, the current worksheet is the one that displays the cell pointer. Note: You can change 1-2-3 so that the date and time, rather than the file name, are displayed in the lower-left corner of the screen.

Formulas are operations or calculations that you want 1-2-3 to perform on the data. Formulas make 1-2-3 an electronic worksheet, not just a computerized method of displaying data. You enter the numbers and the formulas, and 1-2-3 performs the calculations. If you change a number, 1-2-3 changes the results of all the formulas that use that number. If you change the number in C3 or C4 in figure 3.1, the results of all the cells containing formulas that depend on these cells change automatically.

Introducing Multiple Worksheets

You use multiple-worksheet files in two basic situations. First, multiple-worksheet files are ideal for consolidations. If you need a worksheet for many departments, you can build a separate, identical worksheet for each department. Each worksheet is smaller and easier to understand and use than a large single worksheet that contains all the data for each department. One of the worksheets can be a consolidation that combines the data from the individual departments. For example, you can put a formula in a cell in one worksheet that refers to cells in other worksheets. An example of this technique is found in the section "Using Multiple Worksheets" later in this chapter. Use multiple-worksheet files for any consolidations that contain separate parts, such as products, countries, or projects.

Second, you can use multiple-worksheet files to put separate sections into separate worksheets. You can put input areas, reports, formulas, notes, assumptions and constants, and macros in separate worksheets. Each worksheet, which is therefore smaller and more manageable, can be customized for its particular purpose. This technique includes using global formats and setting column widths as described in Chapters 4 and 5.

Using separate worksheets has other advantages. You can make changes to one worksheet without risking accidentally changing the other worksheets. When the entire file is comprised of one worksheet, you can insert or delete a row or column in one area and accidentally destroy part of another area that shares the same row or column. With multiple-worksheet files, you can design each worksheet so that you can insert and delete rows and columns anywhere and not affect any other part of the file.

Another common error is to accidentally write over formulas that are part of input areas. With multiple worksheets, you can separate input areas and formulas so that this error is less likely.

Linking Files

Using multiple-worksheet files is just one way to work with multiple worksheets. You can also work with worksheets in separate files. You can put a formula in a cell in one worksheet that refers to cells in worksheets in another file. This is called *file-linking*.

With this capability, you can consolidate data in separate files easily. You might, for example, receive data from separate departments or divisions to consolidate. Each department's data is in a separate file. Your consolidation file can use formulas to combine the data from each separate file. The process also works in reverse. You can have a central database file as well as separate files to distribute to each department. The individual department files can contain formulas that refer to data in the central database file.

Using linked files instead of one large file has several advantages:

- You can use file-linking to build large worksheet systems that are too large to fit into memory all at once.

- You can link files that come from different sources.

- You can more easily build formulas in one file that refer to cells in another file if both files are in memory at one time.

- You can develop a separate macro library file. (See Chapter 11 for more information on creating macros and macro libraries.

Using the Workspace

The *workspace* is made up of the worksheets and files that you have in memory at any one time. The potential size of your workspace is formidable. With 256 columns and 8192 rows, you can visualize the size of a single worksheet as a piece of paper almost 20 feet wide and over 110 feet long. At its maximum, the worksheet can be over 500 feet wide. This large work area gives you flexibility when you design your worksheets. You do not have to crowd everything together to save space. You can lay out different parts of the worksheet in different places to make the data easier to use and understand.

If you try to build a single worksheet that uses all possible rows and columns, you will have produced a worksheet that is complex, difficult to use, and possibly too large for your computer's memory. A more typical large worksheet might contain information about thousands of employees or inventory items. This type of worksheet uses a few columns and many rows. Another worksheet might contain a series of related reports that uses many columns but just a few rows.

You start out building small, simple worksheets. As you increase your skills using 1-2-3, you will feel comfortable building larger, more complex worksheets. The generous workspace lets you build your worksheets without worrying about running out of room.

When you start to build more complex models, you want to use multiple-worksheet files. Just as you can have horizontal rows and vertical columns, multiple-worksheet files give you a third dimension.

You can have a total of up to 256 worksheets in memory at one time. This can be one file with 256 worksheets or many files each containing one or more worksheets. In most cases, you are limited by the amount of memory in your computer.

This potential workspace is enormous. You have available 256 columns by 8192 rows by 256 worksheets—over 500 million cells! Obviously, you cannot use all this space at one time. No computer has that much memory. 1-2-3 does give you the flexibility to build files with many small worksheets or a few large worksheets, or to build many small files and have them all in memory at the same time.

Understanding the Display with Multiple Worksheets

You can change the screen to view one worksheet or multiple worksheets in different ways. These window options are covered in detail in Chapter 4. The default screen display is a single window that shows part of one worksheet (see fig. 3.1). The worksheet in figure 3.1 could be a single-worksheet file or part of a multiple-worksheet file. In figure 3.2, the screen is changed to perspective view. Perspective view lets you see parts of up to three worksheets at one time.

Cue:
You can view multiple worksheets at one time with window options.

Because this file contains only two worksheets, the last one (on top) is blank. In this file, worksheet B is used for assumptions and notes. This is a typical use for multiple-worksheet files.

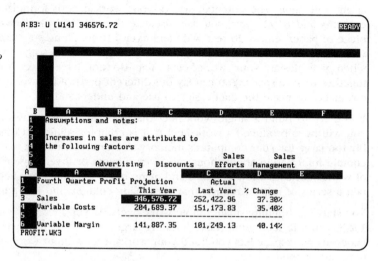

Fig. 3.2.
A file with two worksheets in perspective view.

```
A:B3:  U [W14] 346576.72                                              READY

 B     A          B          C          D          E          F
 1 Assumptions and notes:
 2
 3 Increases in sales are attributed to
 4 the following factors
 5                                        Sales      Sales
 6             Advertising  Discounts     Efforts  Management
 A     A                   B               C            D           E
 1 Fourth Quarter Profit Projection      Actual
 2                         This Year   Last Year  % Change
 3 Sales                  346,576.72  252,422.96    37.30%
 4 Variable Costs         204,689.37  151,173.83    35.40%
 5                        -----------------------------------
 6 Variable Margin        141,887.35  101,249.13    40.14%
PROFIT.WK3
```

The name of the current file is displayed in the lower-left corner of the screen once you've saved the file. In figure 3.2, the current file is PROFIT.WK3. The current worksheet is the one displayed on-screen. If you use the window options to display more than one worksheet, the current worksheet is the one that displays the cell pointer. In figure 3.2, the current worksheet is A, and the current cell is A:B3.

Reminder:
The current worksheet is the one that displays the cell pointer.

To determine the current worksheet in figure 3.2, you can make several observations: the cell pointer is in worksheet A; the row and column borders in worksheet A show the coordinates of the cell pointer; and the cell address in the control panel begins with A:. If a file has more than three worksheets, there is no way to see all the worksheets at the same time.

Most features of 1-2-3 apply to either a single worksheet or to multiple worksheets in a file. In this and later chapters, you learn to use 1-2-3 with one worksheet first, and then extend your knowledge to work with multiple-worksheet files, linked files, and multiple files in memory.

Moving Around the Worksheet

You can use several methods to move the cell pointer quickly anywhere in the worksheet. Remember that moving around the worksheet means moving the cell pointer. The *cell pointer* is the bright rectangle that highlights—and identifies—an entire cell. In figure 3.2, the cell pointer is in cell A:B3. Characters within the cell pointer appear in reverse video on the highlighted background.

Any data typed into the worksheet goes into the cell at the location of the cell pointer. The *cursor* is the blinking line in the control panel when you enter or edit data in a cell. The cursor shows you the position of the next character typed. Within a menu, the *menu pointer* is the highlighter used to select a command.

The current cell address is displayed in the upper-left corner of the display in the following format: **A:B3**. This format represents the worksheet letter, the column letter, and the row number (see fig. 3.2). When you work with one worksheet, the worksheet letter is always A. When you work with multiple worksheets, the worksheet letter displayed in the upper-left corner of the reverse-video border indicates the currently active worksheet or the worksheet where the cell pointer is currently located. In figure 3.2, the worksheet at the bottom of the screen is A; the one in the middle is B; and the one on top is C.

You can also find the current location of the cell pointer by observing the reverse-video border. In figure 3.2, the border for column B and row 3 contrasts with the rest of the border. Exactly how it contrasts depends on the type of monitor.

Because you can enter data only at the location of the cell pointer, you must know how to move the cell pointer to the location you want before you enter the data. Because you can display only a small part of the worksheet at any one time, you must know how to move the cell pointer so that you can see different parts of the worksheet at different times.

Reminder:
The same keys are used to move the cell pointer and the cursor, depending on the current mode.

Table 3.1 lists the keys that move the cell pointer. Table 3.2 lists the movement keys that move the cursor in EDIT mode. Many of the same keys move either the cell pointer or the cursor, depending on the current mode. These keys are often called pointer-movement keys when they move the cell pointer, and cursor keys when they move the cursor. This can be confusing if you do not realize that these terms refer to the same keys.

The function of movement keys varies depending on the mode that is currently active:

Mode	*Function of Movement Keys*
READY or POINT	The movement keys move the cell pointer.
LABEL or VALUE	The movement keys end the entry, return to READY mode, and move the cell pointer.
EDIT	Some movement keys move the cursor in the control panel; other movement keys end the edit, return to READY mode, and move the cell pointer.
MENU	The movement keys move the menu pointer to menu choices.

This section covers moving the cell pointer around one worksheet. Later in this chapter, you learn to move around multiple-worksheet files and multiple files. This section also discusses the movement of the cell pointer. Cursor movement is covered later in this chapter during the discussion of editing data in the worksheet, and menu-pointer movement for commands is discussed in Chapter 4.

Using the Basic Movement Keys

The four directional-arrow keys that move the cell pointer are located on the numeric keypad and on the separate pad of the Enhanced Keyboard. The cell pointer moves in the direction of the arrow on the key. If you hold down the arrow key, the cell pointer continues to move in that direction. When the pointer reaches the edge of the screen, the worksheet continues to scroll in the direction of the arrow. If you try to move past the edge of the worksheet, 1-2-3 beeps a warning.

You can use several other keys to page through the worksheet by moving the cell pointer one screenful at a time. Press the PgUp and PgDn keys to move up or down one screenful. Press Ctrl-right arrow or Tab to move one screenful to the right; press Ctrl-left arrow or Shift-Tab (hold down the Shift key and press Tab) to move one screenful to the left. The size of one screenful depends on the type of display driver in your system and whether one or more windows are present on-screen. (Windows are discussed in Chapter 4.)

Table 3.1 summarizes the action of the movement keys. Press the Home key to move the cell pointer directly to the home position—usually cell A1. In Chapter 4, you learn how to lock titles on-screen. Locked titles can change the home position. The other keys listed in table 3.1 are covered in the following sections.

Table 3.1
Movement-Key Operation with One Worksheet

Key	Description
→	Moves the cell pointer one cell to the right
←	Moves the cell pointer one cell to the left
↑	Moves the cell pointer one cell up
↓	Moves the cell pointer one cell down
Ctrl→ or Tab	Moves the cell pointer right one screen
Ctrl← or Shift-Tab	Moves the cell pointer left one screen
PgUp	Moves the cell pointer up one screen
PgDn	Moves the cell pointer down one screen
Home	Moves the cell pointer to the home position (usually A1)
End Home	Moves the cell pointer to the lower-right corner of the active area

Key	Description
End→, End↓, End←, End↑	Moves the cell pointer in the direction of the arrow to the next cell that contains data; (the intersection between a blank cell and a cell that contains data)
F5 (GoTo)	Prompts for a cell address or range name, and then moves the cell pointer directly to that cell
F6 (Window)	If the window has been split, moves the cell pointer to the next window
Scroll Lock	Toggles the scroll function on and off; when on, moves the entire window when you press one of the four arrow keys

Using the Scroll Lock Key

The Scroll Lock key toggles the scroll function on and off. When you press the Scroll Lock key, you activate the scroll function, and the SCROLL status indicator appears at the bottom of the screen. When you press an arrow key with Scroll Lock on, the cell pointer stays in the current cell, and the entire window moves in the direction of the arrow key. When the cell pointer reaches the end of the display, and if you continue to press the same arrow key, the cell pointer moves to the next cell as the entire window scrolls. If the SCROLL status indicator is on, press the Scroll Lock key again to turn it off.

Use the scroll function if you want to see part of the worksheet that is off the screen without moving the cell pointer from the current cell. For example, in figure 3.2, the cell pointer is in B3. Suppose that you want to see the data in column G before you change the contents of B3. If you turn on the scroll function and press the right-arrow key once, the entire window moves to the right. You can see column G, and the cell pointer stays in B3 (see fig. 3.3). To get the same result without using Scroll Lock, you press the right arrow five times to display column G, and then press the left arrow five times to return to B3.

Reminder:
Check the SCROLL indicator if the cell pointer does not move the way you expect.

Scroll Lock has no effect on the other movement keys. If the cell pointer does not move the way you expect, check to see whether Scroll Lock has been accidentally turned on. Check for the SCROLL indicator in the lower-right corner of the screen, as shown in figure 3.3. Press Scroll Lock again to turn it off.

Using the End Key

The End key is used in a special way in 1-2-3. When you press and release the End key, the END status indicator appears on the last line of the display. If you then press one of the arrow keys, the cell pointer moves in the direction of the

Fig. 3.3.
The Scroll Lock key used to move an entire window.

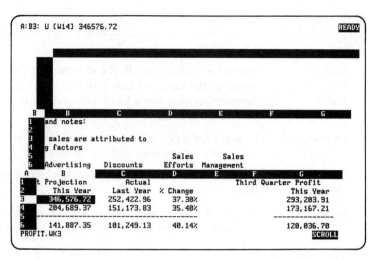

```
A:B3: U [W14] 346576.72                                          READY


  B       B           C          D          E          F          G
  1  and notes:
  2
  3     sales are attributed to
  4  g factors
  5                                  Sales      Sales
  6  Advertising    Discounts     Efforts   Management
  A       B           C          D          E          F          G
  1  t Projection      Actual                         Third Quarter Profit
  2     This Year    Last Year  % Change                        This Year
  3     346,576.72   252,422.96    37.30%                        293,203.91
  4     204,689.37   151,173.83    35.40%                        173,167.21
  5  --------------------------------------            --------------
  6     141,887.35   101,249.13    40.14%                        120,036.70
  PROFIT.WK3                                                       SCROLL
```

arrow key to the next intersection of a blank cell and a cell that contains data. The cell pointer always stops on a cell that contains data if possible. If there are no cells that contain data in the direction of the arrow key, the cell pointer stops at the edge of the worksheet.

For example, figure 3.4 shows the cell pointer in cell B3. The END status indicator at the bottom-right corner of the screen shows that the End key has been pressed. If you now press the right-arrow key, the cell pointer moves right to the first cell that contains data. In this case, the cell pointer moves to D3, as shown in figure 3.5. If you press the End key, and then the right-arrow key again, the cell pointer moves to the last cell that contains data before a blank cell. In this case, the cell pointer moves to G3, as shown in figure 3.6.

Fig. 3.4.
The END key status indicator.

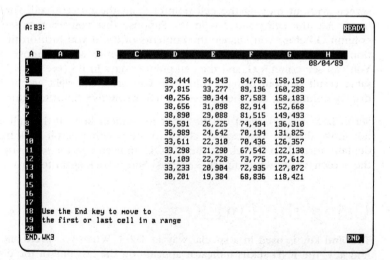

```
A:B3:                                                            READY

  A       A         B          C         D         E         F         G         H
  1                                                                        08/04/89
  2
  3                                     38,444    34,943    84,763   158,150
  4                                     37,815    33,277    89,196   160,288
  5                                     40,256    30,344    87,583   158,183
  6                                     38,656    31,098    82,914   152,668
  7                                     38,890    29,088    81,515   149,493
  8                                     35,591    26,225    74,494   136,310
  9                                     36,989    24,642    70,194   131,825
 10                                     33,611    22,310    70,436   126,357
 11                                     33,298    21,290    67,542   122,130
 12                                     31,109    22,728    73,775   127,612
 13                                     33,233    20,904    72,935   127,072
 14                                     30,201    19,384    68,836   118,421
 15
 16
 17
 18  Use the End key to move to
 19  the first or last cell in a range
 20
 END.WK3                                                           END
```

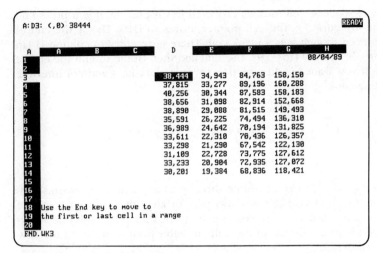

Fig. 3.5.
The cell pointer moved to the first cell that contains data after End-right arrow was pressed.

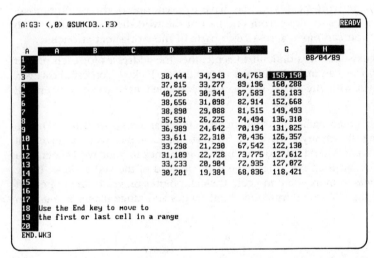

Fig. 3.6.
The cell pointer moved to the last cell that contains data after End-right arrow was pressed again.

If no other data is in the worksheet and you press the End key and then the right-arrow key again, the cell pointer moves to the end of the worksheet to cell IV3. If you press End and then press the down-arrow key from G3, the cell pointer moves to G14.

Cue:
Use the End key to move directly to the end of a list of data.

The End key works the same way with the left- and up-arrow keys. In figure 3.6, End and left arrow takes you to D3. From D3, End and up arrow takes you to D1 (the edge of the worksheet). After you press the End key, the END indicator stays on only until you press an arrow key or the End key again. If you press End in error, just press End again and the END status indicator goes off.

If you press the End key and then the Home key, the cell pointer moves to the lower-right corner of the active area. The active area includes all rows and all columns that have data or cell formats (covered in Chapter 5). If you press End and then Home in figure 3.6, the cell pointer moves to H19. This is the end of the active area even though it is a blank cell. There is an entry in column H (in H1) and an entry in row 19 (in A19). Use End and then Home to find the end of the active area if you want to add a section to your worksheet and not interfere with any existing data.

Using the GoTo Key To Jump Directly to a Cell

You can use the GoTo (F5) key to jump directly to any cell in the worksheet. When you press GoTo (F5), 1-2-3 prompts you for an address. When you type the cell address, the cell pointer moves directly to that address. With one worksheet, the address is in the format of the column letter from A to IV and the row number from 1 to 8192.

If you have a large worksheet, you may have to press one of the pointer-movement keys many times to move from one part of the worksheet to another. With the GoTo key, you can move across large parts of the worksheet at once.

With a large worksheet, it is difficult to remember the addresses for each part of the worksheet. This can make it difficult to use the GoTo key. You can, however, use range names with the GoTo key so that you don't have to remember cell addresses.

Cue:
You can use range names with the GoTo (F5) key.

You can give a range name to a cell or a rectangular group of cells. A *range name* is an English synonym for a cell address; for example, you can give cell B56 the range name PROFIT. If you include range names in your worksheet, you can press GoTo, and then type the range name instead of the cell address. If the range name refers to more than one cell, the cell pointer moves to the upper-left corner of the range. More information about ranges and range names is found in Chapter 4.

Entering Data into the Worksheet

To enter data into a cell, move the cell pointer to that cell, type the entry, and then press Enter. As you type, the entry appears on the second line of the control panel. When you press Enter, the entry appears in the current cell and on the first line of the control panel. If you enter data into a cell that already contains information, the new data replaces the earlier entry.

Cue:
Use the movement keys to complete an entry and move to the next cell.

If you plan to enter data into more than one cell, you do not need to press Enter and then move the cell pointer to the next cell. You can type the entry into the cell and move the cell pointer with one keystroke; just press one of the pointer-movement keys (such as the arrow keys, Tab, or PgDn) after typing the entry.

The two types of cell entries are labels and values. A *label* is a text entry. A *value* is either a number or a formula. 1-2-3 determines the type of cell entry from the first character that you enter. 1-2-3 treats your entry as a value (a number or a formula) if you begin with one of the following numeric characters:

0 1 2 3 4 5 6 7 8 9 + − . (@ # $

If you begin by entering any other character, 1-2-3 treats your entry as a label. As soon as you type the first character, the mode indicator changes from READY to either VALUE or LABEL.

Entering Labels

Labels make the numbers and formulas in your worksheets understandable. The labels in figures 3.1 and 3.2 tell you what the data means. In figures 3.3 through 3.6, the numbers and formulas have no labels, and you have no idea what this data represents.

Because a label is a text entry, it can contain any string of characters and can be up to 512 characters long. Labels can include titles, headings, explanations, and notes, all of which can help make your worksheet more understandable.

When you enter a label, 1-2-3 adds a label prefix to the beginning of the cell entry. The label prefix is not visible on the worksheet, but is visible in the control panel (see fig. 3.7). 1-2-3 uses the label prefix to identify the entry as a label and determine how it is displayed and printed.

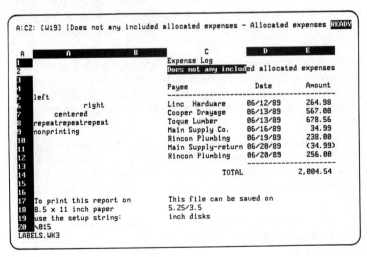

Fig. 3.7.
Examples of different label prefixes.

You can assign one of the following five label prefixes:

'	Left-aligned (default)
"	Right-aligned
^	Centered
\	Repeating
|	Left-aligned and nonprinting

When you enter a label, 1-2-3 by default adds the apostrophe (') for a left-aligned label. To use a different label prefix, you type the prefix as the first character of the label.

In figure 3.7, column A shows examples of the different label prefixes so that you can compare how they display. Columns C through E show how to use these label prefixes in a typical worksheet. A column of descriptions such as in C6..C11 usually looks best if left-aligned—the normal way to line up text. Column headings should align with the data below. The heading in C4 is left-aligned to match the Payee descriptions. When the entries fill the cell width, as do the dates in column D, the column heading can be aligned either left, right, or center. In this example, the Date heading is centered. A centered label is best when the column heading is shorter than the data below it. Because numbers and numeric formulas are always right-aligned, the Amount column heading in E4 is also right-aligned.

The dashed lines in rows 5 and 13 are repeating labels. The repeating labels fill the entire width of the cell. If you change the column width, the label changes length to fill the new column width.

The note in C2 has a nonprinting label prefix. The prefix displays left-aligned but does not print if the print range starts in the same row as the label. In this example, if the print range starts in C1, the note in C2 does not print. If the print range starts in A1, the note does print. Printing and nonprinting labels are covered in more detail in Chapter 8.

To use a label prefix as the first character of a label, first type a label prefix, and then type the label prefix as the first character of the label (see cell A20 in fig. 3.7). If you type \015 into A20, the cell displays 0150150015015015015 as a repeating label. You must first type a label prefix, in this case an apostrophe, and then \015.

You must type a label prefix if the first character of the label is a numeric character. If not, as soon as you type the numeric character, 1-2-3 switches to VALUE mode and expects a valid number or formula. If the label is a valid formula, 1-2-3 evaluates it. If it is invalid, 1-2-3 refuses to accept the entry and places you in EDIT mode. (EDIT mode is explained in a later section of this chapter).

In C18 in figure 3.7, you must type a label prefix to precede the label 5.25/3.5. If you do not, 1-2-3 treats the entry as a formula and displays the result of 5.25 divided by 3.5, which is 1.5.

Cue:
Use right-aligned labels for column headings over columns of numbers or numeric formulas.

Reminder:
A repeating label automatically changes length to match the column width.

Reminder:
You must type a label prefix to make another label prefix the first character of the label.

In A18 in figure 3.7, you must type a label prefix to precede the label 8.5 × 11 inch paper, or 1-2-3 treats it as an invalid formula. You often encounter this problem when you enter an address such as **11711 N. College Ave**.

If a label is longer than the cell width, the label displays across the cells to the right as long as these cells are blank (see cells B17..B19 in fig. 3.7). The cell display can even continue into the next windows to the right as long as all these cells are blank.

The label in C2 in figure 3.7 is longer than what can be displayed in the window. You can see the continuation of the label in the next window to the right (see fig. 3.8).

Reminder:
A long label displays across blank cells to its right.

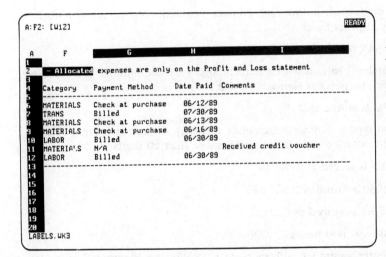

A:F2: [W12]   READY

```
   A      F           G              H              I
1
2         - Allocated expenses are only on the Profit and Loss statement
3
4       Category   Payment Method   Date Paid  Comments
5       ------------------------------------------------------------------
6       MATERIALS  Check at purchase  06/12/89
7       TRANS      Billed             07/30/89
8       MATERIALS  Check at purchase  06/13/89
9       MATERIALS  Check at purchase  06/16/89
10      LABOR      Billed             06/30/89
11      MATERIALS  N/A                          Received credit voucher
12      LABOR      Billed             06/30/89
13      ------------------------------------------------------------------
14
15
16
17
18
19
20
LABELS.WK3
```

Fig. 3.8.
A long label continuing into the next window.

1-2-3 includes several commands that can change many label prefixes at one time. This subject is covered in Chapter 5.

Entering Numbers

To enter a valid number, you can type any of the 10 digits (0–9) and certain other characters according to the following rules:

1. The number can start with a plus sign (+); the sign is not stored when you press Enter.

    +123 is stored as 123.

2. The number can begin with a minus sign (−); the number is stored as a negative number.

    −123 is stored as −123.

3. The number can be placed within parentheses [()]; the number is stored as a negative number. The parentheses are dropped, and the number is preceded by a minus sign.

   (123) is stored as −123.

4. The number can begin with a dollar sign ($); the sign is not stored when you press Enter.

   $123 is stored as 123.

5. You can include one decimal point.

   .123 is stored as 0.123.

6. Three digits must follow each comma included; commas are not stored when you press Enter.

   123,345,789 is stored as 123456789.

7. The number can end with a percent sign (%); the number is divided by 100, and the percent sign is dropped.

   123% is stored as 1.23.

8. You can type a number in scientific notation. A number is stored in scientific notation only if it requires more than 20 digits.

   123E3 is stored as 123000.

   1.23E30 is stored as 1.23E+30.

   123E−4 is stored as 0.0123.

   1.23E−30 is stored as 1.23E−30.

9. If you enter a number with more than 18 digits, it is rounded off to 18 digits.

   12345678998765432198 is stored as 12345678998765432200.

10. If you enter a number with more than 20 digits, it is stored in scientific notation.

   123456789987654321987 is stored as 1.23456789987654322E+20.

If the number is too long to display normally in the cell, 1·2·3 tries to display what it can. If the cell uses the default general format and the integer part of the number can fit in the cell width, 1·2·3 rounds off any part of the decimal part of the number that will not fit. In figure 3.9, the numbers in all three columns are the same; only the column widths are different. In E5, 25.54321 displays rounded off to 26. In C6, 1675.123456789 displays rounded off to 1675.123. Cell formats are described in detail in chapter 5.

Caution:
If the column width is too narrow to display a number, 1·2·3 displays asterisks.

If the cell uses the default general format and the integer part of the number does not fit in the cell, 1·2·3 displays the number using scientific notation. Examples are C4, C7, and C9 in figure 3.9. If the cell uses a format other than general

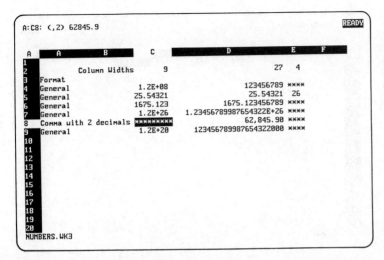

Fig. 3.9.
Asterisks
displayed in
place of a
number too
long for the
cell width.

or the cell width is too narrow to display in scientific notation, and the number cannot fit into the cell width, 1-2-3 displays asterisks (see fig. 3.9).

Entering Formulas

The real power of 1-2-3 comes from its capability to perform calculations on formulas you enter. In fact, formulas make 1-2-3 an electronic worksheet—not just a computerized way to assemble data for reports. You enter the numbers and formulas into the worksheet; 1-2-3 calculates the results of all the formulas. As you add or change data, you never have to recalculate the effects of the changes; 1-2-3 does it automatically for you. In figure 3.2, if you change the Sales or Variable Costs, 1-2-3 automatically recalculates the Variable Margin. In figure 3.7, the total expense in E14 is recalculated each time you add or change an expense amount.

You can enter formulas that operate on numbers, labels, and other cells in the worksheet. Like labels, a formula can be up to 512 characters long.

There are three different types of formulas: numeric, string, and logical. Numeric formulas work with numbers, other numeric formulas, and numeric functions. String formulas work with labels, other string formulas, and string functions. Logical formulas are true/false tests that can test either numeric or string values. Functions are covered in Chapter 6. This chapter covers each type of formula.

Formulas can operate on numbers in the cell, such as 8 + 26. This formula uses 1-2-3 just as a calculator. A more useful formula uses cell references in the calculation. The formula in cell F1 in figure 3.10 is +B1+C1+D1+E1. The control panel shows the formula. The worksheet shows the result of the calculation; in this case, 183. The power and usefulness of this formula is that the result in F1 changes automatically any time you change any of the numbers in the other cells. This single fact is behind the power of the 1-2-3 electronic worksheet.

Reminder:
The formula
displays in the
control panel; the
result of the
calculation displays
in the worksheet.

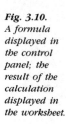

Fig. 3.10.
*A formula
displayed in
the control
panel; the
result of the
calculation
displayed in
the worksheet.*

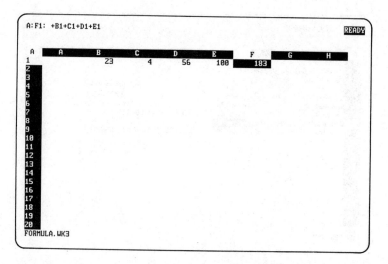

Note that the formula begins with a plus sign (+B1). If a formula begins with B1, 1-2-3 assumes that you are entering a label, and no calculation is performed.

Using Operators in Numeric Formulas

A formula is an instruction to 1-2-3 to perform a calculation. You use operators to specify the calculations to perform. The numeric operators are addition, subtraction, multiplication, division, and exponentiation (raising a number to a power). The formula in figure 3.10 uses the plus sign—the addition operator. The simplest numeric formula uses just the plus sign to repeat the value in another cell. In figure 3.9, D4 and E4 both contain the formula +C4. The other cells in columns D and E are also formulas that refer to the cell in column C. In each case, the values of the cell on column C is repeated in columns D and E.

When 1-2-3 evaluates a formula, it calculates terms within the formula in a specified sequence. Following are the arithmetic operators listed in order of precedence:

Operator	Meaning
^	Exponentiation
+, −	Positive, Negative
*, /	Multiplication, Division
+, −	Addition, Subtraction

Cue:
*Use parentheses in
a formula to
change the order
of precedence of
the calculations.*

If a formula uses all these operators, 1-2-3 calculates the exponentials first, and then works down the list. If two operators are equal in precedence, it makes no difference which is calculated first. This order of precedence has a definite effect on the result of many formulas. To override the order, use parentheses. Operations inside a set of parentheses are always evaluated first.

The following examples show how 1-2-3 uses parentheses and the order of precedence to evaluate complex formulas. In these examples, numbers are used instead of cell references to make it easier to follow the calculations.

Formula	Evaluation	Result
5+3*2	5+(3*2)	11
(5+3)*2	(5+3)*2	16
−3^2*2	−(3^2)*2	−18
−3^(2*2)	−(3^(2*2))	−81
5+4*8/4−3	5+(4*(8/4))−3	10
5+4*8/(4−3)	5+((4*8)/(4−3))	37
(5+4)*8/(4−3)	(5+4)*8/(4−3)	72
(5+4)*8/4−3	(5+4)*(8/4)−3	15
5+3*4^2/6−2*3^4	5+(3*(4^2)/6)−(2*(3^4))	−149

Using Operators in String Formulas

String formulas have different rules than numeric formulas. A string is either a label or string formula. There are only two string formula operators. You can repeat another string, or you can join (*concatenate*) two or more strings.

The simplest string formula uses only the plus sign to repeat the string in another cell. In figure 3.11, the formula in A6 is +A3. The formula to repeat a numeric cell and to repeat a string cell is the same. In figure 3.9, the formula is considered a numeric formula because it refers to a cell with a number. In figure 3.11, the formula is considered a string formula because it refers to a cell with a string.

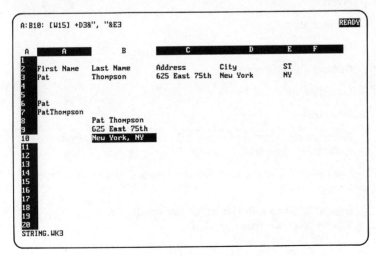

Fig. 3.11.
String formulas used to repeat or concatenate strings.

Reminder:
*A string is treated
as a value of zero
in numeric
formulas.*

The string concatenation operator is the ampersand (&). The formula in A7 in figure 3.11 is +A3&B3. The first operator in a string formula must be a plus sign; any other operators in the formula must be ampersands. If you do not use the ampersand, but use any of the numeric operators, 1-2-3 treats the formula as a numeric formula. A cell that contains a label has a numeric value of zero. The formula +A3+B3 in the worksheet in figure 3.11 is treated as a numeric formula and evaluates to zero.

If you use an ampersand in a formula, 1-2-3 treats it as a string formula. If you also use any numeric operators (after the plus sign at the beginning), 1-2-3 considers it an invalid formula. The formulas +A3&B3+C3 and +A3+B3&C3 are invalid. When you enter an invalid formula, 1-2-3 puts you in EDIT mode. EDIT mode is covered later in this chapter.

Cue:
*You can insert a
string directly into
a string formula if
you enclose it in
quotation marks.*

In figure 3.11, the names run together in A7, so you want to put a space between the first and last names. You can insert a string directly into a string formula by enclosing the string in quotation marks ("). The formula in B8 is +A3&" "&B3. The formula in B10 is +D3", "&E3.

You can write more complex string formulas with string functions, which are covered in Chapter 6.

Using Operators in Logical Functions

Logical formulas are true/false tests. They compare two values and evaluate to 1 if the test is true and 0 if the test is false. Logical formulas are used mainly in database criteria ranges. Logical formulas are covered in more detail in Chapters 6 and 10.

The logical operators include the following:

Operator	Meaning
=	Equal
>	Greater than
<	Less than
>=	Greater than or equal to
<=	Less than or equal to
<>	Not equal
#NOT#	Reverses the results of a test (changes the result from true to false or from false to true)
#OR#	Logical OR to join two tests; the result is true if either test is true.
#AND#	Logical AND to join two tests; the result is true if both tests are true.

Figure 3.12 shows examples of logical formulas.

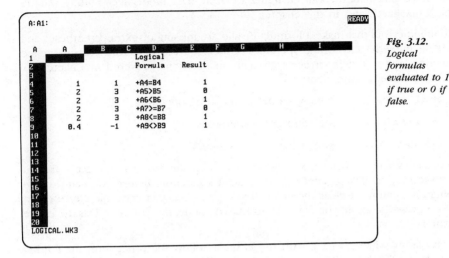

Fig. 3.12.
Logical formulas evaluated to 1 if true or 0 if false.

Pointing to Cell References

Formulas consist mainly of operators and cell references. The formula in figure 3.10 has four cell references. You can type each address, but there is a better way. Whenever 1-2-3 expects a cell address, you can use the movement keys to point to the cell. As soon as you move the cell pointer, 1-2-3 changes to POINT mode, and the address of the cell pointer appears in the formula in the control panel.

Move the cell pointer until it is on the correct cell address in the formula. If this location marks the end of the formula, press Enter. If there are more terms in the formula, type the next operator and continue the process until you are finished; then press Enter. You can type some addresses and point to others. There is no way to tell if the cell references in the formula in figure 3.10 were entered by typing or pointing.

It is very easy to type an incorrect address in a formula. Pointing to cells is not only faster but more accurate than typing. The only time it is easier to type an address than point to the cell is when the cell reference is very far from the current cell and you happen to remember the cell address. For example, if you enter a formula in Z238 and you want to refer to cell I23, it may be faster to just type **I23** than point to it. Experienced 1-2-3 users rarely type addresses.

Cue:
For speed and accuracy, use POINT mode to enter cell references in formulas.

Correcting Errors in Formulas

If, in error, you enter a formula that 1-2-3 cannot evaluate, the program beeps, changes to EDIT mode, and moves the cursor to the place in the formula where it encountered an error. You cannot enter an invalid formula into a worksheet. For more information about changing a cell in EDIT mode, see "Editing Data in the Worksheet" later in this chapter.

Common errors that make a formula invalid are missing or extra parentheses and mixing numeric and string operators. Other sources of errors are misspelled function names and incorrect arguments in functions (covered in Chapter 6). Some common simple errors are

+A1+A2&A3	Mixing numeric and string operators
+A1/(A2−A3	Missing right parentheses
@SIM(A1..A3)	Misspelled @SUM function

You may not know what is wrong or how to fix the formula. You may want to use the Help facility to check the format of a function. Before you can do anything else, you must clear the error. If you press Esc, you erase the entire entry. If you press Esc again, you are back to READY mode, but you have lost the entire formula.

If you know what is wrong with the formula, follow the procedures in "Editing Data in the Worksheet" later in this chapter. If you do not know how to correct the formula, convert it to a label. Because all labels are valid entries, this technique clears the error and lets you continue working. Follow these steps to convert a formula to a label, clear EDIT mode, and return to READY mode:

1. Press Home to move to the beginning of the formula.

2. Type an apostrophe as the label prefix (1-2-3 accepts anything preceded by an apostrophe as a label).

3. Press Enter.

Cue:
To fix a formula that is in error, temporarily convert it to a label and move it to another cell.

You can now use the Help facility or look at another part of the worksheet that has a similar formula. When you find the error, correct the formula and remove the apostrophe. (Refer to the "Troubleshooting" section's data-entry problem #2 for more details.)

Addressing Cells

A cell address in a formula, such as the one in figure 3.10, is known as a cell reference. The formula in F1 has four cell references. Normally, when you Copy a formula from one cell to another cell, the cell references adjust automatically. If you Copy the formula in F1 of figure 3.10 to F2, the cell references change to +B2+C2+D2+E2. This is called *relative addressing*.

You can use cell references in formulas that are absolute instead of relative. An absolute address in a formula does not change when you Copy the formula to another cell. You specify an absolute address when you type a formula by preceding the column and row address with a dollar sign ($). For example, +A:$A$1 is an absolute address. If this address were in cell C10 and you copied it to cell E19, the cell reference would still be +A:$A$1. To specify an absolute cell address in POINT mode, press the ABS (F4) key.

In addition to relative and absolute cell addresses, there are also mixed cell addresses. In a mixed cell address, part of the address is relative and part is fixed. For example, +A$1 is a mixed address.

Whether a cell reference is relative, absolute, or mixed has no effect on the how the formula is calculated. This type of addressing matters only when you copy the formula to another cell. Copying and cell addressing are covered in detail in Chapter 4.

Changing Cell Formats

Several commands change the way numbers and formulas display in the worksheet. These commands, /Worksheet Global Format and /Range Format, are covered in detail in Chapter 5.

For example, you can force a fixed number of decimal digits so that the numbers in a column line up; add commas and currency symbols; show numbers as percents; and even hide the contents of the cell. The values in column E in figure 3.13 are formatted to include commas between thousands and to show 2 decimal places.

In addition, 1-2-3 includes special formats and functions to handle dates and times. These topics are explained in Chapters 5 and 6.

Adding Notes to a Cell

You can add a note to a cell that contains a value. This technique is useful to explain a number or a formula. Immediately after the number or formula, type a semicolon (;); then type the note. The note cannot begin with a space. A note displays in the control panel but not in the worksheet.

In figure 3.13, the note in cell A:B3 reminds anyone who looks at this cell that the calculations include only data from domestic regions. There may also be a similar file containing international data and a third file containing both domestic and international data.

Editing Data in the Worksheet

After you make an entry in a cell, you may want to change it. You may have misspelled a word in a label or created an incorrect formula. You can change an existing entry in two ways.

You can replace the contents of a cell by typing a new entry. The new entry completely replaces the old entry.

You can also change (edit) the contents of the cell. To edit a cell's contents, move the cell pointer to the cell and press the Edit (F2) key to go into EDIT mode. You can also press Edit (F2) while you are typing an entry. If you make an error entering a formula, 1-2-3 forces you into EDIT mode.

If the cell entry can fit on one line, the entry displays on the second line in the control panel. If the entry is too large to display on one line, the entire worksheet area drops down to enlarge the entry area to display a full 512-character entry.

Table 3.2 describes the action of keys in EDIT mode. While in EDIT mode, a cursor is in the entry area in the control panel. You use the keys in table 3.2 to move the cursor. While you edit the cell, the contents of the cell as displayed in the first line of the control panel and in the worksheet do not change. The cell's contents change only when you press Enter to complete the edit. Any key that moves the cell pointer in EDIT mode first completes the entry, and then moves the cell pointer.

Cue:
Press Esc twice to cancel the edit and restore the cell to its original contents.

If you press Esc while in EDIT mode, you clear the edit area. If you then press Esc or Enter with a blank edit area, you do not erase the cell; you cancel the edit, and the cell reverts back to the way it was before you pressed Edit (F2).

Using the Undo Feature

When you type an entry or edit a cell, you change the worksheet. If you change the worksheet in error, you can press the Undo (Alt-F4) key to reverse the last change. For example, if you type over an existing entry, you can Undo the new entry and restore the old one.

Caution:
To use Undo, you must enable it.

Initially, the Undo feature in disabled, so you must use commands to enable Undo. To turn on the Undo feature, choose /Worksheet Global Default Other Undo Enable. To make this change permanent, choose /Worksheet Global Default Update. When Undo is enabled, 1-2-3 must remember the last action that changed the worksheet. This action requires memory. How much memory Undo requires changes with different actions. You should enable Undo on your system and disable it again with /Worksheet Global Default Other Undo Disable only if you get low on memory.

Caution:
You can Undo only the last change.

When you press Undo (Alt-F4), you get a menu with two choices: No and Yes. You must press Y at the menu to actually Undo the last change. In this book, when you are asked to Undo or press the Undo key, remember that you must also press Y.

Remember that you can Undo only the last change; if you make an error, Undo it immediately or the old data may be lost.

If you Undo a change in error, you cannot Undo the Undo. If you press Undo at the wrong time and Undo an entry, you cannot recover it.

Caution:
You cannot reverse the effect of Undo.

Undo is very useful and powerful. It is also tricky and can surprise you, so you must use Undo carefully. 1-2-3 remembers the last change to the worksheet and

Table 3.2
Key Action in EDIT Mode

Key	Action
←	Moves the cursor one character to the left
→	Moves the cursor one character to the right
↑	If the entry fits on one line, completes the edit and moves the cell pointer up one row. If the entry is on more than one line, moves the cursor up one line.
↓	If the entry fits on one line, completes the edit and moves the cell pointer down one row. If the entry is on more than one line, moves the cursor down one line.
Ctrl← or Shift-Tab	Moves the cursor left five characters
Ctrl→ or Tab	Moves the cursor right five characters
Home	Moves the cursor to the beginning of the entry
End	Moves the cursor to the end of the entry
Backspace	Deletes the character to the left of the cursor
Del	Deletes the character at the cursor
Ins	Toggles between insert and overtype mode
Esc	Clears the edit line
Esc Esc	Cancels the edit and makes no change to the cell
F2 (Edit)	Switches to VALUE or LABEL mode
Enter	Completes the edit

reverses this change when you press Undo. You must understand what 1-2-3 considers a change.

A change occurs between the time 1-2-3 is in READY mode and the next time it is in READY mode. Suppose, for example, that you press Edit (F2) to go into EDIT mode to change a cell. You can make any number of changes to the cell, and then press Enter to save the changes and return to READY mode. If you press Undo now, 1-2-3 returns the worksheet to the way it was at the last READY mode. In this case, it returns the cell to the way it was before you edited it.

You can change many cells at one time or even erase everything in memory with one command. These commands are covered in Chapter 4. If you press Undo after a command, you Undo all the effects of the command.

With some commands, such as /Print (Chapter 8); /Graph (Chapter 9); and /Data (Chapter 10), you can execute many commands before you return to READY mode. If you press Undo then, you reverse all the commands executed since the last time 1-2-3 was in READY mode.

For example, suppose that you type an entry into cell K33, press Enter, and then press Home. The cell pointer moves to A1. If you press Undo now, you not only Undo the Home, you Undo the entry in cell K33 as well.

A change can refer to either a change to one or more cells or a change to command settings. For example, to print a report, you must specify a **Print Range**. This does not change any data in the worksheet, but it changes a setting. If you press Undo the next time you are in READY mode, you Undo the **Print Range**.

Caution:
What 1-2-3
considers the last
change may not be
the last action you
performed, so you
may be surprised
by the effects of
the Undo.

Some commands do not change any cells or settings. Examples of such commands are /**File Save**, /**File Xtract**, /**File Erase**, and /**Print Printer Page**. If you make an entry in a cell, then save the file, then press Undo, you Undo the last change, which is the cell entry.

The more extensive a change, the more memory 1-2-3 needs to remember the status of the worksheet before the change. If there is not enough memory to save the status before the change, 1-2-3 pauses and presents you with the following menu:

> **Proceed   Disable   Quit**

Choose **Proceed** to disable Undo temporarily and complete the command. You will not be able to Undo this command, but Undo is re-enabled as soon as the command completes.

Choose **Disable** to disable Undo and complete the command. You will not be able to Undo this command. Undo remains disabled until you **Quit** and restart 1-2-3 or enable Undo again with /**Worksheet Global Default Other Undo Enable**.

Caution:
If 1-2-3 runs out
of memory in the
middle of a
command, part
of the command
may have been
completed.

Choose **Quit** to cancel the command in progress. You do not **Quit** 1-2-3; you return to READY mode. The command may have been partially completed before 1-2-3 ran out of memory. For example, if you **Copy** a range multiple times (explained in Chapter 4) and you run out of memory and choose **Quit** from this menu, the range may have been copied to part of the range you specified as the range to copy to. Check your work carefully to determine the effects of the last command.

In most cases, choose **Proceed**. Be sure, however, that you want to perform the command, because you cannot Undo it. If you execute the command in error, choose **Quit** now, and then immediately Undo whatever the command changed. If you get this menu repeatedly and it is slowing you down, choose **Disable**. You won't be stopped by this menu again, but you won't be able to use Undo.

Using Multiple Worksheets

Multiple-worksheet files make it much easier to organize large, complex files. If you are new to 1-2-3, get comfortable with the basics by starting with one worksheet. When you are ready to design worksheets that are more complex than simple reports, you can use multiple-worksheet files, file linking, and multiple files in memory at the same time.

This section covers moving around multiple worksheets as well as data entry and formulas with multiple worksheets and files. Chapter 4 discusses the commands needed to create and use multiple-worksheet files. Chapter 7 introduces the commands to read files into memory and save them.

Some commands related to multiple worksheets include the following:

Command	Action
/Worksheet Insert Sheet	Adds one or more new worksheets to the current file
/Worksheet Delete Sheet	Deletes one or more existing worksheets from the current file
/File Open	Reads a file from disk and adds it to memory; does not replace existing files in memory
/File New	Opens a new, blank file and adds it to memory; does not replace existing files in memory
/Worksheet Delete File	Removes an active file from memory when more than one file is in memory at the same time
/Worksheet Window Perspective	Displays three worksheets at once in a perspective view
/Worksheet Global Group Enable	Changes the scope of many /Worksheet commands such as Insert, Global Format, and Global Col-Width so that they affect all worksheets in the file together, not just the current worksheet

Moving Around Multiple Worksheets

All the movement keys in table 3.1 work the same way with multiple-worksheet files and multiple files in memory; however, these keys keep the cell pointer in the current worksheet. Table 3.3 shows the additional keys needed with multiple-worksheet files and multiple files in memory. The most important key combinations in table 3.3 are Ctrl-PgUp (to move to the next worksheet) and Ctrl-PgDn (to move to the previous worksheet). Do not be concerned with the other movement keys at this time. You can learn them when you build large worksheet files.

RELEASE 3

Table 3.3
Movement-Key Operation with Multiple Worksheets

Key	Description
Ctrl-PgUp	Moves the cell pointer to the next worksheet
Ctrl-PgDn	Moves the cell pointer to the previous worksheet
Ctrl-Home	Moves the cell pointer to the home position in the first worksheet in the file (usually A:A1)
End Ctrl-Home	Moves the cell pointer to the end of the active area for the file itself in the last worksheet in the file
End Ctrl-PgUp or End Ctrl-PgDn	Moves the cell pointer through the worksheets to the next cell that contains data (the intersection between a blank cell and a cell that contains data)
Ctrl-End Ctrl-PgUp	Moves the cell pointer to the next file
Ctrl-End Ctrl-PgDn	Moves the cell pointer to the previous file
Ctrl-End Home	Moves the cell pointer to the first file in memory
Ctrl-End End	Moves the cell pointer to the last file in memory
F5 (GoTo)	Prompts for a cell address or range name, and then moves the cell pointer directly to that cell (which can be in another worksheet or file)
F6 (Window)	If the window has been split, moves the cell pointer to the next window (which can contain another worksheet or file)

Cue:
Use multiple-
worksheet files for
consolidations.

Figure 3.13 displays a multiple-worksheet file. Worksheet A is the consolidation worksheet. Worksheet B contains the detail data for Region 1, and worksheet C contains the detail data for Region 2. So that you can see the entire set of worksheets in perspective view, this file contains only three worksheets; each contains very little data. Press Ctrl-PgDn to move the cell pointer to B:B3.

Cue:
Use file-links for
consolidations.

Figure 3.14 shows a different way to get the same consolidation as the one in figure 3.13 with multiple files. Each worksheet in figure 3.14 is a separate file. The consolidated file is named CONSOL. The other two files are named REGION1 and REGION2. The file names are in D1 of each file. Because the cell pointer is in CONSOL, this is the file name listed in the lower-left corner of the screen. Press Ctrl-PgUp to move the cell pointer to A:B3 in the file REGION1.

Cue:
Use GoTo to
move between
worksheets.

The GoTo (F5) key works the same within a worksheet or with multiple worksheets. If you press GoTo, and then type a cell address that includes only the column and row, the cell pointer moves to that address in the current work-

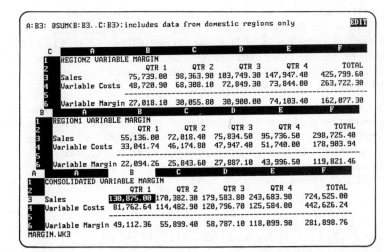

```
A:B3: @SUM(B:B3..C:B3);includes data from domestic regions only        EDIT

C         A          B          C          D          E          F
1  REGION2 VARIABLE MARGIN
2                      QTR 1      QTR 2      QTR 3      QTR 4      TOTAL
3  Sales           75,739.00  98,363.30 103,749.30 147,947.40 425,799.60
4  Variable Costs  48,720.90  68,308.10  72,849.30  73,844.00 263,722.30
5
6  Variable Margin 27,018.10  30,055.80  30,900.00  74,103.40 162,077.30
B         A          B          C          D          E          F
1  REGION1 VARIABLE MARGIN
2                      QTR 1      QTR 2      QTR 3      QTR 4      TOTAL
3  Sales           55,136.00  72,018.40  75,834.50  95,736.50 298,725.40
4  Variable Costs  33,041.74  46,174.80  47,947.40  51,740.00 178,903.94
5
6  Variable Margin 22,094.26  25,843.60  27,887.10  43,996.50 119,821.46
A         A          B          C          D          E          F
1  CONSOLIDATED VARIABLE MARGIN
2                      QTR 1      QTR 2      QTR 3      QTR 4      TOTAL
3  Sales          130,875.00 170,382.30 179,583.80 243,683.90 724,525.00
4  Variable Costs  81,762.64 114,482.90 120,796.70 125,584.00 442,626.24
5
6  Variable Margin 49,112.36  55,899.40  58,787.10 118,099.90 281,898.76
MARGIN.WK3
```

Fig. 3.13.
A file with three worksheets used to consolidate regional data.

```
A:B3: +<<E:\DATA\123\REGION1.WK3>>A:B3..A:A:B3+<<E:\DATA\123\REGION2.WK3>>A:B READY

A         A          B          C          D          E          F
1  REGION2 VARIABLE MARGIN            REGION2
2                      QTR 1      QTR 2      QTR 3      QTR 4      TOTAL
3  Sales           75,739.00  98,363.30 103,749.30 147,947.40 425,799.60
4  Variable Costs  48,720.90  68,308.10  72,849.30  73,844.00 263,722.30
5
6  Variable Margin 27,018.10  30,055.80  30,900.00  74,103.40 162,077.30
A         A          B          C          D          E          F
1  REGION1 VARIABLE MARGIN            REGION1
2                      QTR 1      QTR 2      QTR 3      QTR 4      TOTAL
3  Sales           55,136.00  72,018.40  75,834.50  95,736.50 298,725.40
4  Variable Costs  33,041.74  46,174.80  47,947.40  51,740.00 178,903.94
5
6  Variable Margin 22,094.26  25,843.60  27,887.10  43,996.50 119,821.46
A         A          B          C          D          E          F
1  CONSOLIDATED VARIABLE MARGIN       CONSOL
2                      QTR 1      QTR 2      QTR 3      QTR 4      TOTAL
3  Sales          130,875.00 170,382.30 179,583.80 243,683.90 724,525.00
4  Variable Costs  81,762.64 114,482.90 120,796.70 125,584.00 442,626.24
5
6  Variable Margin 49,112.36  55,899.40  58,787.10 118,099.90 281,898.76
CONSOL.WK3
```

Fig. 3.14.
Three separate files in memory at the same time.

sheet. Include a worksheet letter in the cell address to move the cell pointer to another worksheet in the file. To move the cell pointer to B:A1 in the file in figure 3.13, press GoTo (F5), and then type **b:a1** and press Enter.

To move the cell pointer to the current cell in worksheet B, press GoTo (F5), type **b:**, and then press Enter. 1-2-3 remembers a current cell for every worksheet in memory. In some cases, this is the last location of the cell pointer in the worksheet. For example, if you are in cell A:B3 in figure 3.13 and press F5 to go to B:C15, the cell pointer jumps to C15 in worksheet B, but it remembers the last location in worksheet A. If you then press F5 to go to A:, the cell pointer returns to cell B3 in worksheet A.

When you use the window options, such as perspective view in figures 3.13 and 3.14, the current cells in each worksheet can be synchronized or unsynchronized. This process is explained in detail in Chapter 4. When synchronized, the current cell for all worksheets on-screen is the same address as the current location of the cell pointer. If you are in cell A:B3 in figure 3.13 and press F5 to go to B:C15, the cell pointer jumps to C15 in worksheet B, but it remembers the last location in worksheet A. If you then press F5 to go to A:, the cell pointer moves to cell C15 in worksheet A.

To go to another active file in memory, press GoTo (F5), and then type the name of the file surrounded by double-angle brackets (<< >>). To move directly to REGION2 in figure 3.14, press GoTo (F5), type <<**REGION2**>>, and then press Enter. To move to a specific worksheet and cell in REGION2, include the worksheet and cell address. To move to cell A:F6 in REGION2, press GoTo (F5), type <<**REGION2**>>**A:F6**, and then press Enter.

Entering Formulas with Multiple-Worksheet Files

A formula can refer to cells in other worksheets. To refer to a cell in another worksheet, include the worksheet letter in the address. If the cell pointer is in A:A1, to refer to cell C4 in worksheet B, type **+B:C4**. To point to a cell in another worksheet, type **+**, and then use the movement keys, including Ctrl-PgUp and Ctrl-PgDn, to move to the cell in the other worksheet.

To see how three-dimensional files are used for consolidations, consider figure 3.13. The formula in A:B3 in figure 3.13 sums the sales data in the other two worksheets. Similar formulas in the range A:B3..A:E4 sum the data for the other quarters and for costs. Writing formulas using multiple-worksheet files is much like writing formulas with a single worksheet. The only difference is that you must include the worksheet letter when you use an address in another worksheet.

Entering Formulas that Link Files

A formula can refer to cells in other files. This is called *file-linking*. Figure 3.14 shows three separate files in memory. The formula in A:B3 in CONSOL refers to cell A:B3 in REGION1 and cell A:B3 in REGION2. This powerful feature lets you consolidate data from separate files automatically.

You can use file-linking on a network or other multiuser environment. If you believe that one or more of these linked files were updated since you read the file that contained the links, use /File Admin Link-Refresh to update these formulas.

When you write a formula that refers to a cell in another file in memory, you can point to the cell just as if it were a worksheet in the same file. 1-2-3 includes the path and file name as part of the cell reference (see fig. 3.14). If the file is not in memory, you must type the entire cell reference including the file name and extension inside double angle brackets, as in the following example:

+<<REGION1.WK3>>A:B3

If the file is in another directory, you must include the entire path, as in the following example:

+<<E:\DATA\123\REGION1.WK3>>A:B3

As you can see, a formula that links files is very long. If possible, when you build a formula that refers to a cell or a range in another file, try to have that file in memory so that you can point to the cells instead of typing the complete address. Once the formulas are built, the linked files do not all have to be in memory at the same time. Because formulas are longer and more complex with multiple worksheets and files, try to use POINT mode whenever you enter a formula.

Cue:
For speed and accuracy, use POINT mode to enter cell references in formulas.

Whenever you read from the disk a file containing formulas that refer to cells in another file, 1-2-3 automatically reads the referenced cells from each linked file and recalculates each linked formula. The linked files are not read into memory. This means that you can build worksheet systems that are linked but are too large to fit into memory all at the same time. This feature allows you to build large consolidation models that update automatically without running out of memory.

You can read the CONSOL file in figure 3.14 without reading the REGION1 and REGION2 files (see fig. 3.15). As you read the file, 1-2-3 updates the formulas in CONSOL that refer to cells in other files. You can update REGION1 and save it, and then update REGION2 and save it. When you retrieve CONSOL, you get the correct consolidated data.

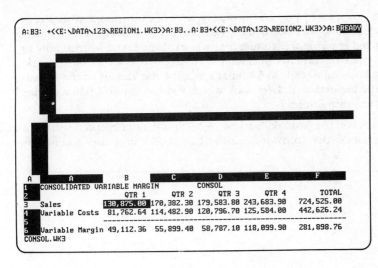

Fig. 3.15.
A formula that refers to cells in files which are on disk and not in memory.

Choosing Between Multiple-Worksheet Files and Linked Files

Figure 3.13 shows a consolidation using a multiple-worksheet file. Figure 3.14 shows the same consolidation using linked files. The method you choose depends on the specific circumstances. If each regional worksheet is updated by a different person, separate files are necessary. If each regional file is so large that you don't have enough memory to put them all into one file, separate files are required.

If you have many regions but each regional worksheet is small, it is easier to use a single, multiple-worksheet file. It is easy to sum a range of any size in a multiple-worksheet file (see fig. 3.13). Ranges, however, cannot include multiple files, so you must write long formulas with individual cell addresses as shown in figure 3.14. A formula can be no more than 512 characters long. You can exceed this amount with about 16 regions, depending on the names of the path to the subdirectories you use to store your worksheet files.

Another consideration might be recalculation times. A multiple-worksheet file takes longer to recalculate than separate linked files.

If memory and recalculation time are not at issue, and you do not have to distribute parts of the file to others, multiple-worksheet files are easier to build and update in most cases.

Chapter Summary

In this chapter, you learned how to organize your work into single worksheets, multiple-worksheet files, and linked files. The process of moving around worksheets and files and entering and editing data was explained. You learned how to build different types of formulas, including formulas that refer to other worksheets and files. Pointing to cells in formulas and using the various operators was also covered. The important Undo feature, which you can use to Undo a change made in error, was introduced.

This chapter gives you the basic skills to use 1-2-3. In the next chapter, you learn the basic commands that provide the tools to build and use worksheets effectively.

4

Using Fundamental
1-2-3 Commands

Much of the power of 1-2-3 comes from your use of its commands. You use commands to tell 1-2-3 to perform a specified task or sequence of tasks. Commands can change the operation of the 1-2-3 program itself, or they can operate on a file, a worksheet, or a range. You use commands to change how data displays in the cell, to arrange the display of worksheets in windows on-screen, to print reports, to graph data, to save and retrieve files, to copy and move cells, and to perform many other tasks.

1-2-3 includes over 800 commands. Certain commands are used every time you use the program; others are used rarely, if ever. Some commands perform general tasks that apply to all worksheets; other specialized commands apply only to special circumstances. This chapter covers using command menus and the most fundamental 1-2-3 commands. Later chapters cover more specific commands.

You also learn the limitations on these commands. Certain actions, such as formatting a backup diskette, you cannot do within 1-2-3. In this chapter, you learn how to access the operating system and return to 1-2-3.

In addition to the detailed explanation of the most important commands in this chapter, this book includes a separate Command Reference that lists and describes all the commands in alphabetical order. A tear-out Command Menu Map at the back of the book shows all the menus.

This chapter shows you how to do the following:

- Use command menus
- Save your files
- Use ranges and range names

- Set column widths
- Clear data from rows, columns, and worksheets
- Insert rows, columns, and worksheets
- Use window options
- Freeze titles on-screen
- Protect and hide data
- Control recalculation
- Move and copy data
- Reference cells with relative and absolute addressing
- Find and replace particular data
- Access the operating system without quitting 1-2-3

Selecting Commands from Command Menus

Reminder:
You can access the
command menu
from READY mode
only.

You execute 1-2-3 commands through a series of menus. To access the main menu, which displays in the second line of the control panel, press the slash (/) key from READY mode. The mode indicator changes to MENU (see fig. 4.1). This menu gives you access to over 800 commands.

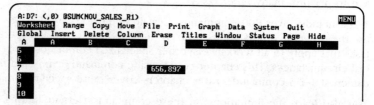

Fig. 4.1.
The main
command
menu.

One command in a command menu is highlighted. When you first press the slash key, Worksheet is highlighted. Below the menu options, on the third line, is either an explanation of the highlighted menu option or a list of the options in the next menu. In figure 4.1, the third line lists the Worksheet menu options.

To select a menu option, point to the choice and press Enter. Table 4.1 shows the keys that move the menu pointer, also called the highlighter. As you highlight each menu item, the next set of commands displays on the screen's third line. Figure 4.2 shows the menu after you select /Worksheet. Notice that the third line in figure 4.1 has moved up to become the menu line in figure 4.2. Continue to make menu selections until you get to the command you want. With some commands, you are prompted to specify ranges, file names, values, or other information.

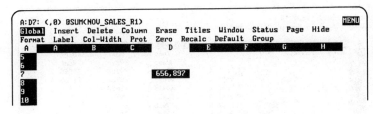

Fig. 4.2.
The /Worksheet menu.

Table 4.1
Menu Pointer Movement Keys

Key	Function
→	Moves the pointer one command to the right. If at the last command, wraps to the first command.
←	Moves the pointer one command to the left. If at the first command, wraps to the last command.
Home	Moves the pointer to the first command
End	Moves the pointer to the last command
Enter	Selects the command highlighted by the menu pointer
Esc	Cancels the current menu and moves to the previous menu. If at the main menu, cancels the menu and returns to READY mode.
Ctrl-Break	Cancels the menu and returns to READY mode

Once you become familiar with the command menus, you can use a faster method to select commands. Just type the first letter of each command. This is the same as highlighting the command and pressing Enter. Every option on a menu begins with a different character, so 1-2-3 always knows which menu option you want. Most users type the first letter of the commands they know well and point to commands they don't often use.

Cue:
Type the first character of a command name to select the command from a menu.

One of the first commands you use is /**R**ange **E**rase. To erase a cell or a range of cells, first press / from READY mode. Select **R**ange, and then select **E**rase. The prompt Enter range to erase: appears (see fig. 4.3). If you want to erase just the current cell, press Enter (see fig. 4.4). If you want to erase a range, specify the range to erase and press Enter. You learn how to specify ranges in the section "Using Ranges" later in this chapter.

You can point to each menu option or type the first letter of the option. In this book, the entire command name is shown; the first letter is in boldface. You type only the first letter. For example, to erase a range, you type /re (/**R**ange **E**rase).

Reminder:
Press Esc to return to the previous command menu; press Ctrl-Break to return to READY mode.

As you make menu selections, you can make an occasional error. If this happens, press Esc to return to the previous menu. If you press Esc at the main menu, you clear the menu and return to READY mode. If you press Ctrl-Break from any menu, you return directly to READY mode.

Fig. 4.3.
The /Range Erase prompt.

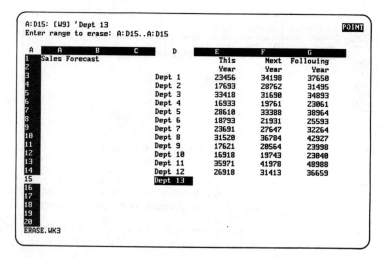

Fig. 4.4.
The current cell erased with /Range Erase.

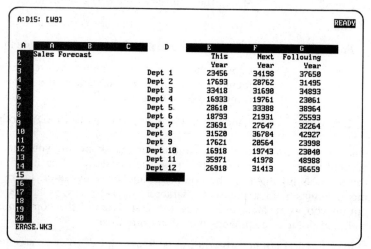

You can explore the command menus without actually executing the commands. Highlight each menu option in the main menu (see fig. 4.1) and read the third line in the control panel to find out more about the option or to see the next menu. Then select each menu option to get to the next menu (see fig. 4.2). Continue to select the menu options you want to explore until there are no more menus. Use the Command-Menu Map at the back of this book to help guide you through the menus. Figure 4.5 shows the /Worksheet Window Display menu. This menu shows you that you can select one of two display options.

Use the Esc key to back out of a menu to the next higher menu without actually executing the command. Figure 4.6 shows the result after you press Esc at the /Worksheet Window Display menu in figure 4.5. You can now explore another /Worksheet Window option.

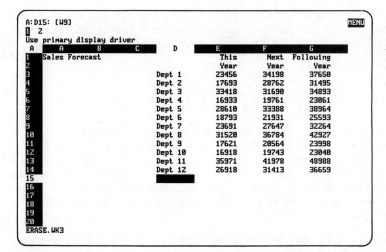

Fig. 4.5.
The /Worksheet
Window
Display menu.

Fig. 4.6.
The /Worksheet
Window menu
after you press
Esc from the
/Worksheet
Window
Display menu.

You can continue this process to explore any or all the command menus. Just remember to press Esc to move up one menu. To return directly to READY mode from any menu, press Ctrl-Break.

The names of the main menu choices (see fig. 4.1) help guide you to the correct command. For example, all the graph commands are accessed through /Graph, and all the data-management commands are accessed through /Data. There is one important exception: The /Worksheet commands can refer to a single worksheet, to a file, or to 1-2-3 as a whole. For example, you use /Worksheet Global Default to change overall 1-2-3 defaults, such as the choice of printer. With previous versions of 1-2-3, you could only work with one worksheet and one file at a time. /Worksheet was the highest level. These highest-level commands are still accessed through the /Worksheet command.

If you execute a command in error, you can Undo it. For example, if you erase a range in error (see figs. 4.3 and 4.4), you can press Undo (Alt-F4) and select **Yes** to recover the erased range. See Chapter 3 for a complete discussion of Undo.

Saving Your Files

A file you build exists only in the computer's memory. When you use /**Q**uit to exit 1-2-3 and return to the operating system, you lose your work if you did not first save it to disk. When you save a file, you copy the file in memory to the disk and give it a file name. The file exists in memory and remains on disk after you quit 1-2-3 or turn off the computer. When you make changes to a file, these changes are made only in the computer's memory until you save the file again with the changes.

More information on file operations is included in Chapter 7. In that chapter, you learn how to read in, use, and save multiple files in memory at the same time. For now, you can learn to save your work by using the /**F**ile **S**ave command. This chapter covers saving only one file in memory.

First, choose /**F**ile **S**ave from the command menu. If you have only one file in memory, 1-2-3 prompts for the name of the file to save and displays a default path and file name for the file. If you have never saved the file before, 1-2-3 assigns a default file name such as FILE0001.WK3 (see fig. 4.7). Do not use this name, but type a meaningful file name, such as DEPT1BUD (a budget file for Department 1). If you have more than one file open in memory, see Chapter 7 for more information.

Fig. 4.7.
The default file name assigned by 1-2-3.

Once you have saved a file, the next time you save it, the default file name is the name you supplied the last time you saved the file, such as DEPT1BUD (see fig. 4.8). To save the file again and keep the same name, just press Enter.

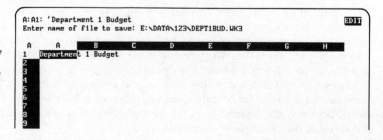

Fig. 4.8.
The default file name as the file name used the last time the file was saved.

To save the file with a different name, type the file name. The file name you type replaces the existing name. If the file already exists on the disk, 1-2-3 displays a menu with the following options (see fig. 4.9):

Cancel   **Replace**   Backup

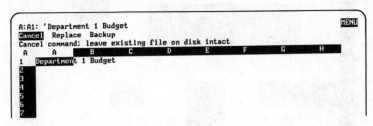

Fig. 4.9.
The /File Save menu when the file already exists.

Choose **Replace** to write over the previous file. Once you choose **Replace**, you lose the previous file. If you make an error in a file, and then save it with the same name and choose **Replace**, you cannot read in the previous file.

Choose **Cancel** to cancel the **/File Save**. If you type a file name in error that matches another file name, **Cancel** the command so that you do not lose the other file.

If you choose **Backup**, 1-2-3 renames the existing file on disk with a .BAK extension, and then saves the new file. With this choice, you have both the new file and the previous file on disk.

*Caution:
If you choose
Replace from the
/File Save menu,
the previous file
with that name is
lost.*

*Cue:
Choose Backup to
keep a backup
copy of your file
before you save a
new version.*

Using Ranges

A *range*, a rectangular group of cells, is defined by the cell addresses of two opposite corners and is separated by two periods. As shown in figure 4.10, a range can be a single cell (E1..E1), part of a row (A1..C1), part of a column (G1..G5, D13..D20, and F14..F15), or a rectangle that spans multiple rows and columns (B4..E9 and A13..B15). A range can also span multiple worksheets. A range can be an entire worksheet or file, but it cannot span multiple files.

Many commands act on one or more ranges. For example, the **/Range Erase** command in figure 4.3 prompts you for the range to erase. In this example, the range is a single cell. You can respond to a prompt for a range in three different ways. At different times, each one of these methods may be the most convenient. To specify a range, you can use any of the following methods:

- Type the addresses of the corners of the range.

- Highlight the cells in the range in POINT mode.

- Type the range name or press Name (F3) and point to the range name if one has been assigned.

Each method is covered in the following sections.

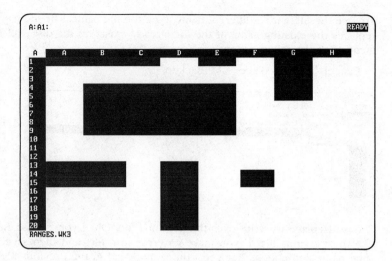

Fig. 4.10.
A sample of 1-2-3 ranges.

Typing the Addresses of the Range

The first method, typing the addresses of the range, is used the least because it is the most prone to error. With this method, you type the addresses of any two opposite corners of the range.

You specify a range by typing the address of the upper-left and lower-right corners; separate the two addresses with one or two periods. 1-2-3 always stores a range with two periods to separate the addresses, but you need to type only one period.

For example, to specify the range B4..E9 in figure 4.10, you can type B4..E9 or B4.E9 or E9..B4 or E9.B4. You can also use the other two opposite corners: E4..B9 or B9..E4. In all cases, 1-2-3 stores the range as B4..E9.

You type cell addresses to specify a range in several situations: when the range does not have a range name; when the range you want to specify is far from the current cell and it is not convenient to use POINT mode; and when you happen to know the cell addresses of the range. Experienced 1-2-3 users rarely type cell addresses; they use one of the other two methods: specifying a range in POINT mode or using range names.

Specifying a Range in POINT mode

The second method, highlighting the cells in the range in POINT mode, is the most common.

You can point to and highlight a range in commands and functions just as you can point to a single cell in a formula. Any special considerations for highlighting ranges in functions are covered in Chapter 6.

Highlighting a Range

Figure 4.11 is a sample sales forecast. Suppose that because of a reorganization, you have to erase all the forecasts and enter new data. Figure 4.11 shows the Enter range to erase: prompt that appears when you execute /**R**ange Erase. The default range in the control panel is the address of the cell pointer, in this example A:E3..A:E3. The single cell is shown as a one-cell range. When the prompt shows a single cell as a one-cell range, the cell is said to be *anchored*. With /re and with most /**R**ange commands, the default range is an anchored, one-cell range. When the cell is anchored, as you move the cell pointer, you highlight a range.

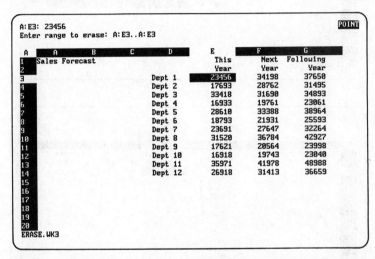

Fig. 4.11.
A one-cell range at the location of the cell pointer.

Figure 4.12 shows the screen after you press End-down arrow and then End-right arrow. You can also press End-Home, which is quicker and uses fewer keystrokes. As you move the cell pointer, the highlight expands from the anchored cell. The highlighted range becomes A:E3..A:G14; this is the range that appears in the control panel. When you press Enter, 1-2-3 executes the command using the highlighted range (see figure 4.13).

Cue:
Check the control panel to see whether the cell is anchored.

Pointing and highlighting in this typical example is faster and easier than typing the range addresses E3..G14. Also, because you can see the range as you specify it (see fig. 4.12), you make fewer errors pointing than typing.

Use the End key when you highlight ranges. The End key moves to the end of a range of occupied cells. To highlight the range from A:E3..A:G14 in figure 4.12, you can press End-down arrow and End-right arrow, as in the previous example. Without the End key, you have to press the right arrow twice and the down arrow 11 times.

Cue:
Use the End key to highlight ranges quickly.

With some commands, such as /**R**ange Erase in this example, the anchored cell starts at the position of the cell pointer. You should move the cell pointer to the

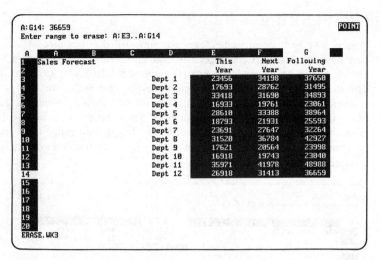

Fig. 4.12.
A range highlighted as the cell pointer is moved.

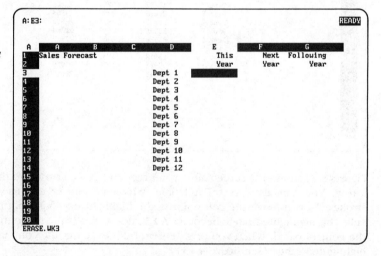

Fig. 4.13.
The highlighted range erased.

upper-left corner of the range before you start the command. In figure 4.11, the cell pointer started at A:E3, the upper-right corner of the range to erase.

Figure 4.14 shows what happens if the cell pointer is in the wrong cell when you start a /Range Erase. The cell pointer was in F4; after you press End-down arrow and End-right arrow, the range A:F4..A:G14 is highlighted.

Whenever you highlight a range, the cell opposite the anchored cell is called the *free cell*. You can identify the position of the free cell by observing the contrasting row and column borders. In figure 4.14, the free cell is G14. The highlight expands or contracts from the free cell when you use one of the movement keys. If the wrong cell is anchored, as in figure 4.14, you can move the anchor cell and the free cell by pressing the period key (.). Every time you press the period key

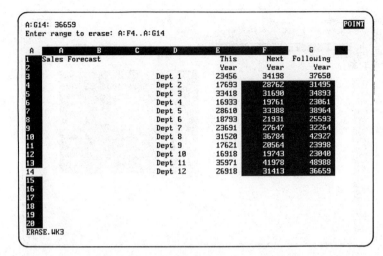

Fig. 4.14.
The wrong
range
highlighted.

while in POINT mode, the free cell moves to another corner of the highlighted range.

To highlight the correct range in figure 4.14, first press the period key twice. You can tell that the free cell moves from G14 to F4 (see fig. 4.15) by observing the contrasting borders for column F and row 4. Now you can press the up- and left-arrow keys to highlight the correct range (see fig. 4.16).

Cue:
Press the period
key to move the
free cell to another
corner˙ of the
range.

With /**R**ange Erase, 1-2-3 expects the range to start at the current location of the cell pointer and starts with an anchored cell. This is true of certain other commands, including all the /**R**ange commands (except /**R**ange Search), /**C**opy, and /**M**ove.

With other commands (including /**D**ata, /**G**raph, /**P**rint, and /**R**ange Search), at the Enter range: prompt, 1-2-3 does not expect the range to start at the current

```
A:F4: 28762                                               POINT
Enter range to erase: A:G14..A:F4

   A      A        B        C        D        E       F        G
1        Sales Forecast                            This    Next    Following
2                                                  Year    Year    Year
3                                   Dept 1        23456   34198   37650
4                                   Dept 2        17693   28762   31495
5                                   Dept 3        33418   31690   34893
6                                   Dept 4        16933   19761   23061
7                                   Dept 5        28610   33388   38964
8                                   Dept 6        18793   21931   25593
9                                   Dept 7        23691   27647   32264
10                                  Dept 8        31520   36784   42927
11                                  Dept 9        17621   20564   23998
12                                  Dept 10       16918   19743   23040
13                                  Dept 11       35971   41978   48988
14                                  Dept 12       26918   31413   36659
15
16
17
18
```

Fig. 4.15.
The free cell
moved to F4.

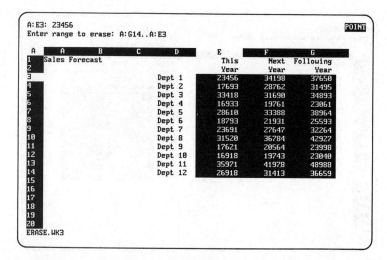

Fig. 4.16.
The correct range highlighted after the free cell is moved to E3.

location of the cell pointer. The control panel shows the current cell address, A:M1, as a single address (see fig. 4.17). This means that the cell pointer is not anchored. When you use the movement keys, the address in the control panel changes to the single address of the current location of the cell pointer. To anchor the first corner of the range, press the period key. Figure 4.18 shows the screen after moving the cell pointer to A:M3 and pressing the period key. The address in the control panel changes to a one-cell range. If you want a larger range than A:M3, move the cell pointer to highlight the range and press Enter.

Cue:
Press Esc or Backspace to clear a highlighted range.

You can press Esc or Backspace to clear an incorrectly highlighted range. The highlight collapses to the anchor cell only, and the anchor is removed. If you press Esc or Backspace in figure 4.14, the highlight becomes just F4 and the cell

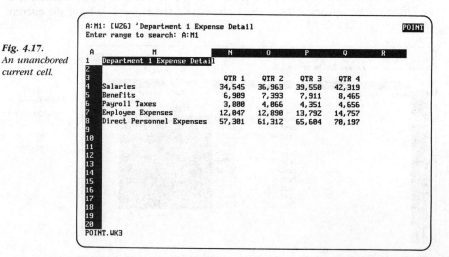

Fig. 4.17.
An unanchored current cell.

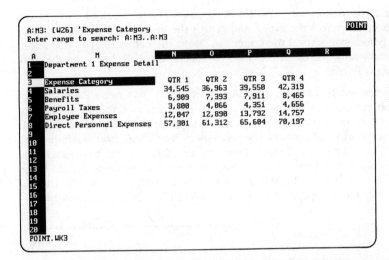

Fig. 4.18.
An anchored cell after the period key is pressed.

becomes unanchored (see fig. 4.19). Observe that the cell address in the control panel in figure 4.19 is the single address A:F4, not the one-cell range A:F4..A:F4.

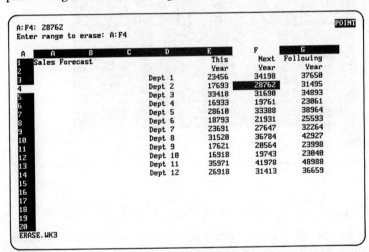

Fig. 4.19.
The highlighted range and the anchor cleared.

You can now move the cell pointer to E3 and press the period key to anchor the cell again. The control panel shows the one-cell range A:E3..A:E3. This is the same situation as figure 4.11. You can now highlight the range A:E3..A:G14 and complete the command.

Dealing with Remembered Ranges

When you specify a range with some commands, such as /Data, /Graph, /Print, and /Range Search, 1-2-3 remembers the range. When you repeat the command, 1-2-3 highlights the previous range.

Cue:
1-2-3 remembers the previous range with some commands.

If this is what you need, just press Enter. If you want to specify a new range, press Backspace to cancel the range and return the cell pointer to the cell that was current before you started the command. Move the cell pointer to the beginning of the new range, press the period to anchor the cell, highlight the new range, and press Enter.

You can also use Esc to cancel a previous range. When you press Esc to cancel the range, the cell pointer moves to the upper-left corner of the old range, not the current cell in the worksheet. For example, suppose the cell pointer is in M1, and you want to print this part of the worksheet. The range previously printed was A:A2..A:G18. When you choose /**P**rint **P**rinter **R**ange, 1-2-3 remembers the old range (see fig. 4.20). If you press Backspace now, 1-2-3 cancels the old range and returns the cell pointer to M1. If you press Esc now, 1-2-3 cancels the old range but moves the cell pointer to A2, the upper-left corner of the old range.

Fig. 4.20.
A previously
remembered
range.

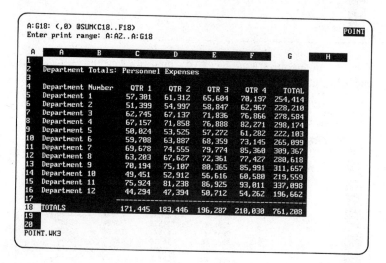

Specifying a Range with Range Names

Another method for specifying a range at the prompt involves giving the range a name. Range names, which should be descriptive, can include up to 15 characters and can be used in formulas and commands.

Using range names has a number of advantages. Range names are easier to remember than addresses. It is sometimes faster to use a range name rather than point to a range in another part of the worksheet. Range names also make formulas easier to understand. For example, if you see the range name NOV_SALES_R1 in a formula, you have a better chance of remembering that the entry represents "November Sales for Region 1" than C:D7..C:D10 (see fig. 4.21).

If you have more than one file in memory, 1-2-3 displays a list of range names in the current file, as well as a list of the other files in memory. To select a range

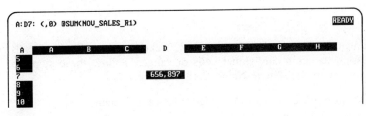

Fig. 4.21.
A formula that
uses a range
name.

name in another file, you first select the file name to see the display of range
names in that file. You can then select the range name in that file.

Whenever 1-2-3 expects a cell or range address, you can specify a range name.
There are two ways to specify a range name. You can type the range name, or
you can press Name (F3) and point to the range name. When you press Name,
the third line of the control panel lists the first four range names in alphabetical
order. Use the movement keys to point to the correct range name and press
Enter. If you have many range names, press Name (F3) again; 1-2-3 displays a full
screen of range names (see fig. 4.22).

Cue:
*You can use the
Name (F3) key in
commands,
functions, and
multiple
worksheets in
conjunction with
the GoTo (F5) key.*

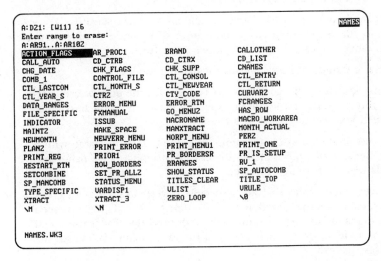

Fig. 4.22.
A full-screen
display of
range names.

If the command calls for a single cell address, such as with /Data Sort Primary-
Key or GoTo (F5), 1-2-3 can specify a range whether you type an English name
or a cell address. If the prompt calls for a single cell address, such as with /dspk
or GoTo (F5), and you type a range name that applies to a multiple-cell range,
1-2-3 uses the upper-left corner of the range. If you type a non-existent range
name, 1-2-3 displays an error message. Press Esc or Enter to clear the error and
try again.

Cue:
*You can use a
range name any
time 1-2-3 expects
a range or cell
address.*

Because a single cell is considered a valid range, you can name a single cell as a
range. Whenever 1-2-3 expects a cell address, you can type the address, point to
the cell, or type the single-cell range name.

Creating Range Names

To create range names, you use the /**R**ange Name Create or /**R**ange Name Labels commands to assign names to individual cells or ranges. Follow these steps to create range names with the /**R**ange Name Create command:

1. Move to the top-left corner of the range you want to name.

2. Choose /**R**ange Name Create.

3. Type the name, and then press Enter at the Enter name: prompt. 1-2-3 displays the Enter range: prompt.

   If you type a new range name, 1-2-3 shows the current cell as an anchored range. Highlight the range or type the address or addresses of the cell or range; then press Enter.

   If you type an existing range name, 1-2-3 highlights the existing range. Use the arrow keys to extend the range or press Esc to cancel the range and specify a new range. Press Enter.

Cue:
You can specify range names using any combination of uppercase and lowercase letters.

Range names can include up to 15 characters and are not case-sensitive. You can type or refer to the name using any combination of uppercase and lowercase letters, but all range names are stored as uppercase letters.

Following are a few rules and precautions for naming ranges:

- Do not use spaces or special characters (except for the underscore character [_]) in range names. If you use special characters, you can confuse 1-2-3 when you use the name in formulas.

- You can use numbers in range names, but don't start the name with a number. Because of a quirk in 1-2-3, you cannot type a range name into a formula that starts with a number.

- Do not use range names that are also cell addresses (such as P2), key names (such as GoTo), function names (such as @SUM), or advanced macro command keyword names (such as BRANCH). If you use a cell address as a range name, when you type the range name, 1-2-3 uses the cell address instead.

Certain other errors can occur when you use range names in formulas. These errors are covered in Chapter 6.

You can also create range names with the /**R**ange Name Labels command. With this command, you can assign range names to many individual cells at one time. You can use /**R**ange Name Labels to assign range names only to single-cell ranges. With /rnl, you use labels already typed into the worksheet as range names for adjacent cells. In figure 4.23, for example, you can use the labels in cells B5..B8 to name the cells with sales data in C5..C8. Because you want to name the cells to the right of the labels, use /**R**ange Name Labels **R**ight. Specify a range of B5..B8 and press Enter. Now C5 has the range name Dept_1.

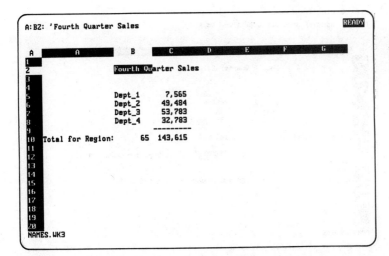

Fig. 4.23.
Labels that can
be used for
range names.

The other options with /**R**ange **N**ame **L**abels are **L**eft, **D**own, and **U**p. These commands only assign range names to labels in the range you specify. If you specified
a range of B2..B10 in figure 4.23, the blank cells in B3, B4, B9, and the number in
B10 are ignored. The first fifteen characters in the label in B2 become the range
name for C2: Fourth Quarter. You do no harm if you include cells that are blank,
or include numbers or formulas in a /**R**ange **N**ame **L**abels range, but do not
include other labels; you will end up with unwanted range names.

Adding Notes about Ranges

Once you create a range name, you can append a note to a range name with
/**R**ange **N**ame **N**ote **C**reate. First, select the range name you want to annotate, and
then type a note of up to 512 characters. You can use this feature to explain the
meaning of the range or how it is used. You can also use this command to
change an existing note. You can list these notes with /**R**ange **N**ame **N**ote **T**able.

Listing All Range Names and Notes

1-2-3 includes two commands that can create a table of named ranges in your
worksheet. /**R**ange **N**ame **T**able creates a list of range names and addresses.
/**R**ange **N**ame **N**ote **T**able creates a list of range names, addresses, and notes.
Using these commands is the only way you can see your range-name notes (see
fig 4.24). This table is part of the documentation for the worksheet file and can
be put in a worksheet separate from the actual data.

To delete an unwanted range name, use /**R**ange **N**ame **D**elete. Use caution when
using the /**R**ange **N**ame **R**eset command, however. The command immediately
deletes all the range names in the file.

Caution:
The /Range Name
Reset command
deletes all range
names.

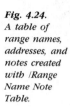

Fig. 4.24.
A table of
range names,
addresses, and
notes created
with /Range
Name Note
Table.

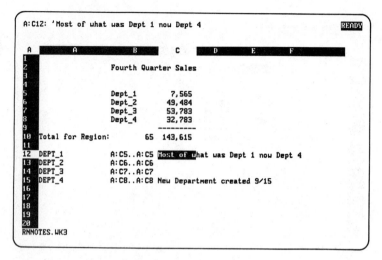

Using Ranges in Files with Multiple Worksheets

If your file has more than one worksheet, you can specify three-dimensional ranges. A three-dimensional range must have the shape of a three-dimensional rectangle. A range cannot span more than one file, but you can specify a range in one file that refers to a two- or three-dimensional range in another file.

For example, you can specify a /Data Query Input range in FILEA that refers to a range in FILEB. When you execute /Data Query Extract in FILEA, the input range used is in FILEB. This enables you to use /Data Query to use data from a number of files. More information on this process is found in Chapter 10.

You can also print a range in FILEA that refers to a range in FILEB. This enables you to print a report that combines data from multiple files. This process is covered in Chapter 8.

Figures 4.25, 4.26, and 4.27 display examples of three-dimensional ranges. To create the range B:B2..D:B2 in figure 4.25, start in B:B2 and press the period key to anchor the range. Then press Ctrl-PgUp twice to move up to worksheet D. To create the range B:B2..C:B4 in figure 4.26, start in B:B2 and press the period key to anchor the range. Press the down-arrow key twice to highlight B:B2..B:B4, and then press Ctrl-PgUp to move up to worksheet C. To create the range B:B2..D:D5 in figure 4.27, start in B:B2 and press the period key to anchor the range. Press the down-arrow key three times and the right-arrow key twice to highlight B:B2..B:D5, and then press Ctrl-PgUp twice to move up to worksheet D.

Three-dimensional ranges can be useful with consolidation worksheets. *Consolidations* are worksheets that combine data from many different worksheets that each contain data from one department, region, product, and so on.

It is much easier to highlight a range than type the corner addresses. If you do type the address, make sure that you use the correct worksheet letters. The corners are the upper left of the first worksheet and the lower right of the last worksheet.

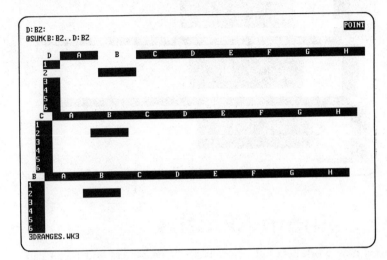

Fig. 4.25.
A three-dimensional range that includes a single cell across three worksheets.

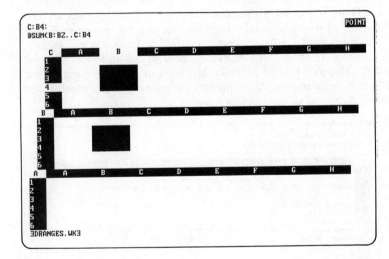

Fig. 4.26.
A three-dimensional range that includes three cells in a column across two worksheets.

Fig. 4.27.
A three-dimensional range that includes a rectangular range across three worksheets.

Setting Column Widths

When you start a new worksheet, all columns are 9 characters wide. You can change this default column width and the width of each individual column to best accommodate your data. If columns are too narrow, numbers display as asterisks, and labels are truncated if the adjacent cell is full. If columns are too wide, you cannot see as much on-screen or print as much on one page. Figure 4.28 shows a worksheet with a default column width of 5 characters and an individual column width of 13 for column A. The number in cell J8 is too wide for the column and displays as a row of asterisks. The label in A5 is too long for the column width and is truncated by the number in B5. Any column width other than the default is displayed in the control panel.

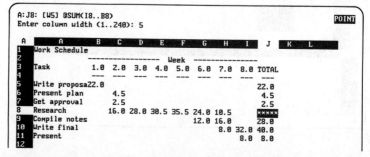

Fig. 4.28.
A worksheet with a global column width of 5 and individual column widths.

Whether a number can fit into a cell depends on both the column width and the format. In general, a number's width must be one character less than the column width. Some negative numbers display with parentheses, which take two extra characters. If a number displays as a row of asterisks, change either the column width, the format, or both.

Use /Worksheet Global Col-Width to change the default column width for the entire worksheet. At the prompt, type a number between 1 and 240 and press Enter.

To set the width of one column, move the cell pointer to the column you want to change and use /Worksheet Column Set-Width (see fig. 4.28). At the prompt, type a number between 1 and 240 and press Enter. To change multiple-column widths at the same time, use /Worksheet Column Column-Range Set-Width. At the first prompt, highlight the range of columns to set; then type the column width and press Enter. /Worksheet Column Column-Range Set-Width operates on a consecutive set of columns only.

An individual column width overrides the global column width. If you change the global column width shown in figure 4.28, the width of column A does not change.

If you are not sure of the exact column width you want, use the left- and right-arrow keys instead of typing a number. Each time you press the left-arrow key, the column width decreases by one. Each time you press the right-arrow key, the column width increases by one. When the display looks the way you want, press Enter. This technique works for both individual, column-range, and global column widths.

Cue:
Use the arrow keys to set column widths.

Use /Worksheet Column Reset-Width and /Worksheet Column Column-Range Reset-Width to remove an individual column width and reset the width to the global default.

If the window is split when you change column widths, the column width applies only to the current window. When you clear a split window, the column widths in the upper or left window are saved. Any column widths in the lower or right window are lost. Column widths and global column widths apply to just the current worksheet unless you turn on GROUP mode with /Worksheet Global Group. In GROUP mode, all worksheets in the file change column widths at the same time.

Use GROUP mode when all the worksheets in a file have the same format, for example, when each worksheet contains the same data for a different department or division (see fig. 4.32). In GROUP mode, any formatting change (such as setting column widths) that you make to one worksheet in the file affects all the worksheets in the file.

Erasing and Deleting Rows, Columns, and Worksheets

You can clear parts or all of your work in several ways. Any data that you clear is removed from the workspace in memory, but does not affect the files on disk until you use the /File commands explained in Chapter 7. There are two ways to clear part of your work in memory. If you erase the work, you remove all the contents of the cells. If you delete the work, you remove the cells themselves from the workspace.

Erasing Ranges

Use the /**R**ange **E**rase command to erase sections of a file in memory. You can erase a single cell, a range within one worksheet, or a range that spans multiple worksheets in one file. You cannot, however, erase cells in more than one file with one /**R**ange **E**rase command.

When you erase a range, only the contents are lost. Characteristics, such as format, protection status, and column width, remain.

After you choose /**R**ange **E**rase, 1-2-3 prompts you for the range to erase. You highlight a range or type a range name and press Enter. You can also press Name (F3) for a list of range names. To erase only the current cell, press Enter.

Deleting Rows and Columns

After you erase a range, the cells remain but are now blank. In contrast, when you delete rows or columns, 1-2-3 deletes the entire row or column and updates the addresses of the rest of the worksheet to reflect their removal. To delete a row, use /**W**orksheet **D**elete **R**ow. You are then prompted for the range of rows to delete. To delete one row, press Enter. To delete more than one row, use the movement keys to highlight the rows you want to delete; then press Enter. You only need to highlight one cell in each row—not the entire row (see fig. 4.29).

Fig. 4.29.
One cell in
each row
highlighted for
deletion.

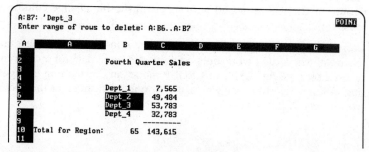

When you press Enter, the rows that contain highlighted cells are deleted (see fig. 4.29). The rest of the worksheet then moves up (see fig. 4.30). 1-2-3 automatically adjusts all addresses, range names, and formulas. You can follow the same procedure to delete columns.

If you delete rows or columns that are part of a range name or a range in a formula, 1-2-3 automatically adjusts the range. If the deleted rows or columns contain formulas that refer to single cells, the reference changes to ERR and the

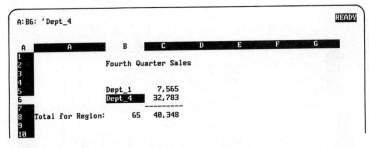

Fig. 4.30.
The worksheet after rows are deleted.

formulas become invalid (see fig. 4.31). This action can be a serious consequence of deleting rows and columns. These formulas do not have to be visible on-screen; they can be anywhere in the file, or even in other worksheets or files.

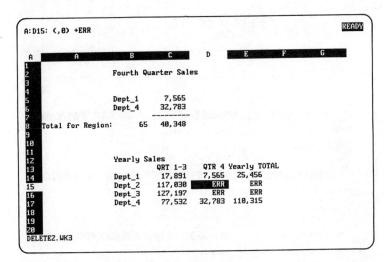

Fig. 4.31.
ERR replacing cell addresses in formulas referring to deleted cells.

Using GROUP Mode To Change All the Worksheets in a File

Normally, deleting rows or columns affects only the current worksheet. However, if you have multiple worksheets in the file and GROUP mode is turned on, when you delete (or add) rows or columns to one worksheet, you delete (or add) the same rows of columns in all worksheets in the file.

Choose /Worksheet Global Group Enable to turn on GROUP mode. The GROUP status indicator appears on the status line (see fig. 4.32). If you now delete the columns highlighted in figure 4.32, you delete the same columns in all worksheets (see fig. 4.33).

GROUP mode applies to all commands that affect the status of a worksheet, such as /Worksheet Global Col-Width discussed in this chapter and /Worksheet Global Format, covered in Chapter 5.

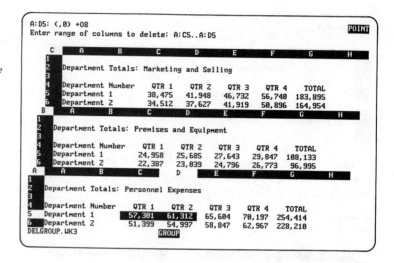

Fig. 4.32.
A multiple-worksheet file in GROUP mode before columns are deleted.

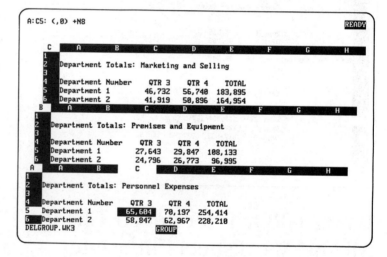

Fig. 4.33.
The multiple-worksheet file in GROUP mode after columns are deleted.

Deleting Worksheets and Files

If the file has multiple worksheets, you can delete an entire worksheet the same way you delete a row or a column. Use /Worksheet Delete Sheet to delete one or more worksheets from a file. You cannot delete all the worksheets from a file; at least one worksheet must remain after the deletion.

If you try to delete all worksheets in a file, you receive an error message, and no worksheets are deleted.

If you have multiple files in memory, you can remove a file from the workspace with /Worksheet Delete File. Point to the file from the list of active files in memory and press Enter. Up to three single worksheet files can be visible at one time (see fig. 4.34), but more files can be active in memory. At the Enter name of file in memory to delete: prompt, up to the first four files in memory are listed on the third line. Press Names (F3) to see the names of all the files in memory. If you have not saved the file, all changes you made to the file are lost. (See Chapter 7 for more information on files.) After you delete a file from memory, more memory is available; you can add data to the existing files in memory or open another file.

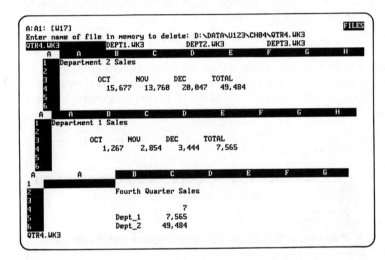

Fig. 4.34.
The list of file names presented at the prompt.

Clearing the Entire Workspace

You can clear all files from memory with /Worksheet Erase Yes. The command deletes *all* worksheets and files from memory. This command's name, which is confusing, is a holdover from previous versions of 1-2-3, in which only one file and one worksheet could be in memory at one time. /Worksheet Erase Yes also restores all the default global settings. The effect is the same if you quit 1-2-3 and restart it from the operating system.

When you are finished working on a system with multiple files in memory, you can use /Worksheet Erase Yes to clear them all from memory. You can then retrieve another file or read in another worksheet system. Remember to use /File Save before you use /Worksheet /Erase Yes. 1-2-3 provides no method of reclaiming worksheets after /wey is executed.

Caution:
/Worksheet Erase Yes deletes all files in memory, not just the current worksheet.

Inserting Rows, Columns, and Worksheets

You can delete rows, columns, and worksheets; you can also insert them any-where in the file. You insert rows with /Worksheet Insert Row and columns with /Worksheet Insert Column. You can insert one or more rows or columns at one time. At the Enter insert range: prompt, highlight the numbers of rows or columns you want to insert and press Enter.

Reminder:
When you insert columns, all addresses in formulas and range names adjust automatically.

When you insert rows, all rows below the cell pointer are pushed down. When you insert columns, all columns to the right of the cell pointer are pushed to the right. All addresses in formulas and range names adjust automatically. Figure 4.35 shows the file from figure 4.33 after one column has been inserted between columns C and D. Because GROUP mode is still on, a column is inserted in every worksheet in the file.

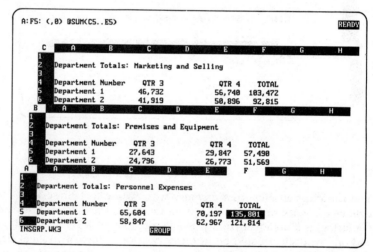

Fig. 4.35.
Addresses automatically adjusted after column insertion.

If you insert a row or column in the middle of a range, the range expands to accommodate the new rows or columns. In figure 4.33, the formula in E5 is @SUM(C5..D5). In figure 4.35, the formula is pushed to F5 when the column is inserted and now is @SUM(C5..E5), which includes the columns in the old range as well as the inserted column.

Use /Worksheet Insert Sheet to insert one or more new worksheets into the file. 1-2-3 then prompts you to insert the new worksheets either Before or After the current worksheet. In most cases, you insert the worksheet After the current worksheet. Figure 4.36 shows the file from figure 4.35 after one worksheet was inserted after worksheet A.

If you insert worksheets in the middle of a multiple-worksheet file, all the work-sheets behind the new ones receive new worksheet letters. As in figure 4.36, if

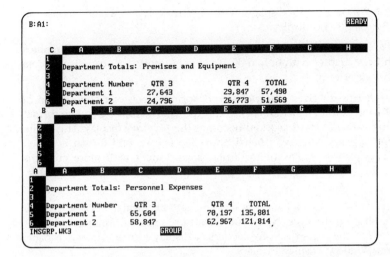

Fig. 4.36.
Addresses of
worksheets
behind the
inserted
worksheet
adjusted
automatically.

you insert a new worksheet after worksheet A, and worksheet B already exists, the new worksheet becomes B, and the old worksheet B becomes C. All addresses and formulas adjust automatically. If you insert a worksheet in the middle of a range that spans worksheets, the range expands automatically to accommodate the new worksheet.

Using Window Options

You can change the way you view the worksheets in memory in a number of different ways. You can change the display format to view more rows and columns at one time. You can split the screen into two windows either vertically or horizontally, and you can view parts of three worksheets at once in perspective, three-dimensional view. These options give you the ability to see different parts of your work at the same time.

Changing the Display Format

When you work with large databases, reports, or tables of data, such as the one in figure 4.41, you cannot see all the data at one time. If your display hardware supports it, you can change the display to view more columns and/or more rows of data at the same time. The more data you can see at one time, the easier it is to compare different months or different departments.

Many displays give you a choice of formats besides the standard 80-character by 25-line (80×25) display. You choose these display formats when you install 1-2-3 (see Appendix A). For example, with a Hercules Monochrome Graphics Card, you can choose an 80×25 or 90×43 display. With an EGA card, you can choose an 80×25 or 80×43 display. With a VGA card, you can choose an 80×25, 80×34, or 80×60 display.

If you have a monochrome display adapter (no graphics), a Color/Graphics adapter, or an EGA adapter with only 64K of video memory, you can display data in the 80×25 format only.

Cue:
Use /Worksheet
Window Display
Secondary to view
more data at one
time if your
hardware
permits it.

If your display hardware gives you a choice of formats, you can choose two of them at installation and then switch back and forth from within 1-2-3. The format you choose first is marked with a 1 and becomes the *primary* display. This is the way the screen appears when you first load 1-2-3. The second format is called the *secondary* display. If you want to display a worksheet with more columns than the default, you can use the /Worksheet Window Display Secondary command.

You may want to do most of your work at the 80×25 format because it's the sharpest and easiest on the eyes. When you want to see more of the worksheet at one time, switch to the higher density secondary display format. To switch back, use /Worksheet Window Display Primary.

Splitting the Screen

You can split the screen either horizontally or vertically into two windows with /Worksheet Window Horizontal or /Worksheet Window Vertical. These commands are useful when you are using large, single worksheet applications; /wwh and /wwv enable you to see different parts of the worksheet at the same time.

Split the screen vertically when you want to see the totals columns to the right of the data, as in figure 4.37. Split the screen horizontally when you want to see the totals rows at the bottom of the data. With a split screen, you can change data in one window and at the same time see how the totals change in the other window. This capability is very handy for "what-if" analysis.

A split screen also comes in handy when you write macros. You can write the macro in one window and see the data that the macro operates on in the other window. Macros are covered in Chapter 11.

Reminder:
Move the cell
pointer to the
position where you
want the screen to
split.

The window splits at the position of the cell pointer, so be sure that you move the cell pointer to the correct position first.

When you split the screen vertically, the left window includes the columns to the left of the cell pointer. In figure 4.37, the cell pointer was in column E when the window was split. Columns A-D (the columns to the left of the cell pointer) became the left window. The right window was then scrolled to display the TOTAL and VARIANCE in columns O and P. These columns are always visible as you scroll the left window.

When you split the screen horizontally, the top window includes the rows above the cell pointer. To display rows 10-20 in the upper window, scroll the display so that row 10 is at the top of the display, and then move the cell pointer to row 21 and select /Worksheet Window Horizontal.

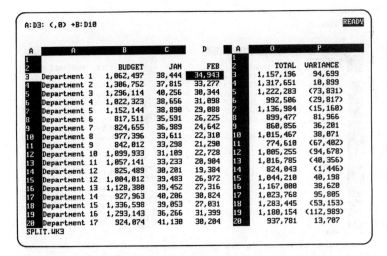

Fig. 4.37.
The screen split vertically.

A:D3: (,0) +B:D10   READY

	A	B	C	D		A	O	P
1					1			
2		BUDGET	JAN	FEB	2		TOTAL	VARIANCE
3	Department 1	1,062,497	38,444	34,943	3		1,157,196	94,699
4	Department 2	1,306,752	37,815	33,277	4		1,317,651	10,899
5	Department 3	1,296,114	40,256	30,344	5		1,222,283	(73,831)
6	Department 4	1,022,323	38,656	31,098	6		992,506	(29,817)
7	Department 5	1,152,144	38,890	29,088	7		1,136,984	(15,160)
8	Department 6	817,511	35,591	26,225	8		899,477	81,966
9	Department 7	824,655	36,989	24,642	9		860,856	36,201
10	Department 8	977,396	33,611	22,310	10		1,015,467	38,071
11	Department 9	842,012	33,298	21,290	11		774,610	(67,402)
12	Department 10	1,099,933	31,109	22,728	12		1,005,255	(94,678)
13	Department 11	1,057,141	33,233	20,904	13		1,016,785	(40,356)
14	Department 12	825,489	30,201	19,384	14		824,043	(1,446)
15	Department 12	1,004,012	39,483	26,972	15		1,044,210	40,198
16	Department 13	1,128,380	39,452	27,316	16		1,167,000	38,620
17	Department 14	927,963	40,206	30,824	17		1,023,768	95,805
18	Department 15	1,336,598	39,053	27,031	18		1,283,445	(53,153)
19	Department 16	1,293,143	36,266	31,399	19		1,180,154	(112,989)
20	Department 17	924,074	41,130	30,204	20		937,781	13,707

SPLIT.WK3

Because a split screen has two borders, you cannot display quite as much data at one time as you can with a full screen.

As you move down the worksheet in figure 4.37, both windows scroll together. If you move the cell pointer below row 20, both windows scroll up so that you can see row 21. In this case, this is what you want. No matter where the cell pointer is in the left window, you can see the total for that department in the right window. This is called *synchronized scrolling.*

At other times, you may want to see two unrelated views of the same worksheet, for example, when one window contains data and the other window contains macros. In this case, you want the two windows to scroll separately. Use /Worksheet **W**indow **U**nsync to stop the synchronized scrolling and /Worksheet **Win**dow **S**ync to restore it.

In figure 4.37, the two windows display different parts of the same worksheet. If you have multiple worksheets or files in memory, you can use the split screen to display different worksheets. When you use Ctrl-PgUp, Ctrl-PgDn, or the other movement keys to move between worksheets and files, you affect only the current window. The file in figure 4.37 has multiple worksheets. With the cell pointer in the left window, if you press Ctrl-PgUp, the left window displays worksheet B; the right window is unchanged (see fig. 4.38).

You use synchronized scrolling to see two parts of the same table or report at the same time, as in figure 4.37. The data in the two windows are part of the same table. If you scroll down to row 22 in the left window, you want to see the total in row 22 in the right window.

When the two windows display different worksheets, you are looking at different data in the two windows, as in figure 4.38. Notice that if you scroll down to row 22 in the right window in figure 4.38, you do not want to scroll down to row 22 in the left window.

```
B:D3: 3170                                                          READY

B        A             B        C        D    ║ A      O        P
1  Department 1                                 ║1
2                     BUDGET      JAN      FEB   ║2          TOTAL  VARIANCE
3  Product 1         112,243    4,428    3,170  ║3      1,157,196   94,699
4  Product 2         118,236    4,664    3,340  ║4      1,317,651   10,899
5  Product 3         191,618    9,197    6,328  ║5      1,222,283  (73,831)
6  Product 4         202,239    7,563    6,651  ║6        992,506  (29,817)
7  Product 5         254,547    7,519    5,896  ║7      1,136,984  (15,160)
8  Product 6         183,614    5,073    9,558  ║8        899,477   81,966
9                                               ║9        860,856   36,201
10                 1,062,497   38,444   34,943  ║10     1,015,467   38,071
11                                              ║11       774,610  (67,402)
12                                              ║12     1,005,255  (94,678)
13                                              ║13     1,016,785  (40,356)
14                                              ║14       824,043   (1,446)
15                                              ║15     1,044,210   40,198
16                                              ║16     1,167,000   38,620
17                                              ║17     1,023,768   95,805
18                                              ║18     1,283,445  (53,153)
19                                              ║19     1,180,154 (112,989)
20                                              ║20       937,781   13,707
SPLIT.WK3
```

Fig. 4.38.
Two different
worksheets
displayed in a
split window.

Cue:
In perspective
view, each window
displays a separate
worksheet.

To clear a split screen, use /Worksheet Window Clear. No matter what window you are in, the cell pointer moves to the left or upper window when you clear a split screen.

You can also split the screen with /Worksheet Window Perspective. Figure 4.36 displays three worksheets as if they were stacked up on your desk. With /wwp, you always see exactly three worksheets. If there are less than three worksheets in memory, you see blank worksheets. In perspective view, each window displays a separate worksheet.

You can have a split screen or a perspective view, but not both at the same time. To go from one option to the other, first use /Worksheet Window Clear, and then choose the other window option.

Zooming and Moving between Windows

To move between windows, use the Window (F6) key. With a split screen, you move back and forth between the two windows. In perspective view, you move up from the first to the second to the third, and then back down to the first worksheet again. Window (F6) moves only between windows on-screen. If you have worksheets that are not visible in a window, use Ctrl-PgUp and Ctrl-PgDn (or other worksheet-movement keys) to get to these other worksheets. Ctrl-PgUp and Ctrl-PgDn also move through the visible worksheets in perspective view.

Cue:
Use Zoom (Alt-F6)
to enlarge a
window to full-
screen size.

You can make the current window expand to full-screen size with the Alt-F6 (Zoom) key. The ZOOM status indicator appears in the status line at the bottom of the display. To return to the separate windows, press Alt-F6 again.

When you use a split screen or perspective view, the view in each window is smaller than a full screen. Perspective view is handy when you move among different worksheets in memory (see fig. 4.36), but you can see only six rows in each worksheet at one time. When you want to work with one of the worksheets for a while, use Zoom to display the worksheet in a full-screen view so that you can see a full 20 rows. In figure 4.38, you can see only two months in the left window. If you want to work on the data in the left window, you can use Zoom to see five months at once (see fig. 4.39).

```
B:D3: 3170                                                      READY

  B       A         B         C         D         E         F         G
1      Department 1
2                  BUDGET     JAN       FEB       MAR       APR       MAY
3      Product 1  112,243    4,428     3,170     7,035     9,829     9,815
4      Product 2  118,236    4,664     3,340     7,410    10,354    10,338
5      Product 3  191,618    9,197     6,328    13,623    17,181    20,338
6      Product 4  202,239    7,563     6,651    15,779    21,130    22,994
7      Product 5  254,547    7,519     5,896    15,208    20,245    20,726
8      Product 6  183,614    5,073     9,558    25,708    18,119    18,997
9
10               1,062,497  38,444    34,943    84,763    96,858   103,208
11
12
13
14
15
16
17
18
19
20
SPLIT.WK3                    ZOOM
```

Fig. 4.39.
A window expanded to full-screen size after Zoom (Alt-F6) is pressed.

When you are in ZOOM mode, you can use the F6 key to move between windows as if they were all on-screen at the same time. This technique provides a way to move quickly between full-screen windows. F6 requires only one keystroke with one hand; Ctrl-PgUp requires two hands.

Displaying a Graph in a Worksheet

The /Worksheet Window Graph command applies only when you are using graphs. Use /Worksheet Window Graph to split the screen into a data window and a graph window. The graph changes automatically as you change the data in the worksheet. Figure 4.40 shows a display with a graph window. You cannot use /Worksheet Window Graph with a color/graphics adapter (CGA) because of the CGA's low resolution. Graphing is covered in detailed in Chapter 9.

Freezing Titles on the Screen

Most worksheets are much larger than can be displayed on-screen at any one time (see fig. 4.41). As you move the cell pointer, you scroll the display. New data appears at one edge of the display while the data at the other edge scrolls

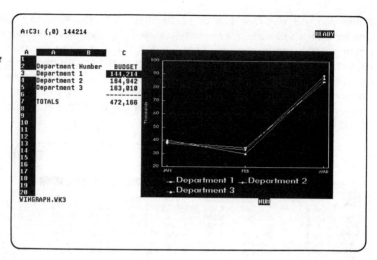

Fig. 4.40.
The screen split
into a data
window and a
graph window.

out of sight. This scrolling can be a problem when titles at the top of the worksheet and descriptions at the left also scroll off the screen (see fig. 4.42). You can
no longer tell what month and what departments the worksheet contains.

Cue:
Use the /Worksheet
Titles command to
prevent titles from
scrolling off the
screen.

To prevent the titles from scrolling off the screen, you can use the /Worksheet
Titles command to lock titles on-screen.

To lock titles, follow these steps:

1. Position the display so that the titles you want to lock are at the top and
   left of the display (see fig. 4.41).

Fig 4.41.
Part of the data
visible on the
worksheet.

A:B4: (,0) [W10] +B:B10   READY

	A	BUDGET	JAN	FEB	MAR	APR	MAY
4	Department 1	1,062,497	38,444	34,943	84,763	96,858	103,208
5	Department 2	1,306,752	37,815	33,277	89,196	102,014	114,444
6	Department 3	1,296,114	40,256	30,344	87,583	99,494	100,902
7	Department 4	1,022,323	38,656	31,098	82,914	81,070	82,164
8	Department 5	1,152,144	38,890	29,088	81,515	84,552	94,339
9	Department 6	817,511	35,591	26,225	74,494	71,451	77,039
10	Department 7	824,655	36,989	24,642	70,194	69,684	70,397
11	Department 8	977,396	33,611	22,310	70,436	80,645	85,278
12	Department 9	842,012	33,298	21,290	67,542	65,139	63,960
13	Department 10	1,099,933	31,109	22,728	73,775	80,675	87,451
14	Department 11	1,057,141	33,233	20,904	72,935	76,787	76,582
15	Department 12	825,489	30,201	19,384	68,836	66,229	64,752
16	Department 12	1,004,012	39,483	26,972	88,458	86,954	85,819
17	Department 13	1,128,380	39,452	27,316	77,631	84,475	84,958
18	Department 14	927,963	40,206	30,824	83,885	85,593	83,618
19	Department 15	1,336,598	39,053	27,031	79,099	88,476	96,329
20	Department 16	1,293,143	36,266	31,399	83,595	96,031	102,120
21	Department 17	924,074	41,130	30,204	76,311	76,666	78,599

TITLES.WK3

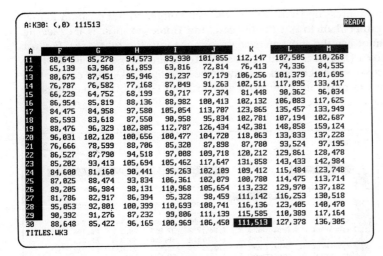

```
A:K30: (,0) 111513                                              READY
A     F       G       H       I       J       K       L       M
11  80,645  85,278  94,573  89,930 101,855 112,147 107,505 110,268
12  65,139  63,960  61,859  63,816  72,814  76,413  74,336  84,535
13  80,675  87,451  95,946  91,237  97,179 106,256 101,379 101,695
14  76,787  76,582  77,168  87,049  91,263 102,511 117,095 133,417
15  66,229  64,752  68,199  69,717  77,374  81,448  90,362  96,034
16  86,954  85,819  88,136  88,982 100,413 102,132 106,083 117,625
17  84,475  84,958  97,580 105,054 113,707 123,865 135,457 133,949
18  85,593  83,618  87,550  90,958  95,834 102,781 107,194 102,687
19  88,476  96,329 102,805 112,787 126,434 142,381 148,858 159,124
20  96,031 102,120 100,656 100,477 104,720 118,063 133,833 137,228
21  76,666  78,599  88,706  85,320  87,898  87,780  93,524  97,195
22  86,527  87,790  94,518  97,008 109,718 120,212 129,861 128,478
23  85,202  93,413 105,694 105,462 117,647 131,858 143,433 142,984
24  84,600  81,160  90,441  95,263 102,109 109,412 115,484 123,748
25  87,025  88,474  93,834 106,361 102,079 100,780 114,475 113,714
26  89,205  96,984  98,131 110,968 105,654 113,232 129,970 137,182
27  81,786  82,917  86,394  95,328  98,459 111,142 116,253 130,518
28  95,053  92,801 100,399 110,693 108,741 116,136 123,405 140,470
29  90,392  91,276  87,232  99,806 111,139 115,585 110,389 117,164
30  88,648  85,422  96,165 100,969 106,450 111,513 127,378 136,305
TITLES.WK3
```

Fig 4.42.
Titles scrolled off the worksheet.

2. Move the cell pointer to the first row below the titles and the first column to the right of the titles. In figure 4.41, the titles are in rows 2-3 and column A; the cell pointer is in B4.

3. Choose /Worksheet Titles Both to lock both horizontal and vertical titles.

Once these titles are locked, the data below row 3 and to the right of column A can scroll off the screen, but the locked titles in rows 2-3 and column A remain on-screen (see fig. 4.43).

```
A:K30: (,0) 111513                                              READY
A      A          G       H       I       J       K       L
2                MAY     JUN     JUL     AUG    SEPT     OCT
3                ------  ------  ------  ------  ------  ------
13 Department 10  87,451  95,946  91,237  97,179 106,256 101,379
14 Department 11  76,582  77,168  87,049  91,263 102,511 117,095
15 Department 12  64,752  68,199  69,717  77,374  81,448  90,362
16 Department 12  85,819  88,136  88,982 100,413 102,132 106,083
17 Department 13  84,958  97,580 105,054 113,707 123,865 135,457
18 Department 14  83,618  87,550  90,958  95,834 102,781 107,194
19 Department 15  96,329 102,805 112,787 126,434 142,381 148,858
20 Department 16 102,120 100,656 100,477 104,720 118,063 133,833
21 Department 17  78,599  88,706  85,320  87,898  87,780  93,524
22 Department 18  87,790  94,518  97,008 109,718 120,212 129,861
23 Department 19  93,413 105,694 105,462 117,647 131,858 143,433
24 Department 20  81,160  90,441  95,263 102,109 109,412 115,484
25 Department 21  88,474  93,834 106,361 102,079 100,780 114,475
26 Department 22  96,984  98,131 110,968 105,654 113,232 129,970
27 Department 23  82,917  86,394  95,328  98,459 111,142 116,253
28 Department 24  92,801 100,399 110,693 108,741 116,136 123,405
29 Department 25  91,276  87,232  99,806 111,139 115,585 110,389
30 Department 26  85,422  96,165 100,969 106,450 111,513 127,378
TITLES.WK3
```

Fig 4.43.
Locked titles on-screen.

With locked titles, pressing Home moves the cell pointer to the position following the titles rather than to A1. In this case, the Home position is B4 (see fig. 4.41). You cannot use the movement keys to move into the titles area, but you can use the GoTo (F5) key. When you use GoTo to move to a cell in the titles area, the title rows and/or columns display twice (see fig. 4.44). This can be very confusing. You can move into the titles area in POINT mode and see the same doubled display as in figure 4.44.

Fig. 4.44.
Doubled
display with
the cell pointer
in the titles
area.

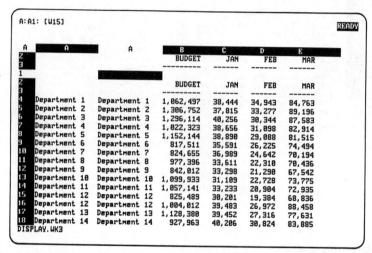

Use /**Worksheet Titles Clear** to cancel the locked titles so that you can move freely in the titles area. You can also lock just the rows at the top of the screen with /**Worksheet Titles Horizontal** or just the columns at the left with /**Worksheet Titles Vertical**. To change the locked titles, you must use /**Worksheet Titles Clear** first, and then specify the new locked titles.

With a split screen, locking titles affects only the current window. With a multiple-worksheet file, locking titles affects only the current worksheet unless you are in GROUP mode.

Protecting and Hiding Worksheet Data

A typical 1-2-3 file contains numbers, labels, formulas, macros, and at least one worksheet. When you first build a file, you may lay out the worksheets for an entire year (see fig. 4.41). The budget model in figure 4.41 contains all the labels and formulas for a yearly budget. Once you build this file, you do not want the labels and formulas to change. However, the detailed budget figures may change many times as different versions are submitted for approval or submitted to different departments for revision.

Once the budget is approved, you may add actual expense data each month. Each time someone changes the detailed data, you run the risk of accidentally changing a formula or a label. If a formula is changed, all the totals can be wrong.

If different people add data to the file, an individual may want to change a formula that seems incorrect. For example, a model may use factors for inflation, growth, or foreign exchange rates. These factors may be decided by the Finance Department and should apply equally to all departments. Some department heads, however, may want to use their own factors. This can invalidate the overall budget that is submitted for approval.

1-2-3 includes a number of features that protect data from accidental or deliberate change. For example, parts of a file might contain confidential data such as salaries or cost factors. 1-2-3 includes features that let someone use the file but not see certain areas of the file. Unfortunately, none of these features can stop persons from finding this hidden information if they know enough about 1-2-3.

You can also password-protect a file that contains confidential data when you save it. This completely prevents access to the file by anyone who does not know the password.

Protecting Cells from Change

Every worksheet has areas containing formulas and labels that do not change over time. Other areas of the worksheet contain data that can change. You can protect the cells that should not change and still allow changes to other cells by using two related commands: /**R**ange Unprot marks the cells that allow changes; /**W**orksheet Global **P**rot Enable turns on protection for all other cells.

You must tell 1-2-3 to use the cell-protection feature. When you start a new worksheet, protection is disabled. This means that you have complete access to all cells in the worksheet. To enable the protection feature, use /**W**orksheet Global **P**rot Enable. Initially, all cells in the worksheet are protected. If you enable protection and try to change a protected cell, 1-2-3 displays an error message and does not make the change. When protection is enabled, the symbol PR appears in the control panel for every protected cell.

You must unprotect the cells you want to change when worksheet protection is enabled. Use /**R**ange Unprot. At the Enter range to unprotect: prompt, highlight each range of cells. U appears in the control panel for every unprotected cell. Cells that contain data and are unprotected display in green on color monitors and in boldface on monochrome monitors.

Once you unprotect a range of cells, you can protect them again with /**R**ange Prot. You can protect or unprotect ranges with global protection either enabled or disabled.

Typically, when you build a new worksheet, you leave global protection disabled. When you finish the worksheet, and you feel that all the formulas and labels are correct, you can unprotect the data input areas and enable global protection.

/Worksheet **G**lobal **P**rot affects only the current worksheet in a multiple-worksheet file. You can have some worksheets in a file with global protection enabled and other worksheets with global protection disabled. If you are in GROUP mode, you change the global protection status of all worksheets at the same time. When you enable GROUP mode, all worksheets change to the global protection status of the current worksheet.

As you build a worksheet, you want protection disabled so that you can change all cells. When the worksheet is complete and you enable protection, you might build another worksheet in the same file, perhaps for macros, a consolidation, or a summary report. You want to leave protection disabled in this new worksheet until you are finished building it. Or, you might have some worksheets in a file that are used as input areas. You want these worksheets unprotected to let users add data and to insert rows and columns. The other worksheets in the file with formulas, reports, and macros would have protection enabled.

Caution:
Protection does not stop anyone from deliberately tampering with a file unless the file is sealed.

If you need to change a protected cell for any reason, you can unprotect the cell, change it, and then protect it again. You can also disable global protection, change the cell or cells, and then enable it again. Because of this, 1-2-3's protection features protect only against accidental change, not from deliberate alteration of the worksheet by an unauthorized person. To prevent unauthorized tampering, you must seal the file as explained in the section on sealing files found later in this chapter.

Using /Range Input

When you use /**W**orksheet **G**lobal **P**rot **E**nable, you restrict changes to cells that are range-unprotected. You can go one step further and restrict the cell pointer to unprotected cells in a specified range by using the /**R**ange **I**nput command.

You use /**R**ange **I**nput with data entry areas or forms, such as the one in figure 4.45. The range K28..K34 is unprotected; the other cells are protected. Typically, you use /ri when you build worksheets for others to use for data entry. In this case, you want whoever will do the data entry to see the entire range I22..L34 but to be able to move the cell pointer only in the range K28..K34.

When you choose /**R**ange **I**nput, the Enter data-input range: prompt appears; you specify the input range and press Enter. In figure 4.45, the data-input range is I22..L34. 1-2-3 positions the display at the beginning of the data-input range and moves the cell pointer to the first unprotected cell in the range, in this case K28.

While /**R**ange **I**nput is active, you can move the cell pointer only to unprotected cells in the input range. If you press Home, the cell pointer moves to K28; press End to go to K33. If you are in K33 and press the down-arrow key, you "wrap" to K28. If you are in K29 and press the right-arrow key, there are no unprotected cells to the right of K28; the cell pointer moves to K29.

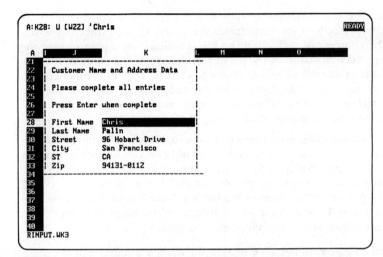

A:K28: U [W22] 'Chris   READY

```
 A  I    J          K            L   M      N        O
21 |-------------------------------------------|
22 | Customer Name and Address Data            |
23 |                                           |
24 | Please complete all entries               |
25 |                                           |
26 | Press Enter when complete                 |
27 |                                           |
28 | First Name   Chris                        |
29 | Last Name    Palin                        |
30 | Street       96 Hobart Drive              |
31 | City         San Francisco                |
32 | ST           CA                           |
33 | Zip          94131-0112                   |
34 |-------------------------------------------|
35
36
37
38
39
40
RINPUT.WK3
```

Fig. 4.45.
An input form used with /Range Input.

While /**R**ange **I**nput is active, you can type entries and edit any unprotected cells. You cannot, however, execute commands. If you press the slash key, you enter the slash character into a cell. To deactivate /**R**ange **I**nput, press Enter or Esc in READY mode. The cell pointer moves to its position before /**R**ange **I**nput was selected.

Reminder:
You cannot execute commands while /Range Input is active.

You can use /**R**ange **I**nput for convenience as well as security. /**R**ange **I**nput can be used if you work with novice users who know little about 1-2-3. Because these users can only move the cell pointer to unprotected cells while /**R**ange **I**nput is in effect, they will not accidentally try to change protected cells. /ri is almost always executed by a macro as part of a data entry system. (Macros are covered in Chapters 11 and 12). The advanced macro command {FORM} is another way to create and use data entry forms.

RELEASE 3

Hiding Data

Sometimes you want to do more than just stop someone from changing data or formulas; you want to prevent others from even seeing the information. To do this, you can hide cells, columns, and worksheets.

You can hide data so that the data is not easily visible, but you cannot hide data to prevent someone from seeing confidential data if that person knows how to use 1-2-3.

Caution:
You cannot hide data from someone who knows how to use 1-2-3.

To hide a cell or range of cells, use /**R**ange **F**ormat **H**idden. Hidden cells display as blank cells in the worksheet. If you move the cell pointer to a hidden cell, and the cell is protected with global protection enabled, the cell contents will not display in the control panel. To display the cell contents again in the worksheet, use any other range format as described in Chapter 5. Or, use /**R**ange **F**ormat **R**eset to reset the cell to the global format.

RELEASE 3

You cannot use the hidden format to hide data completely unless the file contains no unprotected cells. If you can change the format or the protection status, you can see the contents of the cell. If the file is sealed, you cannot change the format or the protection status, but you can still determine the value in the hidden cell. Just enter a formula in an unprotected cell that refers to the hidden cell. If you want to determine the formula in the hidden cell, you can use the {CONTENTS} macro command. These techniques are discussed in Chapter 5. The {CONTENTS} macro command is covered in Chapter 12.

To completely hide columns, use /**W**orksheet **C**olumn **H**ide and highlight the columns you want to hide. You need to highlight only one cell in each column. A hidden column does not display in the window but retains its column letter. Figure 4.46 shows a worksheet with some columns about to be hidden. Figure 4.47 shows the worksheet after the columns are hidden. Note that in the column borders, column letters D..F are skipped. The columns are still there, but they do not display, and you cannot move the cell pointer to them.

When you print a range with hidden columns, the hidden columns will not print. Although you can change the appearance of the display and reports with hidden columns, this is not an effective way to hide sensitive information. Whenever you are in POINT mode, 1-2-3 displays the hidden columns so that you can include cells in the hidden columns in the ranges. This is true even if the file is sealed as described in the following section.

To hide a worksheet in a multiple-worksheet file, use /**W**orksheet **H**ide **E**nable and highlight the worksheets you want to hide. The worksheets and all the data still exist, but you cannot move the cell pointer to a hidden worksheet. Figure 4.48 shows a file similar to the one in figure 4.47, but the monthly detail has been moved to worksheet B, and the other columns moved to the left to fill in the gap. Figure 4.49 shows the file after worksheet B is hidden.

Fig. 4.46.
/Worksheet
Column Hide
used to hide
columns.

```
A:F3: (,0) 84763                                                    POINT
Specify columns to hide: A:D3..A:F3

A     A         B      C        D        E      F       G        H
1
2                            BUDGET     JAN     FEB     MAR    TOTAL  VARIANCE
3     Department 1       144,214   38,444  34,943  84,763  158,150   13,936
4     Department 2       164,942   37,815  33,277  89,196  160,288   (4,654)
5     Department 3       163,010   40,256  30,344  87,583  158,183   (4,827)
6     Department 4       156,855   38,656  31,098  82,914  152,668   (4,187)
7     Department 5       154,556   38,890  29,088  81,515  149,493   (5,063)
8     Department 6       128,374   35,591  26,225  74,494  136,310    7,936
9     Department 7       114,947   36,989  24,642  70,194  131,825   16,878
10    Department 8       133,835   33,611  22,310  70,436  126,357   (7,478)
11    Department 9       119,778   33,298  21,290  67,542  122,130    2,352
12    Department 10      116,507   31,109  22,728  73,775  127,612   11,105
13    Department 11      116,584   33,233  20,904  72,935  127,872   10,488
14    Department 12      116,221   30,201  19,384  68,836  118,421    2,200
15
16
17
18
19
20
HIDECOL.WK3
```

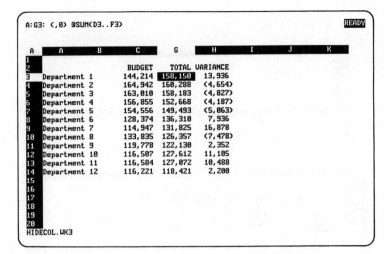

Fig. 4.47.
The worksheet
with hidden
columns.

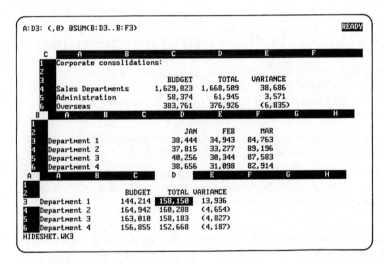

Fig. 4.48.
A multiple-
worksheet file
with details in
worksheet B.

Like hidden columns, you can't use hidden worksheets to hide sensitive data. Whenever you are in POINT mode, 1-2-3 displays the hidden worksheets. This is true even if the file is sealed as described in the next section.

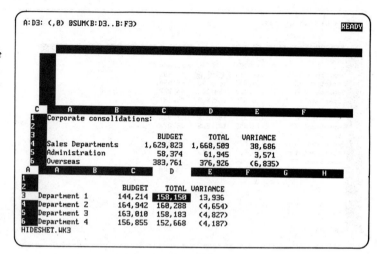

Fig. 4.49.
The worksheet
file with
worksheet B
hidden.

Sealing a File To Prevent Tampering

/File Admin Seal File provides the maximum protection for a file that is used by others. Even someone who is very knowledgeable about 1-2-3 cannot tamper with a sealed file. You can be sure that the protected formulas and labels, the formats, and the worksheet and range settings are not changed.

To protect a file, you enable global protection and unprotect only the cells that should be changed. Then you seal the file with a password.

Once you seal the file, no one can change the protection status or format of any cells or change the global protection. This means that protected cells are really secure. Only unprotected cells can be changed.

To seal a file, choose /File Admin Seal File. 1-2-3 prompts you for a password. The password can include up to 15 characters and cannot contain spaces. The password does not display as you type it. 1-2-3 then prompts you for the password again. If you type the same password again, 1-2-3 seals the file.

If you need to change the file, you must first unseal the file with /File Admin Seal **Disable**. 1-2-3 prompts you for the password. You must type the original password or you cannot unseal the file and change it. Passwords are case-sensitive. A lowercase letter does not match an uppercase letter. You should write the password down and keep it in a safe place.

Cue:
Seal a file if it will
be used by others.

Caution:
If you lose the
password, you
cannot unseal the
file and change it.

Saving a File with a Password To Prevent Access

To completely prevent access to a file, you can save the file with a password. Without the password, no one can read the file or get any information from the file. If you lose the password, you cannot access any information in the file.

You can seal a file with a password and also save a file with a password. These two actions and the two passwords are completely independent. If you seal a file, you can read the file, but you cannot change any protected cells or settings without the seal password. If you save the file with a password, you need the password to read in the file, but once you have read the file into memory, you can change the file.

You can seal the file and save it with a different password. For example, you might want to do this with a confidential personnel file. Someone must have the file password to even read the file. If the file is also sealed, that person can then change only the unprotected cells. You can be the only person who can unseal the file to change it.

More information on password-protection of files is found in Chapter 7.

Controlling Recalculation

The commands discussed so far have shown you how to view, clear, and protect data in worksheets and files. This section covers how you can control how 1-2-3 updates the file as you change it.

Whenever a value in a file changes, 1-2-3 recalculates all other cells that depend on the changed value. This is the essence of an electronic worksheet. 1-2-3 provides a number of recalculation options for different circumstances.

Understanding Recalculation Methods

Normally, 1-2-3 recalculates the file whenever any cell changes. This feature is called *automatic recalculation*. With previous versions of 1-2-3, large worksheets could take a long time to recalculate, slowing down work greatly. With Release 3, however, recalculation is now optimal and background.

Optimal recalculation means that the only cells recalculated are those cells containing formulas that refer to the changed cell. If you change a cell in a large file, and that cell is used in only one formula, only that one formula is recalculated. Recalculation is therefore very fast.

Background means that you can continue to work while 1-2-3 recalculates the file. You may have many numbers to add or change, and they each can affect hundreds of calculations in the file. As you enter each number, 1-2-3 starts a recalculation, but you are not locked out of continuing to enter numbers to the worksheet. As long as you change cells faster than 1-2-3 can recalculate the file, the CALC indicator stays on in the status line at the bottom of the display. As soon as 1-2-3 completes the recalculation, the CALC indicator disappears.

Because of these recalculation routines, recalculation is best left in the default automatic mode most of the time. You can tell 1-2-3 not to recalculate the worksheet when there is a change by using /Worksheet Global Recalc Manual. To force a recalculation, press the Calc (F9) key. Pressing F9 produces a foreground calculation. Until the recalculation is complete, the mode indicator is set to WAIT, and you cannot use 1-2-3.

Automatic recalculation can slow down macro execution because the recalculation is not done in the background. If you use macros, you may prefer to have the macro set the recalculation to manual while the macro executes, and then reset recalculation to automatic before the macro ends. There are special considerations for macros when recalculation is manual. These are covered in Chapter 12.

During recalculation, 1-2-3 determines which formulas depend on which cells and sets up a recalculation order to ensure the correct answer. This process is called the *natural order of recalculation*. Spreadsheet programs before 1-2-3 could not do this and sometimes required many successive recalculations before they arrived at the right answer in all cells.

These early spreadsheet programs could only recalculate either columnwise or rowwise. Columnwise recalculation starts in cell A1 and calculates the cells down column A, then down column B, and so on. Rowwise recalculation starts in cell A1 and calculates the cells across row 1, then across row 2, and so on. Columnwise and Rowwise are options in the /Worksheet Global Recalc menu, but you should ignore them and leave recalculation on Natural.

Using Iteration To Solve Circular References

In one situation, the *circular reference*, the natural order of recalculation does not ensure the correct answer for all cells. A circular reference is a formula that depends, either directly or indirectly, on its own value. Usually a circular reference is an error, and you should eliminate it immediately. Whenever 1-2-3 performs a recalculation and finds a circular reference, the CIRC indicator appears in the status line at the bottom of the display. Figure 4.50 shows a typical erroneous circular reference in which the @SUM function includes itself.

Cue:
Use /Worksheet Status to find the location of a circular reference.

If you are not sure of the reason when the CIRC indicator appears, use /Worksheet Status for a basic status display (see fig. 4.51). This display points out one of the cells that caused the circular reference. In this case, you can fix the error. In other cases, the source of the problem may be less obvious and you may have to check every cell referred to in the cell that contains the formula.

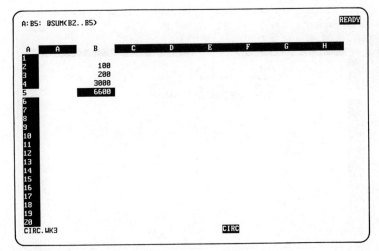

Fig. 4.50.
A circular reference that produces the CIRC indicator.

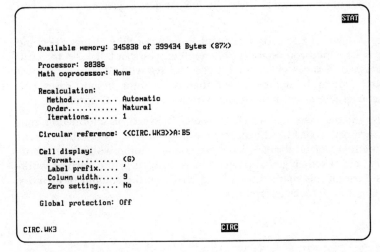

Fig. 4.51.
The circular reference displayed by the /Worksheet Status screen.

In some special cases, a circular reference is deliberate. Figure 4.52 shows a worksheet with a deliberate circular reference. In this example, a company sets aside ten percent of its net profit for employee bonuses. The bonuses themselves, however, represent an expense that reduces net profit. The formula in C5 shows that the amount of bonuses is net profit in D5 × .1, or 10%. But net profit is profit before bonuses − bonuses (B5 − C5). The value of Employee Bonuses depends on the value of Net Profit and the value of Net Profit depends on the value of Employee Bonuses. In figure 4.52, C5 depends on D5 and D5 depends on C5. This is a classic circular reference.

Each time you recalculate the worksheet, the answers change by a smaller amount with a legitimate circular reference. Eventually, the changes become insignificant. This is called *convergence*. Note that the erroneous circular refer-

Fig. 4.52.
A worksheet
with a
deliberate
circular
reference.

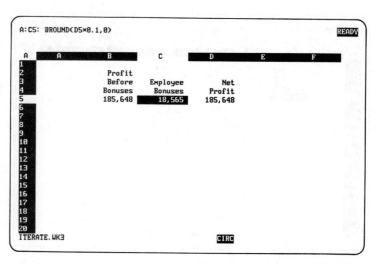

ence in figure 4.50 never converges, and the @SUM gets bigger every time you recalculate.

The worksheet in figure 4.52 needs 5 recalculations before the changes become less than one dollar. Once you establish this number, you can tell 1-2-3 to recalculate the worksheet 5 times every time it recalculates with /Worksheet Global Recalc Iteration. Type in the number 5, and then press Enter. In most cases, you can handle a converging circular reference with a macro (see Chapter 12).

Use /Worksheet Status (see fig. 4.51) to see a mixture of information that includes the memory available, the processor in your computer, the current recalculation method, default formats, label prefix and column width for the current worksheet, and whether global protection is enabled in the current worksheet. The main use of this status display is to check on the amount of memory available and to locate circular references.

Moving the Contents of Cells

When you build worksheets, you often enter data and formulas in one part of the worksheet and later want to move them somewhere else. Use the /Move command to move the contents of a cell or range from one part of a worksheet file to another. You can move the cell or range to another part of the same worksheet or a different worksheet in the same file. Unfortunately, you cannot move a range from one file to another.

Use /Move to move other data out of the way so that you can add to a list, a report, or a database. You also use /Move to rearrange a report so that it prints out in the exact format you want. When you first start to lay out a report, you are often not sure how you want it to look. After some trial-and-error and moving the data around, you get the report format you want.

When you move a range, you also move the format and protection status. You do not, however, move the column width. The original cells still exist after you move their contents, but they are blank and any unprotection or formatting is removed.

Moving the Contents of a Single Cell

Figure 4.53 shows three numbers in column B and their sum in B5. These cells are formatted to display with commas and two decimal places. The numbers are unprotected. To move the sum in B5 to D6, move the cell pointer to B5 and start the /Move command. The Enter range to move FROM: prompt asks you what cells you want to move. To move just the one cell, press Enter. The next prompt, Enter range to move TO: asks where you want the cells to go. Move the cell pointer to D6 and press Enter. The result is shown in figure 4.54. The exact formula that was in B5 is now in D6.

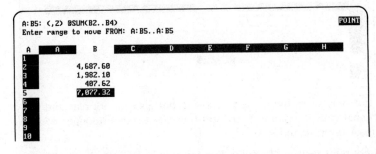

Fig. 4.53.
A formula before being moved.

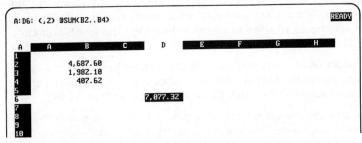

Fig. 4.54.
The formula after being moved.

Moving the Contents of a Range

To move a range, move the cell pointer to the upper-left corner of the range and start the /Move command. At the Enter range to move FROM: prompt, highlight the range of cells to move as in figure 4.55. This prompt starts with the address of the cell pointer as an anchored range. When you move the cell pointer, you highlight the range starting at the original location of the cell pointer to the corner you move to. Press Enter to lock in the FROM: range. At the Enter range to move TO: prompt, move the cell pointer to the upper-left corner of the new location and press Enter. This prompt's address is not anchored. In figure 4.56, the range was moved to C1. Like all commands that prompt for ranges, you can type addresses, point and highlight, or use range names.

Fig. 4.55.
A range of numbers before being moved.

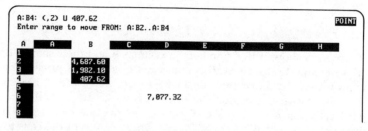

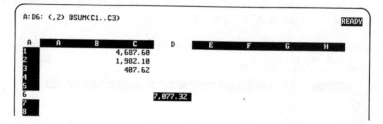
Fig. 4.56.
The formula adjusted after the numbers are moved.

In figure 4.56, not only were the contents moved, but also the formats and protection. The original cells in column B are still there, but they no longer contain data, formatting, or unprotected status.

This is a very important feature of /Move. The formula in D6 still shows the sum of the three numbers. When you move data, all formulas that refer to that data adjust their cell references to refer to the new location. The formula in D6 is now @SUM(C1..C3).

You can move ranges of any size; you can also move them between worksheets. If you build a large model by starting with one worksheet, you can move parts of it into different worksheets as the model grows (see figs. 4.57 and 4.58).

When you move a range, you completely eliminate anything that was in the destination range before the move. You lose the data, the format, and the protection status. If any formulas refer to those cells, the references change to ERR.

In figure 4.59, you want to replace the numbers in C1..C3 with the numbers in H1..H3. Figure 4.60 shows the result if you move H1..H3 to C1..C3. The formula in D6 changes from @SUM(C1..C3) to @SUM(ERR).

This change is permanent unless you immediately press Alt-F4 to Undo the move. Otherwise, you must manually re-enter the formula in D6. You can have hundreds of formulas all over the file that refer to the cells C1..C3, and every one must be corrected. (You don't have to type every formula; you can use the /Copy command as explained in the next sections.) Because of this, be very careful with /Move; you can destroy a worksheet if you use /Move incorrectly.

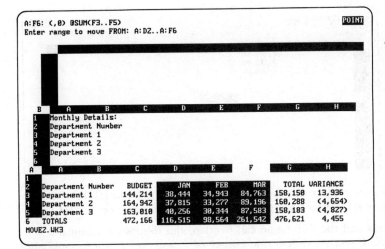

Fig. 4.57.
The worksheet
before data is
moved to
another
worksheet.

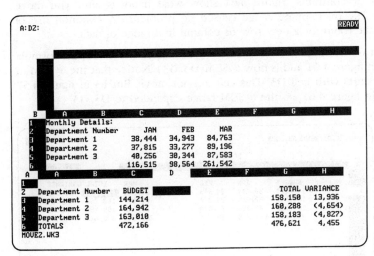

Fig. 4.58.
The worksheet
after data is
moved to
another
worksheet.

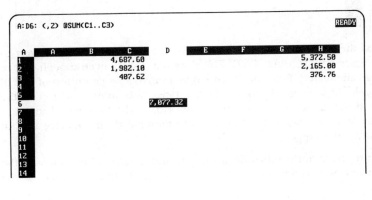

Fig. 4.59.
The worksheet
before data is
moved into
cells already
used in a
formula.

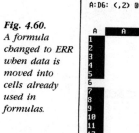

Fig. 4.60.
A formula
changed to ERR
when data is
moved into
cells already
used in
formulas.

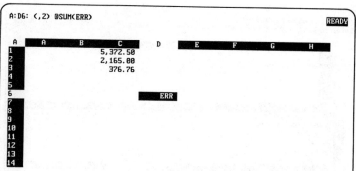

The correct way to replace the data in C1..C3 with the data in H1..H3 (see fig. 4.59) is to /Copy H1..H3 to C1..C3, and then use /Range Erase on H1..H3.

The FROM: range and the TO: range can overlap, and the /Move command still works correctly. If you move just one corner of a range used in a formula, the range expands or contracts. Figure 4.61 show what happens after you move F2..H6 to G2. The overlapping range caused no problems. A common use of /Move is to make room for a new row or column in a range of data.

The formula in G3 in figure 4.57 is @SUM(D3..F3). After the move, the formula moved to H3 in figure 4.61 and is now @SUM(D3..G3). Notice that the @SUM in both formulas starts with cell D3. This cell did not move. But F3 in figure 4.57 moved to G3 in figure 4.61, so the @SUM range expanded to D3..G3.

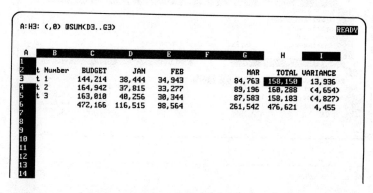

Fig. 4.61.
The range
expanded and
formulas
adjusted
automatically
as one corner
of the range is
moved out.

If you moved the range G2..I6 in figure 4.61 back to F2, the formulas revert to the ones in figure 4.57 (see fig. 4.62). ERR does not display even though part of the range was eliminated. ERR only occurs if you move a range on top of one of the corner cells in a range. In figure 4.60, a range was moved on top of the corner cells in the range in the formula in row D6, so the formulas changed to ERR. In figure 4.62, a range moved on top; the formulas do not change to ERR but just contract the range.

The cell pointer does not need to be at the top of the range when you start the /Move command. Sometimes it's easier to start at the destination range. At the

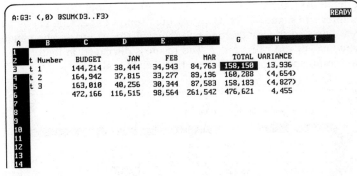

Fig. 4.62.
The range
contracted and
the formulas
adjusted
automatically
as one corner
of the range is
moved in.

Enter range to move FROM: prompt, press Esc to unanchor the range. Move the cell pointer to the range that you want to move; press the period key to anchor the range; highlight the range to move; and then press Enter. At the Enter range to move TO: prompt, 1-2-3 moves back to the original location of the cell pointer. Press Enter to complete the move operation.

Copying the Contents of Cells

You use /**Move** to rearrange data in a file. You use /**Copy** to make duplicate copies of a range in a file, or to copy from one file to one other file. In a typical file, most formulas are duplicated many times. For example, in figure 4.62, the formula in G3 is duplicated in G4..G6. The same is true for the formulas in column H. This list could include hundreds of rows. It is long and tedious to type each formula separately. Fortunately, if you need the same number, label, or formula in a number of places in a file, you can enter them once and copy them.

You can copy a single cell or a range to another part of the worksheet, to another worksheet in the file, or to another worksheet in another file. When you copy, you can make a single copy or many copies at the same time. When you copy a range, you also copy the format and protection status. You do not, however, copy the column width. The original cells are unchanged after you copy them. When you copy, the duplicate cells overwrite anything that was in the destination range before the copy. You lose the data as well as the format and protection status.

Copying the Contents of a Single Cell

The simplest example is to copy a label from one cell to another. Figure 4.63 shows the beginnings of a budget appliction. A repeating label in C6 separates the department detail from the totals in row 7. To copy this label from C6 to D6, move the cell pointer to C6 and select /Copy. At the prompt Enter the range to copy FROM:, press Enter to specify the one-cell range at C6. At Enter the range to copy TO:, move to D6 and press Enter. The result is displayed in figure 4.64. Unlike the /Move command, /Copy produces the label in both places.

Fig. 4.63.
A worksheet before a label is copied.

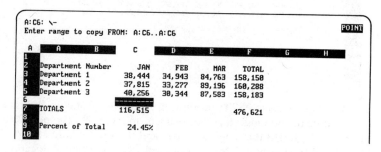

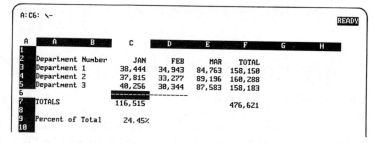
Fig. 4.64.
The worksheet after a label is copied.

Copying a Formula with Relative Addressing

The real power of /Copy shows up when you copy a formula. The formula in C7 is @SUM(C3..C5). When you copy C7 to D7, the formula in D7 is @SUM(D3..D5) (see fig. 4.65). This concept, *relative addressing*, is one of the most important concepts in 1-2-3. When you copy a formula, 1-2-3 adjusts the new formula so that its cell references are in the same relative location as they were to the original formula.

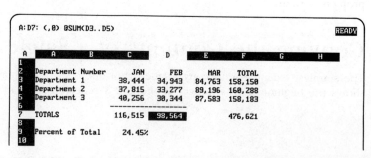
Fig. 4.65.
The addresses adjusted automatically when a formula is copied.

The best way to understand relative addressing is to understand how 1-2-3 actually stores addresses in formulas. The formula in C7 is @SUM(C3..C5). In other words, this formula means "sum the contents of all the cells in the range from C3 to C5." But that is not the way 1-2-3 really stores this formula. To 1-2-3, the formula is "sum the contents of all the cells in the range from the cell 4 rows above this cell to the cell 2 rows above this cell." When you copy this formula to D7, 1-2-3 uses the same relative formula but displays it as D3..D5.

In most cases, when you copy a formula, you want the addresses to adjust automatically. Sometimes, you do not want some addresses to adjust, or you want part of an address to adjust. These situations are examined separately.

Copying a Formula with Absolute Addressing

The formula in C9 in figure 4.65 is +C7/F7. This figure represents January's sales as a percent of the total. If you copy this formula to D9, you get +D7/G7. The D7, the sales for February, is correct. G7, however, is incorrect; G7 is a blank cell. When you copy the formula in C9, you want the address F7 to copy as an absolute address. This means that you do not want it to change after you copy it to D9.

To specify an absolute address, type a dollar sign ($) before each part of the address you want to remain "absolutely" the same. The formula in C9 should be +C7/$F$7. When you copy this formula to D9, the formula becomes +D7/$F$7.

Instead of typing the dollar signs, you can press the Abs (F4) key after you type the address; the address changes to absolute. In this case, the complete formula becomes +D7/$A:$F$7 (see fig. 4.66). 1-2-3 stores addresses in a peculiar way. If an address is in the same worksheet as the cell that contains the formula, and the worksheet reference is relative, 1-2-3 does not store the worksheet letter in the address, such as the D7 part of the formula in D9. If the worksheet reference is absolute, the worksheet letter is stored in the formula, such as the $A:$F$7 part of the formula in D9.

Cue:
Specify absolute addresses when you write the formula, not when you copy it.

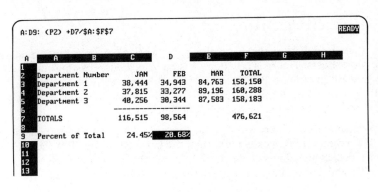

Fig. 4.66.
An absolute address that remains unchanged when copied.

You can enter dollar signs while pointing to addresses in a formula. As you point to a cell to include it in a formula, press the Abs (F4) key to make the address absolute. If you make an error and forget to make an address absolute, just press F2 to go into EDIT mode, move the cursor in the control panel to the address you want to make absolute, and then press F4.

If you want to change an absolute reference (with dollar signs) back to a relative reference, press F2, move the cursor to the reference, and then press F4 a number of times until there are no dollar signs. Press Enter to reenter the formula.

Another kind of addressing is called *mixed addressing*. Mixed addressing can be very complex and is covered later in this chapter.

Copying One Cell's Contents a Number of Times

In figure 4.65, one cell was copied one time. The idea, however, is to copy the formula in C7 to D7 and E7. You can do this in one copy operation. The FROM: range is still C7, but at the Enter range to copy TO: prompt, move the cell pointer to D7, press the period to anchor the cell and highlight E7 as well, and then press Enter. The formula in C7 is copied to both cells (see fig. 4.67).

Fig. 4.67.
A cell copied to a number of cells in one copy.

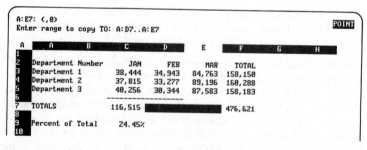

Copying One Cell's Contents to a Range of Cells

Caution:
Avoid overlapping FROM: and TO: ranges. Unless the overlapping cell is the first cell of both the FROM: and TO: ranges, you can destroy the data before you copy it.

You can copy a single cell to a range on the same worksheet or a range that spans multiple worksheets. Figure 4.68 shows a simple price-forecasting model. The current prices are in column B. The formula in C3 increases the price by the amount in B1. To copy this formula through the table in worksheet A, copy FROM: C3 TO: C3..G10. The result is displayed in figure 4.69.

When you copy a single cell, there is no harm if you include the FROM: cell in the TO: range, as in figure 4.68. As a general rule, the first cell in the FROM: range can be the same cell as the first cell in the TO: range. In most other cases, an overlapping FROM: and TO: range can destroy the data before it is copied.

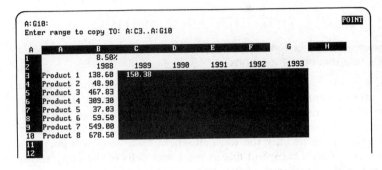

Fig. 4.68.
A cell copied to a number of rows and columns in one copy.

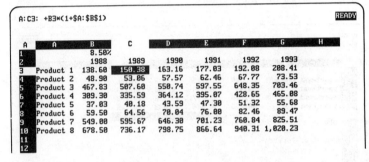

Fig. 4.69.
The worksheet after the copy.

If the same pricing model for different departments is found in different worksheets, for example, you can fill in multiple worksheets with one three-dimensional copy. Figure 4.70 is the result of copying FROM: A:C3 TO: A:C3..C:G10. To highlight the TO: range across multiple worksheets, highlight the TO: range on the first sheet being copied to—in this example, A:C3..AG10. Press Ctrl-PgUp to copy this same range through to the next worksheet. In this example, press Ctrl-PgUp twice to extend the range to A:C3..C:G6.

Fig. 4.70.
A cell copied to to multiple rows, multiple columns, and multiple worksheets in one copy.

Copying the Contents of a Range

In previous examples, one cell at a time was copied. You can copy a row or a column of cells to a number of locations.

In figure 4.71, suppose that you want to copy the label in C6 and the formula in C7 across the other columns. Copy FROM: C6..C7 TO: D6..F6. Figure 4.71 shows the screen after the TO: range is highlighted. In this example, a range down one column is copied a number of times across a row. Note that the TO: range is only across row 6. This highlights only the top cell where each copy will go. 1-2-3 remembers the size of each copy and fills in the lower cells of the copy accordingly. The result is displayed in figure 4.72.

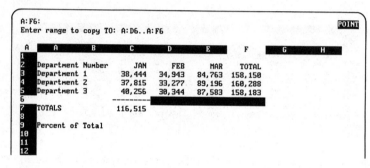

Fig. 4.71.
A range down a column copied a number of times across a row in one copy.

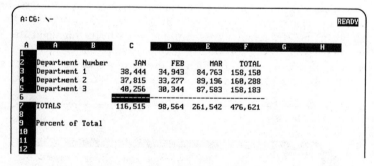

Fig. 4.72.
The worksheet after two cells down a column are copied across three columns.

You can also copy a range across one row down a number of columns. In figure 4.73, you want to copy the TOTAL in G3 and the VARIANCE in H3 down the column. Copy FROM: G3..H3 TO: G4..G6. Figure 4.73 displays the screen after the TO: range is highlighted. The result is displayed in figure 4.74.

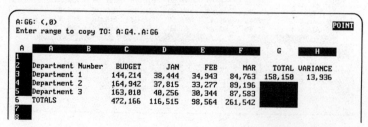

Fig. 4.73.
A range across a row copied a number of times down a column in one copy.

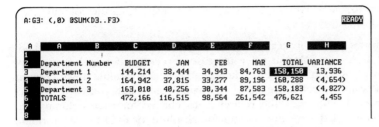

```
A:G3: (,0) @SUM(D3..F3)                                        READY

    A      A         B        C        D        E        F        G        H
1
2          Department Number  BUDGET      JAN      FEB      MAR    TOTAL VARIANCE
3          Department 1      144,214   38,444   34,943   84,763  158,150   13,936
4          Department 2      164,942   37,815   33,277   89,196  160,288  (4,654)
5          Department 3      163,010   40,256   30,344   87,583  158,183  (4,827)
6          TOTALS            472,166  116,515   98,564  261,542  476,621    4,455
7
8
```

Fig. 4.74.
The worksheet after two cells across a row are copied down two columns.

Copying a range a number of times is very useful. When you build worksheets, you will use this technique often. The technique, however, does have limitations. Following is the general rule: If the FROM: range is only one-cell wide in a dimension, you can copy it a number of times in that dimension.

Cue:
If the FROM: range is only one-cell wide in a dimension, you can copy it a number of times in that dimension.

A single cell is one-cell wide in all directions; it is part of one row, one column, and one worksheet. You can copy a single cell across a row, down a column, and through multiple worksheets, as shown in figures 4.68–4.70.

Because the FROM: range in figure 4.71 (C6..C7) occupies 2 rows, you can copy this range across columns (see fig. 4.71) or through multiple worksheets. You cannot copy this range down rows. If you specified a TO: range in figure 4.71 of D6..F7 or even D6..F100, you will get the same result in figure 4.72. The rows are ignored in the TO: range because they are fixed in the FROM: range.

A two-dimensional range can be copied only once to each worksheet in the file. If you copy more than once, any data from the previous copy operation will be overwritten. For example, the range C3..G10 in figure 4.69 can be copied anywhere on this worksheet one time. If you highlight more than a single cell as the TO: range, 1-2-3 uses the upper-left corner and ignores the rest. You can also copy this range through multiple worksheets. If the price forecasts in worksheets B and C in figure 4.70 are blank, you can copy FROM: A:C3..A:G10 TO: B:C3..C:C3 to complete the other two worksheets.

A three-dimensional range, such as A:C3..C:G10, can be copied only once. The three-dimensional range of the copy is successful only if there are enough worksheets in the file.

In figure 4.70, you can copy the range A:C3..C:G10 to any position in worksheet A, such as A:I3. This process duplicates the data in all three worksheets. If you try to copy the range A:C3..C:G10 to any position in worksheet B or C, such as B:I3, 1-2-3 displays the error message Cannot Move or Copy data beyond worksheet boundaries. The TO: range is three worksheets deep. You are trying to copy data from worksheets A-C into worksheets B-D. Because no worksheet D exists, the copy fails.

Copying with Mixed Addressing

In some cases, you must use formulas with a mix of both absolute and relative references if you want the formula to copy correctly. The following example shows you how to keep a row reference absolute while letting the column reference change during the copy.

Figure 4.75 shows a price-forecast worksheet similar to the one in figure 4.68, but this time there is a different price increase percentage for each year. Now the formula in C3 is more complex. When you copy this formula down column C, you do not want the reference to C1 to change, but when you copy the formula across row 3, you want the reference to change for each column. The mixed reference is relative for the column and absolute for the row. The formula in C3 is +B3*(1+$A:C$1). When you copy this down one row to C4, the formula becomes +B4*(1+$A:C$1). The relative address B3 became B4, but the mixed address $A:C$1 is unchanged. When you copy this formula to D3, the formula becomes +C3*(1+$A:D$1). The relative address B3 becomes C3, and the mixed address becomes $A:D$1. You can copy FROM: C3 TO: C3..G10 and create the correct formula throughout the worksheet.

Fig. 4.75.
A mixed
address in a
formula
adjusted when
copied in one
direction and
remaining the
same when
copied in
another
direction.

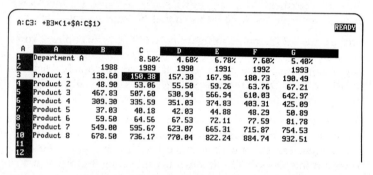

To make an address mixed without typing the dollar signs, use the Abs (F4) key. The first time you press F4, the address becomes absolute. As you continue to press F4, the address cycles through all the possible mixed addresses and returns to relative. The complete list of relative, absolute, and mixed addresses is found in table 4.2. To obtain the address in figure 4.75, press F4 twice.

Caution:
Decide whether
you want the
worksheet part of
the address to be
absolute with
absolute and mixed
addresses.

When you work with multiple worksheets, you must be very careful with absolute and mixed addresses. When you first press F4, the first absolute and mixed addresses make the worksheet absolute. In many cases you do not want this. Consider the worksheet in figure 4.75. The term $A:C$1 in cell C3 forces the C$1 reference to always look at sheet A. If you plan to expand this model to multiple worksheets, as in figure 4.70, you want each worksheet to reference the growth range for that sheet. You want the worksheet letter to change relative to its new worksheet; you therefore want a term of A:C$1 and not the original $A:C$1. In this case, the correct formula in C3 would be +B3*(1+A:C$1). To get the last address in the formula correct, you press the F4 key six times.

Table 4.2
Using Abs (F4) To Change Address Type

Number of Times Needed To Press Abs (F4):	Result	Explanation
1	$A:$D$1	Completely absolute
2	$A:D$1	Absolute worksheet and row
3	$A:$D1	Absolute worksheet and column
4	$A:D1	Absolute worksheet
5	A:$D$1	Absolute column and row
6	A:D$1	Absolute row
7	A:$D1	Absolute column
8	A:D1	Returned to relative

Using Range Names with /Copy

With all commands that prompt for a range, you can use range names for the FROM: range, the TO: range, or both. Just type the range name or press the Name (F3) key and point to the range name. Unfortunately, 1-2-3 makes it impossible to use range names with mixed addresses.

To specify an absolute address, you must type the dollar sign before the range name. To use the range name SALES in a formula as an absolute address, you type **$SALES**. You cannot use Abs (F4) with range names. You cannot specify a range name and make it a mixed address. You must use the actual cell addresses.

Using /Range Value To Convert Formulas to Values

/**R**ange **V**alue is a special type of copy command. When you use /**R**ange **V**alue on a cell that contains a label or a number, this command works exactly like /**C**opy. When you use /**R**ange **V**alue on a cell that contains a formula, the current value, not the formula, is copied. You use /rv to freeze the value of formulas so that they won't change. Figure 4.76 shows a model that forecasts profits for future years. You update the forecasts each quarter, but you want to keep track of the forecasts from the previous quarter for comparison. You can do this by converting the formula results in row 16 into values in row 18. In this way, next quarter's changes won't affect row 18.

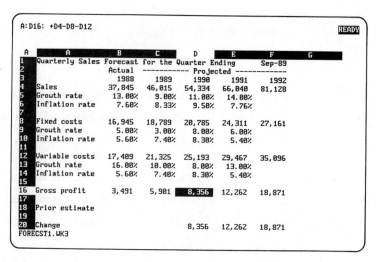

Fig. 4.76.
A worksheet
before a /Range
Value.

The profit figures in figure 4.76 are formulas. To obtain the previous estimate in row 18, use /Range Value FROM: B16..F16 TO: B18. The previous estimate is a copy of the gross profit converted to numbers.

The result is shown in figure 4.77. The numbers in row 18 are the current values of the formulas in row 16.

Fig. 4.77.
The worksheet
after the /Range
Value that
locked in the
previous profit
figures.

In figure 4.78, the various rates were updated, and 1-2-3 calculated new gross profits. Because the previous estimates in row 18 did not change, you can compare the newest estimate with the previous one and calculate the difference in row 20.

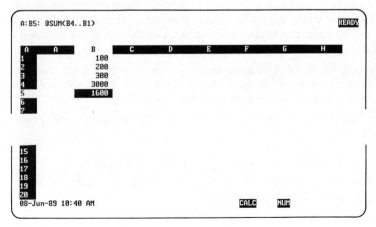

```
A:D18: 8356                                                    READY

A        A         B        C        D        E        F        G
1   Quarterly Sales Forecast for the Quarter Ending    Sep-89
2                   Actual  ---------- Projected ------------
3                   1988     1989     1990     1991     1992
4   Sales           37,845   46,015   54,534   64,492   77,836
5   Growth rate     13.00%   8.30%    8.00%    12.00%
6   Inflation rate  7.60%    9.43%    9.50%    7.76%
7
8   Fixed costs     16,945   18,789   21,087   25,701   28,985
9   Growth rate     5.00%    4.50%    12.54%   7.00%
10  Inflation rate  5.60%    7.40%    8.30%    5.40%
11
12  Variable costs  17,409   21,325   24,873   29,550   34,572
13  Growth rate     16.00%   8.60%    9.70%    11.00%
14  Inflation rate  5.60%    7.40%    8.30%    5.40%
15
16  Gross profit    3,491    5,901    8,574    9,241    14,279
17
18  Prior estimate  3,491    5,901    8,356    12,262   18,871
19
20  Change                            218      (3,021)  (4,592)
FORECST2.WK3
```

Fig. 4.78.
The worksheet with new profit figures after the rates are updated.

Formulas take more memory than numbers; they also take time to recalculate. You can convert (to numbers) formulas that will never change. For example, the years for projections in row 3 in figure 4.78 are formulas that add 1 to the previous year. The formula in C3 is +B3+1. To convert these formulas to numbers, use /**R**ange **V**alue FROM: C3..F3 TO: C3. The trick here is to use /**R**ange **V**alue to convert the formulas to themselves.

Cue:
Use /Range Value to convert formulas to numbers.

There is a danger with /**R**ange **V**alue if you have recalculation set to manual. If you use /**R**ange **V**alue on a formula that is not current, you freeze the old value. This problem is even worse if you convert formulas to numbers and the formulas are not current. You lose the formulas, and the resulting numbers are wrong. In figure 4.79, the CALC indicator shows that the worksheet is not current. If you use /**R**ange **V**alue on the formula in B5, you freeze an incorrect value. If your worksheet is set to manual recalculation and the CALC indicator is on, press Calc (F9) before you use /**R**ange **V**alue.

Caution:
Don't use /Range Value if the CALC indicator is on; you can freeze an incorrect value.

```
A:B5: @SUM(B4..B1)                                            READY

A        A         B        C        D        E     F     G     H
1                  100
2                  200
3                  300
4                  3000
5                  1600
6
7




15
16
17
18
19
20
08-Jun-89 10:40 AM                              CALC     NUM
```

Fig. 4.79.
An incorrect value locked in when /Range Value is issued while the CALC indicator is on.

Using /Range Transpose

/Range Transpose is another special type of copy command. **/Range Transpose** converts rows to columns, columns to rows, and changes formulas to values at the same time. In figure 4.80, the range F12..N19 is the result of the command **/Range Transpose** FROM: A2..H10 TO: F12. The rows and columns are transposed and the formulas in row 10 become numbers in column N.

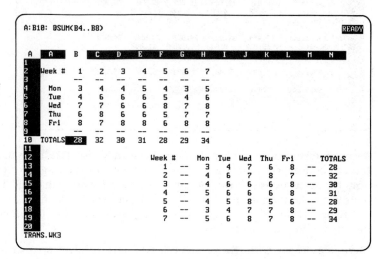

Fig. 4.80.
A table after
/Range
Transpose was
used to
transpose the
rows and
columns.

As with **/Range Value**, you can freeze incorrect values if recalculation is set to manual. Make sure that the CALC indicator is off before you transpose a range.

Finding and Replacing Data

/Range Search searches a range of cells to find a string of characters in labels and formulas. This feature works much like the search-and-replace feature in many word processors. An incorrect search and replace can destroy a file, so always save the file first.

Suppose that you had a list of department names as labels (see fig. 4.81), and you want to shorten the labels from "Department" to "Dept." To search and replace a label, choose **/Range Search**, and then follow these steps:

1. At the prompt, highlight the range to search, A3..A10 (see fig. 4.81), and then press Enter.

2. Type the search string (**department**), and then press Enter.

3. At the menu (see fig. 4.82), choose to search **Formulas**, **Labels**, or **Both**. Choose **Labels** to replace cells with labels.

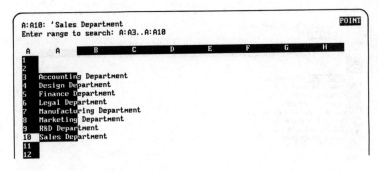

Fig. 4.81.
A column of labels before a /Range Search to replace Department with Dept.

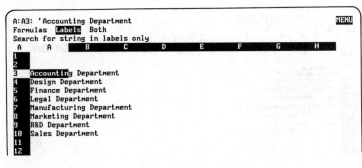

Fig. 4.82.
The /Range Search menu with Labels selected.

4. At the menu, (see fig. 4.83) choose to either **Find** or **Replace**. Choose **Replace**.

5. At the prompt, type the replacement string (**Dept**), and then press Enter.

6. The cell pointer moves to the first cell with a matching string (A3) and gives you the following menu (see fig. 4.84):

    Replace   All   Next   Quit

Choose **Replace** to replace Department with Dept in this one cell and move to the next matching cell. Choose **All** to replace Department with Dept in all cells in the range. Choose **Quit** to stop the search and replace and return to READY mode. Choose **Next** to skip the current cell without changing it and move to the next matching cell. A good idea is to choose **Replace** for the first cell and make sure that the change is correct. If it is correct, choose **All** to replace the rest. If you made an error on the first **Replace**, choose **Quit** and redo the command.

The result is shown in figure 4.85. Case is not used with a search string (department matches Department, for example), but case is important in the replacement string.

If you choose **Find** instead of **Replace** in the menu in figure 4.83, the cell pointer moves to the first cell in the range with a matching string and gives you a menu with the options **Next** or **Quit**. Choose **Next** to find the next occurrence or **Quit** to return to READY mode. If there are no more matching strings, 1-2-3 stops with an error message.

Fig. 4.83.
The /Range Search menu with Replace selected.

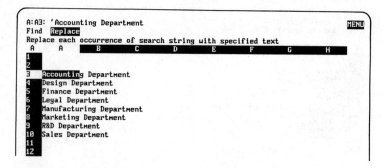

Fig. 4.84.
The /Range Search menu after Replace is selected.

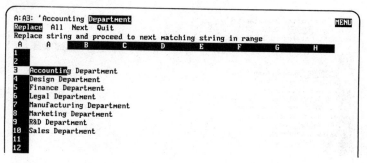

Fig. 4.85.
The labels after the /Range Search Replace command is used.

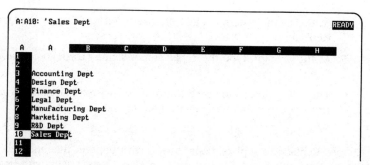

You can also use /Range Search to modify formulas. If you have many formulas that round to 2 decimal places, such as @ROUND(A1*B1,2), you can change the formulas to round to 4 decimal places with a search string of ,2) and a replace string of ,4). You must be very careful when you replace numbers in formulas. If you try to replace 2 with 4 in the last example, the formula @ROUND(A2*B2,2) becomes @ROUND(A4*B4,4).

If your replacement makes a formula invalid, 1-2-3 cancels the replacement and returns to READY mode with the cell pointer at the cell that contains the formula it could not replace.

At the end of a **R**eplace, the cell pointer is at the last cell replaced.

Accessing the Operating System

In this chapter, you learned how to use many different 1-2-3 commands to build and modify your worksheet files. At times, however, you may need to perform a function that you cannot do in 1-2-3, but one which requires you to use the operating system or another program. For example, suppose that you want to save a file on a diskette, but you have no formatted diskettes available. In this case, you want to use the DOS or OS/2 FORMAT commands. Or, while you are working in 1-2-3, someone may ask you to print a copy of a letter you created with a word processor.

In these situations, you can save your files and /Quit 1-2-3. Then, when you are finished with the other task, you can restart 1-2-3 and read in the files again. However, you do not have to /Quit 1-2-3; there is a faster way.

Use /System to temporarily suspend 1-2-3 and access the operating system (DOS or OS/2). Once in the operating system, you can copy files, format diskettes, execute other system functions, or even execute another program such as a word processor, if you have enough memory available. To return to 1-2-3, type **exit**, and then press Enter. You return to 1-2-3 with the exact same status that you left. The same worksheets and files are in memory, and the cell pointer is in the same place. Window settings and any other defaults are exactly as you left them.

If enough memory is not available, 1-2-3 cannot invoke the operating system. You can recover some memory if you save your files and close them as described in Chapter 7.

Always save your files before you use /System. If you execute any program that remains in memory (memory-resident), you will not be able to re-enter 1-2-3. Examples of memory-resident programs include SideKick and SideKick Plus from Borland International, Lotus Magellan, the DOS MODE and PRINT commands, print spoolers, and many other programs. If you do not save your files and you cannot re-enter 1-2-3, all your work will be lost.

Caution:
Save your work
before you use
/System. You
might not be able
to return to 1-2-3.

Chapter Summary

In this chapter, you learned to use the fundamental 1-2-3 commands that work with most worksheets and files. You learned how to use command menus, how to specify and name ranges, and how to save files. The process of controlling how data is displayed on-screen was discussed, and you learned how to change column widths, split the screen into windows, and lock titles. Erasing ranges and inserting and deleting rows, columns, and worksheets was presented as a means of changing the layout of your worksheets and files.

You learned how to protect and hide data and files. Just as important, you learned the limitations of these techniques and how they can be overridden.

You learned how to use /Move and /Copy, two basic commands that are used when you rearrange data and build worksheets and files. You also learned how to use 1-2-3's search and replace feature to find data or to change it.

Finally, you learned how to suspend 1-2-3 so that you can perform actions that you cannot do in 1-2-3, and then return to the program just as you left it.

Learning all the commands in 1-2-3 is a formidable task. Fortunately, many commands perform very specialized tasks; you can learn them as you need to perform these tasks. These more specialized commands are covered in the following chapters.

5

Formatting Cell Contents

Using 1-2-3 to manipulate data is only the first step in using an electronic work-sheet. Making the results clear and easy to understand can be as important as calculating the correct answer. In this chapter, you learn to use the tools that control how data within cells is displayed on-screen. Changing how data displays is called *formatting*. There are two types of formatting commands. The /Range commands, such as /Range Format, affect the display of individual cells. The /Worksheet Global commands affect the display of an entire worksheet or file. You use both types of commands to customize the display of data.

When you format data, you change only the way the data displays. You do not change the value of the data itself. Other advanced formatting capabilities that apply only when you print reports are also available. Those printing capabilities are covered in Chapter 8.

This chapter shows you how to do the following:

- Set worksheet global defaults

- Set range and worksheet global formats

- Use the format commands to change how cells display

- Change label alignment in the cell

- Justify long labels across columns

- Suppress the display of zeros within cells

Setting Worksheet Global Defaults

1-2-3 includes a number of overall settings that define how 1-2-3 operates or how the screen looks. These settings can be changed. Some settings must be selected with the Install program (see Appendix A). For example, you use Install to specify the type of display and the printers that are connected to your computer. Others can be changed as you work in 1-2-3. The main command to change these settings while you are in 1-2-3 is /Worksheet Global Default (see fig. 5.1). Choose **Printer** from the menu in figure 5.1 to change the printer defaults, as described in Chapter 8. Choose **Dir** and **Ext** to change the defaults for directories and files (see Chapter 7). Choose **Graph** to change the graphing defaults (see Chapter 9). Choose **Autoexec** to control the Autoexec macros (see Chapter 11).

Fig. 5.1.
The /Worksheet
Global Default
menu.

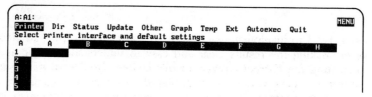

Choose **Other** from the menu in figure 5.1 for additional choices (see fig. 5.2). Choose **Clock** to change the default file and clock indicator at the lower-left corner of the screen, as described in the Command Reference. Choose **Undo** to enable Undo (Chapter 3). **Help** is an obsolete command and should be ignored.

Fig. 5.2.
The /Worksheet
Global Default
Other menu.

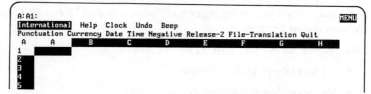

Choose **International** for the International menu (see fig. 5.3). You use this menu for additional formatting options.

Fig. 5.3.
The /Worksheet
Global Default
Other
International
menu.

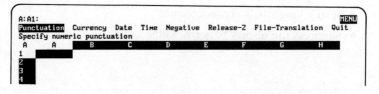

Another selection from the **Other** menu is **Beep**. Normally, 1-2-3 Release 3 beeps when you make an error. You can turn off the beep with /**Worksheet Global Default Other Beep No** and turn the beep back on with /**Worksheet Global Default Other Beep Yes**.

You might want to turn off the beep when you work in an area where the beep would disturb others, such as on an airplane. You might also turn off the beep when you demonstrate a 1-2-3 system to others so that it's not so obvious if you press a key in error.

To see the current status of all these settings, use /**Worksheet Global Default Status** (see fig. 5.4).

Cue:
Use /Worksheet Global Default Status to see all the global defaults at one time.

```
                                                                    STAT

   Printer:                         International:
      Interface..... Parallel 1        Punctuation..... A
      Auto linefeed. No                       Decimal Period
                                              Argument Comma
      Margins                                 Thousands Comma
         Left 4          Top 2        Currency........ $ (Prefix)
         Right 76        Bottom 2     Date format D4.. A (MM/DD/YY)
                                      Date format D5.. A (MM/DD)
      Page length... 66               Time format D8.. A (HH:MM:SS)
      Wait.......... No               Time format D9.. A (HH:MM)
      Setup string..
      Name.......... HP LaserJet II Add Mem None
                                      Negative........ Parentheses
      Automatic graph: Columnwise     Release 2....... LICS
                                      File translate.. Country
      File list extension: WK*
      File save extension: WK3        Clock on screen: Standard
      Graph save extension: CGM       Undo: No     Beep: Yes
                                      Autoexec: Yes
      Default directory: C:\123R3
      Temporary directory: C:\123R3

   23-May-89 09:11 AM



                        default screen
```

Fig. 5.4.
The /Worksheet Global Default Status screen.

Any setting changes you make are effective only until you /**Quit** 1-2-3. The next time you start 1-2-3, these settings revert to their original values. To permanently update the changed settings, choose /**Worksheet Global Default Update**. This command updates a configuration file called 123.CNF. 1-2-3 uses this file to determine the default for these settings.

Caution:
Update the global defaults, or all changes are lost when you quit 1-2-3.

Use /**Worksheet Status** (see fig. 5.5) to see a mixture of information that includes the memory available, the processor in your computer, the current recalculation method, default formats, label prefix and column width for the current worksheet, and whether global protection is enabled in the current worksheet. The main use of this status display is to check on the amount of memory available and to find circular references. (See Chapter 4 for more information on circular references.)

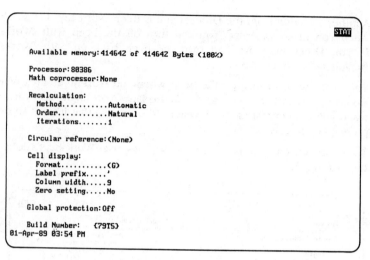

Fig. 5.5.
The /Worksheet Status screen.

Setting Range and Worksheet Global Formats

Data in a cell has two characteristics: its contents and how it displays. These two characteristics are related, but they are not the same. The contents of the current cell are shown in the control panel; the formatted display of the contents shows in the worksheet (see fig. 5.6). A cell may contain a formula, such as +B8 in cell C8, but the current value of the formula displays in the cell. The formula in C8 displays as 1,234.30. Other factors, such as the column width, can affect how a cell displays, but the cell format is the most important.

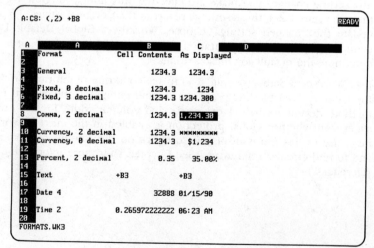

Fig. 5.6.
A worksheet demonstrating various formats.

The Available Formats

You can display data in a cell in a number of different formats. Table 5.1 lists the available formats.

Table 5.1
Available Display Formats

Format	Example	Application
General	1234.5	Numeric data
Fixed	1234.50	Numeric data
Comma (,)	1,234.50	Numeric data
Currency	$1,234.50	Numeric data
Percent	35.4%	Numeric data
Scientific	1.2345E + 03	Numeric data
+/−	+ + + + +	Numeric data
Date	10/10/89	Special date serial numbers
Time	06:23 AM	Special time fractions
Text	+ C6	All formulas
Hidden	No display	All data
Label	57 Main St.	Blank cells before labels are entered
Automatic	1,234.50	Blank cells before data is entered
Parentheses	(1,234.50)	Numeric data

Most formats apply only to numeric data (numeric formulas and numbers). If you format a label as **Fixed** or **Currency**, for example, the format has no effect on how the label displays. A few formats, such as **Hidden**, can apply to labels and string formulas. Figure 5.6 shows examples of some of the possible formats.

No matter what the format, numeric data is right-aligned. The rightmost digit always displays in the second position from the right. The extreme right position is reserved for a percent sign or right parentheses. The result of string (text) formulas is always left-aligned, even if the formula refers to a label with another alignment.

The width of a cell is controlled by the column width setting, as described in Chapter 4. If the column is not wide enough to display a numeric entry, asterisks fill the cell (see C10 in fig. 5.6). To display the data, you must either change the format or change the column width.

Because the extreme right position is reserved for a percent sign or right parentheses, a number must fit into the cell using one character less than the column width. If the column width is 9, the formatted number must fit into 8 positions not counting a percent sign or right parenthesis. Negative numbers display with either a minus sign or parentheses. This means that a negative number requires an extra character to display. With a column width of 9, a negative number must fit into 7 positions.

The Contents versus the Format of a Cell

Remember that formatting changes how the data displays, not the data itself. For example, the number 1234 can display as 1,234, $1,234.00, 123400% and many other combinations. No matter how the number displays, it remains the same number.

Some formats display a number as if it were rounded. If you format 1234.5 in Fixed format with zero decimal places, the number displays as 1235, but the actual value of 1234.5 is used in formulas. In figure 5.7, the sales total in C8 looks like an addition error. Actually, the formula in C6 is +B6 × 1.1, projecting 10% higher sales next year. The value of the formula in C6 is 95.7. The display, however, shows 96 formatted Fixed with zero decimal places. The value of the formula in C7 is 83.6, but the display shows 84. The value of the sum in C8 is 179.3, but the display shows 179. The value appears as 96 + 84 = 179. This is an apparent rounding error produced by rounding the display.

Fig. 5.7.
An apparent rounding error caused by formatting.

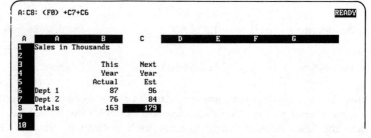

To avoid rounding errors, you need to round the actual value of the formulas in figure 5.7, not just the display. To round the value of a formula, use the @ROUND function, as explained in Chapter 6.

Using the Format Commands

You change the format of a cell or range of cells with the /Range Format command (see fig. 5.8). You then pick one of the formats from the menu or choose

Other for additional choices (see fig. 5.9). For comma format, you press the comma key (,).

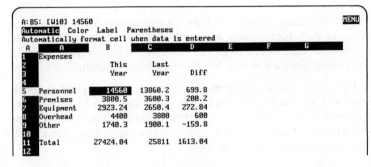

Fig. 5.8.
The /Range
Format menu.

Fig. 5.9.
The /Range
Format Other
menu.

If you choose Fixed, Sci, , (comma), **Currency**, or **Percent**, you are prompted for the number of decimal places (see fig 5.10). Whenever this prompt appears, 1-2-3 shows a default of 2 decimal places. Press Enter to accept the default, or type another number between 0-15 and press Enter. The **Date** and **Time** formats have additional menus that are covered later in this chapter. The **Time** format is an option in the **Date** menu.

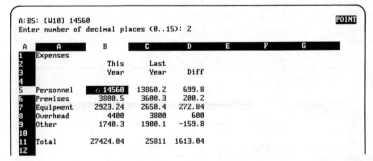

Fig. 5.10.
The prompt to
enter the
number of
decimal places.

After you select a format and any options, you are prompted for the range to format. Highlight the range and press Enter. Figure 5.11 shows the result after you use /**R**ange **F**ormat **F**ixed with 2 decimal places on the range B5..B11. An abbreviation of the format appears in the control panel when the current cell has a range format. In figure 5.11, (F2) displayed in the control panel indicates that B5 has been range formatted as Fixed with 2 decimal places. If the cell has no range format, no format indicator appears in the control panel.

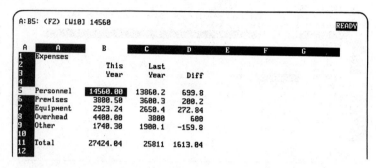

Fig. 5.11.
A range formatted as fixed with 2 decimal places.

When you start a new file, none of the cells have a range format. For example, in figure 5.10, none of the cells have a range format. In figure 5.11, only the cells in the range B5..B11 have a range format. When a cell does not have a range format, the cell takes the format specified in the /Worksheet Global Format.

When you start a new file, the global format is General. To change the global format, use /Worksheet Global Format (see fig. 5.12). Figure 5.13 shows the worksheet after changing to comma format with 2 decimal places. Notice that the format in B5..B11 did not change. These cells have a range format; the global format affects only the cells with no range format.

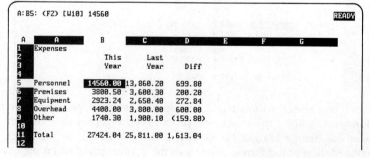

Fig. 5.12.
The /Worksheet Global Format menu.

Fig. 5.13.
The worksheet with a global format of comma (,) with 2 decimal places.

If you want a cell or range that has a range format to have the same format as the global format, you can remove range formatting with /Range Format Reset. Figure 5.14 shows the worksheet after /Range Format Reset in the range B5..B11. This range now displays with the global comma format. If you want a cell or range with a range format to have a different range format, execute the /Range Format command again and choose a different format.

Use the global format for the format that you expect to use the most in the worksheet. Then use /Range Format to format ranges you want to display with other formats. Most worksheets look best if a variety of formats are used to match the data. Figure 5.14 shows a worksheet with a global format of comma, as well as Currency, Percent, and Date range formats.

```
A:E5:  (P2) +D5/C5                                          READY

A       A          B          C          D       E    F         G
1    Expenses                                         05/16/89
2                    This      Last               %
3                    Year      Year     Diff     Diff
4
5    Personnel  $14,560.00 $13,860.20  $699.80    5.05%
6    Premises     3,800.50   3,600.30   200.20    5.56%
7    Equipment    2,923.24   2,650.40   272.84   10.29%
8    Overhead     4,400.00   3,800.00   600.00   15.79%
9    Other        1,740.30   1,900.10  (159.80)  -8.41%
10
11   Total      $27,424.04 $25,811.00 $1,613.04    6.25%
12
```

Fig. 5.14.
A worksheet with a variety of formats.

/Worksheet Global Format applies to the current worksheet. If you change the /Worksheet Global Format in a file with multiple worksheets, you change only the current worksheet. If you want all the worksheets in the file to have the same global format, turn on GROUP mode with /Worksheet Global Group. If every worksheet in the file has the same layout, such as the file in figure 5.15, you use GROUP mode so that changes to one worksheet affect all worksheets. If each worksheet in the file has a different layout, such as situations in which separate worksheets are used for input areas, notes and assumptions, reports, and macros, you want GROUP mode off so that you can format each worksheet separately.

Reminder:
In GROUP mode, /Worksheet Global Format applies to all worksheets in the file.

GROUP mode also affects the /Range Format command. With GROUP mode enabled, if you format a range in one worksheet, the same range is range formatted in all worksheets in the file. Figure 5.16 shows the effects of /Range Format Percent with 4 decimal places on the range A:E5..A:E11. Even though the range includes only worksheet A, the same range in the other worksheets also changes formats.

The following sections describe each format in detail. Each format can be a /Worksheet Global Format or a /Range Format.

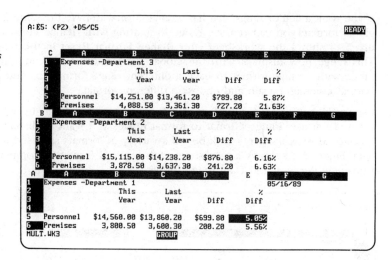

Fig. 5.15.
All worksheets with the same global format in GROUP mode.

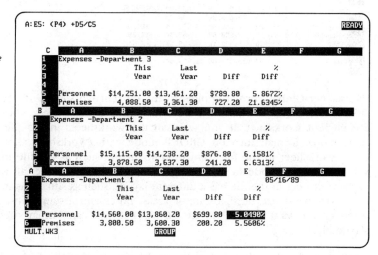

Fig. 5.16.
The same range in all worksheets range formatted at the same time.

General Format

General format, the default for all new worksheets, displays only the number. If the number is negative, it is preceded by a minus sign; if the number contains decimal digits, it can contain a decimal point. If the number contains too many digits to the right of the decimal point to fit in the column width, the decimal portion is rounded. If the number is too large or small to display normally, it displays in scientific format. 123400000 displays as 1.2E+08, and 0.0000000012 displays as 1.2E−09. Negative numbers in scientific format display with a leading minus sign.

Following are several examples of General format in cells that have a column width of 9:

Typed Entry	Cell Format	Display Result
123.46	(G)	123.46
− 123.36	(G)	− 123.36
1.2345678912	(G)	1.234568
150000000	(G)	1.5E + 8
− .00000002638	(G)	− 2.64E − 8

(G) appears in the control panel of cells that have been formatted with /Range Format General.

Fixed Format

Use the Fixed format when you want a column of numbers to line up on the decimal point. 1-2-3 displays a fixed number of decimal places, from 0–15, that you specify. If the number has more decimal digits than the number you specify in the format, the number is rounded on the display, but not in the value used for calculation.

Following are several examples of Fixed format in cells that have a column width of 9:

Typed Entry	Cell Format	Display Result
123.46	(F0)	123
123.46	(F1)	123.5
− 123.46	(F2)	− 123.46
123.46	(F4)	123.4600
− 123.46	(F4)	********
12345678	(F2)	********

In all cases, the full number in the cell is used in calculations. Negative numbers display with a leading minus sign.

(Fn) appears in the control panel of cells that have been formatted with /Range Format Fixed. n represents the number of decimal places.

Comma Format

Like the Fixed format, the comma format (,) displays data with a fixed number of decimal places (from 0-15). In addition, the comma format separates the thousands with commas. Positive numbers less than 1,000 display the same way in Fixed format and comma format. The comma format is used most often for financial data.

If the number has more decimal digits than the number you specify in the format, the number is rounded on the display. The full value in the cell is used in calculations.

Use the comma format instead of Fixed format for large numbers. It is easier to read 12,300,000.00 than 12300000.00. With comma format, negative numbers display in parentheses. −1234 displays as (1,234) with 0 decimal places.

You can change the setting so that negative numbers display with a leading minus sign by using /Worksheet Global Default Other International Negative Sign (/wgdoins). −1234 then displays as − 1,234. To return to parentheses for negative numbers, use /Worksheet Global Default Other International Negative Parentheses. This default applies to 1-2-3 as a whole, not to any one worksheet or file.

(,n) appears in the control panel of cells that have been formatted with /Range Format ,. n represents the number of decimal places.

Following are several examples of comma (,) format in cells that have a column width of 9:

Typed Entry	Cell Format	Display Result
123.46	(,0)	123
1234.6	(,2)	1,234.60
− 1234.6 (if /wgdoins)	(,0)	(1,235) − 1,235
− 1234	(,2)	********

Currency Format

Currency format works much like comma format but includes a leading dollar sign. Because of the dollar sign, an extra position in the column width is needed to display a number in Currency format. Negative numbers are handled the same as with comma format.

The dollar sign, the default currency symbol, can be changed if you are using a different currency. Use /Worksheet Global Default Other International Currency to specify a different currency symbol and whether the symbol is a prefix or a suffix. This default applies to 1-2-3 as a whole, not to any one worksheet or file.

Caution:
If you change the currency symbol, the change affects all open files on your computer.

For example, suppose that you create a file using Currency format for U.S. dollars and save the file. You later create a file that uses the British Pound (£). You can change the /Worksheet Global Default Other International Currency to the British pound. When you later retrieve another file, any cells formatted Currency display the pound as the currency symbol.

(Cn) appears in the control panel of cells formatted with /Range Format Currency. n represents the number of decimal places.

Following are several examples of Currency format in cells that have a column width of 9:

Typed Entry	Cell Format	Display Result
123	(C2)	$123.00
(if /wgdoic)		£123.00
−123.124	(C2)	($123.12)
(if /wgdoins)		−$123.12
1234.12	(C0)	$1,234
1234.12	(C2)	*********

Percent Format

Use the **Percent** format to display percentages. You specify the number of decimal places from 0–15. The number displayed is the value of the cell multiplied by 100, followed by a percent sign.

If the number has more decimal digits than the number you specify in the format, the number is rounded on the display.

Note that the number of decimal places you specify is the number as a percent, not as a whole number. Only 2 decimal places are needed to display .2456 as a percent.

The number displays as multiplied by 100, but the value of the cell is unchanged. To display 50% in a cell, you type **.5** and format for percent. If you type **50** and format for **Percent** with zero decimal places, 5000% displays.

(Pn) appears in the control panel of cells formatted with /Range Format Percent. n represents the number of decimal places.

Reminder:
Enter percentages as decimal fractions, not as whole numbers.

Following are several examples of **Percent** format in cells that have a column width of 9:

Typed Entry	Cell Format	Display Result
.2	(P2)	20.00%
−.3528	(P2)	−35.28%
30	(P0)	3000%
30	(P4)	*********

Scientific Format

Use Scientific format (**Sci**) to display very large or very small numbers. Very large and very small numbers usually have a few significant digits and many zeroes as place holders to tell you how large or how small the number is.

A number in scientific notation has two parts; a *mantissa* and an *exponent*. The mantissa is a number from 1-10 that contains the significant digits. The exponent tells you how many places to move the decimal point to get the actual value of the number. You specify the number of decimal places in the mantissa from 0-15. If the number has more significant digits than the number you specify in the format, the number is rounded on the display.

1230000000000 displays as $1.23E+12$ in scientific format with 2 decimal places. $E+12$ signifies that you must move the decimal point 12 places to the right to get the actual number. 0.000000000237 displays as $2.4E-10$ in scientific format with 1 decimal place. $E-10$ means that you must move the decimal point 10 places to the left to get the actual number.

A number too large to display in a cell in **General** format displays in scientific format.

(Sn) appears in the control panel of cells formatted with **/Range Format Sci**. n represents the number of decimal places.

Following are several examples of **Sci** format in cells that have a column width of 9:

Typed Entry	Cell Format	Display Result
1632116750000	(S2)	$1.63E+12$
1632116750000	(S0)	$2E+12$
−1632116750000	(S1)	$-1.6E+12$
−1632116750000	(S2)	********
.00000000012	(S2)	$1.20E-10$
−.00000000012	(S0)	$-1E-10$

The +/− Format

The **+/−** format creates a horizontal bar chart based on the number in the cell. A positive number displays as a row of + signs; a negative number displays as a row of − signs; a zero displays as a period. The number of pluses or minuses can be no wider than the cell.

This format was originally devised to create imitation bar charts in spreadsheets that had no graphing capability. The format has little use today.

(+) appears in the control panel of cells formatted with **/Range Format +/−**.

Following are several examples of **+/−** format in cells that have a column width of 9:

Typed Entry	Cell Format	Display Result
6	(+)	+ + + + + +
4.9	(+)	+ + + +
−3	(+)	− − −
0	(+)	.
17.2	(+)	*********

Date and Time Formats

All the formats mentioned so far deal with regular numeric values. Use **Date** and **Time** formats when you deal with date and time calculations or time functions. These functions are covered in Chapter 6.

Choose **/Range Format Date** or **/Worksheet Global Format Date** (see fig. 5.17) for the five **Date** format options, or to choose a **Time** format. Choose **/Range Format Date Time** or **/Worksheet Global Format Date Time** (see fig. 5.18) for the four **Time** format options.

Date Formats

When you use date functions, 1-2-3 stores the date as a serial number representing the number of days since December 31, 1899. The serial date number for January 1, 1900 is 1. The serial date number for January 15, 1990 is 32888. The latest date that 1-2-3 can handle is December 31, 2099, with a serial number of 73050. If the number is less than 1 or greater than 73050, a **Date** format displays as asterisks. **Date** formats ignore any fraction. 32888.99 with format D4 (long international) displays as 01/15/90. The fraction represents the time, a fractional portion of a 24-hour clock.

Don't be concerned about which serial date number refers to which date. Let 1-2-3 format the serial date number to appear as a textual date.

Actually, all the date serial numbers starting with March 1, 1900, are off by one day. The calendar inside 1-2-3 treats 1900 as a leap year; it is not. A date serial number of 60 displays as 02/29/00—a date that does not exist. Unless you compare dates before February 28, 1900, to dates after February 28, 1900, this error has no effect on your worksheets. However, dates can be off by one day if you export data to a database.

Caution: Lotus 1-2-3 is one day off in serial-number calculations starting with March 1, 1900. This makes a difference when you export 1-2-3 data to a database.

When you choose **/Range Format Date**, the **Date** menu appears: (see fig. 5.17). Five **Date** formats can format serial numbers to look like dates. Table 5.2 lists these formats. Long international and short international have four different possible formats each. The defaults are those that are most common in the United

States. If you prefer one of the other international **D**ate formats, use /**W**orksheet **G**lobal **D**efault **O**ther International **D**ate and choose from formats **A** through **D**.

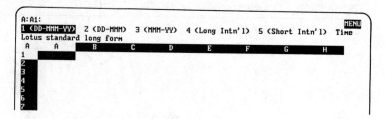

Fig. 5.17.
The /Range
Format Date
menu listing
the possible
Date formats.

Table 5.2
Date Formats

Menu Choice	Format	Description	Example
1	(D1)	Day-Month-Year DD-MMM-YY	01-Jan-90
2	(D2)	Day-Month DD-MMM	01-Jan
3	(D3)	Month-Year MMM-YY	Jan-90
4	(D4)	Long International *	
A		MM/DD/YY	01/15/90
B		DD/MM/YY	15/01/90
C		DD.MM.YY	15.01.90
D		YY-MM-DD	90-01-15
5	(D5)	Short International *	
A		MM/DD	01/15
B		DD/MM	15/01
C		DD.MM	15.01
D		MM-DD	01-15

* Use the /**W**orksheet **G**lobal **D**efault **O**ther International **D**ate command to select one of the international formats (A, B, C, or D).

You can enter serial date numbers without using date functions. You simply type what looks like a date; 1-2-3 converts it to a serial date number. This is often the fastest way to enter dates. You can enter a date in either **D**ate 4 format, such as **1/15/90**, or **D**ate 1 format, such as **15-Jan-90**; 1-2-3 converts the entry to the date serial number 32888. If you enter a date in **D**ate 2 format, such as **15-Jan**, 1-2-3 assumes that you want the current year. If the internal clock in the computer says it is 1990, **15-Jan** converts to 32888, the date serial number for January 15, 1990. If you type **15-Jan** during 1989, you get 32523, the date sequence number for January 15, 1989.

RELEASE 3

However, 1-2-3 does not format the cell. For this number to display as a date, either the global format or the range format must be a **Date** format. You can use **/Range Format** on the cell either before or after you enter the date in the cell. If you know that you will enter dates in certain cells, format the blank cells with a **Date** format. You won't see the date serial numbers, just the formatted dates.

Cue:
Format blank cells with a Date format before you enter dates.

You cannot enter dates as date serial numbers using the other date formats. If you enter a date in **Date** 3 format, such as **Jan-90**, 1-2-3 treats the entry as a label. If you enter a date in **Date** 5 format, such as **1/15**, 1-2-3 treats it as a formula and converts it to a number, in this case 0.066667. This can be confusing.

For example, suppose that a cell is formatted as (D4). You type the following and press Enter:

1/15/90

Caution:
If you enter a date in Date 5 format, 1-2-3 treats it as a formula and converts it to a number.

1-2-3 converts the entry to the serial date number 32888.

(Dn) appears in the control panel of cells formatted with **/Range Format Date**. n represents the **Date** format selection (1-5) in the **Format Date** menu (see fig. 5.17).

Following are several examples of **Date** format in cells that have a column width of 9:

Typed Entry	Cell Format	Display Result	Cell Contents
10/12/89	(D1)	*********	32793
10/12/89	(D2)	12-Oct	32793
10/12/89	(D3)	Oct-89	32793
10/12/89	(D4)	10/12/89	32793
10/12/89	(D5)	10/12	32793
15	(D4)	01/15/00	15
32888	(D4)	01/15/90	032888
32888.4538	(D4)	01/15/90	32888.4538
−32888	any date	*********	−32888
12-Oct-89	(D4)	10/12/89	32793
12-oct	(D4)	10/12/89 (during 1989)	32793
Oct-89	any date	Oct-89	'Oct-89
10/12	any date	*********	0.833333

Cue:
Date 1 format cannot display in a cell with the default column width of 9.

Following are several examples of **Date** 1 format in cells that have a column width of 10 (**Date** 1 format cannot display in a cell with a default column width of 9):

Typed Entry	Cell Format	Display Result	Cell Contents
10/12/89	(D1)	12-Oct-89	32793
12-Oct-89	(D1)	12-Oct-89	32793
12-oct	(D1)	12-Oct-89 (during 1989)	32793

Time Formats

1-2-3 maintains times in a special format called *time fractions*. You can then format these time fractions so that they look like a time of the day.

When you enter a time function, 1-2-3 stores the time as a decimal fraction from 0-1 that represents the fraction of the 24-hour clock. The time fraction for 3 a.m. is 0.125; the time fraction for noon is 0.5; and the time fraction for 6 p.m. is 0.75. You can ignore the actual fractions and let 1-2-3 display the fraction as a time.

When you choose /**R**ange **F**ormat **D**ate **T**ime, the **T**ime menu appears (see fig. 5.18). 1-2-3 includes four **T**ime formats that display fractions as times. Table 5.3 lists these formats. Long international and short international have four different possible formats each. The defaults are those most common in the United States. If you prefer one of the other international time formats, use /**W**orksheet **G**lobal **D**efault **O**ther **I**nternational **T**ime and choose from the formats A-D, which represent the four choices.

Fig. 5.18.
The /Range
Format Date
Time menu
listing the
possible Time
formats.

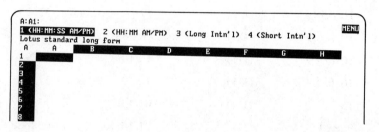

Cue:
Type an entry that
looks like a time;
1-2-3 converts it to
a time fraction
automatically.

You can enter a time fraction without using time functions. You simply type what looks like a time; 1-2-3 converts it to a time fraction. You can enter a time in any **T**ime format. You can use regular time (AM/PM) or 24-hour military time. Seconds are optional. This is often the fastest way to enter times.

If you enter **6:23**, **6:23:00**, **6:23AM**, or **6:23:00 am**, 1-2-3 converts the entry to the time fraction 0.265972. (Actually, 1-2-3 stores fractions with up to 18 or 19 significant digits but 6-8 are shown in these examples.) If you enter **6:23:57** or **6:23:57 AM**, 1-2-3 converts the entry to the time fraction 0.266632. If you enter **6:23 pm** or **18:23**, 1-2-3 converts the entry to the time fraction 0.765972.

You do not have to type **AM** for times before noon. For times after noon, type **PM** or type the hour from 12-23. The AM or PM can be in uppercase or lowercase and can follow a space after the time.

Table 5.3
Time Formats

Menu Choice	Format	Description	Example
1	(D6)	Hour:Minute:Second HH:MM:SS AM/PM	06:23:57 PM
2	(D7)	Hour:Minute HH:MM AM/PM	06:23 PM
3	(D8)	Long International *	
A		HH:MM:SS	18:23:57
B		HH.MM.SS	18.23.57
C		HH,MM,SS	18,23,57
D		HHhMMmSSs	18h23m57s
4	(D9)	Short International *	
A		HH:MM	18:23
B		HH.MM	18.23
C		HH,MM	18,23
D		HHhMMm	18h23m

* Use the /Worksheet Global Default Other International Time command to select one of the international formats (A, B, C, or D).

Cue:
Format blank cells with a Time format before you enter times.

However, 1-2-3 does not format the cell. For this number to display as a time, either the global format or the range format must be a **Time** format. You can use **/Range** Format on the cell either before or after you enter the time in the cell. However, if you enter the time into a cell with **General** format, the time fraction can be confusing. If you know that you will enter times in certain cells, format the blank cells with a **Time** format. You won't see the time fractions, just the formatted times.

If the number is greater than 1, **Time** formats ignore the integer portion. **32888.75** with format D7 (**Time** 2 or Lotus standard short form) displays as 06:00 PM. Negative numbers represent the fraction of a day before midnight. **−0.75** (or **−32888.75**) is the same as **0.25** and displays as 06:00 AM; **−0.125** is the same as **0.875** and displays as 9:00 PM.

(Dn) appears in the control panel of cells range formatted with **/Range** Format **Date Time**. n represents the **Time** format selection (6-9).

1-2-3 identifies **Time** formats in a confusing way. If you choose **Date Time 1**, 1-2-3 displays (D6) in the control panel, not (T1). **Date Time 2** displays (D7), **Date Time 3** displays (D8), and **Date Time 4** displays (D9).

Following are several examples of **Time** format in cells that have a column width of 9:

Typed Entry	Cell Format	Display Result	Cell Contents
6:23	(D6)	********	0.265972
6:23	(D7)	06:23 AM	0.265972
6:23	(D8)	06:23:000	.265972
6:23 AM	(D9)	06:230	.265972
6:23:57	(D7)	06:23 AM	0.266632
6:23:57	(D8)	06:23:57	0.266632
6:23pm	(D7)	06:23 PM	0.765972
6:23:57 pm	(D8)	18:23:57	0.766632
18:23	(D7)	06:23 PM	0.765972
2	(D7)	12:00 AM	2
−.25	(D7)	06:00 PM	−.25

Cue:
Time 1 format cannot display in a cell with the default column width of 9; a column width of 12 is required.

Following are several examples of **Time 1** (D6) format in cells that have a column width of 12 (**Time 1** format cannot display in a cell with the default column width of 9.):

Typed Entry	Cell Format	Display Result	Cell Contents
6:23	(D6)	06:23:00 AM	0.265972
6:23:57	(D6)	06:23:57 AM	0.266632
18:23:57	(D6)	06:23:57 PM	0.766632

Text Format

Use the **Text** format to display in a cell both numeric and string formulas instead of their current value. Numbers formatted for **Text** display in the **General** format. If the formula is too long to display in the column width, it is truncated; it does not display across blank cells to the right like a long label. If you attach a note to the number or formula in a cell, the note displays if the column is wide enough.

All the entries in figure 5.19 are formatted as **Text**. The labels are unaffected. The numbers in B3..B4 display in **General** format. The number in B5 has a note attached and displays with the note left-aligned. The formula and note in B7 display instead of the current value of the formula.

One use of the **Text** format is for criterion ranges with /**Data Query** commands, which are covered in Chapter 10. You can also use **Text** format when you enter or debug complex formulas or to see formulas with /**Data Table**. You can temporarily change the format of a formula to text so that you can see the formula in

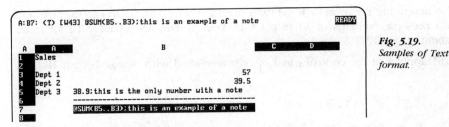

Fig. 5.19.
Samples of Text
format.

one cell while you build a similar formula in another cell. You may need to widen the column temporarily while you do this.

(T) appears in the control panel of cells formatted with /**Range Format Text**.

Hidden Format

A cell formatted as **Hidden** displays as blank no matter what the cell contains. Use this format for intermediate calculations that you don't want to display or to hide sensitive formulas. The contents of a hidden cell do not display in the control panel when you move the cell pointer to that cell if the cell is protected and global protection is enabled. In other cases, you can see the contents of the cell in the control panel. Hidden format is also discussed in Chapter 4.

You cannot use **Hidden** format to completely hide data unless the file contains no unprotected cells. If you can change the format or the protection status, you can see the contents of the cell. If the file is not sealed (see Chapter 4), you can use /**Range Format** to change the format; the contents of the cell then become visible.

Caution:
Don't rely on
Hidden formats to
hide sensitive
information, even if
the file is sealed.

If the file is sealed, you cannot change the format or the protection status, but you can use a formula in any unprotected cell to determine the value in the hidden cell.

The worksheet in figure 5.20 has /**Global Protection Enabled**; the file is sealed with /**File Admin Seal File**. /**Range Prot** and /**Range Format Hidden** have been used on Cell A2. The range C1..C5 is unprotected. The formula in C1 is +A1. This simple formula shows you the value of the hidden cell.

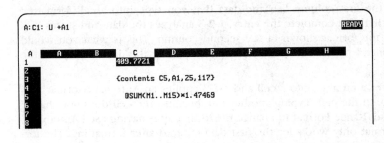

Fig. 5.20.
The appearance
of the
worksheet
changed by use
of Hidden
format.
Sensitive data
or formulas
remain open.

To determine the formula in A1, you need a macro. The {CONTENTS} macro in C3 puts the contents of A1 into C5 in Text format. See Chapter 12 for more about {CONTENTS}.

(H) appears in the control panel of cells formatted with **/R**ange Format **H**idden.

Label Format

Use **/R**ange Format **O**ther **L**abel to assign the Label format. Use this format on blank cells to make it easier to enter labels. With this format, all entries are considered labels; 1-2-3 precedes the entry with the default label prefix. This makes it easier to enter labels that look like numbers or formulas that begin with a numeric character.

As an example, suppose that you typed the following label and pressed Enter:

57 Main Street

1-2-3 considers the entry an invalid numeric entry and puts you in EDIT mode. You must manually type the label prefix. In the next example, suppose you typed the following label and pressed Enter:

10/15

1-2-3 considers **10/15** a formula, converts it to a number, and displays 0.666667. To make this entry a label, you must reenter the label with a label prefix. In both cases, if you format the range as **L**abel before you type the entry, 1-2-3 precedes the entry with a label prefix, and the entry becomes a text label. If you change existing numeric entries to Label format, they do not become labels; the number displays in General format. The Label format has no effect on existing labels.

(L) appears in the control panel of cells formatted **/R**ange Format **O**ther **L**abel.

RELEASE
3

Automatic Format

Use **/R**ange Format **O**ther **A**utomatic to assign the Automatic format. When you enter data into a cell with an Automatic format, 1-2-3 analyzes the format of the data and selects a format. Table 5.4 lists examples of Automatic formatting.

In table 5.4, the first column lists the data that you type into a cell formatted Automatic. When you complete the entry, 1-2-3 analyzes the data and stores it in the cell with the format shown in the second column. This is what you would see in the control panel. The third column shows how the data displays in the worksheet.

Once you enter a number into a cell and 1-2-3 applies an Automatic format, this format stays with the cell. Typing another number into the cell does not change the format. Use **/R**ange Format to change the format after having used Automatic. Automatic format only works for the first data entered after formatting. The format does not change when a number with a different format is entered.

Table 5.4
Automatic Formatting Examples

Data Entered	Format	Data Stored	Data Displayed
57 Main	(A)	'57 Main	57 Main
@SUM(xxxx	(A)	'@SUM(xxxx	@SUM(xxxx
258	(F0)	258	258
258.46	(F2)	258.46	258.46
258.00	(F2)	258	258.00
1,258	(,0)	1258	1,258
1,258.69	(,2)	1258.69	1,258.69
0,087.00	(,2)	87	87.00
$258.00	(C2)	258	$258.00
25%	(P0)	0.25	25%
2.50%	(P2)	0.025	2.50%
1.2E4	(S1)	12000	1.2E+04
2.587E-16	(S3)	2.587E-16	2.587E-16
25.87E-17	(S2)	2.587E-16	2.59E-16
15-jan-90	(D1)	32888	15-Jan-90
15-jan	(D2)	32888*	15-Jan
jan-90	(A)	'jan-90	jan-90
1/15/90	(D4)	32888	01/15/90
10/15	(A)	0.6666666667	0.666667
6:23:57 am	(D6)	0.2666319444	06:23:57 AM
6:23:57	(D8)	0.2666319444	06:23:57
6:23:57 pm	(D6)	0.7666319444	06:23:57 PM
6:23 am	(D7)	0.2659722222	06:23 AM
6:23	(D9)	0.2659722222	06:23
6:23 PM	(D7)	0.7659722222	06:23 PM
18:23:57	(D8)	0.7666319444	018:23:57
18:23	(D9)	0.7659722222	18:23

*If the current year is 1990

If you enter an invalid number or formula, 1-2-3 makes it a label without Automatic format. Consider the following label:

57 Main Street

Also consider the following invalid formula:

@SUM(ABCD

1-2-3 considers these entries invalid numeric entries and changes to EDIT mode. With Automatic formatting, 1-2-3 precedes the entry with a label prefix and considers it a label.

If you type a number containing decimal places, 1-2-3 formats it with that number of decimal places. If you use no other formatting characters, 1-2-3 uses the Fixed format. If you type **123.4**, 1-2-3 makes the format fixed with 1 decimal place (F1). If you type **123.40**, 1-2-3 drops the last zero in the control panel but makes the format fixed with 2 decimal places (F2).

If you precede the number with a dollar sign (or other one-character currency symbol specified with /Worksheet Global Default Other International Currency), 1-2-3 formats the cell as Currency. If you type a number with commas, 1-2-3 drops the commas but formats the cell with comma format. If you follow the number with a percent sign (%), 1-2-3 drops the percent sign, divides the number by 100, and formats the cell with **Percent** format.

If the number looks like one of the long **Date** or **Time** formats, 1-2-3 uses that **Date** format. 1-2-3 does not recognize the short **Date** formats D3: MMM-YY or D5: MM/DD (see table 5.3).

Cue:
Use the Automatic format before you make cell entries.

1-2-3 applies a format to a cell only when you enter a number. If you enter a formula or label into a cell, the format stays **Automatic** and a numeric formula displays in **General** format. If you enter a number into the cell later, 1-2-3 applies a format. If the cell contains a numeric formula and you convert it to a number with Edit (F2) or Calc (F9), 1-2-3 applies a format at that time.

(A) appears in the control panel of cells formatted with /Range Format Other Automatic. When you first enter a number into the cell, the format changes to match the numeric entry.

Parentheses Format

Use the Parentheses format to enclose numbers in parentheses. In certain situations, you want a number to appear in parentheses, but you do not want to enter it as a negative number. In these cases, use /Range Format Other Parentheses Yes. You can combine this format with the other formats. Use /Range Format Other Parentheses No to remove the parentheses.

/Worksheet Global Format Other Parentheses Yes results in parentheses around all numbers in the default format only. The command does not affect numbers with range formats or labels. Use /Worksheet Global Format Other Parentheses No to remove the parentheses from all numeric cells with the default format.

As you will see, this format can be confusing, so use it with care. For example, 456 displays as (456). If you apply this format to a negative number, the number still shows as negative. In General format, −1234 displays as (−1234). In comma format with 2 decimal places, −1234 displays as ((1,234.00)). The double set of parentheses is confusing.

(()) appears in the control panel of cells formatted with /**R**ange **F**ormat **O**ther **P**arentheses in addition to any other format.

Color Format

Use /**R**ange **F**ormat **O**ther **C**olor **N**egative to display negative numbers in color on a color monitor or in boldface with a monochrome monitor. This is a handy way to make negative numbers stand out. The minus sign or parentheses displays also. As with all formatting options, you can use this option on the entire worksheet or on a range only.

Use /**R**ange **F**ormat **O**ther **C**olor **R**eset to turn off the color display of negative numbers.

(−) appears in the control panel of cells formatted with /**R**ange **F**ormat **O**ther **C**olor **N**egative in addition to any other format.

Cue:
Display negative numbers in color if you want them to stand out.

International Formats

You can change some **D**ate and **T**ime formats and the characters 1-2-3 uses for currency, the decimal point, and the thousands separator. Because different countries have different formatting standards, these are called *international* formatting options. If you work with U.S. dollars in the United States, you can stay with the defaults and ignore these options. Use the /**W**orksheet **G**lobal **D**efault **O**ther **I**nternational command to access the menu to change the defaults (see fig. 5.21). Then use /**W**orksheet **G**lobal **D**efault **U**pdate to make the change permanent.

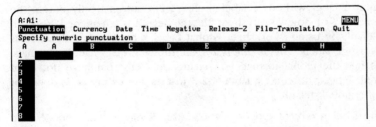

Fig. 5.21.
The /Worksheet Global Default Other International command menu.

Choose **D**ate and **T**ime to change the international **D**ate and **T**ime formats. The format options are listed in Tables 5.2 and 5.3. Choose **C**urrency to change the currency symbol from the dollar sign ($) to another symbol and specify whether it is a prefix or suffix. You can use multiple characters and special Lotus Multibyte Character Set (LMBCS) characters. (For more on LMBCS characters, see Chapter 6 and Appendix B.)

Choose **Punctuation** to change the characters used as a decimal point and as the thousands separator instead of a comma. Eight different combinations are available. Choose **Negative** to specify the way to show negative numbers in comma and **Currency** formats. The default is **Parentheses**, but you can change it to a minus sign.

Changing Label Prefixes

Most formats apply to numeric data. Almost all numeric data formats have one thing in common; the numbers display right-aligned in the cell. With labels or text entries, however, you can align the text in different ways. Label alignment is based on the label prefix. The label prefixes include the following:

Prefix	Alignment
'	left
"	right
^	center
\	repeating
|	nonprinting

Entering labels and label prefixes is covered in Chapter 3. If you want a repeating or nonprinting label, you must type the label prefix. If you type a label with another prefix and you want to change it to repeating or nonprinting, you must edit the cell, delete the old prefix, and type the new one.

You can, however, change the label alignment of a cell or range to left, right, or center with the /**Range Label** command. You can also change the default label prefix that 1-2-3 inserts when you enter a label and do not type a prefix.

When you enter a label without a label prefix, 1-2-3 automatically enters the default label prefix. With a new worksheet file, the default is left-aligned. You can change this default by using /**Worksheet Global Label**. Changing the default has no effect on existing labels. This is different from the way 1-2-3 handles formats. When you change the global format, you change all cells that have not been range formatted. When you enter a label, 1-2-3 inserts a label prefix; it does not change with the global default.

To change the label prefix of existing labels, use /**Range Label**. Choose **Left**, **Right**, or **Center**, and then specify the range. This is usually faster than typing individual label prefixes as you enter labels.

Figure 5.22 shows left-aligned column headings that do not line up with the data. Figure 5.23 shows the headings after /**Range Label Right** is selected. Right alignment starts one position from the extreme right. Right-aligned labels match the alignment of numeric data.

When you work with a multiple-worksheet file, GROUP mode affects the /**R**ange **L**abel command. With GROUP mode enabled, if you use /**R**ange **L**abel to change the label prefix in a range in one worksheet, the label prefix changes in the same range in all worksheets in the file.

```
A:B2: [W10] 'BUDGET                                                      READY

A        A          B         C        D        E        F        G
2                   BUDGET    JAN      FEB      MAR      APR      MAY
3                   ------    ------   ------   ------   ------   ------
4    Department 1   1,062,497 38,444   34,943   84,763   96,858   103,208
5    Department 2   1,306,752 37,815   33,277   89,196   102,014  114,444
6    Department 3   1,296,114 40,256   30,344   87,583   99,494   100,902
7    Department 4   1,022,323 38,656   31,098   82,914   81,070   82,164
8    Department 5   1,152,144 38,890   29,088   81,515   84,552   94,339
9    Department 6     817,511 35,591   26,225   74,494   71,451   77,039
10   Department 7     824,655 36,989   24,642   70,194   69,684   70,397
11   Department 8     977,396 33,611   22,310   70,436   80,645   85,278
12   Department 9     842,012 33,298   21,290   67,542   65,139   63,960
13   Department 10  1,099,933 31,109   22,728   73,775   80,675   87,451
14   Department 11  1,057,141 33,233   20,904   72,935   76,787   76,582
15   Department 12    825,489 30,201   19,384   68,836   66,229   64,752
16   Department 12  1,004,012 39,483   26,972   88,458   86,954   85,819
17   Department 13  1,128,380 39,452   27,316   77,631   84,475   84,958
18   Department 14    927,963 40,206   30,824   83,885   85,593   83,618
19   Department 15  1,336,598 39,053   27,031   79,099   88,476   96,329
20   Department 16  1,293,143 36,266   31,399   83,595   96,031   102,120
21   Department 17    924,074 41,130   30,204   76,311   76,666   78,599
PREFIX.WK3
```

Fig. 5.22.
Left-aligned column headings that do not line up with numeric data.

```
A:B2: [W10] "BUDGET                                                      READY

A        A          B         C        D        E        F        G
2                   BUDGET    JAN      FEB      MAR      APR      MAY
3                   ------    ------   ------   ------   ------   ------
4    Department 1   1,062,497 38,444   34,943   84,763   96,858   103,208
5    Department 2   1,306,752 37,815   33,277   89,196   102,014  114,444
6    Department 3   1,296,114 40,256   30,344   87,583   99,494   100,902
7    Department 4   1,022,323 38,656   31,098   82,914   81,070   82,164
8    Department 5   1,152,144 38,890   29,088   81,515   84,552   94,339
9    Department 6     817,511 35,591   26,225   74,494   71,451   77,039
10   Department 7     824,655 36,989   24,642   70,194   69,684   70,397
11   Department 8     977,396 33,611   22,310   70,436   80,645   85,278
12   Department 9     842,012 33,298   21,290   67,542   65,139   63,960
13   Department 10  1,099,933 31,109   22,728   73,775   80,675   87,451
14   Department 11  1,057,141 33,233   20,904   72,935   76,787   76,582
15   Department 12    825,489 30,201   19,384   68,836   66,229   64,752
16   Department 12  1,004,012 39,483   26,972   88,458   86,954   85,819
17   Department 13  1,128,380 39,452   27,316   77,631   84,475   84,958
18   Department 14    927,963 40,206   30,824   83,885   85,593   83,618
19   Department 15  1,336,598 39,053   27,031   79,099   88,476   96,329
20   Department 16  1,293,143 36,266   31,399   83,595   96,031   102,120
21   Department 17    924,074 41,130   30,204   76,311   76,666   78,599
PREFIX.WK3
```

Fig. 5.23.
Headings aligned after /Range Label Right is executed.

Justifying Text

At times, you want to include in a worksheet several lines, or even a paragraph, that explains a table, graph, or report. 1-2-3 does not include word wrap like a word processor. Everything you type goes into one cell. You use /**R**ange **J**ustify to justify labels.

To justify labels, follow these steps:

1. Move the cell pointer to the first cell in the range of text.

2. Choose /**R**ange **J**ustify.

3. Highlight down the rows that contain labels; allow enough extra rows for the labels to expand into when they are justified.

4. Highlight across the number of columns to show how wide each label can be. In figure 5.24, the text will display from Columns A-F.

You can perform Steps 3 and 4 in either order.

You can type one line of text into each cell, but entering and editing paragraphs in this way is slow and imprecise. You might get something like the ragged text in figure 5.24; some of it is off the screen.

Fig. 5.24.
A column of
long labels for
a note is
difficult to line
up correctly.

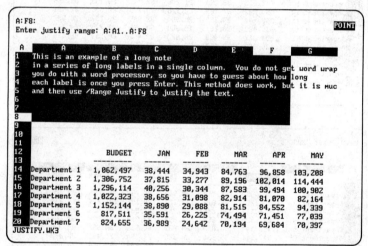

You can type text into one cell or multiple cells down a column as in figure 5.25 and use /**R**ange **J**ustify to arrange it. At the Enter justify range: prompt, highlight the rows down that contain the labels and include any additional rows for the labels to expand into. Highlight across the columns to show how wide each label can be. When you press Enter, 1-2-3 rearranges the text to fit the area you highlighted (see fig. 5.26). Labels are wrapped only at spaces. Where 1-2-3 breaks a label, it eliminates the space. Where 1-2-3 combines all or parts of two labels into one label, it adds a space.

Caution:
Don't use /Range
Justify with a one-
row range if data
is present below
labels.

If you add text in the middle, use /**R**ange **J**ustify again to rejustify the text. If you specify a one-row range, 1-2-3 justifies the entire "paragraph." Figure 5.26 shows the data in figure 5.25 after you use /**R**ange **J**ustify on the range A1..F1. This practice, however, is very dangerous. 1-2-3 justifies the labels and uses as many rows

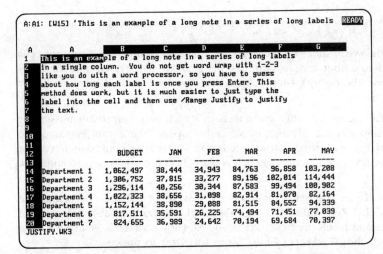

Fig. 5.25.
A series of long labels after /Range Justify.

as it needs, but it moves any data in Column A down to make room. If fewer rows are needed, it moves any data in Column A up. In figure 5.26, the department numbers no longer line up with each department's data.

```
A:A1: [W15] 'This is an example of a long note in a series of long labels   READY

  A         A           B          C       D        E        F         G
1  This is an example of a long note in a series of long labels
2  in a single column.  You do not get word wrap with 1-2-3
3  like you do with a word processor, so you have to guess
4  about how long each label is once you press Enter. This
5  method does work, but it is much easier to just type the
6  label into the cell and then use /Range Justify to Justify
7  the text.
8
9
10
11
12                     BUDGET      JAN     FEB      MAR      APR      MAY
13                     ------      ------  ------   ------   ------   ------
14                     1,062,497   38,444  34,943   84,763   96,858   103,208
15                     1,306,752   37,815  33,277   89,196   102,014  114,444
16  Department 1       1,296,114   40,256  30,344   87,583   99,494   100,902
17  Department 2       1,022,323   38,656  31,098   82,914   81,070   82,164
18  Department 3       1,152,144   38,890  29,088   81,515   84,552   94,339
19  Department 4         817,511   35,591  26,225   74,494   71,451   77,039
20  Department 5         824,655   36,989  24,642   70,194   69,684   70,397
JUSTIFY.WK3
```

Fig. 5.26.
A One-row /Range Justify that pushes down the data below it.

You cannot justify more than one column of labels at one time. When 1-2-3 reaches a blank or numeric cell in the first column, it stops. The labels must all be in the first column of the highlighted range. In figure 5.25, all the labels are in column A. Any labels in column B would be ignored.

Suppressing the Display of Zeros

You can use the /Worksheet Global Zero command to change the display of cells that contain the number zero or formulas that evaluate to zero. To hide the zeros completely, use /Worksheet Global Zero Yes. The zero cells display as if they were blank.

This feature can be useful with worksheets in which zeros represent missing or meaningless information. Making these cells appear blank can improve the appearance of the worksheet. However, it can also cause confusion if you or other users are not sure whether the cell is blank because you forgot to enter the data.

You can also display a label of your choice instead of the zero or blank. Use /Worksheet Global Zero Label and type the label you want to display instead of the zero. Common labels are none, zero, and NA (not available). Figure 5.27 is a worksheet with the /Worksheet Global Zero Label set to none.

Use /Worksheet Global Zero No to cancel the option and display zeros as zeros.

Fig. 5.27.
A worksheet with zero values set to display as none.

A:B9: 0   READY

	A	B	C	D	E	F	G
1	Time Loss Accidents by Department						
2							
3			JANUARY		FEBRUARY		MARCH
4			--------------		--------------		--------------
5		Acci-	Time	Acci-	Time	Acci-	Time
6		dents	Lost	dents	Lost	dents	Lost
7							
8	Department 1	1	7	none	none	1	4
9	Department 2	none	none	none	none	none	none
10	Department 3	2	12	1	4	3	17
11	Department 4	none	none	none	none	2	19
12	Department 5	4	11	2	15	2	15
13	Department 6	1	9	none	none	1	7
14	Department 7	1	6	2	5	none	none
15	Department 8	none	none	1	3	none	none
16	Department 9	3	13	2	4	2	4
17	Department 10	2	18	none	none	1	9
18	Department 11	6	48	4	28	2	8
19	Department 12	none	none	1	3	1	8
20	Department 12	2	4	1	7	none	none

ZERO.WK3

When you work with a multiple-worksheet file, GROUP mode affects the /Worksheet Global Zero command. With GROUP mode disabled, /wgz affects only the current worksheet. With GROUP mode enabled, the /wgz command affects all worksheets in the file.

Chapter Summary

In this chapter, you learned how to display numeric data in a variety of different formats and options, to display formulas as text, and to hide the contents of cells.

Entering and formatting dates and times and how to change the international Date and Time formats were also discussed. You learned how to format blank cells for Automatic and Label formats to make data entry easier and how to change the alignment of labels and justify blocks of text.

You can now build and format worksheets and reports as you now have the basic skills to use 1-2-3 constructively. The next chapter extends your skills to perform data analysis. Chapter 6 covers the extensive library of functions that you use to manipulate data beyond simple formulas, and opens up the vast analytical power of 1-2-3.

6

Using Functions in the Worksheet

In addition to the worksheet formulas you can construct from scratch, you can take advantage of a variety of preconstructed formulas that 1-2-3 provides. Typically, you will find these built-in formulas—called *functions*—a welcome substitute to constructing your own formulas.

In total, 1-2-3 provides 108 functions that can be broken down roughly into seven categories:

- Mathematical and trigonometric
- Statistical
- Financial and accounting
- Logical
- Special
- Date and Time
- String

The mathematical functions, which include logarithmic and trigonometric functions, should prove a necessity for engineering and scientific applications. Don't, however, assume that you won't have use for these powerful tools in simpler worksheets. The functions also provide convenient tools you can use easily to perform a variety of standard arithmetic operations such as rounding values or calculating square roots.

A set of 10 statistical and 11 database statistical functions round out the data analysis capabilities of 1-2-3 by allowing you to perform all the standard statistical calculations either on data in your worksheet or in a 1-2-3 database. You can

185

find minimum and maximum values, calculate averages, and compute standard deviations and variances. (Sometimes, the database statistical functions are listed as a separate function type; in practice, however, they are used as specialized versions of the statistical functions that apply only to 1-2-3 databases. The database statistical functions aren't described here, but rather in Chapter 10, "Managing Data.")

The financial and accounting functions allow you to perform a series of discounted cash flow, depreciation, and compound interest calculations that ease considerably the burden and tediousness of investment analysis and accounting or budgeting for depreciable assets.

The logical functions let you add standard Boolean logic to your worksheet and use the logic either alone or as part of other worksheet formulas. Essentially, each of the logical functions allows you to test whether a condition—it can be either one you've defined or one of 1-2-3's predefined conditions—is true or false.

1-2-3 also provides a set of what it calls *special* functions. You use these special tools for dealing with the worksheet itself. For example, one special function returns information about specific cells. Others count the number of rows, columns, or worksheets in a range.

The date and time functions allow you to convert dates, such as November 26, 1959, and times, such as 6:00 p.m., to serial numbers and then use these serial numbers to perform date arithmetic and time arithmetic. These functions are a valuable aid when dates and times affect worksheet calculations and logic.

The seventh and final set of 1-2-3 functions are the string functions, which manipulate text. You can use string functions to repeat text characters (a handy trick for creating worksheet and row boundaries and visual borders), to convert letters in a string to upper- or lowercase, and to change strings into numbers and numbers into strings.

This chapter describes the generic steps for using 1-2-3 functions and then goes on to provide you with the precise steps for using specific functions. Each function description is accompanied by examples of its use.

How To Enter a 1-2-3 Function

Entering a 1-2-3 function is a three-step process:

1. Type the @ sign to tell 1-2-3 that you want to enter a function.

2. Type the function name.

3. Enter any information, or arguments, the function needs to make its calculations.

An example of a function is @AVG. If you enter the function @**AVG(1,2,3)**, for instance, 1-2-3 returns the calculated result 2, which is the average of the three numbers 1, 2, and 3.

All functions begin with—and are identified by—the @ character. In effect, by typing @, you tell 1-2-3 that what you are entering is a function.

The next step is to enter the name of the function. With more than 100 functions, you probably are not going to be able to remember every name. Fortunately, 1-2-3 uses short, three-to-five character abbreviations for functions. These abbreviations should allow you to identify and remember those you use most frequently. For example, the function to calculate the average, a statistical function, is AVG; the function to calculate the internal rate of return, a financial function, is IRR; and the function to round numbers, a mathematical function, is ROUND.

A new feature of Release 3 lists along the top of the screen all the 1-2-3 functions, from which you can make a selection. To display the list of functions, press F3 after you type the @ symbol. To select a function from the list, highlight it and press Enter.

The third step is to enter any of the arguments, or inputs, the function needs to perform its calculations. You enter a function's arguments inside parentheses that immediately follow the function's name. If the function has multiple arguments, you separate them with commas. If you want to use a semicolon or period to separate function arguments, you have that option. (Use the menu commands /Worksheet Global Default Other International Punctuation to change the default from commas to semicolons or periods.)

Functions provide you with an extremely powerful and timesaving set of tools if you just follow the three steps outlined. Entering functions should always be straightforward. For example, suppose that you want to calculate the average age of your four children, ages 1, 5, 6, and 8. If you remember that the function name to calculate an average is AVG, you can easily write the 1-2-3 function to make the calculation. To perform the calculation, you enter the following:

@AVG(1,5,6,8)

1-2-3 returns the result, 5, which is the average of the numbers entered as arguments. Notice that the function begins with the @ character, followed by the function name AVG, and that the function's arguments are included inside parentheses and separated by commas.

In the preceding example, actual numeric values are used as the arguments. You also can use cell addresses and range names as arguments. For example, if you store the ages of your four children in worksheet cells B1, B2, B3, and B4, you alternatively can enter the function as

@AVG(B1,B2,B3,B4)

Or, if you name each of the four cells that contain the children's ages with the child's first name, you instead could enter the function as

@AVG(Robert,Sarah,Emil,Maria)

A few of the functions don't require arguments, or inputs. Therefore, you don't use any parentheses. For example, the mathematical function to return π is entered simply as

@PI

And the mathematical function to produce a random number is entered as

@RAND

Nevertheless, the first two steps—identify the function with an @ symbol and type the function's name—are the same for each of the 108 functions. In addition, you usually enter any required arguments inside parentheses. You will discover some subtleties and nuances when you use some of the functions. Those variations in particular functions are described in the text that follows.

Mathematical Functions

1-2-3 provides 17 mathematical functions that allow you to perform most of the common—and some of the more specialized—mathematical operations. The operations you can perform include general, logarithmic, and trigonometric calculations.

General Mathematical Functions

1-2-3 offers nine general mathematical functions: @ABS, @EXP, @INT, @LN, @LOG, @MOD, @ROUND, @RAND, @SQRT. Table 6.1 lists these functions and provides brief descriptions of what they do. The text that follows goes on to give you all the detailed information you need to begin using these functions.

Table 6.1
General Mathematical Functions

Function	Description
@ABS(number or cell reference)	Computes the absolute value of the argument
@EXP(number or cell reference)	Computes the number *e* raised to the power of the argument
@INT(number or cell reference)	Computes the integer portions of a specified number
@LN(number or cell reference)	Calculates the natural logarithm of a specified number
@LOG(number or cell reference)	Calculates the common, or base 10, logarithm of a specified number

Function	Description
@MOD(number,divisor)	Computes the remainder, or modulus, of a division operation
@ROUND(number or cell reference,precision)	Rounds a number to a specified precision
@RAND	Generates a random number
@SQRT(number or cell reference)	Computes the square root of a number

@ABS—Computing Absolute Value

The @ABS function calculates the absolute value of a number.

@ABS(number or cell reference)

The function has one argument, which can be either a numeric value or a cell reference to a numeric value. The result of @ABS is the positive value of its calling argument. @ABS converts a negative value into its equivalent positive value. @ABS has no effect on positive values. Some examples using @ABS are shown in figure 6.1.

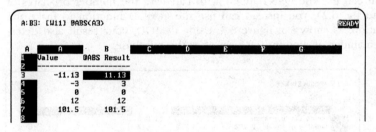

Fig. 6.1.
The results of using @ABS with positive and negative numbers.

@INT—Computing the Integer

The @INT function is used to convert a decimal number into an integer or whole number. The @INT function creates an integer by truncating the decimal portion of a number.

@INT(number or cell reference)

The function has one argument, which can be either a numerical value or a cell reference to a numerical value. The result of applying @INT to the values 3.1, 4.5, and 5.9 yields integer values of 3, 4, and 5.

@INT is useful for computations where the decimal portion of a number is irrelevant or insignificant. Suppose, for example, that you have $1,000 to invest in XYZ company and that shares of XYZ sell for $17 each. You divide 1,000 by 17 to compute the total number of shares that can be purchased. Because you cannot purchase a fractional share, you can use @INT to truncate the decimal portion as shown in figure 6.2.

Fig. 6.2.
The @INT function used to calculate the number of shares that can be purchased.

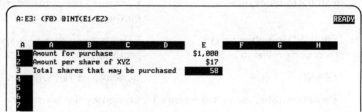

@MOD—Finding the Modulus or Remainder

The @MOD function computes the remainder when the dividend is divided by the divisor. The function is called with two arguments that can either be numerical values or cell references. The function syntax is

@MOD(number,divisor)

Because you can't divide by zero, the divisor argument needs to be something other than a zero value. The result of @MOD will be a value greater than or equal to zero, and less than the divisor.

Although you can use the @INT function to calculate the number of shares of XYZ (refer to fig. 6.2), you instead can use the @MOD function to make the same calculation, as shown in figure 6.3. Using @MOD, your result also determines the remainder or amount left over after the purchase.

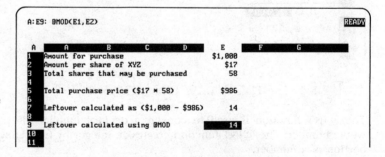

Fig. 6.3.
The @MOD function used to return the remainder, or modulus, from a division.

@ROUND—Rounding Numbers

The @ROUND function performs a standard rounding function using two arguments: the value you want to round, and the precision you want to use in the rounding. The function format is

@ROUND(number or cell reference,precision)

The precision argument determines the number of decimal places and can be a numeric value between −18 and +18. You use positive precision values to specify places to the right of the decimal place and negative values to specify places to the left of the decimal. A precision value of 0 rounds decimal values to the nearest integer. Figure 6.4 demonstrates the use of @ROUND in a few examples.

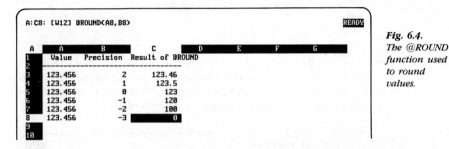

A:C8: [W12] @ROUND(A8,B8)   READY

	A	B	C	D	E	F	G
1	Value	Precision	Result of @ROUND				
2							
3	123.456	2	123.46				
4	123.456	1	123.5				
5	123.456	0	123				
6	123.456	−1	120				
7	123.456	−2	100				
8	123.456	−3	0				
9							
10							

Fig. 6.4.
The @ROUND function used to round values.

Note that the @ROUND function and the /Range Format command perform differently. @ROUND actually changes the contents of a cell, where /Range Format only alters how a cell's contents are displayed.

In 1-2-3, the formatted number you see on-screen or in print may not be the number used in calculations. This difference can cause errors of thousands of dollars in spreadsheets such as mortgage tables. To prevent errors, use the @ROUND function to round formula results to be the same as the display.

Caution:
The formatted number you see on-screen or in print may not be the number used in calculations.

As you work with rounding, keep in mind some general information about how the @ROUND function works. @ROUND rounds a number according to the old standard rule: if the number is less than 0.5, it gets rounded down to 0; if it's 0.5 or more, it gets rounded up to 1. According to this rule, however, the function may not always return a correctly rounded result. Sometimes, as in the earlier example of the @INT function, you should round down to the nearest integer. Then again, at times, you should round up to nearest integer.

For example, suppose that you need to schedule computer time for nine people and that each person usually needs one-fourth of an hour. You calculate the number of hours of computer time to schedule as 1/4 times 9, or 2 1/4 hours of computer time. If you use the @ROUND function, 2 1/4 gets rounded to 2. If you schedule only 2 hours, however, you end up being short by 1/4 hour. By scheduling 3 hours, you end up having three-quarters of an hour left over, but everybody gets the time they need. Accordingly, what you really want to do is round up.

If you need to round up to the nearest integer, you can do so by adding 0.5 to the number you need to round. Figure 6.5 illustrates this technique.

Cue:
Round up to the nearest integer by adding 0.5 to the number you need to round.

@RAND—Producing Random Numbers

@RAND is a random number generator function and uses no arguments.

@RAND

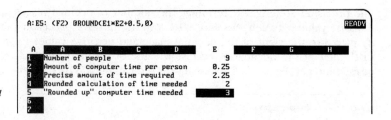

Fig. 6.5.
A result
"rounded up"
by adding 0.5
to the rounded
number.

@RAND returns a randomly generated number between 0 and 1, using 18 digits to the right of the decimal each time the worksheet is recalculated. Figure 6.6 shows @RAND generating 5 random numbers in cells A5 through A9. Note that new random numbers are generated each time you recalculate.

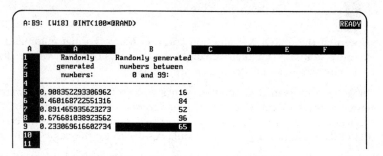

Fig. 6.6.
The @RAND
function used
to produce
random
numbers.

You will find @RAND helpful for modeling problems that involve random occurrences, such as traffic-flow prediction, inventory control, and financial markets analysis. Generally, to simulate random occurrences in these sorts of models, you use random numbers as model inputs.

Reminder:
Use @RAND for
modeling problems
that involve
random
occurrences.

@SQRT—Calculating the Square Root

The @SQRT function calculates the square root of a positive number with an accuracy of 18 digits to the right of the decimal point. The function uses one argument, the number you want to square, and the following format:

@SQRT(value or cell reference)

The value squared must be a non-negative numeric value or a cell reference to such a value. If @SQRT is called with a negative value, the function returns ERR. Figure 6.7 shows some examples of @SQRT.

Logarithmic Functions

1-2-3 has three logarithmic functions—@LOG, @EXP, and @LN. Each function is called with one argument, which can be a numeric value or a cell reference to a numeric value. Figure 6.8 shows examples of @LOG, @EXP, and @LN.

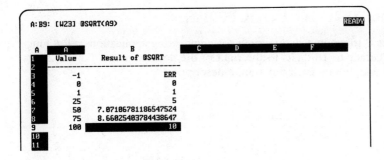

Fig. 6.7.
The @SQRT
function used
to square
numbers.

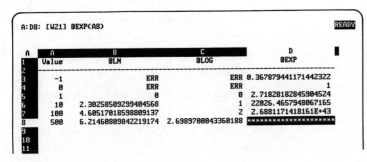

Fig. 6.8.
Examples of
1-2-3's
logarithmic
functions—
@LN, @LOG,
and @EXP.

@LOG—Computing Logarithms

The @LOG function computes the base 10 logarithm.

  @LOG(value or cell reference)

This function may not be called with a negative value. If @LOG is called with a negative value, ERR is returned.

@EXP—Finding Powers of e

The @EXP function computes the power of *e*.

  @EXP(value or cell reference)

With @EXP, you quickly can create very large numbers. If the function's resulting value is too large to be displayed, asterisks are displayed.

@LN—Computing Natural Logarithms

The @LN function computes the natural, or base *e*, logarithm.

  @LN(value or cell reference)

This function may not be called with a negative value. If @LN is called with a negative value, ERR is returned.

Trigonometric Functions

1-2-3 provides 8 trigonometric functions for engineering applications. All 8 functions have accuracy to 18 digits to the right of the decimal point. Table 6.2 lists the functions and, beside each function, a description.

Table 6.2
Trigonometric Functions

Function	Description
@PI	Calculates the value of π
@SIN(angle)	Calculates the sine given an angle in radians
@COS(angle)	Calculates the cosine given an angle in radians
@TAN(angle)	Calculates the tangent given an angle in radians
@ASIN(angle)	Calculates the arcsine given an angle in radians
@ACOS(angle)	Calculates the arccosine given an angle in radians
@ATAN(angle)	Calculates the arctangent given an angle in radians
@ATAN2(number1,number2)	Calculates the four-quadrant arctangent

@PI—Computing Pi

The @PI function computes the value of π. The function is called with no arguments.

    @PI

Reminder:
@PI will return the value 3.14159265358979324.

@PI will return the value 3.14159265358979324. @PI is used in calculating the area of circles and the volume of spheres. In addition, @PI is needed to convert from angle measurements in degrees to angle measurements in radians. Because $2*\pi$ radians are in 360 degrees, you can multiply the number of degrees by $(2*\pi)/360$, and the result represents radians as shown in figure 6.9.

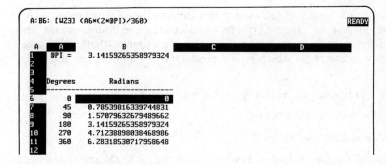

Fig. 6.9.
The @PI function used to convert angles from degrees to radians.

@COS, @SIN, and @TAN—Computing Trigonometric Functions

The @COS, @SIN, and @TAN functions calculate the cosine, sine, and tangent, respectively, for an angle. Each function is called with one argument—an angle calibrated in radians.

@COS(angle in radians)

@SIN(angle in radians)

@TAN(angle in radians)

Be sure to convert angle measurements into radians before using these functions.

Figure 6.10 illustrates these three functions. Notice that in cells D5 and D9, @TAN returns ERR. These errors occur because an angle's tangent equals its sine divided by its cosine. When the cosine is zero, as it is in both of these cases, @TAN returns ERR because the function cannot divide by zero.

Cue:
Convert angle measurements into radians before using these functions.

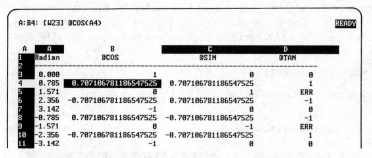

Fig. 6.10.
Examples of the @COS, @SIN, and @TAN functions.

@ACOS, @ASIN, @ATAN, and @ATAN2 —Computing Inverse Trigonometric Functions

The @ACOS, @ASIN, @ATAN, and @ATAN2 functions calculate the arccosine, the arcsine, the arctangent, and the four-quadrant, respectively. @ACOS computes the inverse of cosine; @ASIN computes the inverse of sine; and @ATAN computes the inverse of tangent. @ATAN2 calculates the four-quadrant arc-tangent using the ratio of its two arguments. Given a number, the @ASIN function calculates a radian angle which would produce that number from the @SIN function.

Both @ACOS and @ASIN are called with one argument.

@ACOS(value or cell reference)

@ASIN(value or cell reference)

Reminder:
Because all cosine and sine values lie between −1 and 1, @COS and @SIN can be called only with values between −1 and 1.

Because all cosine and sine values lie between −1 and 1, @ACOS and @ASIN can be called only with values between −1 and 1. Each function returns ERR if you use a value outside this range. @ASIN returns angles between −π/2 and +π/2, while @ACOS returns angles between 0 and π/2. Figure 6.11 shows examples of the @ACOS and @ASIN functions.

Fig. 6.11.
Examples of the @ACOS, @ASIN, and @ATAN functions.

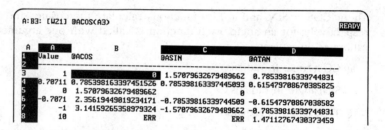

For the @ATAN function, you again use one argument. @ATAN can be called with any number and returns a value between −π/2 and +π/2. The format of the function is

@ATAN(value or cell reference)

@ATAN2 computes the angle whose tangent is specified by the ratio number2/number1—the two arguments. At least one of the arguments must be some number other than zero. @ATAN2 returns angles between −π and +π. The function format is

@ATAN2(number1,number2)

Figure 6.12 gives some examples of the @ATAN2 function.

Fig. 6.12.
Examples of the @ATAN2 function.

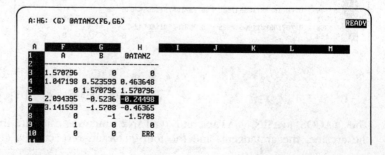

Statistical Functions

1-2-3 provides 10 statistical functions: @AVG, @COUNT, @MAX, @MIN, @SUM, @SUMPRODUCT, @STD, @STDS, @VAR, and @VARS. (Additional statistical functions, which are specifically for databases, are described in Chapter 10, "Managing Data.") Table 6.3 lists the functions, their arguments, and the statistical operations they perform.

Table 6.3
Statistical Functions

Function	Description
@AVG(list)	Calculates the arithmetic mean of a list of values
@COUNT(list)	Counts the number of cells that contain entries
@MAX(list)	Returns the maximum value in a list of values
@MIN(list)	Returns the minimum value in a list of values
@STD(list)	Calculates the population standard deviation of a list of values
@STDS(list)	Calculates the sample population standard deviation of a list of values
@SUM(list)	Sums a list of values
@SUMPRODUCT (range1, range2)	Multiplies range1 by range2 and sums the values
@VAR(list)	Calculates the population variance of a list of values
@VARS(list)	Calculates the sample population variance of a list of values

Every one of the statistical functions except one—@SUMPRODUCT—uses the argument *list*. List can be either individually specified values or cell addresses, a range of cells, or multiple ranges of cells. For example, each of the following formats (or any combination) works:

@SUM(1,2,3,4)

@SUM(B1,B2,B3,B4)

@SUM(B1..B4)

@SUM(B1..B2,B3..B4)

Although the preceding examples use the @SUM function (which totals the values included as arguments), the principles these examples illustrate apply equally to each of the statistical functions.

Reminder:
Every statistical function except @SUMPRODUCT uses the argument list.

Note that some of the statistical functions perform differently when you specify cells individually than when you specify ranges. The functions that perform differently in this case include @AVG, @MAX, @MIN, @STD, @STDS, @VAR, and @VARS. When you specify a range of cells, 1-2-3 ignores empty cells within the specified range. When you specify cells individually, however, 1-2-3 takes empty cells into consideration for the particular functions mentioned.

Suppose, for example, that you are looking for the minimum value in a range that includes an empty cell and cells containing the entries 1, 2, and 3; in this case, 1-2-3 returns the value 1 as the minimum value. Suppose, however, that you instead specify individually a cell that is empty along with cells containing the entries 1, 2, and 3; in this case, 1-2-3 returns the value 0 as the minimum.

The reason that 1-2-3 makes this distinction is that empty cells actually contain zeros, although they are invisible. Accordingly, 1-2-3 assumes that if you go to the extra effort of actually specifying an individual cell—even if it is empty—you must want it included in the statistical calculation.

When you specify cells, keep in mind also that 1-2-3 treats cells holding labels as zeros. This is the case both when the cell is included as part of a range and when the cell is individually specified.

@AVG—Computing the Arithmetic Mean

To calculate the average of a set of values, you add all the values and then divide the sum by the number of values. Essentially, then, the @AVG function produces the same result as if you divided @SUM(list) by @COUNT(list)—two functions described later in this section. You will find the @AVG function a helpful tool for calculating the arithmetic mean—a commonly used measure of a set of values' average. The format of the function is as follows:

@AVG(list)

As noted earlier, the list argument can be values, cell addresses, cell names, cell ranges, range names, or combinations of these.

Figure 6.13 shows an example of the @AVG function calculating the mean price per share of an imaginary company. The figure shows the @AVG function argument as B3..B11. As long as cells B8 and B9 are empty and are included in the list argument only as part of a range, the values of these cells—actually zero—are ignored in the average calculation.

@COUNT—Counting Cell Entries

The @COUNT function totals the number of cells that contain entries. The format for the function is as follows:

@COUNT(list)

The list argument can be values, cell addresses, cell names, cell ranges, range names, or combinations of these.

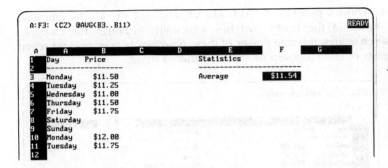

Fig. 6.13.
The @AVG function used to calculate the mean price per share.

For example, you could use the @COUNT function to show the number of share prices included in the @AVG calculation made in figure 6.13. Figure 6.14 shows this calculation being made in cell F4.

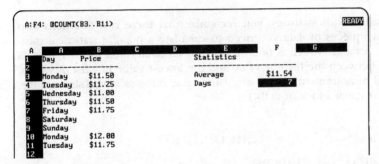

Fig. 6.14.
The @COUNT function used to calculate the number of prices per share in average calculations.

Be sure to include only ranges as the arguments in the @COUNT function. If you specify a cell individually, 1-2-3 counts that cell as if it has an entry even if the cell is empty. If you absolutely must specify a cell individually, but want it counted only if it actually contains an entry, you need to use the @@ function. That function is described along with 1-2-3's other special functions later in this chapter.

@MAX and @MIN—Finding Maximum and Minimum Values

The @MAX function finds the largest value included in your list argument; the @MIN function finds the smallest value included in your list argument. The formats for these functions are as follows:

@MAX(list)

@MIN(list)

Figure 6.15 shows information concerning prices per share of an imaginary company. Using the @MAX and @MIN functions can help you easily find the lowest and the highest prices, respectively. You can see the argument of the @MAX

Reminder:
The @MAX function finds the largest value included in your list.

function in the control panel as B3..B11. The argument of the @MIN function, which isn't shown in the figure, matches identically. Although the example shows only seven values, the true power of these functions is most evident when your list consists of several dozen or several hundred items.

Fig. 6.15.
The @MIN and
@MAX
functions used
to show low
and high prices
per share.

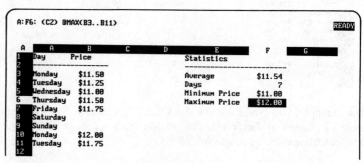

If you are familiar with statistics, you recognize that these two functions also provide the two pieces of data you need to calculate a popular statistical measure—a range. A range, which is one measure of variability in a list of values, is the difference between the highest value and the lowest value in a list of values. (The statistical measurement, range, is not the same thing as a worksheet range, which is a rectangular block of cells.)

@STD and @STDS—Calculating the Standard Deviation

The @STD function calculates the standard deviation of a population, and the @STDS function calculates the standard deviation of a sample. The formats for these functions are as follows:

@STD(list)

@STDS(list)

The precise definitions of the two standard deviation functions are best shown by the formulas 1-2-3 uses to calculate them. These formulas ase as follows:

$$STD = \sqrt{\frac{\sum_{n=1}^{N}(X_n-avg)^2}{N}} \qquad STDS = \sqrt{\frac{\sum_{n=1}^{N}(X_n-avg)^2}{N-1}}$$

where

N = Number of items in list
X_n = The *n*th item in list
avg = Arithmetic mean of list

Essentially, the standard deviation is a measure of dispersion about or around an average. A smaller standard deviation indicates less dispersion, or variation, while a larger standard deviation indicates greater dispersion, or variation. Perhaps not surprisingly, a standard deviation of 0 indicates that there is no dispersion—meaning that every value in the list of values is the same.

To choose the correct function, you also need to know whether you are dealing with the entire population or with a sample. If you are measuring, or including, every value in a calculation, you are working with a *population*. However, if you are measuring, or including, only a subset or portion of the values in a calculation, you are working with a *sample*.

For example, if you are interested only in the variability in price per share over the last seven trading days, you use the @STD function because you are including every value in your calculation. However, if you are interested only in the variability in price over the last month and you are working with only the last seven days' price per share data, you use the @STDS function because you are including only a portion of the values. This might be a case, for instance, when you use the characteristics of the sample to infer the characters of the population. Figure 6.16 shows these additional statistical measures.

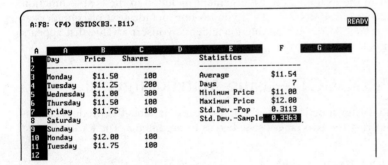

Fig. 6.16.
The @STD and
@STDS
functions used
to calculate
standard
deviation.

@SUM—Totaling Values

The @SUM function provides a convenient way to add a list of values that you specify as the list argument in the following format:

@SUM(list)

Further extending the stock price data example, assume that you have purchased the shares recorded in column C, as shown in figure 6.17. You could create a formula that adds these values, as in the following statement:

+C3+C4+C5+C6+C7+C10+C11

You also could enter the formula as shown in cell C13 in figure 6.17.

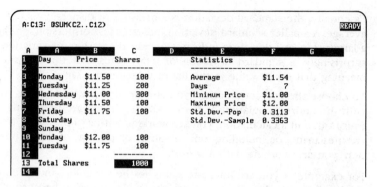

Fig. 6.17.
The @SUM
function used
to calculate the
total shares
purchased.

Of all the statistical functions that 1-2-3 provides, @SUM is the one you probably will use most because it so often provides such a convenient, shorthand way of constructing formulas. Because labels are included in statistical functions as zeros, you should include a cell at both ends of ranges you are summing with the @SUM function. This is a good practice because if rows or columns are inserted at the first or last value in the range, the range included as the function's list argument expands as part of the insertion. For instance, if you insert a row at rows 3 and 11 in the example, the list argument included in the @SUM function expands to become @SUM(C2..C12). If you do not include text placeholders at either end of an @SUM range, you might accidentally insert a value that appears to be in the total, when it is not.

@SUMPRODUCT—Using Matrix Algebra

The @SUMPRODUCT function gets its name because it sums the products calculated by multiplying the two ranges specified as its arguments. The format for the function is

Reminder:
@SUMPRODUCT
multiplies the two
ranges specified as
its arguments.

@SUMPRODUCT(range1, range2)

For example, you could use the @SUMPRODUCT function to calculate the total dollars of stock purchased over a specified period of days, as shown in figure 6.18. In effect, the @SUMPRODUCT function performs the following calculations: B3*C3, B4*C4, B5*C5, B6*C6, B7*C7, B10*C10, B11*C11, and then totals the results—called *products*.

@VAR and @VARS—Calculating the Variance

The variance, like the standard deviation, is a measure of dispersion about, or around, an average. The @VAR function calculates the variance of a population; the @VARS function calculates the variance of a sample. The formats for these functions are as follows:

@VAR(list)

@VARS(list)

```
A:C15: (C2) [W14] @SUMPRODUCT(B2..B12,C2..C12)                    READY

  A      A         B         C      D        E          F        G
 1    Day       Price     Shares         Statistics
 2    ------------------------------     ------------------------
 3    Monday    $11.50      100          Average         $11.54
 4    Tuesday   $11.25      200          Days                 7
 5    Wednesday $11.00      300          Minimum Price   $11.00
 6    Thursday  $11.50      100          Maximum Price   $12.00
 7    Friday    $11.75      100          Std.Dev.-Pop     0.3113
 8    Saturday                           Std.Dev.-Sample  0.3363
 9    Sunday
10    Monday    $12.00      100
11    Tuesday   $11.75      100
12                      ----------
13    Total Shares        1000
14
15    Total Purchases  $11,400.00
16
```

Fig. 6.18.
The
@SUMPRODUCT
function used
to calculate the
total purchases.

Actually, calculating a statistical variance is an intermediate step in calculating the standard deviations described in the discussion of the @STD and @STDS functions. By comparing the two formulas that follow, you can see that the standard deviation is simply the square root of the variance.

$$\text{VAR} = \frac{\displaystyle\sum_{n=1}^{N}(X_n - \text{avg})^2}{N} \qquad\qquad \text{VARS} = \frac{\displaystyle\sum_{n=1}^{N}(X_n - \text{avg})^2}{N-1}$$

where

N = Number of items in list
X_n = The *n*th item in list
avg = Arithmetic mean of list

For explanations of the terms *population* and *sample*, refer to the text about the @STD and @STDS functions.

Figure 6.19 shows the use of the @VAR and @VARS functions to measure the price-per-share variability over the specified period. As the figure illustrates, the @VAR and @VARS functions, along with all the other statistical functions, constitute a valuable set of analytical tools that often will provide valuable insights into data you examine and assess.

Financial and Accounting Functions

Release 3 of 1-2-3 provides 12 financial and accounting functions that perform a variety of discounted cash flow, loan amortization, and asset depreciation calcula-

RELEASE 3

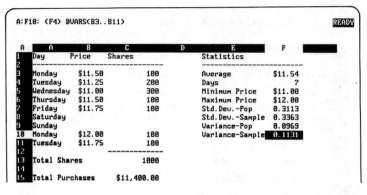

Fig. 6.19.
The @VAR and @VARS functions used to calculate variances.

tions. The 1-2-3 financial functions include two that calculate returns on investments—@IRR and @RATE; one function that calculates loan payments—@PMT; two functions for calculating present values—@NPV and @PV; one function that calculates future values—@FV; two functions that perform compound growth calculations—@TERM and @CTERM; and four functions that calculate asset depreciation—@SLN, @DDB, @SYD, and @VDB. Table 6.4 summarizes the financial and accounting functions available in 1-2-3 Release 3.

Table 6.4
Financial and Accounting Functions

Investment Function	Description
@IRR(guess,cashflows)	Calculates the internal rate of return on an investment
@RATE(future value, present value,term)	Calculates the return on an investment given the present value and the future value
@PMT(principal, interest,term)	Calculates the loan payment amount
@NPV(interest,cashflows)	Calculates the present value of a stream of periodic cash flows—even if the cash flows are not even
@PV(payment,interest, term)	Calculates the present value of a stream of periodic cash flows if the cash flows are even
@FV(payment,interest, term)	Calculates the future value of a stream of periodic cash flows
@TERM(payment,interest, future value)	Calculates the number of times a loan payment is made
@CTERM(interest,future value,present value)	Calculates the number of periods for present value to grow to future value

Depreciation Function	Description
@SLN(cost,salvage,life)	Calculates straight-line depreciation
@DDB(cost,salvage,life, period)	Calculates 200% declining balance depreciation
@SYD(cost,salvage,life, period)	Calculates sum-of-the-years'-digits depreciation
@VDB(cost,salvage,life, period,percent)	Calculates either 200% or another, optionally specified, percent declining balance depreciation

@IRR—Internal Rate of Return

The @IRR function measures the percentage return on an investment. The format for the function is

@IRR(guess,cashflows)

The guess argument typically should be a percent between 0 and 1, and the first cash flow must be a negative amount. 1-2-3 uses the guess argument as the interest rate in the following formula and tests whether the result equals 0.

$$0 = \sum_{n=0}^{N} \frac{C_n}{(1+IRR)^n}$$

where C_n = Cash flow at *n*th period

If the result does not equal 0, 1-2-3 continues to try different interest rates in an attempt to make the equation true—that is, the left side of the equation, 0, equals the right side of the equation. (Notice that the right side of the equation is the formula for calculating the profit measure called the *net present value*.) 1-2-3 attempts to converge to a correct interest, or discount rate, with .0000001 precision within 20 attempts or iterations. If the program cannot do so, the @IRR function returns the ERR value.

Tip: You may need to try several guesses to get one that's close enough for 1-2-3 to converge on the correct internal rate of return. Because the @IRR function finds an internal rate of return below the initial guess easier than one above the initial guess, guessing high is the best practice.

Figure 6.20 illustrates the @IRR function calculating the internal rate of return on a certificate of deposit investment. The purchase amount, a negative cash

Reminder: The guess argument should be a percent between 0 and 1.

flow, is made at time 0. Other cash flows occur at the end of equally spaced periods. Notice that the monthly internal rate of return is converted to an annual rate by multiplying the monthly amount by 12.

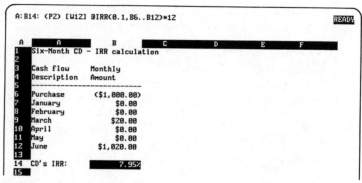

Fig. 6.20.
The internal rate of return calculated on a bank CD with the @IRR function.

Reminder:
An investment may have multiple internal rates of return.

Although the internal rate of return profit measure is widely used, you should be aware that the formula is currently being disputed. Note that the problem is with the internal rate of return formula itself, not the @IRR function, which simply makes using the formula easier.

One problem is evident when you use the internal rate of return measure on an investment that has multiple internal rates of return. In theory, for example, the formula for calculating the internal rate of return for an investment with cash flows over 10 years is a 10th root polynomial equation with up to 10 correct solutions. In practice, an investment will have as many correct internal rates of return as there are sign changes in the cash flows.

A sign change occurs when the previous period's cash flow is a negative amount while the current period's is a positive amount—or vice versa. Accordingly, even if you get the @IRR function to return an internal rate of return with your first guess, try other guesses to see that there's not another correct internal rate of return answer; you probably don't want to use the measure when it delivers multiple solutions. Figure 6.21 shows two, mathematically correct internal rates of return being calculated based on the same set of cash flows shown.

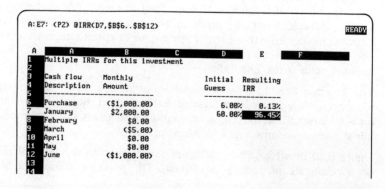

Fig. 6.21.
The @IRR function returning two correct solutions.

A second problem with the internal rate of return measure relates to ranking investments by their internal rates of return. Remember that the internal rate of return measure calculates the percentage profit per period. Typically, however, you are interested in the actual dollars of profit rather than the percentage.

Using the @IRR function measure blindly, for example, you might pick a $1 investment delivering a 50% internal rate of return over a $1,000,000 investment delivering a 49% return; and you might pick a $100 investment that delivers 25% for 1 year over a $100 investment that delivers 24.5% for 25 years. In both of these examples, the internal rate of return possibly may direct you to the correct course of action. However, if you focus exclusively on the internal rate of return percentage, you possibly may miss the better investment opportunity. Again, this isn't the fault of the 1-2-3 function @IRR, but rather a result of the internal rate of return formula itself.

@RATE—Compound Growth Rate

The @RATE function calculates the compound growth rate for an initial investment that grows to a specified future value over a specified number of periods. The rate is the periodic interest rate and not necessarily an annual rate. The format of this function, where n equals the number of periods, is as follows:

Reminder:
@RATE calculates the compound growth rate for an initial investment that grows to a future value over a number of periods.

@RATE(future value,present value,term)

This function's basic formula calculates the future value of an initial investment given the interest rate and the number of periods. For the @RATE calculation, the formula is rearranged to compute the interest rate in terms of the initial investment, the future value, and the number of periods.

Interest rate $= (\text{future value/present value})^{1/\text{term}} - 1$

You could use the @RATE function, for example, to determine the yield of a zero-coupon bond that is sold at a discount of its face value. Suppose that for $350 you can purchase a zero-coupon bond with a $1,000 face value, maturing in 10 years. What is the implied annual interest rate? The answer, shown in figure 6.22, is 11.07 percent.

Reminder:
Use the @RATE function to determine the yield of a zero-coupon bond.

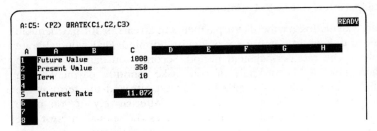

A:C5: (P2) @RATE(C1,C2,C3)

	A	B	C	D	E	F	G	H
1	Future Value		1000					
2	Present Value		350					
3	Term		10					
4								
5	Interest Rate		11.07%					
6								
7								
8								

Fig. 6.22.
The @RATE function used to calculate the zero-coupon bond yield.

The @RATE function is also useful in forecasting applications to calculate the compound growth rate between current and projected future revenues, earnings, and so on.

@PMT—Loan Payment Amounts

You can use the @PMT function to calculate the periodic payments necessary to pay the entire principal on an amortizing loan. All you need to know is the loan amount (or the principal, periodic interest rate, and term) or the number of payment periods. Three arguments are entered into the @PMT function, as follows:

@PMT(principal,interest,term)

The @PMT function assumes that payments are to be made at the end of each period; these payments are called *payments in arrears*. The function uses the following formula to make the payment calculation:

$$PMT = principal * \frac{interest}{1-(1+interest)^{-n}}$$

where n = Number of payments

Figure 6.23 shows the @PMT function being used to calculate the monthly car payment on a $12,000 car loan. The loan is repaid over 60 months and accrues interest at the monthly rate of 1%.

Fig. 6.23.
The @PMT
function used
to calculate
loan payments.

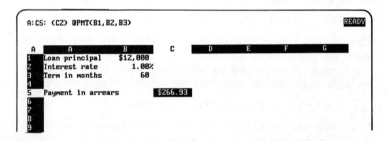

You can modify the calculated result of the @PMT function if payments are to be made at the beginning of the period; these payments are called *payments in advance*. The modified format for the function is as follows:

@PMT(principal,interest,term)/(1 + interest)

Whether you are calculating payments for payments in arrears or for payments in advance, you need to keep two important guidelines in mind. First, you calibrate the interest rate as the rate-per-payment period. Second, you express the loan term in payment periods. Accordingly, if you make monthly payments, you should enter the interest rate as the monthly interest rate and the term as the number of months you will be making payments. Alternatively, if you make annual payments, you should enter the interest rate as the annual interest rate and the term as the number of years you will be making payments.

@NPV—Net Present Value

The @NPV function closely resembles the @PV function except that @NPV can calculate the present value of a varying, or changing, stream of cash flows. The format of the function is

@NPV(interest,cashflows)

The function calculates the following formula:

$$NPV = \sum_{n=1}^{N} \frac{C_n}{(1+i)^n}$$

where
C_n = Cash flow at nth period
i = Discount rate

Figure 6.24 shows how you can use the @NPV function to calculate the present value of a stream of varying cash flows.

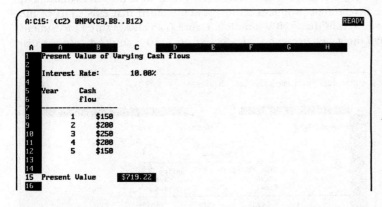

Fig. 6.24.
The @NPV function used to present the value of varying cash flows.

Note that what 1-2-3 labels as the net present value function is not what accountants and financial analysts define as the net present value profit measure. 1-2-3's @NPV assumes that the first cash flow occurs at the end of the first period; therefore, the function actually is only a flexible present value function. In any situation where you might use the @PV function, therefore, you also can use the @NPV function to obtain the same result.

Accountants and financial analysts use the term net present value to refer to a measure of an investment's profitability using the following formula:

Cue:
The @NPV function closely resembles the @PV function.

$$NPV = \sum_{n=0}^{N} \frac{C_n}{(1+i)^n}$$

where

C_n = Cash flow at nth period
i = Discount rate

Cue:
To calculate the actual profitability measure called net present value, subtract the initial investment.

To calculate the actual profitability measure called net present value, you need to subtract the initial investment from the results of the @NPV function. When you construct a formula using the @NPV function this way, essentially you are testing whether or not the investment meets, beats, or falls short of the interest rate specified in the @NPV function.

If the calculated result of the preceding formula is a positive amount, it means that the investment produces an investment return that beats the interest rate specified in the @NPV function. If the calculated result equals zero, it means that the investment produces an investment return that equals the interest rate specified in the @NPV function. If the calculated result is a negative amount, it means that the investment produces an investment return that falls short of the interest rate specified in the @NPV function. Figure 6.25 shows three investment alternatives and their net present values based on a 10% interest rate, or discount rate.

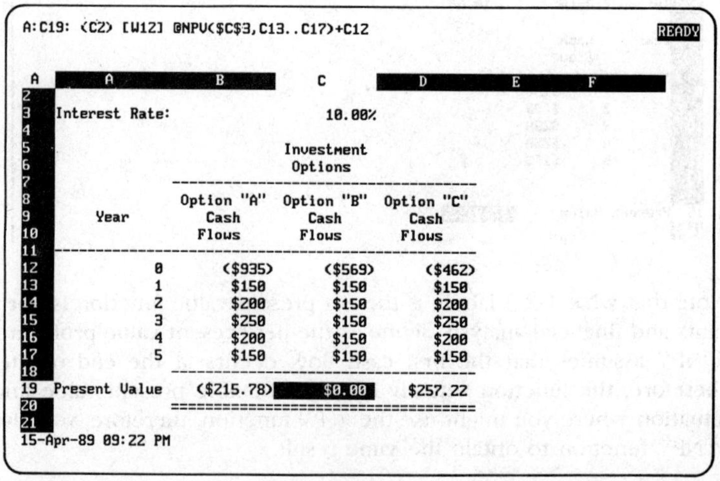

Fig. 6.25.
The @NPV function used to calculate the net present value profit measure.

```
A:C19: <C2> [W12] @NPV($C$3,C13..C17)+C12                          READY

     A          A          B           C           D        E      F
 2
 3   Interest Rate:                  10.00%
 4
 5                                 Investment
 6                                  Options
 7
 8                         Option "A"  Option "B"  Option "C"
 9             Year          Cash        Cash        Cash
10                          Flows       Flows       Flows
11
12              0          ($935)      ($569)      ($462)
13              1           $150        $150        $150
14              2           $200        $150        $200
15              3           $250        $150        $250
16              4           $200        $150        $200
17              5           $150        $150        $150
18
19   Present Value        ($215.78)     $0.00      $257.22
20
21
15-Apr-89 09:22 PM
```

@PV—Present Value of an Annuity

The @PV function closely resembles the @NPV function in that @PV calculates the present value of a stream of cash flows. The difference is that the @PV function calculates the present value of a stream of equal cash flows occurring at the end of the period. This stream of equal cash flows is called an *ordinary annuity*, or *payments in arrears*. The @PV function uses the following format:

@PV(payments,interest,term)

The formula used in the function is

$$PV = payment * \frac{1-(1+interest)^{-term}}{interest}$$

Figure 6.26 shows the result of using the @PV function to calculate the present value of ten $1,000 payments.

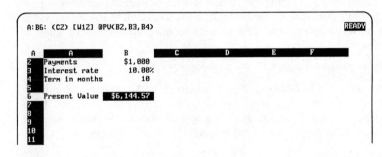

Fig. 6.26.
The @PV function used to calculate the present value of ten $1,000 payments.

Keep in mind that the @PV function assumes that the equal-amount cash flows, or payments, occur at the end of the period. If the cash flows occur at the beginning of the period—called an annuity due or payments in advance, you use the following variation of the function:

@PV(payments,interest,term)*(1+interest)

@FV—Future Value

The future value function calculates to what amount a stated amount will grow based on a specified interest rate and number of years. The function is helpful for estimating the future balances into which current savings and investments will grow. The format of the function is

@FV(payment,interest,term)

The function uses the following formula:

$$Future\ value = payment * \frac{(1+interest)^{term}-1}{interest}$$

You might, for example, use the future value function to calculate the estimated size of your individual retirement account 25 years from now. Figure 6.27 shows such a calculation assuming annual contributions of $2,000 and annual interest rates of 9%.

Fig. 6.27.
The @FV
function used
to calculate a
future IRA
balance.

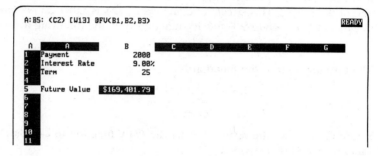

In addition to calculating the future value of a stream of periodic cash-flow payments (using the @FV function), you also may want to calculate the future value of amounts you've already set aside. The formula to calculate the future value of a present value is

Future value = present value * $(1 + \text{interest})^{\text{term}}$

Suppose, for example, that in addition to planning to make $2,000 annual individual retirement account contributions over the next 25 years, you also have $5,000 dollars you've already accumulated. You want to know the future value of this amount. Figure 6.28 shows an example using these assumptions.

Fig. 6.28.
A formula used
to calculate the
future value of
a present value
amount.

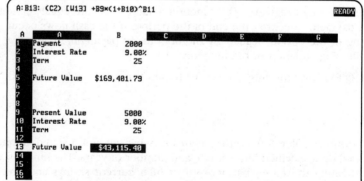

@TERM—Term of an Investment

The @TERM function calculates the number of periods required to accumulate a specified future value by making equal payments into an interest-bearing account at the end of each period. The format of the @TERM function is

@TERM(payment,interest,future value)

The @TERM function is similar to the @FV function except that instead of finding the future value of a stream of payments over a specified period, the @TERM function finds the number of periods required to reach the given future value. The actual equation for calculating the number of periods is

$$\text{Term} = \frac{@LN(1 + (\text{interest*future value})/\text{payment})}{@LN(1 + \text{interest})}$$

Reminder:
The @TERM
function finds the
number of periods
required to reach
the given future
value.

Suppose that you want to determine the number of months required to accumulate $5,000 by making a monthly payment of $50 into an account paying 6 percent annual interest compounded monthly (0.5 percent per month). Figure 6.29 shows how @TERM can help you get the answer, which is slightly more than 81 months (6 years and 9 months) for an ordinary annuity, but slightly less than 81 months for an annuity due. For this account, making the deposit at the beginning of the month makes only a little difference.

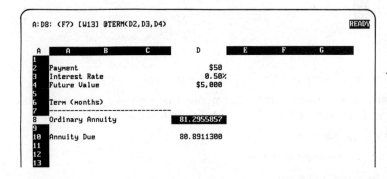

Fig. 6.29.
The @TERM
function used
to calculate the
number of
months to
reach a
specified future
value.

To calculate the term for an annuity due, use the following equation:

Term for an
annuity due = @TERM(payment,interest,future value/(1 + interest))

@CTERM—Compound Term of an Investment

The @CTERM function calculates the number of periods required for an initial investment earning a specified interest rate to grow to a specified future value. While the @TERM function calculates the number of periods needed for a series of payments to grow to a future value at a specified interest rate, the @CTERM function calculates the required number of periods based on the specified present value, future value, and interest rate. The format of the @CTERM function is

@CTERM(interest,future value,present value)

The equation used to calculate @CTERM is

$$\text{Term} = \frac{@LN(\text{future value}/\text{present value})}{@LN(1 + \text{interest})}$$

The @CTERM function is useful for determining the term of an investment necessary to achieve a specific future value. For example, suppose that you want to determine how many years it will take for $2,000 invested in an IRA account at 10 percent interest to grow to $10,000. Figure 6.30 shows how to use the @CTERM function to determine the answer, which is just over 16 years and 10 months.

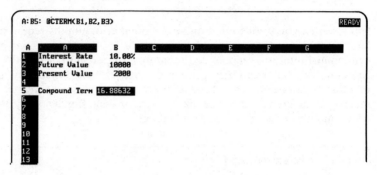

Fig. 6.30.
The @CTERM
function used
to calculate the
number of
years for
$2,000 to grow
to $10,000 at
10%.

@SLN—Straight-Line Depreciation

The @SLN function calculates straight-line depreciation given the asset's cost, salvage value, and depreciable life. The format of the function is

@SLN(cost,salvage value,life)

The formula used to calculate @SLN is

SLN = (cost−salvage value)/ life

The @SLN function conveniently calculates straight-line depreciation for an asset. For example, suppose that you have purchased a machine for $1,000 that has a useful life of 3 years and a salvage value estimated to be 10 percent of the purchase price ($100) at the end of its useful life. Figure 6.31 shows how to use the @SLN function to determine the straight-line depreciation for the machine, which is $300 per year.

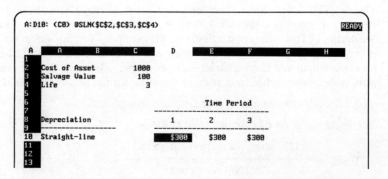

Fig. 6.31.
The @SLN
function used
to calculate
straight-line
depreciation.

@DDB—Double-Declining Balance Depreciation

The @DDB function calculates depreciation using the double-declining balance method, with depreciation ceasing when the book value reaches the salvage value. Double-declining balance depreciation is a method of accelerating depreciation so that greater depreciation expense occurs in the earlier periods rather than the later ones. Book value in any period is the purchase price less the total depreciation in all prior periods.

The format of the @DDB function is

@DDB(cost,salvage,life,period)

In general, the double-declining balance depreciation in any period is

book value*2/n

In this formula, *book value* is the book value in the period, and *n* is the depreciable life of the asset. 1-2-3, however, adjusts the results of this formula in later periods to ensure that total depreciation does not exceed the purchase price less the salvage value.

Figure 6.32 shows how the @DDB function can calculate depreciation on an asset purchased for $1,000, with a depreciable life of 3 years and an estimated salvage value of $100.

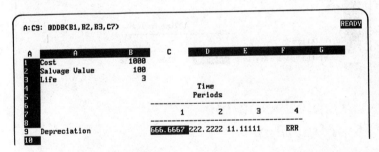

Fig. 6.32. The @DDB function used to calculate a 200% declining balance depreciation.

Keep in mind that when you use the double-declining balance depreciation method for an asset with a small salvage value, the asset will not be fully depreciated in the final year. If this is the case with one of your assets, you need to use the @VDB function, discussed later in this section.

@SYD—Sum-of-the-Years'-Digits Depreciation

The @SYD function calculates depreciation by the sum-of-the-years'-digits method. This method accelerates depreciation so that earlier periods of the item's life reflect greater depreciation than later periods. The format of the function is

@SYD(cost,salvage,life,period)

The cost is the purchase cost of the asset. The salvage is the estimated value of the asset at the end of the depreciable life. The life is the depreciable life of the asset. And the period is the period for which depreciation is to be computed.

@SYD calculates depreciation with the following formula:

$$SYD = \frac{(cost-salvage)*(life\ period+1)}{life*(life+1)/2}$$

The expression in the numerator, life period + 1, shows the life of the depreciation in the first period, decreased by 1 in each subsequent period. This expression reflects the declining pattern of depreciation over time. The expression in the denominator, life*(life+1)/2, is equal to the sum of the digits, as follows:

$$1 + 2 + \ldots + life$$

From this expression, the name *sum-of-the-years'-digits* originated.

Figure 6.33 shows how the @SYD function can calculate depreciation for an asset costing $1,000 with a depreciable life of 3 years and an estimated salvage value of $100.

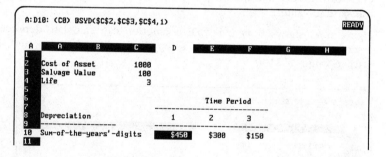

Fig. 6.33. The @SYD function used to calculate sum-of-years'-digits depreciation.

@VDB—Variable-Declining Balance Depreciation

The @VDB function calculates depreciation using the 200%-declining balance method—or optionally, using a different percentage. Depreciation ceases when the book value reaches the salvage value. As stated in the section on the @DDB function, declining balance depreciation is a method of accelerating depreciation so that greater depreciation expense occurs in the earlier periods rather than the later ones.

Essentially, the @VDB function mirrors the @DDB function with two important differences. First, you can choose to specify the percentage used as something other than 200%. Second, the @VDB function—unlike the @DDB function—always will fully depreciate an asset.

The format of the @VDB function is

@VDB(cost,salvage,life,period,percent)

In general, the declining balance depreciation in any period is

book value*percent /n

In this formula, book value is the book value in the period, and *n* is the depreciable life of the asset. 1-2-3, however, adjusts the results of this formula in later periods to ensure that total depreciation does not exceed the purchase price less the salvage value.

Figure 6.34 shows how the @VDB function can calculate depreciation on an asset purchased for $1,000, with a depreciable life of 3 years and an estimated salvage value of $100. The optional percent argument is set as 150%.

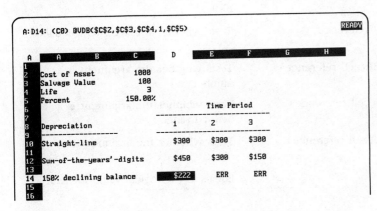

Fig. 6.34. The @VDB function used to calculate 150% declining balance depreciation.

Logical Functions

The logical functions allow you to add standard Boolean logic to your worksheet and use the logic either alone or as part of other worksheet formulas. Essentially, each of the logical functions allows you to test whether a condition is true or false.

Reminder: Logical functions add Boolean logic to your worksheet.

For some of the logical functions, you describe the test and what the function should do based on the test. For example, the @IF function tests any condition you include as an argument and then returns one value or label if the test is true, and another value or label if the test is false. For other logical functions, both the test and what the function returns based on the test are built right into the function itself. The @ISSTRING function is an example of this because it simply tests whether the argument is a string and returns a 1 if the test is true and a 0 if the test is false.

The eight logical functions that 1-2-3 provides are summarized in table 6.5. Rather than describe the logical functions in alphabetical order, as this chapter has done for many of the other function sets, the following text describes the logical functions in order of complexity. Therefore, you probably will want to read the description of the first function and progress from there.

Table 6.5
Logical Functions

Function	Description
@FALSE	Equals 0, the logical value for false
@IF(test,true,false)	Tests the condition and then returns one result if the condition is true and another if the condition is false
@ISERR(cell reference)	Tests whether the argument equals ERR
@ISNA(cell reference)	Tests whether the argument equals NA
@ISNUMBER(cell reference)	Tests whether the argument is a number
@ISRANGE(cell reference)	Tests whether the argument is a defined range
@ISSTRING(cell reference)	Tests whether the argument is a string
@TRUE	Equals 1, the logical value for true

@IF—Creating Conditional Tests

The @IF function represents a powerful tool—one you can use both to manipulate text within your worksheets and to effect calculations. For example, you could use the @IF statement to test the condition "Is the inventory on-hand below 1,000 units?" and then return one value or string if the answer to the question is true, and another if the answer is false. The @IF function uses the format

@IF(test,true,false)

Figure 6.35 shows several examples of the @IF function in action. To show clearly the functions, their arguments, and their results, the first column displays the function (formatted as text so that you can read it), and the second column shows the calculated results of the function.

The first @IF function checks whether the contents of a cell equals a string and produces one of two strings based on whether the test is true or false. Notice that when you include the actual string in the @IF statement test, you include it in quotation marks. Perhaps not surprisingly, you use the equal sign (=) to compare the two strings.

The second @IF function tests whether the contents of the cell named BOBS_SALES exceed 10,000 and returns one string if the test is true and another

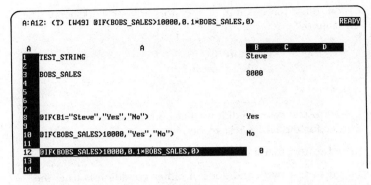

```
A:A12: (T) [W49] @IF(BOBS_SALES>10000,0.1*BOBS_SALES,0)          READY

         A                    A              B    C    D
1   TEST_STRING                          Steve
2
3   BOBS_SALES                           8000
4
5
6
7
8   @IF(B1="Steve","Yes","No")           Yes
9
10  @IF(BOBS_SALES>10000,"Yes","No")     No
11
12  @IF(BOBS_SALES>10000,0.1*BOBS_SALES,0)    0
13
14
```

Fig. 6.35.
Examples of the @IF function using strings and values.

if the test is false. The third @IF function again tests whether the contents of BOBS_SALES exceed 10,000 and then calculates the commission that the salesperson named Bob is entitled to if his sales exceed 10,000. To test for BOBS_SALES exceeding 10,000, the function uses the greater than sign (>).

The @IF function actually performs six logical tests. These are summarized in table 6.6.

Table 6.6
Logical Test Symbols

Symbol	Description
<	Less than
<=	Less than or equal to
=	Equal to
>=	Greater than or equal to
>	Greater than
<>	Not equal to

As figure 6.35 illustrates, the @IF function is a powerful tool for worksheets in that it allows you to add decision-making logic to your worksheets. That logic can be based on strings or numeric values, and the function can return either strings or numeric values. You can further expand the power of @IF functions by using compound tests.

Reminder: The @IF function allows you to add decision-making logic to your worksheets.

If you think about the conditions you test in your worksheet formulas, probably many are made up of two or more individual tests. For example, the following statement illustrates a compound condition:

IF
    (test 1) Company revenues increase and
    (test 2) Company expenses decrease
THEN
    true   Company profits will increase.

You will find occasion to use three complex operators in your worksheets. These are summarized in table 6.7.

Table 6.7
Complex Operators

Operator	Description
#AND#	Used to test two conditions that both must be true in order for the entire test to be true
#NOT#	Used to test that a condition is *not* true
#OR#	Used to test two conditions; if either condition is true, the entire test condition is true

Figure 6.36 illustrates how you might use these three complex operators. In the figure, REVS89 is the name of the cell that contains the 1989 gross revenues, and REVS88 contains the 1988 gross revenues; MARG89 is the cell that contains the 1989 gross margin, and MARG88 contains the 1988 gross margin. The first complex @IF condition tests whether both the conditions REVS89>REVS88 and MARG89>=MARG88 are true. If both tests are true, then the function returns the string "Good"; otherwise, the function returns the string "Bad".

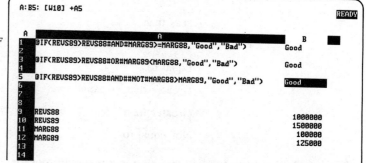

Fig. 6.36.
Compound @IF
conditions
being tested.

The second complex @IF function tests whether either one of the two conditions, REVS89>REVS88 or MARG89<MARG88 is true. If either test is true, then the function again returns the string "Good"; if both are false, the function returns the string "Bad".

The third complex @IF condition tests whether the condition REVS89>REVS88 is true and the condition MARG88>MARG89 is false. When both tests are passed, the function returns the string "Good"; when either of the two tests is false, the function returns the string "Bad".

You also can specify the true or the false argument within an @IF function as another @IF function. Putting @IF functions inside other @IF functions is a common and powerful logical tool. This technique, called a *nested IF*, gives you the capability to construct sophisticated logical tests and operations in your

1-2-3 worksheets. For example, figure 6.37 shows an @IF statement with nested IFs that calculates a sales commission where the salesperson receives a $500 commission if he or she books $10,000 or more in sales and also receives 10% of amounts exceeding $10,000.

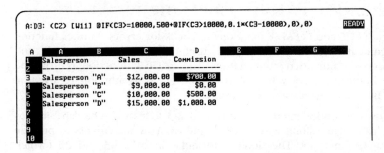

Fig. 6.37.
Nested @IF
statements used
to calculate
sales
commissions.

@ISERR and @ISNA—Trapping Errors in Conditional Tests

The @ISERR function tests whether what you specify as the argument equals ERR. If the test is true, the function returns the value 1; if the test is false, the function returns the value 0. The format for the function is

  @ISERR(cell reference)

The @ISERR function is handy because you can use it to trap errors and thereby keep them from causing other dependent formulas and functions from also returning the ERR value. Figure 6.38 illustrates the mechanics of the @ISERR function and the returned values—both when the test condition is true and when the test condition is false.

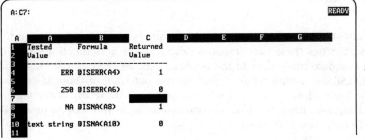

Fig. 6.38.
The @ISERR
and @ISNA
functions used
to test
arguments.

Figure 6.38 also shows the mechanics of the @ISNA function. The @ISNA function works in a fashion similar to that of the @ISERR function. @ISNA tests whether the argument you include is equal to NA. If the test is true, the function returns the value 1; if the test is false, the function returns the value 0. The format for this function is

  @ISNA(cell reference)

You end up using the @ISNA function to trap NA values in worksheets where you have been using the @NA function. The @NA function, which represents "Not Available," is discussed in the "Special Functions" section of this chapter.

@TRUE and @FALSE—Checking for Errors

You use the @TRUE and @FALSE functions to check for errors. Neither function requires arguments. These functions are useful for providing formula and advanced macro command documentation. The @TRUE function returns the value 1, the Boolean logical value for true. The @FALSE function returns the value 0, the Boolean logical value for false.

Figure 6.39 uses an undocumented feature of 1-2-3 Release 3—its capability to perform Boolean logic—along with @TRUE and @FALSE statements to provide easy-to-read @IF functions. The Boolean formulas in cells B3 and B5 (which are displayed because the cell format is Text) perform logical tests just like the @IF statement does. However, rather than returning a user-specified value if the test is true (or false), these formulas return the logical values for true and false: 1 and 0.

Fig. 6.39.
The @TRUE and @FALSE functions used with Boolean logic in @IF statements.

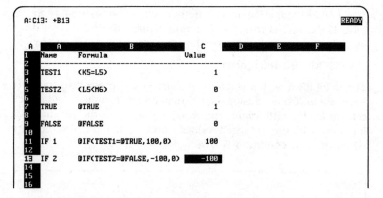

Cells B7 and B9 show the @TRUE and @FALSE functions, and cells C7 and C9 show the logical values these two functions produce. The @IF functions in cells B11 and B13 compare the results of the Boolean logic in TEST1 to @TRUE and TEST2 to @FALSE and return values based on the outcome of these tests. In a sense, Boolean logic allows you to construct logical tests using any of the logical operators, but without using the @IF statement—or, as in this case, a nested IF statement with only one @IF function.

@ISRANGE—Checking for a Range Name

@ISRANGE determines whether the argument that follows the function is a range name. If the argument is a range name, the @ISRANGE function returns a value of 1; if the argument is not a range name, the function returns a value of 0. The format of @ISRANGE is

@ISRANGE(cell reference)

The argument can be either a cell reference to a string or the string itself. The string does not need to be a text label. The string can be either a cell reference containing a text label or a formula that returns a text label.

One of the best uses for @ISRANGE is within macro programs that test for the existence of range names. The following subroutine from a print macro, for example, tests for the existence of the range name INTERRUPT.

```
PRINT    {LOOK INTERRUPT}
         {IF @ISRANGE(INTERRUPT) = 1}{BRANCH ABORT}
         /ppagpq
```

If the range name INTERRUPT exists, then @ISRANGE returns the value 1, making the IF statement true, and the macro branches to another subroutine called ABORT. If INTERRUPT is not a range name, @ISRANGE returns 0, making the IF statement false, and the macro proceeds to the third line of the subroutine.

@ISSTRING and @ISNUMBER—Checking the Cell's Aspect

Before using the contents of a cell, you may want to use functions to test the cell's *aspect*—what type of cell it is, whether contained data is a number or a label, whether the cell is empty. A cell's aspect also concerns the cell's address, the row and column the cell resides in, the cell's label prefix (if any), the width of the cell, and the cell's format. Depending on the characteristics of a cell's aspect, you may need to use different cell-processing methods.

Two functions that help you determine the type of value stored in a cell are @ISSTRING and @ISNUMBER. Although these functions are used most often with the @IF function, they can be used with other types of functions as well. The @ISNUMBER function helps to verify whether a cell entry is a number. The general format of the function is

@ISNUMBER(cell reference)

If the argument is a number, the numeric value of the function is 1 (true)—that is, the argument is a number. If the argument is a string, including the null string (" "), the numeric value of the function is 0 (false)—that is, the argument is not a number.

Suppose, for example, that you want to test whether the value entered in cell B3 is a number. If the value is a number, you want to show the label "number" in the current cell; otherwise, you want to show the label "string". The statement you can use is

@IF(@ISNUMBER(B3),"number","string")

With this statement, you can be fairly certain that the appropriate label will appear in the current cell. The @ISNUMBER function, however, gives the numeric value of 1 to empty cells as well as to numbers, because blank cells actually contain invisible zeros. Obviously, the function itself is incomplete because the function will assign the label "number" to the current cell if cell B3 is empty. For complete reliability, the function must be modified to handle empty cells.

You can distinguish between a number and an empty cell by using the formula that follows. Note that cell AA3 must contain the label B3..B3.

@IF(@ISNUMBER(B3),@IF(@COUNT(@@(AA3)),"number","blank"),"string")

This function first tests whether the cell contains a number or a blank. If so, the function then uses the @COUNT function to test whether the range B3..B3 contains an entry. (Recall that @COUNT assigns a value of 0 to blank cells and a value of 1 to cells with an entry when the argument used is a range rather than a cell reference. See this chapter's discussion of the @COUNT function for a detailed explanation.) If the cell contains an entry, the label "number" is displayed. Otherwise, the label "blank" is displayed. If the cell does not contain a number or a blank, the cell must contain a string with the "string" label displayed.

As an alternative, you may consider using the @ISSTRING function. @ISSTRING works in nearly the same way as @ISNUMBER. @ISSTRING, however, determines whether a cell entry is a string value. The general format of the command is

@ISSTRING(cell reference)

If the argument for the @ISSTRING function is a string, then the value of the function is 1 (true)—the argument is a string. If the argument is a number or blank, however, the value of the function is 0 (false)—the argument is not a string. One nice feature of @ISSTRING is that you can use this function to stop what Lotus calls the "ripple-through" effect of NA and ERR in cells that should have a string value. 1-2-3 considers both NA and ERR as numeric values.

Returning to the earlier example about discriminating between a number and an empty cell, you also can complete the function with the help of @ISSTRING by using the following formula. Note that cell AA3 must contain the label B3..B3.

@IF(@ISSTRING(B3),"string",@IF(@COUNT(@@(AA3))>0,"number","blank"))

The first step that this function performs is to test whether string data is present. If string data is present, then the function assigns the label "string". Otherwise, the @COUNT function is used to determine whether the range B3..B3 contains a number or is empty. If the data is a number, then the label "number" is assigned. Otherwise, the label "blank" is assigned.

@ISNUMBER provides the capability to test for a number, although the function's inability to distinguish between numbers and blank cells is its principal weakness. In many applications, however, @ISNUMBER provides sufficient testing of values, especially when you are certain that a cell is not blank. @ISSTRING provides the capability to test for a string. When used with the @COUNT function, @ISSTRING can distinguish blank cells from strings. The @COUNT function combined with both @ISNUMBER and @ISSTRING can help you distinguish between blank cells and numbers.

Special Functions

The special functions are listed together, in a separate category, because they provide information about cell or range content or worksheet location. @CELL, @CELLPOINTER, and @COORD are three of 1-2-3's most powerful special functions and have many different capabilities. @CELL and @CELLPOINTER can return up to nine different characteristics of a cell. @COORD specifies a cell address as absolute, relative, or mixed. @NA and @ERR allow you to trap errors that might otherwise appear in your worksheet. @ROWS, @COLS, and @SHEETS let you determine the size of a range. The @@ function lets you indirectly reference one cell with another cell within the worksheet. The @CHOOSE, @HLOOKUP, @VLOOKUP, and @INDEX functions let you look up values in tables or lists based on specified keys. Finally, @INFO lets you retrieve system related information. Table 6.8 lists 1-2-3's special functions.

Table 6.8
Special Functions

Function	Description
@@(cell address)	Returns the contents of the cell referenced by the cell address in the argument
@CELL(string,range)	Returns the attribute designated by the string for the cell in the upper-left corner of the range
@CELLPOINTER(string)	Returns the attribute designated by the string for the current cell
@CHOOSE(offset,list)	Locates the specified entry in a list
@COLS(range)	Computes the number of columns in a range
@COORD(worksheet, column,row,absolute)	Constructs a cell address
@ERR	Displays ERR in the cell
@HLOOKUP(key,table, offset)	Locates the specified key in a lookup table and returns a value from that row of the lookup table

Table 6.8—*Continued*

Function	Description
@INDEX(range,column-offset,row-offset,worksheet-offset)	Locates an entry in the specified address in a range
@INFO(attribute)	Retrieves system information
@NA	Displays NA in the cell
@ROWS(range)	Computes the number of rows in a range
@SHEETS(range)	Computes the number of sheets in a range
@VLOOKUP(key,table, offset)	Locates a specified key in a lookup table and returns a value from that column of the lookup table

@@ — Referencing Cells Indirectly

Reminder:
@@ provides a way of indirectly referencing one cell by way of another cell.

The @@ function provides a way of indirectly referencing one cell by way of another cell. The format of the function is

> @@(cell reference)

Simple examples show what the @@ function does. If cell A1 contains the label 'A2, and cell A2 contains the number 5, then the function @@(A1) returns the value 5. If the label in cell A1 is changed to 'B10, and cell B10 contains the label "hi there", the function @@(A1) returns the string value "hi there".

The argument of the @@ function must be a cell reference to the cell containing the indirect address. Similarly, the cell referenced by the argument of the @@ function must contain a string value that evaluates to a cell reference. This cell can contain a label, a string formula, or a reference to another cell, as long as the resulting string value is a cell reference.

The @@ function is useful primarily in situations where several formulas each have the same argument, and the argument must be changed from time to time during the course of the application. 1-2-3 lets you specify the arguments of each formula through a common indirect address, as shown in the example in figure 6.40.

In figure 6.40, column B contains a variety of financial functions, all of which use the @@ function to reference 1 of 7 interest rates in column F indirectly through cell D6. When you are ready to change the cell being referenced, you have to change only the label in cell D6 instead of editing all 6 formulas in column B. Figure 6.41 shows the results of the same formulas after the indirect address has been changed from 'F6 to 'F7.

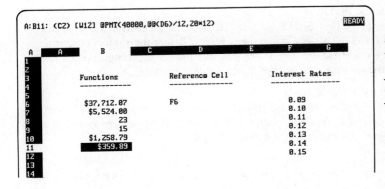

Fig. 6.40.
An example of the @@ function in a series of formulas.

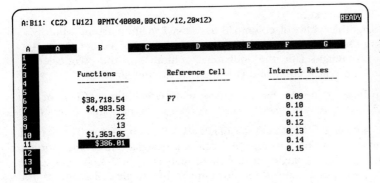

Fig. 6.41.
Formulas using @@ after change of indirect reference.

@CELL and @CELLPOINTER—Checking Cell Attributes

The @CELL and @CELLPOINTER functions provide an efficient way to determine the nature of a cell because these functions return up to nine different characteristics of a cell. The @CELL and @CELLPOINTER functions are used primarily in macros and advanced macro command programs (see Chapters 11 and 12).

Reminder:
@CELL and @CELLPOINTER provide an efficient way to determine the nature of a cell.

The general formats of the @CELL and @CELLPOINTER functions are

@CELL(string,range)

@CELLPOINTER(string)

Both functions have a string argument, which is the aspect of a cell you want to examine. The @CELL function, however, also requires the specification of a range; the @CELLPOINTER function works with the current cell.

The following examples illustrate how the @CELL function can be used to examine some cell attributes:

@CELL("address",SALES)

If the range named SALES is C187..E187, 1-2-3 returns the absolute address $C$187. This is a convenient way of listing the upper-left corner of a range's address in the worksheet. To list all the range names and their addresses, use the /**R**ange **N**ame **T**able command.

@CELL("prefix",C195..C195)

If the cell C195 contains the label 'Chicago, 1-2-3 returns ' (indicating left alignment). If, however, cell C195 is blank, 1-2-3 returns nothing; in other words, the current cell appears blank.

@CELL("format",A10)

1-2-3 changes the second argument to range format (A10..A10) and returns the format of cell A10.

@CELL("width",B12..B12)

1-2-3 returns the width of column B as viewed in the current window regardless of whether that width was set using the /**W**orksheet Column Set-Width command (for the individual column) or the /**W**orksheet Global Column-Width command (for the default column width).

The other attributes that can be examined with either the @CELL or the @CELLPOINTER function are "row", "col", "contents", "type", and "protect".

The difference between @CELL and @CELLPOINTER is important. The @CELL function examines the string attribute of a cell you designate in a range format, such as A1..A1. If you use a single range format, such as A1, 1-2-3 changes to the range format (A1..A1) and returns the attribute of the single-cell range. If you define a range larger than a single cell, 1-2-3 evaluates the cell in the upper-left corner of the range.

On the other hand, the @CELLPOINTER function operates on the current cell— the cell where the cell pointer was positioned when the worksheet was last recalculated. The result remains the same until you enter a value or press the Calc (F9) key if your worksheet is in automatic recalculation mode, or until you press Calc (F9) in manual calculation mode.

For example, to determine the address of the current cell, you can enter @CELLPOINTER("address") in cell B22. If recalculation is set to automatic, the value displayed in that cell is displayed as the absolute address $B$22. This same address remains displayed until you recalculate the worksheet by making an entry elsewhere in the worksheet or by pressing the Calc (F9) key. The address that appears in cell B22 changes to reflect the position of the cell pointer when the worksheet was recalculated. If recalculation is manual, you can change only the address by pressing the Calc (F9) key. Figure 6.42 illustrates the use of the @CELLPOINTER function with all the attributes that can be examined by both the @CELLPOINTER and @CELL functions.

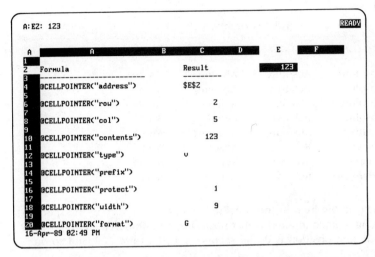

A:E2: 123   READY

A	A	B	C	D	E	F
1						
2	Formula		Result		123	
3	--------------------		---------			
4	@CELLPOINTER("address")		$E$2			
5						
6	@CELLPOINTER("row")		2			
7						
8	@CELLPOINTER("col")		5			
9						
10	@CELLPOINTER("contents")		123			
11						
12	@CELLPOINTER("type")	v				
13						
14	@CELLPOINTER("prefix")					
15						
16	@CELLPOINTER("protect")		1			
17						
18	@CELLPOINTER("width")		9			
19						
20	@CELLPOINTER("format")	G				

16-Apr-89 02:49 PM

Fig. 6.42.
The
@CELLPOINTER
function used
to examine cell
attributes.

@COORD—Creating a Cell Address

Use @COORD to create an absolute, relative, or mixed cell address. The format of @COORD is

@COORD(worksheet,column,row,absolute)

The worksheet argument corresponds to the worksheet containing the cell that is referenced. The column and row arguments refer respectively to the column and row containing the cell address. The last argument, absolute, refers to the exact type of reference—absolute, relative, or mixed—you want the function to return. All of the @COORD function's arguments (worksheet, column, row, absolute) require that you enter numbers:

worksheet   Enter 1–256 (worksheet A = 1, B = 2, C = 3,...IV = 256)

column   Enter 1–256 (column A = 1, B = 2, C = 3,...IV = 256)

row   Enter the row number of the cell (1–8192)

absolute   Enter the number for the type of reference (see table 6.9)

When you use @COORD, the function returns the actual address, not a value.

@CHOOSE—Selecting an Item from a List

The @CHOOSE function selects an item from a list based on the item's position in the list. The format of the function is

@CHOOSE(offset,list)

Reminder:
@CHOOSE selects
an item from a list.

Table 6.9
Values of Absolute

Value	Worksheet	Column	Row	Example
1	Absolute	Absolute	Absolute	$A:$A$1
2	Absolute	Relative	Absolute	$A:A$1
3	Absolute	Absolute	Relative	$A:$A1
4	Absolute	Relative	Relative	$A:A1
5	Relative	Absolute	Absolute	A:$A$1
6	Relative	Relative	Absolute	A:A$1
7	Relative	Absolute	Relative	A:$A1
8	Relative	Relative	Relative	A:A1

The function selects the item in the specified position, or offset, in the specified list. The one thing to keep in mind is that positions are numbered starting with 0. For example, the first position is 0, the second is 1, the third is 2, and so on.

Figure 6.43 shows examples of the @CHOOSE function. The key, or offset, is the specified position. The actual formulas are shown in column B. The list of items, which can be either values or strings, are shown in columns C through F. And the results of the @CHOOSE functions are shown in column H.

Fig. 6.43.
The @CHOOSE function used to select an item from a list.

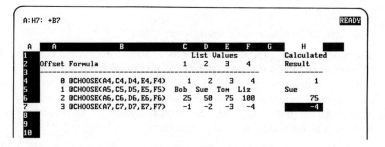

@COLS, @ROWS, and @SHEETS—Finding the Dimensions of Ranges

The @COLS, @ROWS, and @SHEETS functions are used to describe the dimensions of ranges. The general formats of these functions are

@COLS(range)

@ROWS(range)

@SHEETS(range)

Suppose that you want to determine the number of columns in a range called RANDOM, which has the cell coordinates A:D4..C:G9, and display that value in the current cell. The function you enter is @COLS(RANDOM). Similarly, you can enter @ROWS(RANDOM) to display the number of rows in the range and

@SHEETS(RANDOM) to display the number of sheets in the range. Figure 6.44 shows the results of entering @ROWS(RANDOM) in cell B5, @COLS(RANDOM) in cell B7, and @SHEETS(RANDOM) in cell B9.

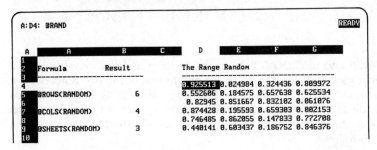

Fig. 6.44.
The @COLS,
@ROWS, and
@SHEETS
functions used
to show range
dimensions.

If you specify a single cell (such as C3) as the argument for the @COLS, @ROWS, or @SHEETS function, 1-2-3 changes the argument to range format (C3..C3) and returns the value 1 for the function.

@ERR and @NA—Trapping Errors

If you find yourself in a situation in which you simply don't know what number to enter for a value, but you don't want to leave the cell blank, you can enter @NA (for "Not Available"). 1-2-3 then displays NA in that cell and in any other cell that depends on that cell.

Another condition that you may encounter, particularly when you are setting up templates for other people, is that of screening out unacceptable values for cells. For example, suppose that you are developing a checkbook-balancing macro in which checks with values less than or equal to zero are unacceptable. One way to indicate the unacceptability of these checks is to use ERR to signal that fact. You might use the following version of the @IF function:

@IF(B9<=0,@ERR,B9)

In simple English, this statement says: "If the amount in cell B9 is less than or equal to zero, then display ERR on the screen; otherwise, use the amount." Notice that the @ERR function controls the display in almost the same way that @NA does in a previous example.

1-2-3 also uses ERR as a signal for unacceptable numbers—for example, a division by zero or mistakenly deleted cells. ERR often shows up temporarily when you are reorganizing the cells in a worksheet. If the ERR message persists, however, you may have to do some careful analysis to figure out why.

As it does for NA, 1-2-3 displays ERR in any cells that depend on a cell with an ERR value. Sometimes many cells display ERR after you delete rows or columns that contain cells on which other formulas depend. To correct the errors, you must trace back through the chain of references to find the root of the problem. Making a change in the worksheet, such as deleting columns and rows, causes cells to display ERR. Use Undo (Alt-F4) to return to the worksheet as it was before the change. See Chapter 3 for more information about Undo.

@HLOOKUP and @VLOOKUP—Looking Up Entries in a Table

The @HLOOKUP and @VLOOKUP functions retrieve a string or value from a table based on a specified key. The operation and format of the two functions are essentially the same except the @HLOOKUP function looks through horizontal tables (hence, the H in the function's name), and the @VLOOKUP function looks through vertical tables (the source of the V in its name). The formats of the two functions are as follows:

@HLOOKUP(key,range row,offset)

@VLOOKUP(key,range column,offset)

Keys are values in labels that the LOOKUP command uses to search through the list. Essentially, what 1-2-3 does is compare the key specified as one of the arguments with the contents of each cell in the first row or column of the table, looking for a cell whose contents match the key.

Cue:
When you use numeric keys, make sure that the key values ascend in order.

When you use numeric keys, make sure that the key values ascend in order. If they don't, you may get an ERR. (In contrast, if the keys are strings, the keys can be listed in any order.) Also, with numeric keys, the LOOKUP function is actually searching for the largest value that is less than or equal to the key. Therefore, if the LOOKUP function can't find a value that is equal, the function will pick the largest value that is less than the key.

The range argument is the area making up the entire lookup table. Offset specifies which row or column contains the data you are looking up. The offset argument is always a number, in ascending order, ranging from 1 to the highest number of columns or rows in the lookup table. Number 1 marks the first column to the right of the column containing key data or the first row below the row containing key data. When you specify an offset number, it cannot be negative or exceed the correct number of columns or rows.

The best way to grasp the mechanics of either LOOKUP function is by reviewing examples. Figure 6.45 shows one @HLOOKUP and two @VLOOKUP functions, which together demonstrate the principles of 1-2-3's LOOKUP functions.

The first function, @HLOOKUP, finds the key E in the range defined as D2..H3. If the LOOKUP is successful, the function retrieves the contents of the offset row numbered 1—the value 4. Notice that as with the @CHOOSE function, offset numbering starts at 0. The result of the @HLOOKUP function in cell B3 is shown in cell B4 as 4.

Keep in mind that both the @HLOOKUP and @VLOOKUP functions just read through and retrieve data from the ranges. The functions make no changes to any of the cells within the range.

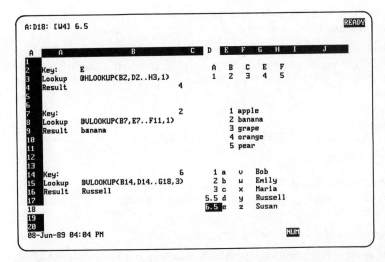

Fig. 6.45.
The
@HLOOKUP
and
@VLOOKUP
functions used
to retrieve
strings and
values from
tables.

Figure 6.45 also shows examples of two @VLOOKUP functions. The first @VLOOKUP, shown in cell B8, looks through the vertical table located in the worksheet range E7..F11 looking for an entry with a numeric key value of 2. The function succeeds and then returns the string from the number 1 offset column—*banana*. The key is shown in cell B7, the @VLOOKUP function in cell B8, and the result of the @VLOOKUP function in cell B9.

The second @VLOOKUP function, shown in cell B15, looks through the vertical table located in the worksheet range D14..G18 looking for an entry with a numeric key value of 6. If you take a look at figure 6.45, you see that no entries in the table have a key value of 6. When this is the case, a LOOKUP function picks the table entry with the largest key value that doesn't exceed the argument key.

Watch for three common errors when you construct @HLOOKUP and @VLOOKUP functions. First, when you use a string as the key argument, the LOOKUP function returns an error if the function can't find the string in the LOOKUP table. If a LOOKUP function with a string key returns ERR, first check that you haven't misspelled the string either in the function or in the LOOKUP table.

A second common error is omitting the columns or rows that contain the key, and value or string, you want returned in the LOOKUP table argument; this situation also generates an ERR condition. The examples in figure 6.45 use cell addresses to specify the table so that the example is easy to understand. However, you probably will want to name your LOOKUP tables, and that can make spotting missing rows or columns tricky.

When you do use named ranges for a table argument, make sure that the named range includes both the key column or row and the offset column or row. Accordingly, if you use an @HLOOKUP function with the offset row argument set to 6, your table range should include at least 7 rows. Alternatively, if you use a

@VLOOKUP function with the offset column argument set to 3, your table range should include at least 4 columns.

A third problem, which is simple to avoid or correct, is to remember that the key strings or values belong in the first column or row, and that column and row numbering starts at 0. Accordingly, the first offset is 0, the second is 1, the third is 2, and so on.

@INDEX—Retrieving Data from Specified Locations

@INDEX, a data management function, is similar to the table-lookup functions described earlier. However, @INDEX has some unique features. The general format of the function is

@INDEX(range,column-offset,row-offset,worksheet-offset)

Like the table-lookup functions, the @INDEX function works with a table of numbers. But unlike the table-lookup functions, the @INDEX function does not use a test variable and a comparison column (or row). Instead, the @INDEX function requires you to indicate the column-offset and row-offset of the range from which you want to retrieve data. For example, the following function, shown in figure 6.46, returns the value 2625:

@INDEX(L142..S145,3,2)

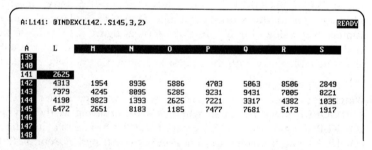

Fig. 6.46.
An example of
the @INDEX
function.

A:L141: @INDEX(L142..S145,3,2)								READY
A	L	M	N	O	P	Q	R	S
139								
140								
141	2625							
142	4313	1954	8936	5886	4703	5063	8506	2849
143	7979	4245	8095	5285	9231	9431	7005	8221
144	4190	9823	1393	2625	7221	3317	4382	1035
145	6472	2651	8183	1185	7477	7681	5173	1917
146								
147								
148								

Notice that the number 0 corresponds to the first column, 1 corresponds to the second column, and so on. The same numbering scheme applies to rows. Using 3 for the column-offset and 2 for the row-offset indicates that you want an item from the fourth column, third row.

Reminder:
With the @INDEX
function, you
cannot use
column, row, or
worksheet numbers
that fall outside the
relevant range.

With the @INDEX function, you cannot use column, row, or worksheet numbers that fall outside the relevant range. Using either negative numbers or numbers too large for the range causes 1-2-3 to return the ERR message.

The @INDEX function is useful when you know the exact position of a data item in a range of cells and want to locate the item quickly. For instance, the @INDEX function works well for rate quotation systems. Figure 6.47 shows an example of a system for quoting full-page magazine advertising rates.

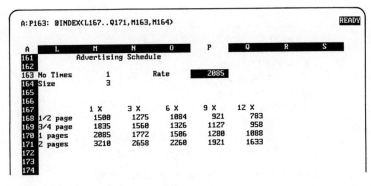

Fig. 6.47.
The @INDEX
function used
for advertising
rate quotations.

In this example, the following function returns a value of 2085:

@INDEX(L167..Q171,M163,M164)

This value corresponds to the amount in the first column and the third row of the index range. If a 6 is entered for the frequency (in this example, the number of times an ad is run), the ERR message appears instead of a valid dollar amount.

The worksheet-offset number allows you to work in three-dimensional ranges. Offset numbering starts at zero: the first worksheet in a range is specified as 0; the second as 1; and so on. The worksheet-offset argument is optional.

@INFO—Getting Current Session System Information

The @INFO function, new to Release 3, allows you to tap 11 types of system information about the current session. Table 6.10 summarizes the 11 attributes you can check using the @INFO function.

Table 6.10
Session Attributes

Attribute	Description
"directory"	Returns the current directory
"memavail"	Returns the memory available
"mode"	Returns numeric code indicating mode:
	0 = WAIT mode
	1 = READY mode
	2 = LABEL mode
	3 = MENU mode
	4 = VALUE mode
	5 = POINT mode
	6 = EDIT mode
	7 = ERROR mode

Attribute	Description
	8 = FIND mode
	9 = FILES mode
	10 = HELP mode
	11 = STAT mode
	13 = NAMES mode
	99 = All other modes (such as those set by the {INDICATE} command)
"numfile"	Returns the number of currently open files
"origin"	Returns the cell address of the first cell in the window with the cell pointer
"osreturncode"	Returns the value returned by the most recent /System or {SYSTEM} command
"osversion"	Returns the current operating system description
"recalc"	Returns the current recalculation setting
"release"	Returns the 1-2-3 release number, upgrade level, and revision number
"system"	Returns the name of the operating system
"totmem"	Returns the total amount of memory

Figure 6.48 shows examples of the @INFO function in action.

Fig. 6.48.
The @INFO
function
returning on
11 system
attributes.

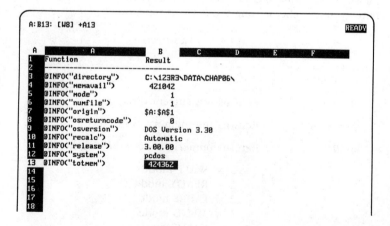

Date and Time Functions

1-2-3's date and time functions allow you to convert dates such as November 26, 1989, and times such as 6:00 p.m. to serial numbers and then use these serial numbers in date arithmetic and time arithmetic—a valuable aid when dates and times affect worksheet calculations and logic.

As you review the examples showing the mechanics of the 1-2-3 date and time functions, you should develop a better appreciation of their potential contributions to your worksheets. The date and time functions available in 1-2-3 are summarized in table 6.11.

Table 6.11
Date and Time Functions

Function	Description
@D360(date1,date2)	Calculates the number of days between two dates based on a 360-day year
@DATE(y,m,d)	Calculates the serial number that represents the described date
@DATEVALUE(date string)	Converts a date expressed as a string into a serial number
@DAY(date)	Extracts the day number from a serial number
@HOUR(time)	Extracts the hour number from a serial number
@MINUTE(time)	Extracts the minute number from a serial number
@MONTH(date)	Extracts the month number from a serial number
@NOW	Calculates the serial date and time from the current system date and time
@SECOND(time)	Extracts the second number from a serial number
@TIME(h,m,s)	Calculates the serial number that represents the described time
@TIMEVALUE(time string)	Converts a time expressed as a string into a serial number
@TODAY	Calculates the serial number for the current system date
@YEAR(date)	Extracts the year number from a serial number

@D360—Dealing with 360-Day Years

The @D360 function allows you to calculate the number of days between two dates based on a 360-day year. Both date arguments must be expressed as valid serial numbers; otherwise, the function returns the ERR value. The format of the function is

@D360(date1,date2)

The @D360 function should prove helpful in those situations where interest calculations are made assuming a 360-day year—as is often the case. Figure 6.49 shows, for example, the number of days between January 1, 1989, and January 1, 1990, and the number of days between January 1, 1989, and July 1, 1990, based on a 360-day year.

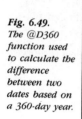

Fig. 6.49.
The @D360 function used to calculate the difference between two dates based on a 360-day year.

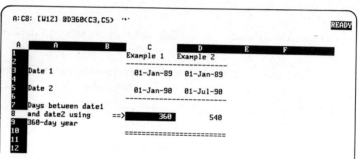

@DATE—Converting Date Values to Serial Numbers

The first step in using dates in arithmetic operations is to convert then to actual numbers, or serial numbers, that you can then use in addition, subtraction, multiplication, and division operations. Given this, probably the most frequently used date function is @DATE. The @DATE function converts any date into a number you can use in arithmetic operations—and, as importantly, that 1-2-3 can view as a date. The @DATE function uses the format

@DATE(year,month,day)

You identify a year, month, or day using numbers. For example, the date November 26, 1959, which also can be expressed as 11-26-59 would be entered into the @DATE function as follows:

@DATE(59,11,26)

The numbers you enter to represent the year, month, and day need to make up a valid date, or 1-2-3 returns an ERR. For example, 1-2-3 is programmed so that you can specify the day argument in February as 29 only during leap years, and you never can specify the day as 30 or 31 for February. When you specify the month as 1, which represents January, 30 and 31 are valid day arguments because January has 31 days.

As you begin using the @DATE function, keep a couple of guidelines in mind. First, the internal 1-2-3 calendar starts with the serial number 1, the first date that 1-2-3 recognizes, and that serial number represents January 1, 1900. A single day is represented by the increment 1; 1-2-3 represents January 2, 1900, as 2.

Second, even though 1900 wasn't a leap year, 1-2-3 assigns the serial number 60 to the date February 29, 1900. Although generally this should not be a problem, you may have problems if you transfer data between 1-2-3 and other programs. If this is the case, you will need to adjust for this error yourself. To do so, subtract 1 from serial numbers that represent dates between January 1, 1900, and March 1, 1900.

Figure 6.50 shows an example of the @DATE function being used to calculate the number of days between the date a loan is originated and the date the loan is paid off. In cases where the lender calculated interest charges using daily compounding, this information would be necessary to calculate the final interest charges.

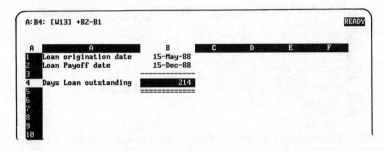

Fig. 6.50.
The @DATE function expressing dates as serial numbers you can use in mathematical operations.

Note that the serial dates used in figure 6.50 appear as dates even though they are actually just numbers. Using the /Range Format Date command sequence, you can format serial numbers that represent dates to appear in one of several ways. When you format the dates, 1-2-3 still works with the dates as serial numbers, but you see the dates in reports and on-screen in formats that you recognize and understand as dates. (The /Range Format commands and the various Date and Time formats available are discussed in detail in Chapter 5, "Formatting Cell Contents.")

@DATEVALUE—Changing Date Strings to Serial Numbers

@DATEVALUE computes the serial number for a string that looks like one of the 1-2-3 date formats you might have set using the /Range Format command. The general format of the function is

@DATEVALUE(date string)

You need to construct the date string by including one of the five 1-2-3 date formats or by referencing a cell that contains one of the valid date formats. If the string doesn't look like a formatted date, 1-2-3 returns the ERR value; if it does, 1-2-3 returns the serial number.

Note: If you have reset the default date format for 1-2-3 using the /Worksheet Global Default Other International Date command, you need to use the International Date format you set as the default as the date string for the @DATEVALUE function. For example, if you reset the default date format to (MM/DD/YY), you need to enter the date December 27, 1982, as @DATEVALUE("12/27/82").

Figure 6.51 shows the @DATEVALUE function converting into serial numbers the date strings that mirror each of the five standard date formats. Column A shows the 1-2-3 date format name; column B shows the date string; column C, the format of the @DATEVALUE function; and column D, the results of the @DATEVALUE function formatted to look like the corresponding date string in column B.

Fig. 6.51.
The
@DATEVALUE
function used
to convert date
strings to serial
date numbers.

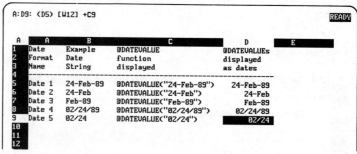

Because no year is included in the date string for the second and fifth date formats, 1-2-3 assumes that the year is the same as the system date year—or in these cases, 1989. Because no day is included in the date string for the third format, 1-2-3 assumes that the day is the first day of the month. You will want to keep these assumptions in mind and verify that they are appropriate for your specific application.

@DAY, @MONTH, and @YEAR—Converting Serial Numbers to Dates

The @DAY, @MONTH, and @YEAR functions convert serial numbers to dates. The formats of those functions are as follows:

@DAY(date)

@MONTH(date)

@YEAR(date)

The @DAY function accepts a valid serial number as its single argument and returns the day of the month—which is a number from 1 to 31. The @MONTH function accepts a valid serial date number as its single argument and returns the month of the year—which is a number from 1 to 12. The @YEAR function accepts a valid serial date number as its single argument and returns the number of the year—which is a number from 0 (1900) to 199 (2099). Figure 6.52 illustrates the mechanics of these three helpful date functions, which let you extract just the component of a date—year, month, or day—that you want to manipulate.

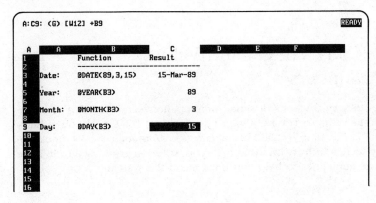

Fig. 6.52.
The @YEAR, @MONTH, and @DAY functions used to extract parts of date serial numbers.

@NOW and @TODAY—Finding the Current Date and Time

1-2-3 provides two functions that extract the date, or date and time information from the system date and time. The @NOW function retrieves both the current system date and current system time as a serial number. The decimal places to the left of the decimal point are used to specify the date; the decimal places to the right of the decimal point are used to specify the time. The @TODAY function is similar to the @NOW function except that it retrieves only the system date, and not the system time. Assuming that you either enter the current date and time when you boot your computer or that you have an internal clock that keeps the date and time for you, these two functions provide a convenient tool for recording the dates and times worksheets are modified or printed. Neither function requires any arguments.

Figure 6.53 illustrates the results of using both functions. Column B shows the serial numbers, which represent the system date and time. Column C shows the two serial numbers formatted as dates. Column D shows the results of the functions, formatted to show the current system time.

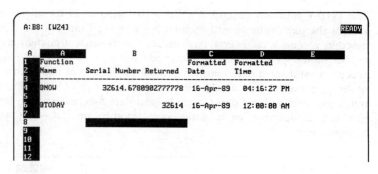

Fig. 6.53.
The @NOW and @TODAY functions used to insert the date and time on a worksheet.

@TIME—Converting Time Values to Serial Numbers

1-2-3 expresses time in fractions of serial numbers between 0 and 1. For example, 0.5 is equal to 12 hours (or 12:00 p.m.). In addition, 1-2-3 works on military time; 10:00 p.m. in U.S. time is 22:00 in military time. Although 1-2-3's timekeeping system may seem a little awkward at first, you will soon grow used to it. Here are some general guidelines to help you understand the system:

Time increment	Numeric equivalent
1 hour	0.0416666667
1 minute	0.0006944444
1 second	0.0000115741

The @TIME function produces a serial number for a specified time of day. The general format of the function is

@TIME(hour number,minute number,second number)

The @TIME function can be used to produce a range of times just as the @DATE function can be used to generate a range of dates. One way to produce a range of times is to use the /Date Fill command. For example, to produce a range of times from 8:00 a.m. to 5:00 p.m. in 15-minute increments, use the following steps:

1. Select /**D**ate **F**ill.

2. Specify the range where you want the times to appear, and then press Enter.

3. Enter @TIME(8,0,0) as the Start value and press Enter.

4. Enter @TIME(0,15,0) as the Step value and press Enter.

5. Enter @TIME(17,0,0) as the Stop value and press Enter.

6. Use /**R**ange **F**ormat **D**ate **T**ime to display the range in whatever time format you choose, and expand the column widths as necessary.

In figure 6.54, B4..D17 was selected as the range for the times to appear, and the results were formatted with **Time 1**.

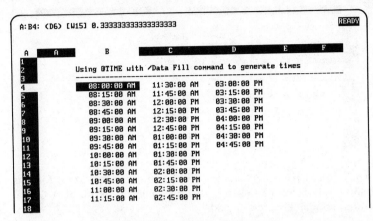

Fig. 6.54.
An example of the @TIME function.

The numeric arguments have certain restrictions. First, the hour number must be between 0 and 23. Second, both the minute number and second number must be between 0 and 59. Finally, although 1-2-3 accepts numeric arguments that contain integers and decimals, only the integer portion is used.

After a time has been interpreted by 1-2-3 as a fraction of a serial number, you can use the /Range Format Date Time command to display the time in a more recognizable way (for example, 10:42 p.m.). 1-2-3's time formats are discussed in the text about @TIMEVALUE that follows.

@TIMEVALUE—Converting Time Strings to Serial Values

Just like @DATEVALUE and @DATE, @TIMEVALUE is a variation of @TIME. Like @TIME, @TIMEVALUE produces a serial number from the hour, minute, and second information you supply to the function. Unlike @TIME, however, @TIMEVALUE uses string arguments rather than numeric arguments. The general format of the function is

@TIMEVALUE(time string)

The time string must appear in one of the four time formats: T1, T2, T3, or T4. If the string conforms to one of the time formats, 1-2-3 displays the appropriate serial number fraction. If you then format the cell, 1-2-3 displays the appropriate time of day. Figure 6.55 shows the results of using the @TIMEVALUE function with the four different acceptable time strings.

The first two time formats, T1 and T2, accept times from 12:00 a.m. to 11:59 a.m., and from 12:00 p.m. to 11:59 p.m. The last two time formats, which Lotus calls International Time formats, accept military time from 00:00 (12 a.m.) to

Reminder:
If the string you supply doesn't conform to an acceptable format, 1-2-3 returns the ERR value.

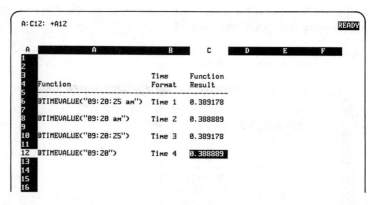

Fig. 6.55.
*An example of
the
@TIMEVALUE
function.*

23:59 (11:59 p.m.). The separator character for the International Time formats defaults to a colon (:), but you can change this by using the /Worksheet Global Default Other International Time command.

@SECOND, @MINUTE, and @HOUR— Converting Serial Numbers to Time Values

The @SECOND, @MINUTE, and @HOUR functions allow you to extract different units of time from a numeric time fraction. The formats of these functions are

@SECOND(time)

@MINUTE(time)

@HOUR(time)

Figure 6.56 shows that these three functions are, in a sense, the reverse of the @TIME function, just as the @DAY, @MONTH, and @YEAR functions are the reverse of the @DATE function.

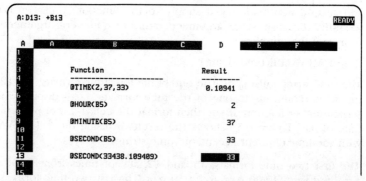

Fig. 6.56.
*The @SECOND,
@MINUTE, and
@HOUR
functions
compared to
the @TIME
function.*

Notice that the argument includes both an integer and a decimal portion. Although the integer portion is important for date functions, it is disregarded for time functions, as illustrated by the last example in the figure. You can use these functions for various time-related chores, such as developing a time schedule.

String Functions

1-2-3 has a variety of functions that give the user significant power to manipulate strings. *Strings* are labels or portions of labels. More specifically, strings are units of data consisting of connected characters (alphabetic, numeric, blank, and special) that are delimited by quotation marks (""). The functions specifically designated as string functions are not the only 1-2-3 functions that take advantage of the power and flexibility of strings. For example, logical, error-trapping, and special functions use strings as well as values. The string functions, however, are specifically designed to manipulate strings. Table 6.12 summarizes the string functions available in 1-2-3.

Table 6.12
String Functions

Function	Description
@FIND(search string, overall string, start number)	Locates the start position of one string within another string
@MID(string,start position,length)	Extracts the specified number of characters from a string, beginning with the character start position
@LEFT(string,length)	Extracts the leftmost specified number of characters from the string
@RIGHT(string,length)	Extracts the rightmost specified number of characters from the string
@REPLACE(original string,start number, length,replacement string)	Substitutes the specified number of characters from the original string, with the replacement string at the character start number
@LENGTH(string)	Displays the number of characters in the string
@EXACT(string1,string2)	Returns TRUE if string1 and string2 are exact matches; otherwise, returns FALSE
@LOWER(string)	Converts all characters in the string to lowercase
@UPPER(string)	Converts all characters in the string to uppercase

Table 6.12—*Continued*

Function	Description
@PROPER(string)	Converts the first character in each word in the string to uppercase, and the remaining characters to lowercase
@REPEAT(string,number)	Copies the string the specified number of times in a cell
@TRIM(string)	Extracts blank spaces from the string
@N(range)	Returns the value contained in the cell in the upper-left corner of the range
@S(range)	Returns the string value of the cell in the upper-left corner of the range
@STRING(number to convert,decimal places)	Converts a value to a string showing the specified number of decimal places
@VALUE(string)	Converts a string to a value
@CLEAN(string)	Removes nonprintable characters from the string
@CHAR(number)	Converts a code number into an ASCII/ LMBCS character
@CODE(string)	Converts the first character in the string into an ASCII/LMBCS code

Reminder:
You can link strings to other strings using the concatenation operator (&). You cannot link strings to blank cells or to cells containing numeric values.

Strings can be linked to other strings by using the concatenation operator (&). The discussion of the individual string functions in this section shows several examples of the use of the concatenation operator. Keep in mind that you can't link strings to cells that contain numeric values or that are empty. If you try, 1-2-3 returns an ERR value.

Avoid mixing data types in string functions. For instance, some functions produce strings, whereas others produce numeric results. Be careful not to combine functions from these two different groups unless you have taken all the precautions regarding string functions discussed throughout this section.

The numbering scheme for positioning characters in a label is also something to watch for when using string functions. These positions are numbered beginning with zero and continuing to a number corresponding to the last character in the label. The following example shows the position numbers (0 to 24) for a long label:

```
          111111111122222
0123456789012345678901234
'two chickens in every pot
```

The prefix (') before the label does not have a number because the prefix is not considered part of the label. Nor are negative position numbers allowed. The importance of position numbers is explained further in the next section.

@FIND—Locating One String within Another

@FIND, one of the simplest string functions, is the best function for showing how position numbers are used in strings. The @FIND function locates the starting position of one string within another string. For instance, you could use this function to find at what position the string "every" occurs within the string "two chickens in every pot". The general format of @FIND is

@FIND(search string,overall string,start number)

The search string is the string you want to locate. In this example, the search string is "every". The overall string is the target string to be searched. In this example, "two chickens in every pot" is the overall string. Finally, the start number is the position number in the overall string where you want to start the search. If you want to start at position 6 and you are using the overall string located in cell A2, the function you use is @FIND("every",A2,6), as shown in figure 6.57.

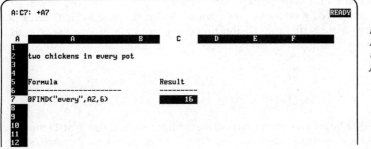

Fig. 6.57.
An example of the @FIND function.

Your result is the number 16—the position of the first (and only) occurrence of "every" in the overall string. If the search string "every" was not found in the overall string, the ERR message would be displayed.

In the example, notice that choosing the start number of 6 has no bearing on the outcome of the function. You could just as easily choose 0 (or any other number less than or equal to 16) for the starting position of the search string. If "every" appeared more than once in the overall string, however, the start number could locate its occurrence elsewhere. Suppose that the following overall string appears in cell A2:

'two chickens in every pot, two cars in every garage

Now suppose that you want to locate all the occurrences of "every" in the overall string. The function @FIND("every",A2,6) returns a value of 16, as before. Try changing the start number by adding 1 to the result of the original function

$(1+16=17)$. The appropriate function is now @FIND("every",A2,17). This new function returns the number 39, the starting location of the second occurrence of "every". Next, add 1 to the second result $(1+39=40)$ and use @FIND("every",A2,40). The resulting ERR message tells you that you have found all the occurrences of the search string. Figure 6.58 shows the results of using different position numbers.

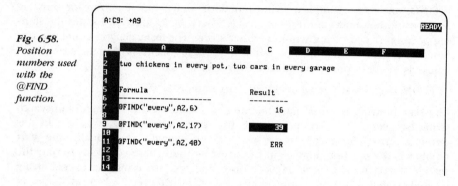

Fig. 6.58.
Position
numbers used
with the
@FIND
function.

```
A:C9: +A9                                                    READY

    A          A            B        C        D       E       F
1
2   two chickens in every pot, two cars in every garage
3
4
5   Formula                          Result
6   ---------------------            --------
7   @FIND("every",A2,6)                 16
8
9   @FIND("every",A2,17)                39
10
11  @FIND("every",A2,40)                ERR
12
13
14
```

Reminder:
@FIND performs
only exact
searches; upper-
and lowercase are
significant.

Keep in mind a few general rules when you use the @FIND function. First, @FIND (like string functions in general) limits a string to 240 characters. Second, any decimals in a start number are ignored by 1-2-3. Finally, any search string must be entered exactly as you want to find it because @FIND does not perform approximate searching. In the preceding example, if you use a search string of "Every" instead of "every", you get the ERR message instead of a number value.

@MID—Extracting One String from Another

Whereas @FIND helps you locate one string within another, the @MID function lets you extract one string from another. This operation is called *substringing*. The general format of the function is

@MID(string,start position,length)

The start position is a number representing the character position in the string where you want to begin extracting characters. The length argument indicates the number of characters to extract. For example, to extract the first name from a label containing the full name "Page Davidson", use

@MID("Page Davidson",0,4)

Cue:
Use @MID with
@FIND to extract
first and last
names from a list
of full names.

This function extracts the string starting in position 0 (the first character) and continuing for a length of 4 characters—the string "Page".

Now suppose that you want to extract the first and last names from a column list of full names and put those two names in a separate column. To accomplish this, use the @MID and @FIND functions together. Because you know that a blank space will always separate the first and last names, @FIND can locate the position of the blank in each full name. Using this value, you can then set up the functions to extract the first and last names.

If cell A8 contains the full name "Ivan Andersen", as shown in figure 6.59, place in cell B8 the function

@MID(A8,0,@FIND(" ",A8,0))

The value of this function will appear as "Ivan" because @FIND(" ",A8,0) will return a value of 4 for the length argument.

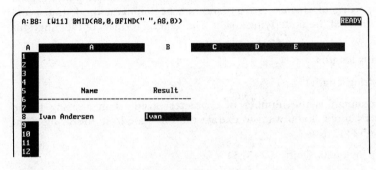

Fig. 6.59.
The @MID
function used
to extract a
substring.

Next place the following function in cell C8, as shown in figure 6.60:

@MID(A8,@FIND(" ",A8,0)+1,99)

The @FIND function indicates that the start position is one character beyond the blank space. In addition, the length of the string to be extracted is 99 characters. Although a length of 99 is greater than you need, there is no penalty for this excess. The string that 1-2-3 extracts is "Andersen".

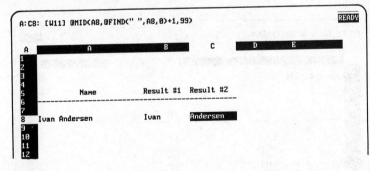

Fig. 6.60.
The @MID and
@FIND
functions used
to locate and
extract first
and last names.

Now that you have seen how the @MID and @FIND functions can separate first and last names, you may want to try using these functions in a case with a name containing a middle initial. Suppose, for example, that you replace the name in figure 6.60 with Ivan G. Andersen—adding the middle initial G. If you want to separate the last name from the first name and middle initial, enter the following formula:

@MID(A8,@FIND(" ",A8,0)+3,99)

In this formula, the @FIND function indicates that the start position is three characters beyond the first blank space—accounting for the middle initial of the last name.

@LEFT and @RIGHT—Extracting Strings from Left and Right

@LEFT and @RIGHT are special variations of the @MID function and are used to extract one string of characters from another, beginning at the leftmost and rightmost positions in the underlying string. The general formats of the functions are

@LEFT(string,length)

@RIGHT(string,length)

Cue:
Use @RIGHT to extract the ZIP code from an address.

The length argument is the number of character positions in a string to be extracted. For example, if you want to extract the ZIP code from the string "Cincinnati, Ohio 45243", use

@RIGHT("Cincinnati, Ohio 45243",5)

@LEFT works the same way as @RIGHT except that @LEFT extracts from the beginning of a string. For instance, use the following function statement to extract the city in the preceding example:

@LEFT("Cincinnati, Ohio 45243",10)

In most cases, use @FIND(",","Cincinnati, Ohio 45243",0) instead of 10 for the length in the function to extract the city from the address. Figure 6.61 shows the results of using @LEFT and @RIGHT with varying length arguments.

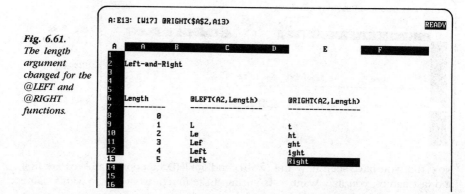

Fig. 6.61.
The length argument changed for the @LEFT and @RIGHT functions.

@REPLACE—Replacing a String within a String

The @REPLACE function removes a group of characters from a string and replaces the characters with another string. The @REPLACE function is a valuable tool for correcting a text entry without retyping the entire string. @REPLACE numbers the character positions in a string, starting with zero and continuing to the end of the string (up to a maximum of 239). The general format of the function is

@REPLACE(original string,start number,length,replacement string)

The start number argument indicates the position where 1-2-3 will begin removing characters in the original string. The length shows how many characters to remove, and the replacement string contains the new characters to replace the removed ones.

Suppose, for example, that the string "This is the original string" appears in cell A2. Figure 6.62 shows several examples of how to use @REPLACE to change words in the string. Notice in the third example in the figure that you can use the @FIND function to locate the string you want to replace instead of starting at 0 and counting the 12 positions to find the start number.

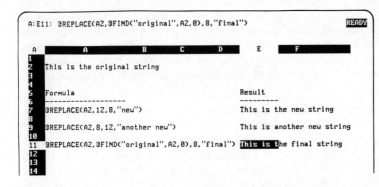

Fig. 6.62.
The @REPLACE function used to alter a string.

@LENGTH — Computing the Length of a String

The @LENGTH function simply indicates the length of your strings. The general format of the function is

@LENGTH(string)

Figure 6.63 shows how @LENGTH can be used to find the length of a string. Notice that the function returns the value ERR as the length of numeric values or formulas, empty cells, and null strings.

@EXACT — Comparing Strings

The @EXACT function compares two strings, returning a value of 1 for strings that are alike and 0 for strings that are not alike. The general format of the function is

@EXACT(string1,string2)

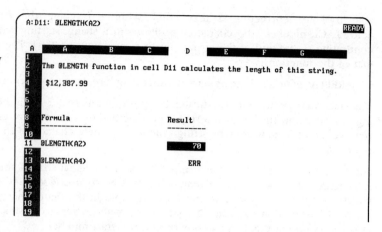

Fig. 6.63.
The @LENGTH function used to find the length of a string.

@EXACT's method of comparison is like the = operator in formulas except that the = operator checks for an approximate match, and the @EXACT function checks for an exact match. For example, if cell A2 holds the string "Marketing Function" and cell B2 holds the string "marketing function", the numeric value of A2=B2 is 1 because the two strings are an approximate match. Conversely, the numeric value of @EXACT(A2,B2) is 0 because the two functions are not an exact match.

Cue:
Use the @S function to ensure that the argument of @EXACT is a string.

The examples in figure 6.64 demonstrate the use of @EXACT. Notice in the third example that @EXACT cannot compare nonstring arguments. If you try to compare the entry in cell A6 with the blank cell C6, the value of @EXACT(A6,C6) is ERR. In fact, if either argument is a nonstring value of any type (including numbers), 1-2-3 returns the ERR value. (Note that you can use the @S function, explained later in this chapter, to ensure that the arguments used with @EXACT have string values.)

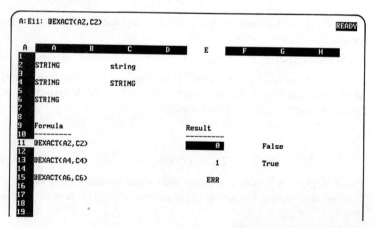

Fig. 6.64.
Strings compared with the @EXACT function.

@LOWER, @UPPER, and @PROPER— Converting the Case of Strings

1-2-3 offers three different functions for converting the case of a string value:

@LOWER(string)   Converts all uppercase letters in a string to lowercase letters

@UPPER(string)   Raises all the letters in a string to uppercase letters; the opposite of @LOWER

@PROPER(string)   Capitalizes the first letter in each word of a label. (Words are defined as groups of characters separated by blank spaces.) @PROPER goes on to convert the remaining letters in each word to lowercase.

Figure 6.65 gives an example of the use of each function.

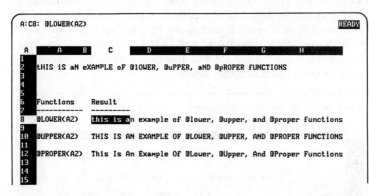

Fig. 6.65. Functions used to convert the case of alphanumeric strings.

As you might expect, none of these three functions works with nonstring values. For instance, if cell E9 contains a number or a null string (" "), 1-2-3 returns ERR for each of these functions. (Note that you can use the @S function, explained later in this chapter, to ensure that the arguments of these functions have string values.)

@REPEAT—Repeating Strings within a Cell

The @REPEAT function repeats strings within a cell much as the backslash (\) repeats characters. But @REPEAT has some distinct advantages over the backslash. @REPEAT lets you repeat the character the precise number of times you want—which may be different than the column width in characters. The general format of the function is

    @REPEAT(string,number)

The number argument indicates the number of times you want to repeat a string in a cell. For example, if you want to repeat the string "COGS" three times, you

Reminder: @REPEAT copies characters beyond the current column width.

can enter @REPEAT("COGS",3). The resulting string will be "COGSCOGSCOGS". This string follows 1-2-3's rule for long labels. That is, the string will be displayed beyond the right boundary of the column, provided that no entry is in the cell to the right. When you use the backslash to repeat a string, however, 1-2-3 will fill the column to the exact column width. If the string doesn't fit within the column width, 1-2-3 truncates it.

You can set up a function to fill a cell almost exactly by using the @CELL and @LENGTH functions. If A3 is the cell you want to fill by repeating the string "COGS", the first step is to enter @CELL("width",A3..A3) in an out-of-the-way cell, such as K4. The next step is to enter @LENGTH("COGS") in K5, another out-of-the-way cell. The final step is to enter the following in cell A3:

@REPEAT("COGS",K4/K5)

If the width of column A is 9 (the default column width), the label that appears in cell A3 is "COGSCOGS". Notice that because @REPEAT uses only the integer portion of the number argument, "COGS" is repeated only twice rather than 2.25 times. The @REPEAT function in figure 6.66 shows you how to generate a dashed line that is one character less than the column width of the current cell. You can enter the formula shown in the figure in one cell and then use the Copy command to copy it to any other appropriate cell in the worksheet. If you use this technique, do not reference in the @CELL function a cell that contains a formula; otherwise, a circular reference may result.

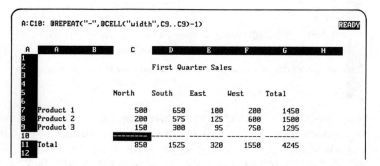

Fig. 6.66.
The @REPEAT
function used
to generate
dashed lines.

@TRIM—Removing Blank Spaces from a String

The @TRIM(string) function can take out unwanted blank spaces from the beginning, end, or middle of a string. The format for the function is

@TRIM(string)

If more than one space occurs consecutively in the middle of a string, 1-2-3 removes all but one of the blank spaces. For example, the @TRIM function in figure 6.67 removes extra spaces from between the words of a sentence.

Notice that the value of @LENGTH(A2) is 69, but the value of @LENGTH(@TRIM(A2)) is 41. (To trim other characters aside from blank spaces, use the @CLEAN function, described later in this chapter.)

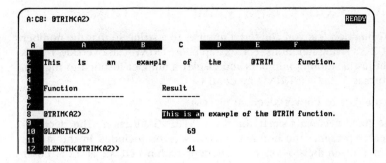

*Fig. 6.67.
Unwanted
spaces removed
with the
@TRIM
function.*

@N and @S—Testing for Strings and Values

The @N and @S functions give you a way to test for the presence of strings or values. @N returns the value of a number or numeric formula found in a cell. If the cell is blank or contains a label, @N returns the value 0. @N always will have a numeric value.

The @S function returns the string value of a cell. If the cell contains a string or a formula that evaluates to a string, then @S returns this string. If the cell contains a number or is empty, @S returns the null string (" "). @S always will have a string value.

The formats of the @N and the @S functions are

@N(range)

@S(range)

The argument must be a range or a single-cell reference. If you use a single-cell reference, 1-2-3 adjusts the argument to range format and returns the numeric or string value of the single cell. If the argument is a multicell range, @N and @S return the numeric or string value of the upper-left corner of the range. Figure 6.68 shows some results of using the @N and @S functions.

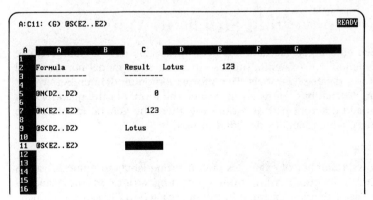

*Fig. 6.68.
String functions
used for string
and numeric
values.*

@STRING—Converting Values to Strings

The @STRING function lets you convert a number to a string so that the number can act with 1-2-3's string functions. For example, @STRING can override 1-2-3's automatic right-justification of numbers and display a number justified to the left. The general format of the @STRING function is

@STRING(number to convert,decimal places)

1-2-3 uses the fixed-decimal format for the @STRING function. The decimal-places argument represents the number of places to be included in the string. For example, if the number-to-convert argument within cell A2 is 22.5, enter @STRING(A2,2) in cell C10. The resulting string "'22.50" is displayed with left-justification, the default setting (see fig. 6.69).

Fig. 6.69.
A number converted to a string.

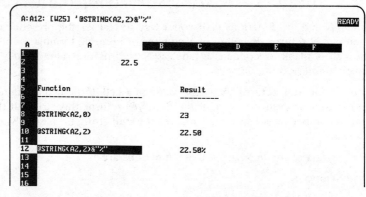

Cue:
Use the @STRING function to display a number as a percentage.

Notice that in the first example in the figure, 1-2-3 rounds the number upward to 23, just as 1-2-3 rounds any number displayed in the fixed-decimal format. The third example shows how to use the @STRING function to show a number as a percentage. The formula @STRING(A2,2)&"%" produces the string "22.50%". Note that to create a string from a number in any format other than fixed decimal, you must add the additional format characters yourself.

@VALUE—Converting Strings to Values

If you have been entering string data but need to use the data as numbers, use the @VALUE function. For example, suppose that you enter model numbers and their quantities in a database as labels. The information on model numbers works fine in the string format; but you want to change the format of the quantity data so that you can add different part quantities together. The general format of the @VALUE function, which handles this kind of task, is

@VALUE(string)

Figure 6.70 shows a number of examples of converting labels to numeric values with the @VALUE function. Aside from converting strings in the standard number format (as in the first example in the figure), @VALUE also can convert strings with decimal fractions as well as numbers displayed in scientific format. In the second example, the string "22 1/2" in cell C10 is converted by the function @VALUE(C10) to the number 22.5. Even if cell C10 contained the string "22 3/2", @VALUE would convert the string to the number 23.5. The final two examples in figure 6.70 show how @VALUE converts strings in percentage and in scientific format.

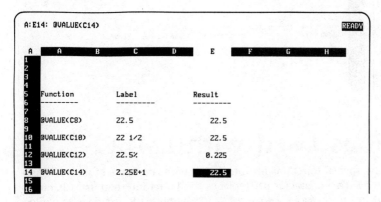

Fig. 6.70.
Labels
converted to
numbers.

A few rules are important when you use @VALUE. Although 1-2-3 usually does not object to extra spaces left in a string, the program has trouble with some extra characters, such as trailing percent signs. Currency signs (such as $) that precede the string are acceptable, however. Try experimenting with different extra characters to see how @VALUE reacts. Another point to remember is that a numeric value supplied as an argument for @VALUE simply will return the original number value.

@CLEAN—Removing Nonprintable Characters from Strings

Sometimes when you import strings with /File Import (see Chapter 7), particularly by way of a modem, the strings will contain nonprintable characters. The @CLEAN function removes the nonprintable characters from the strings (see fig. 6.71). The general format of the function is

@CLEAN(string)

The argument used with @CLEAN must be a string value or a cell reference to a cell containing a string value. 1-2-3 will not accept a cell entry containing @CLEAN with a range argument specified.

Reminder:
@CLEAN removes
nonprintable
characters from
data imported into
your worksheet
from other
sources.

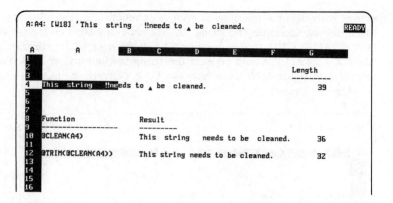

Fig. 6.71.
The @CLEAN function used to remove nonprintable characters.

Functions Used with LMBCS

1·2·3 offers a few special functions for interfacing with the Lotus Multibyte Character Set (LMBCS). This character set replaces the Lotus International Character Set (LICS) used in the previous release of 1·2·3. As with the previous extended character set, LMBCS can best be thought of as a new character set created by Lotus that allows you to display foreign language characters and mathematical symbols.

The complete set of LMBCS characters, listed in Appendix B of this book, includes everything from the copyright sign to the lowercase *e* with the grave accent. The appendix also shows you how to use the Compose (Alt-F1) key to display the LMBCS characters.

@CHAR—Displaying LMBCS Characters

The @CHAR function produces on-screen the LMBCS equivalent of a number between 1 and 6143. The general format of the function is

@CHAR(number)

For example, 1·2·3 represents a ™ sign on-screen with a T. To display the trademark sign on-screen, enter @CHAR(374) in a cell. Furthermore, you can use a string formula to concatenate the trademark sign to a product name. For instance, enter the following formula to produce the string "8080T":

+"8080"&@CHAR(374)

When you print the screen display, this string prints as 8080™. Figure 6.72 shows several other examples of the use of the @CHAR function.

Keep in mind two simple rules when using @CHAR. First, if the numeric argument you are using is not between 1 and 6143, 1·2·3 returns the ERR message. Second, if the argument you use is not an integer, 1·2·3 disregards the noninteger portion of the argument.

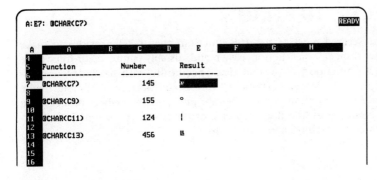

Fig. 6.72.
LMBCS
characters
displayed with
the @CHAR
function.

LMBCS characters also can be displayed using the Compose (Alt-F1) function key together with a compose sequence. See Appendix B for further information and for a list of LMBCS codes.

@CODE—Computing the LMBCS Code

The @CODE function does the opposite of what @CHAR does. While @CHAR takes a number between 1 and 6143 and returns an LMBCS character, @CODE examines a LMBCS character and returns a number between 1 and 6143. The general format of the function is

@CODE(string)

Suppose that you want to find the LMBCS code number for the letter *a*. You enter @CODE("a") in a cell, and 1-2-3 returns the number 97. If you enter @CODE("aardvark"), 1-2-3 still returns 97, the code for the first character in the string. Figure 6.73 shows several other examples of the use of the @CODE function.

Reminder:
@CODE returns
the LMBCS code of
the first character
of the string used
as the argument.

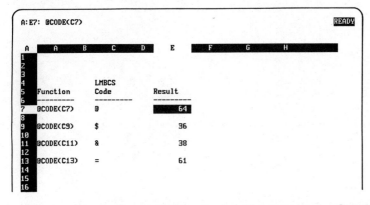

Fig. 6.73.
The @CODE
function used
to find LMBCS
numbers.

Remember that if you specify a number as the argument for @CODE (expressed as a number and not as a string), 1-2-3 returns the ERR message.

Chapter Summary

This chapter described most of the 108 functions that 1-2-3 provides to make formula and worksheet construction easier and, usually, more error-free. (The rest of the 1-2-3 functions, those that deal specifically with databases, are discussed in Chapter 10, "Managing Data.") Even as you become proficient in the use of the functions you regularly incorporate into your worksheet models, you probably will continue to find this chapter a handy resource for functions, function arguments and structure, and sample uses.

7

Managing Files

The commands available when you select /File from 1-2-3's main menu provide a wide range of file management, modification, and protection functions. Some commands, such as /File Erase and /File List, are similar to operating system commands. Other commands are related to specific 1-2-3 tasks and applications. Through the File menu, you can, for example, combine data from several files, extract data from one file to another file, and open more than one file in memory at a time. You can also give a file "reservation" status so that only one user is permitted to write information to and update the file. This chapter covers the /File commands and the topic of good file management in 1-2-3.

This chapter shows you how to do the following:

- Manage the active files in memory
- Name files
- Change directories
- Save files to disk
- Retrieve files from disk
- Extract and combine data
- Use passwords to protect files
- Erase files from disk
- List different types of files
- Transfer files between different programs
- Use 1-2-3 in a multiuser environment

1-2-3's commands for managing worksheet files are accessed from the /File option on the command menu. From that menu option, you can read files, combine information into the current file, and create new files. A brief description of these commands follows. The rest of the chapter covers the /File commands in more detail.

To read a file from disk and make the file active, you can use one of two commands. Use **/File Retrieve** to replace the current file with a new one. Use **/File Open** to add another active file to memory. Any files active before the execution of the **/File Open** command will still be active afterward.

If you want to combine information into the current file, use **/File Combine** or **/File Import**. With the former, you can read all or part of a 1-2-3 worksheet file and combine the data into the current file. With the latter, you can read a text file and combine the data into the current file.

To create a new file, use **/File Save** or **/File Xtract**. **/File Save** saves one or all active files on the disk. **/File Xtract** saves part of a file as a new file.

When you first start 1-2-3, you have a blank worksheet. If you want to build a new worksheet, just use the blank one. If you want to start with an existing file, use **/File Retrieve**. To build a new worksheet file when you have one or more existing files in memory, use **/File New**.

At any one time, you usually work with data files in one directory on your disk. To change the default data directory, use **/File Dir**. To see a list of all or some of the files in the current directory, use **/File List**. To save a list of files as a table in a worksheet, use **/File Admin Table**.

If you want to erase unneeded files on your disk to make room for other files, use **/File Erase**.

If you work with shared files in a network or other multiuser environment, you can use **/File Admin Reservation** to control write-access to files. If you have files with formulas that refer to cells in shared files, use **/File Admin Link-Refresh** to update these formulas manually.

To seal a file so that no one can change the protection settings without giving a password, use **/File Admin Seal**.

Managing Active Files in Memory

In 1-2-3 Release 3, the word *file* refers to two things. A disk-based file stores computer information magnetically for the long term. When you build or change worksheets in memory, the information is lost unless you save it to a disk-based file.

Alternatively, a file can consist of one or more worksheets that form an integral group in the computer's memory, even if the worksheets have not yet been saved to a disk-based file. When you first build a new worksheet, you are starting this second type of file. You can enter data into the worksheet, and you can insert additional worksheets into the same file. When you save a file to disk, you save all the file's worksheets together. When you read a file from disk, you read into memory all the file's worksheets.

Reading a file from disk produces in the computer's memory an exact copy of the disk file. The file still exists unchanged on disk.

When you save a file, you store on the disk an exact copy of the file that is in the computer's memory. The file still exists unchanged in memory. To manage files on disk, you must understand how to manage files in memory.

The computer's memory is your work area. Files in memory are called *active* files. When you use /Quit 1-2-3 or /Worksheet Erase, you lose all active files from memory. When you use /File Retrieve, you replace the current file in memory with another file from the disk. The current file is the file containing the cell pointer. Use /Worksheet Delete File to remove an active file from memory (see "Deleting Worksheets and Files" in Chapter 4). If you save a file before removing it from memory, you can read the file again from disk. If you make changes to a file and do not save it to disk, the changes are lost if you delete the file or replace it in memory.

Naming Files

The exact rules for file names depend on the operating system you use. In this book, the assumption is that you use a version of MS-DOS or PC DOS. File names consist of a 1- to 8-character name plus an optional file extension of 1 to 3 characters. The extension usually identifies the type of file. An example of a file name is BUDGET.WK3. In most cases, you choose the file name, and 1-2-3 supplies the extension.

A file name in DOS can contain letters, numbers, and the following characters:

~ ! @ $ % ^ & ( ) – _ { } # '

Spaces are not allowed. All letters convert automatically to uppercase. A file name should include only letters, numbers, the hyphen (–), and the underline character (_). Other characters may work now but may not work in later versions of DOS or other operating systems. For example, the characters # and ' work with current versions of DOS but not with OS/2. Whether you plan to switch to OS/2 or not, a future release of DOS may well make these two characters invalid in file names.

The standard extension for 1-2-3 Release 3 worksheet files is .WK3. When you type a file name, simply type the 1- to 8-character part of the name. 1-2-3 adds the extension for you. 1-2-3 Release 3 uses the following extensions:

.WK3   For Release 3 worksheet files

.BAK   For backup worksheet files

.WK1   For Releases 2 and 2.01 worksheet files

.PRN   For print-image text files with no special characters

.ENC   For encoded print-image files with graphics and/or formatting characters specific to one printer

.PIC   For files in Lotus graph-image format

.CGM   For files in graphic metafile graph-image format

You can override these standard extensions and type your own.

In addition, 1-2-3 can read worksheets that have the following extensions:

.WKS   For Release 1A worksheet files

.WRK   For Symphony Releases 1 and 1.01 worksheet files

.WR1   For Symphony Releases 1.1, 1.2, and 2 worksheet files

When you execute most file commands, 1-2-3 expects that you want to see the existing files that have .WK* extensions and so lists these files in the control panel. The asterisk (*) means "any character"; .WK*, therefore, designates such extensions as .WK3, .WK1, and .WKS, for example. If you create a file whose extension does not start with .WK, 1-2-3 will not list that file name as a default.

To read a file that has a nonstandard extension, you must type the complete file name and extension. You may want to save a file with a nonstandard extension so that the file does not show up when 1-2-3 lists the worksheet files. For example, you may want to use a nonstandard extension with a file that is part of a macro-controlled system, in which macros retrieve or open the file, so that you do not accidentally retrieve the file outside of the macro. The nonstandard extension "hides" the file from any list of worksheet files. When you want to retrieve the file outside of the macro environment, perhaps to change it, simply type the entire file name and extension.

To change the file lists' default extension from .WK* to something else, use /Worksheet Global Default Ext List and specify the new default extension. To list only Release 3 worksheets, use .WK3. To list 1-2-3 and Symphony worksheet files, use .W*.

You do not have to accept the default .WK3 extension when you save a file. You can type any extension you want. If you use the .WK1 extension, 1-2-3 saves the file in Release 2 format, and the file can be read with either Release 2 or Release 3. This arrangement works only if the file contains just one worksheet and uses only functions or macros available in Release 2.

If you must pass files between Release 2 and Release 3, and you don't use any features, functions, or macros that are not in Release 2, you can change the default extension to .WK1. Use /Worksheet Global Default Ext Save and specify the new default extension—in this case, .WK1. To change these defaults permanently, use /Worksheet Global Default Update.

Changing Directories

A hard disk is logically separated into a number of directories (also called *sub-directories*). The set of directories leading from the root to the directory containing a file you want is called the *path*, or *directory path*. When you perform file operations in 1-2-3, you usually deal with one directory at a time.

To select the default directory when you start 1-2-3, use /Worksheet **Global Default Dir**. Type the path to the directory that contains the files you use most often (see fig. 7.1, which shows the sample path name D:\DATA\123); press Enter. To save the name of the path permanently, use /Worksheet **Global Default Update**.

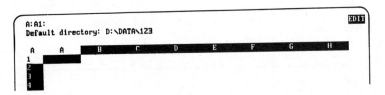

Fig. 7.1.
The sample default directory D:\DATA\123.

To change the current directory, use /File **Dir**. 1-2-3 displays the current directory path (see fig. 7.2). You can ignore the current path and type a new one. As soon as you type a character, the old path clears. To erase part of the path, use the End, left-arrow, right-arrow, Del, and Backspace keys. Type the directory path that you want to use; press Enter. When you perform any other file commands, such as /File **Retrieve**, 1-2-3 assumes that you want to use the current directory and displays the current path.

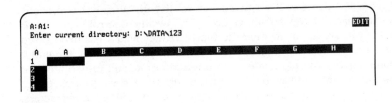

Fig. 7.2.
The current directory, following a prompt for a new current directory.

Saving Files

The /File **Save** command enables you to store on disk a magnetic copy of one or all active files in memory, including all the formats, names, and settings.

When you save a file for the first time, the file has no name. 1-2-3 supplies the default file name FILE0001.WK3 (see fig. 7.3). If this file name already exists in the current directory, 1-2-3 uses FILE0002.WK3, and so on. Do not accept this default file name; instead, type a meaningful name. As soon as you begin to type a new name, 1-2-3 clears the default name but leaves the path. Figure 7.4 shows the control panel after you type the letter *b* as the first character of the file name BUDGET. You do not need to use Backspace to erase the default name. After you type the file name, press Enter.

Fig. 7.3.
The default file name FILE0001.WK3, supplied by 1-2-3.

```
A:A1: [W15] 'Department 1                                              EDIT
Enter name of file to save: D:\DATA\123\FILE0001.WK3
   A          A            B        C        D        E        F       G
1      Department 1       QTR 1    QTR 2    QTR 3    QTR 4    TOTALS
2                         ------   ------   ------   ------   ------
3      Product 1          4,428    3,170    7,035    9,829    24,462
4      Product 2          4,664    3,340    7,410    10,354   25,768
5      Product 3          9,197    6,328    13,623   17,181   46,329
6      Product 4          7,563    6,651    15,779   21,130   51,123
7      Product 5          7,519    5,896    15,208   20,245   48,868
8      Product 6          5,073    9,558    25,708   18,119   58,458
9                         ------   ------   ------   ------   ------
10                        38,444   34,943   84,763   96,858   255,008
11
```

Fig. 7.4.
The clearing of the default file name after the first letter of the file name BUDGET is typed.

```
A:A1: [W15] 'Department 1                                              EDIT
Enter name of file to save: D:\DATA\123\b
   A          A            B        C        D        E        F       G
1      Department 1       QTR 1    QTR 2    QTR 3    QTR 4    TOTALS
2                         ------   ------   ------   ------   ------
3      Product 1          4,428    3,170    7,035    9,829    24,462
4      Product 2          4,664    3,340    7,410    10,354   25,768
5      Product 3          9,197    6,328    13,623   17,181   46,329
6      Product 4          7,563    6,651    15,779   21,130   51,123
7      Product 5          7,519    5,896    15,208   20,245   48,868
8      Product 6          5,073    9,558    25,708   18,119   58,458
9                         ------   ------   ------   ------   ------
10                        38,444   34,943   84,763   96,858   255,008
11
```

When you save a file that has been saved before, the file already has a name. 1-2-3 supplies this name as the default. Figure 7.5 shows the control panel that is on-screen when you are about to save the file BUDGET, which has been saved before. To save the file under the same name, press Enter. To save the file under a different name, ignore the old name, type the new name, and press Enter. To save the file under a name similar to the old name, use the arrow, Backspace, and Del keys to erase any part of the old name; then type any additional characters.

Cue:
Save different versions of your files under different names.

For example, suppose that you build a worksheet and are about to save it for the first time. You don't want the default file name FILE0001.WK3, so you ignore it, type **BUDGET**, and press Enter. Later you add to the worksheet and want to save it again, under the name BUDGET1. You don't want the default file name BUDGET.WK3, so you use the left-arrow key to move the cursor after the *T* in BUDGET, you type **1**, and then press Enter. Renaming different versions of the same worksheet is a good way to keep several backup copies accessible while you build a new worksheet. If you make a catastrophic error and don't discover it until after you have saved the file, you have earlier versions to go back to.

```
A:A1: [W15] 'Department 1                                    EDIT
Enter name of file to save: D:\DATA\123\BUDGET.WK3

   A          A        B        C        D        E        F        G
 1     Department 1     QTR 1    QTR 2    QTR 3    QTR 4    TOTALS
 2                      ------   ------   ------   ------   ------
 3     Product 1        4,428    3,170    7,035    9,829    24,462
 4     Product 2        4,664    3,340    7,410   10,354    25,768
 5     Product 3        9,197    6,328   13,623   17,181    46,329
 6     Product 4        7,563    6,651   15,779   21,130    51,123
 7     Product 5        7,519    5,896   15,208   20,245    48,868
 8     Product 6        5,073    9,558   25,708   18,119    58,458
 9                      ------   ------   ------   ------   ------
10                     38,444   34,943   84,763   96,858   255,008
11
```

Fig. 7.5.
The default
file name
BUDGET.WK3,
supplied by
1-2-3 for a file
previously
saved under
that name.

If a file already exists in the same directory under the same file name you have chosen, 1-2-3 warns you and gives you three options: Cancel, Replace, and Backup (see fig. 7.6). If you do not want to write over the old file on disk, choose Cancel to cancel the command, and start over. You then can save your file under a different name.

RELEASE 3

```
A:A1: [W15] 'Department 1                                    MENU
Cancel Replace Backup
Cancel command; leave existin~ file on disk intact
   A          A        B        C        D        E        F        G
 1     Department 1     QTR 1    QTR 2    QTR 3    QTR 4    TOTALS
 2                      ------   ------   ------   ------   ------
 3     Product 1        4,428    3,170    7,035    9,829    24,462
 4     Product 2        4,664    3,340    7,410   10,354    25,768
 5     Product 3        9,197    6,328   13,623   17,181    46,329
 6     Product 4        7,563    6,651   15,779   21,130    51,123
 7     Product 5        7,519    5,896   15,208   20,245    48,868
 8     Product 6        5,073    9,558   25,708   18,119    58,458
 9                      ------   ------   ------   ------   ------
10                     38,444   34,943   84,763   96,858   255,008
11
```

Fig. 7.6.
The three-item
menu that
appears when
you try to save
a file under a
name that
already exists
in the same
directory.

If you want to write over the old file, choose Replace. The old file with the same name is lost permanently. When you choose Replace, 1-2-3 first deletes the old file from the disk. If you get a Disk full message while saving a file, you must save the file on another disk or erase some existing files to make room to save the file. If you do not successfully save the file, both the new version in memory and the old version on disk are lost.

Cue:
Use the Backup
option to keep the
old version of a file
as a backup copy.

If you want to save your file under the same name but not lose the old file on disk, choose Backup. Backup renames the old file with a .BAK extension, then saves the new file under the same file name, with a .WK3 extension. You thus have both files on disk.

RELEASE 3

You can use the Backup option to save only one file as a backup. If you save the file again and choose Backup, 1-2-3 deletes the current backup file, renames the .WK3 file with a .BAK extension, and saves the new file under a .WK3 extension. If you want to keep the old file with a .BAK extension, you must copy the file to a different disk or directory, or you must rename the file.

RELEASE 3

Retrieving Files from Disk

Two commands enable you to read a file from disk into memory. **/File Retrieve** replaces the current file with the new file. If you just started 1-2-3, or if nothing but a blank worksheet is in memory, use this command. If you have a current file in memory and you changed the file since the last time you saved it, those changes are lost if you use **/File Retrieve** with another file. 1-2-3 gives no warning if you are about to replace a file you have changed.

/File Open reads a file from disk into the computer's memory. Unlike **/File Retrieve**, this command does not replace the current file in memory. With **/File Open**, you can continue to read files into memory until you run out of memory.

When more than one file is in memory, or is active, you can easily move the cell pointer among the files to update one file and then another. As explained in Chapter 3, when both files are in memory, you can more easily create formulas that link files. Also, you can use commands that span multiple files. For example, you can copy data from one file to another, print reports with data from multiple files, graph data in multiple files in the same graph, and use **/Data Query Extract** to move data from one file to another.

After you select **/File Open**, choose either **B**efore or **A**fter to tell 1-2-3 to put the file either before or after the current file. In perspective view, *before* means toward the bottom of the screen, and *after* means toward the top. In figure 7.7, FILE2 is after FILE1 and before FILE3.

Fig. 7.7.
*Three files in
perspective
view.*

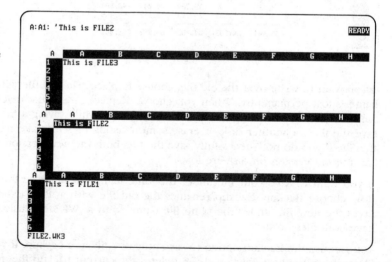

With either **/File Retrieve** or **/File Open**, 1-2-3 lists, at the prompt requesting you to enter the file name, the files on disk. You can either type the file name or point to the file from the list in the control panel. If several files are in the directory, press Name (F3) for a full-screen display of file names (see fig. 7.8). Files are listed in alphabetical order as you read from left to right. Point to the file you want to retrieve; then press Enter.

```
A:A1: [W15] 'Department 1                                          FILES
Enter name of file to retrieve: D:\DATA\123\*.WK*
        BUDGET.WK3      14-Apr-89      12:35 PM      1650
BUDGET.WK3      FILE1.WK3       FILE2.WK3       FILE3.WK3
LINK1.WK3       LINK2.WK3       LINK3.WK3       PARSE2.WK3
PARSE3.WK3      PARSECR.WK3     PARSE.WK3       RESERVE.WK3
SALES2.WK3      SALES.WK3       XCELL.WK3       XFORMULA.WK3
XSALES1.WK3     XTRACT.WK3      XVALUES.WK3
```

Fig. 7.8.
A full-screen list of file names, produced by pressing Name (F3).

Using Wild Cards for File Retrieval

Whenever 1-2-3 prompts you for a file name, you can include the asterisk (*) and the question mark (?) as wild cards in the file name. Wild cards are characters that enable you to make one file name match a number of files. Although wild cards can be used with many of the /File commands, you will probably use these special characters most often with /File Retrieve.

The ? matches any one character in the name (or no character if the ? is the last character in the file name's main part or extension). The * matches any number of characters (or no character).

When you use wild cards in response to a file name prompt, 1-2-3 lists only the files whose names match the wild-card pattern; 1-2-3 does not actually execute the command (unless you use /File List). For example, if you use wild cards after you select /File Retrieve, /File Open, /File Combine, or /File Import, 1-2-3 does not try to read a file but lists only the files that match the wild-card pattern.

Suppose that you type **DEPT?BUD** at the prompt shown in figure 7.8. 1-2-3 lists all file names that start with DEPT, followed by any character, followed by BUD —such as DEPT1BUD, DEPT2BUD, and DEPTXBUD. If you type **BUDGET***, 1-2-3 lists all file names that start with BUDGET, such as BUDGET, BUDGET1, BUDGETX, and BUDGET99.

Retrieving Files from Subdirectories

Whenever 1-2-3 prompts you for a file name and gives you a default, the program also lists the complete path, such as D:\DATA\123\BUDGET.WK3.

To change the current directory, use /File Dir. To retrieve or save a file in another directory without changing the current directory, press Esc twice to clear the old path; then type a new path. You also can edit the existing path in the prompt.

Reminder:
Press Backspace to list a parent directory; select a subdirectory to list the files in that subdirectory.

When 1-2-3 lists the files in the current directory, the program lists any subdirectories below the current directory, placing a backslash (\) before each directory's name. To read a file in one of the subdirectories, point to the subdirectory name and press Enter. 1-2-3 then lists the files and any subdirectories in that subdirectory. To list the files in the parent directory (the directory above the one displayed), press Backspace; 1-2-3 lists the files and subdirectories in the parent directory. You can move up and down the directory structure this way until you find the file you want.

For those who want to learn more about directories, Que Corporation has many books available. Users new to DOS should try *MS-DOS QuickStart*. Intermediate users who want to learn more about DOS or OS/2 file and directory management should consult *Using PC DOS*, 3rd Edition, and *MS-DOS User's Guide*, 3rd Edition, both by Chris DeVoney; *Managing Your Hard Disk*, 2nd Edition, by Don Berliner, or *Using OS/2*, by Caroline Halliday, David Gobel, and Mark Minasi.

Retrieving a File Automatically

Usually, when you first start 1-2-3, you have a blank worksheet. If you are in the default directory and save a file under the name AUTO123, however, 1-2-3 retrieves that file automatically when 1-2-3 starts. This capability is useful if you work with macro-driven worksheet files. You can use the AUTO123 file to provide the first menu of a macro-driven system or a menu of other files to retrieve.

Opening a New File in Memory

Cue:
Use /File New to start a new worksheet and leave the active files in memory.

You can start a new file without clearing any existing files from memory. /File New creates a new, blank file in the computer's memory. Any files that were active before you issued this command remain active after you insert the new file. As with /File Open, described earlier, use /File New when you want to work with more than one active file in memory.

After you select /File New, choose either Before or After to insert the blank worksheet file either before or after the current file. When you start a new file, 1-2-3 prompts you for a file name, offers a default such as FILE0001.WK3 (see the earlier section "Saving Files"), and then writes a blank file to disk.

Figure 7.9 shows the work area in figure 7.7 after the cell pointer has been moved to FILE3 and the /File New After command has been issued to create a new file named FILE4. (Because FILE4 is a new file, it is blank.)

If you want to build a new worksheet file and remove all other files and worksheets, you can clear the work area with /Worksheet Erase. This command clears all files in memory, not just the current worksheet or file. If you changed any files since you last saved them, the changes are lost. 1-2-3 does ask you to confirm No or Yes before it clears the work area. If you changed any active files since you last saved them, 1-2-3 warns you with another No/Yes menu. To save the changes, choose No and save the file; then execute /Worksheet Erase again.

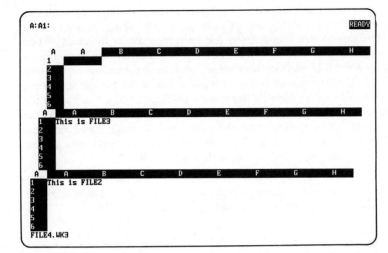

Fig. 7.9.
A new file opened after the existing files in memory.

Extracting and Combining Data

You can take the data from part of a file and use that data to create another, smaller file. For example, you may have a large budget file that contains information from many departments. For each department, you can create an input file that contains only the data for that department.

You then may want to reverse the procedure: you have many departmental input files and want to combine them into one file for company-wide analysis and reporting.

1-2-3 provides the /File Xtract command so that you can save a part of the current file as a new file. 1-2-3 also offers the /File Combine command so that you can combine data from another file into the current file.

Extracting Information

The /File Xtract command enables you to save a range in the current file as a separate file. You can use this command to save part of a file before you change it, to break a large file into smaller files so that it can be read in another computer that has less memory, to create a partial file for someone to work on, or to pass information to another file.

The extracted range can be a single cell or a two-dimensional or three-dimensional range. The extracted file contains the contents of the cells in the range, including the cells' formats and protection status; all range names in the file; and all file settings, such as column widths, window options, print ranges, and graph options.

To extract part of a worksheet, choose /File Xtract and select either Formulas or Values. When you select Formulas, any cells in the extract range in the current file that contain formulas are copied into the extracted file as formulas. When you select Values, any cells in the extract range in the current file that contain formulas are converted into their current values, and these values are copied into the extracted file. 1-2-3 then acts as if you were saving a file for the first time. 1-2-3 prompts for a file name, offering the default FILE0001.WK3. You type a file name and press Enter. Then specify the range to extract and press Enter. For the range, you can type addresses, highlight the range, type a range name, or press Name (F3) and point to a range name. If the file name already exists, you get the same Cancel Replace Backup menu as shown in figure 7.6.

The extracted range can start anywhere in the current file (see fig. 7.10). The upper-left corner of the extracted range becomes cell A:A1 in the new file (see fig. 7.11). All range names adjust to their new positions.

Fig. 7.10.
A highlighted
range to be
extracted.

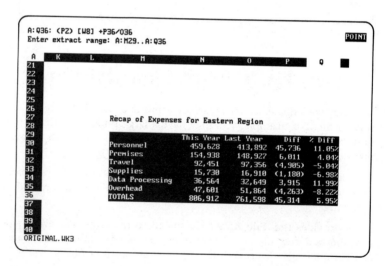

Compare the range name table in the file SALES (see fig. 7.12) with the range name table in the file XVALUES (see fig. 7.13). The XVALUES file was created with /File Xtract Values from the range F1..F9 in the SALES file, and a range name table was added to the extracted file.

In the original file (fig. 7.12), GRAND_TOT refers to F9. In the new file (fig. 7.13), GRAND_TOT refers to A9. All other range names are adjusted as well. Be aware that range names to the left or above the upper left of the extract range "wrap" to the end of the worksheet, as shown in the range name table in figure 7.13. Most of these range names refer to blank cells and really have no meaning in this worksheet. The only meaningful range names are those completely within the extract range—in this case, TOTALS and GRAND_TOT.

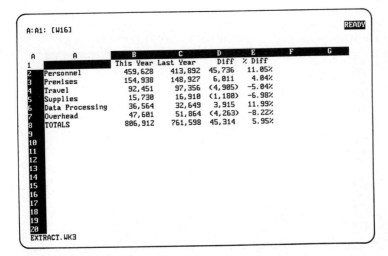

```
A:A1: [W16]                                                    READY

  A         A              B          C          D        E        F        G
1                      This Year  Last Year    Diff     % Diff
2  Personnel           459,628    413,892    45,736     11.05%
3  Premises            154,938    148,927     6,011      4.04%
4  Travel               92,451     97,356   (4,905)     -5.04%
5  Supplies             15,730     16,910   (1,180)     -6.98%
6  Data Processing      36,564     32,649     3,915     11.99%
7  Overhead             47,601     51,864   (4,263)     -8.22%
8  TOTALS              806,912    761,598    45,314      5.95%
9
10
11
12
13
14
15
16
17
18
19
20
EXTRACT.WK3
```

Fig. 7.11.
The extracted
range, which
starts in cell
A:A1 of the
new file.

```
A:F9: (,0) [W10] @SUM(F8..F2)                                 READY

  A         A              B          C          D        E        F        G
1                        QTR 1      QTR 2      QTR 3    QTR 4    TOTALS
2                       ------     ------     ------   ------    ------
3  Department 1         38,444     34,943     84,763   96,858   255,008
4  Department 2         37,815     33,277     89,196  102,014   262,302
5  Department 3         40,256     30,344     87,583   99,494   257,677
6  Department 4         38,656     31,098     82,914   81,070   233,738
7  Department 5         38,890     29,088     81,515   84,552   234,045
8                       ------     ------     ------   ------    ------
9  TOTALS              194,061    158,750    425,971  463,988 1,242,770
10
11
12 Range Name Table
13 GRAND_TOT      A:F9..A:F9
14 NOTES          B:A1..B:A1
15 PAGE1          A:A1..A:F20
16 QTR1           A:B3..A:B7
17 QTR2           A:C3..A:C7
18 QTR3           A:D3..A:D7
19 QTR4           A:E3..A:E7
20 TOTALS         A:F3..A:F7
SALES.WK3
```

Fig. 7.12.
The SALES file.

The extracted file also has all the other settings of the original file, including print, graph, and data ranges. These settings adjust, as do the range names. For example, the print range in SALES (fig. 7.12) is A1..F20. In XVALUES (fig. 7.13), the print range is A1..IR20. The /Graph **X** range is A3..A7 in SALES and IR3..IR7 in XVALUES. As with range names, do not use /**P**rint, /**G**raph, or /**D**ata settings in an extract file unless the entire setting range is within the range extracted. In this example, the /**P**rint and /**G**raph settings are meaningless.

Caution:
*Use /**File X**tract to*
extract data in cells
to a new file, but
do not use range
names or other
settings outside the
extracted range.

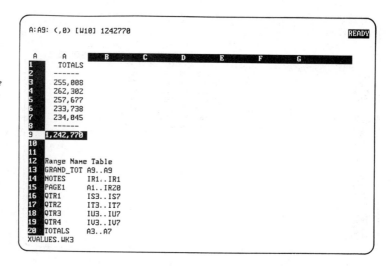

Fig. 7.13.
The extracted file XVALUES, created by /File Xtract Values, with a range name table added.

Extracting Formulas

You should extract formulas only when the formulas in the extract range refer solely to other cells in the extract range. The formulas in figure 7.12 were converted to values in figure 7.13. This fact is important because the formulas in F3..F7 sum a range that was not extracted.

Figure 7.14 shows the XFORMULA file created with /File Xtract Formulas from the range F1..F9 in the SALES file in figure 7.12. This range is the same one extracted with /File Xtract Values in figure 7.13. In the SALES file, the formula in F3 is @SUM(E3..B3). In figure 7.14, this formula becomes @SUM(IV3..IS3). This is because of relative addressing. The formula was summing cells from four cells to the left through one cell to the left. This relative addressing is carried through to the extracted file just at it would if you copied or moved the cells in a worksheet. Notice that the extracted file retains the column width and cell formats as well as the values from the original file.

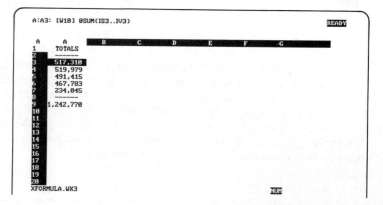

Fig. 7.14.
Meaningless results produced by /File Extract Formulas.

At times you will need to extract formulas. Suppose, for example, that you want to extract one of the worksheets from the file SALES, discussed in the preceding section. Figure 7.15 shows worksheet C of the SALES file. To extract worksheet C and place it in a separate file for Department 1 personnel to complete, use the command /**File Xtract Formulas** and specify the range C:A1..C:F10. You might name this extract file XSALES1 to remind yourself that it is an extract file from SALES for Department 1 (see fig. 7.16). Because all formulas refer to cells in the extracted range, the formulas are still valid. The worksheet in figure 7.16 is identical to worksheet C in figure 7.15.

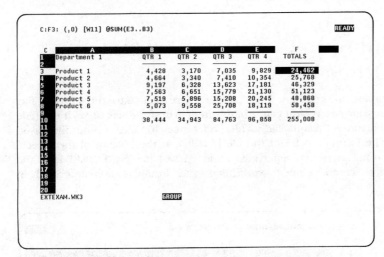

Fig. 7.15.
Worksheet C of
the original
SALES file.

Fig. 7.16.
The XSALES1
file, extracted
from SALES
through the use
of /File Xtract
Formulas.

Cue:
Even absolute
values adjust with
/File Xtract.

When you extract formulas, the formulas adjust even if they are absolute. The resulting formulas are still absolute, but they have new addresses. If the formula in F3 in figure 7.12 were @SUM($E$3..$B$3), the formula in A3 in figure 7.14 would be @SUM($IV$3..$IS$3).

Extracting Values

When you extract values, you get the current value of any formulas in the extract range. If recalculation is set to manual and the CALC indicator is on, press Calc (F9) to calculate the worksheet before you extract a range; otherwise, you may inadvertently extract old values.

Combining Information from Other Files

You can combine information from one or more files into the current file. Depending on your needs, you can do this either with formulas or with the /File Combine command. A formula can include references to cells in other files, as in figure 7.17. The formula in B3 of the file LINKED, at the bottom of the screen, refers to the total sales for Department 1 in B10 of the file LINKED1, in the middle of the screen. Linked worksheets and formulas are described in Chapter 3.

Fig. 7.17.
A worksheet with references to cells in other files.

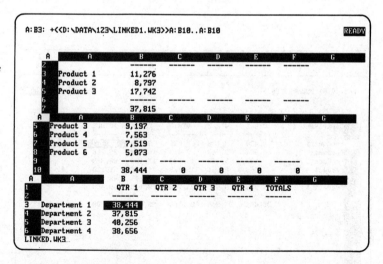

In certain situations, you do not want to use linked files for consolidations. If you use formulas that link many external files, then each time you read in the consolidation file, 1-2-3 must read parts of each linked file to update the linked formulas. This process may take too long.

You may not want to update the consolidation automatically every time you read in the file. You may want to update the consolidation only once a month, for instance, when all the new detail data is available. The rest of the time, you may use the consolidation file for "what if" analysis, using the previous month's data.

When you want manual control over when and how you update a file with data from other files, use /File Combine. This command combines the cell contents of all or part of another file into the current file, starting at the location of the cell pointer.

/File Combine offers three options: Copy, Add, and Subtract. Copy enables you to replace data in the current file with data from an external file. With Add, you sum the values of the cells in the external file with the values of the cells in the current file. Subtract enables you to subtract the data in the external file from the data in the current file.

You can use any of the /File Combine options with either an entire file or a range. The menu choices are Entire-File or Named/Specified-Range. The range can be a single cell, a two-dimensional range, or a three-dimensional range. You can specify range addresses, but you should use range names if possible. You can easily make an error if you specify range addresses, because when you execute the command, you can't see the external file that the data is coming from.

When you use the /File Combine options, blank cells in the external file are ignored. Cells with data in the external file update the corresponding cells in the current file.

Using /File Combine Copy

In the section "Extracting and Combining Data," /File Xtract was used with a consolidated file to create separate files for the individual departments. In this section, the process is reversed. /File Combine Copy is used to update the consolidated file from the individual departmental files. These examples are typical of how you use /File Xtract and /File Combine. You start with the consolidated file, and each month (or other time period) you extract the departmental files for input, then combine them for consolidated analysis and reporting.

You would use /File Combine Copy, for example, if you needed to update the SALES file with new data contained in another file—the file XSALES2, for instance (see fig. 7.18). Making sure that you are in the receiving worksheet, move the cell pointer to the upper-left corner of the range to receive the combined data—in this case, B25 (see fig. 7.19)—and execute /File Combine Copy. After selecting /File Combine Copy, you have the choice of combining the whole file or only a range. If you want to include, for example, only the values in the range B3..E5 in XSALES2, choose Named/Specified-Range; then specify the range B3..E5 and press Enter. Finally, specify the external file—in this case, XSALES2—where the range B3..E5 will come from. Figure 7.20 shows how the data in figure 7.19 has been replaced by the data in figure 7.18.

In this case, the old data and the new data had a known format, with no blank cells. Each cell in the external file replaced the data in the current file. If there

Fig. 7.18.
The XSALES2
file, to be
combined into
SALES.

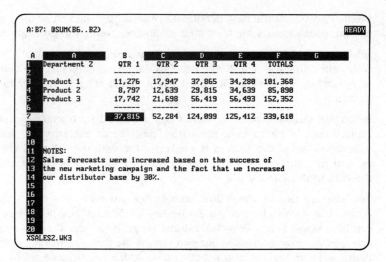

Fig. 7.19.
The SALES file
before the
incorporation
of new data.

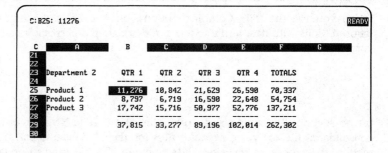

Fig. 7.20.
The SALES file
after the
incorporation
of new data.

Caution:
If there can be
blank cells in the
external file, erase
the data in the
target range before
performing a /File
Combine Copy.

are blank cells in the external file, however, they are ignored, and the corresponding cell in the current file is left unchanged; the corresponding cell is not blanked out.

Figure 7.21 is a variation of the input file shown in figure 7.18. In figure 7.21, Product 3 is canceled and the sales data erased. If you repeat the /File Combine Copy command to update the file in figure 7.20 with the data shown in figure 7.21, you get figure 7.22. Note that the old sales figures for Product 3 are not erased and that the totals for the department are wrong. To avoid this error, erase the range in the current file before you incorporate the new data. In this case, erase C:B25..C:E:27.

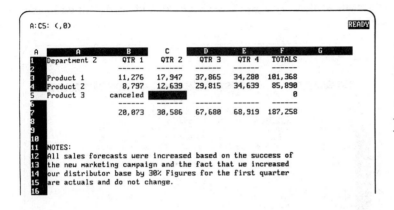

Fig. 7.21.
An input worksheet with blank cells, to be incorporated into the SALES file shown in figure 7.20.

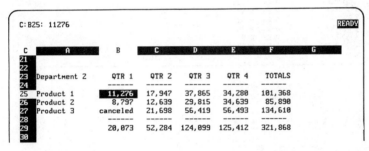

Fig. 7.22.
Incorrect results in the SALES file, produced because the blank cells did not update the file.

In these examples, only numbers, not formulas, were combined. You can combine formulas if you also combine the data referenced in those formulas. From figures 7.18 and 7.21 you could have incorporated B3..F7 and included the TOTALS formulas in row 7 and column F. Because you also combined the data for these formulas, the formulas would have been correct in figures 7.20 and 7.22.

Be careful when you use /File Combine Copy with formulas. Formulas—even absolute ones—adjust automatically to their new location after the execution of /File Combine Copy. In figures 7.18 and 7.21, for example, the formula for the total for QTR 1 in cell A:B7 is @SUM(B6..B2). If you combine this formula into SALES in figures 7.19 and 7.22, the formula adjusts to @SUM(B28..B24) in cell C:B29. If the formula in cell A:B7 were @SUM($B$6..$B$2), the formula would adjust, after the execution of /File Combine, to @SUM($B$28..$B$24) in cell C:B29.

If you simply combine the formulas without the data, the formulas are meaningless, and you get incorrect results. Figure 7.23 shows the master consolidation in worksheet A for the SALES file. Because the detail already exists in another work-

Cue:
Even absolute values adjust with /File Combine Copy.

Caution:
Do not use /File Combine Copy with formulas unless you also incorporate the data referenced by the formulas.

sheet, you could decide to combine only the totals from B7..E7 in figure 7.21 directly into B4..E4. The formula in B7 in figure 7.21 is @SUM(B6..B2). In figure 7.23, the formula adjusts to @SUM(B3..B8191), which is clearly wrong. This formula makes the figures for Department 2 wrong and causes a circular reference. To get what you want in this case, use **/File Combine Add**, as described in the text that follows.

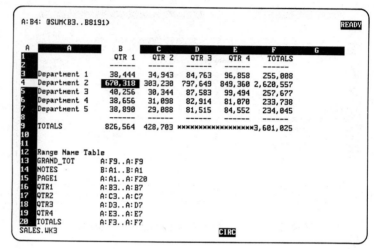

Fig. 7.23.
An erroneous
formula in the
SALES file,
caused by the
omission of
data when /File
Combine Copy
was used with
formulas.

Using /File Combine Add and /File Combine Subtract

/File Combine Add works somewhat like **/File Combine Copy** but differs in some important ways. **/File Combine Subtract** is identical to **/File Combine Add** except that you subtract instead of add. With that exception, everything that follows about **/File Combine Add** applies to **/File Combine Subtract** as well.

Instead of replacing the contents of cells in the current file, **/File Combine Add** adds the values of the cells in the external file to the values of cells in the current file that contain numbers or are blank. In other words, this command adds a number or a formula result to a number or a blank cell. If the cell in the current file contains a formula, the formula is unchanged by **/File Combine Add**.

To update the totals correctly for Department 2 in figure 7.23, move the cell pointer to B4 and use **/Range Erase** to erase B4..E4. Then use **/File Combine Add** Named/Specified-Range to add B7..E7 from file XSALES2 in figure 7.21. The result is shown in figure 7.24.

/File Combine Add adds to the current file the current value of any formulas in the external file. Because you erased the range B4..E4 in SALES in figure 7.23, these blank cells are treated as zeros.

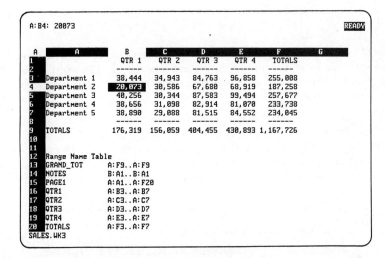

```
A:B4: 20073                                                          READY

A         A          B        C        D        E        F        G
          1                    QTR 1    QTR 2    QTR 3    QTR 4    TOTALS
2                             ------   ------   ------   ------   ------
3         Department 1       38,444   34,943   84,763   96,858  255,008
4         Department 2       20,073   30,586   67,680   68,919  187,258
5         Department 3       40,256   30,344   87,583   99,494  257,677
6         Department 4       38,656   31,098   82,914   81,070  233,738
7         Department 5       38,890   29,088   81,515   84,552  234,045
8                            ------   ------   ------   ------   ------
9         TOTALS            176,319  156,059  404,455  430,893 1,167,726
10
11
12        Range Name Table
13        GRAND_TOT     A:F9..A:F9
14        NOTES         B:A1..B:A1
15        PAGE1         A:A1..A:F20
16        QTR1          A:B3..A:B7
17        QTR2          A:C3..A:C7
18        QTR3          A:D3..A:D7
19        QTR4          A:E3..A:E7
20        TOTALS        A:F3..A:F7
SALES.WK3
```

Fig. 7.24.
The SALES file after being updated with /File Combine Add.

If you had specified a /File Combine Add range of B7..F7 instead of B7..E7, you would have gotten the same result. The total in F7 in figure 7.21 would not be added to the contents of F4 in figure 7.23 because F4 contains the formula @SUM(E4..B4). This formula remains @SUM(E4..B4) after the /File Combine Add because this command has no effect on formulas in the current file.

Be aware that with /File Combine Add, you can add incorrect formula results. Because /File Combine Add converts formulas in the external file to their current values before the command adds them, these values must be current in order for you to get the correct result. If XSALES2 in figure 7.21 were set to manual calculation and the CALC indicator had been on the last time the file was saved, incorrect data could have been added during the execution of the /File Combine command. You can do nothing about this problem when you issue the /File Combine Add command. You must press Calc (F9) to calculate the external file before it is saved.

Caution:
Make sure that the CALC indicator is off before you save a file that might be used for a /File Combine Add or Subtract.

The other way to use /File Combine Add is to sum the values from two or more files into one consolidation. If all you wanted was the single row of totals in B9..F9 in figure 7.24, you could add the totals from all the input worksheets directly. First use /Range Erase to erase A3..F7, because you won't be keeping department totals in this example. Make sure that F9 contains @SUM(B9..E9). Then move the cell pointer to B9 and use /Range Erase on B9..E9. Finally, use /File Combine Add to add the totals from each input file (XSALES1, XSALES2, and so on). This process accumulates the totals from each department.

If you have a separate file for credits or returns, you can use /File Combine Subtract to subtract these returns. If the returns are entered as negative numbers, however, you should use /File Combine Add to add the negative numbers and thereby correctly decrease the sales totals.

Protecting Files with Passwords

You can protect worksheet files by using passwords. Once a file is password-protected, no one can read the file without first issuing the password. This restriction applies to /File Retrieve, /File Open, /File Combine, and Translate (from the 1-2-3 Access System menu).

You password-protect a file when you specify the file name during a /File Save or /File Xtract. Type the file name, press the space bar once, type **p** (see fig 7.25), and then press Enter. 1-2-3 prompts you to type a password of 1 to 15 characters. The password cannot contain spaces. As you type, asterisks (*) appear on the screen so that no one can look over your shoulder to find out the password.

Fig. 7.25.
The file name followed by the letter p, which tells 1-2-3 to password-protect the file.

```
A:B4: 20073                                                              EDIT
Enter name of file to save: D:\DATA\123\sales p

A           A           B         C         D         E         F     *  G
                       QTR 1     QTR 2     QTR 3     QTR 4     TOTALS
1
2                      ------    ------    ------    ------    ------
3  Department 1        38,444    34,943    84,763    96,858    255,008
4  Department 2        20,073    30,586    67,680    68,919    187,258
5  Department 3        40,256    30,344    87,583    99,494    257,677
6  Department 4        38,656    31,098    82,914    81,070    233,738
7  Department 5        38,890    29,088    81,515    84,552    234,045
8                      ------    ------    ------    ------    ------
9  TOTALS             176,319   156,059   404,455   430,893  1,167,726
10
11
12 Range Name Table
13 GRAND_TOT     A:F9..A:F9
14 NOTES         B:A1..B:A1
15 PAGE1         A:A1..A:F20
16 QTR1          A:B3..A:B7
17 QTR2          A:C3..A:C7
18 QTR3          A:D3..A:D7
19 QTR4          A:E3..A:E7
20 TOTALS        A:F3..A:F7
SALES.WK3
```

After you type the password, press Enter; you are prompted to type the password again. Type it again (see fig. 7.26, which shows asterisks where the words have been typed); press Enter. If both passwords are identical, the file is saved in a special format, and neither you nor anyone else has access to the file without first giving the password. If the two passwords do not match, 1-2-3 gives you an error message, and you must type the passwords again.

Passwords are case-sensitive: if a password includes a lowercase letter, that letter does not match the corresponding uppercase letter. When you first assign a password, check the Caps Lock indicator so that you know how you are entering letters.

*Caution:
If you forget the password, you cannot access a password-protected file.*

When you use **Retrieve**, **Open**, or **Combine** with a password-protected file, 1-2-3 prompts you for the password. Only if you type the password correctly will you have access to the file.

When you save a file that has already been saved with a password, 1-2-3 displays the message [PASSWORD PROTECTED] after the file name (see fig. 7.27). To save

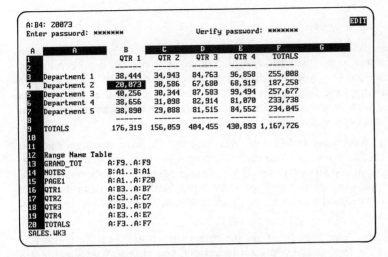

Fig. 7.26.
The control
panel after you
have typed the
password twice.

the file with the same password, just press Enter. To delete the password, press Backspace once to clear the [PASSWORD PROTECTED] message; then press Enter. To change the password, press Backspace once to clear the [PASSWORD PRO-TECTED] message; then press the space bar once, type **p**, and press Enter. Finally, assign a new password.

```
A:B4: 20073                                                         EDIT
Enter name of file to save: D:\DATA\123\SALES.WK3 [PASSWORD PROTECTED]
   A          A          B        C        D        E        F        G
1                                QTR 1    QTR 2    QTR 3    QTR 4    TOTALS
2                                ------   ------   ------   ------   ------
3             Department 1       38,444   34,943   84,763   96,858   255,008
4             Department 2       20,073   30,586   67,680   68,919   187,258
5             Department 3       40,256   30,344   87,583   99,494   257,677
6             Department 4       38,656   31,098   82,914   81,070   233,738
7             Department 5       38,890   29,088   81,515   84,552   234,045
8                                ------   ------   ------   ------   ------
9             TOTALS            176,319  156,059  404,455  430,893 1,167,726
10
11
12            Range Name Table
13            GRAND_TOT  A:F9..A:F9
14            NOTES      B:A1..B:A1
15            PAGE1      A:A1..A:F20
16            QTR1       A:B3..A:B7
17            QTR2       A:C3..A:C7
18            QTR3       A:D3..A:D7
19            QTR4       A:E3..A:E7
20            TOTALS     A:F3..A:F7
SALES.WK3
```

Fig. 7.27.
A password-
protected file
that is about to
be saved again.

If you have several files in memory and you execute /File Save, 1-2-3 displays [ALL MODIFIED FILES] instead of a file name. To save a file and add, delete, or change the password, press Esc or Edit (F2) to change the prompt to the current file name. Then you can proceed as explained earlier.

Erasing Files

Every time you save a file under a different file name, you use up some space on your disk. Eventually you will run out of disk space if you do not occasionally erase old, unneeded files from the disk. Even if you still have disk space left, you will have a harder time finding the files you want to read if the disk contains many obsolete files. Before you erase some old files, you may want to save them to a diskette in case you ever need them again.

Warning:
Once you erase a file from disk, you cannot recover it without using a special utility program.

When you use /Worksheet Delete File, you clear the file from memory, but you do not erase the file from disk. You can still retrieve or open the file. To erase an unneeded file from disk, use /File Erase. This command permanently removes the file from disk and frees up the disk space for other files. You also can use DOS's ERASE or DEL command to erase files on disk. Within 1-2-3, you can erase only one file at a time.

When you choose /File Erase, you get the menu shown in figure 7.28. Use this menu to select the type of file you want to erase. If you choose **Worksheet**, 1-2-3 lists all files in the current directory that have .WK* extensions (unless you change the default with /Worksheet Global Default Ext List). If you choose **Print**, 1-2-3 lists all files contained in the current directory that have .PRN extensions. Choosing **Graph** produces a list of all files contained in the current directory that have .CGM extensions (unless you change the default by using /Worksheet Global Default Graph PIC). Choosing **Other** produces a list of all files in the current directory. "Other," in this case, really means "all."

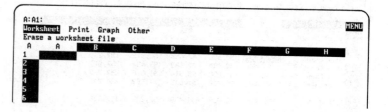

Fig. 7.28.
The /File Erase menu.

To list some other set of files, choose any of the options in figure 7.28; then press Edit (F2) and change the file specification. To list all worksheet files that start with BUDGET, use BUDGET*.WK*; to list all backup files, use *.BAK. When the file you want to erase is listed, highlight the file name and press Enter. Choose **Yes** to confirm that you want to erase the file. 1-2-3 erases the file.

Creating Lists and Tables of Files

1-2-3 provides commands to help you keep track of the files you have on disk. You can either list the files or save a table of files in your worksheet. If you work with many files, you may forget the names of certain files or the times they were last updated. In addition, you can list the files that are active in memory. This capability is handy if you work with many files in memory at the same time.

To see a list of files, use /**File List**. The menu shown in figure 7.29 appears. The **Worksheet**, **Print**, **Graph**, and **Other** options provide the same lists that they provide with the /**File Erase** menu described earlier. Choose **Active** to list all files currently in memory. Figure 7.30 shows a sample active list, which indicates whether an active file has been modified since the last time it was saved. MOD means *modified*; UNMOD means *unmodified*. Choose **Linked** from the /**File List** menu to list all files referenced in formulas in the current file.

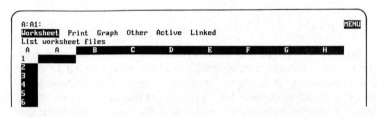

Fig. 7.29.
The /File List or
/File Admin
Table menu.

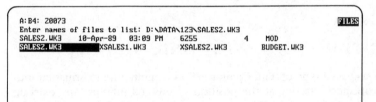

Fig. 7.30.
An active list.

To save a file list as a table in your worksheet, use /**File Admin Table**. You get the same menu as in figure 7.29. If you choose **Active**, you create a table starting at the position of the cell pointer, like the table in figure 7.31. You may have to change the column widths to see all the information.

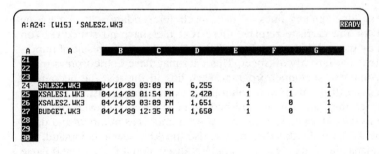

Fig. 7.31.
A table of
active files.

The first column lists the file name. The second column lists the date of the last save. You have to format these cells as a date. The third column lists the time of the last save. You have to format these cells as a time; 1-2-3 does not format them for you. The fourth column lists the size, in bytes, of the file. You get these first four columns by choosing any of the Table options. When you choose Linked, the file name includes the complete path.

With **Active**, you get three additional columns. The fifth column lists the number of worksheets in the file. The sixth column shows a 0 if you have not modified the file since the last save, and a 1 if you have modified it. The seventh column shows a 1, which indicates that you can save the file. A 0 appears in this column only when the file is shared on a network or marked read-only.

Transferring Files

1-2-3 provides a number of ways to pass data between itself and other programs. The simplest file format is straight text; a straight text file also is called an *ASCII file*. Most programs, including spreadsheets, word processors, and database management systems, can create text files. To create a text file in 1-2-3, use /**Print File**, which Chapter 8 covers in detail. To read a text file into a worksheet, use /**File Import**.

Transferring Files with /File Import

/**File Import** is a special type of /**File Combine**. You combine the information into the current worksheet, starting at the position of the cell pointer. Any existing data in these cells is overwritten. When you execute the /**File Import** command, 1-2-3 lists the files contained in the current directory and ending with .PRN extensions. To list files that have another extension—.TXT, for example—type the appropriate characters (such as ***.TXT**) and press Enter.

Importing Unstructured Text Files

The typical text file contains lines of data, each line ending with a carriage return. Except for the carriage returns, these text files have no structure. You combine them by using /**File Import Text**. Figure 7.32 shows the result of importing a typical text file into a worksheet. This data may have come from a mainframe or minicomputer personnel program. Each line in the text file becomes a long label in a cell. All the data is in column A. If you import a list of names or simply want to see this data, you are finished. In most cases, however, you want to work with this data in separate cells; you want numbers as numbers and dates as dates, not labels. To make this data usable, use the /**Data Parse** command. See Chapter 10, "Managing Data," for a complete discussion of the /**Data Parse** command.

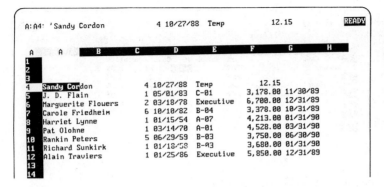

Fig. 7.32.
An unstructured text file imported with /File Import Text as long labels.

Importing Delimited Files

Some ASCII files are in a special format that enables them to be imported into separate cells without being parsed. This special format is called the *delimited* format. There is a delimiter between each field, and labels are enclosed in quotation marks. A delimiter can be a space, comma, colon, or semicolon. If the labels are not enclosed in quotation marks, they are ignored, and only the numbers are imported.

To import a delimited file, use /File Import Numbers. In spite of the name, this command really means "file import delimited." Figure 7.33 is an example of a delimited file. Figure 7.34 shows the results after the execution of /File Import Numbers.

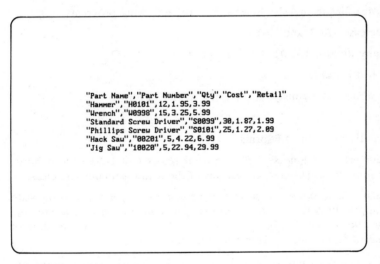

Fig. 7.33.
A delimited ASCII file.

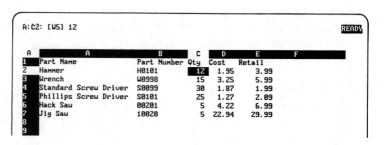

Fig. 7.34.
The delimited
ASCII file after
the execution
of /File Import
Numbers.

Transferring Files with the Translate Utility

Translate is not part of the 1-2-3 worksheet program but is a separate program. Type **trans** from the operating system prompt to execute Translate, or choose **T**ranslate from the 1-2-3 Access System menu.

Use Translate to convert files so that they can be read by a different program. You can convert files to 1-2-3 Release 3 from the following programs:

- dBASE II, III, and III Plus
- DisplayWrite and Manuscript, using the RFT/DCA format
- Multiplan
- Products that use the DIF format

You can convert files from 1-2-3 Release 3 to the following programs:

- 1-2-3 Release 1A, 2, and 2.01
- Symphony Release 1, 1.01, 1.1, 1.2, and 2
- dBASE II, III, and III Plus
- DisplayWrite and Manuscript, using the RFT/DCA format
- Multiplan
- Products that use the DIF format

When you convert 1-2-3 Release 3 files to prior releases of 1-2-3 or Symphony, you will lose some information if you use any of the features unique to Release 3.

To use Translate, first choose the format or program that you want to translate from; then choose the format or program that you want to translate to (see fig. 7.35). Finally, choose the file that you want to translate. Type the file name of the output file to be created by Translate and press Enter.

When you translate from Release 3, you can translate one worksheet in the file or all worksheets into separate files. When you translate to dBASE format, you can translate the entire file or a named range. In most cases, the file contains data

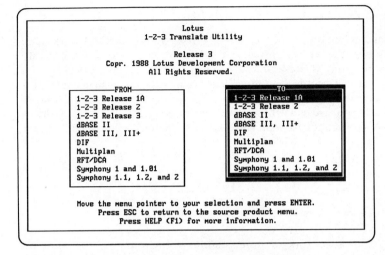

Lotus
1-2-3 Translate Utility

Release 3
Copr. 1988 Lotus Development Corporation
All Rights Reserved.

```
┌─FROM──────────────┐          ┌─TO─────────────────────┐
│ 1-2-3 Release 1A  │          │ 1-2-3 Release 1A       │
│ 1-2-3 Release 2   │          │ 1-2-3 Release 2        │
│ 1-2-3 Release 3   │          │ dBASE II               │
│ dBASE II          │          │ dBASE III, III+        │
│ dBASE III, III+   │          │ DIF                    │
│ DIF               │          │ Multiplan              │
│ Multiplan         │          │ RFT/DCA                │
│ RFT/DCA           │          │ Symphony 1 and 1.01    │
│ Symphony 1 and 1.01│         │ Symphony 1.1, 1.2, and 2│
│ Symphony 1.1, 1.2, and 2│    └────────────────────────┘
└───────────────────┘
```

Move the menu pointer to your selection and press ENTER.
Press ESC to return to the source product menu.
Press HELP (F1) for more information.

Fig. 7.35.
The menu of choices to translate to and from.

in addition to the Input range, so make sure that you use /**R**ange **N**ame to name the database Input range. When you translate a file into dBASE format, the range or entire file must consist only of a database Input range.

Using Earlier 1-2-3 and Symphony Files in Release 3

1-2-3 Release 3 can read files created by all prior releases of 1-2-3 and Symphony. Just use /**F**ile **R**etrieve or /**F**ile **O**pen and specify the complete file name and extension; you do not use Translate. The Translate menu (fig. 7.35) seems to give you the option of translating files to 1-2-3 Release 3 format from the formats for prior releases of 1-2-3 and Symphony. If you choose one of these formats, however, you simply get a message telling you that you do not need to translate the file.

1-2-3 Release 3 can write files in 1-2-3 Release 2 format if you haven't used any features unique to Release 3. Just use /**F**ile **S**ave and specify a file name with a .WK1 extension. Symphony Releases 1.1, 1.2, and 2 also can read these files.

You cannot save a file in Release 2 format if the file contains multiple worksheets or is sealed. Functions that arc new with Release 3 or that contain new arguments are treated like Release 2 add-in functions. New functions or those containing new arguments evaluate to NA in the worksheet. Formats and settings new with Release 3, as well as notes, are lost. Labels larger than 240 characters are truncated. Formulas larger than 240 characters remain in the cell, but the cell cannot be edited in Release 2 or Symphony.

To create a file in Release 3 that can be read by 1-2-3 Release 1A or Symphony Releases 1 or 1.01, you must use Translate.

Using External Databases

You can read and create dBASE III files directly from within the 1-2-3 worksheet. Lotus provides a special "driver" program that enables you to access and create dBASE III files by using /Data External commands. Using /Data External with drivers is covered in Chapter 10. Other vendors of database management programs supply their own drivers that enable 1-2-3 to access and create files from their programs. If you use a database management program and want to share files with 1-2-3, contact the vendor and find out whether it has such a driver available.

Using 1-2-3 in a Multiuser Environment

If you use 1-2-3 in a network or other multiuser environment, you must be aware that two or more people can try to access or update the same file at the same time. The network administrator sets up shared disks so that some files can be shared and some cannot. You do not have to worry about those files on a network server that you alone can read.

Different programs handle the problems of multiple access in different ways. With a database management system such as dBASE III Plus, the program itself controls access so that many users can access the database at the same time. With most programs, such as word processors, the network administrator makes sure that these files are identified as *nonsharable*. This means that only one person can access any one file at one time. If you are working with a word processing file, no one else can read the file until you close it. Then it is available to the next person who wants it.

These techniques do not work with 1-2-3, so Release 3 has a "reservation" system to avoid multiple updates of the same shared file. When you read a file that no one else is using, 1-2-3 gives you a reservation for that file, which means that you can update the file and save it under the same name.

When you read a shared file while someone else is working on it, 1-2-3 prompts you that the file is in use and asks whether you want the file without a reservation (see fig 7.36). If you choose **Yes**, you can access the file in read-only status.

Fig. 7.36.
A file already
in use,
prompting
whether you
want to read it
without a
reservation.

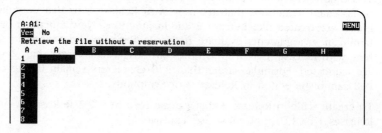

The RO status indicator at the bottom of the screen warns you that you cannot save the file under its current name (see fig. 7.37). If you want to save the file, you must give it a different name.

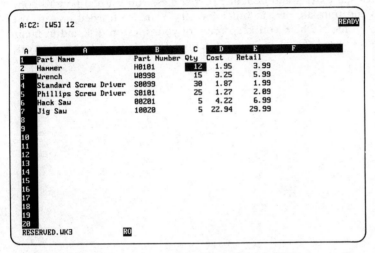

Fig. 7.37.
The RO status indicator, warning you that you cannot save the file under its current name.

If you have the reservation for a file, you keep the reservation until you remove the file (under the same name) from your worksheet. You can remove the file with /Quit, /Worksheet Erase, /Worksheet Delete File, or /File Retrieve. You also can release the reservation with /File Save if you save the file under a different name. You can release the reservation manually with /File Admin Reservation Release. You still have the file in memory, but you cannot save the file.

This reservation system works automatically. If many people can read a file but only one can update it, you can assign the reservation manually. Use /File Admin Reservation Setting Manual so that the first person to read a file does not get the reservation. Everyone who reads the file has read-only access until one person gets the reservation with /File Admin Reservation Get. In general, using manual reservation settings is a bad idea because you cannot enforce that only authorized people get the reservation. The network administrator may be able to set up restricted access for those people who can read but should not write to a file.

When you have a file that contains references to other files, 1-2-3 updates these formulas when you read the file. If you believe that one or more of these external files were updated since you read your file, use /File Admin Link-Refresh to update these formulas.

Although executing the /File Admin Link-Refresh command requires simply selecting the command and pressing Enter, you may need to insert a note in your files reminding you to update files when necessary. See Chapter 3 for more information on linking files and using /File Admin Link-Refresh.

Chapter Summary

In this chapter, you learned how to manage files on disk, and how to save and read whole files and extract and combine partial files. You learned how to combine text files and translate files to other formats. You also learned how to use lists and tables of files to help you keep track of your files on disk and in memory. Finally, you learned the special considerations for using 1-2-3 on a network.

Part II

Creating 1-2-3
Reports and Graphs

Includes

Printing Reports

Creating and Printing Graphs

8

Printing Reports

1-2-3 is a powerful tool for developing and manipulating information in column-and-row format. You can enter and edit your worksheet and database files on-screen, as well as store the data on disk. But to make good use of your data, you often need it in printed form—for example, as an income forecast, a budget analysis, or a detailed reorder list to central stores.

By using 1-2-3's /Print command, you can access several levels of print options to meet your printing needs. You can use the /Print Printer command sequence to send data directly from 1-2-3 to the printer. You can use /Print File *filename* to create a print file (.PRN), which you can incorporate into a word processing file. Or you can use /Print Encoded *filename* to create an encoded file (.ENC), which you can later send to the printer. Either file can be printed from within 1-2-3 or from the operating system prompt.

Note that the /Print menu is one of the most complex menus in 1-2-3. The menu is complex because 1-2-3 gives you considerable control over the design of printed output—from simple one-page reports to longer reports that incorporate data from many worksheets and include sophisticated graphs. Several levels of menus offer commands that you can use to design reports, enhance reports, and control the printer.

Figure 8.1 illustrates the Print menu, with its various menu levels presented as horizontal bars. Notice that the middle portion of the menu contains primarily the commands you use to design your reports, such as commands for setting headers and footers, margins, and page length. The lower left portion of the menu offers commands for enhancing your reports, such as commands for improving the layout, choosing fonts, and selecting color. In the lower right portion of the menu are commands for printing graphs.

295

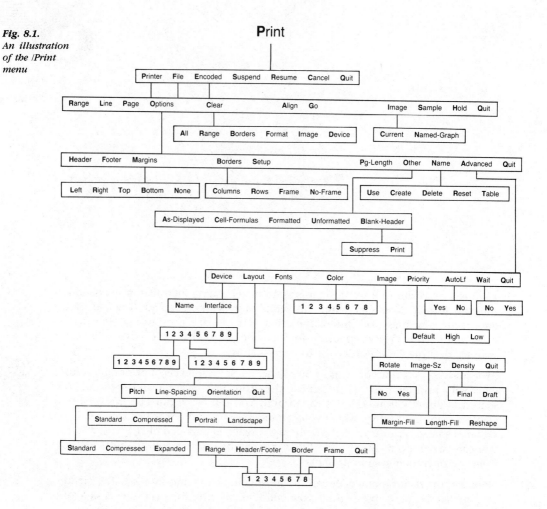

Fig. 8.1.
An illustration of the /Print menu

Although earlier versions of 1-2-3 required the use of a separate program to print graphs, you now can print graphs from the **Print** menu. Graph printing is covered separately in the next chapter.

This chapter shows you how to do the following:

- Print a report immediately, create a file for delayed printing, or create a file for a word processor

- Print a report using 1-2-3's default settings

- Print a multiple-page report

- Print multiple ranges

- Exclude segments within a designated print range

- Change the default settings for page layout and printer control

- Print worksheet formulas

- Enhance the readability and impact of a report with different type styles, sizes, fonts, and colors

- Control paper movement

As indicated in previous chapters, 1-2-3's three-dimensional capability enables you to have as many as 255 worksheets in memory at one time. A printed report can contain data from a single worksheet or from two or more worksheets. Because most print commands work the same whether you are printing from a single worksheet or from multiple worksheets, you will work primarily with one worksheet in this chapter. Techniques for printing from multiple worksheets are covered in the section "Printing Multiple Ranges."

You should know that in 1-2-3 a *print job* can contain data ranges, graphs, and blank lines, which are sent to the printer or a disk file. A job begins when you select **Line**, **Page**, or **Go** from the **/Print Printer**, **/Print File**, or **/Print Encoded** menu. A job ends when you exit the **Print** menu by selecting **Quit**, pressing Esc, pressing **/Print Cancel**, or pressing Ctrl-Break. Later in the chapter, you will learn how to use a **/Print** command sequence to establish your printing priorities. For now, you are ready to begin using the **Print** menu.

Getting Started from the /Print Menu (/Print [P,F,E])

You must start any **/Print** command sequence from the 1-2-3 command menu. Figure 8.2 shows the **Print** option highlighted on the control panel's second line. The third line displays the choices available on the main **Print** menu.

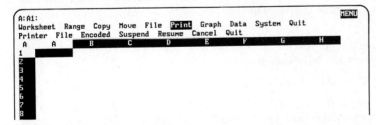

Fig. 8.2.
The 1-2-3 command menu, from which all print operations are accessed.

After choosing **/Print** from the 1-2-3 command menu, you must select one of the first three options shown in figure 8.3: **Printer**, **File**, or **Encoded**. You use the next three options—Suspend, **R**esume, and Cancel—only when a print job is in progress. They will be covered later in the chapter. The seventh option, **Q**uit, returns you to READY mode.

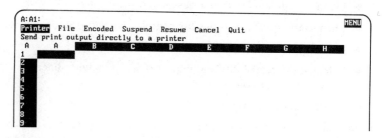

Fig. 8.3.
The initial
print decision:
print to the
printer, a text
file, or an
encoded file.

To indicate that you want to use a printer on-line, choose **P**rinter. Your report will be sent directly to the current printer. (See this chapter's "Choosing a Printer" section for details on how to select a printer.)

To create a text file on disk, select **F**ile. A text file can contain data but no graphs or special printer codes. Later, you can print the text file from within 1-2-3 or from the operating system prompt, or you can incorporate the text file into a word processing file.

To create an encoded file on disk, choose **E**ncoded. An encoded file can contain data, graphs, and printer codes for 1-2-3 print options, such as fonts, colors, and line spacing. An encoded file can be printed from the operating system prompt, but such a file is not suitable for transferring data to another program.

If you choose **F**ile or **E**ncoded, you must respond to the prompt for a file name by typing a name that contains up to eight characters. You do not need to add a file extension because 1-2-3 will automatically assign the .PRN (print file) or .ENC (encoded file) extension. You can specify a different extension if you want.

You use an encoded file for printing at another time or from another computer while preserving all the special print options available in 1-2-3. When you create an encoded file, be sure that the selected printer is the same as the one you will use eventually to print the file. An encoded file contains printer codes that control special printer features, such as fonts and line spacing. Because these codes are printer-specific, an encoded file created for one printer may not print correctly on another printer. The printer control codes embedded in the encoded file ensure that the final output will look the same as output printed directly from 1-2-3.

To print an encoded file, you use the operating system COPY command with the /B option. Consider the following example:

    COPY C:\LOTUS\SALES.ENC/B LPT1:

This command prints the file SALES.ENC, located in directory C:\LOTUS, on the printer connected to the port LPT1 (usually the default printer port). Other printer ports are LPT2, COM1, and COM2.

After you select **Printer**, **File**, or **Encoded**, the second line of the control panel displays a menu with 11 options (see fig. 8.4). Throughout the chapter, this menu is referred to as the /Print [**P,F,E**] menu. The notation /Print [**P,F,E**] indicates that options on this menu are available when you select /Print **Printer**, /Print **File**, or /Print **Encoded**. Occasionally, an abbreviated notation is used in a command sequence, such as /Print [**P,E**] Options Advanced Fonts. This sequence indicates that the option being discussed—in this case, Fonts—will not affect your text file.

The /Print [**P,F,E**] menu offers the following choices:

Menu Item	Description
Range	Indicates what section of the worksheet is to be printed
Line	Advances the paper in the printer by one line
Page	Advances the paper in the printer to the top of the next page
Options	Changes default print settings and offers a number of print enhancements
Clear	Erases some or all of the previously entered print settings
Align	Signals that the paper in the printer is set to the beginning of a page
Go	Starts printing
Image	Selects a graph to print
Sample	Prints a sample worksheet
Hold	Returns to READY mode without closing the current print job
Quit	Exits the **Print** menu and closes the current print job

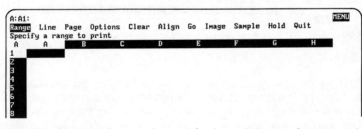

Fig. 8.4.
Options on the
/Print [P,F,E]
menu.

In 1-2-3, the most frequently used (or least dangerous) commands are usually on the left side of a menu. In any print command sequence, you start with /**Print**; branch to **Printer**, **File**, or **Encoded**; and then proceed to the next menu. Regardless of which branch you select, you must specify a **Range** to print, choose **Align**, select **Go** to begin printing, and then select **Quit** or press the Esc key twice to return to the worksheet. All other selections are optional.

Selecting **Align** ensures that printing will begin at the top of all succeeding pages after the first page. Make sure in particular that you reposition your printer paper and use the **Align** command whenever you have aborted a print job.

You use **Page** to move the paper to the top of the next page. **Page** also can be used to eject a blank page, making it easier for you to tear off the last page of your report.

Before you learn which print commands to use for performing specific tasks or operations, you need a general understanding of 1-2-3's default print settings. These settings are discussed in the next section.

Understanding the Default Print Settings

To minimize the keystrokes necessary for a basic print operation, 1-2-3 includes default settings based on certain assumptions about how typical users want to print their reports. The default print operation produces 72 characters per line and 56 lines per page on 8 1/2-by-11-inch continuous-feed paper, and uses the first parallel printer installed. You should check the current settings for your 1-2-3 program, however, for another user may have changed them.

Current Printer Settings

Cue:
Use /Worksheet
Global Default
Printer to check
the current default
print settings.

Check the global default settings before you print. To check these settings, you issue the **/Worksheet Global Default** command, which produces the menu shown in figure 8.5.

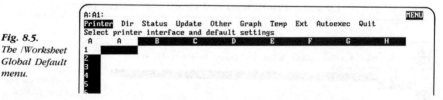

Fig. 8.5.
The /Worksheet
Global Default
menu.

In this menu, three of the options (**Printer**, **Status**, and **Update**) pertain directly to print settings. You use **Printer** to change a setting for the current work session, and **Update** to cause the change to remain in effect every time you reload 1-2-3. To view the current settings, you choose **Status**; the current printer settings will be displayed in a status report similar to that shown in figure 8.6.

The settings relevant to printing are in the upper-left corner of the status screen. The first two settings contain hardware-specific information. The Margins and Page length sections show page layout information. Wait...No is the setting for

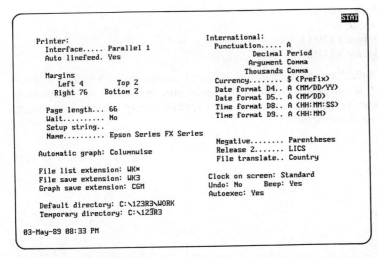

STAT

```
Printer:                          International:
   Interface..... Parallel 1         Punctuation..... A
   Auto linefeed. Yes                        Decimal Period
                                            Argument Comma
   Margins                               Thousands Comma
      Left 4        Top 2            Currency........ $ (Prefix)
      Right 76      Bottom 2         Date format D4.. A (MM/DD/YY)
                                     Date format D5.. A (MM/DD)
   Page length... 66                 Time format D8.. A (HH:MM:SS)
   Wait.......... No                 Time format D9.. A (HH:MM)
   Setup string..
   Name.......... Epson Series FX Series

   Automatic graph: Columnwise       Negative........ Parentheses
                                     Release 2....... LICS
                                     File translate.. Country
   File list extension: WK*
   File save extension: WK3          Clock on screen: Standard
   Graph save extension: CGM         Undo: No      Beep: Yes
                                     Autoexec: Yes
   Default directory: C:\123R3\WORK
   Temporary directory: C:\123R3

03-May-89 08:33 PM
```

Fig. 8.6.
A sample
default status
report.

continuous-feed paper, and no setup string is in effect. Finally, Name indicates which printer is current.

Global Default Hardware-Specific Options

If you want to change any of the print settings shown in the default status report, you issue the /Worksheet Global Default Printer command. Notice in the menu shown in figure 8.7 that the first two options, Interface and AutoLf, are the same as the first two settings in the default status report.

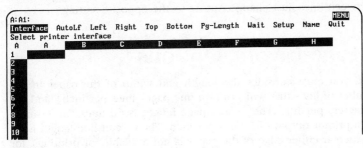

```
A:A1:                                                                  MENU
Interface AutoLf Left Right Top Bottom Pg-Length Wait Setup Name Quit
Select printer interface
A      A          B        C        D        E        F        G        H
1
2
3
4
5
6
7
8
9
10
```

Fig. 8.7.
The /Worksheet
Global Default
Printer menu.

The Interface option specifies one of the following connections between your computer and your printer:

1 Parallel 1 (the default)
2 Serial 1
3 Parallel 2
4 Serial 2
5 Output Device LPT1

6 Output Device LPT2
7 Output Device LPT3
8 Output Device COM1
9 Output Device COM2

Choices 5 through 9 are applicable only if your computer is part of a local area network (LAN). If you select either of the serial port options (2 or 4), another menu will appear. From that menu, you must specify one of the following baud rates (data transmission speeds):

1 110 baud
2 150 baud
3 300 baud
4 600 baud
5 1200 baud
6 2400 baud
7 4800 baud
8 9600 baud
9 19200 baud

For example, a 1200 baud rate equals approximately 120 characters per second.

The baud rate that you select must match the printer's baud rate setting. In addition, the printer must be configured for 8 data bits, 1 stop bit (2 stop bits at 110 baud), and no parity. Check your printer manual for information about the interface and baud rate settings, as well as other print settings.

The AutoLf setting specifies the printer's end-of-line procedure. Yes indicates that the paper is automatically advanced one line when the printer receives a carriage return; No means that a line is *not* automatically advanced when the printer receives a carriage return. With most printers, you should leave AutoLf in its default setting of No. To determine whether the setting is correct, you can print a range of two or more rows. If the output is double-spaced or if the paper does not advance between lines, just change AutoLf to the opposite setting.

Default Page-Layout Options

For page layout, you must consider the length and width of the paper in the printer, the number of lines that will print on one page (lines per inch), and the number of characters per line. The default page length is 66 lines, for 11-inch-long paper and a printer output of 6 lines per inch. The default line length is 80 characters (1/4 inch at either edge of the paper is not available for printing), for 8 1/2-inch-wide paper and a printer output of 10 characters per inch. However, because of 1-2-3's default margin settings (2-line margins at the top and bottom, and 4-character margins at the right and left), the full page width and length are not used. To maximize the amount of information per printed page, set all margins to 0.

Look again at figure 8.7, which shows the /Worksheet Global Default Printer menu. The following options determine default page-layout characteristics:

Menu Item	Message
Left	Default left margin (0..1000):4
Right	Default right margin (0..1000):76
Top	Default top margin (0..240):2
Bottom	Default bottom margin (0..240):2
Pg-Length	Default lines per page (1..1000):66

In each message, the numbers enclosed in parentheses indicate the minimum and maximum values you can select. The number after the colon is the current setting.

Notice that both the left and right margins are given as the number of characters from the left edge of the paper. To calculate the width of your report, subtract the current left margin setting (4) from the current right margin setting (76). Your report will be printed with 72 characters per line.

To calculate how many lines of your worksheet will be printed on each page, you need to subtract not only the lines for the top and bottom margins but also the lines that 1-2-3 automatically reserves for a header and footer (see fig. 8.8). If, for example, you are using all default settings, the actual number of worksheet lines (or rows) that will be printed is 56. You get this number of lines because 1-2-3 assigns 2 lines each for the top and bottom margins, and reserves 3 lines each for the header and footer. These 6 lines are reserved even if you do not supply a header or footer—unless you select /Print [P,F,E] Options Other Blank-Header Suppress. Because the default page length is 66, you subtract 4 lines for the top and bottom margins and 6 lines reserved for the header and footer to get 56 lines printed. (For more information about including headers and footers in your printed reports, refer to the section "Creating Headers and Footers.")

Other Default Options: Wait, Setup, and Name

The final three options for default printer settings control the way paper is fed to the printer (**Wait**), printer-specific options (**Setup**), and the specific printer you use (**Name**).

If you are using continuous-feed paper or a sheet-feeder bin, do not change the **Wait** option's default setting of **No**. If you are hand-feeding single sheets of paper, select **Yes** to change the default setting; printing will pause at the end of each page so that you can insert a new sheet of paper. After you insert the page, select /Print **Resume** to continue printing.

The default setting for **Setup** is no setup string. No special printer-control features, such as underlining or double-striking, are in effect. (For more information about setup strings, see the section "Using Setup Strings.")

The menu that appears after you select **Name** depends on decisions you made during installation. Suppose, for example, that you installed your 1-2-3 program

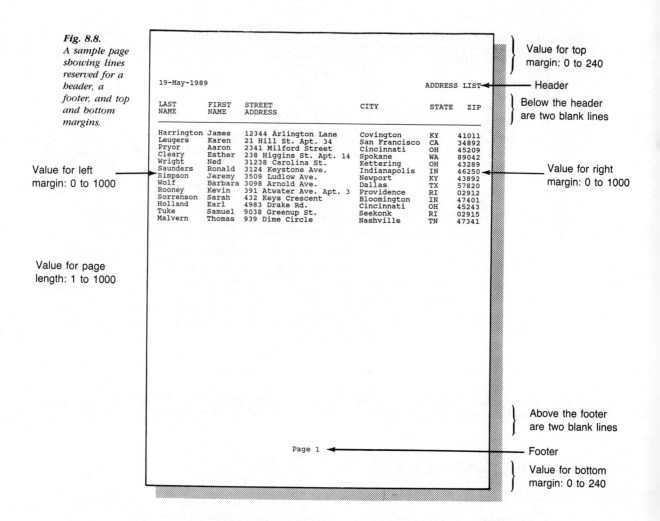

Fig. 8.8.
A sample page showing lines reserved for a header, a footer, and top and bottom margins.

Value for top margin: 0 to 240

Header

Below the header are two blank lines

Value for left margin: 0 to 1000

Value for right margin: 0 to 1000

Value for page length: 1 to 1000

Above the footer are two blank lines

Footer

Value for bottom margin: 0 to 240

```
19-May-1989                                              ADDRESS LIST

LAST       FIRST    STREET
NAME       NAME     ADDRESS                      CITY          STATE   ZIP

Harrington James    12344 Arlington Lane         Covington     KY      41011
Leugers    Karen    21 Hill St. Apt. 34          San Francisco CA      34892
Pryor      Aaron    2341 Milford Street          Cincinnati    OH      45209
Cleary     Esther   238 Higgins St. Apt. 14      Spokane       WA      89042
Wright     Ned      31238 Carolina St.           Kettering     OH      43289
Saunders   Ronald   3124 Keystone Ave.           Indianapolis  IN      46250
Simpson    Jeremy   3509 Ludlow Ave.             Newport       KY      43892
Wolf       Barbara  3098 Arnold Ave.             Dallas        TX      57820
Rooney     Kevin    391 Atwater Ave. Apt. 3      Providence    RI      02912
Sorrenson  Sarah    432 Keys Crescent            Bloomington   IN      47401
Holland    Earl     4983 Drake Rd.               Cincinnati    OH      45243
Tuke       Samuel   9038 Greenup St.             Seekonk       RI      02915
Malvern    Thomas   939 Dime Circle              Nashville     TN      47341




                                    Page 1
```

to print on two different printers: an Epson printer at home and an IBM printer at work. And suppose that because each printer uses a parallel port, you set **Interface** to 1 (parallel 1). In that case, selecting **Name** will produce a menu that offers option 1 (the Epson printer) and option 2 (the IBM printer). If you are at home, choose **1**; if you are at work, choose **2**.

Remember that if you use the /Worksheet Global Default Printer command to change print settings, the new settings remain in effect for the current work session. For the settings to remain the defaults whenever you start 1-2-3, you must use the /Worksheet Global Default Update command after you have made the changes you want.

Reminder:
Select /Worksheet Global Default Update to keep changed default settings in effect for future 1-2-3 sessions.

Printing Your Reports

The 1-2-3 **P**rint menu is designed to accommodate all your worksheet printing needs, from the simplest to the more complex. You need to be concerned with only the /**P**rint [**P,F,E**] menu if you want to print a report quickly—one that does not require changing any default print settings, such as those for paper size, or adding any special enhancements, such as a header, a footer, or a different style of type. If you have special requirements for paper size, margins, or page length, you will need to use the commands available on the menus that follow the /**P**rint [**P,F,E**] menu.

This section shows you how to print reports quickly and efficiently by using a minimum of commands on the /**P**rint [**P,F,E**] menu. First, you will learn how to print a short report of a page or less with only four commands, and then you will learn how to print a multiple-page report. In the next section, you will learn how to include headers and footers in your reports, print worksheet formulas rather than their results, and print borders on each page. Later in the chapter, you will become familiar with the commands that enhance your reports, enabling you to control such features as type style, line spacing, and color.

Figure 8.9 shows a large model, occupying the range A:A1..A:W130. This model, which is referenced throughout the chapter, is used only as an example of a complex worksheet from which you might want to generate reports.

Printing One Screenful of Data (PrtSc)

Before you print any portion of a 1-2-3 worksheet, you need to decide whether the output must be of "report" quality (suitable for official distribution or filing) or whether a "screen dump" (hard copy of the screen's contents) will be adequate. To obtain the printed output shown in figure 8.10, for example, you simply retrieve the Cash Flow Projector worksheet and then press Shift-PrtSc.

Cue:
Pressing Shift-PrtSc for a "screen dump" prints everything on the screen.

The resulting printout captures everything that is on-screen, even such unwanted items as the contents of the highlighted cell A1 and the mode indicator. This kind of "quick and dirty" printout is appropriate for documenting errors, entry data, or model construction.

Whether you can use Shift-PrtSc to obtain a screen dump of a 1-2-3 screen depends on the specifications of your video display and printer hardware. Some

Fig. 8.9.
The Cash Flow Projector worksheet.

CASH FLOW PROJECTOR — Copyright (C) 1989 Que Corporation

BALANCES IN WORKING CAPITAL ACCOUNTS

	Dec	Jan	Feb	Mar	Apr	May	Jun	Jul	Aug	Sep	Oct	Nov	Dec
Assets													
Cash	$17,355	$31,643	$34,333	$36,657	$35,614	$29,146	$20,000	$20,000	$20,000	$76,623	$186,131	$337,995	$582,796
Accounts Receivable	493,151	510,780	533,597	551,287	577,314	614,997	641,802	750,544	879,271	989,501	1,097,516	1,170,846	1,218,036
Inventory	163,833	169,209	176,671	189,246	206,188	228,828	268,990	296,527	324,230	345,629	352,697	358,926	358,926
Liabilities													
Accounts Payable	125,000	130,754	139,851	150,186	163,731	180,350	203,669	225,085	243,320	258,740	267,621	272,747	275,041
Line of Credit	0	0	0	0	0	0	1,834	8,327	2,035	0	0	0	0
Net Working Capital	$549,339	$580,878	$604,750	$627,003	$555,984	$692,620	$726,289	$833,659	$978,146	$1,153,013	$1,368,812	$1,594,820	$1,884,718

SALES

	Oct	Nov	Dec	Jan	Feb	Mar	Apr	May	Jun	Jul	Aug	Sep	Oct	Nov	Dec	Total
Profit Center 1	$27,832	$23,864	$26,125	$31,336	$37,954	$43,879	$51,471	$56,853	$53,145	$54,140	$53,614	$52,015	$48,902	$44,091	$42,536	$570,036
Profit Center 2	13,489	21,444	20,140	22,572	24,888	25,167	32,588	40,140	37,970	34,587	33,463	28,939	24,153	27,060	26,701	358,228
Profit Center 3	126,811	124,382	123,618	131,685	129,044	131,723	139,221	141,879	143,803	147,108	147,032	153,440	149,990	145,198	150,510	1,716,633
Profit Center 4	94,285	92,447	89,010	95,473	98,008	96,986	95,318	103,538	108,146	108,642	106,065	110,401	112,018	111,956	107,522	1,254,073
Profit Center 5										115,000	175,000	225,000	300,000	325,000	350,000	1,490,000
Total Sales	$262,417	$262,137	$256,893	$281,066	$289,894	$297,755	$318,598	$342,510	$349,064	$459,477	$515,174	$569,795	$635,063	$653,305	$677,269	$5,388,970

Percent of Collections

		Oct	Nov	Dec	Jan	Feb	Mar	Apr	May	Jun	Jul	Aug	Sep	Oct	Nov	Dec
	Cash	10%	10%	10%	10%	10%	10%	10%	10%	10%	10%	10%	10%	10%	10%	10%
	30 Days	20%	20%	20%	20%	20%	20%	20%	20%	20%	20%	20%	20%	20%	20%	20%
	60 Days	50%	50%	50%	50%	50%	50%	50%	50%	50%	50%	50%	50%	50%	50%	50%
	90 Days	20%	20%	20%	20%	20%	20%	20%	20%	20%	20%	20%	20%	20%	20%	20%

	Jan	Feb	Mar	Apr	May	Jun	Jul	Aug	Sep	Oct	Nov	Dec	Total
Cash Collections	$263,437	$267,077	$280,066	$292,571	$304,827	$322,258	$350,735	$386,447	$459,566	$526,948	$582,275	$629,878	$4,654,085

PURCHASES

Cost of Goods Sold

		Oct	Nov	Dec	Jan	Feb	Mar	Apr	May	Jun	Jul	Aug	Sep	Oct	Nov	Dec	Total
Profit Center 1	33%	$9,185	$7,875	$8,621	$10,341	$12,525	$14,480	$16,985	$18,794	$17,538	$17,866	$17,693	$17,165	$16,138	$14,550	$14,037	$188,112
Profit Center 2	29%	$3,912	$6,219	$5,841	$6,546	$7,218	$7,298	$9,451	$11,641	$11,011	$10,030	$9,704	$8,392	$7,004	$7,847	$7,743	$103,886
Profit Center 3	50%	$63,406	$62,191	$61,809	$65,843	$64,522	$65,862	$69,611	$70,940	$74,902	$73,554	$73,516	$76,720	$74,995	$72,599	$75,255	$858,317
Profit Center 4	67%	$63,171	$61,939	$59,637	$63,967	$65,665	$64,981	$63,863	$69,370	$72,458	$72,790	$71,064	$73,969	$75,052	$75,011	$72,040	$840,229
Profit Center 5	30%	$0	$0	$0	$0	$0	$0	$0	$0	$0	$34,500	$52,500	$67,500	$90,000	$97,500	$105,000	$447,000
Total Cost of Goods Sold		$139,673	$138,224	$135,908	$146,696	$149,930	$152,621	$159,910	$170,745	$175,908	$208,741	$224,476	$243,746	$263,189	$257,507	$274,075	$2,437,543

Inventory Purchasing Schedule

		Oct	Nov	Dec	Jan	Feb	Mar	Apr	May	Jun	Jul	Aug	Sep	Oct	Nov	Dec
	0 Days in Advance	5%	5%	5%	5%	5%	5%	5%	5%	5%	5%	5%	5%	5%	5%	5%
	30 Days in Advance	50%	50%	50%	50%	50%	50%	50%	50%	50%	50%	50%	50%	50%	50%	50%
	60 Days in Advance	30%	30%	30%	30%	30%	30%	30%	30%	30%	30%	30%	30%	30%	30%	30%
	90 Days in Advance	15%	15%	15%	15%	15%	15%	15%	15%	15%	15%	15%	15%	15%	15%	15%

	Oct	Nov	Dec	Jan	Feb	Mar	Apr	May	Jun	Jul	Aug	Sep	Oct	Nov	Dec	Total
Inventory Purchases	$138,873	$141,363	$148,015	$152,072	$157,391	$165,196	$177,452	$192,785	$217,071	$235,277	$252,180	$265,145	$270,247	$273,747	$274,075	$2,632,637

Payment Schedule

		Oct	Nov	Dec	Jan	Feb	Mar	Apr	May	Jun	Jul	Aug	Sep	Oct	Nov	Dec
	Cash	30%	30%	30%	30%	30%	30%	30%	30%	30%	30%	30%	30%	30%	30%	30%
	30 Days	40%	40%	40%	40%	40%	40%	40%	40%	40%	40%	40%	40%	40%	40%	40%
	60 Days	30%	30%	30%	30%	30%	30%	30%	30%	30%	30%	30%	30%	30%	30%	30%

	Dec	Jan	Feb	Mar	Apr	May	Jun	Jul	Aug	Sep	Oct	Nov	Dec	Total
Payment for Purchases	$142,612	$147,237	$152,451	$158,137	$166,531	$178,375	$195,471	$215,247	$234,886	$250,999	$262,786	$269,766	$272,795	$2,504,680

Preceding block (Oct–Dec)

OPERATING EXPENSES	Oct	Nov	Dec
Profit Center 1	$20,458	$20,760	$20,963
Profit Center 2	14,377	15,002	15,587
Profit Center 3	25,921	26,393	27,339
Profit Center 4	13,922	14,885	15,801
Profit Center 5			
Corporate Overhead	14,944	15,262	15,801
Total Expenses	$89,522	$92,302	$95,491
Payment Schedule Cash	70%	70%	70%
30 Days	20%	20%	20%
60 Days	10%	10%	10%
Total Payment for Expenses			$94,266
Interest Rate			13.50%

Main block (Jan–Dec)

OPERATING EXPENSES	Jan	Feb	Mar	Apr	May	Jun	Jul	Aug	Sep	Oct	Nov	Dec	Total
Profit Center 1	$21,529	$22,329	$22,802	$23,108	$24,099	$24,422	$24,431	$25,060	$25,646	$25,515	$26,639	$26,881	$293,461
Profit Center 2	15,946	16,790	17,355	17,739	18,195	18,610	19,412	19,946	20,348	20,860	21,729	21,785	228,315
Profit Center 3	27,554	28,286	28,464	29,275	29,292	29,578	30,246	30,358	31,041	31,680	32,048	32,525	360,347
Profit Center 4	16,130	16,800	17,651	18,039	18,789	19,704	20,400	20,939	21,589	21,833	22,024	22,154	236,052
Profit Center 5													224,495
Corporate Overhead	16,332	16,474	16,933	17,616	18,575	18,640	19,278	19,544	20,225	21,142	21,565	22,378	228,702
Total Expenses	$97,491	$110,679	$117,205	$123,777	$128,950	$132,954	$136,237	$138,284	$141,844	$145,394	$148,028	$150,529	$1,571,372
Payment Schedule Cash	70%	70%	70%	70%	70%	70%	70%	70%	70%	70%	70%	70%	
30 Days	20%	20%	20%	20%	20%	20%	20%	20%	20%	20%	20%	20%	
60 Days	10%	10%	10%	10%	10%	10%	10%	10%	10%	10%	10%	10%	
Total Payment for Expenses	$96,572	$106,523	$113,928	$121,153	$126,741	$131,236	$134,852	$137,342	$140,571	$143,973	$146,883	$149,515	$1,549,288

CASH FLOW SUMMARY	Jan	Feb	Mar	Apr	May	Jun	Jul	Aug	Sep	Oct	Nov	Dec	Total
Collection of Receivables	$263,437	$287,077	$280,086	$292,571	$304,827	$322,258	$350,735	$386,447	$459,566	$528,948	$580,275	$629,878	$4,664,085
Other Cash Receipts	0	0	0	0	0	0	0	0	0	0	0	50,000	50,000
Cash Disbursements													
Payment for Purchases on Credit	147,237	152,451	158,137	166,531	178,375	195,471	215,247	234,886	250,999	262,786	269,766	272,795	2,504,680
Operating Expenses	96,572	106,523	113,928	121,153	126,741	131,236	134,852	137,342	140,571	143,973	146,883	149,515	1,549,288
Long-Term Debt Service	0	0	0	0	0	0	0	0	0	0	0	0	0
Interest Payment on Line of Credit													
Interest Rate	13.50%	13.50%	13.50%	13.50%	13.50%	13.50%	13.50%	13.50%	13.50%	13.50%	13.50%	13.50%	
Payment	5,340	5,413	5,677	5,930	6,179	6,532	7,109	7,833	9,315	10,681	11,782	12,767	94,538
Income Tax Payments							21	94	23				137
Other													
Total Cash Disbursements	249,149	264,387	277,742	293,614	311,295	333,238	357,228	380,154	400,908	417,440	428,411	435,077	4,148,543
Net Cash Generated This Period	$14,288	$2,690	$2,324	($1,043)	($6,468)	($10,980)	($6,493)	$6,293	$58,658	$109,508	$151,864	$244,801	$565,441

ANALYSIS OF CASH REQUIREMENTS	Dec	Jan	Feb	Mar	Apr	May	Jun	Jul	Aug	Sep	Oct	Nov	Dec
Beginning Cash Balance		$17,355	$31,643	$34,333	$36,657	$35,614	$29,146	$20,000	$20,000	$20,000	$76,623	$186,131	$337,995
Net Cash Generated This Period		14,288	2,690	2,324	(1,043)	(6,468)	(10,980)	(6,493)	6,293	58,658	109,508	151,864	244,801
Cash Balance before Borrowings		31,643	34,333	36,657	35,614	29,146	18,166	13,507	26,293	78,658	186,131	337,995	582,796
Minimum Acceptable Cash Balance		20,000	20,000	20,000	20,000	20,000	20,000	20,000	20,000	20,000	20,000	20,000	20,000
Amount above/(below) Minimum Acceptable Balance		11,643	14,333	16,657	15,614	9,146	(1,834)	(6,493)	6,293	58,658	166,131	317,995	562,796
Current Short-Term Borrowings	0	0	0	0	0	0	1,834	6,493	(6,293)	(2,035)	0	0	0
Total Short-Term Borrowings		0	0	0	0	0	1,834	8,327	2,035		0	0	0
Ending Cash Balance		$31,643	$34,333	$36,657	$35,614	$29,146	$20,000	$20,000	$20,000	$76,623	$186,131	$337,995	$582,796

Fig. 8.10.
The result of
using the Shift-
PrtSc key.

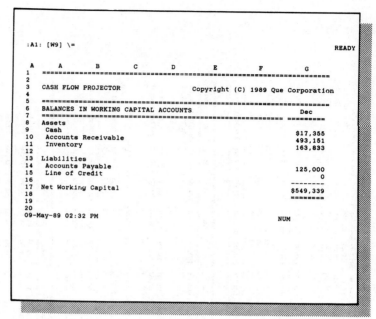

combinations work, and others do not. Here's a rule of thumb: If you can display the worksheet and a graph on-screen at the same time, you cannot use Shift-PrtSc; if you cannot view a worksheet and graph at the same time, you can use Shift-PrtSc. Of course, you must have a printer attached to your computer, and the printer must be turned on and be on-line. Try experimenting. If you cannot get a screen dump, don't worry—you still will be able to print anything you want from within 1-2-3.

Printing a Report of One Page or Less

For most print jobs, when the defaults and the printer are already set up, printing a report of a page or less involves only a few steps. These steps include the following:

1. Choosing to print to the printer or a file

2. Using **Range** to select the worksheet area you want printed

3. Selecting **Align** to signal 1-2-3 that the printer is positioned at the start of a page

4. Choosing **Go** to begin printing

5. Choosing **Page** to eject the paper

If you are certain that all default settings are correct and that no other settings have been provided, you can easily print a report of a page or less by completing the following operations. First, check that your printer is on-line and that your paper is positioned at the top of a page. Next, choose /**P**rint **P**rinter. The following menu will appear:

Range **L**ine **P**age **O**ptions **C**lear **A**lign **G**o **I**mage **S**ample **H**old **Q**uit

Indicate what part of the worksheet you want to print by selecting **R**ange and specifying the rectangular range. You can either type the cell addresses of the range corners or use POINT mode to highlight the area.

You can use the PgUp, PgDn, and End keys to designate ranges when you print. If you want to designate a range that includes the entire active area of the worksheet, first press the Home key, type a period (.) to anchor the corner of the print range, and then press the End key, followed by the Home key again. You must press Enter to finish the selection.

For many reports, a single, two-dimensional range—one rectangular region in a single worksheet—is all you will need. You also can specify multiple ranges for a single print job. (You'll learn how to do that later in the chapter.)

After highlighting the exact range you want printed, select **A**lign and then **G**o. Figure 8.11 shows the Cash Flow Projector worksheet with the range A1..G17 highlighted for printing, and figure 8.12 shows the resulting report. After you select **G**o, choose **P**age to eject the page, and then select **Q**uit to return to READY mode.

Printing a Multiple-Page Report

If your print range contains more rows or columns than can fit on a single page, 1-2-3 will automatically print the report on multiple pages. You follow the same steps for printing a small report, as described in the preceding section. Figure 8.13 shows how 1-2-3 breaks into pages a print range from A1 through X150.

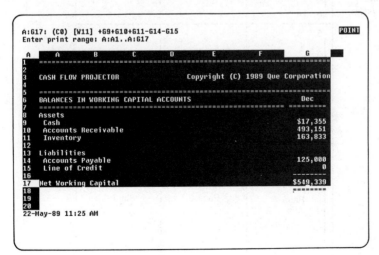

Fig. 8.11.
The Cash Flow Projector worksheet with the range highlighted.

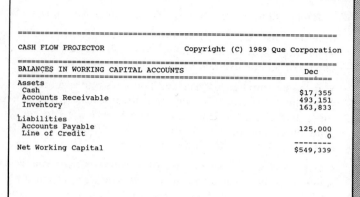

Fig. 8.12.
The report showing the highlighted range.

```
==================================================================
CASH FLOW PROJECTOR              Copyright (C) 1989 Que Corporation
==================================================================
BALANCES IN WORKING CAPITAL ACCOUNTS                         Dec
==================================================================
Assets
  Cash                                                   $17,355
  Accounts Receivable                                    493,151
  Inventory                                              163,833

Liabilities
  Accounts Payable                                       125,000
  Line of Credit                                               0
                                                       --------
Net Working Capital                                    $549,339
```

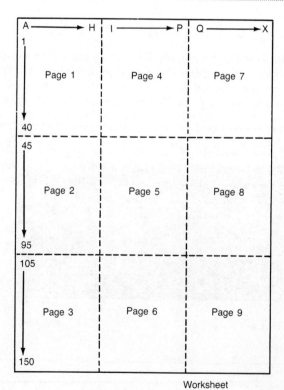

Fig. 8.13.
A large print range automatically printed on multiple pages.

When printing a multiple-page report, you must pay attention to where 1-2-3 will split the worksheet between pages, both vertically and horizontally. 1-2-3 sometimes splits pages at inappropriate locations, resulting in a report that is hard to read. Getting these page breaks to fall exactly where you want them can be a bit tricky.

Horizontal Page Breaks

Horizontal page breaks are always placed between worksheet columns. A single column is never split between two pages. The number of columns that will be printed across a page is determined by the widths of the worksheet columns and the width of the page. As discussed earlier in this chapter, the page width is defined in terms of standard characters and is equal to the right-margin number minus the left-margin number. During printing, a column that would extend past the right margin is made the first column on the next page.

1-2-3's default settings print 8 columns per page (see fig. 8.14). The reason is that the default page width is 72 characters, and the default column width is 9. Because 72 divided by 9 equals 8, 8 columns are printed on a page with no space left over. The ninth column, if included in the print range, will appear at the left edge of a subsequent page.

```
      Jan       Feb       Mar       Apr       May       Jun       Jul       Aug
  ========= ========= ========= ========= ========= ========= ========= =========

  $31,643   $34,333   $36,657   $35,614   $29,146   $20,000   $20,000   $20,000
  510,780   533,597   551,287   577,314   614,997   641,802   750,544   879,271
  169,209   176,671   189,246   206,788   228,828   269,990   296,527   324,230

  130,754   139,851   150,186   163,731   180,350   203,669   225,085   243,320
        0         0         0         0         0     1,834     8,327     2,035
  --------- --------- --------- --------- --------- --------- --------- ---------
  $580,878  $604,750  $627,003  $655,984  $692,620  $726,289  $833,659  $978,146
  ========= ========= ========= ========= ========= ========= ========= =========
```

Fig. 8.14.
Eight worksheet columns printed on a single page.

If the width of the first column in the range is increased to 10, the situation changes. Because the total width of the 8 columns is now 73, they will not fit on a 72-character-wide page. The eighth column is printed on a subsequent page (see fig. 8.15).

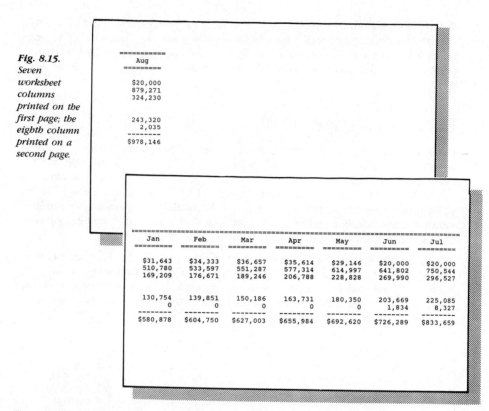

Fig. 8.15.
Seven
worksheet
columns
printed on the
first page; the
eighth column
printed on a
second page.

To determine where a horizontal page break will occur, follow these steps:

1. Determine the page width by issuing /**W**orksheet **G**lobal **D**efault **P**rinter and checking the **Left** and **Right** margin settings. Subtract the left margin from the right margin.

2. Return to your worksheet and, starting in the first column in the print range, move the cell pointer across the worksheet, adding up column widths as you go.

A horizontal page break will be placed before the column that causes the column-width total to exceed the page width.

To move a horizontal page break to the right (that is, to print more columns on a given page), follow these steps:

1. Either decrease the setting of the left margin or increase the setting of the right margin.

2. Decrease the width of one or more columns in the print range.

Finally, to move a horizontal page break to the left (that is, to print fewer columns on a given page), complete these steps:

1. Either increase the setting of the left margin or decrease the setting of the right margin.

2. Increase the width of one or more columns in the print range.

3. Insert one or more blank columns in the print range.

With these techniques, you can position horizontal page breaks to improve the appearance of your reports.

Remember that 1-2-3 treats numbers and labels differently when placing horizontal page breaks. Numbers will be printed complete on a single page because they can span only one cell. A label, however, can span two or more cells if it is wider than the column and if the cell(s) to the right of the label are blank. If a label spans a horizontal page break, part of the label will be printed on one page, and part on another. If you "paste up" several horizontal pages to create a wide report, you may be able to position the pages so that these "split" labels come together again.

Vertical Page Breaks

Vertical page breaks are inserted between worksheet rows; the row just before a vertical page break is printed at the bottom of one page, and the row just below the break is printed at the top of the next page. When printing, 1-2-3 automatically inserts a vertical page break after every *n*th row, where *n* is the setting for lines per page, as discussed earlier in this chapter.

Look again at figure 8.9, which shows the entire Cash Flow Projector worksheet, and at figure 8.16, which shows the report that results from printing range A1..G72 of that worksheet with 1-2-3's default print settings. Note that the Purchases section (which begins in row 42) is split across two pages. 1-2-3 automatically inserted a vertical page break after row 56.

The report would be easier to read if the entire Purchases section were printed on one page. To improve the appearance of the report, you can insert a page break into the worksheet by using a command sequence or by typing a page-break symbol (|::).

To insert a page break by using 1-2-3's commands, you move the cell pointer to the first column in the print range, and then to the row at which you want the page break to occur. Select the /Worksheet **P**age command, which automatically inserts a new blank row containing a page-break symbol (|::).

Suppose, for example, that you want to insert a page break just above the first separating line in the Purchases section of the Cash Flow Projector worksheet. To do this, you position the cell pointer on A42 and then execute the command. Figure 8.17 shows the inserted row with the page-break symbol. To remove the inserted row and the page-break symbol after you finish printing, use the /Worksheet **D**elete **R**ow command.

Fig. 8.16.
The Purchases
section split
between two
pages.

```
Total Cost of Goods Sold           $139,673   $138,224   $135,908
                                   ========   ========   ========

Inventory        0 Days in Advance      5%         5%         5%
Purchasing      30 Days in Advance     50%        50%        50%
Schedule        60 Days in Advance     30%        30%        30%
                90 Days in Advance     15%        15%        15%

Inventory Purchases                $138,873   $141,363   $148,015

Payment          Cash                  30%        30%        30%
Schedule        30 Days                40%        40%        40%
                60 Days                30%        30%        30%
                                                          ---------
Payment for Purchases                                     $142,612
                                                          ========
```

```
===================================================================
CASH FLOW PROJECTOR                  Copyright (C) 1989 Que Corporation
===================================================================
BALANCES IN WORKING CAPITAL ACCOUNTS                       Dec
===================================================================
Assets
  Cash                                                  $17,355
  Accounts Receivable                                   493,151
  Inventory                                             163,833

Liabilities
  Accounts Payable                                      125,000
  Line of Credit                                              0
                                                       --------
Net Working Capital                                    $549,339
                                                       ========


===================================================================
SALES                               Oct       Nov       Dec
===================================================================
Profit Center 1                  $27,832   $23,864   $26,125
Profit Center 2                   13,489    21,444    20,140
Profit Center 3                  126,811   124,382   123,618
Profit Center 4                   94,285    92,447    89,010
Profit Center 5
                                 --------  --------  --------
Total Sales                     $262,417  $262,137  $258,893
                                 ========  ========  ========

                Cash                 10%       10%       10%
Percent of     30 Days               20%       20%       20%
Collections    60 Days               50%       50%       50%
               90 Days               20%       20%       20%

Cash Collections


===================================================================
PURCHASES                           Oct       Nov       Dec
===================================================================
Cost of Goods Sold
  Profit Center 1                    33%       33%       33%
                                  $9,185    $7,875    $8,621
  Profit Center 2                    29%       29%       29%
                                  $3,912    $6,219    $5,841
  Profit Center 3                    50%       50%       50%
                                 $63,406   $62,191   $61,809
  Profit Center 4                    67%       67%       67%
                                 $63,171   $61,939   $59,637
  Profit Center 5                    30%       30%       30%
                                      $0        $0        $0
                                 --------  --------  --------
```

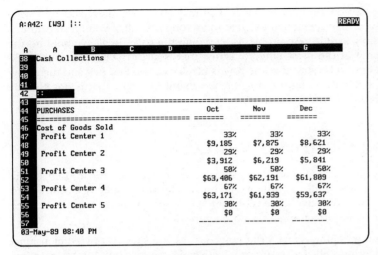

Fig. 8.17.
The result of inserting a page-break symbol in the worksheet.

As an alternative, you can insert a blank row into your worksheet where you want a page break, and then type a page-break symbol (|::) into the leftmost column of the print range in that row. The contents of cells in any row marked by the page-break symbol will not print.

The modified report is shown in figure 8.18. By having the entire Purchases section on one page, readability is greatly improved.

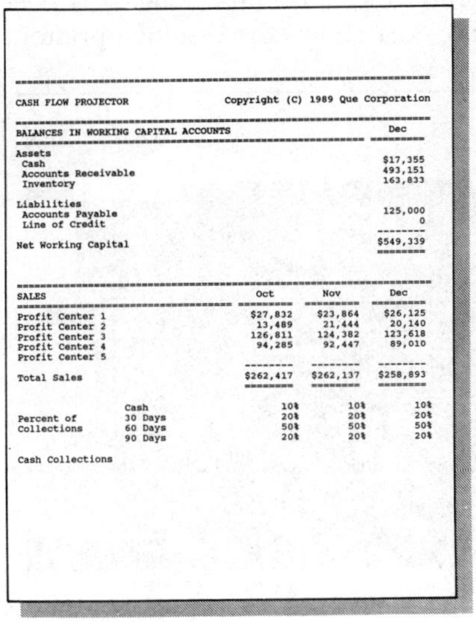

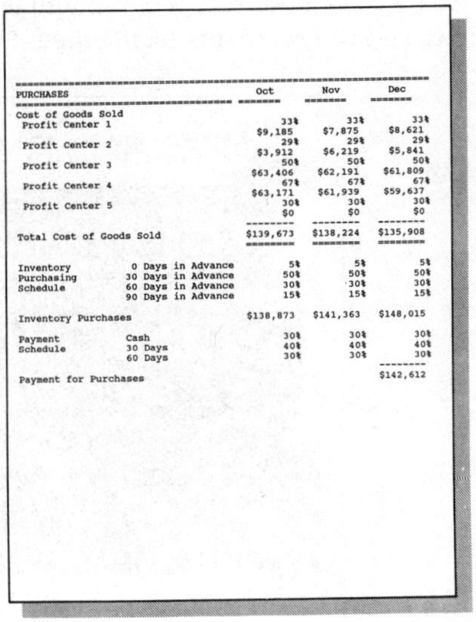

Fig. 8.18.
The Purchases section printed on a single page, following an inserted page-break symbol.

Caution:
Inserting a blank row for a page-break symbol may alter formulas or cause other problems.

Be careful when you alter a worksheet. You may alter formula results by inserting rows, or you may accidentally delete the wrong row after you finish printing. You can possibly avoid these problems by typing the page-break symbol into the leftmost column in the print range of a row that is already blank in your worksheet. Check first to be sure that the row is blank; use the End key and the arrow keys to scan the row. Using the page-break symbol in a row that is not entirely blank will keep that row from printing.

Printing Multiple Ranges

For many reports, a single two-dimensional print range, like those used in the preceding examples, is all you will need. You can, however, specify a print job to include more than one two-dimensional range in one or more worksheets, one or more three-dimensional ranges, or a combination of these.

You specify a three-dimensional print range just as you specify a two-dimensional range—by entering cell addresses or an assigned range name, or by pointing. When pointing, remember that Ctrl-PgUp and Ctrl-PgDn are used to move up and down through active worksheets. Figure 8.19 shows a worksheet with a three-dimensional print range selected, and figure 8.20 shows the resulting printout.

Cue:
To include more than one range in a print job, separate the entered ranges with a range separator symbol (;).

To specify multiple print ranges, enter each range as you would enter a single print range, and enter an argument separator after each range to separate it from the next range. The recommended argument separator is the semicolon (;). Figure 8.21 shows how to specify multiple print ranges; the first range has been entered, and the second is highlighted. Figure 8.22 shows the resulting printout.

Fig. 8.19.
A worksheet with a three-dimensional print range selected.

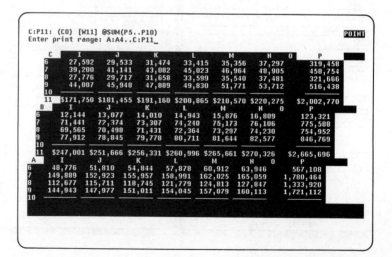

Fig. 8.20.
A printout of
the selected
three-
dimensional
range.

NATIONAL MICRO

	Jan	Feb	Mar	Apr	May	Jun	Jul	Aug	Sep	Oct	Nov	Dec	TOTAL
SALES REPORT													
Northeast	$31,336	$34,370	$37,404	$40,438	$43,472	$46,506	$49,540	$52,574	$55,608	$58,642	$61,676	$64,710	$576,276
Southeast	30,572	33,606	36,640	39,674	42,708	45,742	48,776	51,810	54,844	57,878	60,912	63,946	567,108
Central	131,685	134,719	137,753	140,787	143,821	146,855	149,889	152,923	155,957	158,991	162,025	165,059	1,780,464
Northwest	94,473	97,507	100,541	103,575	106,609	109,643	112,677	115,711	118,745	121,779	124,813	127,847	1,333,920
Southwest	126,739	129,773	132,807	135,841	138,875	141,909	144,943	147,977	151,011	154,045	157,079	160,113	1,721,112
Total Sales	$414,805	$429,975	$445,145	$460,315	$475,485	$490,655	$505,825	$520,995	$536,165	$551,335	$566,505	$581,675	$5,978,880

	Jan	Feb	Mar	Apr	May	Jun	Jul	Aug	Sep	Oct	Nov	Dec	TOTAL
COST OF GOODS													
Northeast	$10,341	$11,274	$12,207	$13,140	$14,073	$15,006	$15,939	$16,872	$17,805	$18,738	$19,671	$20,604	$165,066
Southeast	6,546	7,479	8,412	9,345	10,278	11,211	12,144	13,077	14,010	14,943	15,876	16,809	123,321
Central	65,843	66,775	67,709	68,642	69,575	70,508	71,441	72,374	73,307	74,240	75,173	76,106	775,588
Northwest	63,967	64,900	65,833	66,766	67,699	68,632	69,565	70,498	71,431	72,364	73,297	74,230	754,952
Southwest	72,314	73,247	74,180	75,113	76,046	76,979	77,912	78,845	79,778	80,711	81,644	82,577	846,769
Total Cost of Goods Sold	$219,011	$223,676	$228,341	$233,006	$237,671	$242,336	$247,001	$251,666	$256,331	$260,996	$265,661	$270,326	$2,665,696

	Jan	Feb	Mar	Apr	May	Jun	Jul	Aug	Sep	Oct	Nov	Dec	TOTAL
OPERATING EXPENSE													
Northeast	$21,529	$23,470	$25,411	$27,352	$29,293	$31,234	$33,175	$35,116	$37,057	$38,998	$40,939	$42,880	$386,454
Southeast	15,946	17,887	19,828	21,769	23,710	25,651	27,592	29,533	31,474	33,415	35,356	37,297	319,458
Central	27,554	29,495	31,436	33,377	35,318	37,259	39,200	41,141	43,082	45,023	46,964	48,905	458,754
Northwest	16,130	18,071	20,012	21,953	23,894	25,835	27,776	29,717	31,658	33,599	35,540	37,481	321,666
Southwest	32,361	34,302	36,243	38,184	40,125	42,066	44,007	45,948	47,889	49,830	51,771	53,712	516,438
Total Operating Expenses	$113,520	$123,225	$132,930	$142,635	$152,340	$162,045	$171,750	$181,455	$191,160	$200,865	$210,570	$220,275	$2,002,770

Fig. 8.21.
A worksheet
with multiple
print ranges
specified.

```
G:P29: [W11] @SUM(P23..P28)                                              POINT
Enter print range: sales;G:A22..G:P29_
```

G	J	K	L	M	N	O	P	Q
21								
22								
23	35116	37057	38998	40939	42880		386454	
24	29533	31474	33415	35356	37297		319458	
25	41141	43082	45023	46964	48905		458754	
26	29717	31658	33599	35540	37481		321666	
27	45948	47889	49830	51771	53712		516438	
28								
29	181455	191160	200865	210570	220275		2002770	
30								
31								
32	586	746	906	1066	1226		4152	
33	9200	9360	9520	9680	9840		107520	
34	39408	39568	39728	39888	40048		470016	
35	15496	15656	15816	15976	16136		183072	
36	23184	23344	23504	23664	23824		275328	
37								
38	87874	88674	89474	90274	91074		1040088	
39								

Fig. 8.22.
A printout of
the specified
multiple print
ranges.

NATIONAL MICRO

	Jan	Feb	Mar	Apr	May	Jun	Jul	Aug	Sep	Oct	Nov	Dec	TOTAL
Sales													
Northeast	$31,336	$34,370	$37,404	$40,438	$43,472	$46,506	$49,540	$52,574	$55,608	$58,642	$61,676	$64,710	$576,276
Southeast	30,572	33,606	36,640	39,674	42,708	45,742	48,776	51,810	54,844	57,878	60,912	63,946	567,108
Central	131,685	134,719	137,753	140,787	143,821	146,855	149,889	152,923	155,957	158,991	162,025	165,059	1,780,464
Northwest	94,473	97,507	100,541	103,575	106,609	109,643	112,677	115,711	118,745	121,779	124,813	127,847	1,333,920
Southwest	126,739	129,773	132,807	135,841	138,875	141,909	144,943	147,977	151,011	154,045	157,079	160,113	1,721,112
Total Sales	$414,805	$429,975	$445,145	$460,315	$475,485	$490,655	$505,825	$520,995	$536,165	$551,335	$566,505	$581,675	$5,978,880

	Jan	Feb	Mar	Apr	May	Jun	Jul	Aug	Sep	Oct	Nov	Dec	TOTAL
Operating Expenses													
Northeast	$21,529	$23,470	$25,411	$27,352	$29,293	$31,234	$33,175	$35,116	$37,057	$38,998	$40,939	$42,880	$386,454
Southeast	15946	17887	19828	21769	23710	25651	27592	29533	31474	33415	35356	37297	319458
Central	27554	29495	31436	33377	35318	37259	39200	41141	43082	45023	46964	48905	458754
Northwest	16130	18071	20012	21953	23894	25835	27776	29717	31658	33599	35540	37481	321666
Southwest	32361	34302	36243	38184	40125	42066	44007	45948	47889	49830	51771	53712	516438
Total Operating Expenses	$113,520	$123,225	$132,930	$142,635	$152,340	$162,045	$171,750	$181,455	$191,160	$200,865	$210,570	$220,275	$2,002,770

You can specify any combination of two- and three-dimensional ranges. The following examples are valid multiple print ranges:

A:A1..A:H10;B:C5..B:E12;C:C1..C:D5
A:A1..C:D10;A:F10..D:H20;C:C1..C:H10

In a print job, each range prints below the last, in the order specified when you entered the ranges.

Hiding Segments within the Designated Print Range

Because the print commands require the specification of a range to print, you can print only rectangular blocks from the worksheet. Nevertheless, you can suppress the display of cell contents within the range. You can eliminate one or more rows, exclude one or more columns, or remove from view a segment that occupies only part of a row or column. If you use the default settings, each of the illustrations discussed here is printed on one page.

Excluding Rows

To prevent a row from printing, you type two vertical bars (||) in the row's leftmost cell within the print range. Only one vertical bar appears on-screen, and neither bar appears on the printout. A row marked in this way will not print, but the suppressed data remains in the worksheet and is used in any applicable calculations.

Suppose, for example, that you want to print the Cash Flow Summary line descriptions from the Cash Flow Projector worksheet. When the /Print Printer command prompts you for a range to print, you specify A:A94..A:D111. The resulting printout is shown in figure 8.23.

Fig. 8.23.
A printout of individual cash-disbursements rows.

```
=========================== ==================
CASH FLOW SUMMARY
=========================== ==================
Collection of Receivables
Other Cash Receipts

Cash Disbursements
  Payment for Purchases on Credit
  Operating Expenses
  Long-Term Debt Service
  Interest Payment on Line of Credit
   Interest Rate
   Payment
  Income Tax Payments
  Other

Total Cash Disbursements
```

Now suppose that you do not want the printout to show the cash-disbursements details (rows 100 through 109). Don't use a worksheet command to delete the rows! Instead, keep the rows from printing by typing two vertical bars in the leftmost cell of each row. The simplest method is to insert a new column (column A) at the left edge of the print range and to narrow that column to a width of 1. Then type ǁ (hold down the Shift key and type the backslash twice) in cell A:A100 and copy that entry to cells A:A101..A:A109.

The new column must be included in the print range, or the double vertical bar (ǁ) will have no effect. After you insert the new column A, the print range should be adjusted to A:A94..A:E111 (not A:A94..A:D111 or A:B94..A:E111). Figure 8.24 shows the resulting printout.

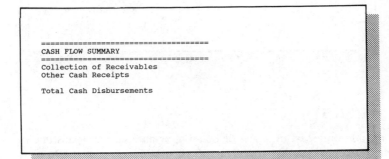

```
================================
CASH FLOW SUMMARY
================================
Collection of Receivables
Other Cash Receipts

Total Cash Disbursements
```

Fig. 8.24.
The printout
with individual
cash-
disbursements
rows omitted.

To restore the worksheet after you have finished printing, you simply delete the column containing the double vertical bar.

Excluding Columns

As you learned in Chapter 4, you can use 1-2-3's /Worksheet Column Hide command to indicate columns that you do not want displayed on-screen. If these marked columns are included in a print range, they will not appear on the printout if **Options Other** is set to **As**-Displayed.

Suppose, for example, that you are working with the Cash Flow Projector worksheet and that you want to print the Sales information for January through March only. That information is contained in range A:A21..A:J40. Issue the /Worksheet Column Hide command and specify columns A:E1..A:G1 to suppress the data for October through December. The resulting printout is shown in figure 8.25.

To restore the columns, select /Worksheet Column **Display**. When the hidden columns (marked with an asterisk) reappear on-screen, you can specify which column or columns to display by highlighting them and pressing Enter.

Fig. 8.25.
The printout
after hiding
columns E, F,
and G.

```
=============================================================
SALES                               Jan       Feb       Mar
=============================================================
Profit Center 1                 $31,336   $37,954   $43,879
Profit Center 2                  22,572    24,888    25,167
Profit Center 3                 131,685   129,044   131,723
Profit Center 4                  95,473    98,008    96,986
Profit Center 5
                                --------  --------  --------
Total Sales                    $281,066  $289,894  $297,755
                                ========  ========  ========

                     Cash           10%       10%       10%
Percent of          30 Days         20%       20%       20%
Collections         60 Days         50%       50%       50%
                    90 Days         20%       20%       20%
                                --------  --------  --------
Cash Collections               $263,437  $267,077  $280,066
                                ========  ========  ========
```

Hiding Ranges

If you want to hide only part of a row or column, or an area that spans one or more rows and columns, you use the /**R**ange Format **H**idden command to mark the ranges.

Perhaps your worksheet includes documentation that you want to save on disk but omit from a printed report. For example, you may want to omit the copyright message in the third row of the Cash Flow Projector worksheet. To omit that message, you issue /**R**ange Format **H**idden and specify cell E3. (Although the message spans several cells, it is entered in E3.) Then print the range A:A1..A:G7 (see fig. 8.26).

Fig. 8.26.
The printout
after hiding
range E3..E3.

```
=============================================================
CASH FLOW PROJECTOR

=============================================================
BALANCES IN WORKING CAPITAL ACCOUNTS                    Dec
=============================================================  =========
```

After you finish printing, you select /**R**ange Format **R**eset and specify the range E3..E3 to restore the copyright message.

If you find yourself repeating certain print operations (such as hiding the same columns or suppressing and then restoring the same documentation messages), remember that you can save time and minimize frustration by developing and using print macros. For more information on using macros, refer to Chapter 11.

Designing Your Reports

As indicated earlier in the chapter, you can use the /Worksheet Global Default Printer command to change the default print settings. Another method is also available for changing the print settings. You can use the /Print [P,F,E] Options menu shown in figure 8.27. The Margins, Setup, and Pg-Length options override the /Worksheet Global Default Printer settings for margins, setup strings, and page length. The Header, Footer, and Borders settings are unique to this menu; they are provided to help you improve the readability of your reports. Two selections, Other and Name, lead to other menus containing a number of options that enable you to design your reports, and to name and save the current settings. All of these menu items are discussed in this section.

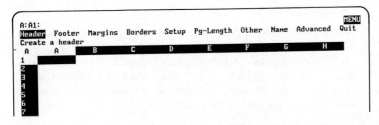

Fig. 8.27.
*The /Print
[P,F,E] Options
menu.*

One menu item—Advanced—leads to additional menus with options for enhancing your worksheet for printing, and controlling the printer. These Advanced options are discussed later in the chapter.

Whatever print settings you select are saved with the worksheet file when you execute /File Save. When you retrieve the file, the settings are still in effect. You also can save sets of printer options with the Name command, which is discussed in the section "Naming and Saving the Current Print Settings."

Creating Headers and Footers

On each page 1-2-3 reserves three lines for a header and an additional three lines for a footer. You can either retain the six lines (regardless of whether you use them) or eliminate all six lines by selecting Other Blank-Header from the /Print [P,F,E] Options menu. Other Blank-Header is discussed later in the chapter.

The header text, which is printed on the first line after any adjustable blank top-margin lines, is followed by two blank header lines (for spacing). The footer text line is printed above the adjustable blank bottom-margin lines and below two blank footer lines (for spacing).

Either the Header or Footer option lets you specify up to 512 characters of text in one line. Portions of the header or footer can be positioned at the left, right, or center of the page. The overall header or footer length, however, cannot exceed the page width.

1-2-3 provides special characters for including in a header or footer a page number, the current date, or the contents of a worksheet cell. Also available are special characters to control the positioning of text within a header or footer. These special characters include the following:

Character	Function
#	Automatically prints page numbers, starting with 1
@	Automatically includes the current system date (in the form 25-Jun-89)
|	Automatically separates text. If this character is not present, the entire header or footer is left-justified. Text to the right of the first | is centered. Text to the right of a second | is right-justified. (You insert a | by pressing the Shift key and typing a backslash.)
\	When followed by a cell address or range name, fills the header or footer with the contents of the indicated cell. After supplying the backslash, you can use POINT mode to indicate the desired cell. When you include a backslash, the contents of the indicated cell will be the only text in the header or footer and will be left-aligned.

To see how these special characters affect a printed report, again print the range A:A1..A:G17 from the Cash Flow Projector worksheet. But first add a header that includes three of the preceding characters.

To add the header, select /Print [**P,F,E**], select **R**ange and specify A:A1..A:G17, and then select **O**ptions **H**eader. At the prompt Enter Header:, type the following:

@|NATIONAL MICRO|#

Then select **Q**uit from the /Print [**P,F,E**] Options menu, choose **A**lign, select **G**o, and select **P**age to eject the paper, if necessary. If you compare the printed report shown in figure 8.28 with that shown in figure 8.12, you can see how the temporary changes, including a printed header line with a company name, improve the report's appearance.

Whenever the print range is too large to fit on a single page, the header will be reproduced on each succeeding page, and the page number will increase by one. If you have used the special character for including page numbers (#) and you want to print your report a second time before you leave the **P**rint menu, you can reset the page number to 1 and set the top of the form by simply selecting **A**lign before you select **G**o.

If you have specified a header line, but the centered or right-justified text doesn't print, make sure that the right-margin setting is appropriate for the current pitch and paper width. To change the header, just repeat the sequence to establish the text, press the Esc key to remove the display of the existing header from the control panel, and then press Enter. (You can delete a header or footer without removing other specified options.)

```
08-May-89              NATIONAL MICRO                    1

========================================================
CASH FLOW PROJECTOR          Copyright (C) 1989 Que Corporation
========================================================
BALANCES IN WORKING CAPITAL ACCOUNTS              Dec
======================================================= =========
Assets
  Cash                                          $17,355
  Accounts Receivable                           493,151
  Inventory                                     163,833

Liabilities
  Accounts Payable                              125,000
  Line of Credit                                      0
                                              --------
Net Working Capital                            $549,339
```

Fig. 8.28.
The result of specifying a header.

Formatted or Unformatted Output

Selecting **U**nformatted from the **/P**rint [**P,F,E**] **O**ptions **O**ther menu suppresses the printing of headers, footers, and page breaks. Unformatted output is often appropriate when you are using **/P**rint **F**ile to create a data file to be imported by another program, such as a word processor. (Exporting data is covered later in the chapter.) You select **F**ormatted to turn the headers, footers, and page breaks back on.

Cue:
When using /Print File to prepare data for other programs, select Unformatted to suppress headers, margins, and other formatting.

Blank-Header

The **B**lank-Header option from the **/P**rint [**P,F,E**] **O**ptions **O**ther menu lets you determine whether 1-2-3 leaves three blank lines at both the top and bottom of each printed page when no header or footer has been specified. If you select **B**lank-Header **S**uppress, the three blank lines are omitted at both the top and bottom of the page, but only if neither a header nor a footer has been provided. You cannot suppress blank lines at only the top or bottom of the page—it's both or neither. The **S**uppress option enables you to print six more lines of data per page. Selecting **B**lank-Header **P**rint reinstates the six blank lines.

RELEASE 3

Reminder:
To print the maximum number of rows on a page, set the top and bottom margins to 0 and select /Print [P, F, E] Options Other Bland-Header Suppress.

Printing a Listing of Cell Contents

Developing and debugging a complex worksheet can take days and weeks of hard work. You should, of course, safeguard your work by making backup disk copies of important files. For both backup and reference purposes, you also can make regular printouts of your worksheet's cell contents, including formulas and formatting information.

Cue:
*Select **C**ell-Formulas to print a listing of the worksheet formulas; **A**s-displayed, the default, prints the range as it is displayed on-screen.*

To print cell contents instead of cell values, you select **C**ell-Formulas from the /**P**rint [**P**,**F**,**E**] **O**ptions **O**ther menu. Choosing **C**ell-Formulas produces a printout that consists of one line for each cell in the print range. The line shows the cell's width (if different from the default), format, protection status, and contents. By subsequently selecting **A**s-Displayed, you restore the default setting that prints the range as it appears on-screen.

Figure 8.29 shows a **C**ell-Formulas printout of the range A:A1..A:G18 from the Cash Flow Projector worksheet. Notice that within the specified print range, all the cells in the first row are listed before the cells in the next row.

Fig. 8.29.
A listing produced with the Cell-Formulas option.

```
A:A1: [W9] \=
A:B1: [W9] \=
A:C1: [W9] \=
A:D1: [W9] \=
A:E1: [W11] \=
A:F1: [W11] \=
A:G1: [W11] \=
A:A3: [W9] 'CASH FLOW PROJECTOR
A:E3: [W11] 'Copyright (C) 1989 Que Corporation
A:A5: [W9] \=
A:B5: [W9] \=
A:C5: [W9] \=
A:D5: [W9] \=
A:E5: [W11] \=
A:F5: [W11] \=
A:G5: [W11] \=
A:A6: [W9] 'BALANCES IN WORKING CAPITAL ACCOUNTS
A:G6: [W11] ^Dec
A:A7: [W9] \=
A:B7: [W9] \=
A:C7: [W9] \=
A:D7: [W9] \=
A:E7: [W11] \=
A:F7: [W11] \=
A:G7: [W11] ' =========
A:A8: [W9] 'Assets
A:A9: [W9] ' Cash
A:G9: (C0) [W11] 17355
A:A10: [W9] ' Accounts Receivable
A:G10: (,0) [W11] 493151
A:A11: [W9] ' Inventory
A:G11: (,0) [W11] 163833
A:A13: [W9] 'Liabilities
A:A14: [W9] ' Accounts Payable
A:G14: (,0) [W11] 125000
A:A15: [W9] ' Line of Credit
A:G15: (,0) [W11] 0
A:G16: [W11] ' --------
A:A17: [W9] 'Net Working Capital
A:G17: (C0) [W11] +G9+G10+G11-G14-G15
A:G18: [W11] ' ========
```

Information within parentheses indicates a range format established independently of the global format in effect. For example, the `(C0)` in cell G17 indicates that the cell was formatted (with a /**R**ange **F**ormat command) as **C**urrency, with zero decimal places. Information within square brackets indicates a column width set independently of the global column width in effect. For example, the `[W11]` in cell G17 indicates that column G was set specifically to be 11 characters wide.

Cell contents are printed after the information for range format and column width. For example, the formula in G17 results in the `$549,339` for Net Working Capital.

Printing Borders

A printed report containing numbers without descriptive headings can be difficult, if not impossible, to interpret. You can make your report easier to understand by using a special 1-2-3 feature that enables you to print specified columns
and/or rows repeatedly on a multiple-page report. In addition, you can include
the worksheet frame (the row numbers located on the left of the screen, and the
column letters located at the top).

Column and Row Borders

If you use the default print settings to print the Cash Flow Projector worksheet,
the report will contain all the necessary information. But without descriptions of
what each line of numbers represents, some pages may be hard to interpret.

To improve the printed report, you can add column and row labels—called *borders* in 1-2-3. With /**Print** [**P,F,E**] **O**ptions **B**orders **C**olumns, you can specify one
or more columns of labels (headings) that will print at the left edge of every
page, serving to identify the rows on the page. Likewise, **B**orders **R**ows designates one or more rows of labels that print at the top of every page, identifying
the columns on the page. Setting borders in a printout is analogous to freezing
titles in the worksheet: **B**orders **C**olumns produces a border like a frozen vertical
title display, and **B**orders **R**ows produces a border like a frozen horizontal title
display.

To understand the process of creating borders, you can modify only a small portion of the Cash Flow Projector worksheet—the Balances in Working Capital
Accounts section, contained in the range A:A1..A:S18. You can omit the blank
columns (E and F) as well as the initial December column (G), and use the **B**orders **C**olumns command to repeat the account names (labels) in columns A
through D.

Select /**Print Printer**, choose **R**ange and specify A:H1..A:S18, and then select
Options **B**orders **C**olumns. When the message Enter Border Columns: appears
in the control panel, specify A1..D1. As you can see from figures 8.30 through
8.33, the account names are repeated to coincide with the dollar amounts for
January through December.

Remember that the print range and the border range must not overlap, or you
will get the borders printed twice on some pages. If you want to print information with a horizontal border on every page, select **B**orders **R**ows. For example,
you can use that option to print only the Liabilities information in rows 13
through 15 (refer to fig. 8.9). To cancel borders, you select /**Print Printer Clear**
Borders.

Fig. 8.30.
Page 1 of a
report printed
with column
borders.

```
===============================================================

CASH FLOW PROJECTOR

===============================================================
BALANCES IN WORKING CAPITAL ACCOUNTS    Jan       Feb       Mar
=============================================  ========  ========  ========
Assets
  Cash                                  $31,643   $34,333   $36,657
  Accounts Receivable                   510,780   533,597   551,287
  Inventory                             169,209   176,671   189,246

Liabilities
  Accounts Payable                      130,754   139,851   150,186
  Line of Credit                              0         0         0
                                       --------  --------  --------
Net Working Capital                    $580,878  $604,750  $627,003
                                       ========  ========  ========
```

Fig. 8.31.
Page 2 of the
report printed
with column
borders.

```
===============================================================

CASH FLOW PROJECTOR

===============================================================
BALANCES IN WORKING CAPITAL ACCOUNTS    Apr       May       Jun
=============================================  ========  ========  ========
Assets
  Cash                                  $35,614   $29,146   $20,000
  Accounts Receivable                   577,314   614,997   641,802
  Inventory                             206,788   228,828   269,990

Liabilities
  Accounts Payable                      163,731   180,350   203,669
  Line of Credit                              0         0     1,834
                                       --------  --------  --------
Net Working Capital                    $655,984  $692,620  $726,289
                                       ========  ========  ========
```

```
===============================================================
CASH FLOW PROJECTOR

===============================================================
BALANCES IN WORKING CAPITAL ACCOUNTS   Jul      Aug      Sep
===============================================================
Assets
  Cash                              $20,000  $20,000   $76,623
  Accounts Receivable               750,544  879,271   989,501
  Inventory                         296,527  324,230   345,629

Liabilities
  Accounts Payable                  225,085  243,320   258,740
  Line of Credit                      8,327    2,035         0
                                  --------- --------- ---------
Net Working Capital               $833,659 $978,146 $1,153,013
                                  ========= ========= =========
```

Fig. 8.32.
Page 3 of the report printed with column borders.

```
===============================================================
CASH FLOW PROJECTOR

===============================================================
BALANCES IN WORKING CAPITAL ACCOUNTS   Oct      Nov       Dec
===============================================================
Assets
  Cash                            $186,131  $337,995   $582,796
  Accounts Receivable            1,097,616 1,170,646  1,218,036
  Inventory                        352,687   358,926    358,926

Liabilities
  Accounts Payable                 267,621   272,747    275,041
  Line of Credit                         0         0          0
                                ---------  --------- ---------
Net Working Capital           $1,368,812 $1,594,820 $1,884,718
                                =========  ========= =========
```

Fig. 8.33.
Page 4 of the report printed with column borders.

Cue:
Select /Print
[P,F,E] Options
Borders Frame to
include the
worksheet frame
on each page of
your printout.

Frame Borders

To include the worksheet frame (vertical row numbers and horizontal column letters) on each page of your printed report, you select **/Print [P,F,E] Options Borders Frame**. Each page will include the worksheet frame (see fig. 8.34). To turn off the frame, you select **Options Borders No-Frame**. The **Frame** option is particularly useful during worksheet development when you want your printouts to show the location of data and formulas within a large worksheet.

Fig. 8.34.
A printed page
that includes
the worksheet
frame.

A						
6	H Jan	I Feb	J Mar	K Apr	L May	M Jun
7	=========	=========	=========	=========	=========	=========
8						
9	$31,643	$34,333	$36,657	$35,614	$29,146	$20,000
10	510,780	533,597	551,287	577,314	614,997	641,802
11	169,209	176,671	189,246	206,788	228,828	269,990
12						
13						
14	130,754	139,851	150,186	163,731	180,350	203,669
15	0	0	0	0	0	1,834
16	--------	--------	--------	--------	--------	--------
17	$580,878	$604,750	$627,003	$655,984	$692,620	$726,289
18	========	========	========	========	========	========

Setting Page Layout: Margins and Page Length

To change page layout temporarily, you use the **/Print [P,F,E] Options** menu. If you want to change the margins, select **Margins** and then choose **Left**, **Right**, **Top**, **Bottom**, or **None** from the menu. The following list indicates the message for each menu item:

Menu Item	Message
Left	Set Left Margin (0..1000):XX
Right	Set Right Margin (0..1000):XX
Top	Set Top Margin (0..240):XX
Bottom	Set Bottom Margin (0..240):XX
None	Clear all margin settings

The numbers in parentheses are the minimum and maximum for each margin setting. The XX at the end of each line denotes the current setting, which you can change. Selecting **None** sets all four margins to 0. Before you make any changes, review the section "Understanding the Default Print Settings" at the beginning of the chapter. Also keep in mind any general layout considerations, such as the number of lines per page, the number of characters per inch, and so on.

Be sure that you set left and right margins that are consistent with the width of your paper and the established pitch (characters per inch). The right margin must be greater than the left margin. Make sure also that the settings for the top and bottom margins are consistent with the paper's length and the established number of lines per inch.

The specified page length must not be less than the top margin *plus* the header lines *plus* one line of data *plus* the footer lines *plus* the bottom margin—unless you use /Print [**P,F,E**] Options Other Unformatted to suppress all formatting. To maximize the output on every printed page of a large worksheet, you can combine the Unformatted option with commands that condence printing and increase the number of lines per inch.

Enhancing Your Reports

Now that you have examined the **Print** menu options for designing your reports, you should become familiar with the menu options for enhancing your printed reports. The /**Print** [**P,E**] Options Advanced menu offers a number of enhancements. Some printers do not support all the advanced options. You can use /**Print** Sample to print a sample printout that will show which of the advanced options your printer supports. Selecting /**Print** Sample and then **Go** will print a sample to the currently selected device or file (encoded or text). This sample includes the following information:

1. A list of your current print settings (see fig. 8.35)

2. A small predefined worksheet printed with the current print options, except **Borders** (see fig. 8.35)

3. Printer capabilities, including fonts 1 through 8, colors 1 through 8, and the various options for pitch and line spacing (see fig. 8.35)

4. A sample graph using the current graph options (see fig. 8.36), plus samples of font options and text sizes for graphs (see fig. 8.37)

The sample shown in figures 8.35, 8.36, and 8.37 was printed with a PostScript laser printer. For more information on designing and printing graphs, refer to Chapter 9.

Improving the Layout

With the /**Print** [**P,E**] Options Advanced Layout menu, you can specify the pitch (character spacing), line spacing, and orientation of your printed pages. These options enable you to modify the layout of your report from the layout provided by 1-2-3's default settings.

Changing the Pitch

The *pitch* affects character size and thus the number of characters printed on each line. The choices available with the **Pitch** option are Standard, Compressed, and Expanded. Again, the actual effect of each of these options depends on your printer. Typical pitch settings are 5 characters per inch (cpi) for **Expanded**, 10 cpi for **Standard**, and 17 cpi for **Compressed**.

Fig. 8.35.
*The first part
of the sample
printout,
showing print
settings, a
predefined
worksheet, and
printer font
and color
capabilities.*

PRINTER SETTINGS

Header =
Footer =
Margins:
  Left = 4 , Right = 76 , Top = 2 , Bottom = 2
Borders:
  Columns = , Rows = , No-Frame
Setup =
Pg-Length = 66
Other:
  Cell-Formulas , Formatted , Print Blank-Header
Device:
  Name = Apple LaserWriter Plus Times/Helvetica
  Interface = Parallel 2
Layout:
  Standard Pitch , Standard Line-Spacing , Portrait
Fonts:
  Range = 0 , Header/Footer = 0 , Border = 0 , Frame = 0
Image:
  No Rotate , Margin-Fill , Final Density

Color = 0 , Default Priority , No AutoLf , No Wait

SAMPLE WORKSHEET

Left-aligned label			
	54	69	$84.00
Right-aligned label	599	614	$629.00
Centered label	-1144	-1159	($1,174.00)

PRINTER CAPABILITIES

FONT 1 and COLOR 1 were used to print this text.
FONT 2 and COLOR 2 were used to print this text.
FONT 3 and COLOR 3 were used to print this text.
FONT 4 and COLOR 4 were used to print this text.
FONT 5 and COLOR 5 were used to print this text.
FONT 6 and COLOR 6 were used to print this text.
FONT 7 and COLOR 7 were used to print this text.
FONT 8 and COLOR 8 were used to print this text.

This text is in STANDARD PITCH.
This text is in COMPRESSED PITCH.
This text is in EXPANDED PITCH.

STANDARD LINE SPACING was used for these three lines of text.
STANDARD LINE SPACING was used for these three lines of text.
STANDARD LINE SPACING was used for these three lines of text.
COMPRESSED LINE SPACING was used for these three lines of text.
COMPRESSED LINE SPACING was used for these three lines of text.
COMPRESSED LINE SPACING was used for these three lines of text.

SAMPLE GRAPH AND GRAPH TEXT OPTIONS

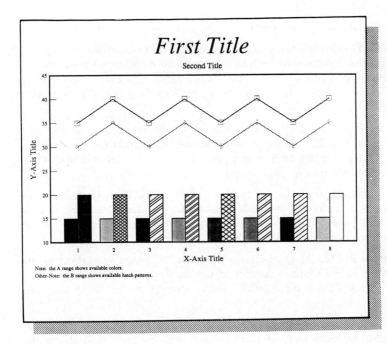

Fig. 8.36.
The second part of the sample printout, showing a predefined graph.

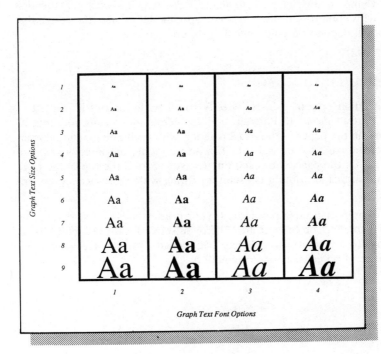

Fig. 8.37.
The third part of the sample printout, showing text sizes and styles available in graphs.

Changing Line Spacing

The Line-Spacing options are Standard (the default) and Compressed. Like pitch, the line spacing that results with each of these options depends on your printer. For many printers, Standard spacing is 6 lines per inch, and Compressed spacing is 8 lines per inch. Changing line spacing also affects the number of lines printed on each page.

Note that when you use the Options Advanced Layout menu to change either line spacing or pitch, 1-2-3 automatically makes an adjustment for the different number of characters per line or lines per page. You do not need to adjust manually the settings for margins or page length.

Suppose that you want to produce a printed report of the Cash Flow Projector worksheet shown in figure 8.9. Because the worksheet is large, printing all of it will require many pages. You can put more data on each printed page by using the Pitch and Compressed menu options.

First, select /Print Printer Range and then designate the entire worksheet as the print range. Next, select Options Advanced Layout Pitch Compressed and then choose Line-Spacing Compressed. Finally, select Quit Quit Quit Align and then Go.

Printing with compressed pitch and line spacing enables you to get considerably more information on each page of your printed report. Figure 8.38 shows the first page of the Cash Flow Projector worksheet printed with standard pitch and line spacing. Compare this figure with figure 8.39, which shows just the first page printed with compressed pitch and line spacing. Of course, the readability of the results will depend on your specific printer.

Choosing Orientation

With the Orientation option, you can specify whether the output is printed in Landscape or Portrait mode. In Portrait mode, which is the default, the lines of text are printed on the paper in the usual manner, with each line extending from the left side of the page to the right. In Landscape mode, the lines of text are printed sideways on the page, with each line extending from the top of the page to the bottom. Landscape printing is useful for fitting wide worksheets onto single pages.

Not all printers support Landscape mode. If your printer does not, selecting this mode will have no effect on the output. When you select Landscape mode, 1-2-3 does not automatically adjust margins and page length; you must change these settings manually to reflect the new orientation.

```
=================================================================
CASH FLOW PROJECTOR              Copyright (C) 1989 Que Corporation
=================================================================
BALANCES IN WORKING CAPITAL ACCOUNTS                        Dec
=================================================================
Assets
  Cash                                                  $17,355
  Accounts Receivable                                   493,151
  Inventory                                             163,833

Liabilities
  Accounts Payable                                      125,000
  Line of Credit                                              0
                                                       --------
Net Working Capital                                    $549,339
                                                       ========


=================================================================
SALES                              Oct       Nov       Dec
=================================================================
Profit Center 1                 $27,832   $23,864   $26,125
Profit Center 2                  13,489    21,444    20,140
Profit Center 3                 126,811   124,382   123,618
Profit Center 4                  94,285    92,447    89,010
Profit Center 5                 --------  --------  --------
                                $262,417  $262,137  $258,893
Total Sales                     ========  ========  ========

                    Cash            10%       10%       10%
Percent of          30 Days         20%       20%       20%
Collections         60 Days         50%       50%       50%
                    90 Days         20%       20%       20%

Cash Collections


=================================================================
PURCHASES                          Oct       Nov       Dec
=================================================================
Cost of Goods Sold
  Profit Center 1                   33%       33%       33%
                                 $9,185    $7,875    $8,621
  Profit Center 2                   29%       29%       29%
                                 $3,912    $6,219    $5,841
  Profit Center 3                   50%       50%       50%
                                $63,406   $62,191   $61,809
  Profit Center 4                   67%       67%       67%
                                $63,171   $61,939   $59,637
  Profit Center 5                   30%       30%       30%
                                     $0        $0        $0
```

Fig. 8.38.
The worksheet page printed with standard line spacing and pitch.

Selecting Fonts

With the /Print [**P,E**] **O**ptions **A**dvanced **F**onts option, you can specify the fonts, or type styles, that will be used to print different sections of each page. 1-2-3 offers 8 different fonts, numbered as shown here:

Font 1   Normal serif
Font 2   Bold serif
Font 3   Italic serif
Font 4   Bold italic serif
Font 5   Normal sans serif
Font 6   Bold sans serif
Font 7   Italic sans serif
Font 8   Bold italic sans serif

Reminder:
To print different sections of each page in different fonts, use the /Print [P,E] Options Advanced Fonts menu.

RELEASE
3

Fig. 8.39.
The worksheet
page printed
with
compressed line
spacing and
pitch.

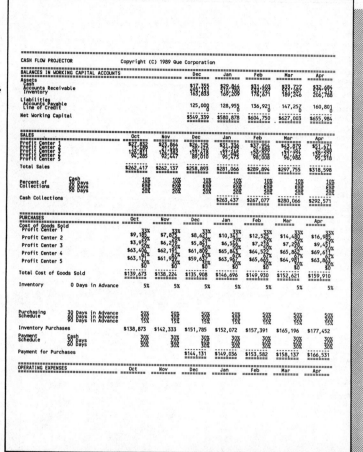

You can see what these fonts look like by referring to figure 8.35. How many of these fonts will be available to you depends on your printer. Some printers have all eight fonts, while other printers have only one or two. To see what fonts your printer supports, select /Print Printer Sample and then Go to produce the sample output, as described earlier in this chapter.

You can specify different fonts for the following parts of each page: main print range, header/footer, border, and frame. After selecting Options Advanced Fonts, select Range, Header, Footer, Border, or Frame. 1-2-3 next displays the numbers 1–8, corresponding to the preceding fonts. Choose the desired font. Selecting Quit returns you to the Options Advanced menu.

Figure 8.40 shows a report printed with font 1 for the range, font 2 for the borders, and font 6 for the header/footer.

National Micro   05-May-89

SALES		Oct	Nov	Dec
Profit Center 1		$27,832	$23,864	$26,125
Profit Center 2		13,489	21,444	20,140
Profit Center 3		126,811	124,382	123,618
Profit Center 4		94,285	92,447	89,010
Profit Center 5				
Total Sales		$262,417	$262,137	$258,893
	Cash	10%	10%	10%
Percent of	30 Days	20%	20%	20%
Collections	60 Days	50%	50%	50%
	90 Days	20%	20%	20%

Fig. 8.40.
A report
printed with
three different
fonts.

If no fonts are specified, or if your printer does not support the specified font, 1-2-3 uses font 1 for all sections of the report.

Using Setup Strings

A *setup string* is a code that you send to the printer to change a printing characteristic, such as compressing the print, underlining, or boldfacing. In 1-2-3, you type a setup string as one or more backslashes (\), each followed by a three-digit decimal number corresponding to the desired code. Because different printers use different codes, you will need to refer to your printer manual (look under the topics of escape codes or printer control codes). A setup string has a maximum length of 512 characters.

You can use one of the following methods to send a setup string from 1-2-3 to your printer:

1. Use the /Print [P,E] Options Setup command to provide a setup string. The setup string will be sent to the printer at the start of every print job. The setup string also will be saved with the worksheet and used the next time you retrieve the worksheet file.

2. Use the /Worksheet Global Default Printer Setup command to provide a default setup string, and then select Update from the /Worksheet Global Default menu. The setup string will be in effect whenever you use 1-2-3. The Options Setup string can be combined with or override the default setup string, depending on the setup strings used.

3. Embed one or more setup strings in the worksheet itself. To use this method, you type two vertical bars (||) and the setup string in the first cell of a blank row in the print range. Because an embedded setup string is sent to the printer only when printing reaches the row that contains the setup string, a setup string can be used to affect only portions of a report. The setup string affects the entire width of all worksheet rows

below the row in which the setup string is located. A second setup string can change or cancel the effect of the first.

You should not use setup strings to change print attributes, such as line spacing and type size, that can be controlled from the /Print [P,E] Options Advanced Layout menu. When you use the Layout menu, 1-2-3 automatically adjusts margins and lines per page to accommodate the new line spacing and type size. If you use setup strings to change either of these settings, you will have to make the adjustments for margins and lines per page. You should use setup strings to make print enhancements not available on 1-2-3 menus, or to change the print style in only part of a report.

To see how setup strings work, try the first and third methods by printing portions of the Sales information from the range A:A21..A:G31 of the Cash Flow Projector worksheet. For these examples, assume that an IBM ProPrinter is being used.

Use the first method to send a setup string that puts the printer in letter-quality mode. Select /Print [P,E] Range and specify the range A:A21..A:G31, choose Options Setup, and then type the following setup string:

\027\073\003

Note that a setup string can consist of one or more numbers. Each number corresponds to a specific code. The special capabilities of your printer and the codes used to control them are detailed in your printer instruction manual. For example, the code \027, which corresponds to ESCAPE, is used as the first element in many setup strings.

Next, select Quit to return to the /Print [P,F,E,] menu, select Align, and choose Go. The printed report is shown in figure 8.41. Compare this report to the one shown in figure 8.42. That report, which was printed without the setup string embedded in the worksheet, displays the printer's default 10 cpi draft-quality output.

Fig. 8.41.
The report
printed in
letter-quality
mode.

SALES	Oct	Nov	Dec
Profit Center 1	$27,832	$23,864	$26,125
Profit Center 2	13,489	21,444	20,140
Profit Center 3	126,811	124,382	123,618
Profit Center 4	94,285	92,447	89,010
Profit Center 5			
Total Sales	$262,417	$262,137	$258,893

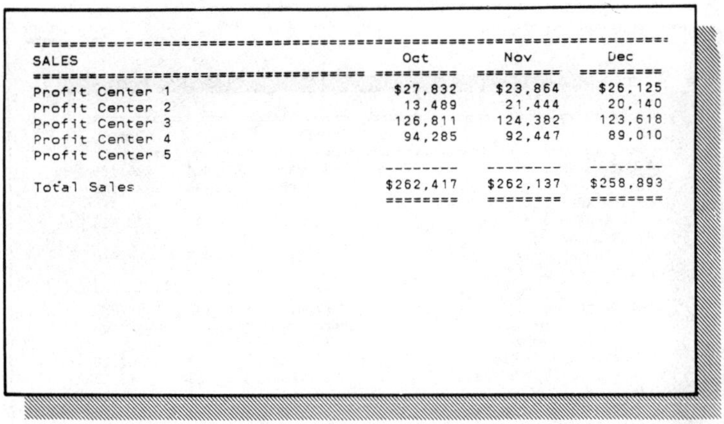

```
================================================================
SALES                              Oct        Nov        Dec
================================== =========  =========  =========
Profit Center 1                     $27,832   $23,864    $26,125
Profit Center 2                      13,489    21,444     20,140
Profit Center 3                     126,811   124,382    123,618
Profit Center 4                      94,285    92,447     89,010
Profit Center 5
                                    --------   --------   --------
Total Sales                        $262,417  $262,137   $258,893
                                    ========   ========   ========
```

Fig. 8.42.
The report
printed in
default draft
mode.

To remove the temporary setup string, select **Setup** from the **/Print [P,E]** Options menu, press Esc, and then press Enter. Exit the **Options** menu by selecting **Quit** or pressing Esc.

A setup string entered in this manner affects all output from the current print operation. In the example, the contents in the entire print range were printed in letter-quality mode. If headers, footers, or borders had been included, they would have been printed in letter-quality mode also.

If you want only selected rows within a print range to reflect a special printing characteristic, you can use the third method—embedding a setup string in the worksheet. In this demonstration, you will include setup strings in the Cash Flow Projector worksheet so that the range printed in figure 8.41 will print with the row for Profit Center 3 underlined.

Cue:
For special print enhancements that affect only part of a report, use embedded setup strings.

First, insert two blank rows—one above and one below row 26. These new rows will be rows 26 and 28. In cell A:A26, type the following control codes to turn underlining on:

||\027\045\001

In cell A:A28, type these codes to turn underlining off:

||\027\045\000

Figure 8.43 shows the worksheet with the control codes (setup strings) included. If you print range A:A21..A:G33, the printout will appear as shown in figure 8.44.

When you have finished printing, just delete the rows containing the setup strings. Remember that these codes are for an IBM ProPrinter; they probably will not work properly on other printers.

When using embedded printer setup strings, keep the following points in mind:

1. The setup string must be inserted in a blank row, in the leftmost column in the print range.

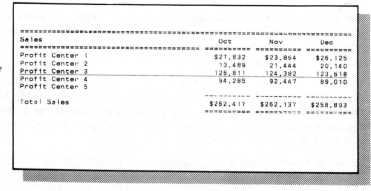

Fig. 8.43.
A worksheet with embedded printer control codes.

```
A:A24: [W9] 'Profit Center 1                                    READY

  A    A        B        C       D        E        F        G
 20
 21 ===========================================================
 22 SALES                                     Oct      Nov      Dec
 23 ===========================================================
 24 Profit Center 1                        $27,832  $23,864  $26,125
 25 Profit Center 2                         13,489   21,444   20,140
 26 |\027\045\001
 27 Profit Center 3                        126,811  124,382  123,618
 28 |\027\045\000
 29 Profit Center 4                         94,285   92,447   89,010
 30 Profit Center 5
 31                                        --------- -------- --------
 32 Total Sales                           $262,417 $262,137 $258,893
 33                                        ========= ======== ========
 34
 35                     Cash                  10%      10%      10%
 36 Percent of          30 Days              20%      20%      20%
 37 Collections         60 Days              50%      50%      50%
 38                     90 Days              20%      20%      20%
 39
 03-May-89 08:38 PM
```

Fig. 8.44.
A printout of the worksheet range, with the data row for Profit Center 3 underlined.

```
=====================================================
Sales                             Oct      Nov      Dec
=====================================================
Profit Center 1                $27,832  $23,864  $26,125
Profit Center 2                 13,489   21,444   20,140
Profit Center 3                126,811  124,382  123,618
Profit Center 4                 94,285   92,447   89,010
Profit Center 5
                               --------- -------- --------
Total Sales                   $262,417 $262,137 $258,893
                               ========= ======== ========
```

2. Any other cell contents in the row containing the setup string are ignored and do not print. The row is not counted as part of the page length.

3. A second setup string is needed if you want to return printing to normal.

RELEASE
3

Selecting Color

With the Color option, you can select whatever color you want to use for your printed report. Headers, footers, and the print range will be printed in the selected color. You can choose from as many as eight colors, depending on your printer. If negative numbers are displayed on-screen in red (in other words, if you have selected /Worksheet Global Format Other Color Negative), those numbers will be printed in red also, if possible.

Printing a Graph with Text (Image)

Thus far, this chapter has dealt with printing text alone (without a graph). You also can include 1-2-3 graphs in your reports, placing a graph on a separate page or on a page containing text. (Graph printing is covered in detail in Chapter 9.) You can use two methods to print a graph as part of a report:

1. After selecting **G**o to print the text portion of the report, select **I**mage from the /**Print [P,E]** menu, specify the graph to print, and then select **G**o again. The selected graph will print immediately after the text.

2. After specifying the worksheet range to print, but before pressing Enter, type a range separator (;) and an asterisk followed by the name of the graph to print. For example, look at the following print range:

   B1..H20;*profits;K10..N15

   This prints the text in B1..H20, followed by the graph named *profits* and the text in K10..N15.

Before printing a graph, you may need to modify its size, rotation, or density. To make these changes, use the /**Print [P,E] O**ptions **A**dvanced **I**mage menu, which is discussed in Chapter 9.

Naming and Saving the Current Print Settings

1-2-3 enables you to save all current print settings under a unique name, recall the settings with that name, and reuse the settings without having to specify them individually. To use this feature, you select /**Print [P,F,E] O**ptions **N**ame. The following choices are presented:

Menu Item	Description
Create	Assigns a name to the current print settings. You select this command and then enter a name in response to the prompt. The name can contain up to 15 characters and can include any combination of letters, numbers, and symbols—except for two "less than" symbols (<<). If you type a print-settings name already in use, the original settings associated with that name are replaced by the current settings.
Delete	Deletes a print-settings name. You select this command and then select the print-settings name to delete.
Reset	Deletes all print-settings names from the current file
Table	Creates a list of all print-setting names in the current file. You select this command and then position the cell

Menu Item	Description
	pointer at the worksheet location where you want the table to appear. The table will occupy one column and as many rows as there are print-settings names.
Use	Makes current the print settings associated with a particular print-settings name

Controlling Your Printer

Some of the print commands deal directly with controlling the printer hardware. You need to understand these commands so that you can create your printed reports efficiently.

Choosing the Printer

/**Print Printer O**ptions **A**dvanced **D**evice enables you to choose the **Name** and the **Interface** of the printer to be used. You select **Device Name** to choose from the list of printers selected during the Install procedure. Next, you select **Device Interface** to indicate the port to which the printer is attached. If the port is a serial port, you also must specify the baud rate.

Reminder:
Use /Print Printer
Options Advanced
Device to select
which installed
printer to use.

Controlling the Movement of the Paper

If you print a range containing fewer lines than the default page length, the paper will not advance to the top of the next page. Likewise, if you print a range containing more lines than the default page length, 1-2-3 will automatically insert page breaks between pages, but the paper will not advance to the top of the next page after the last page has printed. In both cases, the next print job begins wherever the preceding operation ended.

You can use the /**Print [P,E] O**ptions **A**dvanced **AutoLf** option to tell your printer to advance the paper at the end of each line automatically. This option has the same effect as /**Worksheet Global Default Printer Autolf**, but the **Autolf** option from the **Print** menu overrides that **Worksheet** setting.

When you are using a dot-matrix printer and continuous-feed paper, 1-2-3 must be aware of the position of the perforations between pages if the printed output is to be positioned properly on the paper. The top of a page is initially marked by the print head's position when you turn on the printer and load 1-2-3. At the start of each work session, be sure that the paper is positioned so that the print head is at the top of the page, and then turn on the printer. During the work session, do not advance the paper manually. Because 1-2-3 coordinates a line counter with the current page-length setting, any lines you advance manually are not counted, and page breaks will crop up in strange places.

Whenever you or someone else manually advances the paper, 1-2-3 and the printer get "out of sync." When that happens, page breaks may appear midpage, resulting in blank areas in your reports. To prevent this problem, you should select **Align** before selecting **Go** whenever you begin a print job at the top of a page.

As printing progresses, both the printer and 1-2-3 maintain internal line counters that indicate the print head's current position on the page. If these two pointers get "out of sync," you are likely to get output that is printed on top of the perforations while lines in the middle of pages are skipped. If this problem occurs, take the following steps:

1. Turn off the printer.

2. Advance the paper manually until the print head is at the top of a page, and then turn the printer back on.

3. Select **Align** from the /Print Printer menu.

Note that the **Align** command resets 1-2-3's page number counter. If you are including page numbers in your report, you may want to skip the third step.

If you want to advance the paper one line at a time (for example, to separate several ranges that fit on one printed page), you issue the /Print Printer Line command.

If you want to advance to a new page after printing less than a full page, you select /Print Printer Page. Whenever you issue this command, the printer will advance to the start of the next page. (You learned earlier in the chapter how to embed a page-break symbol in the print range in order to instruct 1-2-3 to advance automatically.)

To print an existing footer on the last page of a report, use the **Page** command at the end of the printing session. If you select the **Quit** command from the **Print** menu without issuing the **Page** command, this final footer will not print. However, if you reissue the /Print Printer command and select **Page**, the footer will print when the page ejects.

Reminder:
To print the footer on the last page of a report, issue the /Print [P,F,E] Page command.

Setting Your Printing Priorities

As indicated at the beginning of the chapter, a print job begins when you select **Line**, **Page**, or **Go** from the /Print [**P,F,E**] menu. The print job ends when you exit the **Print** menu by selecting **Quit**, pressing Esc, or pressing Ctrl-Break. When a print job ends, the printing does not stop—you simply have finished defining the job. You can end one print job and then specify additional jobs while the first one is still printing. 1-2-3 automatically puts multiple jobs in a queue and prints them in order.

You can use /Print Printer Options Advanced Priority to set the priority for the current print job within the print queue. If no other jobs are in the queue, this priority setting has no effect (the job is printed immediately). The following **Priority** menu items are available:

Menu Item	Description
Default	Puts the current job ahead of low-priority jobs and behind all other jobs
Low	Puts the current job behind all other jobs
High	Puts the current job behind high-priority jobs and ahead of all other jobs

The **Priority** setting takes effect when you exit the **Print** menu. A job that is actually printing will not be interrupted by a job with a higher priority.

1-2-3 can send data to the printer while you continue to work in the worksheet. This capability is known as *background printing*. If a printer error—for example, running out of paper—occurs during background printing, 1-2-3 displays an error message on-screen. Because this background error does not cause 1-2-3 to go into ERROR mode, you can continue working in the worksheet if you want. You can either correct the printer problem and continue printing with **/Print Resume**, or cancel all print jobs with **/Print Cancel**.

Holding a Print Job (Hold)

The **/Print Printer Hold** option enables you to return to 1-2-3 READY mode while keeping the current print job open. In READY mode, you can perform a number of tasks, including the following:

1. Importing new data into the worksheet
2. Changing column widths, cell formats, or other aspects of worksheet display
3. Modifying **/Worksheet Global** settings

After finishing your tasks in READY mode, you can return to the **/Print [P,F,E]** menu and continue creating the same print job. If you return to READY mode by any means other than **Hold**, the current print job will be closed, and you will have to start again to define the print job.

Note that **Hold** does not affect the printer itself. If a print job is in progress—actually printing—the **Hold** option will not stop the printer. To pause or stop the printer, use **/Print Suspend** or **/Print Cancel**.

Pausing the Printer (Suspend and Wait)

Cue:
Use /Print Suspend to halt printing temporarily. Use /Print Cancel to end all print jobs permanently.

You can temporarily pause the printer by issuing the **/Print Suspend** command. Printing will pause as soon as the printer's internal buffer empties. Do not turn the printer off, or you will lose part of your report! You may lose only a few lines or several pages, depending on the printer. Use **/Print Suspend** to perform such tasks as refilling the paper bin or changing the ribbon.

/Print **Resume** restarts printing that was paused in one of the following ways:

1. You issued a /Print **Suspend** command.

2. You selected /**Print Printer Options Advanced Wait Yes** or /**Worksheet Global Default Printer Wait Yes**, and the printer is therefore at the end of a page, waiting for another sheet of paper.

3. A printer error has occurred. After correcting the error, you issue /**Print Resume** to clear the error message and resume printing.

Select **Wait Yes** if you are hand-feeding paper to the printer; 1-2-3 will stop sending data to the printer at the end of each page. The printer will pause, allowing you to insert a new sheet of paper. **Resume** then continues printing with the next page. This option is different from **Suspend**, which temporarily pauses printing under user control, and from **Cancel**, which permanently ends all print jobs.

Stopping the Printer (Cancel and Quit)

After starting one or more print jobs, you may realize that you have made an error in the worksheet data or print settings and that you need to correct the error before the report is printed. Selecting /**Print Cancel** stops the current print job and removes any other print jobs from the queue. Once you have canceled the current print jobs, you cannot restart them.

When you select /**Print Cancel**, printing may not stop immediately if the printer has an internal print buffer or if a software print spooler has been installed. Turning the printer off for a few seconds will clear the printer buffer. If printing resumes when you turn the printer back on, a print spooler probably is installed (OS/2 automatically installs one). Refer to the documentation for your print spooler for instructions on how to flush it.

The /**Print Cancel** commands resets 1-2-3's page and line counters to 1. If the printer stops in the middle of a page, you will need to take one of the following steps to realign the paper:

1. Turn the printer off, advance the paper manually to the top of the page, turn the printer back on, and select /**Print Printer Align**.

2. With the printer on, use /**Print Printer Line** to advance the paper, one line at a time, to the top of the next page; then select **Align**.

You cannot cancel an individual print job; you must cancel all prints jobs or none.

Clearing the Print Options

With /**Print Printer Clear**, you can eliminate all or some of the **Print** options you chose earlier. When you select **Clear**, the following menu appears:

All Range Borders Format Image Device

You can choose **All** to clear every **Print** option, including the print range, or you can be more specific by using one of the following choices:

Menu Item	Description
Range	Clears existing print range specifications
Borders	Cancels Columns and Rows specified as borders
Format	Eliminates Margins, **Pg**-Length, and **S**etup string settings
Image	Clears graphs selected for printing
Device	Returns device name and interface to defaults

Preparing Output for Acceptance by Other Programs

Many word processing programs and other software packages accept ASCII text files—the kind created by 1-2-3's /**Print File** option. You can maximize your chances of successfully exporting 1-2-3 files to other programs if you use several **Print** command sequences to eliminate unwanted formatting from the output.

You begin by selecting /**Print File** to direct output to an ASCII .PRN file. After specifying a file name and the **Range** to print, you choose **Options Other Unformatted.** Selecting **Unformatted** removes all headers, footers, and page breaks from the output.

You then set the left margin to 0 and the right margin to 255. Do not worry about worksheet lines shorter than 255 characters. The line ends after the last printed character, not at 255.

Next, you select **Quit** to leave the **Options** menu, you create the .PRN file on disk by selecting **Go**, and you select **Quit** to exit the /**Print File** menu. You should then follow the instructions provided with your word processing program or other software package in order to import the specially prepared 1-2-3 disk file.

Refer also to your word processing manual for more information about ASCII or text file retrieval. Before retrieving the .PRN file, be sure that your word processing margins are set as wide as, or wider than, your print range. After retrieving the .PRN file, use a search-and-replace command to remove unwanted hard carriage returns at the end of lines.

To restore the default printing settings for headers, footers, and page breaks, you issue the /**Print Printer Options Other Formatted** command. Ordinarily, you select **Formatted** for printing to the printer or an encoded (.ENC) file, and **Unformatted** for printing to a .PRN file.

Chapter Summary

This chapter showed you how to create printed reports from your 1-2-3 worksheets. You learned first how to print reports with the default settings, and then how to change those defaults through either the **Worksheet** menu or the **Print** menu. To make your reports more readable, you learned how to break the worksheet into pages; provide headers, footers, and borders; and change the margins and page length. You also discovered how to take full advantage of your printer's font, color, and line spacing capabilities by using 1-2-3's advanced print options as well as setup strings.

Using a variety of options to print reports from large worksheets takes practice and careful study of your printer manual. Use this chapter as a reference as you continue to experiment.

The next chapter shows you how to add visual effects to your reports. You will learn how to create graphs, view them on-screen, and print them.

9

Creating and
Printing Graphs

Even if 1-2-3 provided only worksheet capabilities, the program would be extremely powerful. More information can be quickly assembled and tabulated electronically than could possibly be developed manually. But despite the importance of keeping detailed worksheets that show real or projected data, that data can be worthless if it can't be readily understood.

To help decision-makers who are pressed for time or unable to draw conclusions from countless rows of numeric data, 1-2-3 offers graphics capabilities that you can use to display key figures graphically. The program offers seven types of basic business graphs as well as sophisticated options for enhancing the graphs' appearance. Although not quite a match for the capabilities of stand-alone graphics packages, 1-2-3's graphic capabilities are more than adequate in most situations. The real strength of 1-2-3's graphics, however, lies in its integration with the worksheet.

This chapter shows you how to do the following:

- Create graphs from worksheet data
- Use 1-2-3's automatic graphing capability
- Add descriptive labels and numbers to a graph
- Alter the default graph display
- Edit the contents of a graph
- View graphs before you print them
- Save graphs and graph settings for later use
- Reset some or all graph settings

347

- Select an appropriate graph type
- Develop all graph types
- Print graphs that you created in 1-2-3
- Modify the quality, size, and orientation of printed graphs
- Include one or more graphs in a printed report

In this chapter, you will learn how to apply most of 1-2-3's graph options to a single line graph. Then you will learn how to construct all the other types of 1-2-3 graphs. You also will learn how to use 1-2-3's automatic graphing feature. The text shows you how to save a graph in a disk file for use by other programs and how to name a graph for easy recall of its specifications in the current worksheet. Printing graphs is the last subject covered in this chapter.

Basic Hardware and Software Requirements for Creating Graphs

Before creating your first graph, you must determine whether your hardware supports viewing and printing graphs, whether your 1-2-3 software is correctly installed and loaded, and whether the worksheet on-screen contains data you want to graph. You also should be familiar with the various graph types so that you will know which type of graph is best suited for presenting specific numeric data.

This chapter shows you how to use 1-2-3's graphics feature to create and view a graph, store its specifications for later use, save it to disk, and print it. Creating and saving a graph requires only that you have the Lotus system software installed on your computer and that you correctly select options from the /Graph menu.

Reminder:
To view a graph on-screen, you need graphics-capable video hardware.

To view a graph on-screen, you need graphics-capable video display hardware. Almost all systems have such hardware. Without it, you can construct, save, and print a 1-2-3 graph, but you will not be able to view it on-screen. If you have two monitors installed, one monitor will display the worksheet while the other displays the graph.

To print a graph, you need a graphics printer or plotter supported by 1-2-3. Graph printing is described at the end of this chapter.

Understanding Graphs

To understand 1-2-3's graphics capability, you need to be familiar with a few terms concerning plotting a graph. The two basic terms—*x-axis* and *y-axis*—are illustrated in figure 9.1.

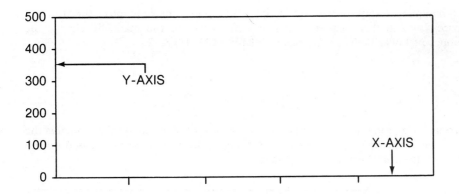

Fig. 9.1.
A graph's x-
and y-axes.

All graphs (except pie graphs) have two axes: the y-axis (the vertical left edge) and the x-axis (the horizontal bottom edge). 1-2-3 automatically provides tick marks for both axes. The program also scales the numbers on the y-axis, based on the minimum and maximum figures included in the plotted data range(s).

Every point plotted on a graph has a unique x,y location. *x* represents the horizontal position, corresponding to the category associated with the data point (for example, Gross Sales, Expenses, or January). *y* represents the vertical position, corresponding to the second value associated with the data point (for example, Dollars or Percent Profit). In figure 9.2, for example, the *x* variable is Month and the *y* variable is a dollar value.

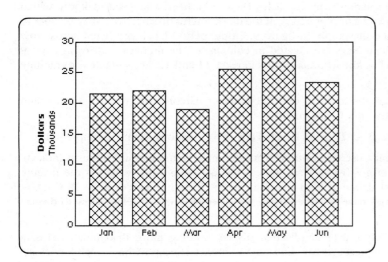

Fig. 9.2.
A basic bar
graph in which
the x variable
is Month and
the y variable
is a dollar
value.

The intersection of the y-axis and the x-axis is called the *origin*. Notice that the origin of the axes in figure 9.2 is zero for both *x* and *y* (0,0). Although graphs can be plotted with a nonzero origin, you should use a zero origin in your graphs to minimize misinterpretation of graph results and to make graphs easier to compare. Later in this chapter, you will learn how you can manually change the upper or lower limits of the scale initially set by 1-2-3.

Creating Simple Graphs

To create a graph, you first must load 1-2-3 and retrieve the file that contains the data you want to graph. Many of the examples in this chapter are based on the Sales Data worksheet shown in figure 9.3.

Fig. 9.3.
A sample sales
data worksheet.

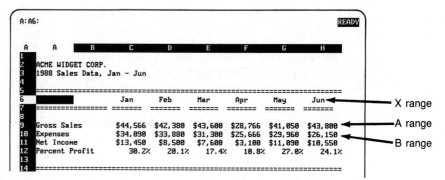

To graph information from the Sales Data worksheet, you need to know which numeric data you can plot and which data (numeric or label) you may be able to use to enhance the graph. In figure 9.3, time period labels are listed across row 6. Category identifiers are located in column A. The numeric entries in rows 9 and 10, as well as the formula results in rows 11 and 12, are suitable for graphing as data points.

To develop graphs to view on-screen, select /Graph from the 1-2-3 command menu to display the Graph menu:

Type **X A B C D E F** Reset View Save Options Name Group Quit

You always must use two options from the main Graph menu. You must indicate which **Type** of graph you want, unless you are using Line, which is the default. And you must define at least one data series from the choices **X, A, B, C, D, E,** and **F**. After you have specified these two options, you can select View to display the graph.

You can quickly create graphs that display nothing more than unlabeled data points in bar or stacked-bar, line or XY, mixed (line plus bar), high-low-close-open (stock market), and pie formats. To do so, select a graph **Type**, specify a data range or ranges from choices **X A B C D E F**, and View the screen output.

X is the range for labels along the x-axis (the horizontal axis). A, B, C, D, E, and F are data ranges that are plotted along the y-axis (the vertical axis). You can plot as many as six sets of data. The result is a basic graph that depicts relationships between numbers or trends across time.

Look at the sample worksheet in figure 9.3. To create a basic graph, suitable for a quick on-screen look at the data, issue the following command sequences. After each range specification, press Enter.

> /Graph **T**ype **B**ar
> > **A** A:C9..A:H9 (Gross Sales, data range A)
> > **B** A:C10..A:H10 (Expenses, data range B)
> > **V**iew

The resulting graph is shown in figure 9.4. In this graph, the six sets of bars represent monthly data. The bars are graphed in order from left to right, starting with the January data. Within each set of bars, the left-hand bar represents the Gross Sales figure and the right-hand bar, the corresponding Expenses figure. This minimal graph shows a fairly steady sales rate over the six-month period, with the exception of the fourth month, which had significantly lower sales. Expenses remained relatively constant.

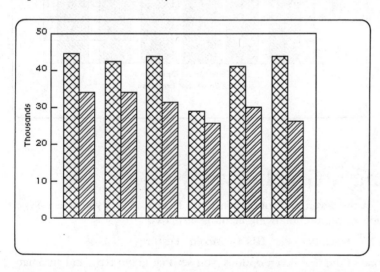

Fig. 9.4.
A basic bar graph.

The graph in figure 9.4 is not, however, something you would want to show to your boss. 1-2-3 has numerous options that let you improve the appearance of your graphs and produce labeled final-quality output suitable for business presentations. To convert the graph in figure 9.4 to presentation-quality, press Esc to return to the worksheet, and then select /**G**raph followed by these commands:

Reminder:
To return to the worksheet when a graph is displayed, press any key.

> **X** A:C6..A:H6 (Monthly headings below x-axis)
> **O**ptions **T**itles **F**irst **ACME WIDGET CORP.**
> > Titles **S**econd **1988 Sales Data, Jan – Jun**
> > Titles **X**-Axis **East Coast Operations**
> > Titles **Y**-Axis **Dollars**
> > **L**egend **A** **Gross Sales**

Legend B Expenses
Grid Horizontal
Scale Y-Scale Format Currency 0
Quit Quit View

The resulting graph is shown in figure 9.5. As you can see, even those who are unfamiliar with the data will be able to understand the contents of an enhanced graph.

Fig. 9.5.
The enhanced,
presentation-
quality graph.

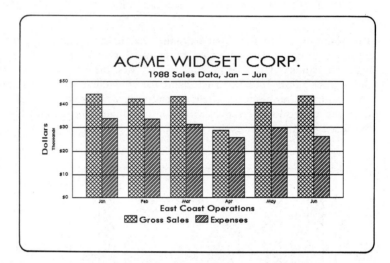

Selecting a Graph Type

Selecting one of the seven available graph types is easy. When you select **Type** from the **/Graph** menu, the following menu is displayed:

   Line   Bar   **XY**   Stack-Bar   Pie   HLCO   Mixed   Features

By selecting one of the first seven options, you set that graph type, and automatically restore the **G**raph menu to the control panel. By selecting **Features**, you go to a submenu that permits setting of certain graph options, which are discussed later in this chapter.

Of the seven 1-2-3 graph types, all but the pie graph display both x- and y-axes. The line, bar, stacked-bar, HLCO (high-low-close-open), and mixed graphs display numbers (centered on the tick marks) along the y-axis only. The x-axis of these graph types can optionally display user-defined labels centered on the tick marks. The XY graph displays numbers on both axes. Some graph types can optionally have a second y-axis, at the right edge of the graph.

Specifying Data Ranges

1-2-3 does not permit you to type data directly to be plotted on a graph. The data to be graphed must be present in the current worksheet, either as values or as the result of formula calculations. Do not confuse the process of specifying data points, which are always numerical, with that of typing descriptions, such as titles. (Typing descriptions is illustrated later in this chapter.)

You must specify which data in the currently displayed worksheet should be graphed. A graph data range consists of one or more rectangular ranges of numbers. If the range contains labels or blank cells, they are ignored. If the data is in adjacent rows or columns, you can let 1-2-3 assign the data ranges with its automatic graph feature, discussed later in this section. Otherwise, you must assign the data ranges manually.

Reminder:
Specify worksheet data to be graphed by entering or highlighting data ranges.

Specifying Data Ranges Manually

To specify a graph data range manually, you first select **A**, **B**, **C**, **D**, **E**, or **F** from the **/Graph** menu, and then specify the range just as you do any other 1-2-3 range—by entering cell addresses or a range name, or by using POINT mode.

The **X** data range option is used for numerical data only with the **XY** graph type. For the other graph types, this option can be used to specify x-axis labels.

Before you start building a graph, read the following general statements about the choice(s) required for each graph type:

Graph type	Option(s)
Line	Enter as many as six sets of data in ranges **A**, **B**, **C**, **D**, **E**, and **F**. 1-2-3 creates one graph line for each range; each point on a line represents one value in the range. The data points in each data range are marked by a unique symbol and/or color when graphed (see table 9.1).
Bar	Enter as many as six data ranges: **A**, **B**, **C**, **D**, **E**, and **F**. 1-2-3 creates one set of bars for each range; each bar in a set represents one value in the range. The bars for multiple data ranges appear within each x-axis group on the graph in alphabetical (A–F) order from left to right. On a monochrome monitor, the bars for each data range are displayed with a unique shading. On a color monitor, they are displayed with a unique color (limited by the maximum number of colors possible on your hardware). Shading and screen colors are summarized in table 9.1.
XY	Choose **X** from the main **Graph** menu and select the data range that contains the independent variable (for example, the x-axis variable). Enter as many as six dependent variable ranges: **A**, **B**, **C**, **D**, **E**, and **F**. 1-2-3 creates one set

Graph type	Option(s)
	of points for each dependent variable range. The data points for each data range are marked by a unique symbol when graphed. The symbols are the same as the **Line** symbols shown in table 9.1.
Stacked-Bar	Follow the bar graph instructions. In a stacked-bar graph, multiple data ranges appear from bottom to top in alphabetical order.
Pie	Enter only one data series by selecting **A** from the main Graph menu. For each value in the **A** range, 1-2-3 creates a pie "slice." (To shade and "explode" pieces of the pie, also select a **B** range, as explained later in this chapter.)
HLCO	The **A**, **B**, **C**, and **D** ranges specify respectively the high, low, closing, and opening values. The **E** range is used for the bars in the lower portion of the graph, and the **F** range is used for the single graph line (see the section on HLCO graphs later in this chapter).
Mixed	Mixed graphs contain bar graphs overlain with line graphs. The **A**, **B**, and **C** ranges are used for the bar portion of the graph, and the **D**, **E**, and **F** ranges for the line portion.

As you build your own graphs, refer to the preceding comments (organized by graph type) and to the information in table 9.1 (organized by data range).

Table 9.1
Graph Symbols and Shading

Data Range	Line Graph Symbols	Bar Graph B&W Shading	On-Screen Color
A	▪	▨	Red
B	◆	▨	Green
C	▼	▨	Blue
D	▫	◇	Yellow
E	◇	▨	Magenta
F	▲	▨	Light Blue

This table shows each data range with the corresponding default assignments for line symbols, bar shading, and color.

Specifying Data Ranges Automatically

In some circumstances, 1-2-3 can automatically perform some or all the work of specifying data ranges for a graph. An automatic graph creates an entire graph with a single keystroke. Group mode lets you specify multiple graph data ranges in one step. These 1-2-3 features can be great time savers.

Automatic Graphs

1-2-3's automatic graph feature lets you create certain types of graphs with a single keystroke. For an automatic graph, the position of the cell pointer, not the settings of the /Graph **X** and /Graph **A** through **F** options, determines which data are included in the graph. Creating an automatic graph requires that two conditions be met:

- The /Graph **X** and **A** through **F** settings are cleared (with the /Graph **R**eset **R**ange command).

- The cell pointer is in a section of the worksheet that can be interpreted as an automatic graph (explained later in this section).

If these conditions are satisfied, displaying an automatic graph requires only that you position the cell pointer anywhere within an automatic graph range and press Graph (F10) or select /Graph View.

The criteria for an automatic graph range are strict, but can be met by many common arrangements of data in a worksheet:

- An automatic graph range must contain data that can be divided, by either rows or columns, into the X and A through F ranges for the graph.

- An automatic graph range must be separated by at least two blank rows and columns from other data in the worksheet.

- The data in an automatic graph range must be arranged by columns or rows with the X data range first, the A data range second, and so on. The first row or column in the range can contain labels.

1-2-3 divides an automatic graph range into rows or columns depending on the setting of /Worksheet Global Default Graph, which can be set to Columnwise or Rowwise. The type of graph created depends on the setting of /Graph Type; if no setting has been made, the default Line graph type is created. Data assignments are made as follows:

- The first column or row that contains numbers is used as the X data range (for XY graphs) or the A data range (for all other graph types). Adjacent columns or rows are used for additional data ranges, in order. Labels in these ranges are treated as zeros.

- For all graph types except XY, a column or row of labels preceding the first numerical data range will be used as the X data range. This range must contain only labels. If such a column or row doesn't exist, no X range assignment is made.

An automatic graph makes use of all current **Graph** menu selections, such as **Type**, **Features**, and **Options**. The only part of an automatic graph that is "automatic" is the assignment of data ranges. Once an automatic graph exists, it can be treated as any other graph—named, saved, printed, and so on.

Consider the worksheet shown in figure 9.6. The data in the range A:A2..A:D6 is a valid automatic graph range. If /Worksheet Global Default Graph Columnwise is in effect (the default), and you have selected /Graph Type Bar, then positioning the cell pointer anywhere in that range and pressing Graph (F10) displays the graph in figure 9.7. Note that the other data ranges in figure 9.6 are not valid automatic graph ranges, because they are not separated by at least two rows or columns from other worksheet data.

Fig. 9.6.
Valid and
invalid
automatic
graph ranges.

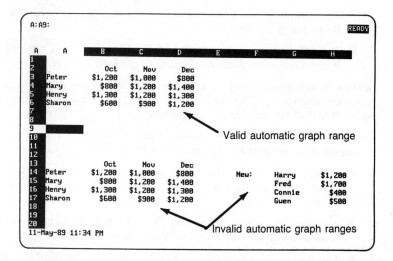

Fig. 9.7.
An automatic
bar graph
created from
the data in
fig. 9.6.

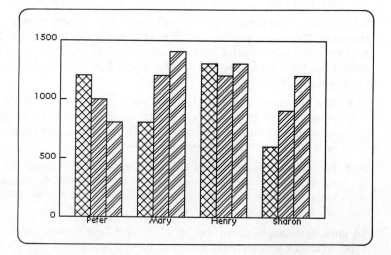

/Graph Group

While the data ranges for 1-2-3 graphs need not be in adjacent worksheet rows or columns, the ranges frequently are. In this situation, using /Graph Group can save a significant number of keystrokes. When all your graph data ranges are in consecutive rows or columns of a rectangular range, the Group option lets you specify all graph data ranges, X and A through F, in one operation. The procedure is as follows:

Cue:
Use /Graph Group to save keystrokes when the X and A–F data ranges are in adjacent rows or columns.

1. Select /Graph Group.

2. Indicate the rectangular range to be divided into data ranges. You can enter cell addresses, a range name, or use POINT mode.

3. Select Columnwise or Rowwise to indicate whether the range should be divided by columns or rows.

Consider the small worksheet shown in figure 9.8. To graph this data as rows in a bar graph, you first set Type to Bar. In this figure, /Graph Group has been selected, and POINT mode has been used to indicate the desired range. After pressing Enter, then selecting Rowwise followed by View, the graph in figure 9.9 is displayed.

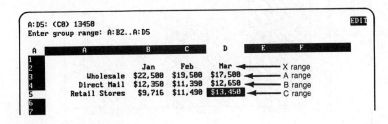

Fig. 9.8.
A group range selected for graphing.

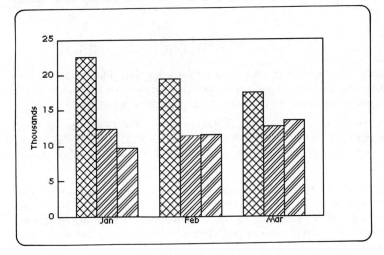

Fig. 9.9.
A Rowwise Group graph created from the data in fig. 9.8.

The following data range assignments have been made automatically:

X A:B2..A:D2
A A:B3..A:D3
B A:B4..A:D4
C A:B5..A:D5

You can graph the same data as columns with the following command sequence:

Group **A:A3..A:D5**
Columnwise
View

The result is shown in figure 9.10.

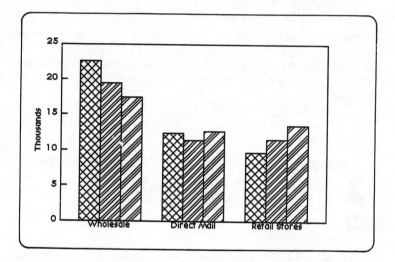

Fig. 9.10.
Group data
graphed
columnwise.

Constructing the Default Line Graph

After you specify the type of graph you want for your data and the location of that data, producing a graph is easy. Using the sales data shown in figure 9.3, you easily can create a line graph of the January through June amounts.

From 1-2-3's command menu, select /Graph to access the Graph menu. Ordinarily, the next step is to select **Type**. But if this is the initial graph created after you load 1-2-3, you don't have to make a selection, because **Line** is the default type.

The next step is to specify the data range(s). You first want to graph the Gross Sales amounts in row 9. To enter the first data range, choose **A** from the main Graph menu and then respond to the control-panel prompt by typing **A:C9..A:H9**. You alternatively can use POINT mode to specify the range, or enter the range name if one has been assigned.

By specifying the type of graph and the location of data to plot, you have completed the minimum requirements for creating a graph manually. If you press View, you see a graph similar to the one shown in figure 9.11.

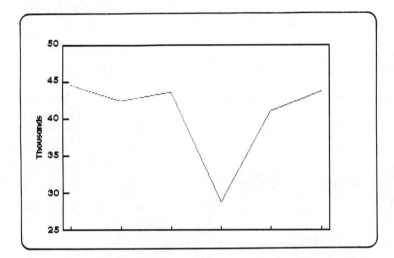

Fig. 9.11.
A basic line
graph.

Although you know what this graph represents, it won't mean much to anyone else. The six data points corresponding to the January-through-June figures have been plotted, but none of the points has been labeled to indicate what it represents. Nor have the graph axes been labeled (except for the Thousands indicator on the y-axis). Notice also that the y-axis origin on this initial graph is not zero, which makes the April decrease seem larger than it really is. Clearly, there's lots of room for improvement here. The text that follows shows you how to enhance this basic graph.

Enhancing the Appearance
of a Basic Graph

Many of 1-2-3's graph features apply equally to all seven graph types. To illustrate, therefore, the next section of this chapter will take you from start to finish, step-by-step, in the creation of a line graph from data in the worksheet in figure 9.3. Later, the chapter covers some graph features that are specific to the other graph types.

Most of the 1-2-3 features for enhancing a graph's appearance are accessed via Options on the Graph menu. Making this selection displays the following menu:

Legend Format Titles Grid Scale Color B&W Data-Labels Advanced Quit

As you work with this menu to add enhancements to your graphs, you should check the results frequently. To see the most recent version of your graph, select **Quit** to return from the **Options** menu to the main **Graph** menu, and then select **View**. Press any key to exit the graph display and restore the **Graph** menu to the screen. Or, depending on your video hardware, you can use the /**Worksheet Window Graph** command to display the graph in a screen window (see this chapter's "Viewing Graphs in a Screen Window" section).

Adding Descriptive Labels and Numbers

To add descriptive information to a graph, you use the **Titles**, **Data-Labels**, and **Legend** options from the **Options** menu. In addition, for all graph types except XY, you can use the **X** data range option. The text that follows covers each of these options.

Using the Titles Option

If you select /**Graph Options Titles**, the following options are displayed in the control panel:

    First Second X-Axis Y-Axis 2Y-Axis Note Other-Note

The **First** and **Second** options are for entering titles that will be displayed centered above the graph. The first title will be in larger type above the second title. After selecting **First** or **Second** from the /**Graph Options Titles** menu, you can either type the desired title in response to the prompt or enter a backslash followed by the address of the worksheet cell containing the label or number to be used as the title.

The **X-Axis**, **Y-Axis**, and **2Y-Axis** options are for labeling the graph axes. **X-Axis** centers a horizontally oriented label below the x-axis. **Y-Axis** places a vertically oriented label just to the left of the left y-axis. **2Y-Axis** positions a vertically oriented label just to the right of the right y-axis. You can type the labels directly, or enter a cell address or range name preceded by a backslash.

The **Note** and **Other-Note** options are for entering "footnotes" that appear in the lower-left corner of the graph. Again, the notes can be typed directly or as a cell address.

Figure 9.12 shows the positions of the various titles as they appear on a graph.

Suppose that you want to enhance the basic line graph of the sales data amounts shown in figure 9.3. You can enter four titles by using cell references for two of the titles and typing new descriptions for the others.

First, select **Titles First**. Next, when 1-2-3 prompts you for a title, type **\A:A2** to reference the cell that contains ACME WIDGET CORP., the first title, and then press Enter. The **Options** menu (*not* the Titles menu) will reappear. Next, select

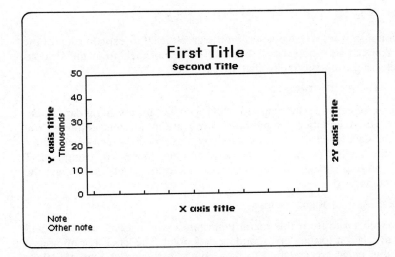

Fig. 9.12.
Graph positions
of the seven
types of titles.

Titles Second and type **\A:A3** to make the label in cell A:A3 the second title centered above the graph.

Then, to label the x-axis, select **Titles X-Axis** and type **MONTH**. To enter the fourth title, select **Titles Y-Axis** and type **Dollars**. Now, to check the graph, select **Quit** (to restore the main Graph menu), and then choose **View**. Your graph should look like the enhanced graph shown in figure 9.13.

Reminder:
The x-axis and
y-axis titles have
no significance
when you
construct a pie
graph.

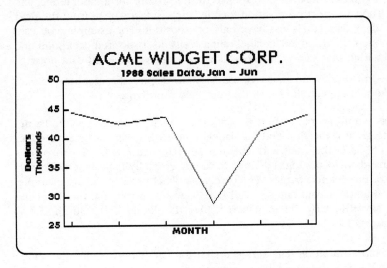

Fig. 9.13.
The line graph
enhanced with
titles.

To edit a title, use the command sequence you used for creating the title. The existing text, cell reference, or range name will appear in the control panel, ready for editing. To eliminate a title, press Esc, and then press Enter.

Entering Data Labels within a Graph

Cue:
Use /Graph Options
Data-Labels to
place descriptive
labels within a
graph.

Sometimes you may want to have labels on the graph itself to explain each of the data points. You can add these labels by selecting **Data-Labels** from the **Options** menu and selecting from the menu that appears:

A   B   C   D   E   F   Group

From this menu, select the data range to which you are are assigning data labels. Select **Group** if the data labels for multiple ranges are in adjacent columns. You cannot type the data labels directly; instead, you must specify a worksheet range that contains the labels. You can give the range as a cell address, by using POINT mode, or by entering a range name. After you specify the data label range, the following menu appears:

Center   Left   Above   Right   Below

The selection you make from this menu determines where each data label will be displayed in relation to the corresponding data point. The labels (or numbers) in the data label range are assigned to data points in the order that the labels appear in the worksheet.

Continue to enhance your sample line graph by entering as data labels the Jan–Jun headings from row 4 of the worksheet. First, select **/Graph Options Data-Labels**, and then select **A** to assign labels to the A range (the only range on the graph).

To enter the six abbreviated monthly headings from row 6 of the worksheet, select **A**, then type **A:C6..A:H6** in response to the prompt for a label range, and press Enter. Then, to specify a position for the labels, select **Above** from the next menu. Each set of data labels can have only one position. For example, you cannot position one cell within a data-label range *above* its associated data point and another cell within that same data-label range *below* its associated data point.

Now, select **Quit** twice, and then choose **View** to display the graph on-screen. Your graph should appear similar to the one shown in figure 9.14.

Cue:
Include blank cells
in data ranges to
alter the spacing of
graph elements.

Placing labels within a graph often produces less than desirable results. Particularly on line graphs, the first and last labels tend to overlap the graph's edges and be cut off, as is the case with the Jun label in figure 9.14. To solve this problem, expand any data ranges defined for a line graph by including blank cells at each end of the defined ranges. To correct the label problem in the example, you can redefine the A data range as **A:B9..A:I9**, and then redefine the data-label range for **A** as **A:B6..A:I6**. When you redisplay the graph, it should appear as shown in figure 9.15.

If you graph more than one data series, attach the data labels to the data range that includes the largest values. Then select **Above** to position the data labels above the data points. If you want to use the data label text itself as the plotted points, select **Neither** from the **/Graph Options Format** menu (which results in neither lines nor symbols being plotted for the specified data range), and then

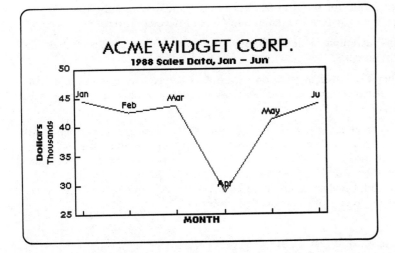

Fig. 9.14.
The line graph
with data
labels added.

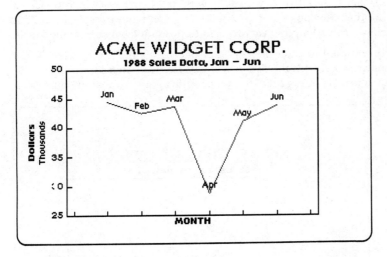

Fig. 9.15.
The same line
graph with the
data and data
label ranges
expanded to
include blank
cells at each
end.

select Center for the data label position. This technique used with a "dummy" data range allows placement of labels anywhere on the graph.

If you graph more than one data series, attach the data labels to the data range that includes the largest numerical values. Then select **Above** to position the data labels above the data points. These steps place the data labels as high as possible in the graph, where they won't obscure the data points.

Another possibility is to use the data label text itself as the plotted points by following these steps:

1. Select **Neither** from the /Graph Options Format menu, which results in neither lines nor symbols being plotted for the specified data range.

2. Select **C**enter for the data label position, which centers the labels over the positions where the data points would have appeared.

By using this technique with a "dummy" data range, you can place labels anywhere on the graph.

To edit either the range or position of the data labels, use the same command sequence you used to create them. Enter a different data-label range or specify a different position.

Reminder:
You cannot use the
Data-Labels option
with a pie graph.

To remove data labels from a data range, follow the same steps used when first creating them, but this time specify a single empty cell as the data-label range. You cannot eliminate the existing range by pressing Esc, as you did to eliminate an unwanted title. Alternatively, you can remove data labels by resetting the data range. Be careful, because this method removes not only the data labels but also the data range and any other associated options.

Entering Labels Below the X-Axis

Instead of placing descriptive information within a graph, you may prefer to enter label information along the x-axis. With all graph types except pie and XY, the main **Graph** menu's **X** option can be used to position labels below the x-axis.

You probably will want to enter the Jan–Jun labels below the x-axis. Select **X** and enter the range that contains the data labels: **A:C6..A:H6**. Then select **V**iew. Your graph should appear as in figure 9.16. Compare this graph to that in figure 9.14.

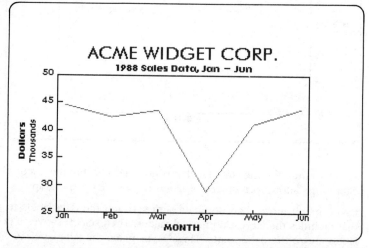

Fig. 9.16.
The graph with
an X range
specified.

The cells you specify for the X range or for a data-label range can contain either labels or values. If values, they are displayed on the graph in the same format as they are displayed on the worksheet. If a label used for a data label won't fit on the graph, the label is truncated (as in fig. 9.14). If a value used as a data label won't fit on the graph, a series of X's is displayed in its place.

Keep the X labels for now. If you later need to eliminate the x-axis labels, select /Graph **Reset X**.

Using the Legend Option

A *data legend* is a key or label on the graph that explains the meaning of a symbol, line color, or hatch pattern. Data legends are particularly useful on graphs that include multiple data ranges.

When a graph contains more than one data range, you need to be able to distinguish between the different ranges. If you are using a color monitor and select Color from the main **Graph** menu, 1-2-3 differentiates data ranges with color. If the main **Graph** menu's **B&W** (black and white) option is in effect, data ranges are marked with different symbols in line graphs and with different hatching patterns in bar-type graphs. (Refer to table 9.1 for a summary of the assignments specific to each data range.)

To print the graph on a black-and-white printer, first choose **B&W**, even if you have a color monitor. A graph created under the Color option will not print properly on a black-and-white printer.

To add data legends to a graph, select **Options Legend** from the main **Graph** menu. The following menu appears:

A B C D E F Range

Select the data range to which you are assigning a legend. Then, in response to the prompt, type the text for the legend or enter a backslash followed by the address of the worksheet cell containing the legend text. Select **Range** to specify a worksheet range containing legend text for all the data ranges.

To illustrate the use of legends, you can add a second data range to the Sales Data line graph, and then add data legends to identify the two data ranges. Suppose, for example, that you want to change the data ranges so that the graph reflects two items: Gross Sales and Expenses.

To add the second data range, select /Graph, choose **B**, and then enter the range for the Expenses data: **A:C10..A:H10**. Next, select **Options Legend**, and choose **A** to specify the legend for the first data range. Enter **Gross Sales** or, alternatively, **\A:A9**. The program returns to the Options menu. To specify the legend for the second data range, again select **Legend**, choose **B**, and enter either **Expenses** or **\A:A10**. Finally, select **Quit** and **View** to display the graph. The modified graph should appear similar to the one shown in figure 9.17.

To edit a legend, use the same command sequence you used to create the legend. The existing text, cell reference, or range name will appear in the control panel, ready for you to edit. To eliminate a legend, press Esc, and then press Enter.

Legends are appropriate only for graphs with two or more data series. You cannot use the **Legend** option for pie graphs, which can have only one data series.

Cue:
To edit a data legend or a graph label, follow the same steps used to create the label or legend.

Fig. 9.17.
A graph with
two data
ranges and
data legends.

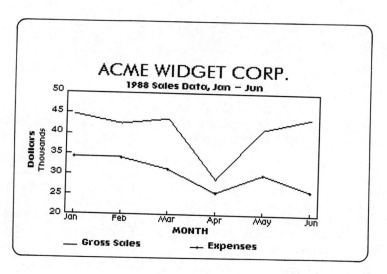

Altering the Default Graph Display

The graph enhancements discussed so far all involved making additions to a basic, simple graph. Other enhancements are possible by modifying the default settings 1-2-3 uses to create a simple graph. In this section, you learn to enhance the basic line graph by changing some of 1-2-3's defaults. This chapter's "Building All Graph Types" section discusses some default settings that apply to other graph types.

Selecting the Format for Data in Graphs

The /Graph Options Format selection lets you specify the format of the data display in graphs that include lines: line, XY, mixed, and HLCO graphs. (The option affects only the line portions of mixed and HLCO graphs.) When you select Format from the Options menu, the following menu appears:

Graph **A B C D E F** Quit

Select the data range whose format you want to specify, or select Graph to set the format for all data ranges. Next, the following menu appears:

Lines Symbols **B**oth **N**either **A**rea

The selections have the following effects:

Lines   The data points are connected by lines, but no symbols are
             displayed.

Symbols   A symbol is displayed at each data point, but the symbols are
             not connected by lines.

Both   Both symbols and connecting lines are displayed. This is the default.

Neither   Neither symbols nor lines are displayed. (This option is used with centered data labels, as described in a preceding section).

Area   The space between the indicated line and the line below it (or the x-axis) is filled with a color or hatch pattern. If Area format is specified for more than one data range, the lines are stacked. Negative values in the line are treated as zeros.

Experiment with these settings to see the effect. For example, selecting **Options Format Graph Area** results in the sample graph appearing as shown in figure 9.18.

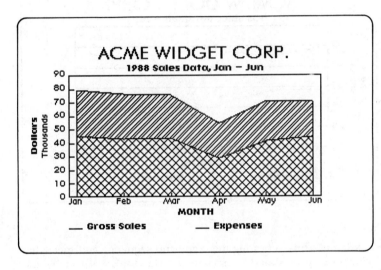

Fig. 9.18.
An area graph with the data format modified.

Setting a Background Grid

Ordinarily, you use the default (clear) background for your graphs. At times, however, you may want to impose a grid on a graph so that the data-point values are easier to read.

Selecting **/Graph Options Grid** produces the following menu:

   Horizontal   Vertical   Both   Clear   Y-Axis

The selections on this menu have the following effects:

Horizontal   Draws across the graph a series of horizontal lines, spaced according to the tick marks on the y-axis

Vertical   Draws across the graph a series of vertical lines, spaced according to the tick marks on the x-axis

Reminder:
Use /Graph Options Grid to display a vertical grid, horizontal grid, or both on your graph.

Both	Draws both horizontal and vertical lines	
Y-Axis	Determines whether Horizontal grid lines are drawn according to tick marks on the left y-axis, the right y-axis, or both	
Clear	Clears all grid lines from the graph	

Reminder:
You cannot add a grid to a pie graph.

To add horizontal lines to the sample graph, select /**Graph** Options Grid Horizontal. Then select **Quit** from the Options menu and press **View**. The graph should look like the one shown in figure 9.19 (assuming that you first selected Options Format Graph **Both** to turn off the area graph option).

Fig. 9.19.
A graph with horizontal grid lines.

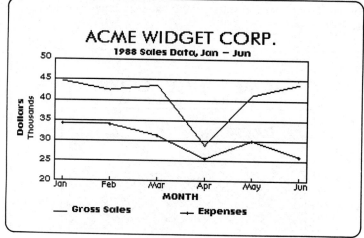

Experiment with different grids, repeating the command sequence and specifying other options. Whenever you want to eliminate a grid display, select /**Graph** Options Grid Clear.

Modifying the Graph Axes

Reminder:
Use the /Graph Options Scale menu to control the scale and labeling of the graph's x- and y-axes.

The Scale option takes you to a series of menus that let you control various aspects of how the graph's axes are displayed. When you select /**Graph** Options Scale, the following menu appears:

   Y-Scale   **X**-Scale   **Skip**   **2Y**-Scale

Reminder:
Scale options do not apply to pie graphs.

If you choose Skip, you can specify that you want the graph to display only every *n*th data point in the X range. The *n* variable can range from 0 to 8192, although you almost always will use low values such as 2 or 5.

If you select /Graph Options Scale Skip and enter a value of 2, the resulting graph will look similar to the one shown in figure 9.20. Notice that only Jan, Mar, and May are displayed on the x-axis scale; Feb, Apr, and Jun have been skipped. In this case using Skip does not make a significant difference in the graph's appearance. If the month names were spelled out in full, however, they would overlap if all were displayed. Using Skip then would make the x-axis more legible.

Cue:
Use /Graph Options Scale Skip when you have too many x-axis values to display together.

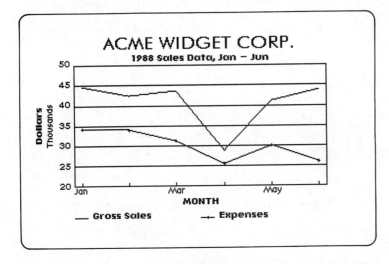

Fig. 9.20.
The graph displayed with Skip set to 2.

The other three options on this menu are for selecting which axis to change: the y-axis, the x-axis, or the second (right) y-axis. Whichever axis you select, the series of menus and options that appears after you select an axis is the same:

Reminder:
1-2-3 automatically includes a y-axis scale.

Automatic Manual Lower Upper Format Indicator Type Exponent Width Quit

Remember that any changes made from this menu apply only to the specific graph axis selected in the previous step.

Minimum and Maximum Axis Values

When you create a graph with 1-2-3, the program automatically sets the scale, or minimum-maximum range, of the y-axis based on the smallest and largest numbers in the data range(s) plotted. This default applies as well to the 2Y-axis when it is used. For XY graphs, 1-2-3 also automatically establishes the x-axis scale based on values in the X data range.

To specify an axis range manually, you first select Manual from the preceding menu. Next you select Lower and enter the minimum axis value. Finally, you select Upper and enter the maximum axis value. Selecting Automatic returns 1-2-3 to the default automatic scaling.

Cue:
You can specify the maximum and minimum values for both the x- and y-axes.

While you can change the minimum and maximum axis values, you cannot determine the size of the tick mark increment; this is set automatically by 1-2-3. Also, be aware that it is possible to set an axis range that is too small to include all the data points. If this happens, some data points will not be plotted. 1-2-3 does not warn you when this happens.

Suppose that you want to change the y-axis origin on the sample graph. First, select /Graph Options Grid Clear to get rid of the grid lines. Next, select Scale Y-Scale Manual. Select Lower and enter 0, and then select Upper and enter 50000. Finally, select Quit Quit View to display the graph shown in figure 9.21.

Fig. 9.21.
The graph with
the y-axis scale
set to 0–50000.

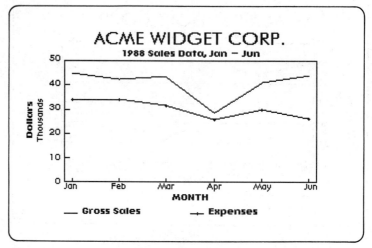

Notice how the perspective of the graph has changed. Earlier, with automatic scaling, the y-axis range was from 20000 to 50000. The April dip in sales appeared more severe than it actually is. By setting the scale manually so that the y-axis origin is at 0, the visual impression of the graph more accurately reflects the actual figures.

Axis Number Format

1-2-3's default is to display the axis scale values in General format, the same format that is the default for the screen display of worksheet values. You can display axis scale values in any of 1-2-3's numeric formats. Select Format from the /Graph Options Scale menu, and the following choices appear:

   Fixed Sci Currency , General +/– Percent Date Text Hidden

Making a format choice here is exactly like selecting a format for a worksheet range with /Range Format. This process includes specifying the number of decimal places and the particular Date or Time format desired (refer to Chapter 5 for details). Note that /Graph Options Scale Format is a distinct command from /Graph Options Format, which controls the way lines are displayed.

For the sample graph, a currency format would be appropriate for the y-axis. Select Scale Y-Scale Format Currency and enter 0 for the number of decimal places. Selecting Quit Quit View displays the graph as shown in figure 9.22.

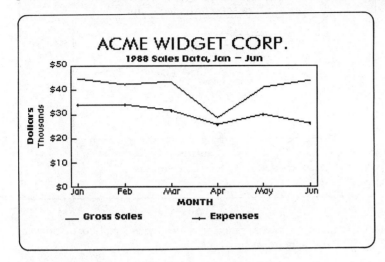

Fig. 9.22.
The graph
displayed with
the y-axis scale
values in
Currency
format.

Axis Scale Indicator

When axis scale values are some multiple of 10, 1-2-3 automatically displays a scale indicator, such as *Thousands* or *Millions*, between the axis and the axis title. You can suppress display of the scale indicator or enter your own scale indicator text. After selecting Indicator from the /Graph Options Scale menu, you have three choices. None suppresses display of the scale indicator. Manual lets you define the indicator; you can type the scale indicator text or specify a cell address preceded by a backslash. Yes turns the automatic indicator display back on.

Suppose that you change the y-axis indicator in the sample graph. Select Scale Y-Scale Indicator Manual, and then enter X 1000. You alternatively could specify a cell address or a range name for the indicator text, preceded by \. If you View the graph by selecting View from the Graph menu, the graph appears as shown in figure 9.23.

Axis Type

The Type command on the /Graph Options Scale menu lets you specify whether the graph axis will have a linear scale (the default) or a logarithmic scale. On a linear scale, equal distances on the axis correspond to linear increments in value—10, 20, 30, and so on. On a logarithmic scale, equal distances on the axis correspond to logarithmic (base 10) increments in value—10, 100, 1000, and so on. Although you generally use linear scales, logarithmic scales are appropriate

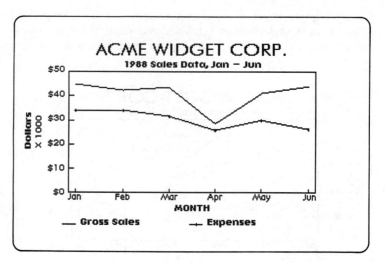

Fig. 9.23.
The graph with
a manual
Y-Scale
indicator.

for graphing data sets that span a wide range of values when small fluctuations at the lower end of the data range must be visible.

Consider the data shown in figure 9.24. If you graph this data as a line graph with a linear Y-scale, you get the graph shown in figure 9.25. The small values A through H are essentially hidden in this graph. Changing the y-axis to a logarithmic scale yields the graph shown in figure 9.26. This graph shows the entire range while preserving the minor fluctuations of points A through H.

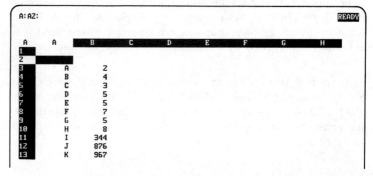

Fig. 9.24.
Sample
worksheet data
for linear and
logarithmic
plots.

Scale Number Exponent

The *scale number exponent* is the power of 10 by which scale numbers must be multiplied to reflect the actual values in the graph. In the sample sales data graph, 1-2-3 automatically has selected an exponent of 3. The scale values—for example, 30, 40, and 50—must be multiplied by 1000 (10 to the third power) when you read the graph values. If you don't like 1-2-3's automatic selection

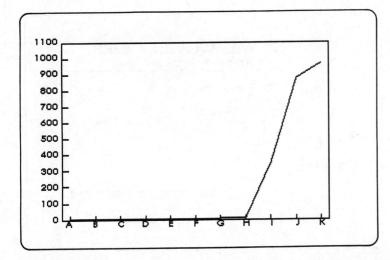

Fig. 9.25.
*The data from
fig. 9.24 plotted
on a linear
y-axis.*

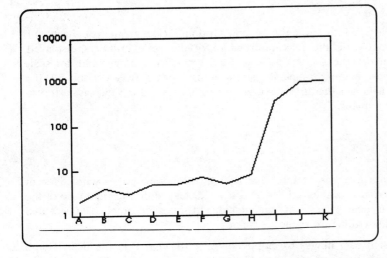

Fig. 9.26.
*The data from
fig. 9.24 plotted
on a
logarithmic
y-axis.*

(which is usually the most appropriate), you can manually select a scale exponent. Your choices are −9, −6, −3, 0, 3, and 6.

To change the exponent on the Sales Data graph, select Scale Y-Scale Exponent Manual and enter an exponent of **0**. You also need to select Scale **Y**-Scale Indicator **Yes** to remove the manual scale indicator **X 1000** entered earlier. The graph now should appear as shown in figure 9.27.

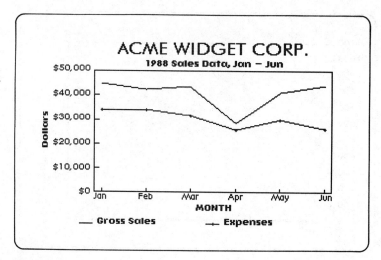

Fig. 9.27.
The Y-Scale
exponent set
manually to 0.

Scale Number Width

When you select **Width** from the /Graph Options Scale menu, you have two choices for specifying the maximum width of the scale numbers displayed. Choose **Automatic** (the default) to have 1-2-3 set the maximum width for scale numbers. Choose **Manual** to specify a maximum width between 0 and 50. If a scale number is longer than the maximum width minus 1, 1-2-3 displays asterisks instead of the number.

Adding a Second Y Scale

1-2-3 allows you to create graphs that have two separate y-axes with different scales. The second y-axis, called the 2Y-axis, is displayed on the right side of the graph. By using dual y-axes, you can include on the same graph data sets that encompass widely different ranges of values.

Cue:
Use dual y-axes to
plot data ranges
that differ widely.

When you assign data ranges to graph ranges **A** through **F** in the main Graph menu, the ranges automatically are assigned to the first y-axis. To create a 2Y-axis, select /Graph Type Features. You are presented with the following menu:

    Vertical Horizontal Stacked 100% 2Y-Ranges Y-Ranges Quit

The fifth and sixth options are relevant to double y-axis graphs. (The other menu options are covered in the next section.) Select **2Y-Ranges** to display the following menu:

    Graph **A** **B** **C** **D** **E** **F** Quit

Selecting **Graph** assigns all data ranges (which you initially selected from the main Graph menu) to the 2Y-axis. Selecting **A** through **F** assigns the indicated data range to the 2Y-axis. Note that you don't enter actual ranges here—you do that from the main **Graph** menu. The choices made here only move existing ranges from the first to the second y-axis.

If you select **Y-Ranges** from the **Features** menu, the same menu appears:

  Graph A B C D E F Quit

The selections here are used to move data ranges back from the 2Y-axis to the y-axis.

To illustrate the advantages of having dual y-axes, you can modify the sample graph to display Gross Profit and Percent Profit. Select **/Graph B**, press Esc to cancel the current B range, and enter **A:C12..A:H12** as the B range. Next, select **Options Legend B** and change the B legend to read **Percent Profit**. When you display the graph by selecting View from the **Graph** menu, the graph will appear as shown in figure 9.28.

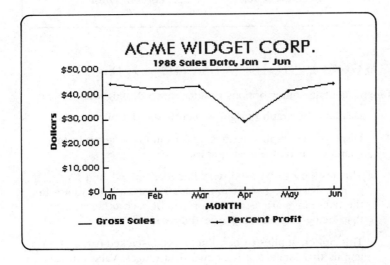

Fig. 9.28.
Gross Sales and
Percent Profit
graphed on a
single y-axis.

Where are the data points for Percent Profit? These data points are in the range 10–30, while the y-axis is scaled from 0 through 50000. Because the Percent Profit data points are plotted almost right on top of the x-axis, you don't see them.

To rectify this problem, return to the main **Graph** menu by pressing Esc, and then select **Type Features 2Y-Ranges B** to assign the B data range (Percent Profits) to the 2Y-axis. Next, select **Options Scale 2Y-Scale Format Percent** and enter 0 for the number of decimal places. Then select **Options Titles 2Y-Axis** and enter **% Profit**. Finally, choose **Quit View**, and the graph shown in figure 9.29 will be displayed. With dual axes, both the Gross Sales and the Percent Profits data ranges can be displayed clearly.

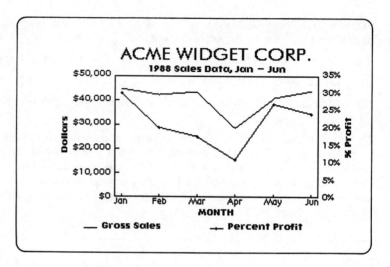

Fig. 9.29.
Gross Sales and
Percent Profit
graphed on
dual y-axes.

Using Other Features Menu Options

The **Features** menu contains other options besides those dealing with 2Y-axes:

Vertical	Displays the graph upright, which is the default
Horizontal	Displays the graph sideways. (An example is given in this chapter's section on bar graphs.)
Stacked	This option can be used with line, bar, mixed, and XY graphs that have two or more data ranges. All the values in the data range are "stacked" on top of each other rather than being plotted relative to the x-axis.
100%	This option applies to bar, line, mixed, stacked-bar, and XY graphs that include at least two data ranges. Values in each data range are plotted as a percentage of the total value.

Figure 9.30 shows an example of a graph created without the Stacked option. The graph shows Expenses plotted as range A and Net Income plotted as range B, with Stacked (the default) turned off. After displaying this graph, return to the **Graph** menu, select **Type Features Stacked Yes**, and redisplay the graph. The graph then should appear as shown in figure 9.31. Note that the B range, Net Income, is stacked on, or added to, the A range. Because Net Profits plus Expenses equals Gross Sales, this graph actually is displaying three sets of information, even though Gross Sales is not an explicitly selected data range. Continue to enhance the graph by selecting **Options Format Graph Area**. The result is shown in figure 9.32.

To illustrate the type of graph produced with the **100%** option on the Features menu, consider the budget worksheet shown in figure 9.33.

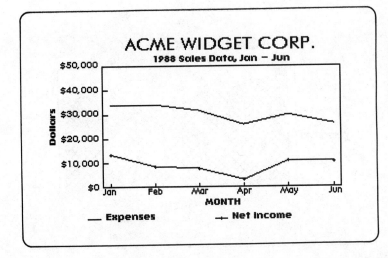

Fig. 9.30.
Expenses and
Net Income
plotted on a
nonstacked line
graph.

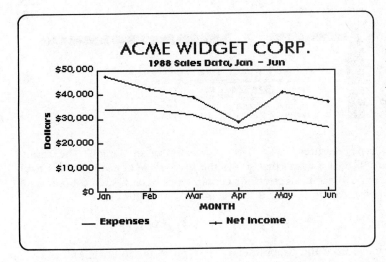

Fig. 9.31.
Expenses and
net income
plotted as a
stacked line
graph.

You can create a bar graph from the budget worksheet data using the following command sequence:

```
/Graph Type Bar
        X A:C18..A:E18
        A A:C20..A:E20
        B A:C21..A:E21
        C A:C22..A:E22
        D A:C23..A:E23
        Options Legend Range A:B20..A:B23
```

The resulting graph, shown in figure 9.34, shows for each month the total dollar amount spent in each of the four categories. Now, return to the main **Graph**

Reminder:
*Use the **T**ype*
Features 100%
option to plot each
data range as a
percentage of the
total.

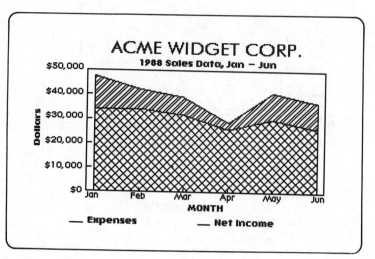

Fig. 9.32.
An area format
specified to
further enhance
the graph.

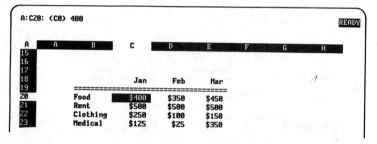

Fig. 9.33.
A three-month
household
expenses
worksheet.

menu, select **Type Features 100% Yes**, and redisplay the graph. The result, shown in figure 9.35, is a graph that shows the *percentage* of each month's total expenses that went to each category. For certain types of data, such as sources of income or expense categories, the 100% graph can be quite useful.

Using Advanced Graph Options

Selecting **Advanced** from the **Graph** menu takes you to the following menu:

    Colors   Text   Hatches   Quit

You need not use any of the **Advanced** options when creating a graph. The **Advanced** options do not add any new data or information to a graph; rather, they modify certain aspects, such as colors and text size, of the way existing information on the graph is displayed and printed.

Reminder:
Use the /Graph
Options Advanced
Text menu to
control the size,
font, and color of
text used in
various sections of
the graph.

Colors

Selecting **Advanced Colors** specifies colors for the A through F data ranges and also allows one or more of the A through F ranges to be hidden. The colors

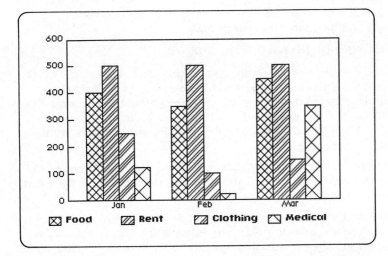

Fig. 9.34.
The budget
worksheet
graphed as a
normal bar
graph.

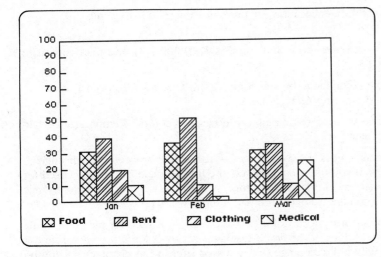

Fig. 9.35.
The budget
worksheet
graphed as a
100% bar
graph.

specified here are used in the graph display and also during printing (if you have a color printer). After selecting Colors, the following menu appears:

A B C D E F

Select the range whose color you want to specify. After you specify the range, the following menu is displayed:

1 2 3 4 5 6 7 8 Hide Range

The effects of these choices are as follows:

1–8   The color that corresponds to the selected number is used for all values in the specified data range. The particular colors that correspond to the numbers 1 through 8 depend on your graphics hardware and your printer.

Hide   The selected data range is not displayed.

Range   This option lets you specify a worksheet *color range* that contains the color numbers to be assigned to individual values in the selected data range. The color range must be the same size as the data range, and can contain values from 1 through 14. The color values are assigned, in order, to the values in the data range.

Using a color range lets you specify 14 different colors, while the Advanced Colors menu provides only 8 colors. Actual display or printing of these 14 colors again depends on your hardware.

By using a conditional @ function in the color range, you can display data points in a color that depends on their value. For example, to display values above 10000 in color 4 and values less than or equal to 10000 in color 7, follow these steps (assuming that the data range is A:C4..A:C13):

1. Select a worksheet location for the color range—for example, A:D4..A:D13.

2. In cell A:D4, enter the formula **@IF(C4>10000,4,7)**, and then copy it to A:C4..A:C13.

3. Assign the color range by selecting /Graph Options Advanced Colors Range and entering **A:D4..A:D13**.

By using formulas in your color range, you can use colors to emphasize certain aspects of your data.

Note: The default colors for data ranges A through F are colors 2 through 7, respectively. When you use a color range, the first color in the range is used for the legend key (if any) for that data range. A negative value in the colors range hides the corresponding value in the data range.

The /Graph Options Advanced Colors **A** Range setting is used for pie graphs only under certain conditions. If the graph display is set to Color and colors have not been specified with a B data range (as discussed later in this chapter's section on pie graphs), then the /Graph Options Advanced Colors **A** Range setting controls the colors used to display a pie graph. Otherwise, the setting is ignored.

Hatches

The Hatches menu choice is used to specify the hatch patterns used for the bars in bar, stacked-bar, mixed, and HLCO graphs; the areas between lines in area graphs; and the slices in pie graphs. You use this option similar to the way you set Advanced Colors. Select Advanced Hatches, and then select the desired data range **A** through **F**. Next, select **1** through **8** or **Range**.

1–8   Assigns the corresponding hatch pattern to the selected data range. Displayed hatch patterns **1** through **8** are the same for all monitors, but printed hatch patterns may differ depending on your printer.

Range   Lets you specify a worksheet *hatch range* that contains the hatch numbers to be assigned to individual values in the selected data range. The hatch range must be the same size as the data range, and can contain values from 1–14. The hatch values are assigned, in order, to the values in the data range.

Using a hatch range lets you specify 14 different hatch patterns, while the **Advanced Hatch** menu provides only 8 patterns. The 6 additional selections are gray scales. Negative numbers in the hatch range hide the corresponding data value. The first hatch pattern in the hatch range is used for the legend key of the corresponding data range.

By using a conditional formula in the hatch range, you can display individual data values in different hatch patterns depending on their value. This is done in the same way as for the color range, explained previously.

The **/Graph Options Advanced Hatches A Range** setting controls pie graph hatch patterns only when graph display is set to **Color** or when graph display is set to **B&W** and hatch patterns are not specified with a B range (as discussed later in this chapter's section on pie graphs).

Cue:
You can display and print colored hatches by using both Advanced Colors and Advanced Hatches.

Text

The **Advanced Text** selection lets you specify attributes for the text displayed and printed on graphs. When you select **Advanced Text**, the following menu appears:

     First   Second   Third   Quit

Use this menu to specify the exact text whose attributes you want to change:

First   The first line of the graph title

Second   The second line of the graph title, the axis titles, and legend text

Third   The scale indicators, axis labels, data labels, and footnotes

After selecting the text group to be changed, the following menu appears:

     Color   Font   Size   Quit

The **Color** option selects the color to be used for the specified text group. The settings made here are displayed only when the graph display is set to **Color**, and are printed only on a color printer. After selecting **Color**, select color **1** through **8**, or **Hide**. As before, the colors that correspond to the color numbers 1–8 depend on your graphics hardware and your printer. **Hide** suppresses display of the selected text whether display is set to **Color** or **B&W**.

The **Font** option lets you select the font, or typestyle, that will be used for the specified text group. After selecting **Advanced Text Font**, you next select either the **First**, **Second**, or **Third** text group. You then can select font **1** through **8**, or **Default** to use the default font for that text group. The defaults are font 1 for the first text group and font 3 for the second and third text groups.

The **Size** menu choice is used to specify the size of text to be used in the graph. After selecting **Advanced Text Size**, you next select either the **First**, **Second**, or **Third** text group, and then select a size (**1** through **9**), or **Default** to use the default size for that text group. The defaults are size **7** for the first text group, size **4** for the second text group, and size **2** for the third text group. Larger numbers correspond to larger type size.

Note: While you can specify nine text sizes, 1-2-3 uses only three of them for screen display. Settings **1–3** display in the smallest text size, settings **4–6** in the medium size, and settings **7–9** in the largest size. The sizes available for printed graphs depend on your printer and on the font selected with **Advanced Text Font**. You can use **/Print Printer Sample** (see Chapter 8) to get an indication of your printer's font capabilities.

If the text size you specify won't fit on the graph (both displayed and printed), 1-2-3 automatically reduces the text size (if a smaller size is available). If the text still won't fit, it is truncated.

Figure 9.36 displays a graph using 1-2-3's defaults for all features that can be changed on the Advanced menu. Compare that figure with figure 9.37, which displays some changes in hatching and text size. These figures should give you some idea of the flexibility that 1-2-3's Advanced graph options provide.

Fig. 9.36.
A bar graph
displayed with
all default
settings.

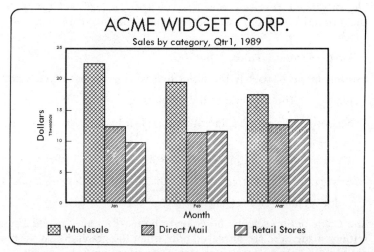

The Advanced options allow you a great amount of control over the final appearance of printed graphs. The options allow you just a bit less control over displayed graphs. Of course, a lot depends on your specific hardware setup. If you

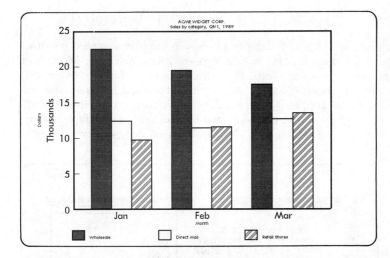

Fig. 9.37.
The same graph
with some
changes in text
size and hatch
styles.

have a VGA graphics display and a laser printer, you will have a lot more flexibility than if you have a CGA display and a dot-matrix printer. The best approach is to use this chapter as a guide as you experiment with your setup.

Viewing Graphs

Several options are available in 1-2-3 for viewing a graph on-screen. You can view a graph from within the worksheet, using the entire screen to display the graph. Depending on your video hardware, you may be able to display a graph in a screen "window," leaving the worksheet visible in the remainder of the screen. You also can decide whether to view the graph in color or in black and white.

Viewing Graphs from the Worksheet

While working in a worksheet, you can view a graph in two ways. You either can press Graph (F10) or issue the /Graph View command. If a graph is currently defined, 1-2-3 will clear the screen and display the graph. If no graph is defined, 1-2-3 will attempt to create an automatic graph (discussed earlier in this chapter) based on the position of the cell pointer. If the cell pointer is in a valid automatic graph range, the automatic graph will be displayed. If not, 1-2-3 will beep and display a blank screen. Pressing Esc returns you to your worksheet.

After you have defined a graph, you can use the Graph (F10) and Esc keys to alternate quickly between the worksheet and the graph. This technique can be used for "what-if" scenarios; as you modify worksheet data, you can quickly see the effects of the changes graphically.

Cue:
Use the Graph
(F10) key to toggle
between graph
display and
worksheet display.

Viewing Graphs in a Screen Window

One useful feature of 1-2-3 is the ability to view a graph in a screen window. This option is accessed via the /Worksheet Window menu. Selecting /Worksheet Window Graph splits the screen vertically at the column to the right of the cell pointer. The current graph, if any, is displayed in the right window, and the worksheet remains displayed in the left window. Any changes made in the worksheet data or in the graph settings are reflected immediately in the graph display. Figure 9.38 shows a 1-2-3 screen with a graph displayed in a window.

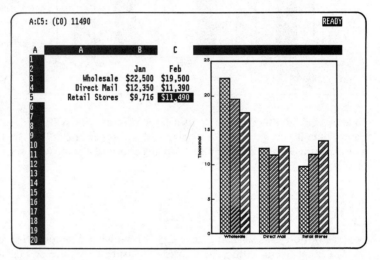

Fig. 9.38.
The /Worksheet Windows Graph command used to display the current graph in a screen window.

Displaying a graph in a window can be extremely useful during graph development. You can see on-screen the effects of changes in data ranges, options, or graph types instantly. Note that /Worksheet Window Graph does not work with all video hardware. With certain video adapters, you will be able to display graphs full-screen, but not in a window.

Viewing a Graph in Color

The /Graph Options Color and B&W (black and white) options determine whether graphs are displayed in monochrome or color. For color display, of course, you need a color monitor. You can select B&W with either a color or monochrome monitor.

When a graph is displayed in color, different data ranges are differentiated by the colors. When displayed in monochrome, data ranges are differentiated by symbols, shapes, or shading patterns. Some of 1-2-3's shading patterns are shown in the area graph in figure 9.39. You will see more patterns in this chapter's section on bar graphs.

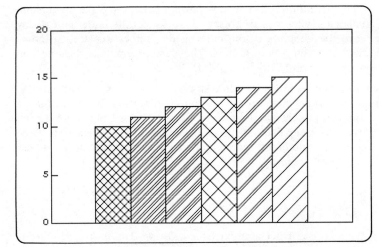

Fig. 9.39.
1-2-3's different
hatch patterns.

Saving Graphs and Graph Settings

You have learned how to create a basic graph and how to use options to enhance the display of that graph. This section shows you how to use the **Save** and **Name** options to save the graph for use by other programs or for recall to the screen. You also can save the settings for one or more graphs for later recall within the worksheet.

Cue:
Use /Graph Name
to save a graph for
later recall in the
worksheet.

Saving Graphs on Disk

Unlike earlier versions of 1-2-3, Release 3 does not require that a graph be saved to disk before printing. You can, however, save a graph in a disk file for later modification by other programs.

1-2-3 can save graphs in either of two file formats: *Picture* file format or *Metafile* format. Which format you use depends on the setting made on the /**W**orksheet **G**lobal **D**efault **G**raph menu. To determine the current setting, select /**W**orksheet **G**lobal **D**efault **S**tatus and look for the entry under Graph save extension:. If PIC is listed, then graphs will be saved in Picture file format. If CGM is displayed, Metafile format will be used. To change the setting, select /**W**orksheet **G**lobal **D**efault **G**raph, and then select **M**etafile or **P**IC.

To save a graph, select /**G**raph **S**ave. You are then prompted for the file name. You either can use the arrow keys to highlight an existing name or type a name that is as many as eight characters long. 1-2-3 automatically will supply the .PIC or .CGM extension, depending on the format selected. If a file by the same name already exists in the current directory, you will see a Cancel/**R**eplace menu similar to that which appears when you try to save a worksheet file under an existing name. To overwrite the contents of the existing file, select **R**eplace. To abort storage of the current graph, select Cancel. The current graph is the one you would see by pressing Graph (F10) from READY mode.

If you have set up subdirectories for disk storage, you can store the current graph to a subdirectory other than the current one without first having to issue a /**File D**irectory command to change directories. To store the graph, select /**G**raph **S**ave. Press Esc twice to remove all existing current directory information. Then type the name of the new subdirectory in which you want to store this particular graph, followed by the file name.

Saving Graph Settings

Although using 1-2-3 to construct a graph from existing data in a worksheet is easy, having to rebuild the graph whenever you want to print or display it on-screen would be tedious. Graphs saved to disk cannot be recalled into 1-2-3. You can, however, save the settings for one or more graphs and recall them later. These settings are not saved in a separate file, but are kept as part of the worksheet itself.

To save the current graph settings, you issue the /**G**raph **N**ame command to access the following menu:

Use **Create** **Delete** **Reset** **Table**

These commands perform the following actions:

Create   Saves the current graph setting under a user-specified name

Use   Displays a list of named graphs, and makes current the one you select

Delete   Deletes a single named graph

Reset   Deletes all named graphs (careful!)

Table   Creates a listing of all named graphs in the current worksheet. Move the cursor to the cell where you want the listing to appear and press Enter. The listing will occupy three columns and as many rows as there are named graphs. For each named graph, the listing gives the name, the type of graph (line, bar, and so on), and the first graph title. This list will overwrite any existing worksheet data.

When designing multiple graphs, be sure to use the Create option to save the settings under a name you specify for each graph before going on to the next. Also, be sure to save the worksheet even if the actual data have not changed.

Resetting the Current Graph

You may have noticed that, throughout this chapter, instructions for editing or removing options have been given at the end of each new topic. These instructions are important because 1-2-3 continues to use an enhancement in the next version of the same graph, or in a new graph, unless you take specific actions to remove that enhancement. For example, you can build a series of six different bar graphs by specifying the graph type (with the **Type** option) for only the first one. Recall, for example, that after you specified the titles in the sample Sales Data graph, you did not have to specify them again for the subsequent versions of the graph.

If you want to make changes to only a few items in a graph's design, you can do so from the **Options** menu. However, if the next graph you will construct is substantially different from the current one, you may want to use the **/Graph Reset** command. Selecting **/Graph Reset** produces the following menu:

> Graph **X A B C D E F R**anges **Options Quit**

You use these menu options in the following ways:

Graph	Cancels all current graph settings. This command resets the type, data ranges, options—everything!
X	Cancels labels displayed below the x-axis, pie-slice labels, and x-axis information for an XY graph. Clears any associated legends.
A–F	Cancels the specified data range and any associated legends
Ranges	Cancels all data ranges, including **Group** ranges, without affecting **Options**
Options	Cancels all **/Graph Options** settings, returning them to their defaults where appropriate

To illustrate the total graph-reset operation when a graph is defined, select **/Graph Reset Graph**. If you then select **View** from the main **Graph** menu, you hear a beep and see a blank screen. If your cell pointer is on a range with numbers, however, 1-2-3 sets the data range automatically. By removing the graph's data ranges, you eliminate the essential ingredients for graph production.

Developing Alternative Graph Types

You can use 1-2-3 to build seven types of graphs: line, bar, XY, stacked-bar, mixed, HLCO, and pie. In some cases, more than one graph type can accomplish the desired presentation. Choosing the best graph for a given application can sometimes be strictly a matter of personal preference. For example, selecting **Line**, **B**ar, or **P**ie would be appropriate if you plan to graph only a single data range. At other times, however, only one graph type will do the job. For instance, HLCO graphs are specialized for presenting certain types of stock market information. Before you work through the remainder of this chapter, take a moment to learn or review the primary uses of each graph type. Then go on to learn how to construct each type of graph.

Selecting an Appropriate Graph Type

A brief summary of the use of each graph type follows. This list in not exhaustive, of course. Your creativity and ingenuity are the only real limiting factors when applying 1-2-3's graph types to your data.

Type	*Purpose*
Line	To show the trend of numeric data across time
Bar	To compare related data at one point in time, or to show the trend of numeric data across time
XY	To show the relationship between one numeric *independent variable* and one or more numeric *dependent variables*
Stack-Bar	To show two or more data ranges in terms of the proportion of the total contributed by each data point
Pie	To graph a single data series, showing what percentage of the total each data point contributes. Do not use this type of graph if your data contains negative numbers.
HLCO	To show fluctuations in a stock's high-low-close-open prices over time
Mixed	A combination of line and bar graphs, to combine in a single graph data best shown in bar format and data best shown in line format

Building All Graph Types

Throughout this chapter, examples of line graphs have been used to illustrate most of 1-2-3's graph enhancements. Most of the options described can be used for all the other graph types as well. This section focuses briefly on each of the graph types, giving an example and discussing any enhancements that apply particularly to that type. In this section, each of the example graphs are based on the worksheet shown in figure 9.40.

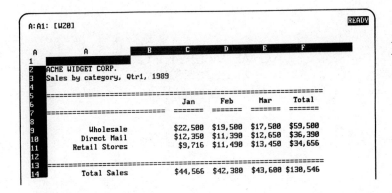

Fig. 9.40.
A sales-by-category worksheet.

Line Graphs

Suppose that you want to create a line graph that shows the steady increase in retail store sales during the 1st quarter. To create this graph, first select /**Graph Reset Graph** to reset any existing graph settings. Next, use the following command sequence to select the graph type and the data ranges:

> **Type Line**
> **A A:C11..A:E11**

Next, select the X data range:

> **X A:C6..A:E6**

Finally, enter the graph titles:

> **Titles First \A:A2**
> **Titles Second \A:A11**

When you select **Quit** and then **View**, the graph shown in figure 9.41 is displayed.

Bar Graphs

Suppose that you want to create a bar graph that shows each month's sales by category. A bar graph is appropriate for this data because the differences in sales figures can be clearly shown by the different bar heights.

First, select /**Graph Reset Graph** to reset any existing graph settings. Next, use the following command sequence to select the graph type and the data ranges:

> **Type Bar**
> **A A:C9..A:E9**
> **B A:C10..A:E10**
> **C A:C11..A:E11**

Next, select an X data range and specify a range for data legends:

> **X A:C6..A:E6**
> **Options Legend Range A:A9..A:A11**

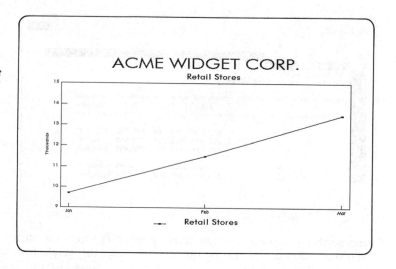

Fig. 9.41.
A line graph depicting first quarter retail sales.

Finally, specify graph titles and a y-axis title:

Options Titles First \A:A2
           Titles Second \A:A3
           Titles Y-Axis Dollars

The resulting graph, shown in figure 9.42, illustrates that Wholesale sales have been decreasing, Retail Store sales have been holding about steady, and Direct Mail sales have been increasing. In this graph, each of the three bars clustered around a tick mark on the x-axis represents sales from a certain category for that month. In each set of bars, the leftmost bar represents data range A; the next, data range B; and the next, data range C. Monthly headings are centered under the x-axis tick marks.

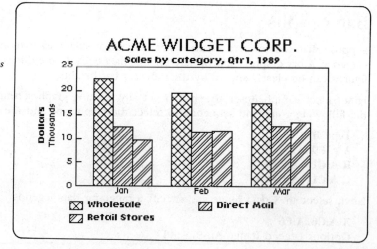

Fig. 9.42.
Data from fig. 9.40 graphed as a bar graph.

Because you will need this graph for later examples, assign it a name by selecting /Graph Name Create and entering **Q1SALES**. Now you will be able to modify the graph in the next examples, then recall it in its original form when needed.

Suppose that you want to display this graph in horizontal orientation. To do so, select **Type Features Horizontal**. The graph now is displayed as shown in figure 9.43. Horizontal display can be used with other graph types (except pie), but seems particularly appropriate for bar graphs. Selecting between **Vertical** and **Horizontal** is usually a matter of personal preference.

Reminder:
A bar graph can be displayed either vertically or horizontally.

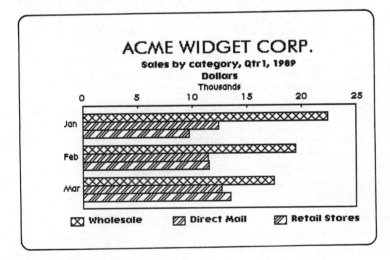

Fig. 9.43.
The graph in fig. 9.42 graphed horizontally.

Stack-Bar Graphs

You may want to experiment with different graph types when you plot multiple time-series data. If the data ranges combine in amount to produce a meaningful figure (for example, the total monthly sales for the Acme Widget Corp.), try using **Stack-Bar** as a graph type. The data ranges in a stacked-bar graph appear as bars; these bars are plotted in the order A B C D E F, with the A range closest to the x-axis. After having entered the command sequences to create figure 9.42, for example, you could create the stacked-bar graph shown in figure 9.44 by selecting **Type Features Vertical** to return to vertical graph display. Then select **Type Stack-Bar** from the main Graph menu, and select **View** to display the graph on-screen.

All the options you set to produce the bar graph in figure 9.42 are carried over to the new stacked-bar graph. 1-2-3 also adjusts automatically the upper and lower limits of the y-axis. In a stacked-bar graph, the lower limit must always be zero.

Distinguishing between certain patterns of crosshatches can be difficult if those patterns appear next to each other. For example, look at the patterns that repre-

Fig. 9.44.
The graph in fig. 9.42 displayed as a stacked-bar graph.

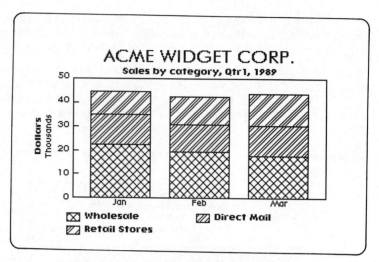

sent Retail Stores and Direct Mail—the uppermost two bar sections for each month. To solve this problem, assign the data ranges differently: assign the data for Direct Mail to range D instead of range B. Assuming that the current graph is shown in figure 9.44, use the following command sequences to produce the graph shown in figure 9.45:

```
/Graph Reset B Quit
        D A:C10..A:E10
        Options Legend D Direct Mail
Quit View
```

Fig. 9.45.
Ranges D and B exchanged for increased legibility.

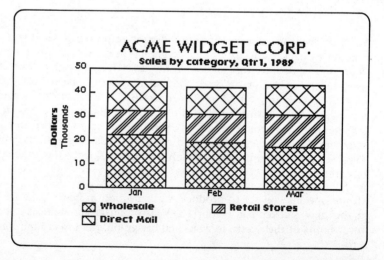

Cue:
To view a stacked-bar graph in color, assign different colors to consecutive bars.

If you compare figures 9.44 and 9.45, you can see that changing the patterns of crosshatches by carefully selecting data ranges makes the information easier to read. If you intend to view the stacked-bar graph in color, be sure to assign different colors to consecutive bars; otherwise, you will not be able to differentiate between two distinct data items. Hatch patterns can also be changed from the **Options Advanced** menu, discussed in this chapter's earlier section on "Using Advanced Graph Options."

Mixed Graphs

A mixed graph is nothing more than a combination of the line and bar types. Data ranges A, B, and C are plotted as bars, while ranges D, E, and F are plotted as lines. Otherwise, all graph options and restrictions apply.

Suppose that you want to modify the graph in figure 9.42 to be a mixed graph that displays individual sales categories as bars and total sales as a line. First, recall the settings (remember, you saved them as a named graph) by selecting /Graph **Name Use**, then highlighting **Q1SALES**, and pressing Enter. The graph is displayed as shown in figure 9.42. Return to the Graph menu, select **Type Mixed**, and redisplay the graph. You may be surprised to see that it hasn't changed!

The graph didn't change because only the "bar" ranges, A–C, have been assigned. If no "line" ranges are assigned, a mixed graph displays just as a bar graph does. The converse is true as well: if line ranges but no bar ranges are assigned, a mixed graph displays as a line graph does.

You can complete the mixed graph by entering the following commands from the main **Graph** menu:

> **D A:C14..A:E14**
> **Options Legends D \A:A14**
> **Quit View**

The result is the graph shown in figure 9.46. The message of this graph is that while individual sales categories are changing, Total Sales are remaining relatively constant.

Pie Graphs

You use a pie graph only for plotting a single data range that contains only positive numbers. Many of the **Graph** menu's options, including all those dealing with graph axes, do not apply to pie graphs.

Suppose that you want to construct a pie graph from the data shown in figure 9.41, and that you want to graph the percentage of Total Sales for the quarter from each category. You start by selecting /Graph **Reset Graph**. Next, you select **Type Pie** and specify **A:F9..A:F11** as data range A. When you display the graph, it appears as shown in figure 9.47.

1-2-3 automatically calculates and displays parenthetically the percentage of the whole represented by each pie wedge. These percentage values can be suppressed by using a C range, as described in the text that follows.

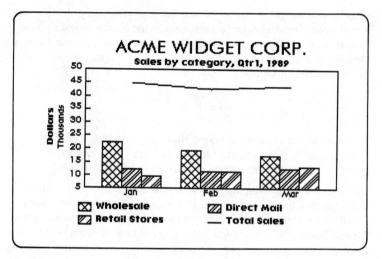

Fig. 9.46.
A mixed graph.

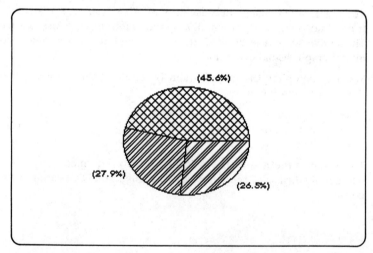

Fig. 9.47.
*An unenhanced
pie graph.*

You can enhance this basic pie graph by adding titles and an X range of explanatory labels. For example, you can use the labels in column A as the X range by entering the following command sequence:

X A:A9..A:A11
Options Titles First \A:A2
        Titles Second Total Sales by Category
Quit View

The resulting graph is shown in figure 9.48.

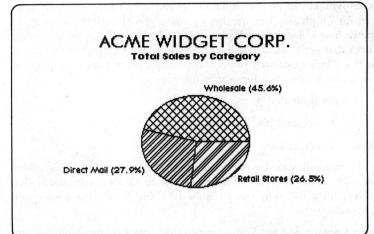

Fig. 9.48.
A pie graph
enhanced with
titles and
labels.

1-2-3 provides eight different shading patterns for monochrome display, eight different colors for EGA color display, and four colors for CGA color display. Figure 9.49 shows the pie graph shading patterns associated with each code number.

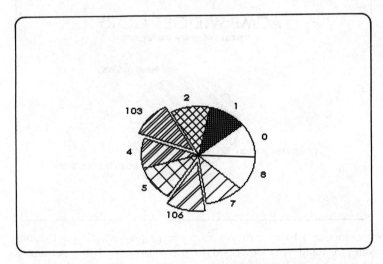

Fig. 9.49.
The pie graph
hatch patterns
associated with
each code
number.

To suppress the display of percentage values on the pie graph, assign a C range in the same manner as the B range. A value of 0 in a cell in the C range suppresses the percentage display for the corresponding pie slice. A blank cell retains the percentage display. Note: You can have a C range with no B range.

1-2-3 automatically will display the pie wedges in different colors or hatch patterns, depending on whether **Options B&W** or **Options Color** is in effect. You

Cue:
Use the B data
range to specify
colors or hatch
patterns for the
wedges of a pie
graph.

can modify the assignment of colors or hatching, and optionally "explode" individual pie slices for emphasis. You do this by using the B data range to enter codes for the pattern or colors for each pie wedge. The B range can be any range of your worksheet that is the same size as the A data range being plotted as a pie graph. The codes for color *or* hatch pattern, depending on whether the graph is displayed in black and white or color, are as follows:

0 or 8	An unshaded pie slice
1–7	A specified hatch pattern or color
Negative value	A hidden slice

Cue:
Create an "exploded" pie wedge by adding 100 to the wedge's shading code in the B range.

Adding 100 to the preceding codes results in an exploded pie slice. Figure 9.49 shows the effects of different codes in **B&W** mode. In Color mode, each slice would be displayed in a different color (limited by the maximum colors supported by your hardware).

Suppose that you want to add shading or exploding codes to the Sales-by-category worksheet graph. Although you can put the B range anywhere in the worksheet, put it adjacent to the A range for this example. In cells A:G9..A:G11, enter the values **4**, **5**, and **106**, in that order. Then, from the **Graph** menu, specify those three cells as the B range. Selecting **View** displays the graph shown in figure 9.50.

Fig. 9.50.
A pie graph with an exploded slice.

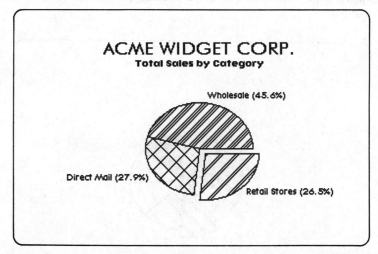

To assign both colors and hatch patterns to a pie graph, use **/Graph Options Advanced Hatches A Range** (as described in this chapter's "Using Advanced Graph Options" section). To hide a pie slice, include a negative number in the corresponding cell of the B range.

XY Graphs

The XY graph, often called a *scatter plot*, is a unique variation of a line graph. In an XY graph, a data point's position on the x-axis is determined by a numerical value rather than by a category. Two or more different data items from the same data range can have the same X value. Rather than showing time-series data, XY graphs illustrate the relationships between different attributes of data items—age and income, for example, or educational achievements and salary. You must think of one data item (X) as the *independent variable* and consider the other item (Y) to be dependent on the first—that is, the *dependent variable*. Use the main **Graph** menu's **X** data range to specify the range containing the independent variable, and one or more of the **A B C D E F** options to enter the dependent variable(s).

Suppose that you want to create a graph which shows the relationship between the amount spent on advertising each month and the sales generated. For the example, you can use the data in figure 9.51, which shows the advertising budget and sales by month for an entire year. Note that a line graph would be an appropriate type for plotting Sales as a function of Month. For Sales vs. Advertising Budget, however, you must use an XY graph.

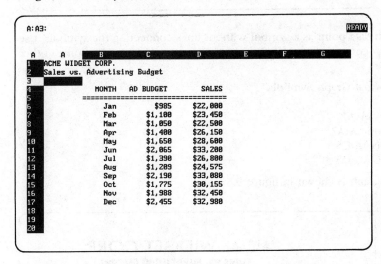

Fig. 9.51.
Data to be plotted on an XY graph.

To create the XY graph, enter the following commands:

```
/Graph Type XY
        X A:C7..A:C18
        A A:D7..A:D18
```

The resulting graph is shown in figure 9.52.

Notice that the data points are connected by lines, making the graph difficult to interpret. This problem results because 1-2-3 orders the data points from right-to-left based on the values in the X range (smallest-to-largest), while the points are connected in the order they appear in your worksheet. Therefore, for XY graphs, you usually will want to set **Format** to **Symbols**. Setting **Format** to Sym-

Cue:
To create a scatter plot, use an XY graph with Format set to Symbols.

Fig. 9.52.
A basic XY
graph.

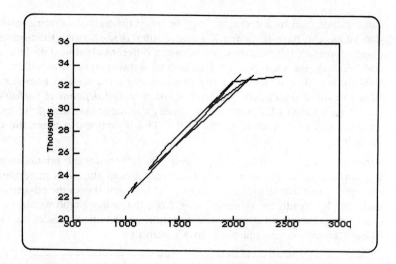

bols plots each data point as a symbol without lines connecting the symbols. Use the following commands to make that change and to add some other enhancements:

Options Format Graph Symbols
Quit
Titles First \A:A1
Titles Second \A:A2
Titles X-Axis \A:C5
Titles Y-Axis \A:D5

The resulting graph is shown in figure 9.53.

Fig. 9.53.
The enhanced
XY graph.

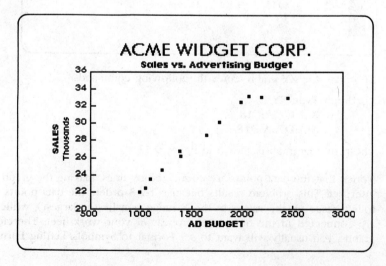

This graph clearly shows a trend between advertising expenditures and sales. As the advertising budget goes up, so do sales. Note, however, that the plot "flattens out" at the top, suggesting that once advertising expenditures increase beyond $2000 per month, they are not having any additional effect on sales.

HLCO Graphs

HLCO stands for high-low-close-open. This is a special type of graph used in graphing data about the price of a stock over time. The meanings of the values are as follows:

High   The stock's highest price in the given time period

Low   The stock's lowest price in the given time period

Close   The stock's price at the end, or close, of the time period

Open   The stock's price at the start, or open, of the time period

Reminder:
Use an HLCO
graph type to plot
stock market
information.

While HLCO graphs are specialized for stock market information, they also can be used to track other kinds of fluctuating data over time, such as daily temperature or currency exchange rates.

Each set of data—four figures representing high, low, close, and open values—is represented on the graph as one vertical line. The vertical extent of the line (that is, the length) is from the low value to the high value. The close value is represented by a tick mark extending right from the line, and the open value by a tick mark extending left. The total number of lines on the graph depends on the number of time periods included.

An HLCO graph also can include a set of bars below the HLCO section of the graph, and a line across the HLCO section. The bars and line can be used for any quantity you want. In the financial world, the bars often are used to illustrate daily trading volume for the stock.

Data ranges for an HLCO graph are assigned as follows:

Range	Values or elements
A	The high values
B	The low values
C	The closing values
D	The opening values
E	The bars
F	The line

You can specify only some of these ranges, and only the corresponding part of the graph will be plotted. The minimum requirements are that the A and B ranges must be specified, *or* the E range, *or* the F range. The graph in figure 9.54, for example, shows an HLCO plot of common stock data for a fictional company. Data ranges A through E were assigned, with range F not used. Graph enhancements, such as an X range, titles, and axis labels, are added, as with the other graph types.

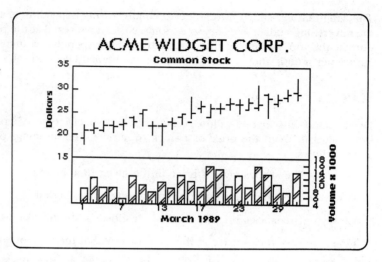

Fig. 9.54.
An HLCO graph
of stock market
information.

Stock market figures are often downloaded from on-line information services as text labels in the form '45 3/8. To change these to values that can be used in an HLCO graph, use the @VALUE function, as described in Chapter 6.

Printing Graphs

The first part of this chapter showed you how to create 1-2-3 graphs that are displayed on the screen. Screen graphs are fine as far as they go, but you will often need to create printed copies that can be distributed to colleagues, used in business presentations, or filed for future reference.

If you have used earlier versions of 1-2-3, you will notice a major change in the way graphs are printed in Release 3. Rather than using a separate PrintGraph program, you now can print graphs from within the main 1-2-3 program itself. Furthermore, 1-2-3's background printing capability permits you to continue working in your worksheet while a graph is printing.

The text in this section shows you how to print graphs you created in 1-2-3. You also learn how to modify the quality, size, and orientation of printed graphs. In addition, you learn how to include one or more graphs in a printed report.

Basic Graph Printing

To print a graph, you must have installed a graphics-capable printer during the 1-2-3 Install procedure, and have it connected to your computer and on-line. If you installed only one printer, you are ready to go.

If you installed more than one graphics-capable printer, you can select the one to be used for graph printing. Issue the /**Print Printer Options Advanced Device Name** command and specify the interface that the selected printer is connected to. You can determine the currently selected printer with /**Worksheet Global Default Status**, which presents a screen display of various default settings, including the selected printer. (See Chapter 8 for more information on the printing commands.)

Reminder:
If you installed more than one graphics-capable printer, select the one to be used for graph printing.

You print graphs from the **Print** menu. A graph, or a report containing a graph, can be sent directly to the printer or to an encoded disk file for later printing. To print immediately, select /**Print Printer**. To send output to an encoded file, select /**Print Encoded**, and then enter the desired file name. Chapter 8 includes detailed information on creating and using encoded files.

Reminder:
To print immediately, select /Print Printer; to send output to an encoded file, select /Print Encoded.

After choosing between /**Print Printer** and /**Print Encoded**, select **Image** from the Print [**P,E**] menu, shown in figure 9.55.

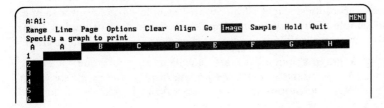

Fig. 9.55.
The Image selection on the /Print [P,E] menu.

Next, select either **Current** or **Named-Graph**. The **Current** option prints the current graph—that is, the graph that would be displayed on-screen by selecting /**Graph View** or pressing Graph (F10) from READY mode. The **Named-Graph** option prints a named graph. Highlight the desired name from the list presented and press Enter. You can select any named graph from any active file.

After specifying the image to print, you are returned to the **Print** [**P,E**] menu. Make sure that the printer is on-line. Align the top of the paper with the top of the hammer plate, and then select **Align** from the menu. Select **Go** to start printing. You then can select **Quit** to return to your worksheet. You can continue working on the worksheet, even specifying additional graphs and reports to print. If you do so, they will be placed in 1-2-3's print queue and printed in order according to their priority.

The procedure for printing a graph is identical in many respects to printing a text-only report. The same principles of background printing, print jobs, headers and footers, margins, and print priority that were covered in Chapter 8 apply to graph printing as well. Before continuing with this chapter, you should therefore be familiar with the material in Chapter 8.

Note: Background printing works only when you have selected /**Print Printer**. If you have selected /**Print Encoded** *filename*, you have to wait until the printing process is completed before being able to perform other worksheet tasks.

If you have a color monitor, you probably are creating and viewing your graphs in color (as selected with /**Graph Options Color**). If you are going to print these graphs on a black-and-white printer, remember to change the display to mono-chrome with /Graph Options **B&W** before printing the graph or before assigning it a name with /Graph Name Create.

Changing the Appearance of Printed Graphs

Most aspects of a graph's appearance are decided when you initially design the graph for screen display. Colors, fonts, text size, and hatch patterns are specified when you first create the graph on the screen. You cannot modify these features during printing. Note, however, that the final appearance of the printed graph may differ somewhat from its appearance on the screen, particularly with regard to fonts and, if using a color printer, colors. The printed appearance of fonts and colors depends to a large extent on the specifics of your printer. To get an idea of your printer's capabilities, select /**Print Printer Sample Go** to print a sample worksheet and sample graph, containing graph, color, and font examples. Keep this sample worksheet available for reference when you create your next graph.

Reminder:
Specify some aspects of a graph's appearance at print time.

Some aspects of a graph's appearance are specified at print time. Selecting **Options Advanced Image** from the **Print [P,E]** menu displays the menu shown in figure 9.56. These menu selections work as described in the text that follows.

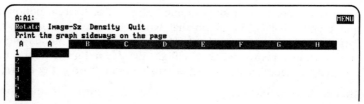

Fig. 9.56.
The /Print [P,E]
Options
Advanced
Image menu.

Image-Sz

Cue:
Use the Image-Sz option to specify the size and shape of printed graphs.

The **Image-Sz** option is used to specify the size and shape of printed graphs. The default graph shape is a rectangle with a 4:3 (width:length) ratio; the default size is a graph that fills the width of the page between the margins. Using the default page margin settings, the result is a graph that is approximately 6 1/2 inches wide and 5 inches high.

The **Image-Sz** options are as follows:

Length-Fill You enter a graph length in standard lines (6 per inch). 1-2-3 creates the largest possible graph using that length, while maintaining the default 4:3 (width:length) ratio.

Margin-Fill 1-2-3 creates a graph of the default shape that fills the page between the left and right margins. This is the default **Image-Sz** setting.

Reshape　　　You enter a graph length in standard lines (6 per inch) and a graph width in standard characters (10 per inch). 1-2-3 creates a graph of the specified size and shape. If the specified width or length exceeds the page size, 1-2-3 resizes the graph to fit on the page.

If you have previously printed a data range or another graph on part of a page, select /Print Printer Page to have the next graph print on a new page. If you do not advance the paper to the next page, and the graph will not fit on the remaining portion of the page, 1-2-3 automatically advances to the next page before starting the new graph.

To print the largest possible graph on its own page, select Reshape, and then enter a length and width that both exceed the dimensions of the page. 1-2-3 will resize the graph to the largest size that will fit on a page.

When Length-Fill or Reshape has been selected and a graph length is entered that is longer than a page, 1-2-3 prints the largest possible graph, centering it both vertically and horizontally on the page. With Margin-Fill, the graph is centered horizontally but not vertically.

Rotate

The Rotate option determines whether your graph is printed upright on the page or sideways. Rotate No, the default setting, prints graphs upright on the page. Select Rotate Yes to print graphs rotated 90 degrees counterclockwise. If your printer cannot rotate graphs, selecting Yes has no effect.

Reminder:
The Rotate option has no effect if your printer cannot rotate graphs.

When you rotate a graph, its size depends on your Image-Sz settings. When you use the default Margin-Fill size, the graph's 4:3 (width:length) ratio does not change when the graph is rotated, but the right-left margin space is considered the length rather than the width. When using the Length-Fill size setting, the length you specified is considered the width when the graph is rotated.

Rotate affects only graphs and does not affect the orientation used to print a data range. To rotate both data ranges and graphs, select /Print [P,E] Options Advanced Layout Orientation Landscape. This command sequence has an effect only if supported by your printer.

Density

The Density option offers you two choices: Draft or Final. Draft produces a lower-density printout with an image that is not as dark as Final. On some printers, graphs in Draft density are printed significantly faster than those in Final density. Draft density also puts less wear on printer ribbons and toner cartridges. While you are experimenting to see how your graphs look on paper, use Draft density; then switch to Final for the final printed copy.

Cue:
Use Draft density while you are experimenting on paper; switch to Final for the final printed graph.

Note: 1-2-3 supports only one density on some printers. In this case, the Image Density selection has no effect.

Printing a Graph with Default Settings

Assuming that your printer is properly installed and connected, printing the current graph with the default settings is simple. Select /Print Printer Image Current Go Quit, and your graph will be printed. Note: With laser printers, you may have to select Page before the graph will print. Using a sample graph from earlier in this chapter, you get output as shown in figure 9.57.

Fig. 9.57.
A graph printed
with the
default /Print
[P,E] Options
Advanced
Image settings.

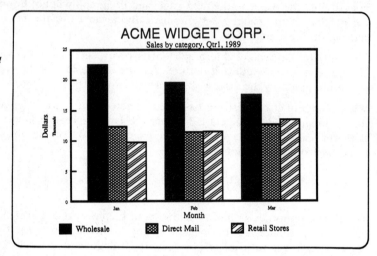

To print a graph that is not current, but is a named graph, the procedure is only slightly different. Select /Print Printer Image Named-Graph, highlight the name of the desired graph, and press Enter. Next, select Go Quit, and the graph is printed.

Printing a Graph with Customized Print Settings

To see the effect of changing the graph size, select /Print Printer Options Advanced Image Image-Sz Reshape, and in response to the prompts, enter 30 for width and 44 for length. Select Quit three times to return to the /Print [P,E] menu, and then select Go Quit. You do not need to specify Image again, because this image is already selected as the one to be printed. The printed graph now looks like the one in figure 9.58.

Cue:
Save graph size
settings as a
named print
setting.

Saving Graph Print Settings

Keep in mind that graph size settings are not saved with the graph. You can, however, save them as a named print setting, as explained in Chapter 8. To save

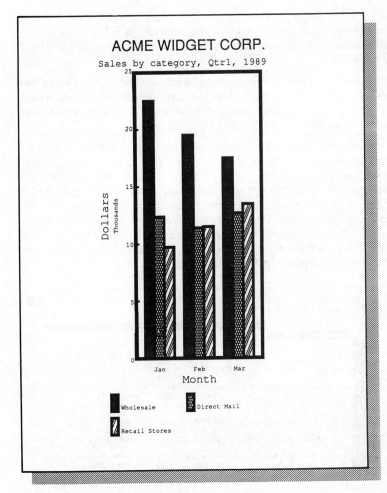

Fig. 9.58.
The graph from
fig. 9.57
printed with
a width of 30
and a length
of 44.

the print settings that produced figure 9.58, for example, you select **Options Name Create** from the /**Print [P,E]** menu. You are prompted for a name to assign to the current print settings. Because these settings produce a tall, narrow graph, enter **narrow** followed by Enter. The print settings will be saved under that name when you save the worksheet with /**File Save**.

The next time you work with this worksheet, you can recall these settings by selecting **Options Name Use** from the /**Print [P,E]** menu, highlighting **NARROW**, and pressing Enter.

Including Graphs in Reports

Printing your graphs on separate pages from the worksheet data and then collating them to produce a report is a simple matter. A more effective approach, how-

Cue:
You can use two methods for printing worksheet data and graphs on a single page.

ever, is to have a graph and its supporting data on one page. If your graph size allows this arrangement, you can accomplish this easily with 1-2-3. You can use two methods for printing worksheet data and graphs on a single page. The first technique always works.

In the first technique, you must specify *both* the graph and the text as part of the same print job. As mentioned in Chapter 8 on printing reports, this is performed by including the name of the graph, preceded by an asterisk, as part of the print range. This method will work with all types of printers.

Figure 9.59, for example, shows the worksheet data from which the graph in figure 9.57 was generated. In this worksheet, the command sequence /**Graph Name Create** was used to assign the name DEFAULT to this graph. Figure 9.59 shows the screen after issuing /**Print Printer Range** and entering a two-part range specification. The range consists of the worksheet data range A1..F19 followed by a semicolon and the graph name DEFAULT preceded by an asterisk. This range specification tells 1-2-3 to print the worksheet range A1..F19 and then print the graph DEFAULT. Note that the worksheet range specified includes a couple of blank lines at the end to separate it from the graph.

Fig. 9.59.
A print range specified that includes worksheet data and a named graph.

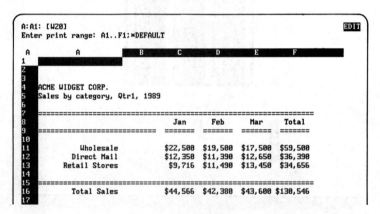

The resulting output is shown in figure 9.60. The graph provides a quick visual view of the data, while the worksheet figures provide the details. This sort of dual presentation can be very effective when used properly.

A second technique works only with dot-matrix printers. Recall that when 1-2-3 is finished printing a print job, the paper is *not* automatically advanced to the start of the next page. If you immediately start another print job, even if it is a graph, printing will begin on the paper just after the previous job left off.

The procedure for printing with dot-matrix printers is as follows:

1. Print the first part of the report (text or graph).

2. Do *not* issue **Page Align** to advance the paper.

3. Print the second part of the report (graph or text).

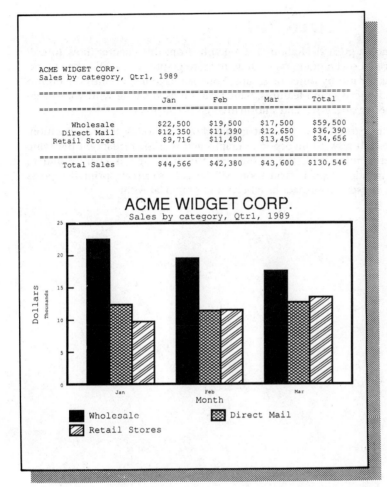

ACME WIDGET CORP.
Sales by category, Qtr1, 1989

	Jan	Feb	Mar	Total
Wholesale	$22,500	$19,500	$17,500	$59,500
Direct Mail	$12,350	$11,390	$12,650	$36,390
Retail Stores	$9,716	$11,490	$13,450	$34,656
Total Sales	$44,566	$42,380	$43,600	$130,546

Fig. 9.60.
A worksheet range and a graph printed on the same page.

An exception to these steps is when the second job is a graph that will not fit in the space remaining on the page. In this situation, 1-2-3 automatically advances the paper to the top of the next page. By adjusting the size of the graph and text portions, you can ensure that both fit on one page. The default graph size is about half of a standard page. Specifying a worksheet data range of 20 lines or fewer should enable both to fit on one page. Another alternative is to make the graph smaller.

This second technique does not work with laser printers. Because laser printers are page printers rather than line printers, they eject the final page at the end of a print job even when blank space is remaining.

Chapter Summary

You have learned a great deal about 1-2-3 graphs from this chapter: how to create and enhance all seven graph types, how to store graphs for recall in the worksheet as well as for use by other programs. You also have had an introduction to 1-2-3's many advanced graph features, which can be used, along with your imagination, to produce attractive and informative graph displays.

In addition, you learned how to print graphs, how to modify their orientation, size, and shape, and how to incorporate graphs and worksheet data on the same page. By experimenting with the techniques presented in this chapter and in Chapter 8 on printing reports, you soon will be able to create printed reports that effectively present your data in tabular and graphical form.

Part III

Customizing 1-2-3

Includes

Managing Data

Using Macros

Introducing the Advanced Macro Commands

409

CHAPTER

10

Managing Data

In addition to the electronic spreadsheet and business graphics, 1-2-3 has a third element: data management. Because the entire 1-2-3 database resides in the worksheet within main memory (RAM), 1-2-3's database feature is fast, easy to access, and easy to use.

The speed results from a reduction in the time required to transfer data to and from disks. By doing all the work inside the worksheet, 1-2-3 saves the time required for input and output to disk.

The 1-2-3 database is easily accessed because Lotus Development Corporation has made the entire database visible within the worksheet. You can view the contents of the whole database by using worksheet windows and cursor-movement keys to scroll through the database.

The ease of use is a result of integrating data management with the program's worksheet and graphics functions. The commands for adding, modifying, and deleting items in a database are the same ones you have already seen for manipulating cells or groups of cells within a worksheet. And creating graphs from ranges in a database is as easy as creating them in a worksheet.

This chapter shows you how to do the following:

- Understand the advantages and limitations of 1-2-3's database
- Create, modify, and maintain data records
- Sort, locate, extract, and edit data entries
- Create three-dimensional and labeled data tables
- Use database functions
- Load data from ASCII files and other programs
- Access and manipulate data in a table within an external database

411

What Is a Database?

A *database* is a collection of data organized so that you can list, sort, or search its contents. The list of data might contain any kind of information, from addresses to tax-deductible expenditures.

In 1-2-3, the word *database* means a range of cells that spans at least one column and more than one row. This definition, however, does not distinguish between a database and any other range of cells. Because a database is actually a list, its manner of organization sets it apart from ordinary cells. Just as a list must be organized to be useful, a database must be organized to permit access to the information it contains.

The simplest database organization in 1-2-3 is a single database contained in a single worksheet. In most of the examples in this chapter, as well as in most real-world applications, this organization is used. You also can have multiple databases, each one occupying a different portion of one worksheet. Finally, with Release 3's three-dimensional capabilities, you can have multiple databases in two or more worksheet "levels." Note, however, that a single database cannot span different worksheet levels; the database must be located entirely within one worksheet level.

Remember nonetheless that in 1-2-3 a database is similar to any other group of cells. This knowledge will help you as you learn about the different /Data commands covered in this chapter. In many instances, you can use these database commands in what you might consider "nondatabase" applications.

The smallest unit in a database is a *field*, or single data item. For example, if you were to develop an information base of present or potential corporate contributors for a not-for-profit organization, you might include the following fields of information:

Company Name
Company Address
Contact Person
Phone Number
Last Contact Date
Contact Representative
Last Contribution Date

A database *record* is a collection of associated fields. For example, the accumulation of all contributor data about one company forms one record.

In 1-2-3, a record is a row of cells within a database, and a field is a single cell.

A database must be set up so that you can access the information it contains. Retrieval of information usually involves key fields. A database *key field* is any field on which you base a list, sort, or search operation. For example, you could use ZIPCODE as a key field to sort the data in the contributor database and to assign contact representatives to specific geographic areas. And you could pre-pare a follow-up contact list by searching the database for the key field LAST CONTACT DATE in which the date is less than one year ago.

With Release 3, a new term—*database table*—is often used. Note that the term *database* is used instead in this chapter. Note also that the term *data table* refers only to the data table created with the /**D**ata **T**able command.

What Can You Do with a 1-2-3 Database?

A 1-2-3 database resides within the worksheet's row-and-column format. Figure 10.1 shows the general organization of a 1-2-3 database. Labels, or *field names*, that describe the data items appear as column headings. Information about each specific data item (field) is entered in a cell in the appropriate column. In figure 10.1, the highlighted cell (D6) represents data for the second field name in the database's fourth record. In the Marketing Research database shown in figure 10.2, the highlighted row (row 5) contains all fields of the first record.

Reminder:
The 1-2-3 database resides in the worksheet's row-and-column format.

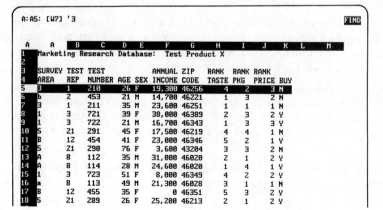

Fig. 10.1.
Organization of a 1-2-3 database.

Fig. 10.2.
A highlighted record in the Marketing Research database.

The major disadvantage of Lotus's approach is the limitation it imposes on the size of the database. With most popular database programs, such as dBASE IV, only portions of your database reside in memory at one time; the entire database resides on disk. With 1-2-3, the entire database must be in memory before you can perform any data management operations. To increase the size of your 1-2-3 database, you must increase the amount of RAM in your computer.

Theoretically, the maximum number of records you can have in a 1-2-3 database corresponds to the maximum number of rows in the worksheet (8,192 rows minus 1 row for the field names). Realistically, however, the number of records in a specific database is limited by the amount of available memory: internal memory (RAM), disk storage, and the room needed within the database to hold data extracted by the /Data Query commands.

If your computer has 2.5M of internal memory, you can store in a single database only about 2,400 400-byte (character) records or 850 1,000-byte records. (To provide a frame of reference, each record in the Marketing Research database shown in fig. 10.2 contains 67 characters.) Disk operating system commands and the 1-2-3 program instructions occupy the remaining memory. Although 1-2-3 requires 1M of memory, you need to extend the internal memory capacity beyond 1M for large databases.

If you use diskettes for external storage of database files, you are limited to files that total approximately 1.2 million characters on a high-density, 5 1/4-inch diskette or that total 1.44M on a high-density, 3 1/2-inch diskette. On a hard disk, a database of 1,500 500-byte records occupies 1 million characters, or 1 megabyte.

When you estimate the maximum database size you can use on your computer equipment, be sure to include enough blank rows to accommodate the maximum output you expect from extract operations. You may be able to split a large 1-2-3 database into separate files if all the data does not have to be sorted or searched as a unit. For example, you may be able to separate a telephone list database by name (A through M in one file; N through Z in another) or area code. If you can deal with 1-2-3's memory constraints and the somewhat time-consuming method of using menu options to manipulate data, you will have a powerful data management tool.

You access the menu of /Data commands from the 1-2-3 command menu. Because all the options (**W**orksheet, **R**ange, **C**opy, **M**ove, **F**ile, **P**rint, and **G**raph) that precede **D**ata on the main menu work as well on databases as they do on worksheets, the power of 1-2-3 is at your fingertips.

If you prefer to use a stand-alone program such as dBASE for your database, you can use 1-2-3's file-translation capabilities (refer to Chapter 7) to take advantage of 1-2-3's data and graph commands. You also can use 1-2-3's /Data External command, covered later in this chapter, to access database files created with certain stand-alone database programs.

When you select /Data from the 1-2-3 command menu, the following options are displayed in the control panel's second line:

   Fill Table Sort Query Distribution Matrix Regression Parse External

The Sort and **Query** (search) options are true data management operations. Both are described in detail early in this chapter. The other options (**Fill**, **Table**, **Distribution**, **Matrix**, **Regression**, and **Parse**) are considered, more appropriately, data-creation and data-manipulation operations. They too are described in this chapter. Finally, the **External** option is used to access database files created with other database programs, such as dBASE III. **External** is discussed in the last section of the chapter.

Creating a Database

You can create a database as a new worksheet file or as part of an existing worksheet. If you decide to build a database as part of an existing worksheet, choose a worksheet area that will not be needed for anything else. This area should be large enough to accommodate the number of records you plan to enter during the current session and in the future. If you add the database to the side of the worksheet, be careful about inserting or deleting worksheet rows that might also affect the database. If you add a database below an existing worksheet, be careful not to disturb predetermined column widths in the worksheet portion when you adjust column widths to the widths of database fields.

Caution: Locate your database where it won't be affected by inserted columns, deleted rows, or changed column widths.

After you have decided which area of the worksheet to use, you create a database by specifying field names across a row and entering data in cells as you would for any other 1-2-3 application. The mechanics of entering database contents are simple; the most critical step in creating a useful database is choosing your fields properly.

Determining Required Output

1-2-3's data-retrieval techniques rely on locating data by field names. Before you begin typing the kinds of data items you think you may need, write down the output you expect from the database. You also will need to consider any source documents already in use that can provide input to the file. For example, you might use the following information from the sample contributor database:

Company Name
Company Address
Contact Person
Phone Number
Contact Date
Contact Representative
Last Contribution Date

When you are ready to set up these items in your database, you must specify for each item of information a field name, the column width, and the type of entry.

You might make a common error in setting up your database if you choose a field name (and enter data) without thinking about the output you want from that key field. For example, suppose that you establish GIFTDATE as a field name to describe the last date a contribution was made. Then you enter record dates as labels, in the general form MMM-DD-YYYY (such as JAN-01-1989). Although you can search for a GIFTDATE that matches a specific date, you will not be able to perform a math-based search for all GIFTDATEs within a specified period of time or before a certain date. To get maximum flexibility from 1-2-3's data commands, you can enter dates in your databases in the following forms (refer to Chapter 6 for more information):

@DATE(year number,month number,day number)

MM/DD/YY

Reminder:
The format of your data (date, labels, or numbers) will affect how the data can be sorted and searched.

You then need to choose the level of detail needed for each item of information, select the appropriate column width, and determine whether you will enter data as a number or a label. For example, if you want to be able to sort by area code all records containing telephone numbers, you should enter telephone numbers as two separate fields: area code (XXX) and the base number XXX-XXXX. Because you will not want to perform math functions on telephone numbers, you can enter them as labels.

To save memory and increase data-entry speed and accuracy, you should code information when possible. For example, if you need to query only about records according to contact representatives, plan to use the first, middle, and last initials of each contact representative in the database instead of printing a list of their full names. If you enter database content from a standard source document, such as a marketing research survey form, you can increase the speed of data entry by setting up the field names in the same order as that of the corresponding data items on the form. Be sure to plan your database carefully before you establish field names, set column widths and range formats, and enter data.

Entering Data

After you have planned your database, you can build it. To understand how the process works, create a Marketing Research database as a new database on a blank worksheet (in READY mode). After you select the appropriate area of the worksheet for the database, enter the field names across a single row (see fig. 10.3).

Fig. 10.3.
Field names entered in a database.

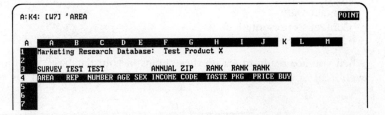

In the figure, row 4—the field name row—is highlighted. The field names must be labels, even if they are the numeric labels '1, '2, and so on. Although you can use more than one row for the field names, 1-2-3 uses only the values that appear in the bottom row. For example, the first field name in the Marketing Research database (rows 3 and 4 of column A) is SURVEY AREA. Only the word AREA (the portion in row 4) will be referenced as a key field in sort or query operations.

Keep in mind that all field names should be unique; any repetition of names confuses 1-2-3 when you search or sort the database. The field names in figure 10.3 are acceptable because, although the words in row 3 are repeated (two TESTs and three RANKs), each field name in row 4 is unique.

To control the manner in which cells are displayed on-screen, you use 1-2-3's /Range Format and /Worksheet Column Set-Width options. In figure 10.2, notice that the range format in column F is , (comma) with zero decimal places, and that column widths on the worksheet vary from four to seven characters.

Note also that whenever a right-justified column of numeric data is adjacent to a left-justified column of label information (such as AGE and SEX, or INCOME and CODE), the data looks crowded. You can insert blank columns to change the spacing between fields; if you plan to search values in the database, however, do not leave any blank rows.

After you have altered the column widths, entered title and field names, and added spacing columns, you can add records to the database. To enter the first record, move the cursor to the row directly below the field-name row, and then enter the data across the row in the usual manner.

In the sample Marketing Research database, the contents of the AREA, REP, NUMBER, SEX, CODE, and BUY fields are entered as labels; the contents of the AGE, INCOME, TASTE, PKG, and PRICE fields are entered as numbers. Figure 10.4 shows the initial data and the column spacing for this sample database.

Reminder:
Keep all field names unique; any repetition of field names will confuse 1-2-3.

Cue:
Insert blank columns between fields to prevent crowding of data.

Fig. 10.4. The newly created Marketing Research database.

This sample Marketing Research database will be used periodically throughout this chapter to illustrate the results of using various /Data commands. In this book, the fields are limited to a single screen display. In "real life" applications, however, you would track many more data items. You can maintain 256 fields (the number of columns available) in a 1-2-3 database.

In the AREA field, letters indicate the shopping-center test locations, and numbers indicate the locations of college-campus product testing. The entries in the TASTE and PKG fields reflect options 1 through 5 (1 = most favorable); the entries in the PRICE field reflect options 1 through 3 (1 = too high).

Modifying a Database

After you have collected the data for your database and decided which field types, widths, and formats to use, creating a database is easy. Thanks to 1-2-3, maintaining the accuracy of the database content is easy also.

To add and delete records in a database, use the same commands for inserting and deleting rows that you use for any other application in 1-2-3. Because records correspond to rows, you begin inserting a record with the /Worksheet Insert Row command. You then fill in the various fields in the rows with the appropriate data. Figure 10.5 shows a record being inserted in the middle of a database. Instead of inserting a record in the middle of a database, however, you probably will add new records at the end, and then use 1-2-3's sorting capabilities, illustrated in the next section, to rearrange the physical order of database records.

Fig. 10.5.
A record row being inserted in the database.

```
A:A10: [W7]                                                    READY

A    A     B    C     D   E F    G        H     I     J     K    L     M   N
1   Marketing Research Database:    Test Product X
2
3   SURVEY TEST TEST                ANNUAL   ZIP   RANK  RANK RANK
4   AREA   REP  NUMBER AGE   SEX    INCOME   CODE  TASTE PKG  PRICE  BUY
5   3      1    210    26    F      19,300   46256   4    2    3     N
6   b      2    453    21    M      14,700   46221   1    3    2     N
7   3      1    211    35    M      23,600   46251   1    1    1     N
8   1      3    721    39    F      38,000   46389   2    3    2     Y
9   1      3    722    21    M      16,700   46343   1    3    3     Y
10
11  5      21   291    45    F      17,500   46219   4    4    1     N
12  B      12   454    41    F      23,000   46346   5    2    1     Y
13  5      21   290    76    F      3,600    43204   3    3    2     N
14  A      8    112    35    M      31,000   46020   2    1    2     Y
15  A      8    114    28    M      24,600   46020   1    4    1     Y
16  1      3    723    51    F      8,000    46349   4    2    2     Y
17  a      8    113    49    M      21,300   46028   3    1    1     N
18  B      12   455    35    F      0        46351   5    3    2     Y
19  5      21   289    26    F      25,200   46213   2    1    2     Y
20
08-May-89 08:21 PM
```

To delete records, move your cell pointer to the row or rows you want to delete, and select the /Worksheet Delete Row command. Be extremely careful when you specify the records to be deleted if you are not using Undo (Alt-F4). If you want to remove only inactive records, consider first using the /Data Query Extract command to store the extracted inactive records in a separate file before you delete the records. (This chapter will show you how.)

Reminder:
Add new fields to
your database with
/Worksheet Insert
Column; delete
fields with
/Worksheet Delete
Column.

The process of modifying fields in a database is the same as that for modifying the contents of cells in any other application. As you learned in Chapter 3, you change the cell contents either by retyping the cell entry or by using the Edit (F2) key and editing the entry.

To add a new field to a database, you position the cell pointer anywhere in the column that will be to the right of the newly inserted column. You issue the /Worksheet Insert Column command and then fill the field with values for each record. For example, to insert a DATE field between the NUMBER and AGE fields in the Marketing Research database, position the cell pointer on any cell in the AGE column, issue the /Worksheet Insert Column command, and then type the new field name in cells D3 and D4 (see fig. 10.6).

Cue:
Use the /Data
Query Extract
command to
archive inactive
records before you
delete them from
the main database.

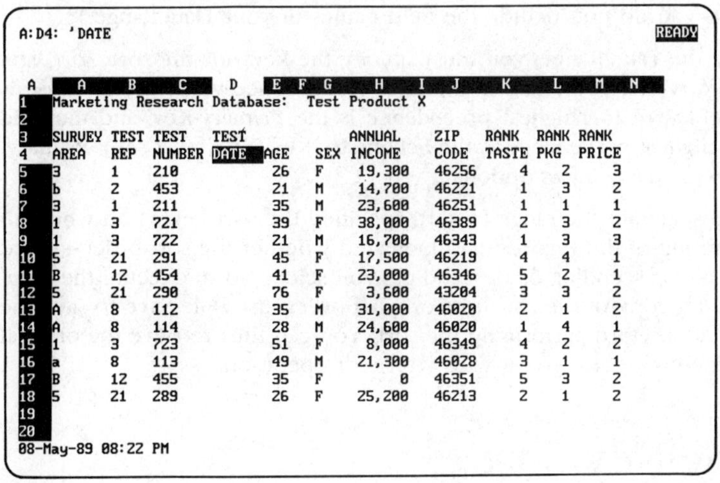

```
A:D4:  'DATE                                                        READY

A    A       B      C      D   E F G      H      I  J    K     L    M    N
1  Marketing Research Database:     Test Product X
2
3  SURVEY TEST  TEST   TEST             ANNUAL    ZIP    RANK  RANK RANK
4   AREA  REP  NUMBER DATE  AGE  SEX  INCOME    CODE   TASTE PKG  PRICE
5  3       1    210         26   F    19,300   46256     4    2     3
6  b       2    453         21   M    14,700   46221     1    3     2
7  3       1    211         35   M    23,600   46251     1    1     1
8  1       3    721         39   F    38,000   46389     2    3     2
9  1       3    722         21   M    16,700   46343     1    3     3
10 5      21    291         45   F    17,500   46219     4    4     1
11 B      12    454         41   F    23,000   46346     5    2     1
12 5      21    290         76   F     3,600   43204     3    3     2
13 A       8    112         35   M    31,000   46020     2    1     2
14 A       8    114         28   M    24,600   46020     1    4     1
15 1       3    723         51   F     8,000   46349     4    2     2
16 a       8    113         49   M    21,300   46028     3    1     1
17 B      12    455         35   F         0   46351     5    3     2
18 5      21    289         26   F    25,200   46213     2    1     2
19
20
08-May-89 08:22 PM
```

Fig. 10.6.
A column
being inserted
for a new field.

Because maintaining data is expensive, you may not feel justified in keeping certain seldom-used data fields in the database. To delete such a field, position the cell pointer anywhere in the column you want to remove, and then select the /Worksheet Delete Column command.

All other commands, such as those for moving cells, formatting cells, and displaying the contents of worksheets, work the same in both database and worksheet applications. Be careful, however, not to interfere with the row/column structure of your database.

Sorting Database Records

1-2-3's data management capability enables you to change the order of records by sorting them according to the contents of the fields. You can use the /Data Sort command only with a worksheet database, not with an external database. Selecting /Data Sort produces the following menu:

Data-Range   Primary-Key   Secondary-Key   Extra-Key   Reset   Go   Quit

To sort the database, you start by designating a Data-Range. This range must include all the records to be sorted and also be wide enough to include all the fields in each record. If you do not include all fields when sorting, you will destroy the integrity of your database. Parts of one record will end up with parts of other records. Remember not to include the field-name row in this range. (If you are unfamiliar with how to designate ranges or how to name them, refer to Chapter 4.)

The Data-Range does not necessarily have to include the entire database. If part of the database already has the organization you want, or if you do not want to sort all the records, you can sort only a portion of the database. (Remember that when you sort, you do not include the field names in your Data-Range.)

After choosing the Data-Range, you must specify the keys for the sort. *Sort keys* are the fields to which you attach the highest precedence when the database is sorted. The field with the highest precedence is the Primary-Key, and the field with the next highest precedence is the Secondary-Key. You must set a Primary-Key, but the Secondary-Key is optional.

After you have specified the range to sort, specified the sort key(s) on which to base the reordering of the records, and indicated whether the sort order—based on the sort key—is ascending or descending, you select Go to execute the command. To retain a copy of the list in its original order, use /File Save to save the worksheet on disk before performing the sort. You can thus retrieve the original database if something goes wrong with your sort operation.

The One-Key Sort

One of the simplest examples of a database sorted according to a primary key (often called a single-key database) is the white pages of the telephone book. All the records in the white pages are sorted in ascending alphabetical order, with the last name used as the primary key. This ascending alphabetical-order sort can be used to reorder the records in the Addresses database shown in figure 10.7.

You can use 1-2-3's sorting capability to reorder records alphabetically on the LAST name field. Select /Data Sort Data-Range. At the prompt for a range to sort, specify A2..F19. After you specify the range, the /Data Sort menu returns to the screen. This is one of 1-2-3's "sticky" menus. (The /Print [P,F,E] menu is another.) Sticky menus remain displayed and active until you select Quit. This sticky menu is helpful because you do not have to specify /Data Sort at the beginning of each command.

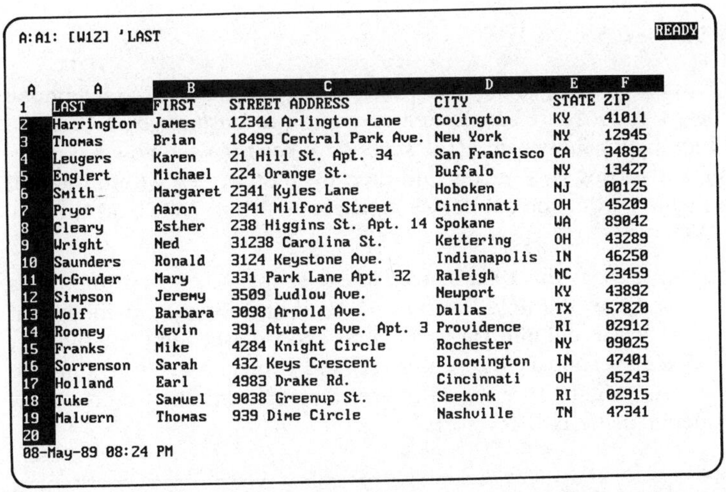

Fig. 10.7.
The unsorted
Addresses
database.

After choosing the **Data-Range**, select **Primary-Key** and then type or point to the
address of any cell (including blank or field-name cells) in the column containing
the primary-key field. For example, type **A1** as the **Primary-Key** in the Addresses
database. 1-2-3 then asks you to enter a sort order (A or D). *A* stands for ascending, and *D* for descending. For this example, choose **A** for ascending order and
press Enter. Finally, select **Go** from the menu to execute the sort. Figure 10.8
shows the Addresses database sorted in ascending order by last name.

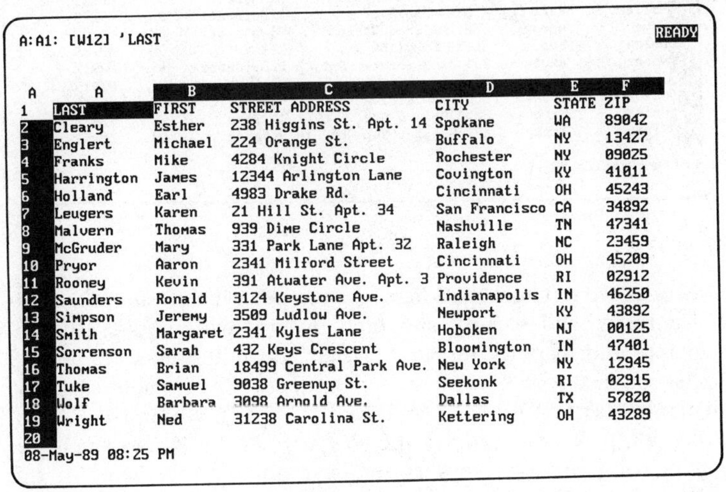

Fig. 10.8.
The Addresses
database sorted
by LAST name.

You can add a record to an alphabetized name-and-address database without hav-
ing to insert a row manually to place the new record in the proper position.
Simply add the new record to the bottom of the current database, expand the
Data-Range, and then sort the database again by last name.

Cue:
*Add a new record
to a sorted
database by
entering the record
at the bottom of
your database and
then re-sorting the
database.*

The Two-Key Sort

A double-key sort uses both a primary and a secondary sort key. In the telephone book's yellow pages, records are sorted first according to business type (the primary key) and then by business name (the secondary key). To see how a double-key sort works (first sorting by one key and then by another key within the first sort order), you can reorder the Addresses database first by STATE and then by CITY within STATE.

Specify the range A2..F19 as the **Data-Range**. Select **Primary-Key** from the **/Data Sort** menu and enter **E1** as the field location of the initial sort. (Remember that you can specify any cell in column E.) Enter **A** to choose ascending for the sort order by STATE. Select **Secondary-Key**, enter **D1**, and choose **A** for ascending for the sort order by CITY. Figure 10.9 shows the results of issuing the **Go** command after you have specified the two-key sort.

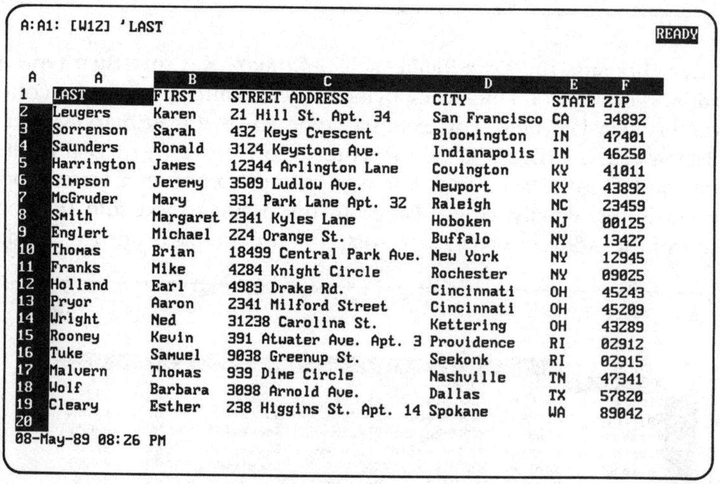

Fig. 10.9.
The Addresses database sorted by CITY within STATE.

```
A:A1: [W12] 'LAST                                                    READY

  A         A          B            C                    D          E      F
  1   LAST        FIRST      STREET ADDRESS         CITY          STATE ZIP
  2   Leugers     Karen      21 Hill St. Apt. 34    San Francisco CA    34892
  3   Sorrenson   Sarah      432 Keys Crescent      Bloomington   IN    47401
  4   Saunders    Ronald     3124 Keystone Ave.     Indianapolis  IN    46250
  5   Harrington  James      12344 Arlington Lane   Covington     KY    41011
  6   Simpson     Jeremy     3509 Ludlow Ave.       Newport       KY    43892
  7   McGruder    Mary       331 Park Lane Apt. 32  Raleigh       NC    23459
  8   Smith       Margaret   2341 Kyles Lane        Hoboken       NJ    00125
  9   Englert     Michael    224 Orange St.         Buffalo       NY    13427
 10   Thomas      Brian      18499 Central Park Ave. New York     NY    12945
 11   Franks      Mike       4284 Knight Circle     Rochester     NY    09025
 12   Holland     Earl       4983 Drake Rd.         Cincinnati    OH    45243
 13   Pryor       Aaron      2341 Milford Street    Cincinnati    OH    45209
 14   Wright      Ned        31238 Carolina St.     Kettering     OH    43289
 15   Rooney      Kevin      391 Atwater Ave. Apt. 3 Providence   RI    02912
 16   Tuke        Samuel     9038 Greenup St.       Seekonk       RI    02915
 17   Malvern     Thomas     939 Dime Circle        Nashville     TN    47341
 18   Wolf        Barbara    3098 Arnold Ave.       Dallas        TX    57820
 19   Cleary      Esther     238 Higgins St. Apt. 14 Spokane      WA    89042
 20
08-May-89 08:26 PM
```

As you can see, records are now grouped first by state in alphabetical order (California, Indiana, Kentucky, and so on), and then by city within state (Bloomington, Indiana, before Indianapolis, Indiana). When you determine whether to use a primary or secondary sort key, be sure to request a reasonable sort. For example, do not try to sort first by CITY and then by STATE within CITY. Also, whenever possible, you may want to have the sort keys as the leftmost fields in your database. By having the sort keys as the first one or two fields in the database, you will not have to hunt for the results of the sort. As in this example, however, you may find that the visual advantage isn't always feasible.

The Extra-Key Sort

Cue:
Use Extra-Key to sort a database on more than two fields.

The **Extra-Key** option enables you to specify as many as 253 sort keys to be used in addition to the primary and secondary sort keys. These extra keys are used to determine the sort order when two or more records contain identical values in both the primary- and secondary-key fields. The extra keys are numbered from 1 through 253 and are applied in order: Extra-Key 1 is used to break ties in the secondary-key field, Extra-Key 2 is used to break ties in extra-key field 1, and so on.

You assign an extra key essentially the same way that you assign primary and secondary keys. Select **Extra-Key** from the /**Data Sort** menu and then enter the number (1–253) of the extra key you are assigning. Next, enter the field (column) to be used for the extra key, followed by the sort order (**A** for ascending or **D** for descending).

To understand how an extra-key sort works, look at the database shown in figure 10.10. Note that several of the records are "tied" in their LAST (name) and ZIP fields. You can sort this database on the LAST and ZIP fields, specifying FIRST as an extra key to break the ties.

```
A:A17: [W12] 'Smith                                              READY

      A            B          C                 D        E     F
1  LAST         FIRST      STREET ADDRESS      CITY      STATE ZIP
2  Smith        John       12 Oak Drive        Amityville NY   11701
3  Adams        Peter      1505 34th Street    Carmel    IN    46032
4  Jones        Jack       1600 Main St., Apt. B Carmel  IN    46032
5  Adams        Arthur     13 Maple Ave.       Durham    NC    27705
6  Jones        Sarah      1200 16th St., Apt 12 Durham  NC    27705
7  Wilson       Henry      P.O. Box 14         Storrs    CT    06268
8  Wilson       William    75 Davis Crescent   Amityville NY   11701
9  Smith        Wendy      101 Talmadge Court  Amityville NY   11701
10 Adams        Amy        45 Seventh St.      Durham    NC    27705
11 Jones        Ned        99 Aspen Avenue     Durham    NC    27705
12 Jones        Mary       2 Maxwell St.       Carmel    IN    46032
13 Wilson       Paul       10 S. Water St.     Amityville NY   11701
14 Smith        Jennifer   119 W. Club Blvd.   Storrs    CT    06268
15 Adams        Kathy      P.O. Box 165        Carmel    IN    46032
16 Wilson       Norman     92 Albany Rd.       Storrs    CT    06268
17 Smith        Fred       400 East Lake Drive Storrs    CT    06268
18
19
20
SORT1.WK3
```

Fig. 10.10.
A database with "ties" in the LAST and ZIP fields.

First, use the procedures outlined earlier in this chapter to specify A2..F17 as the **Data-Range**, column A as the **Primary-Key**, and column F as the **Secondary-Key**, both in ascending order. Next, select **Extra-Key** from the /**Data Sort** menu and enter **1** as the Extra-Key number. Specify column B as the extra-key field and choose ascending order. Finally, select **Go**. The database will be sorted by LAST, then by ZIP within LAST, and finally by FIRST within ZIP (see fig. 10.11).

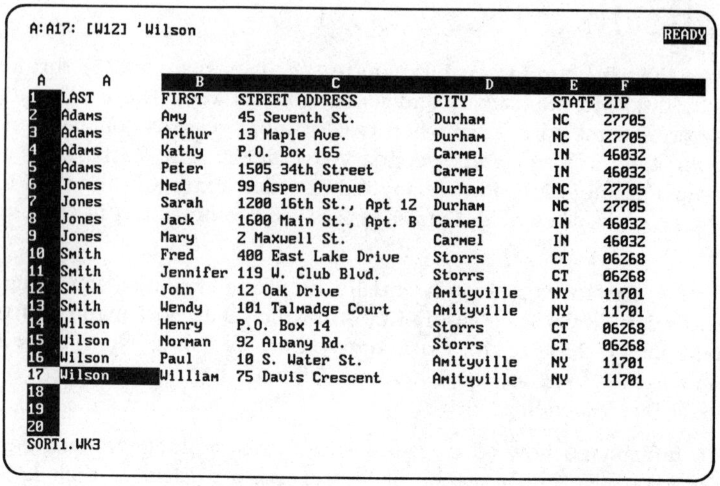

Fig. 10.11.
The database
sorted with
LAST as the
Primary-Key,
ZIP as the
Secondary-Key,
and FIRST as
Extra-Key 1.

```
A:A17: [W12] 'Wilson                                              READY

    A     A          B            C                D       E    F
1     LAST        FIRST     STREET ADDRESS      CITY       STATE ZIP
2     Adams       Amy       45 Seventh St.      Durham     NC   27705
3     Adams       Arthur    13 Maple Ave.       Durham     NC   27705
4     Adams       Kathy     P.O. Box 165        Carmel     IN   46032
5     Adams       Peter     1505 34th Street    Carmel     IN   46032
6     Jones       Ned       99 Aspen Avenue     Durham     NC   27705
7     Jones       Sarah     1200 16th St., Apt 12 Durham   NC   27705
8     Jones       Jack      1600 Main St., Apt. B Carmel   IN   46032
9     Jones       Mary      2 Maxwell St.       Carmel     IN   46032
10    Smith       Fred      400 East Lake Drive Storrs     CT   06268
11    Smith       Jennifer  119 W. Club Blvd.   Storrs     CT   06268
12    Smith       John      12 Oak Drive        Amityville NY   11701
13    Smith       Wendy     101 Talmadge Court  Amityville NY   11701
14    Wilson      Henry     P.O. Box 14         Storrs     CT   06268
15    Wilson      Norman    92 Albany Rd.       Storrs     CT   06268
16    Wilson      Paul      10 S. Water St.     Amityville NY   11701
17    Wilson      William   75 Davis Crescent   Amityville NY   11701
18
19
20
SORT1.WK3
```

To remove an extra sort key, you assign its number to the data field being used by a "higher" sort key. For example, to cancel **Extra-Key 2**, you select **/D**ata **S**ort **E**xtra-Key, type **2**, and specify the column being used by **Extra-Key 1**. To cancel **Extra-Key 1**, you assign it to the data field being used by the **Secondary-Key**.

When sorting a three-dimensional range, 1-2-3 sorts the data in each worksheet independently. Rows are *not* moved from one worksheet to another.

Determining the Sort Order

Certain aspects of the sort order are determined by the collating sequence setting that you established when 1-2-3 was installed on your system. The three options for this setting are Numbers First, Numbers Last, and ASCII. When you select ascending sort order, the effects of each setting are shown in table 10.1 (selecting descending order reverses the orders shown).

For Numbers First and Numbers Last, capitalization is ignored. For ASCII, uppercase letters precede lowercase letters.

When you've specified numbers as labels, a problem can occur because 1-2-3 sorts from left to right, one character at a time. For example, if you were to sort the Marketing Research database in ascending order according to the representative who administered the test (REP, in column B), the results of the sort would resemble those shown in figure 10.12.

Table 10.1
Collating Sequences for Ascending Order

Collating Sequence	Sort Order
Numbers First	Blank cells Labels beginning with numbers in numerical order Labels beginning with letters in alphabetical order Labels beginning with other characters in ASCII value order Values
Numbers Last	Blank cells Labels beginning with letters in alphabetical order Labels beginning with numbers in numerical order Labels beginning with other characters in ASCII value order Values
ASCII	Blank cells All labels in ASCII value order Values

```
A:B4: [W5] 'REP                                              READY

     A       B      C      D  E  F      G       H      J    K    L    M  N
     A       B      C      D  E  F      G       H      I    J    K    L    M  N
 1  Marketing Research Database:    Test Product X
 2
 3  SURVEY  TEST   TEST                ANNUAL   ZIP    RANK RANK RANK
 4  AREA    REP    NUMBER AGE  SEX  INCOME    CODE   TASTE PKG  PRICE   BUY
 5  3       1      211    35   M    23,600    46251    1    1     1     N
 6  3       1      210    26   F    19,300    46256    4    2     3     N
 7  B       12     455    35   F        0     46351    5    3     2     Y
 8  B       12     454    41   F    23,000    46346    5    2     1     Y
 9  b       2      453    21   M    14,700    46221    1    3     2     N
10  5       21     291    45   F    17,500    46219    4    4     1     N
11  5       21     290    76   F     3,600    43204    3    3     2     N
12  5       21     289    26   F    25,200    46213    2    1     2     Y
13  1       3      723    51   F     8,000    46349    4    2     2     Y
14  1       3      722    21   M    16,700    46343    1    3     3     Y
15  1       3      721    39   F    38,000    46389    2    3     2     Y
16  A       8      114    28   M    24,600    46020    1    4     1     Y
17  a       8      113    49   M    21,300    46028    3    1     1     N
18  A       8      112    35   M    31,000    46020    2    1     2     Y
19
20
08-May-89 10:46 PM
```

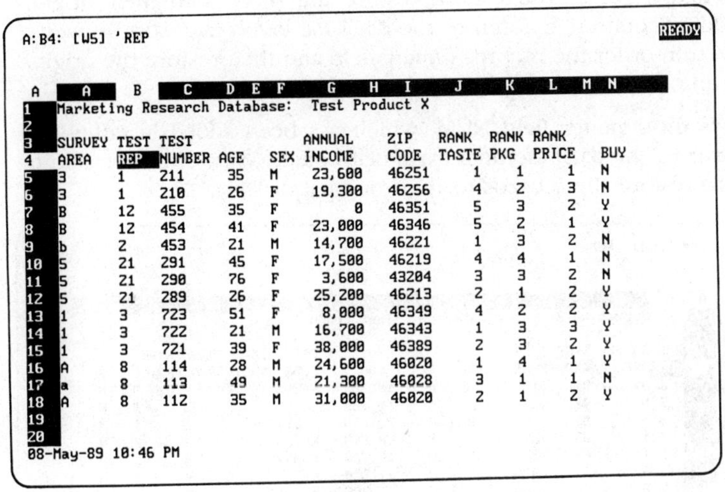

Fig. 10.12.
An erroneous ascending sort.

Although you would expect the records to be sorted in ascending order on the REP field, notice that the 12 in rows 7 and 8 appears before the 2 in row 9, and that 21 appears before 3. This problem occurs because 1-2-3 sorts the numbers one character at a time when sorting labels.

To avoid this problem, you should enter a zero (0) before each single-character REP field. Figure 10.13 shows the corrected sort of the edited single-character REP field.

Fig. 10.13.
The corrected ascending sort.

```
A:B4: [W5] 'REP                                                    READY

A    A    B    C     D    E  F     G        H      I     J     K     L     M  N
1  Marketing Research Database:  Test Product X
2
3  SURVEY TEST TEST              ANNUAL   ZIP    RANK  RANK  RANK
4  AREA   REP  NUMBER AGE  SEX  INCOME   CODE   TASTE PKG   PRICE  BUY
5  3      01   210    26   F    19,300   46256    4     2     3    N
6  3      01   211    35   M    23,600   46251    1     1     1    N
7  b      02   453    21   M    14,700   46221    1     3     2    N
8  1      03   721    39   F    38,000   46389    2     3     2    Y
9  1      03   722    21   M    16,700   46343    1     3     3    Y
10 1      03   723    51   F     8,000   46349    4     2     2    Y
11 a      08   113    49   M    21,300   46028    3     1     1    N
12 A      08   112    35   M    31,000   46020    2     1     2    Y
13 A      08   114    28   M    24,600   46020    1     4     1    Y
14 B      12   455    35   F        0    46351    5     3     2    Y
15 B      12   454    41   F    23,000   46346    5     2     1    Y
16 5      21   291    45   F    17,500   46219    4     4     1    N
17 5      21   290    76   F     3,600   43204    3     3     2    N
18 5      21   289    26   F    25,200   46213    2     1     2    Y
19
20
08-May-89 10:49 PM
```

Restoring the Presort Order

Cue:
Add a "counter" field to your database in case you later want to restore records to their original order.

If you sort the original contents of the database on any field, such as the REP field shown in figure 10.12, you cannot restore the records to their original order. If you add a "counter" column to the database before any sort, however, you will be able to reorder the records on any field and then restore the original order by re-sorting on the counter field.

Fig. 10.14 shows the counter field NUM, which has been added in column A. After you have sorted the database on a particular column, you can sort again on the NUM field to restore the records to their original order.

Fig. 10.14.
The "counter" field added to the original database.

```
A:A4: [W4] 'NUM                                                        READY

A   A    B      C    D      E    F  G    H        I      J     K     L      M   N  O
1        Marketing Research Database:  Test Product X
2
3   REC  SURVEY TEST TEST              ANNUAL   ZIP    RANK  RANK  RANK
4   NUM  AREA   REP  NUMBER AGE  SEX  INCOME   CODE   TASTE PKG   PRICE  BUY
5   1    3      01   210    26   F    19,300   46256    4     2     3    N
6   2    b      02   453    21   M    14,700   46221    1     3     2    N
7   3    3      01   211    35   M    23,600   46251    1     1     1    N
8   4    1      03   721    39   F    38,000   46389    2     3     2    Y
9   5    1      03   722    21   M    16,700   46343    1     3     3    Y
10  6    5      21   291    45   F    17,500   46219    4     4     1    N
11  7    B      12   454    41   F    23,000   46346    5     2     1    Y
12  8    5      21   290    76   F     3,600   43204    3     3     2    N
13  9    A      08   112    35   M    31,000   46020    2     1     2    Y
14  10   A      08   114    28   M    24,600   46020    1     4     1    Y
15  11   1      03   723    51   F     8,000   46349    4     2     2    Y
16  12   a      08   113    49   M    21,300   46028    3     1     1    N
17  13   B      12   455    35   F        0    46351    5     3     2    Y
18  14   5      21   289    26   F    25,200   46213    2     1     2    Y
```

Searching for Records

You have learned how to use the /Data Sort option to reorganize information from the database by sorting records according to key fields. In this section of the chapter, you will learn how to use /Data Query, the menu's other data-retrieval command, to search for records and then edit, extract, or delete the records you find. The /Data Query commands can be used with a 1-2-3 database or an external table. In the latter case, you must first use the /Data External Use command (discussed later in this chapter) to establish a connection to the external table.

The Tools Inventory database shown in figure 10.15 is useful in illustrating the basic concepts of 1-2-3's search (also called *query*) operations. Looking for records that meet certain conditions is the simplest form of searching a 1-2-3 database. To determine when to reorder items, for example, you can use a search operation to find any records with an on-hand quantity of less than four units.

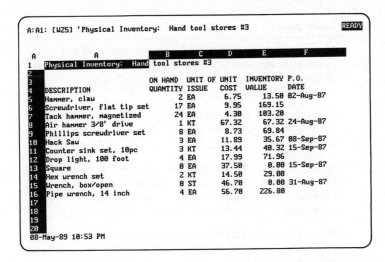

Fig. 10.15.
The initial
Tools Inventory
database.

After you have located the information you want, you can extract the found records from the database and place them in another section of the worksheet, separate from the database. For example, you can extract all records with a purchase order (P.O.) date, and print the newly extracted area as a record of pending purchases.

With 1-2-3's search operations, you also have the option of looking for only the first occurrence of a specified field value in order to develop a unique list of field entries. For example, you can search the ISSUE field to extract a list of the different units of measure. Finally, you can *delete* all inventory records for which quantity on-hand equals zero (if you do not want to reorder these items).

Using Minimum Search Requirements

To initiate any search operation, you need to select the appropriate operation from the /Data Query menu:

Input Criteria Output Find Extract Unique Del Modify Reset Quit

You can use the first three options to specify ranges applicable to the search operations. Input and Criteria, which give the locations of the search area and the search conditions, respectively, must be specified in all Query operations. An output range must be established only when you select a Query command that copies records or parts of records to an area outside the database.

The last two options signal the end of the current search operation. Reset removes all previous search-related ranges so that you can specify a different search location and conditions. Quit returns you to READY mode.

The five options in the middle of the Query menu perform the following search functions:

Option	Description
Find	Moves down through a database, and positions the cell pointer on records that match given criteria. You can enter or change data in the records as you move the cell pointer through them.
Extract	Creates copies, in a specified area of the worksheet, of all or some of the fields in records that match the given criteria.
Unique	Similar to Extract, but recognizes that some of the field contents in the database may be duplicates of other cell entries in the same fields. Eliminates duplicates as entries are copied to the output range.
Del	Deletes from a database all the records that match the given criteria and shifts the remaining records to fill in the remaining gaps.
Modify	Either inserts or replaces records in the input range with records from the output range. This command is used to add new records to a data table, or to extract records from a table, modify them, and then reinsert them.

To perform a Query operation, you must specify both an input range and a criteria range and select one of the four search options. (Before issuing a Unique or Extract command, you must also specify an output range.)

Determining the Input Range

The input range for the /Data Query command is the range of records you want to search. The specified area does not have to include the entire database. In the Tools Inventory database shown in figure 10.15, specifying an input range of A4..F16 defines the search area as the entire database. Entering A1..F9 as the input range for the sorted College database in figure 10.16 limits the search area to the records for the accounting majors.

A:A1: [W7] 'STATUS READY

A	A	B	C	D	E	F	G	H
1	STATUS	MAJOR	SEX	AGE	SORT-KEY			
2	Full	Accounting	F	20	Accounting F 20 Full			
3	Part	Accounting	F	26	Accounting F 26 Part			
4	Full	Accounting	F	27	Accounting F 27 Full			
5	Part	Accounting	F	29	Accounting F 29 Part			
6	Full	Accounting	F	35	Accounting F 35 Full			
7	Full	Accounting	F	42	Accounting F 42 Full			
8	Full	Accounting	M	22	Accounting M 22 Full			
9	Part	Accounting	M	27	Accounting M 27 Part			
10	Part	Administration	M	19	Administration M 19 Part			
11	Full	Administration	M	20	Administration M 20 Full			
12	Part	Finance	F	19	Finance F 19 Part			
13	Part	Finance	F	48	Finance F 48 Part			
14	Full	Finance	M	19	Finance M 19 Full			
15	Part	Finance	M	19	Finance M 19 Part			
16	Full	Finance	M	26	Finance M 26 Full			
17	Full	Finance	M	31	Finance M 31 Full			
18	Full	Marketing	F	19	Marketing F 19 Full			
19	Full	Marketing	F	33	Marketing F 33 Full			
20	Part	Marketing	F	33	Marketing F 33 Part			

08-May-89 10:40 PM

Fig. 10.16. *The sorted College database.*

The input range can contain a single database, or multiple worksheet and/or external databases. Keep in mind that a worksheet database is limited to a single worksheet. An input range can, however, contain multiple databases from different worksheets.

Whether you search all or only a part of a database, you *must* include the field-name row in the input range. (Remember that you must *not* include the field names in a sort operation.) If field names occupy space on more than one row, specify only the bottom row to start the input range. In the Tools Inventory database shown in figure 10.15, for example, because rows 3 and 4 both contain portions of the field names, you would start the input range with row 4 (by entering A4..F16 instead of A3..F16).

Reminder: *You must include the field names in the input range whether you search all or part of a database.*

Select /Data Query Input, and specify the range by typing or pointing to a range name or by using an assigned range name. You do not have to specify the range again unless the search area changes. To search more than one database, you enter the ranges one after the other, separated by a semicolon.

Entering the Criteria Range

In previous 1-2-3 applications, you learned to communicate cell locations to 1-2-3. Similarly, when you want 1-2-3 to search for records that meet certain criteria, you must be able to talk to 1-2-3 in terms the program will understand.

Suppose that you want to identify all records in the Addresses database that contain OH in the STATE field. When the database is on-screen and 1-2-3 is in READY mode, type **STATE** in cell H2 and **OH** in cell H3 (see fig. 10.17). Type **Criteria Range** in cell H1 only if you want the documentation it provides; cell H1 is not directly involved in the search command.

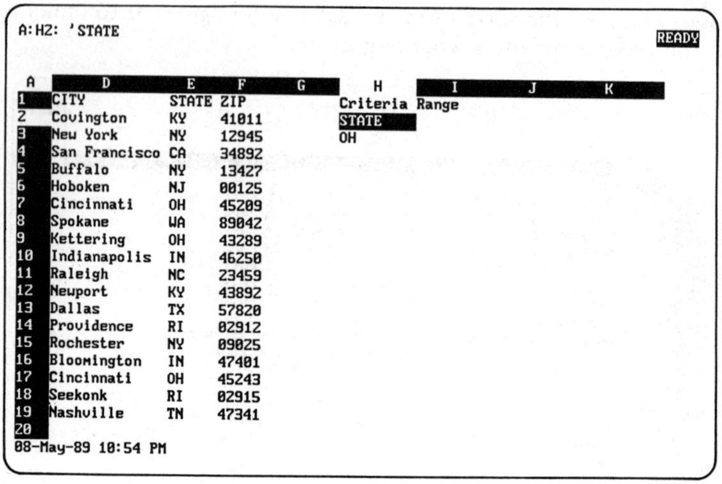

Fig. 10.17.
The Addresses database showing a single search condition.

```
A:H2: 'STATE                                                    READY

A      D            E      F      G        H         I        J        K
1  CITY          STATE  ZIP             Criteria Range
2  Covington     KY     41011           STATE
3  New York      NY     12945           OH
4  San Francisco CA     34892
5  Buffalo       NY     13427
6  Hoboken       NJ     00125
7  Cincinnati    OH     45209
8  Spokane       WA     89042
9  Kettering     OH     43289
10 Indianapolis  IN     46250
11 Raleigh       NC     23459
12 Newport       KY     43892
13 Dallas        TX     57820
14 Providence    RI     02912
15 Rochester     NY     09025
16 Bloomington   IN     47401
17 Cincinnati    OH     45243
18 Seekonk       RI     02915
19 Nashville     TN     47341
20
08-May-89 10:54 PM
```

Select /**D**ata Query, and specify A1..F19 as the input range. The **Query** menu will be displayed in the control panel as soon as you enter the input range. Select Criteria, and then type, point to, or name the range H2..H3 as the location of your search condition. The **Query** menu again will return to the screen.

Reminder:
The criteria range must include the field name(s) in the first row, and criteria in the second row.

You can use numbers, labels, or formulas as criteria. A criteria range can be up to 32 columns wide and 2 or more rows long. The first row must contain the field names of the search criteria, such as STATE in row 2 of figure 10.17. The rows below the unique field names contain the actual criteria, such as OH in row 3. The field names of the input range and the criteria range must match exactly.

By entering one or more criteria in the worksheet and specifying the input and criteria ranges, you have completed the minimum steps necessary to execute a **Find** or **Del** command. Remember that you must enter field names in the first row of the criteria range, above the specific conditions.

Using the Find Command

When you select **Find** from the **Query** menu, a highlighted bar rests on the first record (in the input range) that meets the conditions specified in the criteria range. In the current example, the highlighted bar rests on the first record that includes OH in the STATE field (see fig. 10.18).

```
A:A7: [W12] 'Pryor                                                    FIND

  A        A           B          C                     D           E     F
1  LAST      FIRST      STREET ADDRESS          CITY         STATE ZIP
2  Harrington James     12344 Arlington Lane    Covington    KY    41011
3  Thomas     Brian     18499 Central Park Ave. New York     NY    12945
4  Leugers    Karen     21 Hill St. Apt. 34     San Francisco CA   34892
5  Englert    Michael   224 Orange St.          Buffalo      NY    13427
6  Smith      Margaret  2341 Kyles Lane         Hoboken      NJ    00125
7  Pryor      Aaron     2341 Milford Street     Cincinnati   OH    45209
8  Cleary     Esther    238 Higgins St. Apt. 14 Spokane      WA    89042
9  Wright     Ned       31238 Carolina St.      Kettering    OH    43289
10 Saunders   Ronald    3124 Keystone Ave.      Indianapolis IN    46250
11 McGruder   Mary      331 Park Lane Apt. 32   Raleigh      NC    23459
12 Simpson    Jeremy    3509 Ludlow Ave.        Newport      KY    43892
13 Wolf       Barbara   3098 Arnold Ave.        Dallas       TX    57820
14 Rooney     Kevin     391 Atwater Ave. Apt. 3 Providence   RI    02912
15 Franks     Mike      4284 Knight Circle      Rochester    NY    09025
16 Sorrenson  Sarah     432 Keys Crescent       Bloomington  IN    47401
17 Holland    Earl      4983 Drake Rd.          Cincinnati   OH    45243
18 Tuke       Samuel    9038 Greenup St.        Seekonk      RI    02915
19 Malvern    Thomas    939 Dime Circle         Nashville    TN    47341
20
08-May-89 10:56 PM
```

Fig. 10.18.
The first record highlighted in a Find operation.

By using the down-arrow key, you can position the highlighted bar on the next record that conforms to the criteria. You can continue pressing the down arrow until the last record that meets the search conditions has been highlighted (see fig. 10.19). Notice that the mode indicator changes from READY to FIND during the search.

```
A:A17: [W12] 'Holland                                                 FIND

  A        A           B          C                     D           E     F
1  LAST      FIRST      STREET ADDRESS          CITY         STATE ZIP
2  Harrington James     12344 Arlington Lane    Covington    KY    41011
3  Thomas     Brian     18499 Central Park Ave. New York     NY    12945
4  Leugers    Karen     21 Hill St. Apt. 34     San Francisco CA   34892
5  Englert    Michael   224 Orange St.          Buffalo      NY    13427
6  Smith      Margaret  2341 Kyles Lane         Hoboken      NJ    00125
7  Pryor      Aaron     2341 Milford Street     Cincinnati   OH    45209
8  Cleary     Esther    238 Higgins St. Apt. 14 Spokane      WA    89042
9  Wright     Ned       31238 Carolina St.      Kettering    OH    43289
10 Saunders   Ronald    3124 Keystone Ave.      Indianapolis IN    46250
11 McGruder   Mary      331 Park Lane Apt. 32   Raleigh      NC    23459
12 Simpson    Jeremy    3509 Ludlow Ave.        Newport      KY    43892
13 Wolf       Barbara   3098 Arnold Ave.        Dallas       TX    57820
14 Rooney     Kevin     391 Atwater Ave. Apt. 3 Providence   RI    02912
15 Franks     Mike      4284 Knight Circle      Rochester    NY    09025
16 Sorrenson  Sarah     432 Keys Crescent       Bloomington  IN    47401
17 Holland    Earl      4983 Drake Rd.          Cincinnati   OH    45243
18 Tuke       Samuel    9038 Greenup St.        Seekonk      RI    02915
19 Malvern    Thomas    939 Dime Circle         Nashville    TN    47341
20
08-May-89 10:57 PM
```

Fig. 10.19.
The last record highlighted in a Find operation.

The down-arrow and up-arrow keys let you position the highlighted bar on the next and previous records that meet the search criteria set in the criteria range. The Home and End keys can be used to position the highlighted bar on the first and last records in the database that match the criteria.

Reminder:
Use the up- and down-arrow keys to highlight the previous and next records that meet the search criteria.

In FIND mode, you can use the right-arrow and left-arrow keys to move the single-character flashing cursor to different fields in the current highlighted record. Then enter new values or use the Edit (F2) key to update the current values in the field. One caution: If you change the record so that it no longer satisfies the Find criteria and then move away from that record, you cannot use the down-arrow or up-arrow key to return to the record during the Find operation.

To end the Find operation and return to the Data Query menu, press Enter or Esc. To return directly to READY mode, press Ctrl-Break.

Listing All Specified Records

Cue:
Use /File Xtract to copy extracted records to a new file.

The Find command has limited use, especially in a large database, because the command must scroll through the entire file if you want to view each record that meets the specified criteria. As an alternative to the Find command, you can use the Extract command to copy to a blank area of the worksheet only those records that meet the conditions. (Before you issue the command, you must define the blank area of the worksheet as an output range.) You can view a list of all the extracted records, print the range of the newly extracted records, or even use the /File Xtract command to copy only the extracted record range to a new file on disk.

Defining the Output Range

Choose a blank area in the worksheet as the output range to receive records copied in an extract operation. Designate the range to the right of, or below, the database. In figure 10.20, for example, both the criteria range and the output range have been placed below the records in the Addresses database.

Fig. 10.20.
The criteria and output ranges below the database.

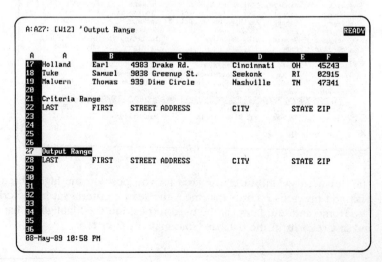

In the first row of the output range, type the names of only those fields whose contents you want to extract. You do not have to type these names in the same order as they appear in the database. (In fig. 10.20, the Output Range entry in cell A27 is for documentation purposes only, and all field names in row 28 have been reproduced in the existing order of the database.)

The field names in both the criteria and output ranges must match exactly the corresponding field names in the input range. If you center a database field name and left-justify the corresponding field name in the output range, for example, an extract operation based on that field name will not work. To avoid mismatch errors, use the /Copy command to copy the database field names in the criteria and output ranges.

Select /Data Query Output; then type, point to, or name the range location of the output area. You can create an open-ended extract area by entering only the field-name row as the range, or you can set the exact size of the extract area.

To limit the size of the extract area, enter the upper-left to lower-right cell coordinates of the entire output range. The first row in the specified range must contain the field names; the remaining rows must accommodate the maximum number of records you expect to receive from the extract operation. Use this method when you want to retain additional data that is located below the extract area. For example, as you can see in figure 10.20, naming A28..F36 as the output range limits incoming records to eight (one row for field names and one row for each record). If you do not allow sufficient room in the fixed-length output area, the extract operation will abort and the message too many records will be displayed on-screen.

To create an open-ended extract area that does not limit the number of incoming records, specify as the output range only the row containing the output field names. For example, by naming A28..F28 as the output range in figure 10.20, you define the area to receive records from an extract operation without limiting the number of records.

An extract operation first removes all existing data from the output range. If you use only the field-name row to specify the output area, all data below that row will be destroyed to make room for the unknown number of incoming extracted records.

Executing the Extract Command

To execute an Extract command, you must type the search conditions in the worksheet, type the output field names in the worksheet, and set the input, criteria, and output ranges from the **Data Query** menu. With /**Data Query Extract**, you also can specify an output range in another worksheet or in an external table.

To accelerate what seems to be a time-consuming setup process, you should establish standard input, criteria, and output areas, and then store the range names for these locations. Keeping in mind the limit of 32 criteria fields, you might establish a single criteria range (such as the range A22..F23 in fig. 10.20) that encompasses all the key fields on which you might search. By establishing such a range, you will save the time needed to respecify a criteria range for each extract on different field names; but if the criteria range contains many unused field names, you will lose some speed of execution.

You can apply the extract process to the Addresses database by creating a list of all records with OH in the STATE field. Assuming that rows 22 and 28 contain the field names, enter **OH** in cell E23. Select /**D**ata **Q**uery and specify the input (A1..F19), criteria (A22..F23), and output (A28..F28) ranges. Then choose **Extract** from the **Q**uery menu. The output range shown in figure 10.21 contains three extracted records, each of which meets the condition of STATE = OH.

Fig. 10.21.
A full-record
extract on an
"exact match"
label condition.

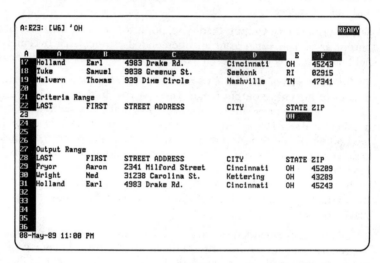

You do not have to extract entire records or maintain the order of field names within the extracted records. For example, you can combine the first- and last-name fields in a new field (NAME) and then extract only the NAME and CITY information from records that have OH in the STATE field. To do this, type **NAME** in cell G1, and then type the string formula **+B2&" "&A2** in cell G2 (see fig. 10.22).

After you have copied the contents of cell G2 to the range G3..G19, use the /**R**ange **V**alue command to convert the formulas in G2..G19 to values.

Next, select /**R**ange **E**rase to delete the field names in row 28. Type the new field **NAME** in cell A28, skip column B (for spacing purposes), and enter the second output field **CITY** in cell C28. If you want to include the new field in the criteria range, type **NAME** in cell G22 also. Then respecify the output range as A28..C28. Expand both the input and criteria ranges to include the new column G. This operation extracts the name and city information for all records of individuals living in Ohio (see fig. 10.23).

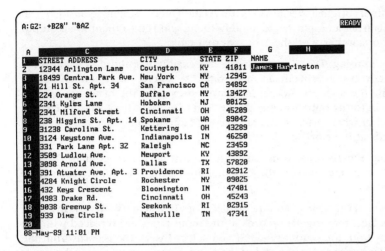

Fig. 10.22.
The NAME field created in the Addresses database.

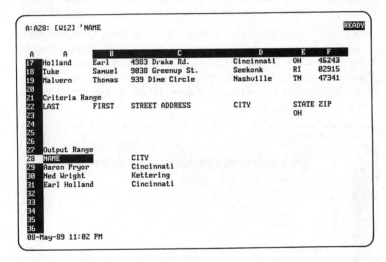

Fig. 10.23.
A partial-record extract on a single label condition.

When extracting from an external table to a worksheet, cells in the output range that receive date or time values are formatted with the Date and Time formats. When the output range is an external table, the formats used are determined by the database driver being used.

Modifying Records

You can use the /Data Query Modify command to extract records from an input range for modification and then return the modified records to the input range. You can insert the modified records in the input range as new records, or you can replace their original versions. With /Data Query Modify, you also can extract records from an input range, modify them, and return them to an output range located in another worksheet or external table.

Reminder: */Data Query Modify inserts or replaces records in the input range with records from the output range.*

The first steps in using /Data Query Modify are exactly like those in using /Data Query Extract. You must specify an input range, a criteria range, and an output range. Selecting /Data Query Modify Extract then extracts the matching records and copies them to the output range. Unlike /Data Query Extract, Modify Extract keeps a record of where each extracted record came from so that you can reinsert the records at their original location.

After extracting the records, you can perform any necessary editing. Do not, however, add or delete rows in the output range, or 1-2-3 cannot replace the records correctly.

Caution: *1-2-3 does not replace records correctly if you add or delete rows in the output range when you use /Data Query Modify.*

Next, you select /Data Query Modify Replace or /Data Query Modify Insert. If you select Replace, the original records in the input range are replaced with the edited versions from the output range. If you select Insert, the records from the output range are appended at the end of the input range, and the original records remain in place. In both cases, the records in the output range are not deleted.

Figures 10.24, 10.25, and 10.26 show an example of using /Data Query Modify. In this example, a sales representative, Wilson, has just gotten married and is changing her name to Hanson. Figure 10.24 shows the criteria range and the output range. You need to edit her sales records to reflect the name change. Figure 10.25 shows the edited records, and figure 10.26 shows the replaced records.

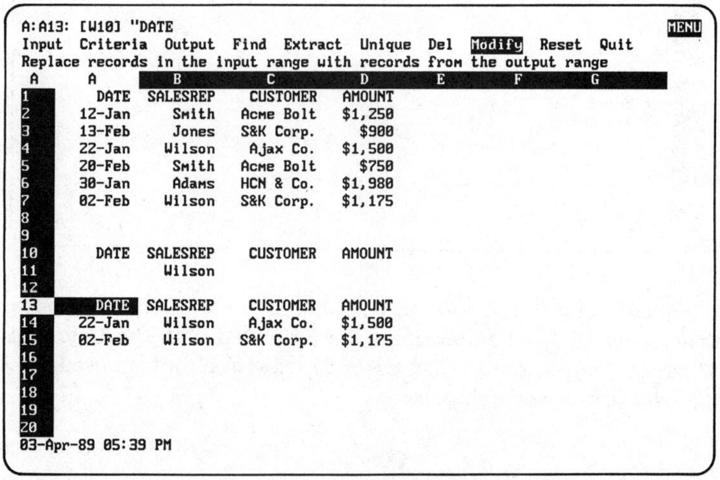
A:A13: [W10] "DATE
MENU
Input Criteria Output Find Extract Unique Del Modify Reset Quit
Replace records in the input range with records from the output range
A A B C D E F G
1 DATE SALESREP CUSTOMER AMOUNT
2 12-Jan Smith Acme Bolt $1,250
3 13-Feb Jones S&K Corp. $900
4 22-Jan Wilson Ajax Co. $1,500
5 20-Feb Smith Acme Bolt $750
6 30-Jan Adams HCN & Co. $1,980
7 02-Feb Wilson S&K Corp. $1,175
8
9
10 DATE SALESREP CUSTOMER AMOUNT
11 Wilson
12
13 DATE SALESREP CUSTOMER AMOUNT
14 22-Jan Wilson Ajax Co. $1,500
15 02-Feb Wilson S&K Corp. $1,175
16
17
18
19
20
03-Apr-89 05:39 PM

Fig. 10.24. *A worksheet data table after /Data Query Modify Extract has been executed.*

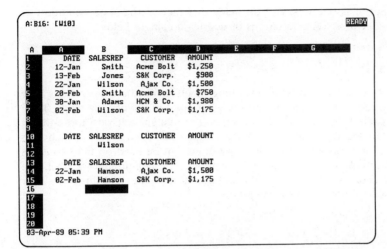

Fig. 10.25.
The same data table after the extracted records have been edited.

Fig. 10.26.
The data table showing the replaced records.

Note that when you use /**D**ata **Q**uery **M**odify **I**nsert, the records being inserted (those in the output range) do not need to have been originally extracted from the database into which they are being inserted.

Handling More Complicated Criteria Ranges

In addition to an "exact match" search on a single label field, 1-2-3 permits a wide variety of record searches: on exact matches to numeric fields; on partial matches of field contents; on fields that meet formula conditions; on fields that meet all of several conditions; and on fields that meet either one condition or another. Consider first some variations of queries on single fields.

Wild Cards in Criteria Ranges

Cue:
Use wild cards to match labels in database operations.

You can use 1-2-3's wild cards for matching labels in database operations. The characters ?, *, and ~ have special meaning when used in the criteria range. The ? character instructs 1-2-3 to accept any character in that specific position, and can be used only to locate fields of the same length. The * character, which tells 1-2-3 to accept any and all characters that follow, can be used on field contents of unequal length. By placing a tilde (~) symbol at the beginning of a label, you tell 1-2-3 to accept all values *except* those that follow. Table 10.2 illustrates how you can use wild cards in search operations.

Table 10.2
Using Wild Cards in Search Operations

Enter	To Find
N?	NC, NJ, NY, and so on
BO?L?	BOWLE but not BOWL
BO?L*	BOWLE, BOWL, BOLLESON, BOELING, and so on
SAN*	SANTA BARBARA, SAN FRANCISCO
SAN *	SAN FRANCISCO only
~N*	Strings in specified fields that *do not* begin with the letter *N*

Use the ? and * wild-card characters when you are unsure of the spelling used in field contents. Be sure that the results of any extract operation which uses a wild card are what you need. And be extremely careful when you use wild cards in a **Del** command. If you are not careful, you may remove more records than you intend.

Formulas in Criteria Ranges

To set up formulas that query numeric or label fields in the database, you can use the following relational operators:

>	Greater than
>=	Greater than or equal to
<	Less than
<=	Less than or equal to
=	Equal to
<>	Not equal to

Create a formula that references the first field entry in the numeric column you want to search. 1-2-3 will test the formula on each cell down the column until the program reaches the end of the specified input range.

You can place the formula anywhere below the criteria range's field-name row (unlike text criteria, which must appear directly below the associated field name). For example, you can use a formula based on information already in the Marketing Research database shown earlier in figure 10.4 to extract the records of test participants who are at least 45 years old. First, type the formula **+D5>=45** in cell D22 (see fig. 10.27).

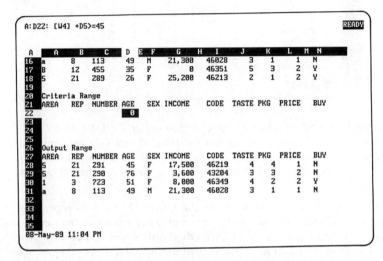

Fig. 10.27.
A relational formula condition to extract records.

Notice that the formula is displayed in the control panel and that a zero (0) is displayed in cell D22. The formula checked whether the contents of cell D5 (in which AGE equals 26) were greater than or equal to 45 and returned the zero (0) to indicate a false condition. (To better understand the search condition, you could use the /Range Format Text command to change the display from 0 to the formula. But the AGE column in this example is so narrow that the full formula cannot be displayed in the cell.)

After you have specified the input, criteria, and output ranges correctly, executing an extract operation produces 4 records for which AGE equals or exceeds 45 years. A criterion of +D5>45 would extract only 3 records; the formula +D5=45 would extract only 1 record.

To reference cells outside the database, use formulas that include absolute cell addressing. (For addressing information, refer to Chapter 4.) For example, suppose that immediately after you issue the preceding command (to extract records based on AGE), you want to extract the records of those Marketing Research database respondents whose income exceeds the average income of all respondents. To do this, you first must return to READY mode. Then determine the average income by entering **@AVG(G5..G18)** in a blank cell (G24) away from all database ranges.

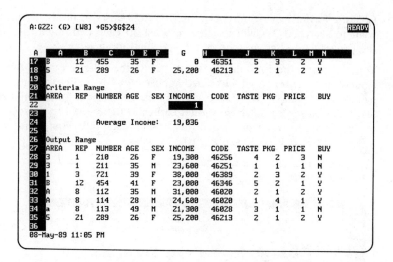

Fig. 10.28.
A mixed formula condition to extract records.

```
A:G22: (G) [W8] +G5>$G$24                                        READY

A    A       B     C     D E F     G      H I    J    K    L    M  N
17  B       12    455    35 F        0   46351    5    3    2   Y
18  5       21    289    26 F    25,200   46213    2    1    2   Y
19
20  Criteria Range
21  AREA   REP  NUMBER AGE    SEX INCOME   CODE TASTE PKG  PRICE   BUY
22                                      1
23
24                    Average Income:   19,036
25
26  Output Range
27  AREA   REP  NUMBER AGE    SEX INCOME   CODE TASTE PKG  PRICE   BUY
28  3       1    210    26 F    19,300   46256    4    2    3   N
29  3       1    211    35 M    23,600   46251    1    1    1   N
30  1       3    721    39 F    38,000   46389    2    3    2   Y
31  B       12   454    41 F    23,000   46346    5    2    1   Y
32  A       8    112    35 M    31,000   46020    2    1    2   Y
33  A       8    114    28 M    24,600   46020    1    4    1   Y
34  a       8    113    49 M    21,300   46028    3    1    1   N
35  5       21   289    26 F    25,200   46213    2    1    2   Y
36
08-May-89 11:05 PM
```

Next, type the formula **+G5>$G$24** as the criterion under INCOME in cell G22 (see fig. 10.28). The +G5 tells 1-2-3 to test (starting in cell G5) income contents against the average income in cell G24 and to continue down column G to the end of the input range (row 18), testing each subsequent income cell against the average income in cell G6.

With the program still in READY mode, press the Query (F7) key to repeat the most recent query operation (**Extract**, in this example) and eliminate the need to select **/Data Query Extract**. Use the shortcut method only when you do not want to change the locations of the input, criteria, and output ranges. As you can see from figure 10.28, the extracted records indicate that eight of the Marketing Research database participants have incomes greater than the average income of all respondents.

AND Conditions

Now that you have seen how to base a **Find** or **Extract** operation on only one criterion, you will learn how to use multiple criteria for your queries. You can set up multiple criteria as AND conditions (in which *all* the criteria must be met) or as OR conditions (in which any *one* criterion must be met). For example, searching a music department's library for sheet music requiring drums AND trumpets is likely to produce fewer selections than searching for music appropriate for drums OR trumpets.

Indicate two or more criteria, *all* of which must be met, by specifying the conditions on the criteria row immediately below the field names. The multiple criteria in row 24 of the College database request those records for which MAJOR equals Accounting and SEX equals Male (see fig. 10.29). If you then issue an **Extract** command, 1-2-3 will extract two records that meet both conditions.

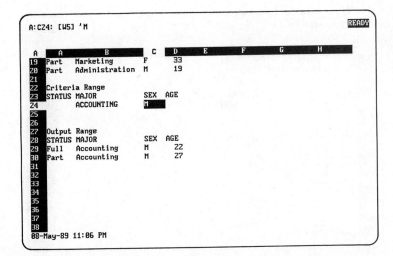

Fig. 10.29.
An initial two-field logical AND search.

When you maintain a criteria range that includes many fields, you can quickly extract records based on an alternative condition. For example, access READY mode, change **M** to **F** in cell C24 (under SEX), and press the Query (F7) key. 1-2-3 immediately copies the records of female accounting majors to the output range (see fig. 10.30).

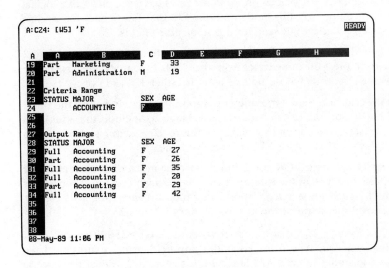

Fig. 10.30.
A revised two-field logical AND search.

You can continue to add conditions that must be met. Enter the additional criteria only in the row immediately below the field-name row. For example, the extracted records in figure 10.31 are limited to female accounting majors under 30 years old.

*Fig. 10.31.
A three-field
logical AND
search.*

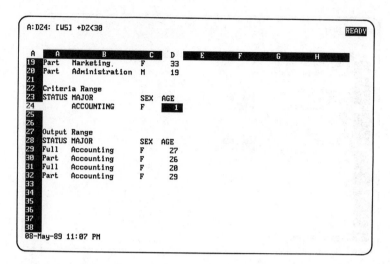

```
A:D24: [W5] +D2<30                                              READY

   A        A          B          C   D    E      F      G      H
  19    Part    Marketing.        F     33
  20    Part    Administration    M     19
  21
  22    Criteria Range
  23    STATUS  MAJOR             SEX   AGE
  24            ACCOUNTING        F      1
  25
  26
  27    Output Range
  28    STATUS  MAJOR             SEX   AGE
  29    Full    Accounting        F     27
  30    Part    Accounting        F     26
  31    Full    Accounting        F     28
  32    Part    Accounting        F     29
  33
  34
  35
  36
  37
  38
  08-May-89 11:07 PM
```

OR Conditions

Criteria placed on the *same* row have the effect of a logical AND; they tell 1-2-3 to find or extract on this field condition AND this field condition AND this field condition, and so on. Criteria placed on *different* rows have the effect of a logical OR; that is, find or extract on this field condition OR that field condition, and so on. You can set up a logical OR search on one or more fields.

Searching a single field for more than one condition is the simplest use of an OR condition. For example, you can extract from the Tools Inventory database (refer to fig. 10.15) those records whose unit of issue is either KT (kit) or ST (set).

Under the ISSUE criterion field, type one condition immediately below the other (see fig. 10.32). Be sure to expand the criteria range to include the additional row. As you can see from the output range in figure 10.32, four records in the Tools database have either KT or ST for a unit of issue.

You also can specify a logical OR condition on two or more different fields. For example, suppose that you want to search the Marketing Research database for records in which age is greater than 50 OR in which income exceeds $25,000. Figure 10.33 shows the setup of the criteria in rows 22 and 23.

Type **+D5>50** in cell D22. In the next row, enter **+G5>25000** in cell G23. (Remember that you can type formulas under any field name; you could have entered the two formulas in cells A22 and A23, for example). Adjust the criteria range to include the specified OR condition by expanding the criteria range down a row. When you issue the **Extract** command, five records are copied to the output range. Although rows 29 and 31 in figure 10.33 do not reflect INCOME contents exceeding $25,000, they do contain AGE contents over 50. Only one condition OR the other had to be met before the copy was made.

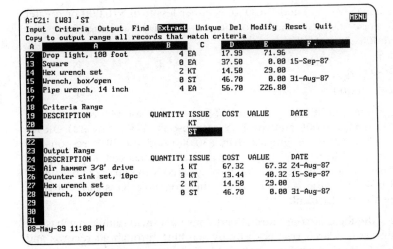

Fig. 10.32.
A logical OR search within a single field.

Fig. 10.33.
A logical OR search on two fields.

To add additional OR criteria, drop to a new row, enter each new condition, and expand the criteria range. If you reduce the number of rows involved in an OR logical search, be sure to contract the criteria range.

Although no technical reason prevents you from mixing AND and OR logical searches, the results of such a mixed query operation may not be of much use. Follow the format of placing each AND condition in the row immediately below the criterion field-name row, and each OR condition in a separate row below. For example, if you want to search the Marketing Research database for records in which BUY equals Y (Yes) and INCOME is either less than $10,000 or greater than $30,000, erase the AGE search condition in cell D22 and then enter the AND/OR conditions in the following cells:

	G	H	I	J	K	L	M	N
22	+G5<10000							Y
23	+G5>30000							Y

By specifying these conditions, you tell 1-2-3 to search for records in which INCOME is less than $10,000 and the BUY response is "Yes" (row 22) OR for records in which INCOME is greater than $30,000 and the BUY response is "Yes" (row 23). The criteria range (A21..N23) remains unchanged. Repeating the Y in cell N23 is critical (even though you have entered Y in cell N22) because if 1-2-3 finds a blank cell within a criteria range, the program selects all records for the field name above that blank cell.

You should test the logic of your search conditions on a small sample database in which you can verify search results easily by scrolling through all records and noting which of them should be extracted. For example, if the Marketing Research database contained hundreds of responses, you could test the preceding AND/OR search conditions on the small group of 14 records shown earlier in figure 10.4. (Issuing an **Extract** command should copy to the output area only the records in rows 8, 13, 15, and 17.)

String Searches

If you want to search on the partial contents of a field, you can use functions in a formula. For example, suppose that you can remember only the street name "Keystone" for a record you want to extract from the Addresses database. If you can safely assume that all street addresses start with a number and have a space before the street name (XXX Streetname), you can use the formula shown in the control panel of figure 10.34 as the search criterion in cell C23.

Fig. 10.34.
*A function
condition used
for a string
search.*

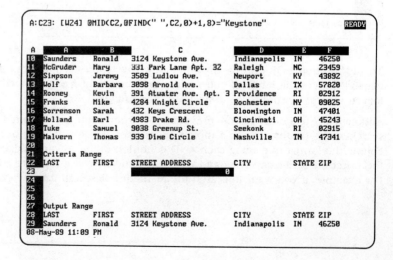

The double quotation marks (" ") in the formula instruct 1-2-3 to start the search after a blank space is encountered (between the street number and street name). The `1,8` portion of the formula instructs the program to search on the first through the eighth character positions matching "Keystone," thereby eliminating any need to know whether "Street," "Ave.," or "Avenue," is part of the field. Issuing the **Extract** command produces one record in the output range (row 29). You also could use compound criteria and search on both CITY and part of the STREET ADDRESS field. (See Chapter 6 for an in-depth description of 1-2-3 functions.)

Special Operators

To combine search conditions within a single field, use the special operators #AND# and #OR#. Use the special operator #NOT# to negate a search condition.

Use #AND# or #OR# to search on two or more conditions within the same field. For example, suppose that you want to extract from the Tools Inventory database all records with an August, 1987, purchase-order date (DATE). Establish the criteria by requesting an extract of all dates later than July 31, 1987, AND earlier than September 1, 1987. In figure 10.35, the formula condition has been entered in cell A20. (Keep in mind that you do not have to type a formula under the associated field name—DATE, in this example.) The extracted records are displayed in rows 25 through 27.

```
A:A20: [W25] +F5>@DATE(87,7,31)#AND#F5<@DATE(87,9,1)                    READY

 A          A                          B        C       D         E        F
10 Hack Saw                                3 EA     11.89     35.67 08-Sep-87
11 Counter sink set, 10pc                  3 KT     13.44     40.32 15-Sep-87
12 Drop light, 100 foot                    4 EA     17.99     71.96
13 Square                                  0 EA     37.50      0.00 15-Sep-87
14 Hex wrench set                          2 KT     14.50     29.00
15 Wrench, box/open                        0 ST     46.70      0.00 31-Aug-87
16 Pipe wrench, 14 inch                    4 EA     56.70    226.80
17
18 Criteria Range
19 DESCRIPTION                      QUANTITY ISSUE   COST   VALUE      DATE
20                                1
21
22
23 Output Range
24 DESCRIPTION                      QUANTITY ISSUE   COST   VALUE      DATE
25 Hammer, claw                            2 EA      6.75     13.50 02-Aug-87
26 Air hammer 3/8' drive                   1 KT     67.32     67.32 24-Aug-87
27 Wrench, box/open                        0 ST     46.70      0.00 31-Aug-87
28
29
08-May-89 11:10 PM
```

Fig. 10.35. *The special operator #AND# used for extracting records.*

You use the #AND#, #OR#, and #NOT# operators to enter (in one field) conditions that could be entered some other way (usually in at least two fields). For example, you could enter **+C5="KT"#OR#C5="ST"** in a single cell in row 20 (any cell in the criteria range A19..F20) as an alternative criterion entry for producing the output shown in figure 10.32 (unit of issue as KT or ST in the Tools Inventory database).

Use #NOT# at the beginning of a condition to negate that condition. For example, if the Tools Inventory database had only three units of issue—KT, ST, and EA (each)—you could produce the results shown in figure 10.32 by specifying the criterion **#NOT#EA** in cell C20 of the criteria range A19..F20.

Performing Other Types of Searches

Cue:
Use the /Data Query Unique command to copy only the first occurrence of a record in the output range.

In addition to the /Data Query Find commands, you can use the Data Query menu's Unique and Del commands for searches. By issuing the Unique command, you can produce (in the output range) a copy of only the first occurrence of a record that meets a specified criterion. And you can update the contents of your 1-2-3 database by deleting all records that meet a specified criterion. After entering the conditions, you need to specify only the input and criteria ranges before you issue the Del command.

Extracting Unique Records

Ordinarily, the Unique command is used to copy into the output area only a small portion of each record that meets the criterion. For example, if you want a list of measurements used in the Tools Inventory database, set up an output range that includes only the unit of ISSUE (see fig. 10.36). To search all records, leave blank the row below the field-name row in the criteria range A19..F20. Then, with the input range defined as A4..F16 and the output range set at A24, select /Data Query Unique to produce (in rows 25 through 27) a list of the three units of measure.

Fig. 10.36.
The results of issuing a /Data Query Unique command.

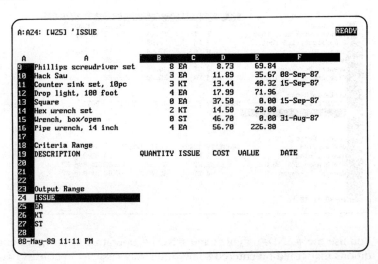

As another example, you can produce (from the College database) a list of the majors selected by current students. To do so, you specify in the output area only the field name MAJOR, leave blank the row under field names in the criteria range, and execute the Unique command.

As with /Data Query Extract and /Data Query Modify Extract, you can specify as the output range an external table where 1-2-3 should place the results of a /Data Query Unique operation.

Deleting Specified Records

As you learned in Chapter 4, you can use the /Worksheet Delete Row command sequence to remove rows from a worksheet. If you want a fast alternative to this "one by one" approach, use the /Data Query Del command to remove unwanted records from your database files. Before you select Del from the Query menu, simply specify the range of records to be searched (input range) and the conditions for the deletion (criteria).

For example, suppose that you want to remove from the Addresses database all records with a STATE field beginning with the letter N. To do so, specify an input range of A1..F19, a criteria range of A22..F23, and use the criterion N* in cell E23. Then issue the /Data Query Del command to remove all records for states that begin with N. As you can see from the figure, the remaining records pack together in rows 2 through 14, and the input range automatically adjusts to A1..F14 (see fig. 10.37).

```
A:E23: [W6] 'N*                                              MENU
Input  Criteria  Output  Find  Extract  Unique  Del  Modify  Reset  Quit
Delete all records that match criteria
A        A          B          C                   D            E     F
1  LAST        FIRST      STREET ADDRESS      CITY         STATE ZIP
2  Harrington  James      12344 Arlington Lane Covington    KY    41011
3  Leugers     Karen      21 Hill St. Apt. 34  San Francisco CA   34892
4  Pryor       Aaron      2341 Milford Street  Cincinnati   OH    45209
5  Cleary      Esther     238 Higgins St. Apt. 14 Spokane   WA    89042
6  Wright      Ned        31238 Carolina St.   Kettering    OH    43289
7  Saunders    Ronald     3124 Keystone Ave.   Indianapolis IN    46250
8  Simpson     Jeremy     3509 Ludlow Ave.     Newport      KY    43892
9  Wolf        Barbara    3098 Arnold Ave.     Dallas       TX    57820
10 Rooney      Kevin      391 Atwater Ave. Apt. 3 Providence RI    02912
11 Sorrenson   Sarah      432 Keys Crescent    Bloomington  IN    47401
12 Holland     Earl       4983 Drake Rd.       Cincinnati   OH    45243
13 Tuke        Samuel     9038 Greenup St.     Seekonk      RI    02915
14 Malvern     Thomas     939 Dime Circle      Nashville    TN    47341
15
20
21 Criteria Range
22 LAST        FIRST      STREET ADDRESS      CITY         STATE ZIP
23                                                         N*
24
08-May-89 11:11 PM
```

Fig. 10.37.
The results of issuing a /Data Query Del command.

Be extremely careful when you issue the /Data Query Del command. To give you the opportunity to verify that you indeed want to select the Del command, 1-2-3 displays the following menu, on which the leftmost, least dangerous command is highlighted:

Cancel Delete

Choose Cancel to abort the Del command. Select Delete to verify that you want to execute the delete operation.

Although you cannot view the exact rows to be deleted, you can guard against deleting the wrong records by doing one (or both) of two things. Before you issue a /Data Query Del command, do either of the following:

- /File Save the database, using a name such as TEMP, to create a copy of the original. Then, if the logic of the delete conditions proves faulty, you will be able to retrieve this copy.

- Perform an Extract on the delete conditions, view the records to verify that they are to be removed, and then perform the delete operation.

Joining Multiple Databases

Cue:

Join multiple databases by using one or more key fields that the databases have in common.

A powerful feature of Release 3 is its capability to create an output range that contains fields and/or calculated columns based on records contained in two or more databases. Performing a *join*, as it is called, is based on relating two or more databases on the basis of one or more key fields they have in common. A *key field* is one whose content is unique for each record in the database. For an employee database, for example, Social Security number is a key field because every individual has a different Social Security number. Address is not a key field because two employees might live at the same address.

The first step in joining multiple databases is to enter a *join formula* in the criteria range. The join formula specifies the relationship that must be satisfied between the key fields in the databases. In most applications, the required relationship will be that the key fields are equal (=). Suppose, for example, that you have two databases, with the range names PERSONAL and SALARY, which contain different information about your employees. Both databases have a Social Security number, SSNUM, as a key field. To join these two databases, you use the following join formula:

PERSONAL.SSNUM = SALARY.SSNUM

This join formula will join from the two databases any records that have the same value in the SSNUM field.

Next, you specify the input and output ranges. In the first row of the output range, enter the names of the fields you want included in the output range. These fields can include calculated or aggregate columns (but not both in the same output range).

Finally, select /Data Query Extract or /Data Query Unique. Release 3 goes through the records in the input range and compares the contents of the key fields specified in the join formula. For each set of records whose key fields match the join formula criterion, a new record is written to the output range.

The worksheet in figure 10.38, for example, contains two small databases. TABLE1, in the range A1..B5, contains the key field PARTNO (part number) and the field COUNT (number of each part on-hand). TABLE2, in the range D1..E5, also contains a PARTNO key field, plus a COST field that gives the unit cost of each part. TABLE1 and TABLE2 are range names that have been assigned to the databases.

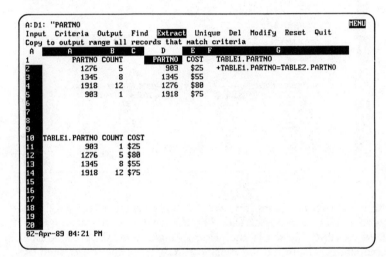

Fig. 10.38.
A join of two
data tables.

To join these two databases, first use the /Range Name Create command to assign the range name TABLE1 to the range A1..B5, and the range name TABLE2 to the range D1..E5. Type a heading for the criteria range. Notice that the heading is made up of one of the database's range names, a period, and the name of the key field. Then enter the following formula to create a criteria range:

+ TABLE1.PARTNO = TABLE2.PARTNO

Next, create an output range with column headings for the fields you want included. As for the criteria range, the output range must include one of the database's range names, a period, and the name of the key field. In this case, include all three field names.

After creating the output range, specify both databases as the input range. Select /Data Query Input, and in response to the prompt, enter **TABLE1;TABLE2**.

Finally, select Extract. The results are shown in figure 10.38. The output range contains COUNT and COST information for each matching PARTNO in the input range.

The output range of a join operaion can contain computed or aggregate columns (but not both). Examples of a computed column and an aggregate column are shown in figure 10.39. Since you cannot have a computed column and an aggregate column in the same output range, figure 10.39 shows two output ranges. Each extract was done separately.

Fig. 10.39.
A computed column in an output range.

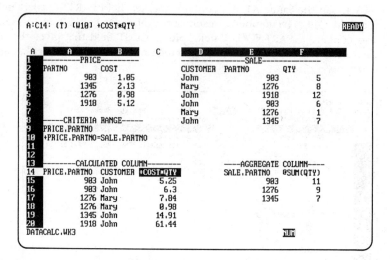

Once again, there are two databases, one with a range named PRICE (A2..B6) and the other with a range named SALE (D2..F8). The databases are joined by the part number field PARTNO, shown in the criteria range (cells A9..A10). Notice that in the computed-column output range of A14..C14, the third field is +COST*QTY. Type this formula in the cell as you would any formula. In the figure, the cell was formatted as **Text** to show the formula. Otherwise, you would see the formula's result, which is ERR. As the records are extracted, 1-2-3 makes each calculation, using the quantity from the SALE database and the cost from the PRICE database.

You may use nearly any valid formula in creating a computed column. The exceptions are formulas containing the functions @AVG, @COUNT, @MIN, @MAX, @SUM, and any of the database @ functions, such as @DSUM. All these functions, except the database @ functions, will create an aggregate column. Notice in figure 10.39 that the aggregate column uses the @SUM function. With the same input and criteria ranges set, the output range is E14..F14. When you choose **Extract**, the unique part numbers are extracted to the ouput range with a summation of each part number sold. The summation is done with the column heading of the @SUM(QTY) function. The computed and aggregate columns can be used with an output range for a single database, as well as in the output range of joined multiple databases.

When creating join formulas, keep in mind the following guidelines:

- Key field names used in a join formula cannot contain special characters, such as commas, spaces, or pound signs (#). If they do, 1-2-3 cannot calculate the formula properly.

- Key field names do not have to be the same in order to be used to join two databases. The names must only be key fields that contain the same type of data. Therefore, the Social Security number field can be called SSNUM in one table and EMPLOYEENUM in another and still be used as the basis for a join formula. If the field names are different, you do not need to include the database range names in the join formula:

  EMPLOYEENUM = SSNUM

- You can use more than one set of key fields in a join formula. For example, the following join formula links both the CUSTOMER and PARTNO fields in the two databases:

  + TABLE1.CUSTOMER = TABLE2.CUSTOMER#AND#
  TABLE1.PARTNO = TABLE2.PARTNO

- You can use any of the logical operators (>, <, <>, >=, <=) in a join formula. 1-2-3 compares the join formula fields in every combination of records from the input ranges and creates a new record in the output range each time the join formula is TRUE.

Reminder:
You cannot use key fields that contain special characters in a join formula.

Creating Data Tables

In many situations, the variables used in your worksheet formulas are known quantities. Last year's sales summary, for example, deals with variables whose exact values are known. The results of calculations performed using those values contain no uncertainties. Other situations, however, involve variables whose exact values are not known. Worksheet models for financial projections often fall into this category. Next year's cash flow projection, for example, depends on prevailing interest rates. While you can make an educated guess at what interest rates will be, you cannot predict them exactly.

/Data Table commands are designed for the latter category. The /Data Table commands let you create tables that show how the results of formula calculations vary as the variables used in the formulas change.

Here's a common example. You have decided to purchase a new car, and you will be taking out a $12,000 loan. The area banks offer several combinations of loan periods and interest rates. You can use a data table to calculate the monthly payment that would result from each combination of period and interest rate. Figure 10.40, for example, shows how you can use a 1-2-3 data table to determine the monthly payment on the $12,000 loan at different interest rates and loan periods. Cell C3 has been formatted as Text to display the formula it contains.

Cue:
Use /Data Table to create tables that show how formula results vary as variables change.

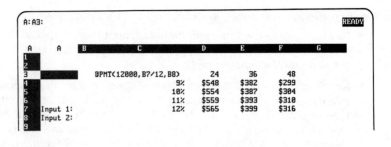

Fig. 10.40.
A data table to determine the monthly payment on a loan at different interest rates and loan periods.

Another function of the /**Data Table** commands is to create *cross-tabulation* tables. A cross-tabulation table provides summary information categorized by unique information in two fields. Look at the data table in figure 10.41. The cross-tabulation table in the range A13..E17 shows the total amount of sales each sales representative made to each customer.

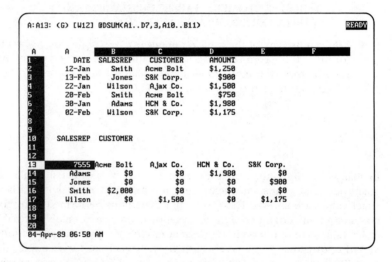

Fig. 10.41.
An example of cross-tabulation analysis.

This section shows you how to use the /**Data Table** commands to perform "sensitivity" or "what if" analysis, and to cross-tabulate information in data tables. First, however, you need to understand some terms and concepts.

General Terms and Concepts

A *data table range* is a worksheet range that contains a data table. A *data table* contains the results of a /**Data Table** command plus some or all of the information that was used to generate the results.

A *variable* is a formula component whose value can change. In figure 10.40, the formula in cell C3 contains two variables: B7 (interest rate) and B8 (loan term).

An *input cell* is a worksheet cell used by 1-2-3 for temporary storage during calculation of a data table. One input cell is required for each variable in the data table formula. The cell addresses of the formula variables are the same as the input cells.

An *input value* is a specific value that 1-2-3 uses for a variable during the data table calculations. The data table in figure 10.40 has two sets of input values: the interest rates in the range C4..C7 and the loan periods in the range D3..F3.

The *results area* is the portion of a data table where the calculation results are placed. One result is generated for each combination of input values. In figure 10.40, for example, one result (such as a monthly payment amount) is calculated for each combination of interest rate and loan period. The results area of a data table must be unprotected.

The formulas used in data tables can contain values, strings, cell addresses, and @ functions. You should not use logical formulas, because this type of formula always evaluates to either 0 or 1. Although using a logical formula in a data table will not cause an error, the results generally will be meaningless.

The Four Types of Data Tables

When you select /Data Table, the following menu appears:

    1 2 3 Labeled Reset

The first four menu selections correspond to the four types of data tables that 1-2-3 can generate. The four table types differ in the number of formulas and variables they can contain. In brief, the table types are these:

Data Table 1	One or more formulas with one variable
Data Table 2	One formula with two variables
Data Table 3	One formula with three variables
Data Table Labeled	One or more formulas with an unlimited number of variables

The text that follows describes each type of data table in turn, showing how it can be used to perform what-if analysis and to create cross-tabulation tables.

Creating a Type 1 Data Table

A data table created with the /Data Table 1 command shows the effects of changing one variable on the results of one or more formulas. Before using this command, you must set up the data table range and a single input cell.

The input cell can be a blank cell anywhere in the worksheet. The best practice is to identify the input cell by entering an appropriate label either above the input cell or to the left.

The data table range is a rectangular worksheet area. It can be placed in any empty worksheet location. The size of the data table range can be calculated as follows:

- The range will have one more column than the number of formulas being evaluated.

- The range will have one more row than the number of input values being evaluated.

The general structure of a type 1 data table range is as follows:

- The top-left cell in the data table range is empty.

- The formulas to be evaluated are entered across the first row. Each formula must refer to the input cell.

- The input values to be plugged into the formulas are entered down the first column.

- After the data table is calculated, each cell in the results range contains the result obtained by evaluating the formula at the top of that column with the input value at the left of that row.

Suppose, for example, that you are planning on purchasing a house in the $75,000–90,000 range, and you will be able to obtain either a 10% or 11% mortgage interest rate. You want to determine, for each interest rate, the monthly mortgage payment that would result at each price.

For the example, you can use cell B2 as the input cell, and identify it with a label in cell A2. You need one formula for each interest rate. Using the @PMT function, enter the following in cell D2:

@PMT(B2,0.1/12,360)

In cell E2, enter the following:

@PMT(B2,0.11/12,360)

Because payments are monthly, each annual interest rate is divided by 12 to get the monthly interest rate. The 360 is the term of the loan in months.

Next, enter the four possible prices in cells C3 through C6. Select /Data Table 1, specify C2..E6 as the table range, and enter B2 as the input cell. The resulting table, which calculates the mortgage payments on four different house prices at two interest rates, is shown in figure 10.42. Cells D2 and E2 have been formatted as Text so that you can see the formulas they contain.

Creating a Cross-Tabulated Table with /Data Table 1

/Data Table 1 also can be used with a data table to create a cross-tabulation table. To create this kind of table, you need to be familiar with 1-2-3 data tables and

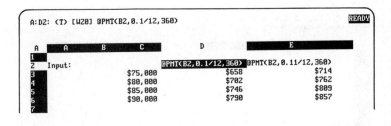

```
A:D2: (T) [W20] @PMT(B2,0.1/12,360)                    READY

A      A       B       C          D                E
1
2    Input:                      @PMT(B2,0.1/12,360) @PMT(B2,0.11/12,360)
3                    $75,000           $658              $714
4                    $80,000           $702              $762
5                    $85,000           $746              $809
6                    $90,000           $790              $857
7
```

Fig. 10.42.
/Data Table 1 used to calculate mortgage payments on four different house prices at two interest rates.

the related terms and concepts, as discussed earlier in this chapter. You also should be familiar with the database @ functions, discussed later in this chapter.

This type of analysis requires an input cell, which can be anywhere in the worksheet. For a cross-tabulation analysis, the cell immediately above the input cell must contain the name of the data table field on which the analysis is being based.

The structure of a data table range for a cross-tabulation analysis is similar to that for a what-if analysis. The upper-left cell is empty, and the top row contains the formula(s) that are to be evaluated. In most cases, these formulas will contain one or more database @ functions.

The left column of the data table range again contains input values. Rather than being values that are plugged directly into the formulas, however, the input values for a cross-tabulation analysis are the values or labels that will be used as *criteria* for the analysis.

After the data table has been calculated, each cell in the results range contains the result of the formula at the top of the column applied to those database records that meet the criterion at the left of the row.

Imagine, for example, that you are the director of a week-long fishing tournament, and you are keeping a database of each contestant's catches. Each "catch" goes into one database record, which contains the contestant's name and the weight of the fish. At the end of the tournament, you want to calculate for each contestant the total weight and the maximum weight of a single catch. The database that handles this application is shown in figure 10.43.

To construct the data table, you can use B13 as the input cell. Because you want to select records based on the NAME field, enter the label NAME above the input cell, in cell B12.

The data table will be in the range D12..F15. The three contestants' names will be in the range D13..D15. The formulas are entered in cells E12 and F12.

In cell E12, for the total weight caught by each contestant, enter

    @DSUM(B1..C10,1,B12..B13)

In cell F12, for the maximum weight of a single catch for each contestant, enter

    @DMAX(B1..C10,1,B12..B13)

Fig. 10.43.
*/Data Table 1
used to perform
a cross-
tabulation
analysis on
data in a data
table.*

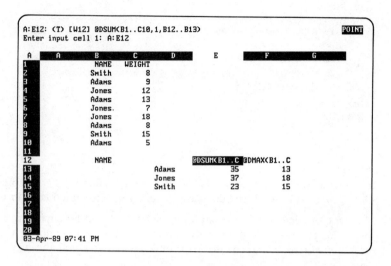

```
A:E12: (T) [W12] @DSUM(B1..C10,1,B12..B13)                      POINT
Enter input cell 1: A:E12

A      A          B        C        D       E          F          G
1                 NAME   WEIGHT
2                 Smith      8
3                 Adams      9
4                 Jones     12
5                 Adams     13
6                 Jones.     7
7                 Jones     18
8                 Adams      8
9                 Smith     15
10                Adams      5
11
12                NAME                      @DSUM(B1..C @DMAX(B1..C
13                          Adams    35           13
14                          Jones    37           18
15                          Smith    23           15
16
17
18
19
20
03-Apr-89 07:41 PM
```

Note that each of these database @ functions refers to the range containing the input cell (B13) and its identifying field name (B12) as the criteria range.

Select /Data Table 1, specify D12..F15 as the table range, and enter **B13** as the input cell. The table of results appears, as shown in figure 10.43. Cells E12 and F12 have been formatted as Text, but the entire formulas are not visible because they are too wide for the column width.

Creating a Type 2 Data Table

The type 2 data table lets you evaluate a single formula based on changes in two variables. The examples shown in figures 10.40 and 10.41 are type 2 data tables.

To use /Data Table 2, you need two blank input cells, one for each variable. They can be located anywhere in the worksheet, and need not be adjacent to each other. The input cells can be identified with an appropriate label in a cell next to or above each input cell.

The size of the data table range depends on the number of values of each variable you want to evaluate. The range will be one column wider than the number of values of one variable, and one row longer than the number of values of the other variable.

The upper-left cell of the data table range contains the formula to be evaluated. This formula must refer to the input cells.

The cells below the formula contain the various input values for one variable. These values will be used for input cell 1. The cells to the right of the formula contain the various input values for the other variable. These values will be used for input cell 2. Be sure that the formula refers correctly to the two input cells so that the proper input values get plugged into the correct part of the formula.

After the data table has been calculated, each cell in the results range contains the result of evaluating the formula with the input values in that cell's row and column.

Suppose, for example, that you want to create a data table which shows the monthly payments on a $12,000 loan at four interest rates—9%, 10%, 11%, and 12%—and three loan periods of 24, 36, and 48 months.

First, decide on a location for the two input cells. You can use cells B7 and B8. Put identifying labels in the adjacent cells A7 and A8.

Because you have three values of one variable and four values of the other, the data table range will be four cells by five cells in size. You can use the range C3..F7. Enter the following @PMT formula in cell C3:

   @PMT(12000,B7/12,B8)

Next, enter the values in the data table range. Enter the four interest rates in the range C4..C7, and the three loan terms in D3..F3.

Now, select /Data Table 2, specify C3..F7 as the table range, enter B7 as input cell 1, and enter B8 as input cell 2. 1-2-3 calculates the data table, as shown in figure 10.44.

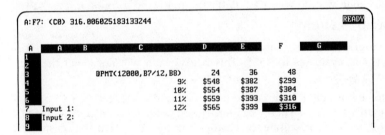

Fig. 10.44.
A table of loan payment amounts created with /Data Table 2.

If you create a data table larger than the screen, you can use /Worksheet Titles to freeze the input values on the screen as you scroll through the results cells.

Creating a Cross-Tabulated Table with /Data Table 2

/Data Table 2 can be used to create a cross-tabulation analysis of records in a data table. To perform this kind of analysis, you need to be familiar with 1-2-3 data tables and the related terms and concepts, and with the database @ functions.

A type 2 cross-tabulation analysis requires two blank input cells, which can be anywhere in the worksheet as long as they are in adjacent columns of the same row. The cell immediately above each input cell must contain the name of the data table field for which that input cell will serve as a criterion.

The structure of a data table range for a type 2 cross-tabulation analysis is similar to that for a type 2 what-if analysis. The upper-left cell contains the formula to be evaluated. When using a database @ function, the function argument that specifies the criteria range should refer to the two input cells *and* the field names above them. The top row and left column contain the values or labels that will be used as criteria when database records are selected for the formula calculations. The contents of the cells in the left column of the data table range will be used as criteria in input cell 1, while the contents of the cells in the top row of the data table range will be used as criteria in input cell 2. Be sure that the data table range input values correspond correctly with the input cells; otherwise, the analysis will produce erroneous results.

After the data table has been calculated, each cell in the results range contains the result of the formula at the top left of the data table range applied to those database records that meet the criteria in that cell's row and column headers.

Suppose that you want to create the type 2 cross-tabulation table shown in figure 10.41. To create a data table showing each sales representative's total sales to each customer, you need a type 2 data table that is cross-tabulated based on the SALESREP and CUSTOMER fields of the database table. Use cells A11 and B11 for the input cells, and put the field names above them in cells A10 and B10.

The data table range will be A13..E17. Enter the following formula in cell A13:

@DSUM(A1..D7,3,A10..B11)

Because the criteria range is empty, the formula sums the AMOUNT column for all the records and evaluates to 7555. This is okay, and will not affect the creation of the data table.

The criteria for input cell 1 (that is, the input cell under SALESREP) will be the sales representatives' names. There are four names; enter them in cells A14..A17. For input cell 2, the criteria will be the customer names. Enter the four customer names in B13..E13.

Note that the values or labels used as criteria in a type 2 cross-tabulation table *must* exactly match the entries in the database. When working with a large database, you can use /Data Query Unique to extract a nonduplicating list of all entries in a particular field, and then use this list as the left column or (after transposing) the top row of the data table range.

The next step is to select /**D**ata **T**able **2** and specify A13..E17 as the table range, **A11** as input cell 1, and **B11** as input cell 2. The results are shown in figure 10.45.

Creating a Type 3 Data Table

A type 3 data table shows the effects of changing three variables in a single formula. The "third dimension" of a type 3 data table is represented by a three-dimensional worksheet range; the table spans two or more worksheets.

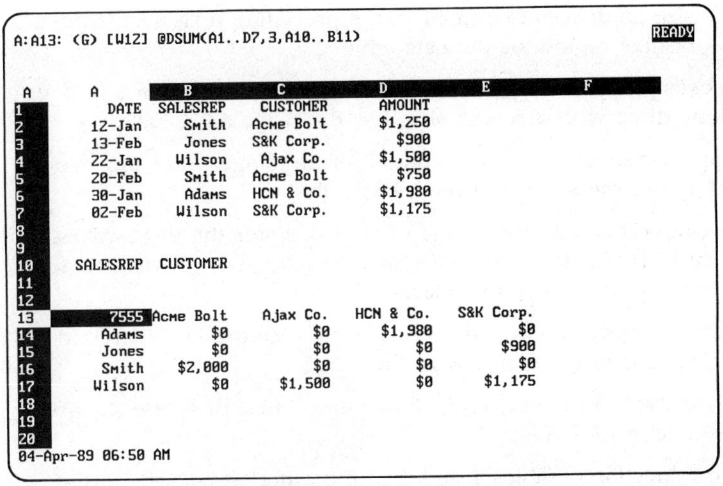

```
A:A13: (G) [W12] @DSUM(A1..D7,3,A10..B11)                    READY

 A      A           B          C          D          E          F
 1          DATE   SALESREP   CUSTOMER    AMOUNT
 2         12-Jan   Smith     Acme Bolt   $1,250
 3         13-Feb   Jones     S&K Corp.     $900
 4         22-Jan   Wilson    Ajax Co.    $1,500
 5         20-Feb   Smith     Acme Bolt     $750
 6         30-Jan   Adams     HCN & Co.   $1,980
 7         02-Feb   Wilson    S&K Corp.   $1,175
 8
 9
10        SALESREP  CUSTOMER
11
12
13            7555 Acme Bolt  Ajax Co.   HCN & Co.   S&K Corp.
14         Adams      $0         $0      $1,980         $0
15         Jones      $0         $0         $0        $900
16         Smith   $2,000        $0         $0          $0
17         Wilson     $0      $1,500        $0      $1,175
18
19
20
04-Apr-89 06:50 AM
```

Fig. 10.45.
/Data Table 2
used to create a
cross-
tabulation
analysis of
data contained
in a data table.

The structure of a type 3 data table is an extension of the type 2 data table structure. The different values of variables 1 and 2 are represented by different rows and columns. The new variable, the third one, is located in the upper-left corner of the data table range; the different values of variable 3 are represented by different worksheets.

Reminder:
A type 3 data table shows the effects of changing three variables in a single formula.

A type 3 data table range spans a three-dimensional region. The size of the region is determined as follows:

Number of rows = (values of variable 1) + 1
Number of columns = (values of variable 2) + 1
Number of worksheets = (values of variable 3)

You also need three input cells. These cells can be located anywhere in any worksheet, but are often grouped together for convenience. You should identify the input cells with labels in adjacent cells.

The formula evaluated in a type 3 data table must refer to all three input cells. Remember that a strict correlation exists between the input cells and the variables they represent. Input cell 1 refers to the variable whose values are located in the first column of the data table range. Input cell 2 refers to the variable whose values are located in the first row of the data table range. Input cell 3 refers to the variable whose values are located in the upper-left corner of the data table range in each worksheet. If the formula does not refer to the input cells correctly, the data table produces erroneous results.

Calculating loan payments is a perfect application for a type 3 data table because the relevant formula uses three variables: principal, interest rate, and term. You can create a data table that calculates monthly payments for three principal amounts, three interest rates, and three loan periods. To establish a type 3 data table range for this application, follow these steps:

1. Using the size guidelines explained in the preceding text, decide on an empty worksheet region for the data table.

   For this example, you need a data table range that is four rows by four columns by three worksheets in size. Use the range A:C2..C:F5.

2. In the top worksheet in the first column of the range, enter the values for variable 1 in the second through last cells.

   In this example, the interest rate is variable 1. Enter the three values for interest rate—**10%**, **11%**, and **12%**—in cells A:C3..A:C5. Format these cells as **Percent** with 0 decimal places.

3. In the same worksheet, enter the values for variable 2 in the second through last cells in the first row in the range.

   Term is variable 2 in the example. Enter the values for term—**24**, **36**, and **48**—in cells A:D2..A:F2.

4. Copy the values for variables 1 and 2 to the other worksheets in the range.

   You need two other worksheets for this data table. To insert these other worksheets, select /Worksheet Insert Sheet After and enter **2**. Next, select /Worksheet Window Perspective to view all three active worksheets. Your screen should appear as shown in figure 10.46.

   When using a type 3 data table for what-if analysis, the values for variables 1 and 2 usually will be the same in each worksheet. You therefore can use the Copy command to copy the information entered in Steps 2 and 3 to the other worksheets in the data table range.

   Now, copy the values you entered in worksheet A to worksheets B and C. To do so, press Ctrl-PgDn to move the cell pointer to worksheet A, and then select Copy and enter A:C2..A:F5 as the FROM range. Next, enter B:C2..C:C2 as the TO range. Figure 10.47 shows the worksheet after performing these copy operations.

5. In the top-left cell of the data table range, enter the values for variable 3. Enter a different value in the corresponding cell in each worksheet.

   Principal is variable 3. Enter the values for principal—**10000**, **15000**, and **20000**—in cells A:C2..C:C2. Format these cells as Currency with 0 decimal places.

The range for the data table is now established. Next, you need to select the input cells. Use cells A:B2..A:B4 for input cells 1–3. Also, put identifying labels in cells A:A2..A:A4. The worksheet now appears as shown in figure 10.48.

Enter the payment formula in any cell outside the data table range—for example, B6. Use the following 1-2-3 function for calculating loan payments:

payment = @PMT(A,B,C)

Cue:
Use the Copy command to copy the variable information to other worksheets in the data table.

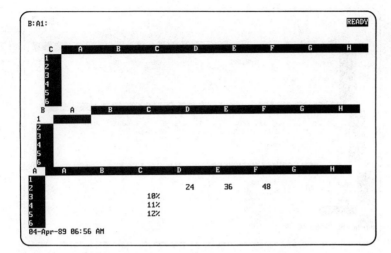

Fig. 10.46.
Three active worksheets, with data table values entered in worksheet A.

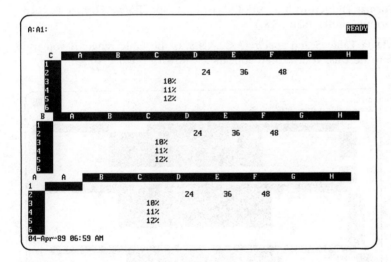

Fig. 10.47.
The data table values from worksheet A copied to worksheets B and C.

In this function, payment is the periodic loan payment, A is the principal amount, B is the interest rate per period, and C is the number of payment periods. For your formula, enter the following:

@PMT(A:B4,A:B2/12,A:B3)

Because payment periods are expressed in months, you divide the annual interest rate by 12 to obtain the monthly interest rate. (Note that when you enter the @PMT function in B6, you will see ERR. This is normal, as the function is not

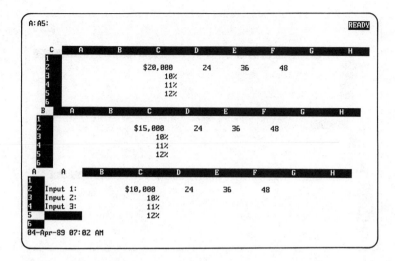

Fig. 10.48.
The input cells and input values.

meant to return a value. The function is to be used in the data table. You may use /**R**ange **F**ormat **H**idden to hide the ERR from B6, or /**R**ange **F**ormat **T**ext to display the formula rather than ERR.)

Now, select /**D**ata **T**able **3** and specify A:C2..C:F5 as the table range. If you use POINT mode to do this, your screen appears as shown in figure 10.49.

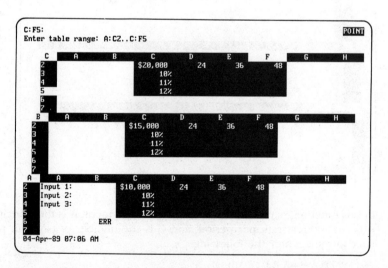

Fig. 10.49.
A three-dimensional data table range specified with POINT mode.

Finally, specify **A:B6** as the formula cell, **A:B2** as input cell 1, **A:B3** as input cell 2, and **A:B4** as input cell 3. Format the results range A:D3..C:F5 as Currency. The results are shown in figure 10.50.

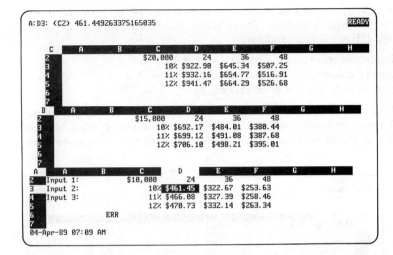

Fig. 10.50.
The three-dimensional table showing the loan payment amount for different interest rates, loan periods, and loan amounts.

Creating a Three-Dimensional Cross-Tabulated Table

Using a type 3 data table for cross-tabulation analysis is analogous to using this table for what-if analysis. Instead of representing three variables plugged into a formula, the three dimensions of a type 3 cross-tabulation analysis hold labels or values. These labels or values are used as criteria to select records from a data table based on three of the table's fields. The cells in the results area each contain the result of a calculation, and the calculation is based on those database records that meet the three criteria for that cell. For example, with information in a sales database, a manager of a car dealership could use a type 3 cross-tabulation analysis to determine the total dollar sales for each car model, by each salesperson, for each month of the year.

As with the type 1 and 2 cross-tabulation tables, you need to be familiar with 1-2-3 data tables and the database functions before you can use type 3 cross-tabulation tables effectively.

To create a type 3 cross-tabulation table, you need three blank input cells in adjacent columns of the same row. The cell immediately above each input cell must contain the name of the database field for which that input cell serves as a criterion.

You also need a formula; this formula can be located in any worksheet cell outside the data table range. When you use a database function, refer to the six-cell range that contains the input cells and field names as the criteria range.

The structure of a type 3 data table for cross-tabulation analysis is similar to the structure for type 3 what-if analysis. The structure also spans a three-dimensional region with the following size guidelines:

Number of rows = (# criteria for field 1) + 1
Number of columns = (# criteria for field 2) + 1
Number of worksheets = (# criteria for 3)

Figure 10.51 shows a 1-2-3 database of sales records. Each record shows the salesperson's name, the month and state of the sale, and the sale amount. You can create a table that summarizes each individual's total sales in each state for each month.

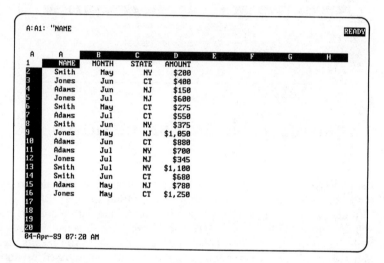

Fig. 10.51.
A database containing information to be analyzed with /Data Table 3.

Use the following steps to establish a type 3 cross-tabulation data table range for this application:

1. Using the preceding size guidelines, decide on an empty worksheet region for the data table.

   Move to the blank area of the worksheet where you will set up the data table. For this example, use A:A23..C:D26 as the data table range.

2. In the top worksheet, enter the values or labels to be used as criteria for the field (input cell 1). Make these entries in the second through last cells of the first column of the range.

   Copy the field names to A:A20..A:C20 and use this as the input cell range for the example.

3. In the same worksheet, enter the values or labels to be used as criteria for the field (input cell 2). Make these entries in the second through last cells of the first row of the range.

   For the example, enter the labels for the NAME and STATE criteria as shown in figure 10.52.

4. Copy the values or labels for input cells 1 and 2 to the other worksheets.

   When using a type 3 data table for cross-tabulation analysis, the criteria for the fields associated with input cells 1 and 2 do not need to be the same in each worksheet, but they usually are. You therefore can use the Copy command to copy the information entered in Steps 2 and 3 to the other worksheets in the data table range.

   Using the procedures described for creating a type 3 what-if analysis, create two more worksheets for the example, switch to perspective view, and copy the NAME and STATE criteria to worksheets B and C.

5. In the top left cell of the data table range, enter the values or labels to be used as criteria for the field (input cell 3). Enter a different criterion in the corresponding cell in each worksheet.

   For the example, enter the MONTH criteria in cells A:A23..C:A23.

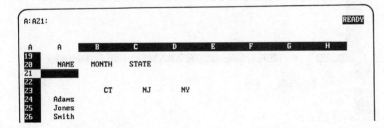

Fig. 10.52.
The data table range for a type 3 cross-tabulation analysis.

The data table range is now established. Your screen should appear as shown in figure 10.53. In this example, the default label prefix is set for right-justification.

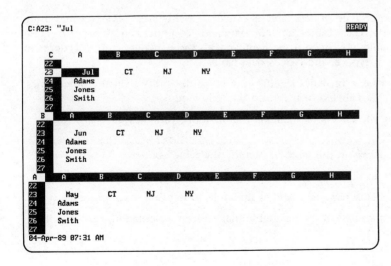

Fig. 10.53.
The three-dimensional data table range.

Return the cell pointer to worksheet A and enter the required formula in cell E20:

@DSUM(A1..D16,3,A20..C21)

Select /**D**ata **T**able **3** and enter A:A23..C:D26 as the table range. Enter **A:E20** as the formula cell, **A:A21** as input cell 1, **A:C21** as input cell 2, and **A:B21** as input cell 3. After formatting the result cells as Currency with 0 decimal places, your screen should look like the one shown in figure 10.54.

Fig. 10.54.
The completed three-dimensional cross-tabulation analysis.

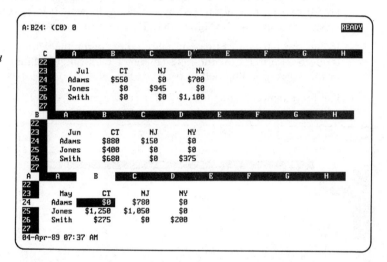

Creating a Labeled Data Table

The most flexible type of data table is called a *labeled data table*, created using Release 3's new /**D**ata **T**able **L**abeled command. To understand how to create a labeled data table, you need to be familiar with the concepts and procedures in creating type 1, type 2, and type 3 data tables.

Cue:
For more flexibility in creating data tables, use the /Data Table Labeled command.

A labeled data table provides significantly more flexibility than the other types. With /**D**ata **T**able **L**abeled, you can do the following:

- Examine the effects of changing one or more variables on one or more formulas

- Include labels in the table to identify the table contents

- Use data in different worksheet areas as input for the data table

- Include blank rows and text in the table to improve its appearance

- Include formulas in the data table that perform calculations on the table results

Figures 10.55 and 10.56 show a table created with /**D**ata **T**able **L**abeled. Figure 10.55 shows only one worksheet of a two-worksheet table. Figure 10.56 shows both worksheets.

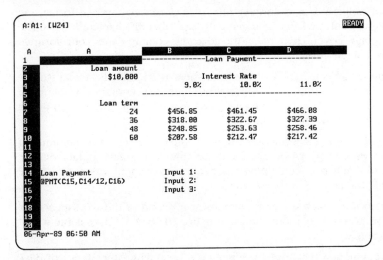

Fig. 10.55.
One worksheet in a two-worksheet table created with /Data Table Labeled.

Fig. 10.56.
Both worksheets in the two-worksheet table.

When creating a labeled data table, keep in mind the terms that follow.

The *formula range* is the worksheet range that contains the formula(s). This formula(s) calculates the data table results, plus contains labels that identify the formulas. In figure 10.55, A14..A15 is the formula range.

The *formula-label range* contains copies of the labels in the formula range. The formula-label range also may contain blank cells, other labels, and values. The placement of labels in the formula-label range is used to determine the following:

which formula is used with the various input values of the data table, and where the calculation results are placed. In figure 10.55, B1..D1 is the formula-label range.

A formula-label range also can contain *label-fill characters*, special formatting characters used to center a label. You generally use label-fill characters when the formula-label range covers two or more adjacent columns and your formula range contains a single formula.

A *row-variable range* is a region of the worksheet that contains rows of input values, organized by columns. A row-variable range may contain one or more columns, with each column containing a separate set of input variables. In figure 10.55, A7..A10 is the row-variable range.

A *column-variable range* is a region of the worksheet that contains columns of input values, organized by rows. A column-variable range may contain one or more rows, with each row containing a separate set of input values. In figure 10.55, B4..D4 is the column-variable range.

A *worksheet-variable range* is a three-dimensional region of the worksheet that contains one or more sets of input values. In figure 10.56, A:A3..B:A3 is the worksheet-variable range.

The *input cells* function just like the input cells used with other types of data tables. You need one input cell for each variable. In figure 10.55, C14..C16 are the input cells.

/Data Table Labeled does not require you to specify a data table range. The location of the results area is determined by the locations of the input ranges.

The specific variable ranges you need to create a labeled data table depend on the number of variables being evaluated by the table formulas and on the layout of the results. For example, a labeled data table that evaluates three variables can use all three types of variable ranges—column, row, and worksheet. You also can create a three-variable table by using any two of the three variable range types. A labeled data table that evaluates two variables can have any two variable ranges—a row-variable range and a column-variable range, for example, or a column-variable range and a worksheet-variable range.

Positioning the Results Area

The placement and structure of the variable ranges are important factors in determining the location and layout of the labeled data table. By changing the placement and structure of the variable ranges, you can control the location of the results area, and you can include blank rows, columns, and/or worksheets in the results area.

The results of labeled data table calculations are placed in the worksheet cells at the intersection of the row(s) that contains the nearest vertical range and the column(s) that contains the nearest horizontal range. A vertical range is one arranged in columns, such as a row-variable range. A horizontal range is one arranged in rows, such as a column-variable range. A formula-label range can be either vertical or horizontal.

To determine the placement of the results area, extend the rows that contain the row-variable range horizontally, both left and right, across the worksheet. Then extend the columns that contain the column-variable range, both up and down, along the worksheet. The cells where these "extended" rows and columns intersect are where 1-2-3 places the results area of the labeled data table.

Figure 10.57 shows a slightly modified version of the labeled data table in figure 10.55. The row- and column-variable ranges are adjacent to each other; therefore, there are no blank rows between the ranges and the results area.

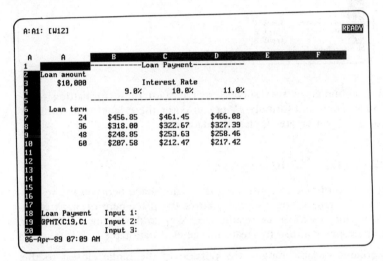

Fig. 10.57.
A labeled data table with no blank rows.

Figure 10.58 shows the same table with the locations of the row- and column-variable ranges changed. The results are placed at the intersection of the rows and columns that contain these variable ranges. This placement inserts blank rows and columns between the variable ranges and the results area.

By placing the vertical and horizontal variable ranges adjacent to each other, you leave no space between the variable ranges and the results area. By placing the variable ranges in separate worksheet regions, you can leave blank rows and/or columns between the variable ranges and the results area.

The same principle applies when working in three dimensions (when using a worksheet-variable range). The results area is placed at the intersection of the rows, columns, and worksheets that contains the variable ranges. By controlling the worksheets in which the variable ranges are placed, you can include blank worksheets between some of the variable ranges and the results area. In a four-worksheet file, for example, you can place the row- and column-variable ranges in worksheet D and the worksheet-variable range in worksheets A and B. 1-2-3 places the results in worksheets A and B only, leaving worksheet C blank.

Cue:
Place blank rows and columns between the variable ranges and the results area.

*Fig. 10.58.
Blank rows
included in the
results area.*

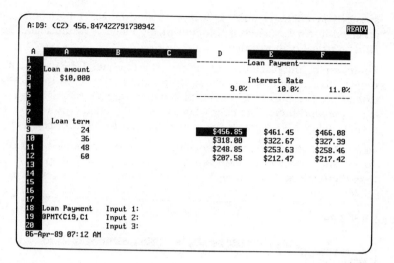

The blank rows, columns, or worksheets created with these formatting techniques can contain labels and formulas. You can enter these labels and formulas either before or after you create the labeled data table.

Formatting the Results Area

The preceding section discussed controlling the blank space *between* the results area and the variable ranges. You also can control the placement of blank rows, columns, and worksheets *within* the results area. You do this by including blank cells in the input ranges you use to create the labeled data table.

For row- and column-variable ranges, the portion of the range closest to the results area is important. If the labeled data table includes a column-variable range, its bottom row is checked for blank cells. If the labeled data table includes a row-variable range, its rightmost column is checked for blank cells. If the formula-label range is the only vertical range or the only horizontal range in the labeled data table, this range is checked for blank cells. A blank cell or cells in any of these places results in the corresponding row(s) and/or column(s) of the results area being left blank (see fig. 10.59).

You can use an analogous procedure to leave worksheets blank within the results area. A blank cell in the bottom or rightmost section of the worksheet-variable range causes the results area in the corresponding worksheet to be left blank. The same applies to a formula-label range that spans multiple worksheets.

You can obtain the same effect you get by including blank cells in the formula-label range by including *dummy labels* in the formula-label range. A dummy label is any label that does not match one of the labels in the formula range.

The blank portions of the results area you create with the preceding techniques can contain labels or formulas. You can enter these labels or formulas either before or after you create the labeled data table.

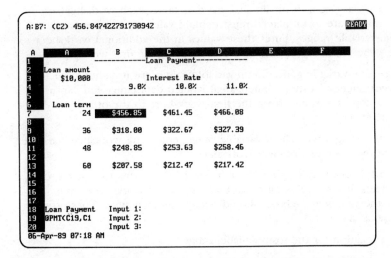

Fig. 10.59.
Blank cells
included in the
column-
variable range.

Creating a Sample Labeled Data Table

This section shows you how to create a labeled data table. The following steps outline the procedure for specifying the variable ranges. After you understand what to enter for each range, you learn the steps you follow in 1-2-3 to enter these ranges.

1. Select a location for the labeled data table.

    The table's *minimum* size (rows × columns × worksheets) is determined by the number of values of each variable being evaluated. The actual size of the results area depends on its specific formatting (for example, inclusion of blank rows and/or columns).

2. Select a location for the input cell(s) and optionally identify the cells with labels in adjacent cells. You need one input cell for each variable being analyzed.

3. Select a worksheet area to hold the formula range.

    The size of this range is two rows by as many columns as you have formulas. Enter the formula(s) in the second row of this range and the formula label(s) in the top row. The formula range must be outside the region that contains the results and the input values.

4. If you are using a row-variable range, enter it either to the right or to the left of the results area. If you are using more than one set of row input values, enter them in adjacent columns in the range.

5. If you are using a column-variable range, enter it either above or below the results area. If you are using more than one set of column-variable range, enter them in adjacent rows in the range.

6. If you are creating a three-dimensional data table, each worksheet in which results are to be placed must contain values in the row- and/or column-variable ranges. Enter these values in the additional worksheet(s) in the same relative positions as they occupy in the first worksheet.

Because row-variable and column-variable values are usually identical in each worksheet of a three-dimensional labeled data table, you can use Copy to copy the values from the first worksheet to the other worksheet(s).

7. If you are using a worksheet-variable range, enter one worksheet-variable value in the same cell of each worksheet.

The worksheet-variable values form a "stack" that spans two or more worksheets. If you are using more than one set of worksheet input values, the values in each set should occupy its own stack. These stacks must be adjacent.

8. Select a location for the formula-label range.

The formula-label range can be located in a row above or below the column-variable range. If you are using a column-variable range, the formula-label range must span the same number of columns as the column-variable range. If you have only one formula label and more than one column, enter the formula and label-fill characters in the first cell of the formula-label range.

The formula-label range also can be located in a column to the left or right of the row-variable range, or in a three-dimensional range between the worksheet-variable range and the results area. If the formula-label range does not span the same number of cells as the corresponding variable range, use the label-fill character.

At this point, you are ready to start working with the /Data Table commands to create the labeled data table. Select /Data Table Labeled and the following menu is displayed:

Formulas Down Across Sheets Input-Cells Label-Fill Go Quit

Table 10.3 explains the functions of these commands.

The following text describes how to create a payment table with /Data Table Labeled. First, start with a blank worksheet and select /Worksheet Global Group Enable to turn on GROUP mode. Next, select /Worksheet Insert Sheet After 1 to insert a single worksheet (worksheet B) in the current file. Now, set the global

Table 10.3
Data Table Labeled Commands

Command	Description
Formulas	Specifies the formula range and the formula-label range
Down	Specifies the row-variable range and input cells
Across	Specifies the column-variable range and input cells
Sheets	Specifies the worksheet-variable range and input cells
Input-Cells	Verifies and/or edits the input cells specified with **Down, Across,** or **Sheets**
Label-Fill	Specifies the label-fill character
Go	Calculates the results and generates the labeled data table
Quit	Returns you to READY mode

column width to 14 and the width of column A to 22. Also, set the global label prefix to **Right**.

Next, enter the following labels in the indicated cells of worksheet A:

B1:	**------------Loan Payment------------**
A2:	**Loan amount**
A6:	**Loan term**
A14:	**Loan Payment**
B14:	**Input 1:**
B15:	**Input 2:**
B16:	**Input 3:**
C3:	**Interest Rate**
B5..D5:	**\-**

After you enter the labels, you can enter the variable values. In cells B4..D4, enter **9%, 10%,** and **11%**; then format those cells as **Percent** with 1 decimal place. Next, in cells A7..A10, enter the term values: **24, 36, 48,** and **60**. The format of these cells does not need to be changed. In cell A3, enter **10000** and format the cell as **Currency** with 0 decimal places.

Next, select **Copy** and enter A:A1..A:D10 as the FROM range and **B:A1** as the TO range. Press Ctrl-PgUp to move the cell pointer to worksheet B and change the value in cell B:A3 to **20000**.

Press Ctrl-PgDn to return the cell pointer to worksheet A. Select **/Worksheet Global Group Disable** to turn off GROUP mode.

In cell A15, enter the following calculation formula:

@PMT(C15,C14/12,C16)

Format that cell as **Text** so that the formula is displayed on-screen.

To create the actual labeled data table, follow these steps:

1. Select **Formulas**, and then specify the formula range and the formula-label range.

   For the example, select **/Data Table Labeled Formulas** and enter A:A14..A:A15 as the formula range and A:B1..A:D1 and the formula-label range.

2. If you are using a row-variable range, select **Down** and specify the row-variable range. If you specify a single-column row-variable range, you next specify a single input cell for the row variable. If you specified a multicolumn row-variable range, 1-2-3 prompts you to specify an input cell for each set (for example, column) of row input variables.

   For the example, select **Down** and enter A:A7..A:A10 as the row-variable range. Press Enter to accept the highlighted range, and then enter **A:C16** as the corresponding input cell.

3. If you are using a column-variable range, select **Across** and specify the column-variable range. If you specify a single-row column-variable range, you next specify a single input cell for the column variable. If you specified a multirow column-variable range, 1-2-3 prompts you to specify an input cell for each set of column input variables.

   For the example, select **Across** and enter A:B4..A:D4 as the column-variable range. Press Enter to accept the highlighted range, and then enter **A:C14** as the corresponding input cell.

4. If you are using a worksheet-variable range, select **Sheets** and specify the worksheet-variable range. If your worksheet-variable range contains only a single "stack," specify the input cell for the worksheet variable. If the worksheet-variable range contains more than one set of variables (for example, multiple "stacks"), 1-2-3 prompts you to specify an input cell for each set of worksheet input variables.

   For the example, select **Sheets** and enter A:A3..B:A3 as the worksheet-variable range. Press Enter to accept the highlighted range, and then enter **A:C15** as the corresponding input cell.

   Worksheet A now looks like figure 10.60, whereas worksheet B looks like figure 10.61.

5. If you want, select **Input-Cells** to verify and edit the addresses of variable ranges and input cells. 1-2-3 cycles through each set of variable ranges and input cells, displaying the addresses you initially entered. Press Enter to accept the original entries or specify new addresses.

6. If you are using label-fill characters but do not want to use the default hyphen (−), select **Label-Fill** and enter the character you want to use (for example, = or *).

7. Select **Go**.

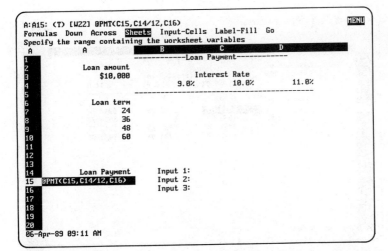

Fig. 10.60.
Worksheet A,
while setting
up /Data Table
Labeled.

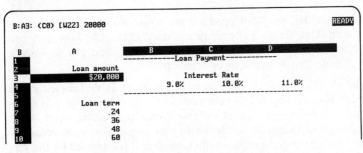

Fig. 10.61.
Worksheet B,
while setting
up /Data Table
Labeled.

1-2-3 evaluates the formulas using the input values in the input ranges. The result of each calculation is placed in the location defined by the intersection of the corresponding row, column, and worksheet.

After formatting the results range A:B7..B:D10 as Currency with 2 decimal places, the data table is completed (see figs. 10.62 and 10.63).

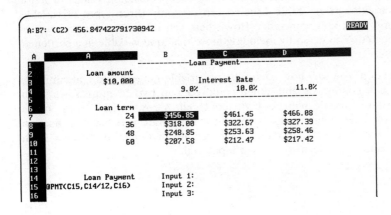

Fig. 10.62.
Worksheet A of
the completed
data table.

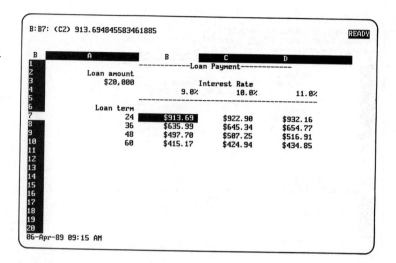

Fig. 10.63.
Worksheet B of
the completed
data table.

You may have noticed that you can produce the same information in figures 10.62 and 10.63 with /**Data Table 3.** By using a labeled data table, however, you have more flexibility than you do with a type 3 data table. You can produce a formatted, labeled table that is easier to understand.

After creating a labeled data table, if you return to the /**Data Table Labeled** menu and select **Down, Across,** or **Sheet,** 1-2-3 remembers the variable range you originally specified. If you accept the original variable range by pressing Enter, 1-2-3 "forgets" the input cell originally associated with that range. You must respecify the input cell. As an alternative, specify another input cell referenced by the formulas used in another data table. This method allows you to use the same sets of input values in different labeled data tables with only a few keystrokes.

Using More Than Three Variables

Reminder:
You can use more
than three variables
in a data table.

A labeled data table can calculate formulas based on changing values of more than three variables. /**Data Table Labeled** can use only three types of variable ranges: column, row, and worksheet. How, then, can more than three variables be accommodated? You do so by including more than one variable in a particular variable range.

In the last section, you saw how each type of variable range could contain more than one part. A column-variable range could contain two or more rows. Each row is a separate variable with its own input cell. A row-variable range could contain two or more columns. Each column is a separate variable with its own input cell. A worksheet-variable range could contain two or more "stacks." Each stack is a separate variable with its own input cell.

When setting up a variable range that contains more than one variable, you must organize the values in a certain way. For the three types of variable input ranges, note the following guidelines:

- For row-variable ranges, the values that change with the greatest frequency must be in the rightmost column.

- For column-variable ranges, the values that change with the greatest frequency must be in the bottom row.

- For worksheet-variable ranges, the values that change with the greatest frequency must be the bottom or rightmost group of cells, depending on the orientation of the range.

Figure 10.64 shows two row-variable ranges, each containing two variables. The row-variable range in B3..C11 is valid because the variable that changes fastest $(10,20,30)$ is in the rightmost column. The values in F3..G11 do *not* constitute a valid row-variable range because the variable that changes the fastest is in the leftmost column.

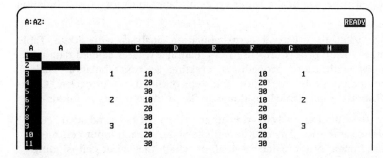

Fig. 10.64. Valid and invalid row-variable ranges.

Figure 10.65 shows a labeled data table that uses one variable range which contains two variables. This labeled data table provides the same information as the labeled data table in figures 10.62 and and 10.63, but does so in a single worksheet. While this table contains only three variables, the principles are easily extended to four or more variables.

In this worksheet, the row-variable range is C7..D15. The input cell for the first row variable, Loan Amount, is B15. The input cell for the second row variable, Loan Term, is B16.

Creating a Cross-Tabulated Table with /Data Table Labeled

As with /**Data Table 3**, you can use /**Data Table Labeled** to perform a cross-tabulation analysis of data contained in a data table. Before reading this section,

Fig. 10.65.
A variable
range with two
variables used
to construct a
three-variable
labeled data
table in a
single
worksheet.

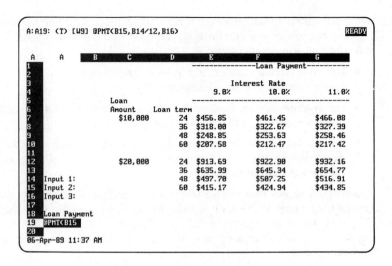

you need to be familiar with the structure of 1-2-3 databases, with the database functions, and with the use of the other types of data tables for cross-tabulation analysis.

The procedure used to create a cross-tabulation analysis with /**Data Table Labeled** is similar to the procedures used in creating a what-if labeled data table. If you're familiar with those procedures, creating a cross-tabulation analysis should not present any problems. Follow the steps outlined in the section "Creating a Sample Labeled Data Table." In doing so, keep these points in mind:

- For a cross-tabulation analysis, the input cells must be in adjacent columns of the same row. The cell immediately above each input cell must contain the name of the database field for which that input cell is going to serve as the criterion.

- For cross-tabulation analysis, the formulas are database functions. Each formula must refer to the input cells as the criteria range.

- When performing a cross-tabulation analysis, the variable ranges can contain multiple variables, as described in the previous steps for a /**Data Table Labeled** what-if analysis.

- 1-2-3 evaluates the formulas based on the database records that meet the criteria in the input ranges. The result of each calculation is placed in the location defined by the intersection of the corresponding row, column, and worksheet.

- If, when creating either type of labeled table, you select **G**o and no error message appears, but the results area remains blank, compare the spelling of the labels in the formula range with those in the formula-label range. They must match exactly for /**Data Table Labeled** to work. Also, if you are using label-fill characters, check to see that the fill character you are using is correct.

Cue:
If the results area
of a labeled table
is blank, check the
spelling of the
labels in the
formula and
formula-label
ranges.

- Because of its complexity, /Data Table Labeled offers many opportunities for error. You may obtain results that appear to be fine, but which are incorrect because of a misassigned input cell or some other error. Before staking your or your company's future on the results of a /Data Table Labeled analysis, check the results carefully.

Caution:
Check the results of a labeled table carefully; if the table is not set up correctly, errors may result.

Using Database Functions

1-2-3's database functions are similar to the worksheet functions but have been modified to manipulate database fields. Like the standard functions, the database functions perform in one simple statement calculations that would otherwise require several statements. This efficiency and ease of application make these functions excellent tools. The database functions are described in table 10.4.

Cue:
Use the database functions to summarize your database selectively.

Table 10.4
Database Functions

Function	Description
@DCOUNT	Gives the number of items in a list
@DSUM	Sums the values of all the items in a list
@DMIN	Gives the minimum of all the items in a list
@DMAX	Gives the maximum of all the items in a list
@DSTD	Gives the standard deviation of all the items in a list
@DVAR	Gives the variance of all the items in a list
@DAVG	Gives the arithmetic mean of all the items in a list
@DGET	Extracts a value or label from a field in a database
@DQUERY	Sends a command to an external data management program
@DSTDS	Calculates the sample standard deviation of values in a field of a database
@DVARS	Calculates the sample variance of values in a field of a database

The general format of these functions is

@DSUM(input range,offset,criteria range)

The one exception to this format is @DQUERY, which is discussed later in this section.

The input and criteria ranges are the same as those used by the /Data Query command. The input range specifies the database or part of a database to be scanned, and the criteria range specifies which records are to be selected. The offset indicates which field to select from the database records; the offset value must be either zero or a positive integer. A value of zero indicates the first column in the data table, a one indicates the second column, and so on.

Suppose that you want to compute the mean, variance, and standard deviation of the average interest rates offered by money market funds for a given week. (If you are unfamiliar with the terms *mean*, *variance*, and *standard deviation*, you can read more about them in Chapter 6.) This chapter shows you how to use the database functions for database applications.

Figure 10.66 shows the Money Market database and the results of the various database functions. Notice that the functions to find the maximum and minimum rates of return are also included.

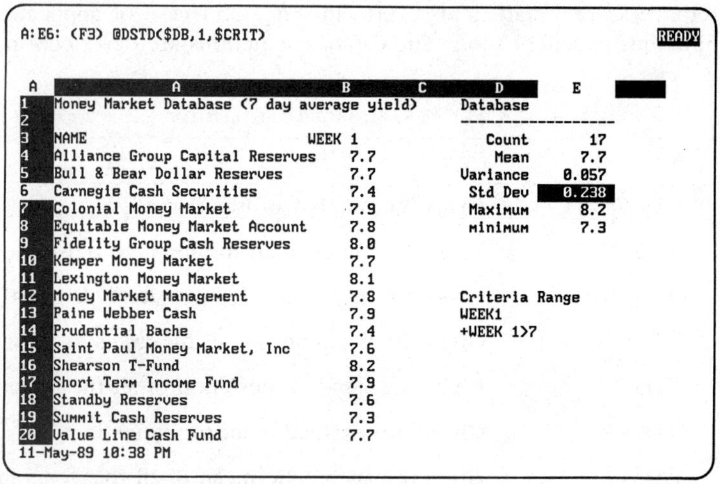

Fig. 10.66.
Database
functions used
with the Money
Market
database.

```
A:E6: (F3) @DSTD($DB,1,$CRIT)                                        READY

A              A                        B        C        D         E
1  Money Market Database (7 day average yield)         Database
2                                                       ------------------
3  NAME                           WEEK 1                    Count      17
4  Alliance Group Capital Reserves   7.7                    Mean      7.7
5  Bull & Bear Dollar Reserves       7.7                 Variance    0.057
6  Carnegie Cash Securities          7.4                  Std Dev    0.238
7  Colonial Money Market             7.9                  Maximum     8.2
8  Equitable Money Market Account    7.8                  Minimum     7.3
9  Fidelity Group Cash Reserves      8.0
10 Kemper Money Market               7.7
11 Lexington Money Market            8.1
12 Money Market Management           7.8            Criteria Range
13 Paine Webber Cash                 7.9            WEEK1
14 Prudential Bache                  7.4            +WEEK 1>7
15 Saint Paul Money Market, Inc      7.6
16 Shearson T-Fund                   8.2
17 Short Term Income Fund            7.9
18 Standby Reserves                  7.6
19 Summit Cash Reserves              7.3
20 Value Line Cash Fund              7.7
11-May-89 10:38 PM
```

In the example, the following functions and ranges are used:

Count	@DCOUNT(A3..B20,1,D13..D14)
Mean	@DAVG(A3..B20,1,D13..D14)
Variance	@DVAR(A3..B20,1,D13..D14)
Std. Dev.	@DSTD(A3..B20,1,D13..D14)
Maximum	@DMAX(A3..B20,1,D13..D14)
Minimum	@DMIN(A3..B20,1,D13..D14)

Figure 10.66 shows that the week's mean return for 17 different money market funds works out to an annual percentage rate of 7.7 (cell E4) with a variance of .057 (cell E5). One standard deviation below a mean of 7.7 is 7.46. One standard deviation above a mean of 7.7 is 7.94.

The result of the @DMIN function (cell E8) shows that Summit Cash Reserves returns the lowest rate at 7.3 percent. This value is almost two standard deviations below the mean. That figure—two standard deviations below the mean—is computed as follows:

Two Std. Devs. below mean 7.7 − (2 × .238) = 7.22

Because approximately 95 percent of the population falls within plus or minus two standard deviations of the mean, Summit Cash Reserves is close to being in the lowest 2.5 percent of the population of money market funds for that week; 5 percent is divided by 2 because the population is assumed to be normal. (See Chapter 6 for further discussion of how to interpret the statistical functions.)

Conversely, the Shearson T-Fund returns 8.2 percent, the highest rate. The @DMAX function has determined the highest rate (cell B16) to be just over two standard deviations above the mean, the highest 2.5 percent of the population.

By setting up the proper criteria, you can analyze any portion of the database you want. How do the statistics change if funds returning less than 7.5 percent are excluded from the statistics? Figure 10.67 gives the answer.

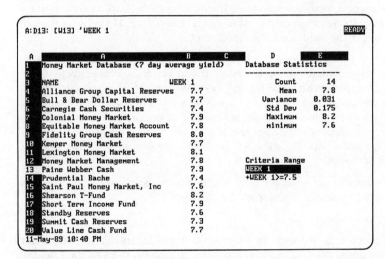

Fig. 10.67. Money fund analysis with funds earning less than 7.5 percent excluded.

Obviously, the database functions can tell you a great deal about the database as a whole and about how to interpret the values contained in it. If you add several more weeks' data to the database, as shown in figure 10.68, the database functions also can be used to analyze all or part of the larger database.

You can use all the methods you have seen so far to interpret the statistics in figure 10.68. The input, offset, and criteria ranges used for the data from the third week of the example are the following:

Input range   A3..G20

Offset   3 (for the fourth column)

Criteria range   I13..I14

Fig. 10.68.
Additional
money fund
data.

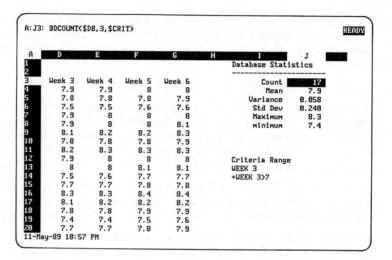

From this information, you can determine how the formulas have been set up for each week. The criteria range displayed in figure 10.68 (I13..I14) shows the criteria used to select the values for the third week.

Two database @ functions new with Release 3 are @DSTDS and @DVARS, which calculate the sample standard deviation and variance, respectively. Compare these @ functions with @DSTD and @DVAR, which calculate the population standard deviation and variance, respectively. When you are evaluating a small number of observations, the sample standard deviation and variance values will give more accurate results than the population values. Chapter 6 explains the statistical formulas used for these @ functions; the formulas are the same as for @STDS and @VARS.

Another new database @ function is @DGET, which extracts a value or label from a field in the database. The format for @DGET is

@DGET(input,field,criteria)

Input, field, and criteria are used in exactly the same manner as for the other database @ functions. @DGET returns the value or label in the specified field of the record that matches the specified criteria.

To see how @DGET works, return to the database first shown in figure 10.66. Suppose that you want to find the name of the firm, if any, offering an 8.2 percent return. In cell D14, enter the criterion **+WEEK 1=8.2**. In cell D4, enter the following formula:

@DGET(A3..B20,"NAME",D13..D14)

The @DGET function returns Shearson T-Fund, which is the only firm on the list that offers an 8.2 percent return (see fig. 10.69). If no elements in the database match the criteria, @DGET returns ERR. More important, @DGET returns

ERR if more than one element in the database matches the criteria. Therefore, if you use @DGET and it returns ERR, you must determine what has caused the error.

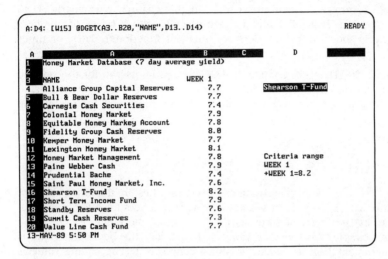

Fig. 10.69.
The results of
the @DGET
function.

A function for use with external tables is @DQUERY, which is similar to the /Data External Other Control command (see the section "Working with External Databases"). With @DQUERY, you may use in the criteria range for record selection a function that belongs to the external database management program. The @DQUERY function, however, will not work with the sample driver supplied with Release 3 of 1-2-3. Other drivers that support this function may become available.

You use the following format for @DQUERY:

  @DQUERY (external function,arguments,arg2...)

The external function is the name of the function in the external database management program, and the arguments are the values that the external function uses. You can include any additional arguments (arg2...) required by the external function; the arguments are separated by a comma.

To understand how @DQUERY works, suppose that your database management program contains a function to match data phonetically. The function is called LIKE, and it has one argument: the data you are matching. For example, LIKE("SMITH") will match the names Smith, Smyth, and Smythe.

In the criteria range, you type @**DQUERY("LIKE","SMITH")**. The @DQUERY function causes the matches to be phonetic because of the use of the LIKE function from the external database management program.

When you enter the @DQUERY function in the cell, the result that you see in the cell is the external function name. In other words, when you type the function @**DQUERY("LIKE","SMITH")**, LIKE is displayed in the cell.

Filling Ranges

Cue:
*Use /Data Fill to
enter a series of
numbers or dates
that increment at
the same value.*

/Data Fill, the command for filling ranges, is useful when combined with the other database commands mentioned earlier in this chapter, particularly /Data Table and /Data Sort. /Data Fill fills a range of cells with a series of numbers (which can be in the form of numbers, formulas, or functions), dates, or times that increase or decrease by a specified increment or decrement.

When you issue the /Data Fill command, 1-2-3 first prompts you for the starting number of the series. The program then asks for the step (or incremental) value to be added to the previous value. Finally, 1-2-3 prompts you for the ending value.

Filling Ranges with Numbers

Consider, for example, the year numbers used as titles in the sales forecast shown in figure 10.70. To enter a sequence of year numbers for a five-year forecast beginning in 1988, you need to start by specifying the range of cells to be filled. In this example, the specified range is B2..F2 and the beginning value is 1988. The incremental or step value in this example is 1. The ending value is 1992 for a five-year forecast.

*Fig. 10.70.
The year
numbers
entered in
B2..F2 with
/Data Fill.*

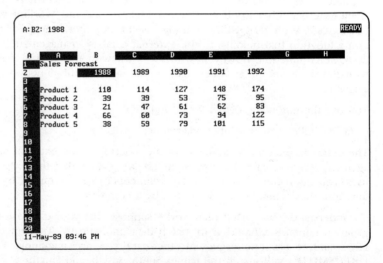

One disadvantage of the /Data Fill command for year numbers is that you cannot center or left-justify the numbers after you have created them. As numbers, they always will be right-justified. If you like the year numbers centered or left-justified, you should type them as labels instead of using this command.

Cue:
*Combine /Data Fill
with /Data Table to
build a list of
interest rates.*

The /Data Fill command also can work with the /Data Table command to build a list of interest rates, as shown in figure 10.71. In the figure, the column of interest rate values was entered with the /Data Fill command. The range B7..B18 was specified for the range of cells to be filled, 0.05 for the starting value, and 0.01 for the step value. For the ending value, 1-2-3 defaults to 8,192, which is far beyond the ending value actually needed. The /Data Fill command, however, fills only the specified range and doesn't fill cells beyond the end of the range.

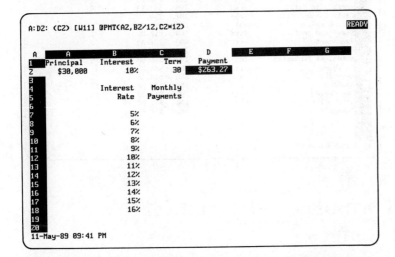

Fig. 10.71.
A worksheet for monthly payment analysis.

The /Data Fill command is useful in combination with /Data Sort. Suppose that you are going to sort a database, and you want to be able to restore the records to their original order if you make a mistake while sorting. All you need to do is add a field to the database and use /Data Fill to fill the field with consecutive numbers. Then you can sort your database. If you find that the results of the sort are unacceptable, you simply sort the database on the new field to return the database to its original order. Figure 10.72 shows an example of a sorted database; figure 10.73 shows the result of the /Data Sort operation.

Cue:
Use /Data Fill with an added field in your database in case you need to restore the original order after sorting.

```
A:D2: (C2) 33                                              READY

      A              A          B        C       D       E        F
    1  COMPANY                 GROUP   SHARES   PRICE  SORT FIELD
    2  Boeheed                 air      100    $33.00     13
    3  Union Allied            chem     100    $61.00     15
    4  Mutual of Pautucket     ins      100    $56.00     10
    5  Rockafella Rail         tran     100    $44.13      4
    6  Rubberstone             rub      200    $23.00      9
    7  Bear and Bull, Inc.     fin      200    $30.75      3
    8  Texagulf                oil      200    $77.00     16
    9  Cable Communications    tele     200    $56.75      5
   10  PetroChem Inc.          oil      200    $61.00      6
   11  Soregums                liq      300    $41.38     11
   12  Pan World               tran     300    $47.88     14
   13  Brute Force Cybernetics tech     400    $11.50      1
   14  Roncomart               ret      400    $31.00      8
   15  Steak and Snail         food     500    $12.00      7
   16  Acme Inc.               tech     500    $16.25      2
   17  Zaymart                 ret      600    $19.25     12
   18
   19
   20
   11-May-89 09:47 PM
```

Fig. 10.72.
The Stocks database sorted by number of shares.

```
A:A1: [W25] 'COMPANY                                            READY

   A              A                B      C      D      E        F
1  COMPANY                        GROUP  SHARES PRICE SORT FIELD
2  Brute Force Cybernetics        tech    400  $11.50      1
3  Acme Inc.                      tech    500  $16.25      2
4  Bear and Bull, Inc.            fin     200  $30.75      3
5  Rockafella Rail                tran    100  $44.13      4
6  Cable Communications           tele    200  $56.75      5
7  PetroChem Inc.                 oil     200  $61.00      6
8  Steak and Snail                food    500  $12.00      7
9  Roncomart                      ret     400  $31.00      8
10 Rubberstone                    rub     200  $23.00      9
11 Mutual of Pautucket            ins     100  $56.00     10
12 Soregums                       liq     300  $41.38     11
13 Zaymart                        ret     600  $19.25     12
14 Boeheed                        air     100  $33.00     13
15 Pan World                      tran    300  $47.88     14
16 Union Allied                   chem    100  $61.00     15
17 Texagulf                       oil     200  $77.00     16
18
19
20
11-May-89 09:48 PM
```

Fig. 10.73.
The Stocks database returned to its original order.

Using Formulas and Functions To Fill Ranges

Reminder:
You can use formulas and functions in beginning and end values in /Data Fill.

In the previous examples, regular numbers have been used for the beginning, incremental, and ending values, but you also can use formulas and functions. If you want to fill a range of cells with incrementing dates, after the range has been set, you can use the @DATE function to set the start value—for example, @DATE(89,6,1). You can use also a cell formula, such as +E4, for the incremental value. In this case, E4 may contain the increment 7 so that you can have increments of one week at a time. You can enter the stop value @DATE(89,10,1), for example; or, if the stop date is in a cell, you can give that cell address as the stop value. 1-2-3 allows many different combinations of commands.

Filling Ranges with Dates or Times

Cue:
Use /Data Fill to enter a series of dates or times in the appropriate format.

The /Data Fill command also lets you fill a worksheet range with a sequence of dates or times without using values, formulas, or functions. You specify the starting and stopping values and the increment between values.

To fill a range with dates or times, you first select /Data Fill. Then you specify the worksheet range to be filled. Next, you enter the start value. To fill a range with dates, enter a start date in any of 1-2-3's date formats except Short International (D5). If you enter a date without the day or the year, 1-2-3 assumes the first day of the month and the current year. To fill a range with times, enter a start time in any of 1-2-3's time formats.

Next, you specify the increment. For dates, enter a value **n** followed by a letter to indicate the increment unit:

d to increment by **n** days
w to increment by **n** weeks
m to increment by **n** months
q to increment by **n** quarters
y to increment by **n** years

For times, enter a value **n** followed by one of the following:

s to increment by **n** seconds
min to increment by **n** minutes
h to increment by **n** hours

Then enter a stop value. For negative increments, the stop value must be smaller than the start value. Enter the stop value as a value or in a valid date or time format.

1-2-3 fills the range top-to-bottom, left-to-right. The first cell is filled with the start value, and each subsequent cell is filled with the value in the previous cell plus the increment. Filling stops when the stop value or the end of the fill range is reached, whichever happens first.

For example, to put a sequence of half-hourly times in column D, select /Data Fill and enter the range D1..D10. For the start value, enter **1:00**; for the increment, enter **30min**; and for the stop value, enter **6:00**.

To put a sequence of biweekly dates in column F, select /Data Fill and enter the range F1..F10. Enter **1-Jan** for the start value, **2w** for the increment, and **07-May** for the stop value.

The results of these commands are shown in figure 10.74. In this worksheet, columns D and F were formatted with /Range Format Other Automatic before the fill operation. When you fill a range formatted as Automatic with a date or time, 1-2-3 formats the range with the same format you use to specify the start and stop date or time.

A:F1: (D2) 32509							READY
A	**A**	**B**	**C**	**D**	**E**	**F**	**G**	**H**
1		10		01:00		01-Jan		
2		11		01:30		15-Jan		
3		12		02:00		29-Jan		
4		13		02:30		12-Feb		
5		14		03:00		26-Feb		
6		15		03:30		12-Mar		
7		16		04:00		26-Mar		
8		17		04:30		09-Apr		
9		18		05:00		23-Apr		
10		19		05:30		07-May		
11								
12								
13								
14								
15								
16								
17								

Fig. 10.74.
The results of using /Data Fill with dates and times.

Note that when you fill with times, 1-2-3 may put in the last cell of the fill range a time that is slightly different from the stop value you specified. A slight loss of accuracy sometimes occurs when 1-2-3 converts between the binary numbers it uses internally and the decimal numbers used for times. To avoid this problem, specify a stop value that is less than one increment larger than the desired stop value. For example, if the increment is 10 minutes and you want the last cell in the range to contain 10:30, specify a stop value between 10:30 and 10:40, such as 10:35.

Creating Frequency Distributions

The command for creating frequency distributions in 1-2-3 is the /Data Distribution command. A *frequency distribution* describes the relationship between a set of classes and the frequency of occurrence of members of each class. A list of consumers with their product preferences illustrates the use of the /Data Distribution command to produce a frequency distribution (see fig. 10.75).

Fig. 10.75.
/Data
Distribution
used to analyze
Taste Preference
data.

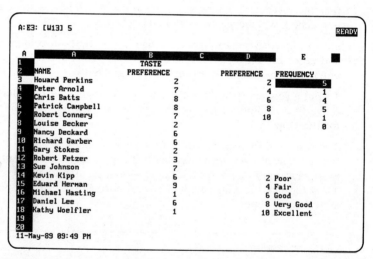

To use the /Data Distribution command, you first specify a values range, which corresponds to the range of Taste Preference numbers in this example. After specifying B3..B18 for the values range, you set up the range of intervals at D3..D7, in what 1-2-3 calls the *bin* range. If you have evenly spaced intervals, the /Data Fill command can be used to enter the values for the bin range. If the intervals are not evenly spaced, you cannot use the /Data Fill command to fill the range.

When you specify these ranges and enter the /Data Distribution command, 1-2-3 creates the results column (E3..E8) to the right of the bin range (D3..D7). The results column, which shows the frequency distribution, is always in the column segment to the right of the bin range and extends one row farther down.

The values in the results column represent the frequency of distribution of the numbers in the values range for each interval. The first interval in the bin range is for values greater than zero and less than or equal to two; the second, for values greater than two and less than or equal to four, and so on. The last value in the results column, in cell E8 just below the corresponding column segment, shows the frequency of leftover numbers (that is, the frequency of numbers that do not fit into an interval classification).

The /**Data** Distribution command can help you create understandable results from a series of numbers. The results are easily graphed, as shown in figure 10.76. A manufacturer looking at this graph would probably start looking for another product or start trying to improve the taste of the current product.

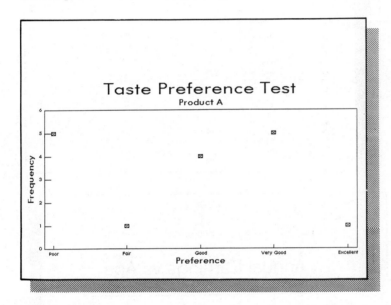

Fig. 10.76.
A graph of the results from the /Data Distribution command.

Using the /Data Regression Command

The /**Data** Regression command gives you a multiple-regression analysis package within 1-2-3. Although most people don't have a need for this advanced feature, if you need to use it, 1-2-3 saves you the cost and inconvenience of buying a stand-alone statistical package for performing a regression analysis.

Use /**Data** Regression when you want to determine the relationship between one set of values (the dependent variable) and one or more other sets of values (the independent variables). Regression analysis has a number of uses in a business setting, including relating sales to price, promotions, and other market factors; relating stock prices to earnings and interest rates; and relating production costs to production levels.

Cue:
Use /Data Regression to determine the relationship between sets of values.

Think of linear regression as a way of determining the "best" line through a series of data points. Multiple regression does this for several variables simultaneously, determining the "best" line relating the dependent variable to the set of independent variables. Consider, for example, a data sample showing Annual Earnings versus Age. Figure 10.77 shows the data; figure 10.78 shows the data plotted as an XY graph.

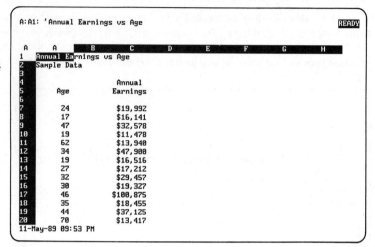

Fig. 10.77.
Annual
Earnings versus
Age data.

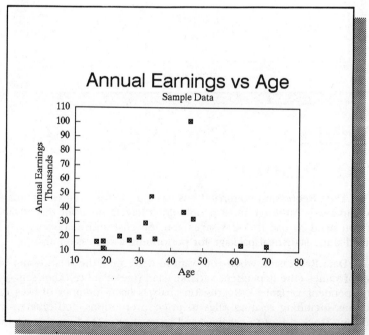

Fig. 10.78.
A graph of
Annual
Earnings versus
Age data.

The /Data Regression command can simultaneously determine how to draw a line through these data points and how well the line fits the data. When you invoke the command, the following menu appears:

X-Range Y-Range Output-Range Intercept Reset Go Quit

Use the X-Range option to select one or more independent variables for the regression. The /Data Regression command can use as many as 75 independent variables. The variables in the regression are columns of values, which means that any data in rows must be converted to columns with /Range Transpose before the /Data Regression command is issued. In this example, the X-Range is specified as A7..A20.

The Y-Range option specifies the dependent variable. The Y-Range must be a single column; in the example, the C7..C20 is specified.

The Output-Range option specifies the upper-left corner of the results range. This should be an unused section of the worksheet, because the output is written over any existing cell contents.

The Intercept option lets you specify whether you want the regression to calculate a constant value. Calculating the constant is the default; in some applications, however, you may need to exclude a constant.

Figure 10.79 shows the results of using the /Data Regression command in the Annual Earnings versus Age example. The results include the value of the constant and the coefficient of the single independent variable that was specified with the X-Range option. The results also include a number of regression statistics that describe how well the regression line fits the data. In this case, the R-Squared value and the standard errors of the constant and the regression coefficient all indicate that the regression line does not explain much of the variation in the dependent variable.

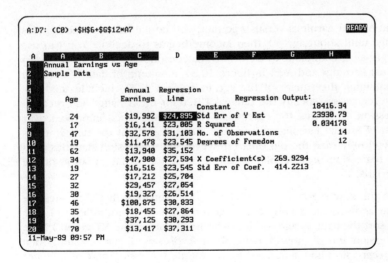

Fig. 10.79.
The results of
/Data
Regression on
Annual
Earnings versus
Age data.

The new data in column D is the computed regression line. These values consist of the constant plus the coefficient of the independent variable times its value in each row of the data. This line can be plotted against the original data, as shown in figure 10.80.

Fig. 10.80.
A plot of
Annual
Earnings versus
Age data, with
a regression
line.

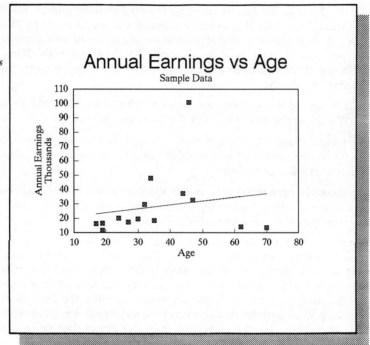

Looking at the Annual Earnings versus Age plot, you notice that income appears to rise with age until about age 50; then income begins to decline. You can use the /Data Regression command to fit a line that describes such a relationship between Annual Earnings and Age. In figure 10.81, a column of data is added in column B containing the square of the age in column A. To include this new column in the regression, specify the range A7..B20 for the X-Range and recalculate the regression. Note that the regression statistics are much improved over the regression of Annual Earnings versus Age. This means that the new line fits the data more closely than the old one. (However, the regression statistics indicate that the regression only "explains" about one-third of the variation of the dependent variable.)

You must add the new regression coefficient to the equation that generates the regression line, and sort the data by age, to generate the new plot in figure 10.82. (You have to sort the data by age to plot the curved line on the XY graph.) Note that the regression line is now a parabola that rises until age 45, and then declines. The regression line generated by a multiple regression may or may not be a straight line, depending on the independent variables that are used.

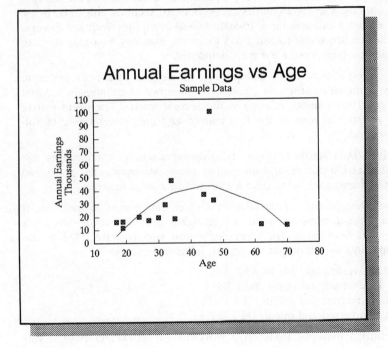

```
A:A1: 'Annual Earnings vs Age                                    READY

     A         B        C        D       E       F       G        H
1  Annual Earnings vs Age
2  Sample Data
3
4              Age X   Annual  Regression
5      Age     AGE    Earnings   Line              Regression Output:
6                                       Constant              -27313.6
7      17      289    $16,141   $5,456  Std Err of Y Est      21359.21
8      19      361    $11,478  $10,789  R Squared             0.294715
9      19      361    $16,516  $10,789  No. of Observations         14
10     24      576    $19,992  $22,373  Degrees of Freedom          11
11     27      729    $17,212  $28,123
12     30      900    $19,327  $32,973  X Coefficient(s)  2712.488 -28.8818
13     32     1024    $29,457  $35,706  Std Err of Coef.  1266.851 14.32767
14     34      156    $47,900  $38,039
15     35     1225    $18,455  $39,056
16     44     1936    $37,125  $43,703
17     46     2116   $100,875  $43,636
18     47     2209    $32,578  $43,452
19     62     3844    $13,940  $28,695
20     70     4900    $13,417  $11,622
11-May-89 10:00 PM
```

Fig. 10.81.
Annual
Earnings versus
Age data, and
the square of
Age.

Fig. 10.82.
A plot of
Annual
Earnings versus
Age data, with
a revised
regression line.

Using the /Data Matrix Command

The /Data Matrix command is a specialized mathematical command that lets you solve systems of simultaneous linear equations and manipulate the resulting solutions. This command is powerful but has limited application in a business setting. If you are using 1-2-3 for certain types of economic analysis or for scientific or engineering calculations, you may find this command valuable.

The /Data Matrix command has a menu with two options: Invert and Multiply. The Invert option lets you invert a nonsingular square matrix of up to 90 rows and columns. Just select the Invert option and highlight the range you want to invert. Then select an output range to hold the inverted solution matrix. You can place the output range anywhere in the worksheet, including on top of the matrix you are inverting.

The time required to invert a matrix is proportional to the cube of the number of rows and columns. A 25-by-25 matrix takes about 10 seconds, and an 80-by-80 matrix takes almost 5 minutes on a 16-MHz 80386 computer with no numeric coprocessor. If you are going to use 1-2-3 to invert matrices, you may want to invest in a numeric coprocessor for your computer.

The Multiply option allows you to multiply two rectangular matrices together in accordance with the rules of matrix algebra. The number of columns in the first matrix must equal the number of rows in the second matrix. The result matrix has the same number of rows as the first matrix, and the same number of columns as the second.

When you select /Data Matrix Multiply, 1-2-3 prompts you for three ranges: the first matrix, the second matrix, and the output range. Multiply is fast compared to Invert, but still may take some time if you multiply large matrices.

Note how the /Data Matrix command affects three-dimensional worksheets. If you specify a three-dimensional input range, 1-2-3 performs inversions on a worksheet-by-worksheet basis. For example, if you specify A:B2..D:D4 as the input range and A:F2 as the output range, the following occurs:

> A:B2..A:D4 is inverted and put in A:F2..A:H4
> B:B2..B:D4 is inverted and put in B:F2..B:H4
> C:B2..C:D4 is inverted and put in C:F2..C:H4
> D:B2..D:D4 is inverted and put in D:F2..D:H4

1-2-3 also performs multiplications on a worksheet-by-worksheet basis if you specify three-dimensional ranges.

Loading Data from Other Programs

Lotus provides several means of importing data from other applications. The Translate utility (see Chapter 7) has options for converting data directly to 1-2-3 worksheets from DIF, dBASE II, dBASE III, and dBASE III Plus files, and from other file formats. You then can access the data by using the /File Retrieve or /File Combine commands from the current worksheet.

Use the /File Import command to read into a current worksheet the data stored on disk as a text file. Depending on the format, these files can be read directly to a range of cells or a column of cells. Specially formatted "numeric" data can be read directly to a range of worksheet cells. ASCII text can be stored as long labels in a single column with one line of the file per cell. You then must disassemble these labels into the appropriate data values or fields by using @ functions or the /Data Parse command.

Finally, you can use certain advanced macro commands (see Chapter 12) to read and write an ASCII sequential file directly from within 1-2-3 advanced macro command programs.

Using the /Data Parse Command

The /Data Parse command is a flexible and easy method of extracting numeric, string, and date data from long labels and placing it in separate columns. For example, suppose that you printed to a disk file a report containing inventory data, and you want to load the print-image file in 1-2-3. After you load the file by using the /File Import command, you must reformat the data with the /Data Parse command.

Cue:
Use /Data Parse to split long labels imported from text files into separate text, number, or date fields.

The /File Import command loads the inventory data into the range A1..A16 (see fig. 10.83). Visually, the data is formatted in a typical worksheet range, such as A1..G16, but the display is misleading. The current cell pointer location is A5; the entire contents of the row exist only in that cell as a long label.

To break the long label columns, move the cell pointer to the first cell to be parsed and select /Data Parse. The following menu then appears:

Format-Line Input-Column Output-Range Reset Go Quit

Use Format-Line to Create or Edit a newly inserted line in the data to be parsed. The Format-Line command specifies the pattern or patterns for splitting the long labels into numbers, labels, and dates.

Use Input-Column to specify the range of cells to be parsed. The input range (contained in just one column) consists of the cell containing the format line, and all cells containing the long labels to be parsed.

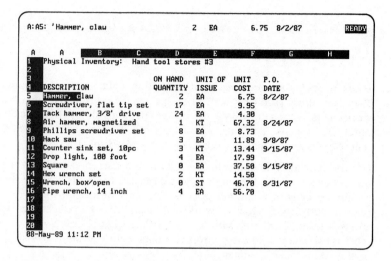

Fig. 10.83.
The results of a
/File Import
command.

Use Output-Range to specify the worksheet range where 1-2-3 will put the parsed data. You can specify a rectangular range or the single cell at the upper left of the range. The output data will have as many rows as there are long labels; the number of columns depends on the format line.

Reset clears the previously set Input-Column and Output-Range. Go performs the parse, based on the specified Input-Column, Format-Lines, and Output-Range.

To parse the data shown in figure 10.83, follow these steps:

1. Move the cell pointer to cell A3, which is the first cell in the range that has the data you want to break into columns. (You do not have to parse the title in cell A1.)

2. Parse the column headings in cells A3..A4, using one format line; and then parse the data in A5..A16, using another format line.

Different format lines are necessary because the data is a mixture of label, numeric, and date data, and because all the headings are labels. Select Format-Line Create. A suggested format line is inserted in the data at A3, in a step that moves the remaining worksheet contents down one line.

After creating a format line, you can edit it by selecting Format-Line again and choosing Edit. Use the format line to mark the column positions and the type of data in those positions. Parse uses the format line to break down the data and move it to its respective columns in the output range.

Combinations of certain letters and special characters comprise format lines. The letters denote the beginning position and the type of data; special symbols define the length of a field and the spacing. Note the following letters and symbols:

Letter/ Symbol	Purpose
D	Marks the beginning of a **D**ate field
L	Marks the beginning of a **L**abel field
S	Marks the beginning of a **S**kip position
T	Marks the beginning of a **T**ime field
V	Marks the beginning of a **V**alue field
>	Defines the continuation of a field. Use one > for each position in the field (excluding the first position).
*	Defines blank spaces (in the data below the format line) that may be part of the block of data in the following cell

Add as many format lines as you need in your data. In the inventory example, you need to enter another format line at cell A6 and specify the format criteria for the data records that follow. Suggested format lines are shown in figure 10.84. To restore the **Parse** menu, press Enter after you finish editing.

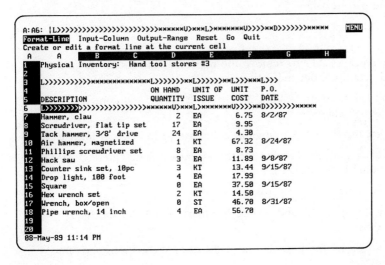

Fig. 10.84.
A format line
edited in a
Parse
operation.

After setting up two format lines in the Physical Inventory example, select **Input-Range** from the **Parse** menu. Point to or type the range A3..A18, which includes format lines, column headings, and data. Continue by selecting **Output-Range** from the **Parse** menu and by specifying A20 as the upper-left corner of a blank range to accept the parsed data. Complete the operation by selecting the **Go** option (see fig. 10.85).

The data displayed in individual cells may not be exactly what you want. You can make a few changes in the format and column width, and you also can add or delete information to make the newly parsed data more usable. These enhance-

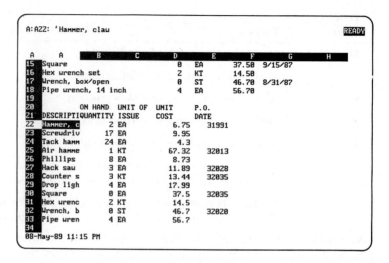

Fig. 10.85.
The results of a
Parse
operation.

```
A:A22: 'Hammer, claw                                                    READY

  A     A          B          C          D          E          F       G          H
 15 Square                               0    EA    37.50  9/15/87
 16 Hex wrench set                       2    KT    14.50
 17 Wrench, box/open                     0    ST    46.70  8/31/87
 18 Pipe wrench, 14 inch                 4    EA    56.70
 19
 20            ON HAND  UNIT OF  UNIT      P.O.
 21 DESCRIPTI QUANTITY  ISSUE    COST      DATE
 22 Hammer, c      2    EA        6.75     31991
 23 Screwdriv     17    EA        9.95
 24 Tack hamm     24    EA        4.3
 25 Air hamme      1    KT       67.32     32013
 26 Phillips       8    EA        8.73
 27 Hack saw       3    EA       11.89     32028
 28 Counter s      3    KT       13.44     32035
 29 Drop ligh      4    EA       17.99
 30 Square         0    EA       37.5      32035
 31 Hex wrenc      2    KT       14.5
 32 Wrench, b      0    ST       46.7      32020
 33 Pipe wren      4    EA       56.7
 34
08-May-89 11:15 PM
```

ments are not part of the **P**arse command, but they usually are necessary after importing and parsed data.

To produce the final inventory database shown in figure 10.86, follow these steps:

1. Delete rows A3..A19 to remove the unparsed data and to move the parsed data up under the title.

2. Expand column A to make it 25 characters wide, and contract column C to make it 8 characters wide.

3. Reformat the P.O. DATE range in column E to the **Date 4** format.

4. Insert at column E a column for the inventory value (the P.O. DATE now should be column F).

5. Widen the new column E to 10 characters.

6. Add the INVENTORY and VALUE headings in cells E3 and E4, respectively.

7. Enter in cell E5 the formula that will compute the inventory value (+B5*D5).

8. Copy the formula in cell E5 to cells E6..E16.

9. Use the /**R**ange Format command to change the format of cells D5..E16 to the comma and 2 decimal places display.

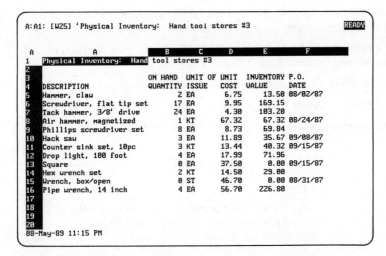

```
A:A1: [W25] 'Physical Inventory:  Hand tool stores #3                    READY

  A            A              B     C     D      E         F
1  Physical Inventory:  Hand tool stores #3
2
3                         ON HAND  UNIT OF UNIT  INVENTORY P.O.
4  DESCRIPTION           QUANTITY ISSUE  COST   VALUE     DATE
5  Hammer, claw                2 EA      6.75    13.50 08/02/87
6  Screwdriver, flat tip set  17 EA      9.95   169.15
7  Tack hammer, 3/8' drive    24 EA      4.30   103.20
8  Air hammer, magnetized      1 KT     67.32    67.32 08/24/87
9  Phillips screwdriver set    8 EA      8.73    69.84
10 Hack saw                    3 EA     11.89    35.67 09/08/87
11 Counter sink set, 10pc      3 KT     13.44    40.32 09/15/87
12 Drop light, 100 foot        4 EA     17.99    71.96
13 Square                      0 EA     37.50     0.00 09/15/87
14 Hex wrench set              2 KT     14.50    29.00
15 Wrench, box/open            0 ST     46.70     0.00 08/31/87
16 Pipe wrench, 14 inch        4 EA     56.70   226.80
17
18
19
20
08-May-89 11:15 PM
```

Fig. 10.86.
The improved
appearance of
parsed data.

Using Caution with /Data Parse

If you are parsing a value that continues past the end of the field, the data is parsed until a blank is encountered or until the value runs into the next field in the format line. This means that if you parse labels, you need to make sure that the field widths in the format line are wide enough so that you can avoid losing data because of blanks. If you parse values, the field widths are less critical.

Caution:
Make sure that the
column widths are
wide enough to
accept the
complete value or
label you want in
the field.

Experiment on small amounts of data until you are comfortable using the /Data Parse command. After you understand how this important command works, you will find many more applications for using it. Every time you develop a new application, you should consider whether existing data created with another software program can be imported and then changed to 1-2-3 format by using the /Data Parse command.

Working with External Databases

Release 3 has added new possibilities with the /Data External feature. You can use the commands on the /Data External menu to access data in tables within an *external* database. An *external table* is a file that is created and maintained by a database program other than 1-2-3, such as dBASE III. Once a connection or link is established between 1-2-3 and an external table, you can perform the following tasks:

- Use /Data Query commands to find and manipulate data in the external table and then work with that data in your worksheet

- Use formulas and database functions to perform calculations based on data in the external table

- Create a new external table that contains data from your worksheet or from an existing external table

When you select /Data External, the following menu appears:

Use List Create Delete Other Reset Quit

The functions of these commands are listed in table 10.5.

Table 10.5
Data External Commands

Command	Description
Use	Establishes a connection to an external table (Use is the first step before using other /**Data External** commands)
List	Displays the names of the tables in an external database, or lists the names of the fields in an external table
Create	Establishes a new table in an external database and copies data from a worksheet data table or another external table to the new table
Delete	Deletes a table from an external database
Other	Includes three functions:
	Control Sends a command to a database management program
	Refresh Sets the interval for automatic updating of worksheet formulas that depend on an external table and for automatic reexecution of /**Data Query** and /**Data Table** commands
	Translation Permits translation of data created with foreign character sets
Reset	Breaks the connection to an external table
Quit	Returns to READY mode

Networks and database programs used on networks usually include mechanisms to limit access to database files. When using 1-2-3 to access external database files, you are under the same restrictions as at other times. When working with 1-2-3's /**Data External** commands under these conditions, you may be prompted to enter your user ID and password. Type each of these, press Enter, and then continue with your 1-2-3 commands. You will have your usual access to the network files. If you encounter problems, see your network administrator.

Understanding External Database Terms

Data management in 1-2-3 becomes more powerful and more flexible with Release 3's capability to use data from tables in external databases. Before you begin working with this new feature, you should be familiar with several terms.

A *database driver* is a program that serves as an interface between 1-2-3 and an external database, allowing 1-2-3 to transfer data to and from the external tables in the database. A separate database driver is required for each external database format you use. As of the first printing of this book, the only database driver supplied with Release 3 is for dBASE III, and the driver name is SAMPLE.

An *external database* is simply the path where the external tables reside.

A *table name* identifies the external table with which you want to work. You must enter the *full* table name before you can access the table from 1-2-3. The full table name consists of three or four parts in the following order:

Reminder:
To access an external table from 1-2-3, you must enter the full table name.

1. The name of the database driver

2. The name of the external database (path)

3. An owner name or user ID, if required by the database program

4. The name of a table in the database, or a 1-2-3 range name that has been assigned to the table

A *table-creation string* contains information used by a database driver to create a new external table. When you create a new external table from within 1-2-3, you may have to specify a table-creation string, depending on the specific database driver in use. The sample driver provided does not require a table-creation string. When in doubt, refer to the database driver documentation.

A *table definition* is a six-column worksheet range that contains information about a new external table. Information in a table definition always includes field names, data types, and field widths, and may include column labels, table creation-strings, and field descriptions.

Using an Existing External Table

Using the data in an external table does not differ much from using a worksheet database. The major difference is that you need to establish a connection to the external table before you use it, and then break the connection when you are finished.

Reminder:
To use an existing table, you must first establish a connection.

To use an existing external table, you must first set up the connection to the external table with the /Data External Use command. This command steps you through the components needed to define the full table name.

First, 1-2-3 displays a list of the available database drivers. After you select a driver, 1-2-3 lists the available external databases you can access with that driver. When you select a database, 1-2-3 displays a list of the table names in that database, with each table name preceded by an owner name if appropriate. You can press the Name (F3) key to display a full-screen list for any of these components. Figure 10.87 shows a full-screen list of available external tables in the database named 123R3, located on drive D.

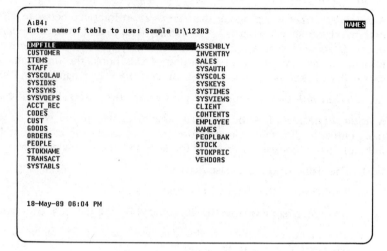

Fig. 10.87.
A list of
available
external tables.

You can enter a table name by typing it or by highlighting each part from the list and pressing Enter. After you establish a connection to an external table, you are prompted to assign the table a 1-2-3 range name. As a default, the table name is supplied for the range name. To use the default, simply press Enter. Otherwise, type the range name you want and then press Enter. The range name is used to refer to the table as if it were a worksheet database.

Note that when you break the connection to an external table, the range name assigned to it is lost. Formulas and functions that reference the range name become undefined when the connection is broken. You must respecify the range name whenever you establish the connection. Be sure to use the same range name each time if your worksheet contains formulas or functions that reference the range.

Using the range name assigned to the table, you can treat the external table as if it were a worksheet database and perform the following tasks:

- Copy some or all records from the external table to your worksheet with /Data Query Extract

- Use /Data Query Extract to copy new records from your worksheet to the external table

- Use formulas and database functions in your worksheet that reference data in the external table

- Modify records in the external table with /Data Query Modify (only if record modification is supported by the database driver in use; as of the first printing of this book, this command is not supported by the sample dBASE III driver)

- Use /Data External Other to perform special database functions not available in 1-2-3

- Terminate the connection to the external table with /Data External Reset

Listing External Tables

/Data External List offers the following options:

Option	Description
Tables	Lists the names of all the tables in an external database
Fields	Lists information about the structure of an external table to which you are connected (with /Data External Use)

A list of the tables in a external database file is useful when you do not remember the exact location of a particular table. To obtain such a list, select /Data External List Tables. You are prompted to supply the database driver name and database name, as for the /Data External Use command. After supplying the appropriate names, you are asked to provide an output range for the list.

Cue:
To find the location of a particular table, use /Data External List Tables.

This list consists of three columns and as many rows as are tables in the database file. Because the list overwrites existing worksheet data, be sure that no important data will be affected. Figure 10.88 shows a sample list. The first column of the list contains the table names, and the second column contains the table descriptions if they are used by the particular database, or NA (not applicable) if they are not. The third column contains the table owner IDs if used, or NA if they are not. The sample dBASE III driver does not use these table descriptions or table owner IDs.

Caution:
An external table list overwrites existing worksheet data.

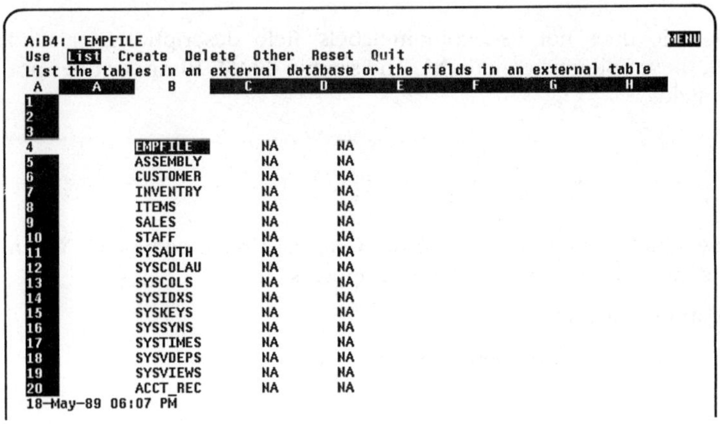

Fig. 10.88.
/Data External List Tables used to create a list of external tables with descriptions.

You can use a list of a table's structure to remind yourself of the contents of a particular external table. You can use this list also as the basis for creating a new table definition, as explained in the next section. To create such a list, select **/D**ata External **L**ist **F**ields. You are first prompted for the range name that identifies the external table, and then for the output range for the list.

The list consists of six columns and as many rows as there are fields in the table. Again, this list overwrites existing worksheet data, so be cautious. Each row in the list contains information about one field in the table (see fig. 10.89). The contents of the columns are the following:

Column 1	Field name
Column 2	Field data type
Column 3	Field width in characters
Column 4	Column label
Column 5	Field description
Column 6	Field-creation string

Fig. 10.89.
The rows containing information about the fields in the table.

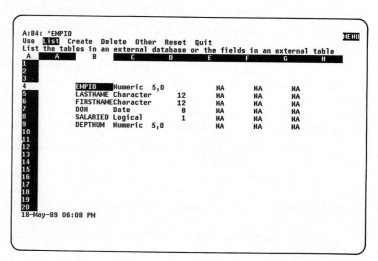

If the external table does not use column labels, field descriptions, or field -creation strings, these columns contain NA. The sample dBASE III driver does not use these three fields.

Creating a New External Table

You create a new external table with the **/D**ata External **C**reate command. When you select this command, the following menu appears:

Name   **D**efinition   **G**o   **Q**uit

Table 10.6 describes each of the menu options.

Table 10.6
Data External Create Commands

Command	Description
Name	Specifies the external database that will contain the new table and specifies the table name
Definition	Specifies the worksheet or external table that will be used as a model for the structure of the new table. The two options are Create-Definition, which creates a table definition based on a range in the model, and Use-Definition, which uses a table definition that already exists in the model.
Go	Creates the external table
Quit	Returns to READY mode

The first step in creating an external table is to use the /Data External Create Name command to name the new external table. You are prompted to supply a name for the new table, followed by a range name to access the table, as for the /Data External Use command. Next, you are prompted for a table-creation string. Because the sample driver does not support the table-creation string, you simply press Enter at this prompt.

To create a new external table, 1-2-3 needs to know the number, order, data types, and names of the fields in the new table. This information is provided in a *table definition*. If the new external table has a structure identical to that of an existing table, 1-2-3 can create the table definition for you automatically. If the new table has a unique structure, you must create and edit a table definition.

Reminder:
To create a new external table, you must enter a table definition.

Duplicating an Existing Structure

You can duplicate the structure of either a worksheet database or an external table. To use a worksheet database, it must be in an active file and must contain a row of field names and at least one data record. When the /Data External Create Definition Create-Definition command prompts you for an input range, you highlight the row of field names and the data record row (see fig. 10.90). Next, the command prompts you for an output range for the table definition (see fig. 10.91). Remember that 1-2-3 will overwrite existing data in this range. Figure 10.92 shows the resulting table definition.

To duplicate an external table, you first must establish a connection to that table and assign it a 1-2-3 range name. Then you simply use /Data External List Fields to create the table definition.

Fig. 10.90.
The prompt for an input range.

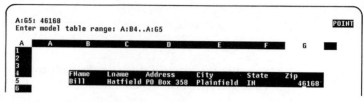

Fig. 10.91.
The prompt for an output range.

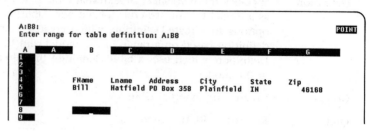

Fig. 10.92.
The resulting table definition.

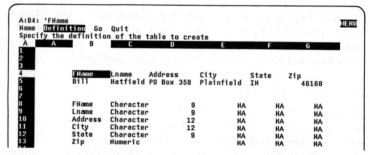

Creating a New Structure

To create a new external table with a new structure, you need to set up a table definition. If you look at figure 10.92, you can see that a table definition contains six columns and one row for each field in the table.

Column 1 contains the field names; this information is required.

Column 2 contains the data type of each field. Although 1-2-3 has only two data types (value and label), some external tables have additional data types. Refer to the database driver documentation for information on the data types supported.

Column 3 specifies the width, in characters, assigned to each field in the external table. Fields with a label data type always require a width; fields with a value data type may or may not require a width, depending on the database driver in use.

Column 4 may contain column labels, again depending on the database driver in use. A *column label* is an alternative label for a database field; such a label provides additional identification of the field. These labels are particularly useful for fields that have been assigned abbreviated field names. For example, the column label *part number* is more informative than the field name *pnum*.

Column 5 may contain field descriptions, depending on the database driver in use. A *field description* is another version of a column label.

Finally, column 6 may contain field-creation strings if they are required by the database driver in use. A *field-creation string* contains information needed by some database drivers to create a field in a new table. If your database driver requires field-creation strings, the details are explained in the database driver documentation.

If the database driver you are using does not require a certain piece of information, the corresponding location in the table description contains NA. The sample dBASE III driver provided does not use column labels, field descriptions, or field-creation strings. Thus, the corresponding locations in figure 10.92 contain NA.

You can use one of two approaches in creating a new table definition range. First, you can copy a table definition from an existing external table and then edit the definition to reflect the structure for the new external table. This method is usually the easier one. Second, you can type the table definition directly into a worksheet range. You use this method to create a new external table only if you know exactly what information is needed by the database driver in use.

Cue:
The easiest way to create a new table definition is to copy and then edit an existing one.

If you want to copy and modify an existing table definition, you can use the /Data External List Fields command to list information about that table. (Listing external tables is described in an earlier section.) The information provided by this command is actually a complete table definition.

The next step is to edit this information to reflect the structure you want the new external table to have. You edit the information as you would any other worksheet data. For example, you may need to make some of the following modifications: change field names, add or delete fields, change the order of the fields, change field widths and/or data types, add or modify column labels and field descriptions, or add field-creation strings if required.

Once the table has been named and the table definition is ready, you use the /Data External Create Go command (see fig. 10.93) to create the external table, and then use /Data External Create Quit to return to READY mode. You can now use the Criteria, Extract, Input, and Output commands on the /Data Query menu to copy data from worksheet databases or other external tables to this newly created table.

Deleting an External Table

You use the /Data External Delete command to delete external tables from the external database. As for the other /Data External commands, you must specify the database driver and database name, and then simply highlight the external table to be deleted (see fig. 10.94). The sample driver provided does not support this command as of the first printing of this book.

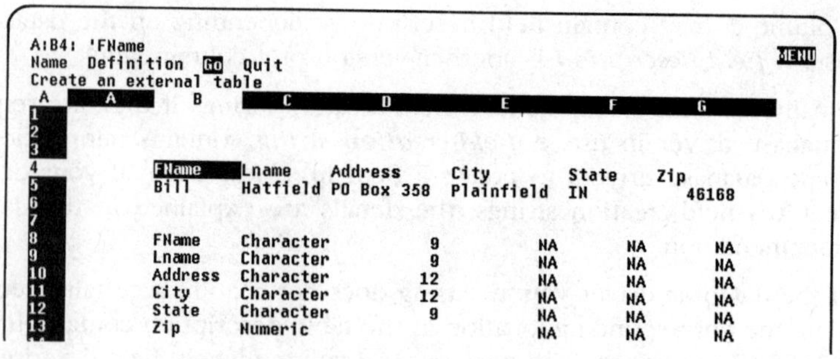

Fig. 10.93.
The /Data
External Create
Go command
used to create
an external
table.

Using Other /Data External Commands

In addition to the /**D**ata **E**xternal commands already discussed, you can use commands to update the table, send commands to the external database program, and use a different character set. When you select /**D**ata **E**xternal **O**ther, the following menu appears:

   Refresh   **C**ontrol   **T**ranslate

These options are discussed in the next sections.

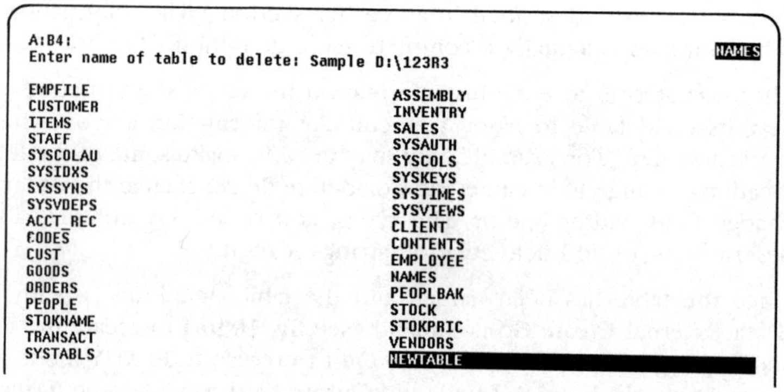

Fig. 10.94.
An external
table
highlighted for
deletion.

/Data External Other Refresh

Reminder:
Use /Data External
Other Refresh to
control the
updating of
worksheet data that
depends on a data
table.

You use /**D**ata **E**xternal **O**ther **R**efresh to specify the time interval at which Release 3 updates those worksheet portions that depend on data in an external table. When you are connected to a network and the external tables you are using may be modified by other users, you can use /**D**ata **E**xternal **O**ther **R**efresh to ensure that the information in your worksheet is up-to-date.

The /**D**ata **E**xternal **O**ther **R**efresh command offers the following options:

Option	Description
Automatic	Automatically updates the worksheet at a certain time interval
Manual	Does not automatically update the worksheet; updates must be done by the user
Interval	Specifies the time interval for **Automatic** refresh. The default is 1 second; you can enter any value from 0 through 3600 seconds (3600 seconds = 1 hour). The **Interval** setting has no effect if **Refresh** is set to **Manual**.

You can divide into two categories the worksheet components that depend on an external table: (1) formulas and database functions that depend on recalculation, and (2) /Data Query and /Data Table commands that do not depend on recalculation.

If you set /Data External Other Refresh to Automatic and set also worksheet recalculation to Automatic, all components of the worksheet are updated at the specified time interval.

If you set /Data External Other Refresh to Automatic but set worksheet recalculation to Manual (with /Worksheet Global Recalc), /Data Query and /Data Table commands are updated at the specified interval, but formulas and database functions are not. Formulas and database functions are updated only when a {CALC} command is executed.

If you set /Data External Other Refresh to Manual, you must update /Data Query and /Data Table commands manually. You must update formulas and database functions by issuing a {CALC} command.

1-2-3's background recalculation permits you to continue working during the recalculation process. If a recalculation cycle takes longer than the refresh interval, the next recalculation cycle begins immediately.

If you change the refresh interval with /Data External Other Refresh Interval, the new value is not saved with the worksheet. For the new value to be in effect for future work sessions, select /Worksheet Global Default Update.

/Data External Other Control

You use /Data External Other Control to send commands to a database management program, permitting you to perform database manipulations not possible with 1-2-3 alone. To use this command, 1-2-3 must be connected to an external table of a database management program having a database driver that supports this command. Again, the sample driver supplied does not support this command as of the first printing of this book.

Reminder:
To send commands to a database program, use /Data External Other Control.

The capabilities of the commands you issue with /Data External Other Control (as well as the command syntax) depend on the database management program—the commands have no relationship to 1-2-3's database management commands. You must be familiar with the commands of the database program to which you want to send a command.

The /Data External Other Control command prompts you first for the external table name, including driver and database, and then for the database command. The database command can be entered as either a string or the address of a cell that contains the command as a label. 1-2-3 sends the command and returns to READY mode.

/Data External Other Translate

Reminder:
To translate a
different character
set, use /Data
External Other
Translate.

When transferring information to and from external tables, 1-2-3 normally copies each character exactly as it is found, with no modification. At times, however, you may be working with a database that was created with a character set different from the one for which your computer hardware is configured. With /Data External Other Translate, you can instruct 1-2-3 to use a different character set to translate between the external table and the worksheet.

To determine whether a particular external table requires translation, use the /Data Query commands to copy records from the external table to your worksheet. Examine the contents of the extracted records for strange-looking characters. If you find such characters, you may need to specify a translation character set. To translate an external table to which you are connected, you supply the full table name to the /Data External Other Translate command. The character sets available will be displayed (see fig. 10.95). After you select the character set, the translation takes place, and 1-2-3 returns to READY mode.

```
A:B4:                                                          NAMES
Enter character set to use: United States (437)

United States (437)          Multilingual (850)
Portuguese (860)             French-Canadian (863)
Nordic (865)
```

Fig. 10.95.
The character
sets available
for translating
the external
table.

If only one character set is available, 1-2-3 automatically selects it. If more than one character set is available for the database in use, you may need to experiment to find the one that translates properly. The selected character set is used to translate all data transferred to and from all tables in the specified database, for the remainder of the current work session.

Disconnecting 1-2-3 and the External Table

/**D**ata **E**xternal **R**eset severs the connection between 1-2-3 and an external table. If only one external table is in use, selecting /**D**ata **E**xternal **R**eset ends the connection to that table. If more than one table is in use, you must specify the database driver, database name, and table name of the specific table whose connection you want to break.

After you break the connection, the range name of the table becomes undefined. Any worksheet formulas or queries that use that range name may produce errors.

Reminder:
To break a connection, use /Data External Reset.

Caution:
Once you break a connection, you lose the table range name; any formulas or queries that use this name may produce errors.

Chapter Summary

The data management chapter addresses all nine options on the /**D**ata menu. **S**ort and **Q**uery, two options described extensively in the first half of the chapter, are true data management commands that require database organization by field name. The other choices—**F**ill, **T**able, **D**istribution, **M**atrix, **R**egression, and **P**arse—manipulate data and can be used in database or worksheet applications. **E**xternal enables you to access and modify data in files created by stand-alone database programs.

Data management is one of the advanced capabilities of 1-2-3. If you have mastered data management, you are a true "power user," and you probably are already using 1-2-3 macros. If not, be sure to continue your learning. Chapter 11 presents the creation and use of keyboard macros, and Chapter 12 introduces you to the powerful advanced macro commands.

11

Using Macros

Although 1-2-3's worksheet, database, and graphics features may provide all the functionality you need, you may find another feature of the program to be invaluable: the macro and advanced macro command programming capabilities. Used in the most basic way, 1-2-3's macros provide a convenient method of automating the tasks you find yourself performing repeatedly, such as printing worksheets or changing global default settings. Macros and the advanced macro commands, however, allow you to do much more. You also can construct sophisticated business applications that function, for example, in the same way as applications written in programming languages such as BASIC, C, or FORTRAN.

This chapter covers the following topics:

- What a macro is

- How to write your first macros

- How to name and run macros

- How to plan the layout of a macro

- How to build a simple macro library

- How to use 1-2-3's Record feature to create and test macros

- How to document macros

The next chapter introduces you to the advanced macro commands (a set of advanced programming commands) and helps you learn the functions and applications of those commands.

What Is a Macro?

The simplest macros are nothing more than short collections of keystrokes that 1-2-3 types for you. 1-2-3 stores this keystroke collection as text in a cell. You can treat it as you would any label. To understand the benefit of this capability, consider the number of times you save and retrieve worksheet files, print reports, and perhaps set and reset worksheet formats. In each case, you perform the operation by typing a series of keys—sometimes a rather lengthy series—on the computer keyboard. Using a macro, however, you can reduce any number of keystrokes to a simple two-keystroke abbreviation.

For example, suppose that you put your company name, *ABC Manufacturing, Incorporated*, in numerous locations throughout your worksheets. You might decide always to type the more than 30 keystrokes that make up this entry. You have the option, however, of storing all 30-plus keystrokes in a macro. Then, the next time you want to type the name into the worksheet, you can execute just two keystrokes—your macro—instead of typing the 30-plus keystrokes. The text that follows describes just such a macro. If you've never written a macro before, why not try the ones that follow as your first?

Writing Your First Macros

The steps for creating any macro are basic:

1. *Plan what you want the macro to do.*

2. *Identify the keystrokes the macro should repeat.*

   Keep in mind that macros are simply text (labels) that duplicate the keystrokes you want to replay.

3. *Find an area of the worksheet where you can enter macros.*

   When you choose the area, be aware that executed macros read text from cells starting with the top cell and working down through lower cells. Macros end when they come to a blank cell or a command that stops macro execution.

4. *Enter the keystrokes, keystroke equivalents, and commands into a cell or cells.*

   You must type an apostrophe (') before a slash (/) or backslash (\) in order for that keystroke to be entered in a cell as text rather than as a command request or as the fill label-prefix. You also must type an apostrophe before a number, +, −, *, or (in order for the keystroke to be entered in a cell as text rather than as a number or formula.

   Use range names rather than addresses in your macros. Addresses entered in the text of a macro do not update when changes are made to the worksheet. As a consequence, moves and inserts or deletions cause a macro to work using incorrect addresses. Creating your macros with range names instead of addresses corrects this problem. The range names in a macro automatically update their meaning when the worksheet changes.

5. *Name the macro in one of three ways:*

   Assign an Alt-letter name, such as \a.

   Choose a descriptive name, such as PRINT_BUDGET.

   Give the name \0 for a macro that runs automatically when the file is loaded.

6. *Document the macro.*

Even when your macros become more complex as your expertise increases, you always will use these same four basic steps to create a macro. Keep in mind that good planning and documentation are important for making macros run smoothly and efficiently.

The text that follows shows you how to write two simple macros. The first macro enters text into a cell. The second macro repeats commands specified in the macro.

Later in this chapter, you learn how to use the Record method of writing macros (see the "Recording and Testing Macros" section).

Writing a Macro that Enters Text

Before you begin building a macro, you need to identify the keystrokes you want the macro to type for you. In the case of a macro that labels worksheets with a company name, you want the macro to type the letters, spaces, and punctuation that make up your company name. Then, and as with any label entry, you want the macro to enter the typed characters into the cell by pressing the Enter key.

Cue:
Identify the keystrokes you want the macro to type for you.

You begin building your macro by storing the keystrokes as text in a worksheet cell. The one keystroke you need to have the macro type is the Enter key. To represent the Enter key, you use a tilde (˜).

Cue:
Store the keystrokes for a macro as text in a worksheet cell.

Cell B3 in figure 11.1 shows the keystrokes, including the Enter (˜), that you want 1-2-3 to type for you as part of the macro:

ABC Manufacturing, Incorporated˜

The next step to writing the macro is to name this sequence of keystrokes as a macro. To name this cell, move the cell pointer to B3 and select /**R**ange **N**ame **C**reate. At the first prompt, type the name **\n**. The backslash (\) represents the Alt key. At the second prompt, specify the range to be named as the cell holding the keystrokes—in this case, cell A:B3.

Be sure to document your macro as shown in figure 11.1. Place the macro name one cell to the left of the first line of the macro—in this case, in cell A3. Documenting the macro in this way will help you remember the macro's name.

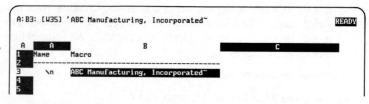

Fig. 11.1.
A simple macro
for entering a
company name.

To execute, or run, this simple macro, all you need to do is move the cell pointer to the cell where you want your company name to appear, hold down the Alt key, and then press N. 1-2-3 enters the sequence of characters identified as the macro \n. Figure 11.2 shows the results of moving the cell pointer to B10 and then running the \n macro. To save this macro for future use, save the file in which the macro is located.

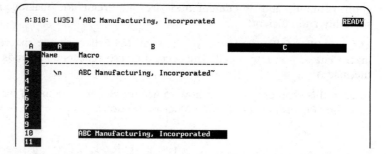

Fig. 11.2.
The results of
running the
\n macro.

Writing a Simple Command Macro

In addition to macros that repeat text, you can write macros that repeat commands. If you follow the same procedure each time, you will find that macro writing can become second nature.

Reminder:
The tilde (˜)
represents pressing
the Enter key.

First, plan what you want your command macro to do. For instance, create a macro that will change the column width from the default 9-character width to 14. The commands for this process are /Worksheet Column Set-Width 14 and pressing Enter. The macro, therefore, is represented as

/wcs14˜

Notice that each character of the macro is what you would press on the keyboard. The tilde (˜) represents pressing the Enter key.

Next, you need to name the macro. Because the macro changes the column width, call the macro \c. (The backslash represents the Alt key.) After the macro is given a name, you can press and hold the Alt key, and press C to start the macro.

Finally, document the macro as shown in figure 11.3. Place the macro name one cell to the left of the first line of the macro—in this case, in cell Z1. Not only does this step document the name of the macro, but it aids you in naming the macro. Choose /**Range Name Labels Right** and press Enter. The label in the cell will be used to create the macro name, one cell to the right—the cell that contains the macro.

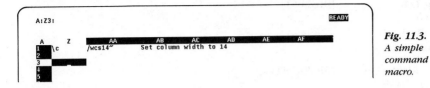

Fig. 11.3.
A simple command macro.

Finally, to document the macro further, type an explanation next to each line of the macro. Place the explanation one cell to the right of each line of the macro.

Using Keywords

Because many keys on your keyboard aren't identifiable by obvious characters, 1-2-3 uses some special characters or words as equivalents for some keys and combinations of keys. Table 11.1 summarizes these keywords—the special characters and words you use in macros to represent keystrokes that don't have obvious alphanumeric characters. Many of these keywords are used in the examples throughout this chapter. (See Chapters 2 and 3 for explanations of the movement and function keys.)

Reminder:
1-2-3 uses some special characters or words as equivalents for some keys and combinations of keys.

Table 11.1
Summary of Macro Keywords

1-2-3 Key	Macro Keyword
/ (slash) or < (less than)	/ or < or {MENU}
˜ (tilde)	{˜}
{ (open brace)	{{}
} (close brace)	{}}
↓	{DOWN} or {D}
↑	{UP} or {U}
←	{LEFT} or {L}
→	{RIGHT} or {R}
Backspace	{BACKSPACE} or {BS}
(No keyboard equivalent; clears entry in EDIT mode)	{CE} or {CLEARENTRY}

Table 11.1—*Continued*

1-2-3 Key	Macro Keyword
Big Left (Ctrl-←) or BackTab (Shift-Tab)	{BIGLEFT}
Big Right (Ctrl-→) or Tab	{BIGRIGHT}
Ctrl-Break in MENU mode	{BREAK}
File (Ctrl-End)	{FILE}
Prev File (Ctrl-End, Ctrl-PgDn)	{PREVFILE} or {PF} or {FILE}{PS}
First File (Ctrl-End, Home)	{FIRSTFILE} or {FF} or {FILE}{HOME}
Last File (Ctrl-End, End)	{LASTFILE} or {LF} or {FILE}{END}
Next File (Ctrl-End, Ctrl-PgUp)	{NEXTFILE} or {NF} or {FILE}{NS}
First Cell (Ctrl-Home)	{FIRSTCELL} or {FC}
Prev Sheet (Ctrl-PgDn)	{PREVSHEET} or {PS}
Next Sheet (Ctrl-PgUp)	{NEXTSHEET} or {NS}
Del	{DELETE} or {DEL}
End	{END}
Last Cell (End, Ctrl-Home)	{LASTCELL} or {LC}
Enter or Return	~
Esc	{ESCAPE} or {ESC}
Help (F1)	{HELP}
Edit (F2)	{EDIT}

RELEASE 3

1-2-3 Key	Macro Keyword
Name (F3)	{NAME}
Abs (F4)	{ABS}
GoTo (F5)	{GOTO}
Window (F6)	{WINDOW}
Query (F7)	{QUERY}
Table (F8)	{TABLE}
Calc (F9)	{CALC}
Graph (F10)	{GRAPH}
Zoom (Alt-F6)	{ZOOM}
App1 (Alt-F7)	{APP1}
App2 (Alt-F8)	{APP2}
App3 (Alt-F9)	{APP3}
Extend (Alt-F10)	{EXTEND} or {APP4}
Home	{HOME}
Ins or Insert	{INS} or {INSERT}
PgDn or PageDown	{PGDN}
PgUp or PageUp	{PGUP}

You may have noticed that a few keys still have neither an obvious alphanumeric character to represent them, nor a keyword to identify them. These include Caps Lock, Compose (Alt-F1), Num Lock, Print Screen, Record (Alt-F2), Run (Alt-F3), Scroll Lock, and Shift. You cannot use these keystrokes in macros.

Naming and Running Macros

Depending on how you name a macro, you execute it in one of the following ways:

Reminder:
You can name and run macros in three ways.

- Macros named with \ and a single letter can be executed with Alt-letter or Run (Alt-F3).

- Macros named with a descriptive name up to 15 characters can be executed with Run (Alt-F3).

- Macros named with \0 are executed with file loading as well as with Run (Alt-F3).

The previous text already described the first way to name and run a macro, which is with the Alt key and a single letter key. Using the second method, you assign the range that holds the macro a descriptive name, and you execute the macro with Run (Alt-F3). The third method creates an automatic macro by the name of \0; the macro is executed automatically when you load the file.

Note that you can run any of these three types of macros with the Run (Alt-F3) key. Depending on how you name a macro, however, the macro also can be executed using alternative keystrokes or automatically.

Invoking a macro in Release 3 with the Run (Alt-F3) key is a much more user-friendly approach than the single Alt-letter method available in early versions of 1-2-3. Selecting Run (Alt-F3) displays a prompt and provides a list of macro names from which you can choose the macro you want to run.

Although you use the \0 name only when you want to invoke a macro automatically as soon as a file is retrieved, you can opt to use either the Alt-letter or descriptive name for any other macro. There are advantages to each type of name, however. Invoking a macro with an Alt-letter name can involve fewer keystrokes (if selected by pressing Alt and the letter) than invoking a macro that has a descriptive name. The disadvantage to using Alt-letter macro names, however, is that you may have difficulty remembering the macros' specific functions, particularly when you have created many macros. Your chances of selecting the right macro are greater when you use descriptive names.

The text that follows describes all three approaches to creating, naming, and running macros.

Alt-Letter Macros that Work with a Key Press

As described earlier, one way to name a macro is using the backslash key (\ ) and a letter character. In the previous releases of 1-2-3, this was the only way you named all macros (except the automatic macros discussed later in this chapter). A simple macro introduced earlier, for example, was named \n. You can use either upper- or lowercase letters to type the name of this macro; 1-2-3 doesn't differentiate between lowercase and uppercase for range names. You do, however, need to limit yourself to letters. Accordingly, \a, \B, and \C all are valid names for Alt-letter macros.

Reminder:
The file containing the macro must be the current file, and an identically named macro can't exist in some other active file.

To run a macro named with the backslash (\ ) and a letter character, hold down the Alt key and press the letter character that identifies the macro. For example, to run a macro named \c, you press Alt-C.

Macros with Descriptive Names

Cue:
*Give macros
descriptive names.*

In Release 3, you also can give macros descriptive names. In previous releases of 1-2-3, you were limited in the number of macros you could create within a worksheet; you could create only 26 macros—one named for each letter of the alphabet. In Release 3, however, you can create as many macros as your file will hold by using up to 15 characters to name a range that stores a macro. As a result, your macro names can be more descriptive.

Rather than naming the macro to print your worksheet \p, for example, you can name it PRINT_BUDGET. Just be careful not to use range names that also are used as 1-2-3 keystroke equivalents, such as CALC or RIGHT, or as one of the advanced macro commands that are listed in Chapter 12. Doing so leads to unpredictable and, often, incorrect results. (For example, you may think that you are running a macro named CALC, but you actually will be selecting the Calc key.)

Figure 11.4 shows a screen comprised of four macros that demonstrate many of the rules and conventions described in the previous text. Each of these macros is discussed in detail in the "Building a Simple Macro Library" section of this chapter. In this section, these macros are used only to demonstrate the three ways to name and run a macro.

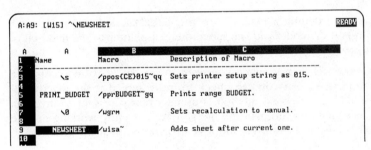

*Fig. 11.4.
Four macros
that
demonstrate
naming rules.*

Cue:
*To run any macro,
press Run (Alt-F3).*

To run a macro to which you've assigned a range name—or, in fact, to run any macro—press Run (Alt-F3). 1-2-3 lists all the range names in the current file. If you have other active files, 1-2-3 also lists these. Figure 11.5 shows the full-screen listing of all macro names that results after pressing Run (Alt-F3) and Name (F3) when the macros shown in figure 11.4 are in the current file. Pressing Name (F3) a second time returns the worksheet display to the screen.

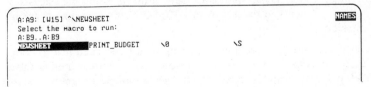

*Fig. 11.5.
A list of range
names in the
current file.*

You can select the macro you want to run in one of three ways. The first way to run a macro is to highlight one of the macro range names appearing in the range names list for the active file and press Enter. If you want to see the range names from one of the other active files, highlight the name of that file and press Enter; 1-2-3 then displays the range names from that file.

Reminder:
Active files are those in memory that you've either retrieved or opened.

The second method is to type the name of the macro or its starting address, and then press Enter. If you type the address without identifying the file, 1-2-3 assumes that you mean the current file. If you type an abbreviated address or one that doesn't include the worksheet letter, 1-2-3 assumes that you mean the current worksheet. If you type a range name without identifying the file, 1-2-3 assumes that you mean a macro on the current file.

Reminder:
The current file and current worksheet are where the cell pointer is located.

When an abbreviated address and/or range will result in an error, you need to prefix the address or name with a worksheet letter and file reference. For example, to execute a macro located in cell A1 in worksheet A in the file named BUDGET90.WK3, you type

   <<BUDGET90.WK3>>A:A1

Suppose that you want to execute a macro in cell A1 in worksheet A in file BUDGET90.WK3, and you are already working in that file. If worksheet B is current, you type

   A:A1

A third approach to running a macro is to press the Esc key twice to enter POINT mode. In POINT mode, you can move the cell pointer to the first cell of the macro and press Enter.

Using the third approach is best when you want to see the actual contents of a macro before running so that you can check to make sure that the macro will perform as it should. The second method is useful when you want to invoke a macro located in a different file than the file you are currently working in. The first method is easiest, most intuitive, and less error prone than the other two.

Automatic Macros that Work When Loaded

You may want some macros to run automatically when the worksheet is retrieved. For example, perhaps you always want to move your cell pointer to the end of a column. A handy trick, then, is to name a macro using the backslash key and the number 0. When you name a macro \0, 1-2-3 runs that macro whenever the file is loaded.

You also can use this feature in more advanced macro and advanced macro command programs. For example, when you've constructed your own menus for a worksheet model, you may want the advanced macro command program to start automatically and place the first custom menu on the screen.

Caution: \0 macros work automatically as long as the /Worksheet Global Default Autoexec setting is **Yes**, which is the default. You can, however, change the setting to **No**, in which case \0 macros are not automatically executed when a file is retrieved or opened.

Figure 11.6 shows an automatic macro that executes the following keystrokes:

{GOTO}D7˜{END}{DOWN 2}

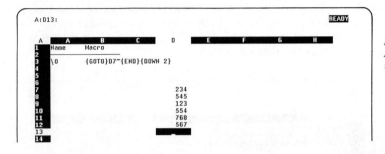

Fig. 11.6.
An automatic
macro, named
\0.

The macro's keystrokes are the same as if you press GoTo (F5), type D7, then press Enter, the End key, and the down-arrow key twice to move to the bottom of the column. However, these keystrokes become automatic when you create the macro.

Notice that the actual contents of cell B3 are

'{GOTO}D7˜{END}{DOWN 2}

Because a macro is actually a text label, it is preceded by a label prefix—in this case, an apostrophe. You can use any of the label prefixes: ', ˆ, ", or \. The most common prefix, however, is the apostrophe.

To practice the method described in the preceding text, type the numbers in cells D7 through D12, as shown in figure 12.6. Next, type through what the macro does. Press F5, D7, and Enter. Press the End key once, and notice the END indicator at the bottom of the screen. Now, press the down-arrow key twice. You have just accomplished what the macro will do.

Now move your cell pointer to cell B3, type the label prefix ' and the characters shown in cell B3 of figure 12.6. 1-2-3 collects your keystrokes as a label. By pressing Enter, you enter the label into cell B3.

Type '\0 in cell A3. Then select /**R**ange **N**ame **L**abels **R**ight and press Enter while your cell pointer is on cell A3. Save the worksheet and then retrieve it. You will see that the macro works automatically. If you want to repeat the macro after it runs automatically when the file is retrieved, press Alt-0, or press Run (Alt-F3) and select \0 from the list of macro range names.

Planning the Layout of a Macro

Although a macro containing fewer than 512 characters can be entered in one cell, you should get into the practice of breaking a long macro apart down a column of cells. By keeping the number of keystrokes in a single cell limited, you can more easily debug, modify, and document a macro.

Figure 11.7, for example, shows two macros that execute the same sequence of keystrokes—the GoTo (F5) key, and then the Name (F3) key twice. One macro is named \a and the other is named \b. In both cases, the range named is only one cell: \a is the range name given to the macro that starts in B3, and \b is the range name given to the macro that starts in B5.

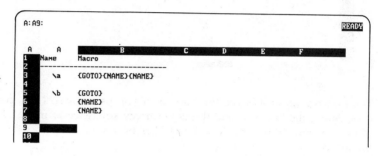

Fig. 11.7.
Two ways to store the keystrokes that make up a macro.

Reminder:
Keystrokes are executed starting at the cell in the upper-left corner of the range.

In the case of the \b macro, you can name either just cell B5 or the range of cells B5..B7, and the macro still works correctly. In fact, you should keep in mind that for both simple macros and advanced macro command programs, the keystrokes are executed starting at the cell in the upper-left corner of the range. After the keystrokes in B5 are executed, the macro moves down one cell and executes any keystrokes in that cell. Similarly, after completing those keystrokes, the macro again moves down one cell. The macro continues to move down and read until it encounters an empty cell, a cell that contains a numeric value, an error, or an advanced macro command that explicitly stops a macro. (These circumstances are discussed in Chapter 12.)

You will find your macros easier to read and understand later if you logically separate keystrokes and keywords into separate cells. One warning, however, is that when you are using keywords, such as {GOTO} and {NAME}, you must keep the entire keyword in the same cell. Splitting the keyword {NAME} into two cells—{NA in one cell and ME} in the cell that follows—doesn't work.

Cue:
Repeat certain keywords by including a repetition factor.

Here's one other helpful hint: 1-2-3 allows you to repeat certain keywords by including a repetition factor. A *repetition factor* tells 1-2-3 that you want a command repeated the number of times you specify. Figure 11.8 shows another example of the same keystrokes performed by the \a and \b macros in figure 11.7. The \c macro uses a repetition factor to repeat the {NAME} keyword. Rather than type {NAME} two times, for example, you can simply type {NAME 2} to repeat the {NAME} keyword. This option is particularly helpful when you need to repeat cursor-movement keys. Rather than type {LEFT}{LEFT}{LEFT}, for instance, you can type {LEFT 3}. When you use a repetition factor, be sure to leave a space between the actual keyword and the number.

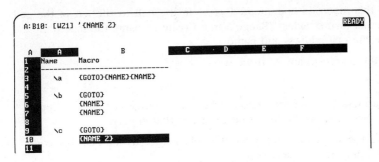

Fig. 11.8.
A repetition factor used in the \c macro to repeat a keyword.

Building a Simple Macro Library

By constructing a separate file that holds commonly used macros or by storing commonly used macros in a separate worksheet within a file, you can run these macros anytime they are loaded—in effect creating a library of macros that you can use over and over again with any of your worksheets. The macros shown earlier in figure 11.4 could be the basis of just such a macro library. Each of these macros is discussed here in turn, along with some additional tips and techniques for writing and using macros.

Cue:
Construct a separate file that holds commonly used macros.

A Macro To Define Printer Setup Strings

The first macro shown in figure 11.4 sets the printer setup string as 015. The actual sequence of keystrokes is stored in cell B3, as follows:

'/ppos{CE}015˜ qq

If you've ever defined a printer setup string, you may be familiar with most of the sequence that makes up this macro. Macro execution starts with an apostrophe (the label prefix), and then the / (slash), which activates the 1-2-3 command menu. The letters **ppos** select the menu commands **P**rint **P**rinter **O**ptions **S**etup.

{CE}, which you also can write as {CLEARENTRY}, is a special macro keyword that doesn't have a keyboard equivalent. {CE} clears the edit line of all data when 1-2-3 is in EDIT mode. In the case of this macro, {CE} clears any printer setup string that already has been entered. The number 015 is, in fact, a common printer setup string to compress print. The ˜ (tilde) enters the setup string. Finally, the letters **qq** quit both the **P**rinter **O**ptions menu and the **P**rint menu.

Reminder:
{CE} doesn't have a keyboard equivalent.

If you have difficulty visualizing the sequence of keystrokes, try typing them yourself starting with the slash key (/), which activates the 1-2-3 command menu. Because {CE} doesn't have a keyboard equivalent, you won't be able to type that part of the macro sequence. Instead, use the Backspace or Esc key to remove any printer setup string you previously defined.

The name of this macro is documented as \s in the cell to the left of the cell storing the actual macro. Select /**R**ange **N**ame **C**reate to name the macro. At the prompts, type the cell address and name.

You can run the macro in any of three ways:

- Press Alt-S.

- Press Run (Alt-F3) and then choose the macro range name \s by highlighting that item on the list of range names that appears.

- Press the Esc key twice and move the cell pointer to the cell that contains the appropriate macro: B3.

A Macro To Print a Report

The second macro shown in figure 11.4 prints the worksheet range BUDGET using the keystrokes stored in cell B5:

'/pprBUDGET˜ gq

The macro starts with an apostrophe (the label prefix) and the / (slash), which activates the 1-2-3 command menu. The letters **ppr** select the menu commands **P**rint **P**rinter **R**ange. BUDGET represents the range that you want to print and that you have previously named using the /**R**ange **N**ame **C**reate command sequence. The ˜ (tilde) sets the print range just as pressing the Enter key does. The letter **g** gives the **G**o print command. The letter **q** quits the menu.

Reminder:
Giving macros
descriptive names
—a feature new to
Release 3—makes
remembering the
names and
purposes of
macros easier.

The name of this macro, PRINT_BUDGET, is defined using the /**R**ange **N**ame **C**reate command sequence and is documented in the cell to the left of the cell storing the actual macro. Because the macro is named with a range name, you run the macro using Run (Alt-F3).

A Macro To Set Worksheet Recalculation

The third macro shown in figure 11.4 sets the worksheet recalculation to manual. The keystrokes, which simply mirror the ones you would use manually, are shown in cell B7:

'/wgrm

Because the macro's name, documented in cell A7, is \0, the macro automatically executes whenever the file that contains this macro is retrieved or opened as long as the /**W**orksheet **G**lobal **D**efault **A**utoexec setting is **Y**es. The macro starts with an apostrophe (the label prefix) and / (slash), which activates the

1-2-3 command menu. The letters **wgrm** select the menu commands **W**orksheet **G**lobal **R**ecalc **M**anual.

In addition to running this macro automatically as part of retrieving or opening the file, you also can run this macro at other times. To run the macro, press Run (Alt-F3), and then choose the macro range name \0 by highlighting that item on the list of range names that appears. If you turn back to figure 11.5, you can see that \0 is one of the range names listed when you press Run (Alt-F3). Another way to run the macro is to press the Esc key twice and move the cell pointer to the cell that contains the appropriate macro: B7.

A Macro To Add a New Worksheet

The fourth macro in figure 11.4, named NEWSHEET, inserts a new worksheet after the current worksheet. The keystrokes for the macro, as shown in cell B9, are as follows:

'/wisa˜

The macro starts with an apostrophe (the label prefix) and / (slash), which activates the 1-2-3 command menu. The letters **wisa** select the menu commands **W**orksheet **I**nsert **S**heet **A**fter, and the ˜ (tilde) represents the press of the Enter key.

Because this macro is named with a descriptive range name, you can run it in either of two ways. The first way is to press Run (Alt-F3) and highlight NEWSHEET on the list of range names that appears. The other way is to press the Esc key twice and move the cell pointer to the cell that contains the appropriate macro: B9.

Recording and Testing Macros

A powerful new feature provided in Release 3 of 1-2-3 is Record (Alt-F2). Note that Record is the only major command not available from the main command menu. The Record feature records your keystrokes, allows you to copy your keystrokes into a worksheet cell as a label, and automatically creates a macro.

Record works by displaying and letting you use information from a special storage area in your computer's memory called the *record buffer*. Not only can you copy keystrokes from the record buffer, but you also can play back the keystrokes from the record buffer, clear the record buffer, and turn on STEP mode— so that a macro can be run one step at a time for testing purposes. The text that follows describes in more detail the steps for using Record to create macros, play back your keystrokes, and step through macros.

Reminder:
Record is the only major command not available from the main command menu.

Creating Macros with Record

Suppose that you want to create a macro that sets the global worksheet format to Currency with two decimal places. To make this setting manually, you select /Worksheet Global Format Currency, type **2**, and then press Enter. You might be able to write this macro easily with what you already know about 1·2·3 macros. 1·2·3, however, gives you an even easier way to write the macro.

To have 1·2·3 record a macro for you, begin by pressing Record (Alt-F2) and selecting Erase from the Record menu. You don't have to erase, but doing so will help you find the characters you need more easily. Keep in mind that the record buffer holds roughly the last 512 characters you've typed. Figure 11.9 shows the command menu that you access by pressing Record (Alt-F2) and from which you select Erase. After selecting Erase, type the keystrokes you want your macro to execute—for the example, type **/wgfc**, type **2**, and press Enter. The Record feature dutifully records your keystrokes in the record buffer.

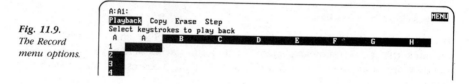

Fig. 11.9.
The Record menu options.

Tip: When you define a range within a macro you are recording, type the range address rather than point with the cursor-movement keys. You can much more easily identify a range in the record buffer from a typed address than from recorded cursor-movement keystrokes.

You next must enter the recorded keystrokes into the worksheet. All you need to do is copy the keystrokes from the buffer to the worksheet and assign a range name to the cell or range containing the keystrokes. To copy the keystrokes from the record buffer into the worksheet, press Record (Alt-F2) and select the **C**opy option from the Record menu. The keystrokes you've typed since the beginning of your 1·2·3 session or since you last selected the **E**rase option appear in the control panel, as shown in figure 11.10.

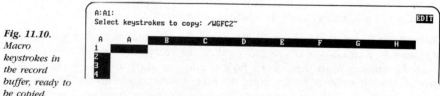

Fig. 11.10.
Macro keystrokes in the record buffer, ready to be copied.

Identify those keystrokes you want to copy using a six-step process:

1. Move the cursor to the first character you want to copy to the worksheet.

2. Press Tab to anchor the cursor.

    Whenever you are in POINT mode, you can unanchor by pressing Esc. Otherwise, the cursor is anchored at the place it was located when you entered POINT mode.

Cue:
Press Esc
to unanchor the
highlight set
with Tab.

3. Use the arrow keys to highlight the remaining keystrokes you want to copy from the record buffer.

    Figure 11.11 shows as highlighted the entire set of keystrokes necessary to set the global format to Currency with two decimal places.

4. After you've highlighted the characters you want to copy, press Enter.

    1-2-3 asks where you want the characters copied (see fig. 11.12).

5. Either move the cell pointer to the appropriate cell or range of cells, or type the cell or range address.

6. Press Enter.

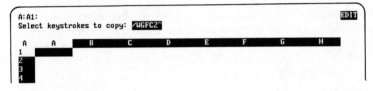

Fig. 11.11.
The highlighted keystrokes selected.

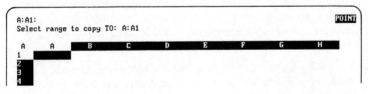

Fig. 11.12.
The prompt that asks where you want the highlighted characters copied.

Tip: You can edit the contents of the record buffer either before or after highlighting the contents, but not while you are highlighting the characters for the copy operation. Use the same editing keys as you would use to edit a formula.

The result of the copy operation will appear as shown in figure 11.13 if you select cell B3 as the range to store the copied characters.

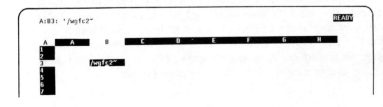

Fig. 11.13.
A recorded macro copied into the worksheet from the record buffer.

To use the macro, you must first name it. Type the label '\f in cell A3, as shown in figure 11.13. Place the cell pointer in cell A3. Select /**R**ange **N**ame **L**abels **R**ight and press Enter. The label \f will be assigned as the range name to the macro in cell B3. You can press Alt-F to start the macro.

You can use the same steps described here to create a simple macro with the Record feature to create more complex and lengthy macros as well. If you do use Record to build larger or more complex macros, however, keep the following information in mind:

- The record buffer is limited in size to 512 bytes. Because a byte is roughly equal in size to one character, you have room only for the last 512 characters in the record buffer. When you type the 513th character, 1-2-3 forgets what your 1st character was--in effect, removing from the record buffer the oldest characters to make room for the newest.

- Because some keys on your keyboard don't have character equivalents, several characters may be required to represent a keystroke. The F5 key, for example, is represented by six characters: {GOTO}.

- The Record feature doesn't record your keystrokes when you press certain keys. These include keys that have neither character symbols nor keywords: Caps Lock, Compose (Alt-F1), Num Lock, Print Screen, Record (Alt-F2), Scroll Lock, and Shift. The Record feature also does not record Ctrl-Break and Ins.

- Fortunately, 1-2-3 uses shortcuts when possible. If you press the right-arrow key 10 times, you might guess that the record buffer records the keyword {RIGHT} 10 times. Instead, 1-2-3 uses a repetition factor and the most abbreviated form of the keyword—in this case, {R 10}—using 6 keystrokes instead of the 10 you actually typed.

- If you execute an Alt-letter macro while you are recording, the name of the macro gets recorded in the record buffer rather than the macro's individual keystrokes. For example, if you execute a macro named \a, the record buffer shows the keystrokes as {\a}. If 1-2-3 encounters {\a} when executing a different macro, the program executes the macro \a and then returns to executing the macro in which {\a} is a step.

Caution:
1-2-3 may copy characters from the record buffer over data in your worksheet.

- You can specify one row or many rows for the range to which you want to copy the characters from the record buffer. 1-2-3 will use as many rows as needed to hold the characters you select to have copied.

- The column width of the range to which you copy the keystrokes affects the number of keystrokes 1-2-3 copies to each cell. If you are copying 20 characters and the cell you specify is 10 characters wide, 1-2-3 attempts to split the keystrokes in half: 10 into the cell you specify and 10 into the cell below. 1-2-3, however, does not split keywords between cells; doing so would create a macro error. Nonetheless, other keystrokes in the macro may be split into illogical segments.

- If you specify a range of cells—not just a single cell—1-2-3 uses the width of the entire range to determine how many characters to put into the top left cell of the range and those below it. For example, if you specify D3..E3 as the range to have 20 keystrokes copied to and the column-width of each column is 10, 1-2-3 copies the full 20 characters into cell D3.

Using Playback To Repeat Keystrokes

An option you have with the Record feature is to "play back," or repeat, your keystrokes. Basically, the steps to play back your keystrokes or some portion of them parallel those used to create a macro. You can play back a sequence of keystrokes as many times as you like. You should find this feature helpful when you want to repeat a sequence of keystrokes, but don't want or need to go to the extra effort to create an actual macro for those keystrokes.

Cue:
Play back a sequence of keystrokes as many times as you like.

Before you play back keystrokes, you need to position your cursor in the specific location where you want the keystrokes to be repeated. Then, to play back the keystrokes, follow these steps:

Reminder:
Before you play back the keystrokes, position the cursor in the specific location where you want the keystrokes repeated.

1. Press Record (Alt-F2) to access the Record menu.

2. Select the **P**layback option.

   The record buffer is displayed.

3. To select the keystrokes you want to repeat, position the cursor at the beginning or end of the sequence of keystrokes you want to repeat, press Tab to anchor the cursor, and then use the left- or right-arrow key to highlight the entire range of keystrokes you want to repeat.

4. Press Enter.

1-2-3 repeats the keystrokes and keystroke equivalents you highlighted. Keep in mind that you can edit the contents of the record buffer either before or after you anchor the cursor.

Using Record To Test Macros

No matter how carefully you construct your macros, they aren't likely to run flawlessly the first time. By taking a series of precautions, however, you can minimize your efforts to get your macros to work correctly.

Probably the first thing you need to do is invest time before you create a macro to design it carefully. Just as a carpenter never would start construction of a house without blueprints, neither should you start construction of a macro without a carefully conceived and well-documented design. Taking the time to map out the detailed steps a macro is supposed to take, to create good documentation of what your macro is supposed to do, and to write descriptions of any range names used in the macro is well worth the effort.

Even if you have a good design and documentation, however, you should plan to test and fix your macros. Testing allows you to verify that your macro works precisely as you want it to. The remaining option on the Record menu provides a valuable aid in locating macro errors: the Step option. This option allows you to execute your macro one keystroke at a time—giving you a chance to see, in slow motion, exactly what your macro does. Even though the Step option is found on the Record menu, you can use Step to test any macro—not just those you record.

Suppose that you want to use the Step option to test the macro shown in figure 11.13, which you created using Record. Follow this procedure to use the Step option to test that macro:

1. Press Record (Alt-F2).

2. Select **Step** to switch to STEP mode.

   The STEP indicator appears at the bottom of the screen, as shown in figure 11.14.

3. Execute the macro that you want to step through one keystroke at a time.

   The SST indicator, which represents Single STep, replaces the STEP indicator.

4. To have the macro begin operation, press any key—for example, the space bar. The first keystroke or keystroke equivalent is executed.

5. To execute each step in sequence, press the space bar after each subsequent step.

Fig. 11.14.
The STEP indicator, which appears when you select the Step option.

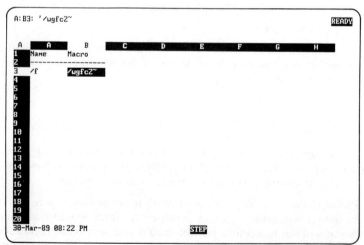

Figure 11.15 shows the first keystroke of the macro from figure 11.13 being executed. The first keystroke of that macro is the slash key (/) and, accordingly, the

1-2-3 command menu is activated. Notice that the STEP indicator now appears as SST.

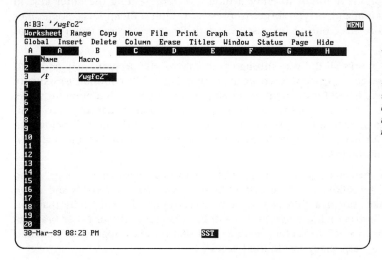

```
A:B3: '/ugfc2~                                                    MENU
Worksheet Range Copy Move File Print Graph Data System Quit
Global Insert Delete Column Erase Titles Window Status Page Hide
 A       A        B        C       D       E       F       G       H
 1    Name     Macro
 2    ----------------
 3    /f       /ugfc2~
 4
 5
 6
 7
 8
 9
10
11
12
13
14
15
16
17
18
19
20
30-Mar-89 08:23 PM                          SST
```

Fig. 11.15.
The SST
indicator,
which appears
when you
begin to step
through the
macro.

If you find your error, terminate the macro by pressing Ctrl-Break, and then Esc or Enter. Edit the macro to correct the error. Then repeat the test procedure in case more errors exist further along in the macro—as is often the case.

Edit macros as you would any label. Move the cell pointer to the cell containing the label you want to edit (in this case, the macro line), press Edit (F2) to go into EDIT mode, and then make your changes to the label. (Using the Edit key is described in detail in Chapter 3.)

When you want to execute the macro without stepping through one keystroke at a time, press Record (Alt-F2) and select Step to turn off the Step option. You also can turn off the option during execution of a macro by pressing Record (Alt-F2) when 1-2-3 is waiting for you to press another key and continue stepping.

Watching for Common Macro Errors

As you test your macros, you should watch for some common errors, described in the text that follows. In addition, refer to the "Troubleshooting" section of this book; that section identifies some of the more common macro problems. You should find that material a helpful companion as you begin testing and debugging, or fixing, your macros.

If 1-2-3 cannot execute your macro as written, the program displays an error message and the cell address where the error is located. Typically, this message should point you to the error. However, the real error—that is, the place 1-2-3 stops executing keystrokes the way you want them—precedes the error identified in the error message.

In the cell identified by the error message, keep your eyes peeled for the chronic macro errors everyone seems to make. If 1-2-3 stops on one of the 1-2-3 commands, you probably forgot to enter a tilde (~), representing the Enter key, to complete a command; or you forget to press Q to quit a menu level. Sometimes you need more than one Q because you actually have several menu levels to quit.

Even if 1-2-3 works all the way through your macro, the program may end with an error message or a beep. Keep in mind that 1-2-3 will continue to execute macro commands until it encounters an empty cell, a cell with a numeric value, or one of the advanced commands that stops macros and advanced macro command programs. Accordingly, use /Range Erase to verify that the cell below the last line of your macro is empty. If the cell is not empty, you've identified at least one of your problems.

If you get a message about an unrecognized macro keyword or range name —which will be followed by the cell address—check your keywords and range names to make sure that they are spelled correctly. In addition, verify that you are using the correct kind of braces—{ }—rather than parentheses ( ) or brackets [ ]; that arguments are correctly specified; and that no extra spaces are included in your macro—especially inside the braces { }.

Documenting Your Macros

Reminder:
Use several
techniques to
document your
macros.

Like every other part of a 1-2-3 worksheet, you need to document your macros. You can document macros using many of the same techniques you use to document worksheets. Use the following techniques to better document your macros:

- Use descriptive names as macro names.
- Use the /Range Name Note feature.
- Include comments within your worksheet.
- Keep any external design notes.

Using Descriptive Names

In previous releases of 1-2-3, you could use only the backslash and a letter to name a macro. You then used this letter and the Alt key to execute the macro. While short, one-letter macros proved easy to execute, the names weren't very descriptive. Because you now can use range names as macro names for macros you will execute with the Run (Alt-F3) key, try to use longer, more meaningful macro names. For example, suppose that you have two identical macros, except one's name is \p and the other's name is PRINT_BUDGET. Clearly the name PRINT_BUDGET does more than just provide a name; it also gives you an idea about what the macro does.

Using the /Range Name Note Feature

Another 1-2-3 feature you can use to document your macros is /**Range Name Note**, which allows you to attach a note to a range name. (Range name notes are described in detail along with other **R**ange commands in Chapter 4.) You should find the /**R**ange Name Note capability particularly valuable in documenting macros originally created in previous releases of 1-2-3, and that are therefore named with the backslash and a single letter. If you have a print macro named \p, for example, you might document the macro with a range name note that gives the description *Prints the 1988 budget*. The note gives you an idea of what the macro does without requiring you to review the macro itself.

Cue:
*Use /Range Name
Note to document
your macros.*

Including Comments in Your Worksheet

Figure 12.4 includes, to the right of the actual macro, descriptions of what each macro does. With simple macros like the ones in the figure, identifying what tasks the macros perform is fairly easy. However, with more complex and longer macros—such as those discussed and demonstrated in the next chapter, you probably will find this sort of internal documentation helpful. Later on, when you want to make changes to the macro, or when someone else wants to make changes, these internal comments provide information on just what a macro is supposed to do and how it is supposed to do it.

Reminder:
*Comments provide
information on
what a macro is
supposed to do
and how it is
supposed to do it.*

Keeping External Design Notes

If you created any paperwork as part of designing and constructing a macro, you should retain it. Don't make the mistake of underestimating the value of this sort of external documentation. As with each form of macro documentation, this material eases considerably the burden of trying later to understand or modify a macro. In general, the more people who use a macro and the more important a macro is, the more critical this sort of external documentation becomes.

Cue:
*Retain any
paperwork you
created as part of
designing and
constructing a
macro.*

The most important piece of external documentation—which never should be neglected—is a hard copy printout of the macro. Examples of other external documentation that may be particularly valuable include notes on who requested a macro and why they requested it, who created a macro and who tested it, the underlying assumptions that determined the overall design, and any diagrams or outlines of macro operations or structure.

Moving Up to the Advanced Macro Commands

If you find yourself writing larger and larger macros—macros that begin to use dozens or hundreds of keystrokes, consider using 1-2-3's advanced macro commands, described in Chapter 12. You use the advanced macro commands in place of 1-2-3's menu commands.

Reminder:
Advanced macro commands are better suited for writing large programs than simple macro commands.

The advanced macro commands are much better suited for writing large programs because the commands are complete words and are much less cryptic than simple macro commands. For example, to erase a range in a macro program, you use the keystrokes /re; in an advanced macro command program, you use the command {BLANK}.

The advanced macro commands also allow you to perform operations that go beyond what's possible from the 1-2-3 command menu—such as reading and writing records to external files and recalculating only a portion of a worksheet. If all this sounds like something you never want to get involved in, don't worry. You don't ever have to use the advanced macro commands. However, if you find yourself more and more restricted and frustrated by the limitations of your macro programs, consider moving up to 1-2-3's advanced macro commands.

Chapter Summary

This chapter has given you the information, and hopefully, the confidence to begin creating your own macros—tools that you can use to save time, reduce repetition, and automate your worksheet models. The chapter defined a macro and walked you through the steps to create some simple macros. The chapter also described the three ways you can name and run macros, explained how to build a simple macro library, showed you how to use 1-2-3 Release 3's new feature—Record—to create and test macros, and reviewed techniques for documenting your macros. The chapter concluded with some ideas on when it's time for you to move up to 1-2-3's advanced macro commands, the subject covered in the next chapter.

12

Introducing the Advanced Macro Commands

In addition to 1-2-3's keyboard macro capabilities, the program contains a powerful set of commands offering many features of a full-featured programming language. This set of commands, which includes the original Release 1A /x commands plus 50 other commands, is called the advanced macro commands (formerly called the Command Language). With the advanced macro commands, you can customize and automate 1-2-3 for your worksheet applications.

In the preceding chapter, you learned how to automate keystrokes to save precious time by streamlining work functions with macros. This chapter explains the various advanced macro commands you can use to perform a variety of programming tasks.

This chapter is not designed to teach programming theory and concepts, but rather to introduce you to the capabilities of programming with the advanced macro commands. If you have a burning desire to try your hand at programming, or if you want to become your company's 1-2-3 expert (creating models to amaze every department), or if you are interested in developing template models to distribute on the open market, you should begin by reading this chapter.

Why Use the Advanced Macro Commands?

Programs created with the advanced macro commands give you added control and flexibility in the use of your 1-2-3 worksheets. With the advanced macro commands, you control such tasks as accepting input from the keyboard during a program, performing conditional tests, repeatedly performing a sequence of commands, and creating user-defined command menus. You can use the advanced macro commands as a full-featured programming language to develop custom worksheets for specific business applications. For example, by developing advanced macro command programs that guide users to enter and change data on a worksheet, you can ensure that data is entered correctly. Even novice users who aren't familiar with all of 1-2-3's commands and operations can use program applications of this type.

After learning the concepts and the parts of the advanced macro commands discussed in this chapter, you will be ready to develop programs that perform the following tasks:

- Create menu-driven spreadsheet/database models

- Accept and control input from a user

- Manipulate data within and between files

- Execute tasks a predetermined number of times

- Control program flow

- Set up and print multiple reports

- Make intelligent decisions based on user input

- Execute multiple programs based on decisions made within programs

As you become more experienced with the advanced macro commands, you will be able to take advantage of its full power to do the following:

- Disengage or redefine the function keys

- Develop a complete business system—from order entry to inventory control to accounting

- Operate 1-2-3 as a disk-based database system—limiting the size and speed of the file operation only to the size and speed of the hard disk

If you want to take 1-2-3 to its practical limits, the set of advanced macro commands is the proper vehicle, and your creativity can be the necessary fuel.

What Are the Advanced Macro Commands?

The 1-2-3 advanced macro commands are a set of 50 invisible commands. These commands are called *invisible* because, unlike the command instructions that are invoked through the 1-2-3 menu and function keys, the advanced macro commands cannot be invoked from the keyboard. These commands can be used only within macro and advanced macro command programs.

The program in figure 12.1 illustrates how you can use the advanced macro commands. With commands such as MENUBRANCH and BRANCH, you can create custom menus to assist and prompt the user. The program in figure 12.1 begins by creating a range name wherever the user has positioned the cell pointer prior to invoking the program. The second line continues by displaying a custom help screen. The third line uses the MENUBRANCH command to display a menu with three options: to select the next help screen, to select the previous help screen, or to return to the original cell-pointer position in the worksheet. The BRANCH command in the last line of the first two options causes the program to redisplay the menu after the user has selected either the next or the previous help screen.

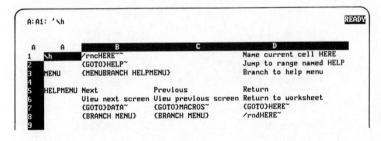

Fig. 12.1.
An advanced macro command program using MENUBRANCH and BRANCH.

Notice that the program branches to range names and not to cell addresses. This is a convention you probably will want to use. Not only does this practice make the program easier to read, but as you move cells, insert and delete rows and columns, and rearrange your worksheet, 1-2-3 updates the range name addresses. Your program, then, continues to operate on the correct cells and ranges.

As you read this chapter, you will learn about the commands for accepting input; for program control; for decision-making operations; for data manipulation; for program enhancement; and for file manipulation. You will find tables that list and describe these commands throughout the text.

1-2-3's /x Commands

In addition to the 50 advanced macro commands, 1-2-3 includes a set of eight /x commands. These commands were included in the original 1-2-3 Release 1A to provide a "limited" programming capability that went beyond simple keystroke macros. All eight /x commands have advanced macro command counterparts. The eight /x commands and their advanced macro command counterparts include the following:

/x Command	Description	Advanced Macro Command Alternative
/xi	Sets up an If-then-else condition	IF
/xq	Quits execution	QUIT
/xg	Instructs a program to continue at a new location	BRANCH
/xc	Runs a subroutine	{subroutine}
/xr	Returns to the next line of the macro calling this subroutine	RETURN
/xm	Creates a menu	MENUBRANCH
/xn	Accepts input of only numeric entries	GETNUMBER
/xl	Accepts input of only labels	GETLABEL

Six of these commands work exactly like their advanced macro command counterparts: /xi, /xq, /xg, /xc, /xr, and /xm. For example, /xq performs exactly like the advanced macro command QUIT. When inserted into a program, both commands will produce the same result.

The remaining /x commands—/xn and /xl—work a little differently than their comparable advanced macro commands. These commands are used to prompt the user for text and numeric data and then place the data in the current cell. Before their advanced macro command counterparts (GETLABEL and GETNUMBER) can do the same tasks, some programming is required. /xn, unlike GETNUMBER, does not allow users to enter alphabetical characters (except for range names and cell addresses), nor does /xn let the user simply press Enter in response to the prompt.

Except in the special instances in which /xn and /xl perform differently from their advanced macro command counterparts, the /x commands should not be used in new programs developed in Release 3. /x commands are beneficial, however, because they enable you to run and easily modify in Release 3 programs originally developed in Release 1A.

The Elements of Advanced Macro Command Programs

In the examples that follow, you will see how you can incorporate macros with the advanced macro commands to produce complete, efficient programs that take 1-2-3's macro capability far beyond simply automating keystrokes. Advanced macro command programs contain the advanced macro commands and all the elements that can be included in macros. Programs can include the following:

- Keystrokes used for selecting 1-2-3 commands (for example, /rfc0)
- Range names and cell addresses
- Keywords for moving the cell pointer (see Chapter 11 for a list of keywords)
- Keywords for function keys (see Chapter 11)
- Keywords for editing (see Chapter 11)
- Key representation for Enter: ~
- Advanced macro commands

Advanced Macro Syntax Command

Like the keywords used in macros (discussed in Chapter 11), all the advanced macro commands are enclosed in braces. Just as you must represent the right-arrow key in a macro as {RIGHT}, you must enclose a command, such as QUIT, in braces: {QUIT}.

Tip: When you write advanced macro command programs, press the Name (F3) key once to enter an open brace ({); 1-2-3 lists all the valid commands and key names, such as {QUIT} and {CALC}. To enter the needed command or key name, highlight it and press Enter.

Some commands amount to just a single command enclosed in braces. For example, to quit a macro during its execution, you use the command {QUIT}; no arguments are given. Many other commands, however, require additional arguments within the boundaries of the braces. The arguments that follow commands have a grammar similar to the grammar used in 1-2-3 functions. The general syntax of commands that require arguments is

{COMMAND argument1,argument2,...,argumentN}

When you use the BRANCH command to transfer program control to a specific location in the program, for example, you must follow the word {BRANCH} with the cell address or range name indicating where the program should branch. In the command {BRANCH rangename}, rangename is the argument.

An argument can consist of numbers, strings, cell addresses, range names, formulas, or functions. The command and the first argument is separated by a space and, for most commands, arguments are separated by commas (with no spaces). As you study the syntax for the specific commands described in this chapter, keep in mind the importance of following the conventions for spacing and punctuation.

Creating, Using, and Debugging Advanced Macro Command Programs

With advanced macro command programs, as with macros, you must keep several considerations in mind to ensure that your programs are efficient and error-free. You begin by defining which actions you want the program to perform and determining the sequence of those actions. Then you develop the program, test it, debug it, and cross-check its results for all possible operations.

If you have created keyboard macros, you have a head start toward creating advanced macro command programs. These programs share many of the conventions used in the keyboard macros presented in Chapter 11. If you haven't yet experimented with 1-2-3 macros, you should take some time to review Chapter 11's simple keystroke macros before you try to develop advanced macro command programs. You also should review Chapter 11's discussions of creating, using, and debugging macros because many of the concepts are related to advanced macro command programs. For users who have created macros and read Chapter 11, the following text gives a brief overview.

Like keyboard macros, advanced macro command programs should be carefully planned and positioned on the worksheet. Locating your macros and advanced macro command programs in a separate worksheet or file is the best practice. If you have macros that you use with many different worksheets, you may want to group them in a separate file. When the time comes to use those macros, issue the /File Open command to activate the macro file. If, however, you have a macro that is specific to one file, create a separate worksheet and store that macro on the separate worksheet in that file.

You enter advanced macro command programs just as you enter macros—as text cells. You must use a label prefix to start any line that begins with a nontext character (such as / or <) so that 1-2-3 does not interpret the characters that follow as numbers or commands. After you decide where to locate your program and begin entering program lines, keep several considerations in mind. Remember to document your advanced macro command programs, as you would document macros, to the right of each program line. Because advanced macro command programs usually are more complex than macros, documenting each line is essential. A documented program (see fig. 12.1) is easier to debug and change than an undocumented one.

As described in Chapter 11, you can invoke macro and advanced macro command programs in one of three ways:

- Macros or advanced macro command programs you named using the backslash key and a letter character can be invoked by pressing and holding the Alt key while pressing the appropriate letter key.

- Macros or advanced macro command programs you named using complete range names can be invoked using the Run (Alt-F3) key. (As noted in Chapter 11, you can actually invoke any macro or advanced macro command program using the Run key.)

- Macros or advanced macro command programs you named using the backslash key and 0 are automatically executed when a file is loaded or opened as long as the /Worksheet Global Default Autoexec setting is Yes—which is the default.

After you have developed and started to run your program, you may need to debug it. Like macros, advanced macro command programs are subject to such problems as missing tildes (˜), and misspelled keywords and range names. Another problem is the use of cell addresses that remain absolute in the program but have changed in a worksheet application. You can solve the cell-address problem by using range names in place of cell addresses wherever possible.

To debug advanced macro command programs, you use 1-2-3's STEP mode as you would for simple keyboard macros. Before you execute the program, press Record (Alt-F2) and select Step to invoke STEP mode. Then execute your advanced macro command program. Press any letter key or the space bar to activate each operation in the program. When you discover the error, press Record (Alt-F2) and select Step to turn off STEP mode, press Esc, and edit your program.

The Advanced Macro Commands

Using the power of the program's advanced macro commands, you can make 1-2-3 applications easier to use, you can enhance the features of 1-2-3's regular commands, and you can customize 1-2-3 for special worksheet applications. In the following sections, the advanced macro commands are grouped into six categories: accepting input, program control, decision-making operations, data manipulation, program enhancement, and file manipulation.

Commands for Accepting Input

The ?, GET, GETLABEL, GETNUMBER, LOOK, and FORM commands provide for all possible types of input into a 1-2-3 file (see table 12.1). These commands can be used also to provide the operator with a more user-friendly interface than that of 1-2-3's standard commands and operations. For example, you can use these commands to create prompts that help the user enter data more easily and quickly. These commands also make performing simple edit checks on the input before storing it in the worksheet easier.

Table 12.1
Commands for Accepting Input

Command	Description
{?}	Accepts any type of input
{GET}	Accepts a single character into the location specified
{GETLABEL}	Accepts a label into the location specified
{GETNUMBER}	Accepts a number into the location specified
{LOOK}	Places the first character from the type-ahead buffer into the location specified
{FORM}	Interrupts macro execution so that data can be entered into an input range's unprotected cells

The ? Command

The ? command causes the program to pause while you enter any type of information. During the pause, no prompt is displayed in the control panel; you can move the cell pointer to direct the location of the input. The program continues executing after you press the Enter key. The format for the ? command is as follows:

{?}   Accepts any type of input

For example, the following one-line program combines macro commands and an advanced macro command to create a file-retrieve program:

```
/fr{NAME}{?}~
```

This program displays all files in the current drive and directory, and then pauses to accept input from the user. In this instance, you can either type the name of a viewed file or simply move the cell pointer to a file name and press Enter.

Tip: Even if you press Enter after you type a {?} entry, you still must include a tilde (˜) at the end of the menu sequence.

The GET Command

The GET command places a single keystroke into a target cell. The keystroke then can be analyzed or tested in a number of ways, and the results of these tests can be used to change the flow of the program. The format for the GET command is as follows:

{GET location}   Accepts single keystroke into range defined by location

In the example shown in figure 12.2, the GET statement traps individual keystrokes in a cell named CAPTURE. The second line evaluates CAPTURE. If the keystroke in CAPTURE is the letter Q, the file is saved automatically. If CAPTURE contains any other keystroke, /fs˜ r is ignored. In either case, control is passed to the third line of the program, which places the cell pointer in cell F25.

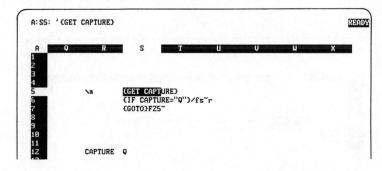

Fig. 12.2.
The GET command used to trap keystrokes.

A more involved use of GET is shown in figure 12.3. Suppose that you are writing an inventory program and want to prompt the user to make a one-keystroke choice to enter data on premium- or regular-quality widgets. Figure 12.3 shows the program you might use in such an application.

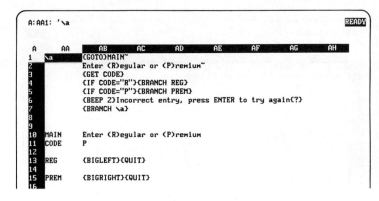

Fig. 12.3.
The GET command used to allow one-character input.

In this example, the GET command is used to pause the program while the user enters a single letter from the keyboard and to store that entry in a cell named CODE. Notice that the program enters the user-prompt in the cell named MAIN. If you want a prompt to appear in the control panel rather than in the worksheet, you must use the GETLABEL or GETNUMBER command.

The GETLABEL Command

The GETLABEL command accepts any type of entry from the keyboard. The prompt, which must be a string enclosed in quotation marks, is then displayed in the control panel. With this command, the entry is placed in the location cell as a label when the user presses the Enter key. The format for the GETLABEL command is as follows:

{GETLABEL prompt,location}   Accepts label into location

In the example in figure 12.4, the GETLABEL statement displays a prompt and accepts a label date into cell R19. The second line places in cell R20 a formula that converts the label date to a numerical date, and then formats the cell to appear as a date.

Fig. 12.4.
The GETLABEL
command used
to allow input
of a label date.

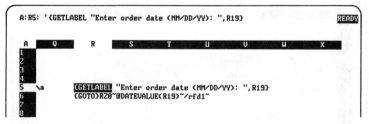

```
A:R5: '{GETLABEL "Enter order date (MM/DD/YY): ",R19}                    READY

        A    Q      R      S      T      U      V      W      X
    1
    2
    3
    4
    5    \a     {GETLABEL} "Enter order date (MM/DD/YY): ",R19}
    6           {GOTO}R20~@DATEVALUE(R19)~/rfd1~
    7
    8
```

Figure 12.5 shows how to use GETLABEL with the IF, BRANCH, and BEEP commands (discussed later in this chapter) to prompt the user for the description of a part. If the user makes an incorrect entry, the second GETLABEL command displays an error message, and the program pauses until the user presses any key. Remember that whatever is entered in response to the prompt is stored in DESC.

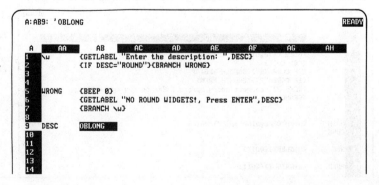

Fig. 12.5.
The GETLABEL
command used
with other
commands to
allow more
complex string
input.

```
A:AB9: 'OBLONG                                                          READY

        A    AA     AB      AC      AD      AE      AF      AG      AH
    1    \w     {GETLABEL "Enter the description: ",DESC}
    2           {IF DESC="ROUND"}{BRANCH WRONG}
    3
    4
    5    WRONG  {BEEP 0}
    6           {GETLABEL "NO ROUND WIDGETS!, Press ENTER",DESC}
    7           {BRANCH \w}
    8
    9    DESC   OBLONG
   10
   11
   12
   13
   14
```

GETLABEL versus /xl

GETLABEL and /xl are identical except for one /xl command feature. Suppose, for example, that you write the /xl command as follows:

```
/xlprompt~~
```

The label entered in response to the prompt is placed at the cell pointer's current location. You cannot write this kind of instruction with the GETLABEL command because 1-2-3 will give you an error message if you don't specify a location for the argument. Using the /xl command is much more convenient than using the GETLABEL command, for example, in a subroutine in which the location of the destination cell changes with each subroutine call. By using /xl in such a situation, you don't have to specify the location at which the label will be placed.

The GETNUMBER Command

The GETNUMBER command accepts only numerical entries. Entering a label results in ERR being displayed in the cell. The prompt, which must be a string enclosed in quotation marks, is displayed in the control panel, and the entry is placed in the cell when you press Enter. The format for the GETNUMBER command is as follows:

{GETNUMBER prompt,location}   Accepts the number into location

In the example in figure 12.6, the GETNUMBER statement displays a prompt and accepts a numerical entry into cell S10. The second line then copies that numerical entry into the next blank row in column A. The @COUNT function finds the next open row in column A.

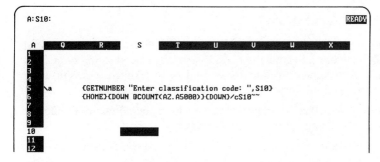

Fig. 12.6.
The GETNUMBER command used to allow numerical input.

Figure 12.7 shows how GETNUMBER can be used in an inventory application. Here GETNUMBER prompts the user for a part number. If the user does not enter a number between 0 and 9999, the program displays the message

INVALID PART NUMBER!, press ENTER

The user is then prompted to enter another number.

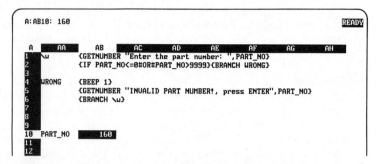

Fig. 12.7.
The
GETNUMBER
command used
in an inventory
application.

GETNUMBER versus /xn

The GETNUMBER and /xn commands work differently. With GETNUMBER, a blank entry or a text entry has a numeric value of ERR. With /xn, however, if the entry is a blank or a text entry, an error message is displayed, and the user is again prompted for a number. This difference can be useful in some applications. If, for example, you accidentally press Q (a letter) instead of the 1 key, the /xn command returns an error message. You can use the /xn command also in the following form:

/xnprompt˜

This command reads a numeric value into the current cell instead of into a specified location. (See the discussion at the end of the GETLABEL section.)

The LOOK Command

The LOOK command checks 1-2-3's type-ahead buffer. If any keys are pressed after the program execution begins, the first keystroke is placed in the target cell location. The LOOK command frequently is used to interrupt processing until you press a key. The general format of the command is as follows:

{LOOK location}   Places the first character from the type-ahead buffer into the location specified

When the LOOK command is executed, the keyboard type-ahead buffer is checked, and the first character is copied into the indicated location. This means that you can type a character at any time, and the program will find it when the LOOK command is executed. The contents of location can then be tested with an IF statement. Because the character is not removed from the type-ahead buffer, you must make provisions to use it or dispose of it before the program needs keyboard input or ends.

In the program in figure 12.8, the LOOK statement examines 1-2-3's type-ahead buffer and places the first keystroke in the cell named CAPTURE. If no keys have been pressed, the LOOK statement blanks the cell, leaving only a label prefix. Although program execution is not halted by this first statement, lines two and three of the sample program force the program to pause. Line three forms a looping structure until a key is pressed, satisfying the IF condition in line two. This is the most common use of the LOOK statement. (For more information, see the discussions of the IF and BRANCH commands.)

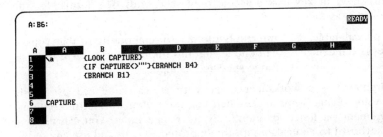

Fig. 12.8.
The LOOK command used to examine the type-ahead buffer and place the first keystroke in the specified location.

As a simple test of the LOOK command, try the example in figure 12.9. This program causes the speaker to beep until you press any key. Each time the LOOK command is encountered, 1-2-3 checks the keyboard buffer and copies into the location INTERRUPT the first character found. Then an IF statement checks the contents of INTERRUPT and branches accordingly. The GETLABEL command at the end of the program serves to dispose of the keystroke that interrupted the loop.

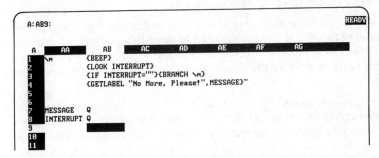

Fig. 12.9.
The LOOK command used to stop a beeping program.

The LOOK command is most helpful when you have built a lengthy program to process, such as a stock-portfolio database, and you want to be able to stop processing at certain points in the program. You can enter a LOOK command followed by an IF statement, similar to that in figure 12.9, at several places in the program. Then, if you press a key, the program stops the next time a LOOK command is executed. If you do not touch the keyboard, the program continues processing. In this example, the LOOK command is preferable to the GET command, which always stops the program to wait for an entry.

The FORM Command

The FORM command interrupts macro execution temporarily so that the user can enter input into the unprotected cells in a specified range. While FORM is similar to the /Range Input command, FORM includes three added options that you may often find useful. First, FORM will branch to another line of advanced macro command instructions if the user enters certain keys. Second, FORM will allow you to specify a set of keystrokes as invalid. And, finally, FORM will allow you to specify a set of keystrokes as the only valid ones. The format for the FORM command is as follows:

{FORM input,call-table, include-keys,exclude-keys}	Interrupts the macro temporarily so that you can enter data into unprotected cells in the range specified as input

The input argument is a worksheet range with at least one cell previously unprotected using /Range Unprotect. When you use FORM without the optional last three arguments, it functions identically to /Range Input: You can use any keys on the keyboard to enter data into the unprotected cells and use any of the cursor-movement keys to move between the unprotected cells. To complete execution of the FORM command, you press Enter or Esc while 1-2-3 is in READY mode. 1-2-3 then continues execution of the advanced macro command program with the cell pointer located wherever it was when you completed FORM.

You can use FORM's three optional arguments—call-table, include-keys, and exclude-keys—either individually or in any combination. Call-table represents a two-column range where the first column lists the names of keys on the keyboard, such as {CALC} or {GRAPH}, and the second column gives the commands that 1-2-3 should execute when you press the key.

Include-keys allows you to specify a range that lists all the keystrokes acceptable during execution of the FORM command. Keep in mind that you will be entering not only keystrokes into the unprotected field in the input range, but also any other keys you need to operate the macro or to deal with an error condition, such as {ESC}.

Exclude-keys allows you to specify a range that lists all the keystrokes unacceptable during the execution of the FORM command. Because by specifying the unacceptable keys you implicitly identify the acceptable keys, you probably will use either the include-keys or the exclude-keys argument, but not both. To omit an optional argument, use one of the following command structures:

{FORM input}
To omit all optional arguments

{FORM input,call-table}
To use only call-table

{FORM input,,include-keys}
To use only include-keys

{FORM input,,,exclude-keys}
To use only exclude-keys

{FORM input,call-table,include-keys}
To use call-table and include-keys

{FORM input,,include-keys,exclude-keys}
To use only include-keys and exclude-keys (although this form is often redundant or illogical)

{FORM input,call-table,,exclude-keys}
To use call-table and exclude-keys

Figure 12.10 shows an example of FORM used to accept data about checks into the unprotected cells B1, B3, B5, and B7 in the range INPUT. The call-table argument, KEYS, specifies additional keystrokes to be executed when certain keys are pressed—in this case, {CALC} and {GRAPH}, a series of beeps. The example doesn't use an include-keys argument, but does use an exclude-keys argument. The range EXCLUDE (E7..E16) shows the excluded keystrokes.

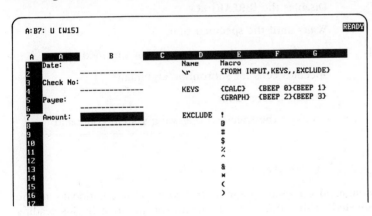

Fig. 12.10.
The FORM command used to collect inputs and specify valid keystrokes.

Commands for Program Control

The commands shown in table 12.2 (BRANCH, MENUBRANCH, MENUCALL, RETURN, QUIT, ONERROR, BREAKOFF, BREAKON, WAIT, DISPATCH, DEFINE, RESTART, and SYSTEM) allow varying degrees of control in 1-2-3 programs. These commands, used alone or in combination with decision-making commands, afford the programmer precise control of program flow.

Table 12.2
Commands for Program Control

Command	Description
{BRANCH}	Continues program execution at the location specified
{MENUBRANCH}	Prompts user with menu found at the location specified
{MENUCALL}	Like MENUBRANCH, except that control returns to the statement after the MENUCALL
{RETURN}	Returns from a program subroutine
{QUIT}	Ends program execution
{ONERROR}	Traps errors, passing control to the branch specified
{BREAKON}	Enables the {BREAK} key
{BREAKOFF}	Disables the {BREAK} key
{WAIT}	Waits until the specified time
{DISPATCH}	Branches indirectly via the location specified
{DEFINE}	Specifies cells for subroutine arguments
{RESTART}	Cancels a subroutine
{SYSTEM}	Executes the specified operating system command

The BRANCH Command

The BRANCH command causes program control to pass unconditionally to the cell address indicated in the BRANCH statement. The program begins reading commands and statements at the cell location indicated in the location argument. Program control does not return to the line from which it was passed unless directed to do so by another BRANCH statement. The general format of the BRANCH command is as follows:

{BRANCH location}   Continues program execution in the cell specified by location

In the example in figure 12.11, the first line places the cell pointer in cell R34 and then enters a @COUNT function. The second line passes program control to cell F13, regardless of any commands that may follow the BRANCH command (in either the same cell location or the cell below). Program commands are read beginning in cell F13.

BRANCH is an unconditional command unless it is preceded by an IF conditional statement, as in the following example:

{IF C22 = "alpha"}{BRANCH G24} {GOTO}S101~

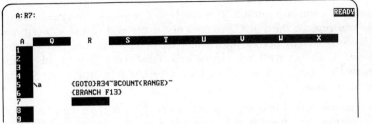

Fig. 12.11.
The BRANCH command used to pass program control to cell F13.

The IF statement must be in the same cell to act as a conditional testing statement. For more information, see the discussion of the IF command.

Suppose, for example, that three separate companies are under your corporate umbrella and that you have written a program for adding and modifying records in a corporate personnel database. Depending on how the user of the program responds to the following prompt, you want the program to branch to a different place in the program and prompt the user further for data specific to that company.

    Enter Company (R, A, or C):

Figure 12.12 shows a portion of the program.

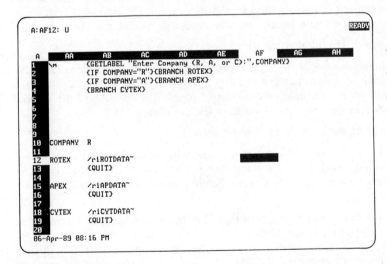

Fig. 12.12.
The BRANCH command used in a database application.

The BRANCH statements in the \m program cause the flow of program execution to shift to the different company routines. In this example, the BRANCH statements are coupled with IF statements to shift execution conditionally, depending on the user's response. After the program executes a company routine, the QUIT statement at the end of the routine causes program execution to stop.

You may prefer that execution return to the \m program or to another program after completing the company routine. This can be accomplished in either of two ways: (1) you can replace the {QUIT} statements at the end of the subroutines with {BRANCH \m} statements to return to \m; or (2) you can replace the BRANCH statements in \m with subroutine calls (discussed later in this chapter); then, in the subroutine, you can include a BRANCH to the point where execution should continue.

You need to remember two important points about BRANCH statements. First, they cause a permanent shift in the flow of statement execution. Second, BRANCH statements are most often used in combination with IF statements.

The MENUBRANCH Command

The MENUBRANCH command defines and displays in the control panel a menu-selection structure from which as many as eight individual programs can be initiated. You select the desired menu item as you would make a selection from a 1-2-3 command menu. The format of the MENUBRANCH command is as follows:

{MENUBRANCH location}   Executes menu structure at location

The menu invoked by the MENUBRANCH command consists of one to eight consecutive columns in the worksheet. Each column corresponds to one item in the menu. The upper-left corner of the range named in a MENUBRANCH statement must refer to the first menu item; otherwise, you will receive the error message

Invalid use of Menu macro command

Each menu item consists of three or more rows in the same column. The first row is the menu option name. Try to keep the option name items short so that they all will fit on the top line of the control panel. If the length of the option name exceeds 80 characters, 1-2-3 displays the error message

Invalid use of Menu macro command

Be careful to choose option names that begin with different letters. If two or more options begin with the same letter and you try to use the first-letter technique to access an option, 1-2-3 selects the first option it finds with the letter you specified.

The second row in the menu range contains descriptions of the menu items. The description is displayed in the bottom row of the control panel when the cell pointer highlights the name of the corresponding menu option. Each description can contain up to 80 characters of text. The description row must be present, even if it is blank.

The third row begins the actual program command sequence. After the individual programs have been executed, program control must be directed by statements at the end of each individual program. No empty columns can exist between menu items; the column immediately to the right of the last menu item must be empty. You can supplement the 1-2-3 menu structure by creating a full-screen menu (for enhancement purposes only).

In figure 12.13, the MENUBRANCH statement produces a menu structure that begins in cell AB4. The individual programs begin in row 6 in each column. Each of these programs must contain a statement to continue after the main task has been completed.

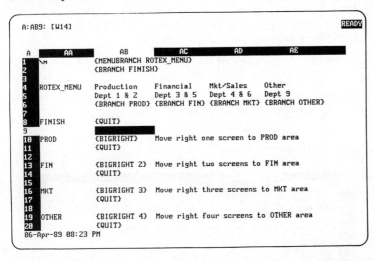

Fig. 12.13.
A program using the MENUBRANCH command.

Suppose, for example, that you are using the corporate personnel database and that you have entered the program shown in figure 12.13. When the MENUBRANCH statement is executed, 1-2-3 displays in the control panel the menu beginning at the cell ROTEX_MENU. (Note: The /**R**ange Name **L**abels **R**ight command was used to assign the name ROTEX_MENU to the cell in which the label Production resides; Production is the first menu item.)

You can select the desired menu item either by moving the cell pointer with the arrow keys or by pressing the first letter of the menu item. The bottom line of the control panel contains a description of the menu item currently highlighted by the user. For instance, when you move the cell pointer to Financial, the third-line description is Dept 3 & 5.

Now suppose that you want to select the second menu item—Financial. You select it the same way you do any 1-2-3 menu item: press Enter after you position the highlighter on your choice, or enter the first letter of the menu item. The menus you create with the MENUBRANCH command are just like the 1-2-3 command menus. After you select Financial from the menu, the next statement to be executed is {BRANCH FIN}. If, instead of selecting a menu item, you press the Esc key, 1-2-3 stops displaying the menu items and executes the next program command after the MENUBRANCH command—{BRANCH FINISH}.

Modeling tip: If you have a multilevel menu structure, you can make the Esc key function as it does in the 1-2-3 command menus (backing up to the previous menu). After the current MENUBRANCH command, place a BRANCH to the previous level's MENUBRANCH. When you press the Esc key, this BRANCH backs you up to the previous menu.

The MENUCALL Command

The MENUCALL command is identical to the MENUBRANCH command except that 1-2-3 executes the menu program as a subroutine. After the individual menu programs have been executed, program control returns to the cell immediately below the cell containing the MENUCALL statement. The format of the MENUCALL command is as follows:

{MENUCALL location}   Like MENUBRANCH except MENUCALL acts as a subroutine

Suppose that you replace the MENUBRANCH command in figure 12.13 with a MENUCALL. The results are shown in figure 12.14.

Fig. 12.14.
Use of the
MENUCALL
command
in place of
MENUBRANCH.

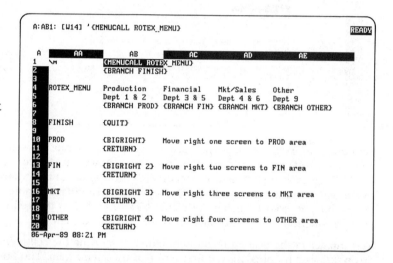

When you use a MENUCALL, 1-2-3 returns to the statement immediately following the MENUCALL whenever it reads a blank cell or a {RETURN}. Suppose, for example, that you select the Financial menu option, which causes 1-2-3 to branch to FIN. The first statement in FIN moves the cell pointer right two screens. When 1-2-3 encounters the {RETURN} statement, however, the flow of execution shifts back to the statement following the MENUCALL: the {BRANCH FINISH} statement.

Keep in mind that pressing Esc has the same effect with MENUCALL as it does with MENUBRANCH. Execution shifts to the statement following the MENUCALL statement. In this situation, you can use the technique described in the MENUBRANCH command modeling tip (using the Esc key).

The advantage of MENUCALL is that you can call the same menu from several different places in a program and continue execution from the calling point after the MENUCALL is finished. This is the advantage you get from using subroutines in general.

Subroutines {name}

A subroutine is an independent program that can be run from within the main program. Calling a subroutine is as easy as enclosing the name of a routine in braces—for example, {SUB}. When 1-2-3 encounters a name in braces, the program passes control to the named routine. Then, when the routine is finished (when 1-2-3 encounters a blank cell or a {RETURN}), program control passes back to the command in the cell below the cell that called the subroutine.

Why use subroutines?

Using subroutines can decrease creation time. For example, rather than include the same program lines to display a help screen in each advanced macro command program you create, type the program lines once to create the help screen, and call those lines as a subroutine from each program.

You will be able to isolate a problem much more easily if you use subroutines. If you suspect that a subroutine is creating a problem, you can replace the call to the subroutine with a {BEEP}. Then run the program. If the program runs correctly, beeping when the subroutine should be called, you know that the problem is in the subroutine.

Subroutines are easy to enhance. If you decide to add new commands, you can modify your subroutine once. All programs that call that subroutine will reflect the new commands.

The greatest benefit of a subroutine, however, is that any program can use it. Simply create the subroutine once, and then call it at any time from any program. When the subroutine is finished, program execution returns to the originating program.

The RETURN Command

The RETURN command indicates the end of subroutine execution and returns program control to the cell immediately below the cell that called the subroutine. When 1-2-3 reads the RETURN, the control returns to the main program (or other subroutine) at the location after the subroutine call. Do not confuse RETURN with QUIT, which ends the program completely. RETURN can be used with the IF statement to return conditionally from a subroutine. The form of this command is as follows:

{RETURN}   Returns control from a subroutine

In figure 12.15, the first line places the cell pointer in AA101 and then calls the subroutine {SUB}. After {SUB} is executed, the RETURN command passes control to the next command after the subroutine call, placing the cell pointer in the

HOME position and then copying the range of cells entered by the subroutine into the range identified by the HOME position as its upper-left corner.

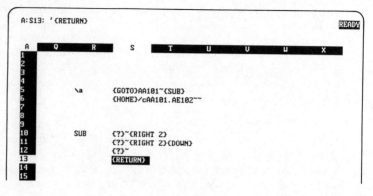

Fig. 12.15.
Use of the
RETURN
command.

1-2-3 also ends a subroutine and returns to the calling routine when the program encounters, while executing the subroutine, a cell that either is blank or contains a numeric value. Although this method of returning from a subroutine works, the RETURN command is preferred because it delimits a particular set of macro keywords and advanced macro command instructions as a subroutine.

The QUIT Command

The QUIT command forces the program to terminate unconditionally. Even without a QUIT command, the program will terminate if it encounters (within the program sequence) a cell that is empty or contains an entry other than a string. A good practice, however, is always to include a QUIT statement at the end of your programs to indicate that you intend execution to stop. (Conversely, do not put a QUIT command at the end of a program that you intend to call as a subroutine.) The form of the QUIT command is as follows:

{QUIT}   Halts program execution

In the following example, the QUIT command forces the program sequence to terminate unconditionally:

{HOME}/fs¯ r{QUIT}

This is not the case when QUIT is preceded by an IF conditional testing statement, as shown in figure 12.16.

The ONERROR Command

The processing of advanced macro command programs normally is interrupted if a system error (such as Disk drive not ready) occurs during execution. By sidestepping system errors that normally would cause program termination,

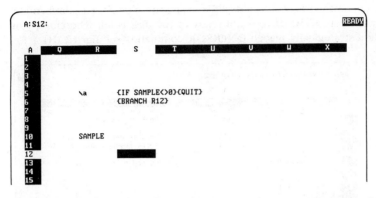

Fig. 12.16.
The QUIT command used with an IF statement.

the ONERROR command allows programs to proceed. The general format of the command is as follows:

{ONERROR branch,message}   Traps errors; program control passes to branch

The ONERROR command passes program control to the cell indicated by the first argument. Any errors can be recorded in the message cell (the optional second argument).

As a general rule, you always should make sure that your ONERROR statement is executed by the program before an error takes place. Therefore, you may want to include an ONERROR statement near the start of your programs. Because you can have only one ONERROR statement in effect at a time, you should take special precautions to write your programs so that the correct ONERROR is active when its specific error is most probable.

In figure 12.17, the ONERROR statement acts as a safeguard against leaving drive A empty or not closing the drive door. If an error occurs, program control passes to S10 and the error message in V10 is displayed. Because S10 is the file-save sequence, this program will not continue until drive A contains a disk and the drive door has been closed.

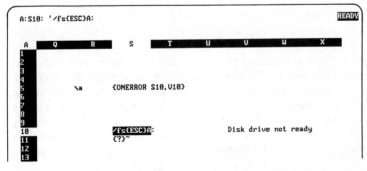

Fig. 12.17.
The ONERROR command used to prompt users to close the drive door.

The best place to put an ONERROR statement is directly above where you think an error may occur. Suppose, for example, that your program is about to copy a portion of the current worksheet to a disk file, using the /File **Xtract** command. A system error will occur if the drive is not ready or the disk is full. Therefore, you should include a strategically placed ONERROR command (see fig. 12.18).

Fig. 12.18.
An ONERROR
statement used
to retry disk
access.

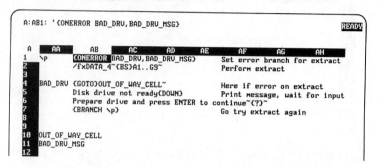

In this example, the ONERROR statement causes the program to branch to a cell called BAD_DRV if an error occurs. A copy of the error message that 1-2-3 issues is entered in a cell called BAD_DRV_MSG. Then, the first statement in the BAD_DRV routine positions the cell pointer in an out-of-the-way cell (cleverly called OUT_OF_WAY_CELL). Next, the following message is entered into the worksheet:

    Disk drive not ready

The preceding message is followed by another message:

    Prepare drive and press ENTER to continue

The program pauses for the user to press Enter. Finally, the program branches back to \p to try again.

Ctrl-Break presents a special problem for the ONERROR statement. Because Ctrl-Break actually causes an error condition, the ONERROR statement is automatically invoked. Therefore, a good technique when you plan to use the ONERROR statement is to disable Ctrl-Break after you have debugged your program. (See the following discussion of the BREAKOFF command.) By disabling Ctrl-Break, you can prevent the confusion that might arise with an untimely error message.

The BREAKOFF Command

The easiest way to stop a program is to issue a Ctrl-Break command. However, 1-2-3 can eliminate the effect of a Ctrl-Break while a program is executing. By including a BREAKOFF command in your program, you can prevent the user from stopping the program before its completion. Note: Before you use a BREAKOFF statement, you must be certain that the program has been fully debugged. Often, while debugging an advanced macro command program, you may need to issue a Ctrl-Break command to halt the program and make a "repair."

The BREAKOFF command disables the Ctrl-Break command during program execution. The format of the BREAKOFF command is as follows:

{BREAKOFF}   Disables Ctrl-Break sequence

Note: When a menu structure is displayed in the control panel, you can halt program execution by pressing Esc, regardless of the presence of a BREAKOFF command.

BREAKOFF is used primarily to prevent the user from interrupting a process and destroying the integrity of data in the worksheet. You will not need to use BREAKOFF unless you are developing extremely sophisticated programs; but, in such applications, BREAKOFF can be an important safeguard against problems caused by users.

The BREAKON Command

To restore the effect of Ctrl-Break, use the BREAKON command. The format of this command is as follows:

{BREAKON}   Enables Ctrl-Break sequence

You probably will want a simple one-line program that issues a BREAKON, just in case something happens to your original program during execution. You may also want to make sure that the last statement in your program before QUIT is BREAKON. Including BREAKON, for example, allows you to use Ctrl-Break to stop program execution or stop command executions.

Because any Ctrl-Break commands in the keyboard buffer are executed as soon as the BREAKON command is executed, be sure that the BREAKON is at a place where the program can stop safely. Figure 12.19 demonstrates how you can use the BREAKOFF and BREAKON commands.

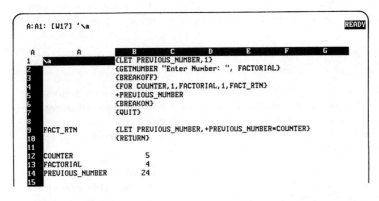

Fig. 12.19.
Use of the
BREAKON and
BREAKOFF
commands.

The WAIT Command

The WAIT command causes the program to pause until an appointed time. The general format of the WAIT command is as follows:

{WAIT argument}   Waits until time or elapsed time specified by argument

The WAIT statement in figure 12.20 allows the message to be displayed for five seconds.

Fig. 12.20. The WAIT command used to display a message.

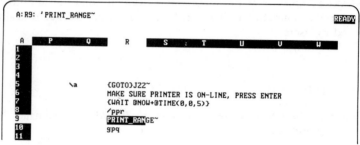

```
A:R9: 'PRINT_RANGE~                                          READY

A     P        Q       R       S    :    T        U        U        W
1
2
3
4
5              \a      {GOTO}J22~
6                      MAKE SURE PRINTER IS ON-LINE, PRESS ENTER
7                      {WAIT @NOW+@TIME(0,0,5)}
8                      /ppr
9                      PRINT_RANGE~
10                     gpq
11
```

The serial time-number must contain a date plus a time. If you want the program to wait until 6:00 p.m. today to continue, you can use the expression

{WAIT @INT(@NOW)+@TIME(18,00,00)}

To make the program pause for 50 seconds, use the expression

{WAIT @NOW+@TIME(00,00,50)}

The DISPATCH Command

The DISPATCH command is similar to the BRANCH command. The DISPATCH command, however, branches indirectly to a location specified by the value contained in the location pointed to by the argument. The format of the command is as follows:

{DISPATCH location}   Branches indirectly to the address stored in location

The location given as the DISPATCH argument should contain a cell address or range name that is the destination of the DISPATCH. If the cell referred to by the location argument does not contain a valid cell reference or range name, an error occurs and program execution either stops with an error message or transfers to the location in the current ONERROR command.

The location must be a cell reference or range name that points to a single cell reference. If the location is either a multicell range or a range that contains a single cell, the DISPATCH acts like a BRANCH statement and transfers execution directly to the location.

In figure 12.21, the DISPATCH statement selects the subroutine to be executed, based on the input in the cell number generated by the GETLABEL statement. The string formula in the DISPATCH command concatenates the word SUB and the menu selection number entered by the user. Because the name of every subroutine begins with the word SUB, the DISPATCH command passes program control to the subroutine specified by the user.

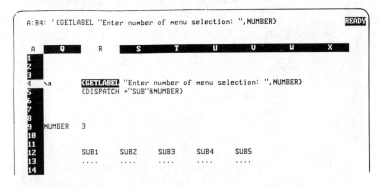

Fig. 12.21.
An example of the DISPATCH command.

The DEFINE Command

An important subroutine feature of 1-2-3 is the capability of passing arguments, using the only keyword version of the subroutine call. A subroutine called with arguments must begin with a DEFINE statement that associates each argument with a specific cell location. The format of the subroutine call with arguments is as follows:

{DEFINE loc1:Type1,... }   Specifies cells for subroutine arguments where loc1, loc2, and so on are names or cell references for the cells in which to place the arguments passed from the main program

One or more arguments, separated by commas, can be used. Type is either STRING or VALUE. Type is optional; if not present, the default is STRING. If an argument is of type STRING, the text of the corresponding argument in the subroutine call is placed in the indicated cell as a string value (label).

If an argument is of type VALUE, the corresponding argument in the subroutine call is treated as a formula, and its numeric or string value is placed in the argument cell. An error occurs if the corresponding argument in the subroutine call is not a valid number, string, or formula. You do not, however, have to put a string in quotation marks or have a leading plus sign (+) in a formula that uses cell references.

Suppose that you have an application where you must repeatedly convert strings to numbers and display the numbers in Currency format. Rather than enter the same code at several different places in the program, you decide to write a subroutine. Figure 12.22 shows how the subroutine might appear. Note that the

/**Range Name Labels Right** command has been used to define all the range names in this example.

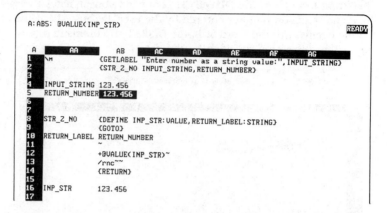

Fig. 12.22.
An example of a subroutine call with parameters.

The first statement in the main part of the program is a GETLABEL statement that reads a string value into the cell named INPUT_STRING. The second statement in the main routine calls a subroutine named STR_2_NO and passes the arguments INPUT_STRING (the name of the cell containing the input string) and RETURN_NUMBER (the name of the cell where the formatted number is to be stored).

The STR_2_NO subroutine begins with a DEFINE statement, which defines where and how the arguments passed to the subroutine from the main part of the program are to be stored. Any subroutine that receives arguments passed from its calling macro must begin with a DEFINE statement.

The DEFINE statement in STR_2_NO specifies two cells, INP_STR and RETURN_LABEL, which will hold the two arguments passed from the caller. Note that if the number of arguments in the subroutine call does not agree with the number of arguments in the DEFINE statement, an error occurs.

The DEFINE statement specifies that the first argument in the subroutine call is to be evaluated and its value placed in INP_STR. Because the first argument is the cell reference INPUT_STRING, the value in cell INPUT_STRING (the string 123.456) is placed in INP_STR.

The DEFINE statement specifies that the text of the second argument in the subroutine call is to be placed into the cell RETURN_LABEL as a string. Because the text of the second argument is RETURN_NUMBER, the string RETURN_NUMBER is placed in cell RETURN_LABEL.

The cell containing the second argument is located in the body of the subroutine. This technique is used to allow the subroutine to return a value to a location designated by the caller. In the example, the location RETURN_NUMBER is passed to the subroutine as a string value. The subroutine uses the passed value as the argument of a {GOTO} statement that places the cell pointer on the output cell.

This technique is one of two primary ways to return information to the calling routine. The other way to return information is to place it in a specified cell that is used every time the subroutine is called. After the subroutine places the cell pointer on the output cell, it continues by converting the string in INP_STR to a number and placing the resulting numeric value in the output cell.

Passing arguments to and from subroutines is important if you want to get the most out of 1-2-3's subroutine capabilities. Subroutines with arguments simplify program coding and make the resulting macros easier to trace. Subroutine arguments are almost essential when you are developing a subroutine to perform a common function you will use again and again. They are also one of the trickiest parts of the 1-2-3 advanced macro commands.

The RESTART Command

Just as you can call subroutines from the main program, you can also call one subroutine from another. In fact, as 1-2-3 moves from one subroutine to the next, the program saves the addresses of where it has been. This technique is called *stacking*, or saving addresses on a stack. By saving the addresses on a stack, 1-2-3 can trace its way back through the subroutine calls to the main program.

If you decide that you don't want 1-2-3 to return by the path it came, you can use the RESTART command to eliminate the stack. In other words, the RESTART command allows a subroutine to be canceled at any time during execution. You will not need to use this command until you are an expert at writing advanced macro command programs. Once you reach this point, however, this command is quite helpful. The RESTART command normally is used with an IF statement under a conditional testing evaluation. The format for this command is as follows:

{RESTART}   Cancels a subroutine

Figure 12.23 illustrates how RESTART can be used to prevent a user from omitting data in a database. This example combines the GETLABEL, GETNUMBER, and BRANCH commands to produce a simple database application for entering product information. GETLABEL and GETNUMBER are used to prompt the user for product data. If the product item number and price are omitted, RESTART prevents the user from continuing to enter new data. In the last line, BRANCH loops to repeat the process for entering a new record.

Consider the program line-by-line. The first line simply begins the subroutine (named SUB) in cell AB3. The subroutine begins by determining exactly where to move the cell pointer in the product database. Notice that @COUNT is used in AB3 to count the number of records in the database. After the cell pointer moves to an empty cell, line AB4 prompts the user for a product description and enters this data in cell D1. The Copy command in AB5 copies the product description to the appropriate cell in the database.

The commands in AB6 through AB11 prompt the user for the product item number and price, copy the data to the appropriate locations in the database, and

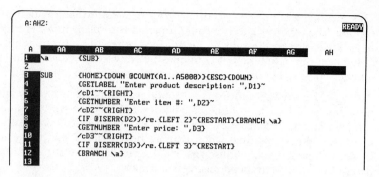

Fig. 12.23.
The RESTART
command used
in a database
application.

check that the item number and price have actually been entered. If the data has not been entered, the RESTART command clears the stack, allowing the subroutine to be canceled. Cell AB8 checks to make sure that item numbers are entered. If a user forgets to include a number, the program prompts the user to reenter product information. Cell AB9 checks price data. If price information is omitted, RESTART again clears the stack, allowing the subroutine to be canceled.

The SYSTEM Command

The SYSTEM command executes any operating system or batch command using the following format:

{SYSTEM command}   Executes the named command

Figure 12.24 shows an example of the SYSTEM command executing the batch command PARK.

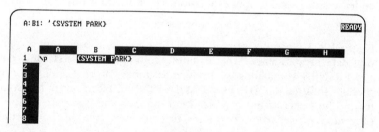

Fig. 12.24.
The SYSTEM
command used
to execute an
operating
system
command.

The operating system command you execute with SYSTEM can be any operating system or batch command, and you have up to 512 characters with which to specify it. Keep in mind some caveats when you use SYSTEM. First, if you attempt to load a memory-resident program, you may not be able to resume 1-2-3. Second, some batch commands may not let you resume 1-2-3. For these two reasons, you will want to be particularly careful to save your files before you begin testing a macro that uses SYSTEM. Also remember that if all you want to do is access the operating system during a 1-2-3 session, the **System** menu command provides a convenient alternative way to do this.

If you do run into problems executing the operating system commands, you can test for successful completion of a command by following the SYSTEM command with @INFO("osreturncode"). See Chapter 6 for a description of this and other @ functions.

Decision-Making Commands

The advanced macro commands for decision-making, shown in table 12.3, give you the capabilities of true programming languages such as BASIC. With the three commands (IF, FOR, and FORBREAK) presented in the following sections, you can test for numeric and string values. The IF command provides the kind of conditional logic available in many high-level languages. FOR and FORBREAK offer a conditional looping capability, allowing you to control how many times a group of commands is activated.

Table 12.3
Decision-Making Commands

Command	Description
{IF}	Conditionally executes statements after IF
{FOR}	Activates a loop a specified number of times
{FORBREAK}	Terminates a {FOR} loop

The IF Command

The IF statement uses IF-THEN-ELSE logic to evaluate the existence of certain numeric and string values. The advanced macro command IF, commonly used to control program flow and enable the program to perform based on criteria provided by the user, is the functional equivalent of the IF command in BASIC. The format of the IF command is as follows:

{IF condition}{true} {false}	Executes true or false statements based on the result of a condition; if the logical expression is true, the remaining commands on the same line are executed

These commands ordinarily include a BRANCH command to skip the {false} statements. If the expression is false, execution skips the commands (after the IF command) on the current line and continues on the next line.

As the following examples illustrate, IF statements can check for a variety of conditions, including the position of the cell pointer, a specific numeric value, or a specific string value. In figure 12.25, for example, the IF statement checks to see whether the current location of the cell pointer is on row 200. If it is, program control is passed to cell R9, where a QUIT command is executed. If the cell pointer is not on row 200, the cell pointer moves down a row, accepts input, and then branches back to cell R6, where the IF statement again checks to see whether the cell pointer is located on row 200.

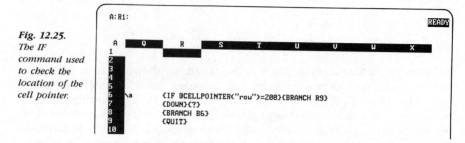

Fig. 12.25.
The IF
command used
to check the
location of the
cell pointer.

Figure 12.26 illustrates how the IF command can be used to evaluate a cell's value. The IF statement evaluates the value in cell R10. If cell R10 contains a negative value, the program converts that value to 0, and program execution is halted. If the value in cell R10 is 0 or greater, the second line of the program replaces the value in cell R10 with the value represented by the equation (R10*.55).

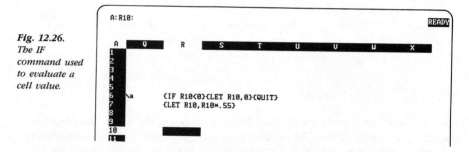

Fig. 12.26.
The IF
command used
to evaluate a
cell value.

The IF command also can evaluate a string value entered by the user. You can, for example, develop IF statements that complete certain operations depending on whether the user enters Y (Yes) or N (No). Suppose, for example, that you want to test the value in a single-cell range called NEW_RECORD. If the value in NEW_RECORD is Y (for Yes), you want to add a new record to a database. Otherwise, you want to modify an existing record in the database. Your program will include the following statements:

```
{IF NEW_RECORD="Y"}{BRANCH NEW_ROUTINE}
{BRANCH MOD_ROUTINE}
```

The first line is contained in a single cell. The part of the cell following the IF portion is called the THEN clause. The THEN clause is executed only if the result of the logical test is true. In this case, the THEN clause contains the keyword BRANCH followed by the range name NEW_ROUTINE. (BRANCH is often used with IF.) The program branches to NEW_ROUTINE if the value of NEW_RECORD is equal to Y (or y; the test is not case-sensitive).

The second line contains the ELSE clause, which is executed only if the result of the logical statement in the IF statement is false (because the THEN clause contains a branch to NEW_ROUTINE). If the program statements in the THEN clause do not transfer control, the line below the IF statement (the ELSE clause) is executed after the statement(s) in the THEN clause. In this example, the ELSE clause also contains a BRANCH statement, but the range to branch to is called MOD_ROUTINE.

The IF statement adds significant strength to 1-2-3's advanced macro commands. However, the one disadvantage of the IF statement is that if you want to execute more than one command after the logical test, the THEN clause must contain a branching statement or a subroutine call. What's more, if the code in the THEN clause does not branch or execute a QUIT command, the program continues its execution right through the ELSE clause.

The FOR and FORBREAK Commands

The FOR command is used to control the looping process in a program by calling a subroutine to be executed a certain number of times. FOR enables you to define the exact number of times the subroutine will be executed. The format of the FOR command is as follows:

{FOR counter,start,stop,step,routine}   Activates a loop a specific number of times

The FOR statement contains five arguments. The first argument is a cell that acts as the counter mechanism for the loop structure. The second argument is the starting number for the counter mechanism; the third is the completion number for the counter mechanism. The fourth argument is the incremental value for the counter mechanism; and the fifth is the name of the subroutine. Arguments 2, 3, and 4 can be values, cell addresses, or formulas. Arguments 1 and 5, however, must be range names or cell addresses. Because multiple loops are permitted, you need to be careful of the logical flow of multiple looping structures.

Notice how FOR is used in the simple example in figure 12.27. The FOR statement, in the first line of the program, controls how many times the program loops to format a column of values. The FOR statement begins by using the range named COUNT, located at B5, as a counter to keep track of how many times the program should loop. The second argument, 1, is the start-number for the counter; the next argument, 5, is the stop-number. The program keeps track of the looping process by comparing the counter against the stop-number, and stops executing if the counter value is larger than the stop-number.

The FOR statement's next argument, 1, is the step-number; this is the value by which the counter is to be incremented after each loop. The last argument, FORMAT, is the name of the routine to be executed.

If you want to end the processing of a FOR command based on something other than the number of iterations, such as a conditional test, you can use the FORBREAK command. When you use this command, 1-2-3 interrupts the pro-

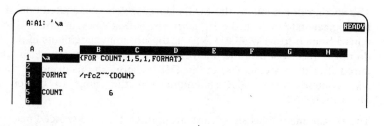

Fig. 12.27.
The FOR
command used
to control the
number of
loops in a
formatting
program.

cessing of the FOR command and continues execution with the command following the FOR statement.

Data Manipulation Commands

The LET, PUT, CONTENTS, BLANK, APPENDBELOW, and APPENDRIGHT commands allow precise placement of data within worksheet files. These commands, described in table 12.4, function similarly to menu commands such as Copy, Move, and Erase but provide capabilities that go beyond these simple operations.

Table 12.4
Data Manipulation Commands

Command	Description
{LET}	Places value of expression in the location specified
{PUT}	Places value into cell within range
{CONTENTS}	Stores contents of the specified source into the specified destination
{BLANK}	Erases the cell or range
{APPENDBELOW}	Places contents of the specified source below the specified destination range and then expands definition of the specified destination range to include the new data
{APPENDRIGHT}	Places contents of the specified source to the right of the specified destination range and then expands the definition of the specified destination range to include the new data

The LET Command

The LET command places a value or string in a target cell location without the cell pointer actually being at the location. LET is extremely useful, for example, for placing criteria in a database criterion range. The format of the LET command is as follows:

{LET location,expression}   Places value of expression in location

In the program in figure 12.28, the LET statement in the first line is executed only if the condition in the IF statement is true. Regardless of the outcome of the first line, the LET statement in the second line is executed. The first line places a label in a cell; the second line places a value representing the formula (in the program) in a cell.

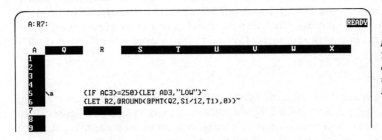

Fig. 12.28.
The LET
command used
with an IF
statement.

You can use a string value with the LET command. In fact, you even can use a string formula. Suppose, for example, that the cell named FIRST contains the string "Robert" and LAST holds the string "Hamer". The following statement, then, will store "Robert Hamer" in NAME:

{LET NAME,first&" "&last}

Like the DEFINE command, the LET command allows you to specify :STRING and :VALUE suffixes after the argument. The :STRING suffix stores the text of the argument in the location, whereas the :VALUE suffix evaluates the argument as a string or numeric formula and places the result in the location. When a suffix is not specified, LET stores the argument's numeric or string value if it is a valid formula; otherwise, the text of the argument is stored. For example, the following statement stores "Robert Hamer" in NAME:

{LET name,first&" "&last:VALUE}

The next statement, however, stores the string *first&" "&last* in NAME:

{LET name,first&" "&last:STRING}

Instead of using the LET command, you could move the cell pointer to the desired location with GOTO and enter the desired value into the cell. The LET command, however, has the major advantage that it does not disturb the current location of the cell pointer. The /Data Fill command also can be used to enter numbers, but not to enter string values. Overall, the LET command is a convenient and useful means for setting the value of a cell from within a program.

The PUT Command

The PUT command places a value in a target cell location determined by the intersection of a row and a column in a defined range. The format of the PUT command is as follows:

{PUT range,col,row,value}   Places value into cell within range

The PUT statement contains four arguments. The first argument defines the range into which the value will be placed. The second argument defines the column offset within the range; the third, the row offset within the range. The fourth indicates the value to be placed in the cell location. The first argument can be a range name or cell address. The second, third, and fourth arguments can be values, cell references, or formulas. Consider, for example, the following PUT statement:

{PUT TABLE,S1,S2,ARG4}

This statement places the contents of the cell named ARG4 in the range named TABLE at the intersection defined by the values in cells S1 and S2. Figure 12.29 shows the results of different variations of this command. Keep in mind that the row and column offset numbers follow the same conventions followed by functions (the first column is number 0, the second is number 1, and so on).

Fig. 12.29.
The PUT
command used
to enter
numbers
and labels.

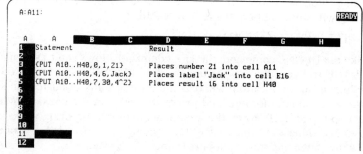

The CONTENTS Command

The CONTENTS command stores the contents of the source cell in the destination cell, optionally assigning an individual cell width and/or cell format. If either width or format is not specified, the CONTENTS command uses the column width or format of the source location to format the string. The format of the CONTENTS command is as follows:

{CONTENTS destination,source,width,format}   Stores contents of
                                                source to destination

Consider, for example, the following CONTENTS statement:

{CONTENTS THERE,HERE,11,121}

This statement places the contents of the cell named HERE in the cell named THERE, gives the individual cell a width of 11, and formats the entry as a full international date (121). Suppose, for example, that you want to copy the number 123.456, which resides in cell A21, to cell B25, and change the number to a string while you copy. The statement for this step is as follows:

{CONTENTS B25,A21}

The contents of cell B25 will be displayed as the string '123.456 with a left-aligned label-prefix character.

Next, suppose that you want to change the width of the string when you copy it. Rather than display the string as 123.456, you want to display it as 123.4. You can get the desired result by changing the statement to

{CONTENTS B25,A21,6}

This second statement uses a width of 6 to display the string. The least significant digits of the number are truncated to create the string. If the number cannot be displayed in the specified width using the specified format, a string of asterisks (*****) is displayed instead of the number. This statement works just like 1-2-3's normal worksheet formatting commands. For example, if you use /Range Format on a cell so that the contents are longer than what can be displayed in the cell, then the cell shows a string of asterisks rather than the value.

Finally, suppose that you want to change the display format of the string while you copy it and change its width. The following string changes the display format to **Currency 0**:

{CONTENTS B25,A21,5,32}

The number used for the format number in this statement is listed among the CONTENTS command format numbers in table 12.5. The result of the statement is the number $123.

In the following examples of the CONTENTS command, with 123.456 as the number in cell A21, the width of column A is 9, and the display format for cell A21 is Fixed 2.

{CONTENTS B25,A21}	Displays the number 123.46 in cell B25, using the **Fixed 2** format
{CONTENTS B25,A21,4}	Displays the number, using a width of 4 and the **Fixed 2** format. The result is ****.
{CONTENTS B25,A21,5,0}	Displays the number 123 in cell B25, using the **Fixed 0** format

The CONTENTS command is somewhat specialized but quite useful in situations that require converting numeric values to formatted strings. Using the Text format, CONTENTS can convert long numeric formulas to strings. This application is particularly useful for debugging purposes.

Table 12.5
Numeric Format Codes for CONTENTS Command

Code	Destination String's Format
0	Fixed, 0 decimal places
1–15	Fixed, 1 to 15 decimal places
16–31	Scientific, 0 to 15 decimal places
32–47	Currency, 0 to 15 decimal places
48–63	Percent, 0 to 15 decimal places
64–79	Comma, 0 to 15 decimal places
112	+/− Bar Graph
113	General
114	D1 (DD-MMM-YY)
115	D2 (DD-MM)
116	D3 (MMM-YY)
121	D4 (Full International)
122	D5 (Partial International)
119	D6 (HH:MM:SS AM/PM time format)
120	D7 (HH:MM AM/PM time format)
123	D8 (Full International time format)
124	D9 (Partial International time format)
117	Text format
118	Hidden format
127	Current window's default display format

The BLANK Command

The BLANK command erases a range of cells in the worksheet. Although this command works similarly to the /Range Erase command, using BLANK has a few advantages over using /Range Erase in your advanced macro command programs. Because BLANK works outside the menu structure, that command is faster than /Range Erase. Going through the sequence of selecting Range from the 1-2-3 command menu and then selecting Erase is a slower process. The format of the BLANK command is as follows:

{BLANK location}   Erases the range defined by location

In the example in figure 12.30, the BLANK statement erases RANGE1. The second line executes the {BLANK RANGE2} statement only if the conditional IF statement tests true.

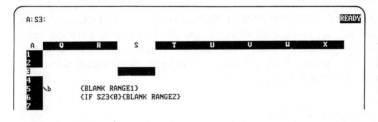

Fig. 12.30.
The BLANK command used to erase a range.

The APPENDBELOW Command

The APPENDBELOW command copies the contents of one range, the source, to the rows immediately below another range, the destination. As part of the copy operation, this command also expands the range of the destination to include the new data. The format of the APPENDBELOW command is as follows:

{APPENDBELOW source,destination}	Copies contents of source to destination and expands destination range to include new data

You will find APPENDBELOW a helpful companion to another new 1-2-3 command—FORM. The two commands provide an easy way of copying data from an input form to a storage table or database range. Figure 12.31 shows a simple example that collects check information, stores that information in a check register, and uses the \a macro (including the APPENDBELOW command) to record data entered into the check form into the check register.

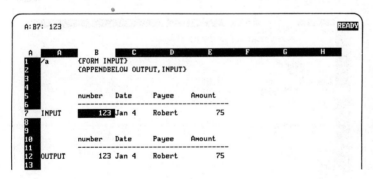

Fig. 12.31.
The APPENDBELOW command used to copy data entered with the FORM command.

Keep in mind two situations that cause the APPENDBELOW command to fail. First, if the number of rows in the specified source exceeds the number of rows left in the worksheet below the specified destination, APPENDBELOW aborts. Obviously, if you have only 10 rows left in your worksheet, you don't have room to copy 11 rows of information. A second condition that causes APPENDBELOW to fail is when executing the command would destroy data in the destination range by overwriting data there. Actually, this condition is a handy safety feature, because APPENDBELOW will not destroy data in your worksheet.

One other subtlety of APPENDBELOW is that when the specified source contains formulas, what ends up being copied to the specified destination are the calculated values—similar to what /Range Value does. This feature is valuable because you don't need to worry about relative cell references changing incorrectly when they are copied to a new location.

The APPENDRIGHT command

APPENDRIGHT's operation mirrors that of APPENDBELOW, with one exception: APPENDRIGHT copies the contents of the specified source to the right of the specified destination. (APPENDBELOW copies the contents of the source to just below the destination.) The APPENDRIGHT command uses the following format:

{APPENDRIGHT source,destination}   Expands the destination range to include newly copied data and converts formulas to values during the copy

APPENDRIGHT ends in an error when there isn't room to copy because of either existing data or insufficient worksheet space. Logically, however, APPENDRIGHT will not run out of space because not enough rows are left; it will run out of space because not enough columns are left. Figure 12.32 shows the APPENDRIGHT command used in an example that mirrors the operation shown in figure 12.31.

Fig. 12.32.
The APPENDRIGHT command used to copy data entered with the FORM command.

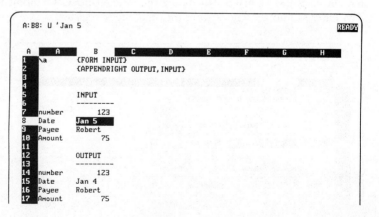

Program Enhancement Commands

The commands shown in table 12.6 (BEEP, PANELOFF, PANELON, WINDOWSOFF, WINDOWSON, FRAMEOFF, FRAMEON, GRAPHON, GRAPHOFF, INDICATE, RECALC, and RECALCCOL) can "dress up" your program or recalculate a portion of your worksheet. With skillful placement, these commands can add the polish that a solid program structure needs to become a smooth, easy-to-use application. This catch-all group of maintenance-oriented commands includes commands to sound your computer's speaker, control the screen display, and selectively recalculate portions of the worksheet. Two commands in this group —WINDOWSOFF and PANELOFF—can significantly increase the execution speed of large advanced macro command programs.

Table 12.6
Program Enhancement Commands

Command	Description
{BEEP}	Sounds one of the computer's four beeps
{PANELOFF}	Suppresses display in the control panel
{PANELON}	Reactivates the display in the control panel
{WINDOWSOFF}	Suppresses redisplay of the current window
{WINDOWSON}	Enables redisplay of the current window
{FRAMEOFF}	Suppresses display of the worksheet frame (worksheet letter, column border letters, and row border numbers)
{FRAMEON}	Displays the worksheet frame (worksheet letter, column border letters, and row border numbers)
{GRAPHON}	Displays the current graph and/or sets the named graph
{GRAPHOFF}	Removes the graph displayed by GRAPHON
{INDICATE}	Resets the control panel indicator to the string specified
{RECALC}	Recalculates a specified portion of the worksheet row-by-row
{RECALCCOL}	Recalculates a specified portion of the worksheet column-by-column

The BEEP Command

The BEEP command activates the computer's speaker system to produce one of four tones. Each argument (1–4) produces a different tone. The BEEP command is commonly used to alert the user to a specific condition in the program or to draw the user's attention. The format of the BEEP command is as follows:

{BEEP number} or {BEEP}   Sounds one of the computer's four beeps

Consider the following BEEP statement:

```
{IF A35>50}{BEEP 2}
```

This statement produces a sound if the condition presented in the IF statement is true. If the condition is not true, program control passes to the next cell below the IF statement.

The PANELOFF Command

The PANELOFF command freezes the control panel, prohibiting the annoying display of program commands in the control panel during program execution. Be aware, however, that the advanced macro commands such as MENUBRANCH, MENUCALL, GETLABEL, GETNUMBER, and INDICATE override the PANELOFF command. This command then can be used effectively to reposition or delete messages from the control panel, regardless of the cell pointer's current location. The format of the PANELOFF command is as follows:

{PANELOFF}   Suppresses display in the control panel

Consider the following example:

```
{PANELOFF}
/cC27..E39~AB21~
```

In this case, the PANELOFF command suppresses display in the control panel of the Copy command in the second line.

The PANELON Command

The PANELON command unfreezes the control panel. This command is commonly used immediately before a GETLABEL or GETNUMBER command. The format of the PANELON command is as follows:

{PANELON}   Reactivates the display in the control panel

In figure 12.33, the PANELON command reactivates the control panel so that the prompt for the GETLABEL statement is displayed.

Fig. 12.33.
The PANELON
command used
with GETLABEL.

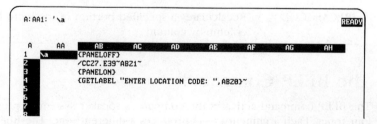

The WINDOWSOFF Command

By using the WINDOWSOFF command, you can freeze the lower part of the screen and have just the control panel show the changes that occur as a result of the commands activated in your program. The WINDOWSOFF command freezes the current screen display, regardless of whether the program is executing. WINDOWSOFF is particularly useful when you are creating applications that will be used by beginning 1-2-3 users. WINDOWSOFF enables you to display only those screen changes that the user must see, freezing other changes that might confuse beginners. The format of the WINDOWSOFF command is as follows:

{WINDOWSOFF}   Suppresses screen display

Consider the following example:

```
{WINDOWSOFF}
/cS24~Z12{CALC}
```

In this example, the WINDOWSOFF command prevents the automatic screen-rebuilding associated with the Copy command or the Calc (F9) key. Using the WINDOWSOFF and PANELOFF commands can have a significant effect on program execution time. In one complex application, use of the WINDOWSOFF and PANELOFF commands to freeze the screen reduced execution time by 50 percent, from 5 to 2 1/2 minutes. Speed improvement depends, of course, on the particular application.

You can use WINDOWSOFF with PANELOFF to create a graph "slide show" for business meetings. These commands allow you to display a sequence of graphs uninterrupted by intervening worksheet screens. The program in figure 12.34 demonstrates how to use the WINDOWSOFF and PANELOFF commands to eliminate screen shifting and to reduce execution time for such a presentation.

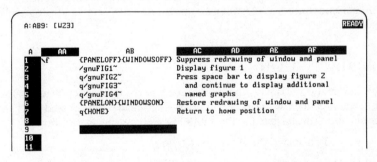

Fig. 12.34.
The
WINDOWSOFF
and PANELOFF
commands
used for a
graphics slide
show.

The PANELOFF and WINDOWSOFF commands in AB1 suppress redrawing of the window and panel. The commands in AB2 through AB5 display four different graphs. In AB6, the PANELON and WINDOWSON commands restore redrawing of the window and panel (see this chapter's section on the WINDOWSON command). The program ends in AB7 by returning the worksheet display with the cell pointer located at the HOME position.

Be aware that if something goes wrong with your program while WINDOWSOFF is in effect, you won't get normal updating of your worksheet window. Unless you have a simple one-line program already preset for issuing the WINDOWSON command (see the following section on WINDOWSON), you may have to reboot 1-2-3 and start your application over in order to recover the use of the screen. Therefore, the wise practice is to develop and test your programs without the WINDOWSOFF and WINDOWSON commands; then add these commands to the debugged and tested program.

The WINDOWSON Command

The WINDOWSON command unfreezes the screen, allowing display of executing program operations. This command is commonly used to allow display of the 1-2-3 menu structures. The format of the WINDOWSON command is as follows:

{WINDOWSON}   Enables redisplay of the current window

In figure 12.34, the WINDOWSON command in AB6 activates display of the worksheet screen after all graphs have been shown.

The FRAMEOFF Command

The FRAMEOFF command removes from the screen display the worksheet letter, column border letters, and row border numbers. The format of the command is as follows:

{FRAMEOFF}   Suppresses display of the worksheet frame

After you execute a FRAMEOFF command within an advanced macro command program, the worksheet frame display continues to be suppressed until either the command program encounters a FRAMEON command or the command program completes execution.

THE FRAMEON Command

The FRAMEON command redisplays the worksheet frame—worksheet letter, column border letters, and row border numbers—originally suppressed by a FRAMEOFF command. The format for the FRAMEON command is as follows:

{FRAMEON}   Redisplays the worksheet frame

Figure 12.35 shows a simple program using FRAMEOFF and FRAMEON. The program initially suppresses display of the worksheet frame until you press a key, then redisplays the worksheet frame until you press a key, and then again suppresses the worksheet frame until you press a key.

If you construct this macro yourself, note that even though the last FRAMEOFF command doesn't have a matching FRAMEON command, the worksheet frame still is redisplayed when the command program ends.

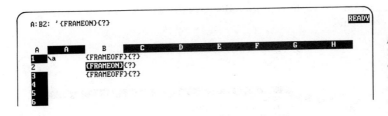

Fig. 12.35.
*The FRAMEOFF
and FRAMEON
commands
used to remove
and replace
the worksheet
letter, column
letters, and
row numbers.*

The GRAPHON Command

The GRAPHON command can set the currently named graph, display the currently named graph, or first set and then display the currently named graph. The format for the GRAPHON command is as follows:

{GRAPHON named-graph,no-display}   Displays the current graph or
another named graph, or sets
the current graph without displaying it

To display a full-screen view of the currently named graph, simply use the command alone—for example:

{GRAPHON}

To display a graph aside from the one currently named, reset the currently named graph and then redisplay it. For example, if you have a graph setting named FIGURE1, you use the following structure:

{GRAPHON FIGURE1}

In either of the preceding two cases, 1-2-3 continues to display a full-sized version of the graph until the command program completes execution or until the command program encounters a GRAPHOFF command, another GRAPHON command, or a command that displays a prompt or menu (such as GETLABEL or MENUCALL).

To change the named graph but not display it, you use the no-display argument. For example, suppose that you have a graph setting named FIGURE1 and you want this as the current graph setting, but you don't want the graph displayed. You use the following structure:

{GRAPHON FIGURE1,no-display}

Figure 12.36 shows these alternative command formats. The first line of the \a program, in cell B1, sets the current graph as FIG1 and displays it for three seconds as indicated by the WAIT command in line 2. The third line in \a, in cell B3, sets the current graph setting as FIG2, but does not display it. The fourth line in \a, in cell B4, displays the current graph—just set as FIG2—for three seconds. The last line of \a, in cell B6, redisplays the worksheet by executing the GRAPHOFF command.

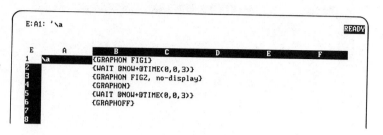

Fig. 12.36.
The GRAPHON and GRAPHOFF commands used to display graphs and change the current graph.

```
E:A1: '\a                                                              READY

E      A       B          C          D          E          F
1    \a      {GRAPHON FIG1}
2            {WAIT @NOW+@TIME(0,0,3)}
3            {GRAPHON FIG2, no-display}
4            {GRAPHON}
5            {WAIT @NOW+@TIME(0,0,3)}
6            {GRAPHOFF}
7
8
```

THE GRAPHOFF Command

The GRAPHOFF command removes the named graph from the display and redisplays the worksheet. The format for using the GRAPHOFF command, illustrated in figure 12.36, is as follows:

{GRAPHOFF}

For more information about the GRAPHOFF command, refer to the preceding section on GRAPHON.

The INDICATE Command

The INDICATE command alters the mode indicator in the upper-right corner of the 1-2-3 screen. This command is commonly used to provide custom indicators. The INDICATE command will accept a string argument as long as the width of your screen. When you use the INDICATE command, you have to enter a string; you cannot use a cell address or range name. The format of the INDICATE command is as follows:

{INDICATE string}   Resets the mode indicator to string

Suppose, for example, that you want to display the message START in the upper-right corner of the screen. You can use the following INDICATE command:

{INDICATE START}

Unless you clear your indicator, using the following command displays the START message until you exit 1-2-3:

{INDICATE}

To blank out the indicator completely, you can use the command

{INDICATE " "}

The RECALC and RECALCCOL Commands

Two macro commands, RECALC and RECALCCOL, allow you to recalculate a portion of the worksheet. This feature can be useful in large worksheets where recalculation time is long and where you need to recalculate certain values in the worksheet before you proceed to the next processing step in your macro. The commands for partial recalculation have the following formats:

{RECALC location,condition,iteration-number}

{RECALCCOL location,condition,iteration-number}

In these commands, location is a range or range name that specifies the cells whose formulas are to be recalculated. The condition and iteration-number arguments are optional.

If the condition argument is included, the range is recalculated repeatedly until the condition has a logical value of TRUE (1). Remember that the condition must be either a logical expression or a reference to a cell within the recalculation range that contains a logical expression. If the condition is a reference to a cell outside the recalculation range, the value of the condition—either TRUE (1) or FALSE (0)—does not change, and the condition does not control the partial recalculation.

If the iteration-number argument is included, the condition argument also must be specified (the value 1 makes the condition always TRUE). The iteration-number specifies the number of times that formulas in the location range are to be recalculated.

The RECALC and RECALCCOL commands differ in the order in which cells in the specified range are recalculated. The RECALC command performs the calculations by row of all the cells in the first row of the range, then all the cells in the second row, and so on. The RECALCCOL command performs the calculations by column of all the cells in the first column of the range, followed by all the cells in the second column, and so on. Using both commands, only cells within the specified range are recalculated.

Use RECALC to recalculate the range when the formulas in the range refer only to other formulas in rows above or to the left of themselves in the same row in that range. Use RECALCCOL to recalculate the range when the formulas in the range refer only to other formulas in columns to the left or to cells above themselves in the same column.

Caution: You may have to use CALC if formulas in the range refer to other formulas located below and to their right, or if formulas refer both to cells in rows above and to the right and to cells in columns below and to the left.

You need to include in the range only those cells you want to recalculate. The formulas in the recalculation range can refer to values in cells outside the range; however, those values are not updated by RECALC or RECALCCOL. When either the RECALC or RECALCCOL command is executed, the partial recalculation occurs immediately. However, the results do not appear on-screen until the screen is redrawn. Program execution may continue for some time before a command that updates the screen is executed. In the interim, the recalculated numbers, although not visible on-screen, are available for use in calculations and conditional tests. If the program ends and you want to be sure that the recalculated numbers are on-screen, use the PgUp and PgDn keys to move the window away from and back to the recalculated range. The act of looking away and back again updates the screen and displays the current values in the recalculated range.

You may need to use CALC, RECALC, or RECALCCOL after commands such as LET, GETNUMBER, and ?, or after 1-2-3 commands such as /Range Input within a program. You do not need to recalculate after invoking 1-2-3 commands such as Copy and Move; 1-2-3 automatically recalculates the affected ranges after such commands, even during program execution.

Caution: Recalculating a portion of the worksheet can cause some formulas (those outside a recalculated range that reference formulas within the range) to fail to reflect current data. If this should occur in your application, be sure to perform a general recalculation at some point before the end of your program.

File Manipulation Commands

Nine commands give 1-2-3 the capability of opening, reading, writing, and closing a sequential data file containing ASCII text data: OPEN, CLOSE, READ, READLN, WRITE, WRITELN, SETPOS, GETPOS, and FILESIZE. This capability allows 1-2-3 applications to read and write files used by other business applications. Although the /File Import and /Print File commands provide a limited capability to manipulate foreign files, the file manipulation commands shown in table 12.7 provide a capability equal to the sequential file commands in BASIC or other programming languages.

Warning: The file manipulation commands are programming commands. To read from and write to foreign files successfully, you must understand exactly how these commands work and how the sequential files you are manipulating are organized. If you write to a file containing another application, be sure to back up the file before trying to write to it from within 1-2-3.

Used with caution, this group of commands can open up the world of outside files to your 1-2-3 applications. If you need to process external data files, these commands make the task possible using 1-2-3.

The OPEN Command

The OPEN command opens a disk file, providing access so that you can write to or read from that file. You can specify in the command's second argument whether you want to read only, write only, or both read from and write to the file.

Table 12.7
File Manipulation Commands

Command	Description
{OPEN}	Opens a file for reading, writing, or both
{CLOSE}	Closes a file opened with {OPEN}
{READ}	Copies specified characters from the open file to the specified location
{READLN}	Copies the next line from a file to the specified location
{WRITE}	Copies a string to the open file
{WRITELN}	Copies a string plus a carriage-return line-feed sequence to the open file
{SETPOS}	Sets a new position for a file pointer
{GETPOS}	Records a file pointer position in the specified location
{FILESIZE}	Records the size of the open file in the specified location

Note that 1-2-3 allows only one file to be open at a time. If you want to work with more than one file in your application, you have to open each file before using it, and then close it again before opening and using the next file.

The format of the OPEN command is as follows:

{OPEN filename,access-mode}   Opens file for reading, writing, or both

The filename argument can be a string, an expression with a string value, or a single-cell reference to a cell that contains a string or a string expression. The string must be a valid operating system file name or path name. A file in the current directory can be specified by its name and extension. A file in another directory may require a drive identification, a subdirectory path, or a complete operating system path in addition to the file name and extension.

The access-mode argument is a single character string that specifies whether you want to read only ("R"), write only ("W"), or both read from and write to the file ("M" or "A").

"R"   Read access opens an existing file and allows access with the READ and READLN commands. You cannot write to a file opened with Read access.

"W"   Write access opens a new file with the specified name and allows access with the WRITE and WRITELN commands. Any existing file with the specified name is erased and replaced by the new file.

"A"

Append access opens an existing file and allows both read (READ and READLN) and write (WRITE and WRITELN) commands. Append access is like Modify access except that Append access places the byte pointer at the end of the file. (Modify places the byte pointer at the beginning of the file.)

"M"

Modify access opens an existing file with the specified name and allows both read (READ and READLN) and write (WRITE and WRITELN) commands. Note that the "M" (Modify) argument cannot create a new file.

The OPEN command succeeds if it is able to open the file with the access you requested. If the OPEN command succeeds, program execution continues with the cell below the OPEN. Any commands after the OPEN in the current cell are ignored.

The OPEN command fails with an ERROR if the disk drive is not ready. You should use an ONERROR command to handle this possibility.

If the access mode is READ or MODIFY but the file does not exist on the indicated directory, the OPEN command fails, and program execution continues with the commands after the OPEN command in the current cell. You can place one or more commands after the OPEN command in the same cell in order to deal with the failure. The most common practice is to place a BRANCH or a subroutine call after the OPEN command to transfer the operation to a macro that deals with the failure.

Here are some examples (with explanations) of the OPEN command:

```
{OPEN "PASTDUE",R}{BRANCH FIXIT}
```

Opens the existing file named PASTDUE in the current directory for reading. If the file cannot be opened, branches to the routine FIXIT.

```
{OPEN "C:\DATA\CLIENTS.DAT",W}
```

Opens the new file named CLIENTS.DAT in drive C, subdirectory DATA, for writing.

```
{OPEN file,A}{BRANCH RETRY}
```

Opens the file whose name is in the cell FILE for Append access. If the file cannot be opened, branches to the routine RETRY.

```
{OPEN file,M}{BRANCH RETRY}
```

Opens the file whose name is in cell FILE for Modify access. If the file cannot be opened, branches to the routine RETRY.

Figure 12.37 shows an example of using all the file commands except the READ and WRITE commands (which are similar to the READLN and WRITELN commands). The program named \o uses the OPEN command to open a user-specified file. This program illustrates how to deal with Disk drive not ready and

File not found errors. After prompting you for the file name, an ONERROR command sets the error jump to the routine that handles such problems as the drive not being ready. Next, the OPEN command is used with the BRANCH that follows it. This BRANCH handles such problems as a File not found error.

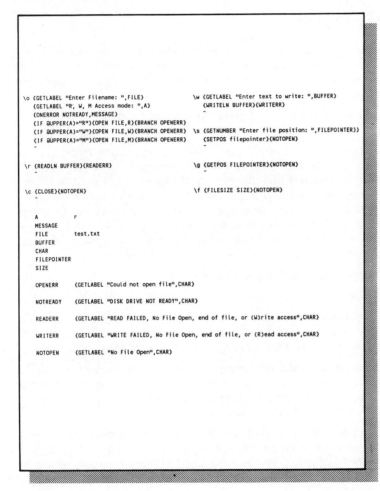

Fig. 12.37.
A program that uses the file manipulation commands.

```
\o {GETLABEL "Enter Filename: ",FILE}          \w {GETLABEL "Enter text to write: ",BUFFER}
   {GETLABEL "R, W, M Access mode: ",A}           {WRITELN BUFFER}{WRITERR}
   {ONERROR NOTREADY,MESSAGE}                      ~
   {IF @UPPER(A)="R"}{OPEN FILE,R}{BRANCH OPENERR}
   {IF @UPPER(A)="W"}{OPEN FILE,W}{BRANCH OPENERR} \s {GETNUMBER "Enter file position: ",FILEPOINTER}}
   {IF @UPPER(A)="M"}{OPEN FILE,M}{BRANCH OPENERR}    {SETPOS filepointer}{NOTOPEN}
                                                      ~

\r {READLN BUFFER}{READERR}                     \g {GETPOS FILEPOINTER}{NOTOPEN}
   ~

\c {CLOSE}{NOTOPEN}                             \f {FILESIZE SIZE}{NOTOPEN}
   ~


   A            r
   MESSAGE
   FILE         test.txt
   BUFFER
   CHAR
   FILEPOINTER
   SIZE

   OPENERR      {GETLABEL "Could not open file",CHAR}

   NOTREADY     {GETLABEL "DISK DRIVE NOT READY",CHAR}

   READERR      {GETLABEL "READ FAILED, No File Open, end of file, or (W)rite access",CHAR}

   WRITERR      {GETLABEL "WRITE FAILED, No File Open, end of file, or (R)ead access",CHAR}

   NOTOPEN      {GETLABEL "No File Open",CHAR}
```

The CLOSE Command

The CLOSE command closes a currently open file. If no file is open, the CLOSE command has no effect. CLOSE does not take an argument. The CLOSE command is particularly important for files that you are writing or modifying; if you don't close a file, you can lose the last data written to the file. The format of the CLOSE command is as follows:

{CLOSE}   Closes a file opened with {OPEN}

Although under most circumstances 1-2-3 automatically closes a file you do not close, you should make it a practice to use CLOSE when you are finished using any file opened with OPEN. (Better safe than sorry.) Use of the CLOSE command is illustrated in the program labeled \c in figure 12.37.

The READ Command

The READ command reads a specified number of characters from the currently open file, beginning at the present file pointer location. The characters read from the file are placed in the worksheet at the cell location indicated. The format of the READ command is as follows:

{READ bytecount,location}   Copies the specified number of characters from a file to the location specified

The bytecount argument is the number of bytes to read, starting at the current position of the file pointer, and location is the cell to read into. READ places the specified number of characters from the file into the location cell as a label. Bytecount can be any number between 1 and 240 (the maximum number of characters in a 1-2-3 label). If bytecount is greater than the number of characters remaining in the file, 1-2-3 reads the remaining characters into the specified location. After the READ command is executed, the file pointer is positioned at the character following the last character read.

Consider, for example, the following statement:

{READ NUM,INFO}

This statement transfers information from the open file into the cell location named INFO. The amount of information transferred is determined by the contents of the cell named NUM, which can contain either a value or a formula.

The READ command is useful primarily when you want to read a specific number of characters into the buffer. A data file that contains fixed-length records, for example, can be read conveniently by a READ command with the bytecount argument specified as the record length.

READ should not be used with ASCII text files from a word processor or text editor. Such files generally have variable-length lines terminated with a carriage-return and line-feed sequence. Instead, use the READLN command, which is described next. READ is used much like the READLN command in the \r program in figure 12.37.

The READLN Command

The READLN command reads one line of information from the currently open file, beginning at the file pointer's current position. The characters read are placed in the cell location in the current worksheet. The READLN command format is as follows:

{READLN location}   Copies the next line from the file to the location

Consider, for example, the following statement:

    {READLN HERE}

This statement copies a line from an open file into the cell named HERE. The line is determined by the SETPOS command. (SETPOS is discussed later in this chapter.)

Use READLN to read a line of text from a file whose lines are delimited by a carriage-return and line-feed combination. You would use READLN, for example, to read the next line from an ASCII text file. ASCII text files are created with 1-2-3's /Print File command. Also referred to as print files, these files are assigned the .PRN file extension by 1-2-3. READLN is best suited to reading files that are print images. The program labeled \r in figure 12.37 illustrates the use of READLN.

Using READ and READLN

If you attempt to read past the end of the file, if no file is open, or if the file was opened with Write access, the READ or READLN command is ignored and program execution continues in the same cell. Otherwise, after the READ or READLN command is completed, program execution continues on the next line. You can place a BRANCH or subroutine call after the READ or READLN to handle the problem of an unexecuted READ or READLN statement.

The WRITE Command

The WRITE command writes a string of text to the currently open file. The WRITE command has the following format:

    {WRITE string}   Copies a string to the open file

The string argument can be a literal string, a range name or cell reference to a single cell that contains a string, or a string expression. Because WRITE does not place a carriage-return and line-feed sequence at the end of the string, multiple WRITE statements can be made to concatenate text on a single line. WRITE is well-suited to creating or updating a file that contains fixed-length database records. The WRITE command is used in much the same way as is the WRITELN command in the \w program in figure 12.37.

If the file pointer is not at the end of the file, 1-2-3 overwrites the existing characters in the file. If the file pointer is at the end of the file, 1-2-3 extends the file by the number of characters written. And if the file pointer is past the end of the file (see the discussion of the SETPOS command later in this section), 1-2-3 extends the file by the amount indicated before writing the characters.

The WRITELN Command

The WRITELN command is identical to the WRITE command except that WRITELN places a carriage-return and line-feed sequence after the last character written from the string. The WRITELN command format is as follows:

{WRITELN string}   Copies a string plus a carriage-return line-feed sequence to the open file

WRITELN is useful when the file being written or updated uses the carriage-return and line-feed sequence to mark the end of its lines or records. In many applications, several WRITE statements are used to write a line to the file; then a WRITELN is used to mark the end of the line. The WRITELN command is illustrated in the \w program in figure 12.37.

The SETPOS Command

The SETPOS command sets the position of the file pointer to a specified value. The format of the command is as follows:

{SETPOS file-position}   Sets a new position for a file pointer

File-position is a number, or an expression resulting in a number, that specifies the character at which you want to position the pointer. The first character in the file is at position 0, the second at position 1, and so on. Suppose, for example, that you have a database file with 100 records which are each 20 bytes long. To access the first record, you can use the following commands:

```
{SETPOS 0}
{READ 20,buffer}
```

To read the 15th record, you can use the following commands:

```
{SETPOS (15-1)*20}
{READ 20,buffer}
```

Nothing prevents you from setting the file pointer past the end of the file. If the file pointer is set at or past the end and a READ or READLN command is executed, the command does nothing, and program execution continues with the next command on the same line (error branch). If the file pointer is set at or past the end and a WRITE or WRITELN command is executed, 1-2-3 first extends the file to the length specified by the file pointer, and then, starting at the file pointer, writes the characters.

Warning: If you inadvertently set the file pointer to a large number with SETPOS and write to the file, 1-2-3 will attempt to expand the file and write the text at the end. If the file will not fit on the disk, the WRITE command does nothing, and program execution continues with the next command on the same line (error branch). If the file will fit on the disk, 1-2-3 extends the file and writes the text at the end.

If a file is not currently open, SETPOS does nothing, and execution continues with the next command on the same line as the SETPOS command. Otherwise, when the SETPOS command is completed, execution continues on the next line of the program. You can place a BRANCH command or a subroutine call after the SETPOS command to handle the problem of an unexecuted statement. SETPOS is illustrated in the \s program in figure 12.37.

The GETPOS Command

The GETPOS command allows you to record the file pointer's current position. The format of this command is as follows:

{GETPOS location}   Records a file pointer position in the specified location

The current position of the file pointer is placed in the cell indicated by location, where location is either a cell reference or a range name. If location points to a multicell range, the value of the file pointer is placed in the upper-left corner of the range.

The GETPOS command is useful if you record in the file the location of something you want to find again. You can use GETPOS to mark your current place in the file before you use SETPOS to move the file pointer to another position. You can use GETPOS to record the locations of important items in a quick-reference index. GETPOS is illustrated in the \g program in figure 12.37.

The FILESIZE Command

Another file-related command, FILESIZE, returns the length of the file in bytes. The format of the command is as follows:

{FILESIZE location}   Records the size of the open file in the specified location

The FILESIZE command determines the current length of the file and places this value in the cell referred to by location. Location can be a cell reference or range name. If location refers to a multicell range, the file size is placed in the cell in the upper-left corner of the range. FILESIZE is illustrated in the \f program in figure 12.37.

Chapter Summary

As you work with the 1-2-3 advanced macro commands, you soon discover that your powerful spreadsheet program has an extremely powerful programming language. Although 1-2-3's advanced macro commands make many things possible, be aware of some practical limitations. For example, because 1-2-3 is RAM-based, you must limit the size of your files. In addition, 1-2-3 may not always execute programming commands with lightning speed. You almost always have a tradeoff of capabilities; the most difficult applications may take a good deal of time to execute.

If you are an adventurer who wants to develop efficient, automated, customized models, and if you can live with the programming limitations, the advanced macro commands are for you. This chapter has provided the groundwork for developing such models. As you become more experienced with the advanced macro commands, turn to other Que titles for help in becoming an expert advanced macro command programmer.

Part IV

Quick Reference Guide to 1-2-3

Includes

Troubleshooting

1-2-3 Command Reference

Troubleshooting

This section addresses many of the problems you can encounter while using 1-2-3 and offers a variety of creative solutions. First-time users of 1-2-3 will find that this section can help them untie knots that seem hopelessly snarled but are really only minor inconveniences when understood correctly.

Experienced users will derive even greater benefit from the problems and solutions presented here. As your use of the program becomes increasingly complex and sophisticated, so do the problems and errors you encounter. Although first-time users face problems that momentarily seem insurmountable, the most perplexing problems in using 1-2-3 are those faced by power users who push the program to its limits.

You can use this section in two different ways:

1. Read the entire section after you have read the rest of the book and have begun to use 1-2-3. Or use the same method segment-by-segment. Most people learn 1-2-3 in segments—learning how to build a simple worksheet before they learn to incorporate complex formulas and functions; then learning how to print reports and create graphs; much later, perhaps, learning how to create and use macros or to use the program's database management capabilities. You can use this section the same way: after you learn the basics of one area of the program, read through the applicable portion of the troubleshooting section. Reading this section before you encounter problems helps you avoid those problems.

2. Refer to this section as you encounter problems. The section is arranged to provide easy reference. The running heads at the upper-right corner of the right page contain the name of the general problem area covered on that page (for example, Worksheet Problems). As each problem is introduced, a more specific designation (for example, DATA-ENTRY PROBLEM #1) appears in the left margin, followed by a brief description of the problem. A quick scan of the heads and the margins takes you to the area that describes your problem. Using this section as a reference is even easier if you have already read the related section, as recommended in the first method.

The topics in this troubleshooting section are arranged in the following order:

1. Installation: Read this section before you install 1-2-3. Some potentially disastrous installation problems cannot be remedied—they can only be avoided. You can remedy some installation problems, however, after they occur. This section covers both initial installation problems and later problems, such as those encountered when you create and use your own driver sets or install different printers.

2. Worksheet: This section covers problems in the basic worksheet environment—the environment in which you will probably encounter your first problems.

3. Commands: This section covers the use of 1-2-3 commands in the worksheet.

4. Functions: This section solves a variety of basic and highly complex problems associated with functions.

5. File Operations: This section particularly addresses problems encountered while transferring and combining data from different files; using different directories; and saving, opening, and retrieving files.

6. Printing: Printing is a troublesome area for most users; they struggle to "get their reports to look exactly like they're supposed to look." This section answers many printing problems and provides creative and useful tips.

7. Graphing: The wide variety of graphing options make this area as difficult as printing. This section leads you through the maze.

8. Data Management: This area is possibly the most troublesome section of all. Many of the highly sophisticated database management systems (DBMS) on the market are much more powerful than this capacity of 1-2-3. Nevertheless, 1-2-3's capabilities are considerable, complex, and unfamiliar to many users. Once you start to use 1-2-3's database capabilities, you quickly and frequently encounter problems. Overcoming these problems, with the help of this section, can open doors to a much more extensive and rewarding use of 1-2-3.

9. Macros: Macros and advanced macro commands are among 1-2-3's most powerful features. Many users benefit from this area because they can learn a little at a time, building their skills slowly. As the skills build, so do the problems. This section helps you with many of those problems.

This troubleshooting reference section cannot be, and is not meant to be, a comprehensive listing of all 1-2-3 problems. This section sometimes echoes and reinforces the explanations given elsewhere in the book. More often, this section extends your knowledge and your skills beyond the explanations given elsewhere. The ultimate solver of problems must be the individual user, but this section can help—by solving specific problems and by showing a pattern of creative thinking for solving problems as they occur.

Troubleshooting Installation

INSTALLATION PROBLEM #1:

When you start 1-2-3, the system hangs at a blank screen after the copyright screen, forcing you to reboot.

EXPLANATION: You create a driver configuration file (DCF) during the install process. If the display in the DCF does not match your actual display, you can hang the program.

SOLUTION: First, if the DCF is not called 123.DCF, make sure that you specified the proper DCF when you executed 1-2-3. Suppose that, for example, 123.DCF is set for monochrome. You also have an EGA monitor driver in a file called EGA.DCF. When you use a color monitor, specify the EGA driver set. To load 1-2-3 with the EGA driver set, enter the following command:

123 EGA.DCF

If you are using 123.DCF, rerun the install program and make sure that the DCF is properly set up for your equipment.

INSTALLATION PROBLEM #2:

You have access to several printers and plotters that you use occasionally for printing worksheets and graphs, but keeping track of all the driver configuration files (DCFs) for these different configurations is difficult.

EXPLANATION: 1-2-3 lets you use only the printers and plotters in your driver configuration file. If you put all your output devices in different DCFs, you must remember which DCF to use when you execute the program.

SOLUTION: Do not set up different driver configuration files for each printer or plotter. Instead, put them all in one file. You can include as many as 16 different devices in one driver configuration file.

If you use different printers and plotters, you can install them all in one driver configuration file. During first-time installation, after you select a printer, you get the prompt Do you want to use another printer? as in figure T.1. Choose **Yes** and select another printer. With some printers, such as the HP LaserJet, you treat different cartridges as if they were different printers.

Repeat this process for any printers or plotters you might attach to your computer. In addition, include any printers attached to other computers you may want to use to print reports or graphs. You can use /**Print Encoded** to create a print image file. To do so, copy this file to the other computer system and use the DOS or OS/2 COPY command to copy the image to the other printer. See Chapter 8 for details on using encoded print image files.

To add printers to an existing driver configuration file, start the install program and choose Change Selected Equipment. Then choose Modify Current DCF to change 123.DCF or Choose Another DCF to Modify to change another DCF on

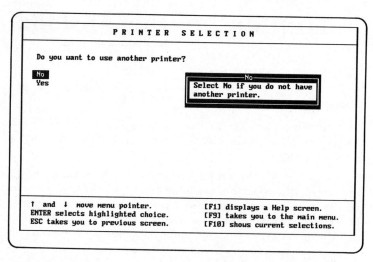

Fig. T.1.
The prompt for
including
another printer
or plotter in
your driver
configuration
file.

disk. Finally, choose Change Selected Printer and select another printer. Repeat the process for every printer you want to add, up to a total of 16.

Choose the default printer within 1-2-3 with /**W**orksheet **G**lobal **D**efault **P**rinter **N**ame. Then choose the default port that this printer is attached to with /**W**orksheet **G**lobal **D**efault **P**rinter **I**nterface. To change the printer for a specific print operation, use /**P**rint **P**rinter **O**ptions **A**dvanced **D**evice **N**ame and /**P**rint **P**rinter **O**ptions **A**dvanced **D**evice **I**nterface. See Appendix A for more details on installing and selecting printers.

Troubleshooting the 1-2-3 Worksheet

Problems with Data Entry

DATA-ENTRY PROBLEM #1:

After you type a label that starts with a number, the program beeps and puts you in EDIT mode.

EXPLANATION: When you begin typing information in a cell, 1-2-3 changes the READY mode indicator in the screen's upper-right corner to either LABEL or VALUE. If the first character you type is a number or a symbol used in a formula, the program assumes that you are typing a value. If you then type any character that is invalid for a value entry, 1-2-3 beeps, moves the cursor to the first character it rejected, and switches to EDIT mode.

SOLUTION: To type a label such as 11711 N. College Avenue, you must first type a label prefix, such as an apostrophe ('), so that 1-2-3 knows you are working with a label. If you forget to enter the prefix and 1-2-3 beeps, press Home and insert the apostrophe.

If the label is a valid numeric entry, instead of an error you get a numeric calculation. For example, if you type **317-842-7162** as a telephone number, 1-2-3 evaluates the entry as a formula and displays –7687. Edit the field and change it from a number to a label.

ALTERNATIVE SOLUTION: If you know in advance that a range will be used for labels, format the blank cells with /**R**ange Format Label. All entries will be preceded with a label prefix. If you format the blank cells in advance with /**R**ange Format Automatic, invalid formulas, such as 11711 N. College Avenue, are treated as labels. Valid formulas, such as 317-842-7162, are still treated as formulas.

DATA-ENTRY PROBLEM #2:

When you finish writing a complex formula, 1-2-3 switches to EDIT mode. If you can't find the error immediately, you have to press Esc. Then you lose the entire formula and have to start again.

EXPLANATION: When you type an invalid formula, the program refuses to accept the entry and switches to EDIT mode. You must provide a valid entry before you can continue.

SOLUTION: Make the formula a valid entry by converting the formula to a label: press the Home key, type an apostrophe, and press Enter. Then you can work on the problem until you find and correct the error. Or you can work on another part of the worksheet and return to the formula later.

Use this method for debugging complex formulas. Suppose that, for example, you enter the following formula in a cell:

@IF(@ISERR(A1/A2),@IF(A2=0),0,@ERR),A1/A2)

When you press Enter, 1-2-3 beeps and switches to EDIT mode. If the error isn't obvious, you cannot exit EDIT mode unless you either fix the error or press Esc, erasing the contents of the cell. Because the program accepts anything as a label, you can insert a label prefix at the beginning of the entry and press Enter. Then copy the formula to another cell and work on the formula until you find the error.

In this case, begin by eliminating the compound @IF from the formula. To do so, copy the formula to a blank cell and then erase the middle @IF statement, replacing it with a zero:

@IF(@ISERR(A1/A2),0,A1/A2)

Because this formula works, the problem must be in the @IF statement you erased. Again, copy the original formula to the work area. Now delete everything except the middle @IF:

@IF(A2=0),0,@ERR)

You can see that you should erase the right parenthesis that follows A2=0. Make the change and test the formula:

@IF(A2=0,0,@ERR)

When this segment works, erase the work cell and correct the original formula:

@IF(@ISERR(A1/A2),@IF(A2=0,0,@ERR),A1/A2)

You may write formulas that are longer and more complex than this example. To debug them, simply convert them to labels and test them, one part at a time. Remember to remove the label prefix after you check the formula.

Problems with Circular References

CIRCULAR REFERENCE PROBLEM #1:

The CIRC indicator suddenly appears after you enter a formula.

EXPLANATION: Whenever the worksheet is recalculated and a CIRC indicator appears on the last line of the screen, 1-2-3 is warning you about a circular reference. Circular references are formulas that refer to themselves, either directly or indirectly. Because these references usually are errors, you should correct them as soon as they occur.

Figure T.2 shows an example of the most common direct circular reference. In this example, the @SUM function includes itself in the range to be summed. Whenever the worksheet recalculates, this sum increases.

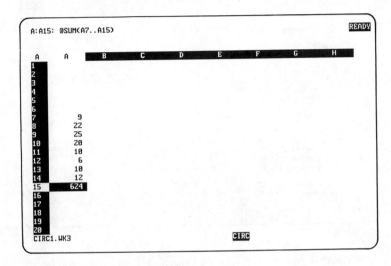

Fig. T.2.
*A direct
circular
reference.*

SOLUTION: Change the formula to @SUM(A7..A14) so that the formula does not refer to itself. The CIRC indicator disappears.

CIRCULAR REFERENCE PROBLEM #2:

The CIRC indicator appears after you enter a formula, but the formula does not refer to itself.

EXPLANATION: 1-2-3 is warning you about an indirect circular reference. This type of reference is tricky to find and fix. No formula refers to itself, but two or more formulas refer to each other. For example, each formula in figure T.3 seems reasonable, but A1 refers to A3, A2 refers to A1, and A3 refers to A2. You have no way of evaluating these formulas. The numbers increase whenever the worksheet recalculates.

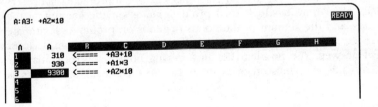

Fig. T.3.
*An indirect
circular
reference.*

SOLUTION: If you cannot find an obvious reason for the CIRC indicator, use /Worksheet Status to find the cell location of one link of the circular reference (see fig. T.4). If, after looking at the formula in the cell, you still cannot find the problem, write down the formula and check the contents of every cell referenced. You eventually will track down the problem.

Fig. T.4.
/Worksheet
Status showing
a circular
reference.

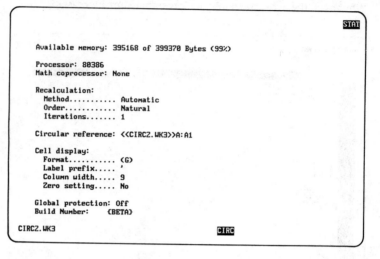

```
                                                                    STAT

        Available memory: 395168 of 399370 Bytes (99%)

        Processor: 80386
        Math coprocessor: None

        Recalculation:
           Method.......... Automatic
           Order........... Natural
           Iterations....... 1

        Circular reference: <<CIRC2.WK3>>A:A1

        Cell display:
           Format.......... (G)
           Label prefix..... '
           Column width..... 9
           Zero setting..... No

        Global protection: Off
        Build Number:     {BETA}

   CIRC2.WK3                                    CIRC
```

ALTERNATIVE EXPLANATION: @CELL("width") can cause a circular reference if you use the cell address that contains this function to determine the width of the column that contains the formula. For example, if cell C9 contains the following formula, it is considered a circular reference:

@CELL("width",C9..C9)

ALTERNATIVE SOLUTION: Because all the cells in the column must be the same width, change the formula to refer to another cell in the same column:

@CELL("width",C8..C8)

CIRCULAR REFERENCE PROBLEM #3:

You have a formula that is supposed to be a circular reference, but you don't know how many times to recalculate to get the correct answer.

EXPLANATION: Even deliberate circular references can be a problem. Figure T.5 shows a profit calculation in which total profit depends on the amount of the executive bonus, and the amount of the bonus depends on profits—a legitimate circular reference. Every time 1-2-3 recalculates, the profit figure comes closer to the correct answer. The problem lies in knowing how many recalculations you need. Generally, you must recalculate until the change in the results is insignificant.

SOLUTION: You can recalculate manually if this is a one-time calculation and the worksheet is small. Use @ROUND to set the required precision. In figure T.5, the bonus is rounded to whole dollars. Then press Calc (F9) to calculate the worksheet until the profit number does not change. In the example shown in figure

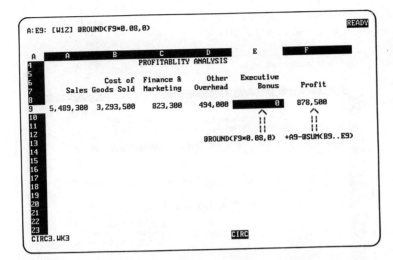

Fig. T.5.
A deliberate circular reference.

T.5, you must calculate the worksheet five times before the profit figure stops changing.

ALTERNATIVE SOLUTION: If the circular reference is part of a large worksheet, recalculation may take an inordinate amount of time. Use the macro in figure T.6 to recalculate only part of the worksheet until you get the correct answer.

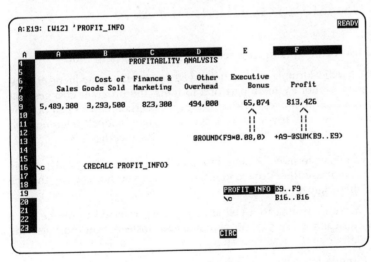

Fig. T.6.
A macro with {RECALC} that helps resolve a circular reference.

If the numbers change often and you want to recalculate automatically, use the macro in figure T.7 to recalculate the profit information until PROFIT is equal to OLD PROFIT in cell F5. Figure T.7 shows the result of executing this macro. In most cases, cell F5 would be hidden. This macro works because {RECALC} proceeds row-by-row and F5 is above PROFIT. If OLD_PROFIT were below PROFIT, this macro would not work because the two numbers would always be the same. The macro would stop at the first {RECALC}.

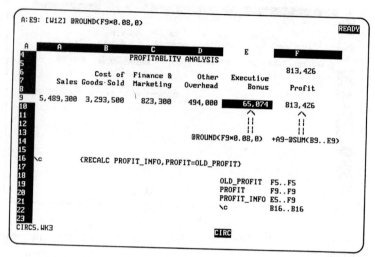

Fig. T.7.
A macro with
{RECALC
condition} that
automatically
solves a
circular
reference.

Problems that Result in ERR

ERR PROBLEM #1:

A formula that had been working correctly suddenly changes to ERR.

EXPLANATION: A valid formula can be destroyed by certain subsequent entries. When the program cannot evaluate part of a formula, the program changes that part of the formula to ERR. Moves, deletes, erases, and certain entries can destroy a formula or make it invalid. If you move a cell or a range to a cell referenced in a formula, the program replaces the reference with ERR (see fig. T.8).

SOLUTION: If you want to move a value into a cell after you refer to that cell in a formula, you cannot use the /Move command. Instead, you must /Copy the cell and then erase the original cell.

If you want to move a formula to a cell after you have referred to the cell in a formula, you again cannot use the /Move command. Instead, you must use the /Copy command, following these four steps:

1. Edit the formula to convert it to a label.

2. Copy the label to the cell.

3. Edit the label to convert it back to a formula.

4. Erase the original cell.

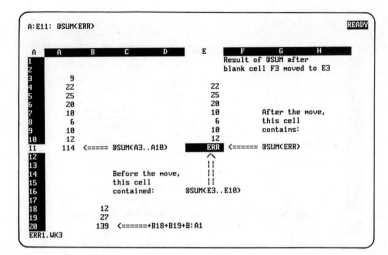

Fig. T.8.
A move that
turns a
formula to
ERR.

You have to convert the formula to a label to prevent relative cell references from changing when you copy the formula. If you want the relative cell references to change when you copy the formula to its new location, just copy the cell as a formula. Absolute cell references (for example, $A$1) do not change when the cell is copied as a formula.

ERR PROBLEM #2:

Formulas change to ERR after you delete a row, a column, or a worksheet somewhere else in the worksheet.

EXPLANATION: Although you seldom deliberately delete a row, column, or worksheet that contains information used in formulas, deleting such information accidentally is not unusual. The /Worksheet Delete command deletes the entire row, column, or worksheet without giving you a chance to inspect the area deleted; you can see only the usual screenful. Information contained in the deleted area may be somewhere off-screen. Figure T.9 shows the effect of deleting row 18 from the worksheet shown in figure T.8. The referenced cell in the formula in B20 (now B19) changes to ERR.

SOLUTION: Avoid this problem by checking the worksheet carefully before you delete. To check a row, move the cell pointer to the row and then press End left-arrow and End right-arrow. If the cell pointer moves from column A to column IV, the row must be empty. Use End up-arrow and End down-arrow to see whether a column is empty from row 1 to row 8192. Use End Home to see whether the worksheet is empty. End Home moves the cell pointer to A1 of an empty worksheet.

Even this method is not foolproof. A formula can legitimately refer to a blank cell in a row, column, or worksheet. Perhaps the cell will contain data that has not

Fig. T.9.
A delete that turns a formula to ERR.

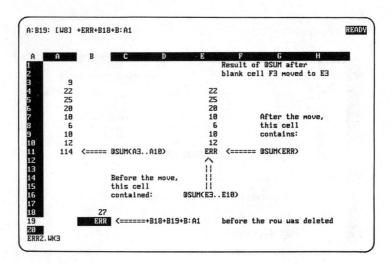

```
A:B19: [W8] +ERR+B18+B:A1                                    READY

 A     A      B      C      D     E       F       G       H
 1                                      Result of @SUM after
 2                                      blank cell F3 moved to E3
 3            9
 4           22                        22
 5           25                        25
 6           20                        20
 7           10                        10            After the move,
 8            6                         6            this cell
 9           10                        10            contains:
10           12                        12
11          114   <===== @SUM(A3..A10) ERR   <====== @SUM(ERR)
12                                      ^
13                                      ||
14                 Before the move,     ||
15                 this cell            ||
16                 contained:      @SUM(E3..E10)
17
18             27
19            ERR  <======+B18+B19+B:A1    before the row was deleted
20
ERR2.WK3
```

yet been entered. If you delete this area, the formula that refers to the cell in that area changes to ERR.

The most foolproof way to avoid this error is to use the following procedure:

1. Save the file.

2. In a blank cell, put an @SUM formula that sums the entire active area (from A:A1 to End Ctrl-Home).

3. Delete the row, column, or worksheet, and if recalculation is set to manual, recalculate the worksheet.

If your @SUM formula changes to ERR, you know that somewhere a cell changed to ERR when you deleted the row, column, or worksheet. Search the worksheet until you find the ERR. If the formula is in error, correct it. If the deleted area is needed, retrieve the worksheet you saved before the deletion or press Undo (Alt-F4) to undo the delete.

ERR PROBLEM #3:

String formulas change to ERR after you erase a cell or a range.

EXPLANATION: With numeric formulas, it usually does not matter whether a cell contains a number or a string, or whether the cell is blank. Blank cells and cells that contain strings are treated as zeros in numeric calculations.

String formulas are not as forgiving as numeric formulas. A string formula results in ERR if any referenced cell is blank or contains numeric values. If you erase a cell used in a string formula, the string formula changes to ERR. This change may be acceptable if you plan to enter new data in the cell. Figure T.10 shows some examples of numeric and string formulas.

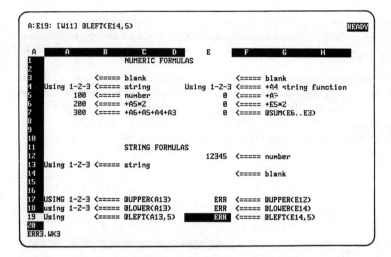

```
A:E19: [W11] @LEFT(E14,5)                                    READY

A          A        B       C       D    E      F      G       H
1                          NUMERIC FORMULAS
2
3                   <===== blank             <===== blank
4    Using 1-2-3    <===== string   Using 1-2-3  <===== +A4 string function
5            100    <===== number            0   <===== +A3
6            200    <===== +A5*2             0   <===== +E5*2
7            300    <===== +A6+A5+A4+A3      0   <===== @SUM(E6..E3)
8
9
10
11                         STRING FORMULAS
12                                  12345  <===== number
13   Using 1-2-3    <===== string
14                                         <===== blank
15
16
17   USING 1-2-3   <===== @UPPER(A13)   ERR  <===== @UPPER(E12)
18   using 1-2-3   <===== @LOWER(A13)   ERR  <===== @LOWER(E14)
19   Using         <===== @LEFT(A13,5)  ERR  <===== @LEFT(E14,5)
20
ERR3.WK3
```

Fig. T.10. ERRs in string functions caused by blank cells and numbers.

SOLUTION: If you are sure that you will complete the blank cells before you print the worksheet, nothing needs to be done. In fact, you can leave the ERR to remind you that data is missing.

If the data is optional, you must trap the possible error in the formula. You can test for a null string in the cell before referencing the cell in the formula. A blank cell is treated as though it contains a null string (" "). For example, the following formula concatenates the strings in A1 and B1 if both contain strings:

  +A1&B1

If A1 always contains a string and B1 can be blank, change the formula to the following:

  +A1&@IF(B1=" "," ",B1)

If A1 is either blank or a number, the result is ERR, and the program warns you that something is wrong. If B1 is blank, no error occurs, and the formula equates to the contents of A1.

The following formula behaves in a similar manner:

  +A1&@S(B1..B1)

The @S function avoids errors, filtering out anything that is not a string. This formula works if B1 contains a label or number, or is blank.

ERR PROBLEM #4:

When you save a file for the first time, formulas in another active file that refer to the new file change to ERR.

EXPLANATION: When a formula refers to a cell or range in another file, the cell reference starts with a file reference in double-angle brackets. For example, you have an active file named CONSOL and another active file named DEPT1. To refer to cell A:B3 in DEPT1 in a formula in CONSOL, use this complete formula:

+<<DEPT1.WK3>>A:B3

You can type this formula or create it in POINT mode if DEPT1 is active. When you first start 1-2-3, you have a blank worksheet file with no name. You can use /File Open or /File New to add another active file to memory. If you open CONSOL and then enter a formula that refers to a cell in the unnamed file, you get a formula with an unnamed file reference. In figure T.11, the formula in CONSOL is the following:

+<<>>A:B3..A:B3

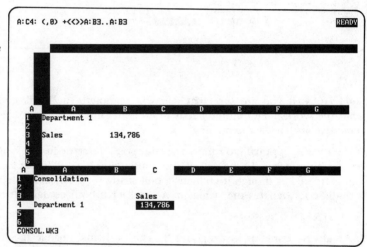

Fig. T.11.
A reference to a cell in a file that has never been saved.

Later, when you save the unnamed file, you assign a name. Unfortunately, 1-2-3 does not adjust the formula in CONSOL. Instead, 1-2-3 makes the formula undefined and displays ERR (see fig. T.12).

SOLUTION: As soon as you start to build a new file, save it and assign a name. Never build a formula in a file that refers to a cell in another file that has never been saved.

ERR PROBLEM #5:

You cannot insert a row—1-2-3 displays a memory error or says that the worksheet is too large.

EXPLANATION: Someone formatted the entire column from row 1 to 8192.

SOLUTION: Go to the last row that contains data and delete all rows below it with /Worksheet Delete Row. To make sure that you don't delete rows that contain data, press End Home to move to the row beyond the last active row in the worksheet.

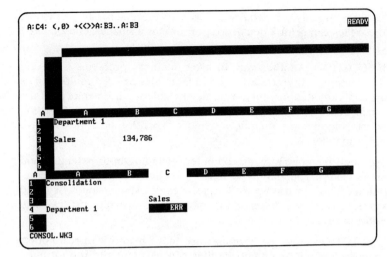

Fig. T.12.
A cell that becomes undefined after you save the file for the first time.

Problems with Memory Management

MEMORY PROBLEM #1:

While working on a large worksheet file or while trying to open another file, you run out of memory.

EXPLANATION: Running out of memory is one of the most common problems in 1-2-3. Some users just keep building larger and larger worksheet files until they eventually run out of memory. Then the users have to redesign their worksheet files. Even if you use relatively small worksheet files, you can run out of memory if you have too many active files in memory at the same time.

SOLUTION: You can use one of several ways to avoid running out of memory. But because none of them is foolproof, use /Worksheet Status to check available memory while you build large worksheet files. You can put a formula in a worksheet that keeps track of available memory. Put @INFO("memavail") in a cell. Then every time the worksheet recalculates, this cell contains the amount of available memory.

Proper worksheet design is the best way to avoid memory problems. Don't try to put an entire accounting system into one worksheet file. And don't try to use one worksheet file for all your product-line forecasts, even if the worksheets for all the product lines are identical. Instead, build separate worksheet files based on a single template. Not only do properly designed worksheet files save memory, they also speed recalculation. (The larger the worksheet, the longer you must wait when you recalculate.)

Sophisticated analysis models can require a dozen or more separate worksheet files. Each of these files can print a detailed report or (for a smaller, consolidated report) extract data to be combined into a summary report.

ALTERNATIVE SOLUTION: Another way to avoid memory problems is to add memory to your computer. If you want to build large files or keep multiple files in memory, just add extended memory. You may be able to add memory on the computer's system board (motherboard) or on an existing memory expansion board. You also can add memory on a new memory expansion board if you have an available expansion slot.

1-2-3 makes use of all memory in your computer, including both extended and expanded memory (EMS). You can use as much extended memory as your computer system allows. You can use up to 8 megabytes of EMS version 3 or up to 32 megabytes of EMS version 4. Extended memory boards usually cost less than expanded memory boards.

ALTERNATIVE SOLUTION: Because formulas use more memory than numbers use, you can convert formulas to numbers after you have entered the formulas needed to build your worksheet. Use the /Range Value command to convert the formulas to numbers. Use this method with any numbers that will not change when you update the worksheet. (Be sure to save the original template with the unconverted formulas in case you discover you need the formulas.)

Because the results of the /Data Table command are numbers, not formulas, you can save memory by converting large tables of formulas to data tables. Then repeat the /Data Table command to recalculate the tables if the values in the input cells change. Do not use this technique in a large worksheet if you frequently need to recalculate the data table; recalculating could take several minutes or even hours.

ALTERNATIVE SOLUTION: If you frequently move, insert, and delete rows and columns when you build large worksheets, you may run out of memory. When you move data or delete rows and columns, not all the memory is recovered. You usually can recover the memory by saving the worksheet and retrieving it again.

ALTERNATIVE SOLUTION: Consider the other programs you may have in memory at the same time as 1-2-3. If you use RAM-resident utilities or a multitasking environment—such as DESQView, Windows, or OS/2—you may have many programs in RAM at the same time. If you remove these programs, you can make more memory available to 1-2-3.

Remove RAM-resident programs if you need memory. The best alternative to doing this is to have two versions of your AUTOEXEC.BAT file—one you use for general computing (with your TSRs) and another you use for 1-2-3 (no TSRs).

ALTERNATIVE SOLUTION: Save and delete some worksheet files in memory. If you have more than one file in memory, you can save the file. Use /Worksheet Delete File to remove the file from memory. This action makes the memory available to expand any active files or open another file.

Troubleshooting 1-2-3 Commands

Problems with Range Names

RANGE NAME PROBLEM #1:

A range name that was valid suddenly results in ERR.

EXPLANATION: Moving and deleting cells and ranges can change formulas to ERR (see the problems in the section "Problems that Result in ERR"). These operations also cause range names to become undefined. Both ranges and range names are identified by the upper-left corner cell and the lower-right corner cell. If you move a cell or a range of cells to one of these corner cells, the range name becomes undefined.

Suppose that, for example, you are working with the range name table shown in figure T.13. After moving A1 to B3 and deleting row 9, your range name table changes (see fig. T.14). If you move to the upper-left or lower-right corner cell of a named range, as in SALES, the range name becomes undefined. The formula still refers to the range name, but the range name does not exist. If you delete an entire named range, as in DEPT7SALES, the range name becomes undefined. If you delete part of a named range, as in EXPENSES, PERCENT, and PROFITS, the named range adjusts automatically, and no ERR occurs.

```
A:B11: (,0) @SUM(SALES)                                          READY

    A         A            B         C          D         E              F
    1                    SALES    EXPENSES    PROFITS   % PROFIT
    2
    3      DEPT 1        171,734   134,464     37,270    21.70%
    4      DEPT 2        188,721   166,332     22,389    11.86%
    5      DEPT 3        130,504    85,280     45,224    34.65%
    6      DEPT 4        155,347   127,667     27,680    17.82%
    7      DEPT 5        149,857   106,888     42,969    28.67%
    8      DEPT 6        129,909   114,287     15,622    12.03%
    9      DEPT 7        134,361   123,487     10,874     8.09%
    10
    11       TOTALS    1,060,433   858,405    202,028    19.05%
    12
    13
    14
    15                                         DEPT7SALES    B9..B9
    16                                         EXPENSES      C3..C9
    17                                         PERCENT       E3..E9
    18                                         PROFITS       D3..D9
    19                                         SALES         B3..B9
    20                                         TOTALS        B11..E11
    NAMES1.WK3
```

Fig. T.13.
A range name table.

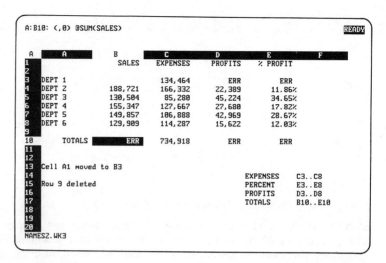

Fig. T.14.
A range name
table after
moving and
deleting.

SOLUTION: Although both ranges and range names are lost in the same manner, using range names provides an easy way to audit these errors. When a range name becomes undefined, it does not show in a range name table. However, if the range name has a note, the name shows up by using /Range Name Note Table (see fig. T.15). Assign a note to all your range names. If you have no reason to assign a note, just assign the range a one-letter note. Keep a current range name note table in all your worksheets. After you make any changes, re-create the range name note table and look for blank ranges.

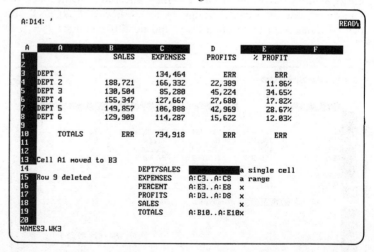

Fig. T.15.
A range name
note table
showing
undefined
range names
with notes.

RANGE NAME PROBLEM #2:

A range name looks correct in the range name table, but the macros and formulas that refer to the named range do not work properly.

EXPLANATION: This problem occurs when you use a range name that is also a cell address. If you set up a complex report and give the individual pages the range names P1, P2, and P3, the printed report contains only the cells P1, P2, and P3. If you give a macro the range name GO2 and then use {BRANCH GO2}, the macro branches to cell GO2 and, probably, stops at a blank cell.

SOLUTION: Never name a range with a combination of one or two letters and a number. Don't even use a range name such as TO4. A range name that is not a valid cell address in the current version of 1-2-3 may be a valid cell address in a future release.

Problems with Relative and Absolute Addressing

ADDRESSING PROBLEM #1:

After you copy a formula to other cells, the copied formulas are incorrect—the addresses are wrong.

EXPLANATION: One of 1-2-3's handiest built-in features is the automatic formula adjustment for relative cell addressing when a formula is copied. Relative addressing is so natural and automatic, you may forget this feature is working.

For example, consider the following formula in cell A4:

+A1+A2-A3

If you copy the formula from A4 to B4, it becomes the following:

+B1+B2-B3

This result depends on what is called relative addressing. Each formula is stored with addresses relative to the cell that contains the formula. Internally, 1-2-3 interprets the formula in A4 as the following: Add the contents of the cell three rows up and the cell two rows up and subtract the contents of the cell one row up. This formula is the same as the one originally in A4 and copied to B4.

You often do not want the cell references to change when you copy a formula. If you copy the cell references as relative addresses, you get the wrong formula. In figure T.16, for example, the formula for percent of total was written in C2 and copied to C3..C14. The relative addressing adjustment changes the formula in C3 from +B2/B14 to +B3/B15.

SOLUTION: Specify an address as absolute when you write the formula, not when you copy it. To make an address absolute, precede the column and the row by a dollar sign ($). If you use the pointing method to specify a range or a cell address, make the address absolute by pressing the Abs key (F4) when you point to the cell. If you type a cell address manually, make the address absolute by pressing the Abs key (F4) after you type the address.

The formula in C2 should be +B2/$B$14. When you copy this formula, the relative address (B2) changes, but the absolute address ($B$14) does not change. The correct formulas are shown in column F of figure T.16.

*Fig. T.16.
Relative and
absolute
addressing.*

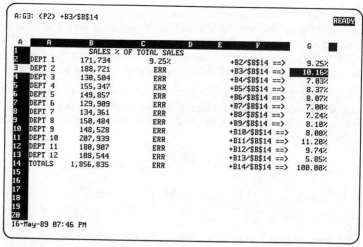

Problems with Recalculation

RECALCULATION PROBLEM #1:

As your worksheets become larger, recalculation takes longer, and some operations have to wait.

EXPLANATION: When you add or change a cell, 1-2-3 recalculates the entire worksheet. This calculation occurs in the background, meaning that you still can work during the recalculation. You know that 1-2-3 is recalculating when the CALC status indicator appears. However, some commands wait for the recalculation to finish. You must wait until both the recalculation and the command finishes. These commands include /**P**rint, /**R**ange Value, and /**F**ile Save.

At first, this recalculation is almost instantaneous, and you can ignore the delay. As you add formulas and include more complex formulas and string functions, the delay increases noticeably. If you have little memory left, 1-2-3 has to swap parts of the program between the disk and memory while it recalculates. This swapping can increase recalculation time greatly.

SOLUTION: Fortunately, you can continue to do most operations while 1-2-3 recalculates. The only operations that have to wait, should wait. Otherwise, you run the risk of printing incorrect values, copying incorrect values, or saving a partially updated file.

You can eliminate the recalculation delays by using the /**W**orksheet Global **R**ecalculation **M**anual command. The next time you change any cell, the CALC status indicator appears at the bottom of the screen to warn you that some cells may be incorrect. You must press the Calc key (F9) when you want the program to recalculate the file. The CALC indicator disappears until you make another entry.

Unless you are sure that you will not use /**P**rint, /**R**ange Value, or /**F**ile Save followed by /**F**ile Combine Add, you should not change recalculation to manual.

RECALCULATION PROBLEM #2:

You use /**File Xtract Values**, and you extract incorrect values.

EXPLANATION: Even with automatic recalculation, if you perform /**File Xtract Values** during a background recalculation, some of the values might be extracted before their correct values are calculated.

SOLUTION: Do not use /**File Xtract Values** with the CALC indicator on. Instead, wait until this indicator goes off.

Miscellaneous Problems

SPLIT SCREEN PROBLEM #1:

When you split the screen into windows to look at different parts of the file or separate files simultaneously, all windows scroll with the window that contains the cell pointer.

EXPLANATION: You split the 1-2-3 screen for one of two basic reasons: to keep part of a large table in sight at all times (for example, the totals) or to look at two completely different parts of a file or two different files at the same time. Figure T.17 shows an example of splitting a screen to display a large table on-screen. The totals are always displayed in the bottom window. When you scroll the top window, the bottom window scrolls with the top, ensuring that the columns in both windows match (see fig. T.18).

This synchronized scrolling is the default (for the **Sync** option) when you split the screen (horizontally or vertically) into two windows. In a vertical split, the same rows are displayed in the left and right windows. In perspective view, you see the same rows and columns in all three worksheets.

```
A:E7: 150222                                              READY

 A      A          B          C          D        E          F          G
 1                BUDGET SUMMARIES
 2
 3
 4
 5             January   February    March    April       May       June
 6             --------  --------   --------  --------  --------   --------
 7  Region 1   129,767   136,256    143,069   150,222   157,733    165,620
 8  Region 2   125,297   131,562    138,140   145,047   152,300    159,915
 9  Region 3   114,807   120,547    126,575   132,903   139,548    146,526
 10 Region 4   121,220   127,281    133,645   140,327   147,343    154,710
 11 Region 5   135,937   142,734    149,871   157,364   165,233    173,494
 12 Region 6   113,055   118,708    124,643   130,875   137,419    144,290
 13 Region 7   130,880   137,424    144,295   151,510   159,085    167,039
 14 Region 8   100,345   105,362    110,630   116,162   121,970    128,068
 15 Region 9   106,299   111,614    117,194   123,054   129,207    135,667
 16 Region 10  125,816   132,106    138,712   145,647   152,930    160,576
 17 Region 11  135,100   141,855    148,948   156,395   164,215    172,426
 18 Region 12  105,713   110,999    116,549   122,377   128,495    134,920
 A      A          B          C          D        E          F          G
 49        TOTALS 4,989,312 5,238,778 5,500,717 5,775,753 6,064,540 6,367,768
WINDOW1.WK3
```

Fig. T.17.
The display split into two windows.

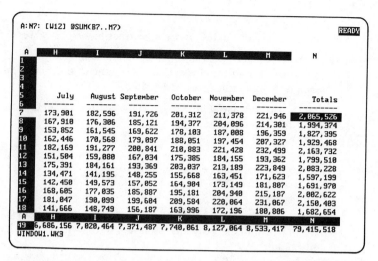

Fig. T.18.
The windows scrolled in sync.

However, when you split the screen to look at two completely different parts of a file (data and macros, for example) or to look at different files, you do not want to use synchronized scrolling. Instead, you want to be able to move the cell pointer around the data area in one window while the other windows remain fixed on a specific area (see fig. T.19).

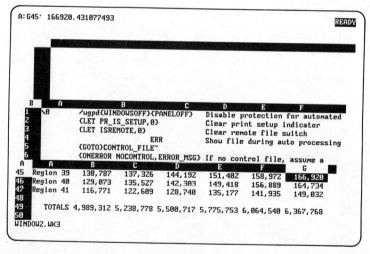

Fig. T.19.
Unsynchronized scrolling.

SOLUTION: To eliminate the default synchronized scrolling, you must specify /Worksheet Window Unsync. As you move down the table in worksheet A in figure T.19, the other windows do not move.

DATA DESTRUCTION PROBLEM #1:

Occasionally, by making a mistake with /Copy, /Move, or /Delete, you destroy part of the worksheet and then must painstakingly reconstruct it.

EXPLANATION: Unlike modeling languages and statistical-analysis packages, spreadsheets such as 1-2-3 do not separate the model from the data. (The model is composed of formulas and macros that do not change. The data is the numbers you enter and change.) When you use 1-2-3 to enter data, you risk accidentally changing the model as well.

SOLUTION: Always keep a backup copy of all worksheets. (Keep two or three backup copies of critical worksheets.) Then, if you destroy a worksheet, you can recover it from the backup file. To save the most recent backup copy every time you save the file, choose the **B**ackup option after /**F**ile **S**ave. The previous version is saved with the same name and a .BAK extension. To save multiple backups, save the file with different names, such as BUDGET1, BUDGET2, and so on.

ALTERNATIVE SOLUTION: You can use the protection option to help prevent the worksheet from being destroyed. Protected cells cannot be changed. If you try to change a protected cell, the program beeps and displays a warning message, and the contents of the cell remain unchanged.

Use the /**R**ange Unprotect command to unprotect the cells you want to change. After you complete the worksheet and are ready to use it, turn on the protection feature by issuing the /**W**orksheet **G**lobal **P**rotection **E**nable command before you enter data. To ensure that no one changes the protection settings, use /**F**ile **A**dmin **S**eal.

TEMPLATE PROBLEM #1:

At the beginning of every month, you must carefully erase all the data from the past month to prepare for the new month. If you leave previous data, the information for the new month is incorrect.

EXPLANATION: This problem is related to the preceding one. Because 1-2-3 does not distinguish between the model and the data, the program cannot present a blank model for the next month's data.

SOLUTION: Although 1-2-3 cannot distinguish between the model and the data, you can. Build a model or template: a worksheet that contains all necessary formulas, formats, and macros—but no data. Save this worksheet and make a backup copy. Then use this model every month to start the new month. After you've added data to the file, always be sure to save the file under a different name from that of the template. For example, you might name a budget template BUDGET. Retrieve BUDGET every month, saving it as BUD0889 in August, 1989; BUD0989 in September, 1989; and so on.

TEMPLATE PROBLEM #2:

You have a large worksheet with many formulas, input areas, and macros. You have difficulty finding all the data input areas until you print the final reports and discover some data is missing.

EXPLANATION: A worksheet can be completely unstructured. You can put input areas, reports, intermediate calculations, and macros anywhere you want in a worksheet file. With this type of unstructured layout, you may find it hard to verify that all required input has been updated.

SOLUTION: Break up the file into separate worksheets. Put all the macros in one worksheet. Put all the input areas in one or more worksheets without other data. Put @NA in input cells. If an input cell is missed, results show as NA. If necessary, use separate worksheets for the reports.

COLUMN WIDTH PROBLEM #1:

You use /Worksheet Insert Sheet to insert a new worksheet, and all the column widths in the new worksheet are the default width. You want both worksheets to have the same custom column widths.

EXPLANATION: You may insert a new worksheet into a file for one of many different reasons. Many times you use each worksheet for a different purpose, such as input, reports, and macros. When each worksheet is different, you do not want to use the same column widths. Therefore, when you insert a new worksheet, you get the default column widths (see fig. T.20).

Fig. T.20.
Default column widths after inserting a new worksheet.

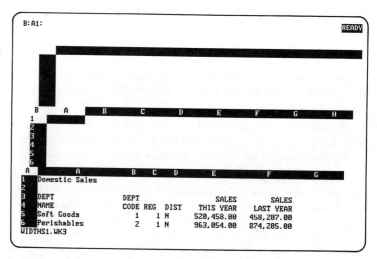

SOLUTION: If you want all worksheets to have the same format, move the cell pointer to the worksheet with the correct column widths and use the /Worksheet Global Group command. All worksheets then will have the same column widths as the current worksheet (see fig. T.21). If you are already in GROUP mode when you insert a new worksheet, it has the same column widths when you create it.

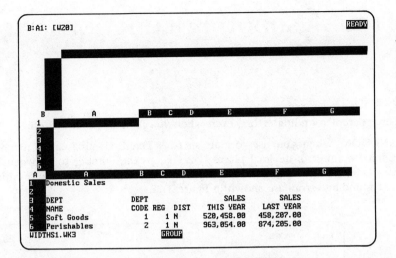

Fig. T.21. Column widths when you insert a new worksheet in GROUP mode.

Troubleshooting Functions

FUNCTION PROBLEM #1:

You get apparent rounding errors, even when you have not rounded off.

EXPLANATION: When you use formats such as Fixed, Comma, and Currency with a fixed number of decimal places, 1-2-3 keeps the number to between 18 and 19 decimal places but rounds off the display. Examples of the resulting apparent rounding errors are shown in figure T.22.

Fig. T.22.
A worksheet
with rounding
errors.

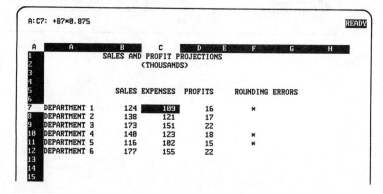

SOLUTION: To avoid such rounding errors, use the @ROUND function to round off numbers to the same precision shown in the display (see fig. T.23).

Fig. T.23.
Rounding
errors
eliminated by
@ROUND.

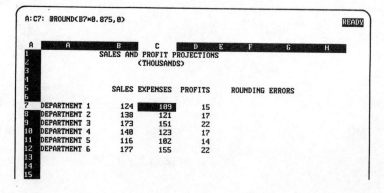

FUNCTION PROBLEM #2:

Two numbers that should be equal sometimes test as unequal.

EXPLANATION: Figure T.24 shows what should be two identical columns of numbers. Column A was created by using /Data Fill starting with 0.1125 and incrementing by 0.0025. Column B contains formulas. The formula in B5 is +A5. The rest of the formulas in column B add 0.0025 to the cell above it.

The @IF formula in column D indicates that the numbers are not equal. Because the formula in B5 is simply +A5, these two numbers are exactly equal. All the other pairs of numbers are not equal. Column I shows the small differences between these numbers. This problem occurs with fractions because computers process numbers in binary and then convert the numbers to decimals to display them. The problem does not occur with integers.

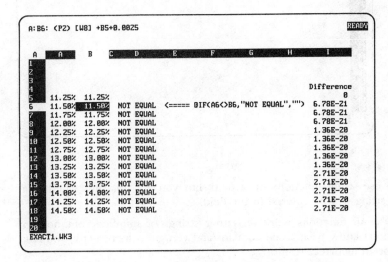

Fig. T.24.
Numbers that
should be
equal but do
not test equal.

SOLUTION: Use @ROUND when you compare two fractions.

FUNCTION PROBLEM #3:

You get ERR when you try to combine numbers and strings.

EXPLANATION: Although 1-2-3 has a full complement of string functions, you cannot mix strings and numbers in the same function. Figure T.25 shows the effect of trying to build an address by using words from strings and a number for the ZIP code.

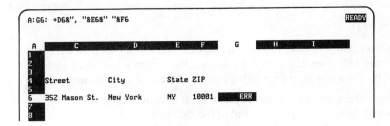

Fig. T.25.
An error when
numbers mix
with strings.

SOLUTION: Use the @STRING function to convert a number to its equivalent string (see fig. T.26). Then you can use the converted number in a string function.

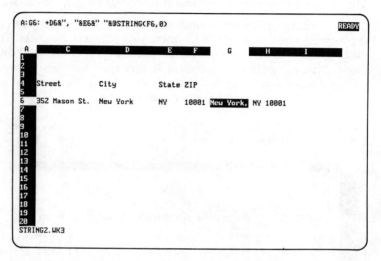

Fig. T.26.
A function that
converts a
number to a
string.

FUNCTION PROBLEM #4:

You want to use string functions on a field, but you are not sure whether a number or a string will be entered in the field.

EXPLANATION: All functions work on either strings or numbers, but not on both. If you don't know what a cell contains and you guess incorrectly, you risk getting ERR or an incorrect result.

SOLUTION: You can test a cell to see whether it contains a number or a string. Then, depending on the contents of the cell, use the appropriate function. Suppose that, for example, you want to concatenate the contents of A1 and B1, using the following formula:

+A1&B1

The ampersand (&), which is a string concatenation operator, causes an error if either A1 or B1 is blank or contains a number. Assume that you are sure A1 contains a string, but you don't know whether B1 contains a string or a number, or is blank. To concatenate B1 to A1 only if B1 contains a string, use the following formula:

+A1&@S(B1)

The @S function (a filter) does nothing if the cell contains a string, but returns a null string if the cell does not contain a string. The formula therefore results in either A1 (if B1 does not contain a string) or in A1&B1 (if B1 contains a string).

To concatenate the contents of B1 regardless of whether it is a number or a string, you need a more complex formula (see fig. T.27).

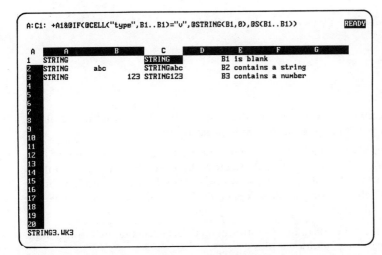

A:C1: +A1&@IF(@CELL("type",B1..B1)="v",@STRING(B1,0),@S(B1..B1))   READY

A	A	B	C	D	E	F	G
1	STRING		STRING		B1 is blank		
2	STRING	abc	STRINGabc		B2 contains a string		
3	STRING		123 STRING123		B3 contains a number		
4							
5							
6							
7							
8							
9							
10							
11							
12							
13							
14							
15							
16							
17							
18							
19							
20							

STRING3.WK3

Fig. T.27.
A formula that handles numbers, strings, or blank cells.

In this formula, if the type is "v" (for value), the contents of the cell are converted to a string. If the cell is blank, the @S function filters out the string, and the cell is ignored. If the cell contains a string, the @S function does nothing, and the two strings are concatenated.

Troubleshooting File Operations

FILE PROBLEM #1:

Your hard disk contains so many files that finding the files you want is difficult. Whenever you perform a file operation, long delays occur.

EXPLANATION: A single hard disk can hold hundreds—even thousands—of files. If that many files are placed in one subdirectory, however, keeping track of them is impossible. And DOS, for example, slows down significantly if you have more than approximately 112 or 224 files (depending on which version of DOS you use) in one subdirectory.

If you try to put all the files in the root directory, DOS reaches an absolute limit and won't let you save additional files.

SOLUTION: Set up separate subdirectories for different applications and users.

The default directory should contain the subdirectory you use most often. To specify the name of this subdirectory, use the /Worksheet Global Default Directory command.

To reach files in other subdirectories, use the /File Dir command. This command changes the directory until you either use /File Dir again or return to the default directory by quitting and reentering 1-2-3.

FILE PROBLEM #2:

You want to retrieve a file that is not in the default directory, but you don't remember which directory contains the file.

EXPLANATION: The file you want is in another subdirectory, but you can see only the files in the current directory.

SOLUTION: Select /File Retrieve to display a list of all worksheet files and all subdirectories of the current directory. To search forward through a chain of directories, point to the directory you want and press Enter. To search backward through the chain of directories, use the Backspace key. When you locate your file, point to it and press Enter. If you want to retrieve other files in this directory, use the /File Dir command to make it the current directory.

ALTERNATIVE SOLUTION: Use the /System command to suspend 1-2-3 temporarily and return to the operating system. Then you can use the TREE, CD, and DIR commands as well as any disk-management utilities you may have to find the subdirectory and file you want.

After you locate the file, type **exit** to return to 1-2-3. Then you can use the /File Dir and /File Retrieve commands to read the file.

FILE PROBLEM #3:

While building a large worksheet file, you fear making a mistake that will destroy part of the worksheet and cost you hours of work.

EXPLANATION: Sooner or later, everyone destroys part or all of an important file. The greater your proficiency in 1-2-3, the larger and more complex the files you can build—and the more disastrous the errors you can make.

SOLUTION: There may be no solution once you destroy the file; you may not be able to restore it. The only solution may be to avoid the problem by preparing for it.

You can best prepare for this problem by saving your file frequently when you make many changes or write macros. Be sure to save the file under a different name. (If you use the same file name, you might save the file two or three times after making a disastrous error before discovering you made that error.)

While you develop a file, save it under a name that includes a sequence number (such as BUDGET1, BUDGET2, BUDGET3, and so on). When you reach BUDGET10 and have done some testing, you can consider erasing BUDGET1. At least once during each development session, save the files to a floppy disk. This backup copy is an additional safeguard.

If you enter data in a worksheet daily, save the worksheet under a name that includes the date (BUD0809 or BUD0810, for example). Remember that time spent storing data is minimal compared to the time you might have to spend reentering lost data and rebuilding lost macro-driven worksheets.

FILE PROBLEM #4:

You want to retrieve a backup copy of a file, but you cannot find the file with /File **Retrieve**.

EXPLANATION: When you save a file with the same name as an existing file, you have the option of saving the previous file as a backup. Instead of erasing the previous file, 1-2-3 renames the file with a .BAK extension. When you use /File **Retrieve**, you see only files with extensions that start with WK.

SOLUTION: After you select /File **Retrieve**, ignore the list of files, type *.**BAK**, and press Enter. You get a list of files in the current directory with a .BAK extension. Point to the file you want and press Enter. Be sure to save the file with a different name after you retrieve it.

FILE PROBLEM #5:

Some of the formulas brought in by /File Combine Copy are meaningless.

EXPLANATION: Using /File Combine Copy is similar to using /Copy within a worksheet. The same rules about relative addressing apply in both instances. If you combine part of another file that contains formulas that refer to cells in the combined area, the formulas stay the same in relation to the cells to which they refer. If you combine formulas that refer to cells outside the combined area, however, these formulas become references to cells somewhere else in the current worksheet. These formulas may become meaningless, leading to incorrect results.

For example, figure T.28 shows the result of combining the data in J10..K15. Because the formula in K10 refers to cell G10, which is a blank cell in this worksheet, the result in K10 is zero. In the original worksheet, the corresponding cell contained a price, and the formula gave a correct result.

Fig. T.28.
Formulas after
/File Combine.

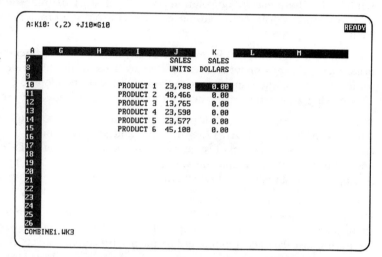

SOLUTION: You can use /File Combine Add to combine the current file with the values from another file. The formulas in the other file are converted to numbers. If you don't want any of the formulas from the other file, simply use /File Combine Add for the entire range. If you want some of the formulas from the other file, first use /File Combine Copy to get the formulas. Then, to get the numbers, use /File Combine Add on a different range.

/File Combine Add has pitfalls of its own. As 1-2-3 executes the /File Combine Add command, the program checks each cell in the current worksheet. If a cell is blank or contains a number, the corresponding value from the file being combined is added to that cell. If the cell in the current worksheet contains a formula, 1-2-3 skips that cell, regardless of what the corresponding cell in the file being combined may contain. And /File Combine Add combines only numeric values—not strings.

FILE PROBLEM #6:

After you use /File Import Numbers to read in an ASCII file, some of the information is lost, and some of it looks scrambled.

EXPLANATION: /File Import Numbers works only when the data in the ASCII file is in a precise format. Each field must be separated by a delimiter such as commas, semicolons, or spaces; each string must be enclosed in double quotation marks. 1-2-3 ignores data that is not in this format, but imports whatever data that it finds and recognizes as numbers. Ordinarily, the result is a useless mess.

SOLUTION: Using /File Import Text, read in the ASCII data as a series of long labels. Then use /Data Parse to separate the data into individual cells that 1-2-3 can use.

FILE PROBLEM #7:

You used /File Import Text and /Data Parse to import a text file, but the dates are not in a format that 1-2-3 recognizes.

EXPLANATION: When you use /Data Parse, 1-2-3 recognizes only numbers and dates with certain formats. If dates are not in a format that the program recognizes, 1-2-3 converts the dates to a string.

SOLUTION: In many cases, no solution is necessary. You can leave the dates as labels unless you plan to use date arithmetic. If you need to convert the labels to dates, however, you can do so by using string functions and @DATEVALUE.

Figure T.29 shows a directory listing that was redirected to a text file, imported into 1-2-3, and parsed. The dates in column L are labels; with hyphens between the date fields, 1-2-3 did not recognize them as dates.

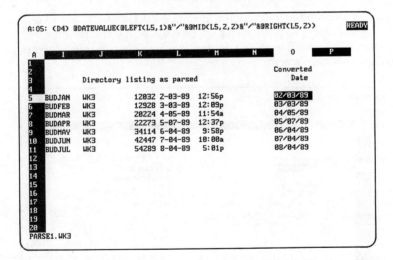

Fig. T.29.
String functions and @DATEVALUE used to convert a date.

The string function in the control panel converts the string to a valid 1-2-3 date format. Next, @DATEVALUE converts to a date the string that looks like a date. Then you use the /Range Format Date command to format the cell so that it looks like a date.

Troubleshooting Printing

PRINTING PROBLEM #1:

You have a multiple-page report that spans different sections of the worksheet. Specifying each of the different print ranges every time you print is a laborious task.

EXPLANATION: The program remembers only the last print range specified. If a report has multiple print ranges, you must specify each one when you print the report.

SOLUTION: You can specify multiple print ranges, and 1-2-3 prints each range. Separate each range with a comma or semicolon. If you want to force a page break after any of the print ranges, move the cell pointer to the first cell of a row you want to start on a new page and use /Worksheet Page to insert a page break.

ALTERNATIVE SOLUTION: Create a macro. If you are not familiar with macros, read Chapters 11 and 12 to learn how to write a simple macro for printing a report and how to use the advanced macro commands.

Assign each page or print range a descriptive name (PAGE1, PAGE2, and so on) and then instruct your macro to print each page (see fig. T.30). The advantage of a macro over specifying multiple ranges is that you can change print options between print ranges with a macro.

Fig. T.30.
A simple print
macro.

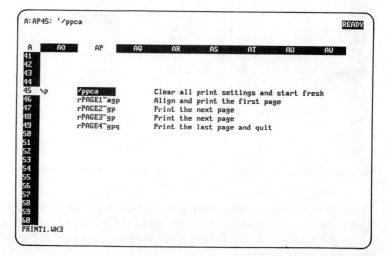

PRINTING PROBLEM #2:

Your print macro usually works as you want, but after you change the print options (to print a different report), the standard reports print incorrectly.

EXPLANATION: 1-2-3 remembers the print settings from the last report you printed. If you print a special report on wider paper or with different margins, headers, footers, and setup strings, for example, these settings affect the next report you print with the macro.

SOLUTION: For each set of print settings you need, specify all the settings and then save them with /Print [P,F,E] Options Name Create, assigning each set of print settings a unique name. To make one of these named settings current, use /Print Printer Options Name Use.

ALTERNATIVE SOLUTION: At the beginning of your print macro, use the /Print Printer Clear All command to reset all printer options to their defaults and to clear everything else. Then have the macro specify the printer options you want. In this way, you can include in one worksheet several print macros that won't interfere with one another. You also can use the /Print [P,F,E] Options Name Use commands in your print macro if you need different print settings.

PRINTING PROBLEM #3:

You tried to print in landscape mode, but the printer printed in normal portrait orientation.

EXPLANATION: In some cases, wide reports are printed across several pages, and you have to tape them together to see the entire report. You want to print the report in landscape mode, down the page instead of across. Therefore, you specify /Print [P,E] Options Advanced Layout Orientation Landscape on your dot-matrix printer, but your printer prints in normal portrait orientation. Landscape applies only to printers that can print characters in landscape orientation; this generally means laser printers. The only way to make a dot-matrix printer print in landscape orientation is in graphics mode where the program composes each letter out of individual dots. Although programs exist that can do this, 1-2-3 does not. The Landscape command is ignored on dot-matrix printers.

SOLUTION: Do not specify Landscape orientation unless your printer is capable of printing that way.

PRINTING PROBLEM #4:

Although you calculated the number of lines per page correctly when you set up your print ranges, the report runs off the end of the page and then skips a page.

EXPLANATION: You must tell the program the exact length (in print lines) of a page. The default for 6 lines per inch on 11-inch paper is 66 lines. But because 1-2-3 automatically reserves 3 lines at the top and 3 lines at the bottom of each page and provides default top and bottom margins of 2 lines each, the maximum print range on a page is only 56 lines. (These extra lines provide 1 line for a header or a footer—even if none is specified—and 2 lines between the print range and the header or footer, plus 4 lines if you don't change the default top and bottom margins.) If you specify top and bottom margins that are different from the default settings, you must subtract them from 60 (not 66) to determine the maximum number of lines in a 1-page print range.

SOLUTION: If you are not trying to pack the maximum number of lines into each page, you can adjust your print ranges to fit the number of available lines.

 Or if you don't use headers or footers, you can recover the use of the six lines by using the /**Print** [**P,F,E**] **O**ptions **O**ther **B**lank-**H**eader **S**uppress command. This print setting eliminates the three blank lines for headers and footers if none are specified.

PRINTING PROBLEM #5:

When you set up your print ranges, you considered margins and the six lines mentioned in the preceding problem. But the program occasionally produces a blank page between printed pages.

EXPLANATION: You can use one of two methods to skip to the next page when you print reports: you can specify a long report and let 1-2-3 skip automatically to a new page whenever it prints a full page or encounters a page-break code, or you can specify individual print ranges for each page and use the **Page** command to tell the program to skip to the next page. Under certain conditions, the two methods conflict, and both send a page break to the printer, resulting in a blank page.

With top and bottom margins of 0, you can have a 1-page print range of as many as 60 lines (or 66 lines if you suppress blank headers). If 1-2-3 encounters a print range of exactly 60 lines, the program automatically tells the printer to skip to the next page. If your macro also sends a page break, you get a blank page.

SOLUTION: Either restrict your print ranges to 59 lines (minus the number of lines for top and bottom margins and borders) or do not issue a **Page** command after a 60-line page.

PRINTING PROBLEM #6:

You do not want to print certain information that falls in the middle of a print range.

EXPLANATION: You've documented assumptions, shown intermediate results that clarify a calculation, and added comments to make your worksheets easier to understand. You may not want to include this information in your final printed reports.

SOLUTION: This problem has several solutions. Pick those that best meet your needs.

1. To skip rows, you can specify multiple print ranges that skip any rows you do not want printed.

2. To skip rows, you can use a special character, usually the vertical bar (|), to tell 1-2-3 not to print a row. (This symbol is located on the backslash key.) Whenever 1-2-3 sees this character in the leftmost cell of a row in a print range, the program skips that row. Except for printing, this character and the left-aligned label prefix (') act in the same way. The contents of the cell are displayed normally.

3. To skip one or more columns in the middle of a print range, use the /Worksheet Column **H**ide command to hide the column before you print it. Then, after you print the range, "unhide" the column by using the /Worksheet Column **D**isplay command.

PRINTING PROBLEM #7:

You want to print a report twice, but the second copy, instead of starting at page 1, begins with the next page number of the first copy.

EXPLANATION: With 1-2-3, you can build a report from many separate sections of a worksheet. If you use page numbers in headers or footers, every page starts with the next page number; the program assumes that you are producing one report.

SOLUTION: Issue the **A**lign command after a **P**age command to instruct 1-2-3 to start again at page 1. Because **A**lign also tells the program you have adjusted the paper to the top of the page, always issue the **P**age command before the **A**lign command to prevent your pages from being misaligned.

PRINTING PROBLEM #8:

You don't want to bother specifying individual print ranges for a long report.

EXPLANATION: If your report is more than five pages long, setting up the range names and writing the macro to print the report can be a tedious process. And if the report will grow longer as time passes (if the report contains year-to-date details, for example), you want to avoid having to continue adding range names and changing the macro.

SOLUTION: Let 1-2-3 automatically break up your report. 1-2-3 forces a page break after every full page and automatically inserts any headers or footers you specify. If you specify borders, 1-2-3 prints them on every page; you simply specify one print range.

1-2-3 also splits vertically a report that is too wide to print on a single page. The program prints as much material as possible on one page and then prints the "right side" of the report on separate pages. You can leave these pages separate or tape them together to make a wide report.

PRINTING PROBLEM #9:

You let 1-2-3 handle page breaks automatically, but the program separates information you want kept on one page.

EXPLANATION: When you specify a long report and let the program separate it automatically into pages, every page has the same number of print lines. However, the report may contain information you do not want separated: paragraphs of explanation or multiple-line descriptions of accounts, for example.

SOLUTION: Leave the report as one print range and insert page-break characters manually wherever you want a page to end. To insert a page-break character, move the cell pointer to the cell in the leftmost column of the row at which you want to start a new page. Then use the /**W**orksheet **P**age command to instruct 1-2-3 to insert a row above the cell pointer and put a page-break character (|::) in the cell.

PRINTING PROBLEM #10:

When you used the /**W**orksheet **P**age command to specify a page break, the command inserted a row through a macro or a database in the same row as the print range.

EXPLANATION: 1-2-3 inserts a page break by inserting a row across the entire worksheet. The blank row is inserted through anything that spans that row.

SOLUTION: Instead of using /**W**orksheet **P**age to insert a page break, you can indicate where you want the new page by typing the page-break character as a label.

In the leftmost column of the row where you want the new page, type the page-break character—a vertical-bar followed by two colons (|::). 1-2-3 treats this label as a page-break character, except that no blank row is inserted in the worksheet. Remember that you must type the page-break character in a blank line in your print range because the row with the page-break character does not print. print.

ALTERNATIVE SOLUTION: Keep macros, databases, and other data that is sensitive to insertions and deletions of rows in separate worksheets.

PRINTING PROBLEM #11:

You used a setup string to tell the printer to print compressed print. But the report wraps to a new line after 72 characters, even though additional space remains on the line.

EXPLANATION: Because 1-2-3 cannot interpret a setup string, it does not recognize either the size of the characters you print or the width of the paper you use. The print settings indicate to the program the amount of material that can fit on a line and on a page.

SOLUTION: Don't use the setup string to change the pitch. Use /**P**rint [**P,E**] **O**ptions **A**dvanced **L**ayout **P**itch to specify the pitch. 1-2-3 automatically adjusts the margins. To change the line spacing, use /**P**rint [**P,E**] **O**ptions **A**dvanced **L**ayout **L**ine-Spacing to adjust automatically the number of lines per page.

ALTERNATIVE SOLUTION: When you change the print pitch with a setup string, change the right margin. With a default left margin of 4 and a default right margin of 76, the 72-character print line matches the standard 72 data characters that 1-2-3 displays on-screen.

If you change the line spacing to something other than six lines per inch, you also must change the **Pg-L**ength to match the new setting.

PRINTING PROBLEM #12:

You use /**Print File** to save a print image to print on a printer attached to another computer. But when you print the image, you get the wrong fonts, pitch, and line spacing. Graphs do not print at all.

EXPLANATION: /**Print File** saves the printer information as an ASCII text file. This file does not include formatting or graphics; therefore, you just get the default values for the printer you use.

SOLUTION: Use /**Print Encoded** to save a print image file with all formatting and graphics information set up for the current printer.

PRINTING PROBLEM #13:

You use /**Print Encoded** to save a print image, but when you print the image, you still get the wrong fonts, pitch, and line spacing. Graphs are either scrambled or do not print.

EXPLANATION: When you use /**Print Encoded**, 1-2-3 uses the printer information for the current printer. The current printer is either the default printer or the printer you used last. Even if you specify another printer with /**Print Encoded Options Advanced Device Name** or /**Print Encoded Options Name Use**, it is too late—1-2-3 sets up the encoded file based on the current printer.

SOLUTION: Use /**Print Printer Options Advanced Device Name** or /**Print Printer Options Name Use** to select the printer you want to use with the encoded file. Then press Esc until you return to the /**Print** menu. Now the other printer is the current printer. Choose **Encoded** again and select **Go** when all settings are correct. Choosing /**Print Printer** the first time through is just a "dummy" menu sequence to choose a different printer. You could choose **Encoded**, but you would have to specify a file name, and 1-2-3 would create a dummy file. It's faster to choose **Printer** when you don't plan to print but just want to change the printer settings.

PRINTING PROBLEM #14:

You tried to print a graph and ran out of memory.

EXPLANATION: 1-2-3 needs extra memory to print a graph. If you have little memory left and try to print a graph, you can run out of memory.

SOLUTION: Save any files in memory and then use /**Worksheet Delete File** to remove one or more files from memory. If only one file is in memory, use /**Worksheet Erase Yes** to remove the file from memory. Even though you remove the file that contains the graph you want to print, 1-2-3 still remembers the information needed to print the graph. Select /**Print Resume** to print the graph.

PRINTING PROBLEM #15:

You start to print a report or graph, realize you made an error, and use /**Print Cancel** to cancel the printing. The printer continues to print.

EXPLANATION: When you use /**Print Cancel**, you tell 1-2-3 to stop sending data to the printer. Many printers have a printer buffer that can hold from 1 line to over 30 pages of information. Once the printer has the data in its buffer, 1-2-3 has no control over the printer.

In addition, programs called *print spoolers* store data to be printed in memory or on disk and send it to the printer when the printer is ready for more data. Once 1-2-3 sends the print data to the spooler, the program thinks that the data is printed and has no control over the printer.

SOLUTION: If the data is in a printer buffer, your printer may have a button or switch that clears the buffer. If there is no way to clear the printer buffer, just turn the printer off and on. All data in the printer buffer is lost.

If you use a print spooler, use /System to go to the operating system. Then follow the instructions for your spooler program to purge the spooler or remove your print entry.

Troubleshooting Graphing

GRAPHING PROBLEM #1:

Because your file uses many different graphs, selecting the graph ranges and other specifications is a slow and tedious process.

EXPLANATION: 1-2-3 has one current active graph. To use many different graphs in one worksheet, you must spend time specifying each one separately.

SOLUTION: Although the program has only one current active graph, you can save a library of graphs within the worksheet. After you have specified a graph completely, use the /Graph Name Create command to save the specification under a name you choose.

Repeat the process for each graph, giving each a different name. Then, to recall any graph, issue the /Graph Name Use command and type the name of the appropriate graph or point to its name in the list of graph names.

When you save the file, you also save the graph names and settings. Be sure that you save the file; if you forget to save it, the names and settings will be lost.

GRAPHING PROBLEM #2:

You don't like the patterns used by some of the graph ranges.

EXPLANATION: 1-2-3 has a default set of hatching patterns for each graph range (A through F). Many users do not like the patterns for the B and C ranges (see fig. T.31).

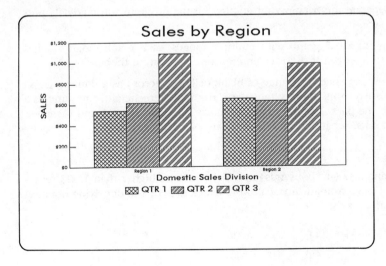

Fig. T.31.
The hatching for A, B, and C ranges in a graph.

SOLUTION: If you have fewer than six ranges to graph, simply skip those ranges whose patterns you don't want to use. You do not have to specify the ranges in order. Figure T.32 shows the preceding graph with ranges A, B, and D specified (no C range).

Fig. T.32.
The A, B, and D
ranges in a
graph.

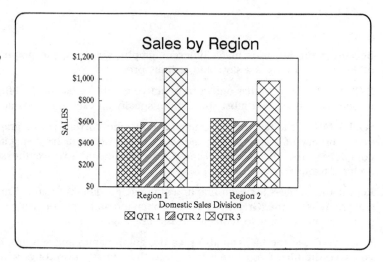

ALTERNATIVE SOLUTION: You can specify the hatching patterns manually with /Graph Options Advanced Hatches. The default hatching patterns for A–F are 2–7, respectively. Pattern 1 is solid; pattern 8 is hollow. You can get the same graph in figure T.32 with ranges A–C if you specify hatching pattern 5 for range C.

GRAPHING PROBLEM #3:

You want to separate the bars in your graphs, but the program automatically puts them side by side.

EXPLANATION: In a bar graph with multiple ranges, each graph range touches the one next to it—even if there is ample room to separate them.

SOLUTION: You can specify a range of blank cells (or zeros) as a dummy graph range. 1-2-3 displays this dummy range as a bar with zero height, the same as a space between the bars. The bar graph in figure T.33 shows the A and C ranges, which contain data, separated by B and D ranges with blank cells.

GRAPHING PROBLEM #4:

You are graphing data (in thousands) in which numbers higher than 1,000 represent millions. 1-2-3 automatically scales the data and adds the deceiving notation Thousands to the y-axis.

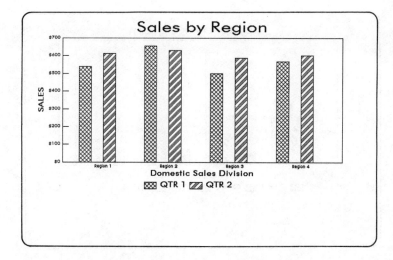

Fig. T.33.
A blank B and
D range used
to space graph.

EXPLANATION: This problem can be extremely confusing. 1-2-3 assumes that all the numbers you graph represent units. If the largest numbers are greater than about 3500, 1-2-3 automatically scales the numbers into thousands and adds the notation Thousands to the y-axis.

If you graph information that is already in thousands (or millions or more) in the worksheet, the Thousands indicator on the graph is incorrect.

Figure T.34 shows a table of sales data for all four quarters. These numbers are in the thousands of dollars. Note that one of the numbers in the table (in cell E6) is larger than 3500. Figure T.35 shows the graph of this data with the incorrect y-axis labels.

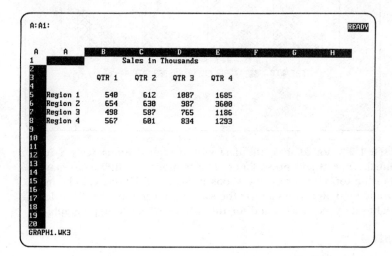

Fig. T.34.
Data with
numbers in
thousands.

Fig. T.35.
An incorrect scaling notation.

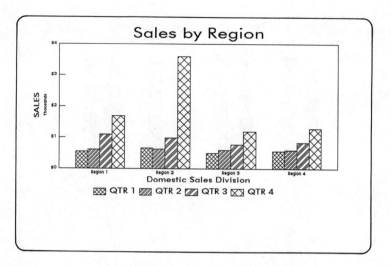

SOLUTION: You can turn off the scaling indicator or type your own. Use the /Graph Options Scale **Y**-Scale Indicator command. To turn off the indicator, choose None. To type your own indicator, choose Manual (see fig. T.36).

Fig. T.36.
A graph with the scaling indicator set manually to Millions.

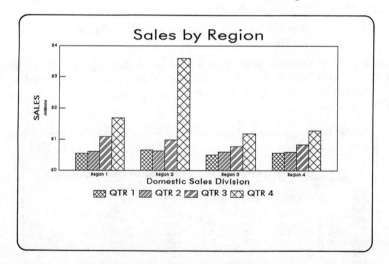

You also can tell 1-2-3 not to scale the data with /Graph Options Scale **Y**-Scale Exponent Manual. Type **0** and press Enter. The numbers on the y-axis stay in units. Instead of the top number on the y-axis in figures T.35 and T.36 being 4, the number would be 4,000. You can use the same command for the **2Y**-Scale (if you use the right-side y-axis scale) and for the **X**-Scale on an XY-type graph.

GRAPHING PROBLEM #5:

Your graph's x-axis labels overlap.

EXPLANATION: You can fit only a limited number of x-axis labels or numbers on a graph before they start to overlap (see fig. T.37).

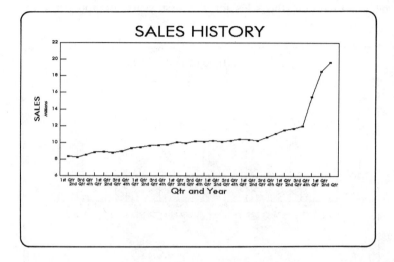

Fig. T.37.
Overlapping
x-axis labels.

SOLUTION: Use the /Graph Options Scale Skip command to skip a specific number of x-axis entries between the entries displayed on the graph. Figure T.38 shows the preceding graph after you have specified Skip **2**.

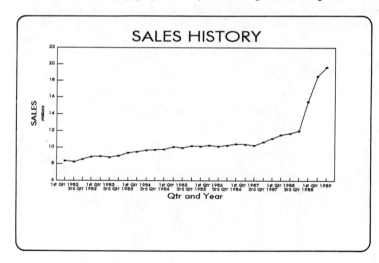

Fig. T.38.
A graph in
which every
second x-axis
label is
skipped.

GRAPHING PROBLEM #6:

You graph numbers with a wide range of values, and the small numbers get scrunched along the x-axis.

EXPLANATION: If some numbers are large and some are small, the small numbers do not show up at all or are close to the x-axis. Figure T.39 shows sales for a company after rapid growth. The graph must accommodate the total sales of over 20 million; therefore, the sales for the first years are too small to distinguish.

Fig. T.39.
Small numbers
and large
numbers in the
same graph.

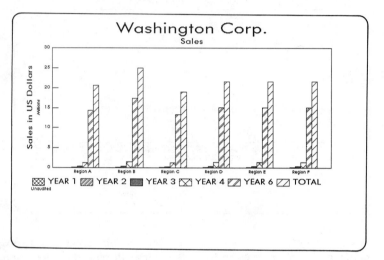

SOLUTION: Use /**Graph O**ption **S**cale **Y**-Scale **T**ype **L**ogarithmic to change the scale to powers of 10 instead of the normal linear scale. With a logarithmic scale, you can graph a wide range of data. Figure T.40 is the graph in figure T.39 with a logarithmic scale and data labels added to the TOTALS. You can use the same command for the **2Y**-Scale (if you use the right-side y-axis scale) and for the **X**-Scale on an XY-type graph.

Fig. T.40.
Small and
large numbers
graphed with a
logarithmic
scale.

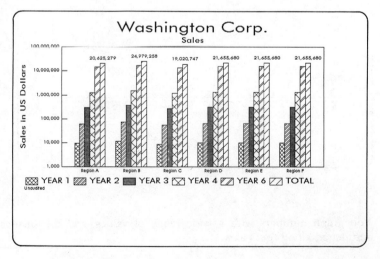

GRAPHING PROBLEM #7:

You want to graph two different but related quantities on one graph, but the resulting graph is confusing.

EXPLANATION: Most 1-2-3 graphs are designed to graph a series of one type of value, such as sales, prices, volumes, or profits. When you combine two different types of data in one graph, the graph can be hard to understand. In figure T.41, ranges A and B graph sales, and ranges C and D graph profits. This graph is not easy to understand.

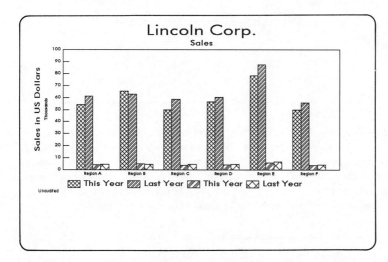

Fig. T.41. Different types of data shown in the same graph.

SOLUTION: A number of graph options can make a graph easier to understand. Figure T.42 graphs the same data as figure T.41 with a number of changes. The C range is used to force a space between sales and profits. Ranges D and E graph profits. Data labels distinguish the sales bars from the profits bars. The hatching patterns were changed with /**Graph O**ptions **A**dvanced **H**atches to make ranges for the same year have the same hatching. Range D has hatching pattern 2 to match range A, and range E has hatching pattern 3 to match range B. The duplicate legends were eliminated.

You can use other options to separate two different types of data. Figure T.43 graphs the same data as figures T.41 and T.42. To create this graph, use /**Graph T**ype **M**ixed to graph ranges A–C as a bar graph (only ranges A and B are used in this example) and ranges D–F as a line graph (only ranges D and E are used in this example). Then use /**Graph T**ype **F**eatures **2Y**-Ranges and assign ranges D and E to a second Y-Scale on the right of the graph. If you viewed this graph now, the lines would overlay the bars, and the result would be more confusing than figure T.43.

To separate these two portions of the graph, use /**Graph O**ptions **S**cale **Y**-Scale **M**anual. Then select **U**pper and type an upper limit about twice the largest sales

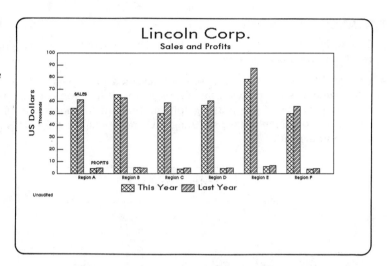

Fig. T.42.
*/Graph options
used to make a
graph clearer.*

value, in this case **200000**. This action forces the bar graph to the lower half of
the graph. Choose **Quit** to move to the **Options** menu and choose **Scale 2Y-Scale
Manual**. Then select **Upper** and type an upper limit slightly larger than the largest
profit value, in this case **7000**. Then choose **Lower** and type the same upper-limit
value as a negative number, in this case − **7000**. The resulting graph in figure
T.43 separates the sales and profits but still shows them on one graph.

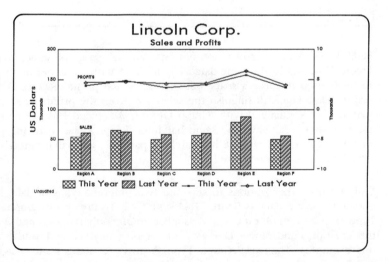

Fig. T.43.
*A mixed graph
with manual
scaling used to
separate two
types of data
on one graph.*

GRAPHING PROBLEM #8:

As you change many different graphing options, you want to see the effects of
the change immediately.

EXPLANATION: Literally hundreds of /Graph menu choices can change the appearance of a graph. It is slow to use Quit or Esc to move up many menu levels in the /Graph menu, to view a graph, and then move down the menus again to make more changes.

SOLUTION: You can see the graph in a window on-screen as you change graph options with /Window Graph. Every time you change data in the worksheet or a graph option, the graph window changes immediately.

ALTERNATIVE SOLUTION: If your monitor cannot display graphs in a graph window or you want a full-screen data display, press Graph (F10) to view a graph at any time. This method works even when you are using the /Graph menu, not just from READY mode.

GRAPHING PROBLEM #9:

After waiting 30 minutes while a graph prints, you discover an error and must print the graph again.

EXPLANATION: The graph display does not show exactly what the printed graph will look like. For example, the display doesn't show all the different type fonts and sizes you can specify for the text portion of your graph. And you easily can overlook missing legends or incorrect data on the display.

SOLUTION: You can use one of two ways to speed a test print. Use draft print and print a small graph. Choose /Print Printer Options Advanced Image Density Draft to print a lower-quality draft. Not all printers have both a draft and final density for graphics. Your printer may print at the same speed in both modes. Choose /Print Printer Options Advanced Image Image-Sz Length-Fill to specify a small test graph. A small graph may lose some detail, but it prints faster. For example, type 12 to print a graph that is only 18 lines high. Because a standard line is one-sixth of an inch, the graph is only 3 inches high. Note that you choose Length-Fill to specify the height of an upright graph.

If you discover an error before the entire graph has printed, use /Print Cancel to cancel the printing.

When you are confident that the graph is correct, choose /Print Printer Options Advanced Image Density Final. Then choose /Print Printer Options Advanced Image Image-Sz Margin-Fill to print the largest draft between the margins.

GRAPHING PROBLEM #10:

When you print a bar graph, you cannot distinguish the bars because there is no hatching.

EXPLANATION: If you display graphs on a color monitor, different ranges display in different colors. Hatching patterns are not used. When you print the graph on a black-and-white printer, all the colors print as black.

SOLUTION: Use /Graph Options B&W to change the graph to black and white with hatching before you print the graph. You also can use /Graph Options Advanced Hatches to add hatching to a color graph.

GRAPHING PROBLEM #11:

You want to print data and a graph on the same page on a laser printer, but 1-2-3 prints them on separate pages.

EXPLANATION: The laser printer automatically ejects the page after each print job—each time you specify **G**o in the /**P**rint menu.

SOLUTION: To print both a data range and a graph on the same page on a laser printer, you must print both with the same **G**o command. To do this, first you must use /**G**raph **N**ame **C**reate to assign a name to the current graph. Then use /**P**rint **P**rinter **R**ange to specify both the data range and the graph name, preceded by an asterisk. For example, to print the range PAGE1 and the graph GRAPH1 on a single page, specify a print range of PAGE1;*GRAPH1.

ALTERNATIVE SOLUTION: On any kind of printer, the graph prints on the same page as the data only if there is enough room for the entire graph. The default size of a graph fills about a half page. If the graph prints on the next page, either print less data on that page or use /**P**rint **P**rinter **O**ptions **A**dvanced **I**mage **I**mage-Sz to make the graph smaller.

Troubleshooting Data Management

DATA MANAGEMENT PROBLEM #1:

You set up a criteria range, but all the records are selected.

EXPLANATION: When you choose /Data Query Find, Extract, Unique, or Del, 1-2-3 uses the criteria range as a filter to select records from the database. If the criteria range is not exact, these /Data Query commands do not work correctly.

SOLUTION: Reissue the /Data Query Criteria command. When 1-2-3 highlights the range, check it carefully, looking for the following errors:

1. Does the criteria range contain a blank row?

2. Does the first row of the criteria range contain field names? If not, the criteria range does nothing.

3. Do the field names match exactly the field names in the database? If any field names in the criteria range do not match the names in the database, the label and number matches in those fields are ignored. Don't take chances with incorrect field names when you build your criteria range. Copy the field names from the database to ensure that the names are identical.

4. Do any compound tests use #NOT# or <> (not equal)? These compound tests, which can be extremely tricky, can produce results that are just the opposite of what you are trying to produce.

For example, note the following erroneous compound test:

+B5<>100#OR#B5<>200

The purpose of this test is to select all records except those in which the value in column B is either 100 or 200. This written statement makes sense, but the effect of the test (the formula) is to select all records in which the value in column B is anything but 100 or 200. The test selects all records because if the value is 100, it passes the test because it is not 200. If the value is 200, it passes the test because it is not 100. The correct way to write the test is

+B5<>100#AND#B5<>200

DATA MANAGEMENT PROBLEM #2:

You set up a criteria range, but none of the records is selected.

EXPLANATION: Each field in a row in a criteria range can be a separate test. To be selected, a record must pass all the tests in the same row. If you write the selection tests incorrectly, it may be impossible for a record to pass all tests. This problem is most common when you use the #AND#, #OR#, and #NOT# operators in your selection tests.

SOLUTION: Carefully check the selection tests in your criteria range for tests such as:

+B5>100#AND#B5<0

This test tells 1-2-3 to select records only when the value in column B is both greater than 100 and less than zero. Because this result is impossible, no records are selected.

Also, make sure that the test's format matches the data in the field you are testing. If you use label matches or string functions on numeric data or if you use number matches on strings, nothing is selected. Use /**Data** Query Criteria and /**Data** Query Input to see whether ranges are specified correctly.

DATA MANAGEMENT PROBLEM #3:

You use a valid formula using field names in a criteria range, but you get an error message when you try to extract records.

EXPLANATION: You can use the field names as if they were range names in formulas in a criteria range. In figure T.44, the criteria range uses the formula +SALES>10000. Even though some records match the criteria, you get an error message that the criteria must contain field references. The reason is that the range name SALES exists somewhere else in the file. The formula refers to the range name SALES, not the field name. A criterion must refer to at least one field in the input range.

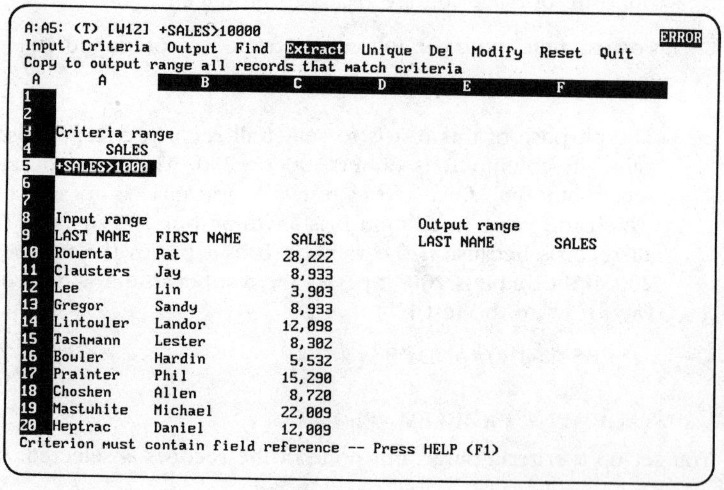

Fig. T.44.
A field name
that is also a
range name
somewhere else
in the file.

```
A:A5: (T) [W12] +SALES>10000                                    ERROR
Input  Criteria  Output  Find  Extract  Unique  Del  Modify  Reset  Quit
Copy to output range all records that match criteria
    A        A          B          C          D          E          F
1
2
3        Criteria range
4             SALES
5        +SALES>1000
6
7
8        Input range                          Output range
9        LAST NAME   FIRST NAME   SALES        LAST NAME        SALES
10       Rouenta     Pat          28,222
11       Clausters   Jay           8,933
12       Lee         Lin           3,903
13       Gregor      Sandy         8,933
14       Lintouler   Landor       12,098
15       Tashmann    Lester        8,302
16       Bouler      Hardin        5,532
17       Prainter    Phil         15,290
18       Choshen     Allen         8,720
19       Mastuhite   Michael      22,009
20       Heptrac     Daniel       12,009
Criterion must contain field reference -- Press HELP (F1)
```

SOLUTION: You can avoid this problem in a number of ways. One way is to make sure that you do not use range names that match database field names. You can avoid using field names by entering the cell address of the first record in the database in the formula, in this case +C10>10000. Another way is to write the formula as a label under the appropriate column in the criteria range. In this case, the formula in A5 would be '>10000. Because this label is in the column headed SALES, 1-2-3 treats this as the formula +C10>10000.

DATA MANAGEMENT PROBLEM #4:

You set up a criteria range, but only the first record is selected, or all the records after the first one are selected.

EXPLANATION: The addresses used in formula matches are treated as relative addresses, based on the first record in the database. Therefore, any cell addresses in formula matches use the first record in the database. Suppose that your criteria range includes the following test (row 9 contains the field names for this database, and row 10 is the first record in the database):

   +C10>10000

When this criteria range is used to select records, 1-2-3 first tests the first record. If the value in C10 is greater than 10000, the record is selected; if not, the record is not selected.

Then 1-2-3 adjusts the formula and moves down one row to the next record. At the second record, the following test is used:

   +C11>10000

The cell addresses change for each record in the database, as though you had copied the formula down one row before making the test. The program handles this step automatically.

Suppose that, for instance, you want to compare a field in the database (C10) to a field outside the database (AG67). The test might be the following:

   +C10>AG67

1-2-3 handles the test on the first record in the manner shown in the preceding example, selecting the record if the test is true. But when the program moves to the second record, the test is changed to the following:

   +C11>AG68

AG68 may either be blank or contain data that does not pertain to the values in column C in your database.

SOLUTION: If you make cell references that address cells outside the database absolute, they won't adjust as 1-2-3 moves down the data records. For example, if you change the test in the preceding example to the following one, 1-2-3 compares all the values in column C to the contents of AG67:

   +C10>$AG$67

DATA MANAGEMENT PROBLEM #5:

A /Data Query Find command works correctly, but /Data Query Extract (or Unique) does not.

EXPLANATION: You can use the same settings for Find, Extract, or Unique. Because Find ignores the output range, you can test whether the problem lies in the criteria range or in the output range. If Find works, but Extract or Unique does not, something is wrong with the output range.

SOLUTION: The field names in the output range must match the field names in the database. If the names do not match, 1-2-3 selects the correct records but does not copy any fields to the output range. To ensure that the field names match, copy them from the database.

DATA MANAGEMENT PROBLEM #6:

As your database grows, the output from Extract commands grows also. You keep filling the output range and getting an error message.

EXPLANATION: When you define an output range, you can define the number of rows you want 1-2-3 to use. If the output of the Extract (or Unique) commands contains more records than you have specified, the query stops and you see an error message:

    Too many records for Output range.

You must enlarge the size of the output range and then rerun the Extract.

SOLUTION: Specify as the output range only the row that contains the field names. 1-2-3 treats this specification as allowing the use of as many rows as necessary for Extract or Unique.

If you use this solution, however, be sure not to put anything below the output range. If you do, you lose valuable data because the next time you issue an Extract or Unique command, 1-2-3 erases everything below the field names before copying the selected records. (The program even erases data that is far below the area needed for copying the selected records.)

The best solution is to put the output range in its own worksheet.

DATA MANAGEMENT PROBLEM #7:

You use Find to move the cell pointer to a certain field, but when you press Enter or Esc, the cell pointer jumps back to its original position.

EXPLANATION: When you start a /Data Query command or press Query (F7), 1-2-3 remembers the original position of the cell pointer. When you end a Find with Enter or Esc, 1-2-3 automatically returns the cell pointer to its original position.

SOLUTION: After using /Data Query Find or pressing Query (F7) to repeat a find, end the find by pressing Query (F7). This action returns you to READY mode and leaves the cell pointer at the cell in the find.

DATA MANAGEMENT PROBLEM #8:

You define what looks like a valid database, but when you try to create an external table, you get an error message.

EXPLANATION: To create an external table, you first create a table definition. Figure T.45 shows an existing 1-2-3 database and a table definition created with /Data External Create Definition Create-Definition. 1-2-3 analyzes the database and creates the external table definition. You then specify Definition Use-Definition Go to create the external table. If the database is valid in 1-2-3 but invalid in the external table, you get an error message.

```
A:A1: [W12] 'LAST NAME                                          ERROR
Name  Definition  Go  Quit
Create an external table
  A        A            B              C       D        E         F
1   LAST NAME     Character          12 NA            NA        NA
2   FIRST NAME    Character          12 NA            NA        NA
3   CITY          Character          14 NA            NA        NA
4   ST            Character           3 NA            NA        NA
5   CUSTOMER_NUM  Numeric              NA            NA        NA
6   1ST_SALE      Date                 NA            NA        NA
7
8
9
10  LAST NAME     FIRST NAME    CITY          ST CUSTOMER_NUMBER 1ST_SALE
11  Rowenta       Pat           San Antonio   TX      100744 02/14/87
12  Clausters     Jay           Philadelphia  PA      100825 12/18/87
13  Lee           Lin           Hercules      CA      100235 09/13/88
14  Gregor        Sandy         Topeka        KS      100878 07/17/86
15  Lintouler     Landor        Flagstaff     AZ      100544 02/01/81
16  Tashmann      Lester        Mobile        AL      100922 07/09/88
17  Bouler        Hardin        Baltimore     MD      100952 12/26/88
18  Prainter      Phil          Jacksonville  FL      200922 04/03/88
19  Choshen       Allen         Washington    DC      200177 12/29/86
20  Mastuhite     Michael       Seattle       WA      100230 12/20/86
Invalid new name for column or table -- Press HELP (F1)
```

Fig. T.45.
A 1-2-3 database that is invalid for an external table definition.

In figure T.45, the name fields contain spaces; the customer number field name is too long; and the 1ST-SALE field name starts with a number.

Even though the field names are valid range names in 1-2-3, they might not be valid field names for the external database driver you are using.

SOLUTION: In general, when you create an external table, you must follow the rules for the driver you are using, not the rules for 1-2-3. Make sure that all the fields, field names, and field definitions follow the rules for the driver. For the sample dBASE III driver, the field names can be up to 10 characters, must start with a letter, and must contain only letters, numbers, and the underline character. A 1-2-3 field can be up to 512 characters, but the maximum dBASE field is 254 characters. A 1-2-3 database can have up to 256 fields, but a dBASE III external table can have up to 128 fields. The maximum dBASE III record is 4K (4096 characters).

DATA MANAGEMENT PROBLEM #9:

You add records to an indexed dBASE III file, and the records are no longer in the correct order when you access the file with dBASE III.

EXPLANATION: You can insert records into an existing dBASE III file with /Data Query Extract, Unique, or Modify Insert. However, 1-2-3 does not update the index file.

SOLUTION: After you add records to an indexed dBASE III file, you must use the REINDEX command from within dBASE III.

DATA MANAGEMENT PROBLEM #10:

You want to use an external table, but you forgot the field names.

EXPLANATION: You can use an external table as either an input or an output range for the /Data Query commands, but you must know the exact names of the fields before you can access any of the data.

SOLUTION: Move the cell pointer to a blank area of your file. Use /Data External Use to gain access to the external table. Then select List Fields to get a definition of the fields in the selected external table (see fig. T.46).

Fig. T.46.
Definitions of
all the fields in
an external
table.

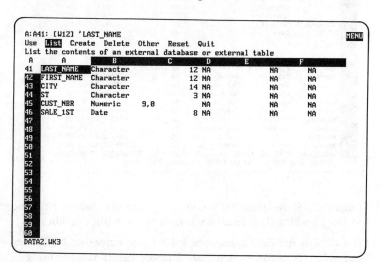

Use /Range Transpose to copy the column of field names into a row of field names you can use for a criteria or output range.

DATA MANAGEMENT PROBLEM #11:

After you extract records to the output range and modify them, you try to replace them in the original database but get an error message.

EXPLANATION: You can modify extracted records and then replace them in the original database with /Data Query Modify Replace. However, this method works only if you extract the records with /Data Query Modify Extract. If you extract the records with /Data Query Extract, 1-2-3 does not keep track of the original location of each extracted record and cannot replace them.

SOLUTION: If you plan to replace records into the original database, extract them first with /**Data Query Modify Extract**. After you modify some or all the records, update the original database with /**Data Query Modify Replace**.

If you already used /**Data Query Extract** and changed the records, you do not have to modify them again. Copy the modified records to a blank area in the worksheet and then use /**Data Query Modify Extract** to extract the records again. Copy the modified records back to the output range, replacing the records you just extracted. Now use /**Data Query Modify Replace** to update the original database.

You cannot use /**Data Query Modify Replace** to replace records in an external dBASE III database with the sample driver supplied with 1-2-3.

Troubleshooting Macros

MACRO PROBLEM #1:

You write an Alt-key macro, and when you try to execute it, nothing happens.

EXPLANATION: You must use a precise name format for macros you execute from the keyboard with the Alt key. The range name must be exactly two characters: the first is always a backslash and the second, a letter (from A to Z). If you name your macro anything else and try to execute it by pressing the Alt key, 1-2-3 cannot recognize it as a macro. A macro you execute with Run (Alt-F3) can have any range name.

SOLUTION: Use /**R**ange **N**ame **C**reate to check the macro's range name. 1-2-3 lists, in alphabetical order, all the range names in the worksheet. Range names that start with a backslash are at the end of the list. Press Name (F3) for a full-screen display of range names. If you don't see the range name listed, you haven't named your macro.

If the range name is in the list, make sure that you have included the backslash. For example, although the letter A is a valid range name, it is not a valid name for a macro activated with the Alt key.

Another common error is to use a slash (/) instead of a backslash (\) when you name a macro. If the range name is in the list, check carefully to make sure that the name starts with a backslash.

If the macro name is listed and looks valid, highlight it and press Enter. 1-2-3 highlights the range with that name. The range should contain only one cell —the first cell of the macro. The contents of the macro must be a label or a string-valued function. If the cell is blank or contains a numeric value, the macro does not work.

MACRO PROBLEM #2:

After you write a few macros, you move some data. The macros now refer to the wrong addresses.

EXPLANATION: Macros are not like formulas; the addresses in macros do not change automatically when you move data that is used by the macro. In fact, in most cases, a macro is nothing more than a label. 1-2-3 does not adjust the contents of labels when you move data.

SOLUTION: Never use cell addresses in macros. Always give range names to all the cells and ranges you use in macros and use these range names in the macros. Then, if you move these ranges or insert and delete rows and columns, the range names adjust automatically, and the macro continues to refer to the correct cells and ranges.

MACRO PROBLEM #3:

Although the logic of your macro appears correct, the macro never works properly. Critical values do not seem to be current, even when recalculation is on automatic.

EXPLANATION: In a large worksheet, macros would execute slowly if 1-2-3 recalculated the entire worksheet after every macro command. 1-2-3 seldom recalculates the worksheet while a macro executes. If critical values change during execution, the macro uses the previous values—not the current ones.

SOLUTION: Determine which cells and ranges must be recalculated to make the macro work correctly, and then add {RECALC} or {RECALCCOL} statements to the macro where necessary. A complete worksheet recalculation with {CALC} works also, but usually is slow.

The macro shown in figure T.47 tests incorrectly for a valid entry. In this macro, {GETNUMBER} finds the previous value because the test in IP_TEST (cell C12) is not updated after {GETNUMBER}. To correct the problem, add a {RECALC} to the macro (see fig. T.48). In this case, a tilde (˜) works if the worksheet is set for automatic recalculation. A {RECALC} or {RECALCCOL} is required in manual RECALC mode.

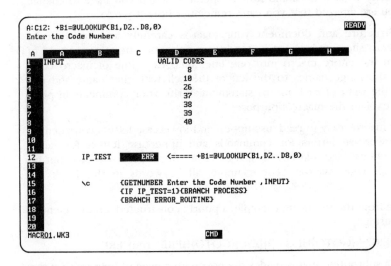

Fig. T.47.
A macro that
requires
recalculation to
work properly.

In figure T.48, the macro branches to PROCESS if the test in C12 is 1 (true) and branches to ERROR_ROUTINE if the test is not 1 (false). These routines perform whatever processing you need in your worksheet.

MACRO PROBLEM #4:

You need to change a macro you wrote earlier, but you cannot remember how it works.

Fig. T.48.
A macro with
{RECALC}.

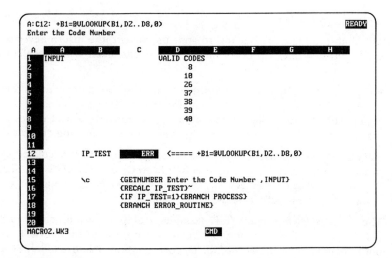

EXPLANATION: This common problem surprises users when they first start to work with macros. After having painstakingly written, tested, and debugged a macro, you use it successfully in your worksheet. Because you wrote the macro, you know exactly what it does and how it operates. When you have to change the macro, you are amazed that you can't remember how it works.

SOLUTION: Structure and document your macros carefully and consistently. Keep each macro short and design it to perform only one operation. Instead of trying to cram the entire macro into one line, keep each line of macro code short. Put all the range names to the left of the cell with that name and put comments to the right of each macro statement. Write your comments in plain language and explain the macro's purpose.

To make your macros easy to read, use upper- and lowercase letters consistently. Always use lowercase letters for commands and uppercase letters for range names and functions. Macro keywords can be either upper- or lowercase, but be consistent in all your macros. (For example, all keywords in this book are uppercase.)

As you can see from the following example, a poorly constructed, undocumented macro is confusing:

\h   /rncHERE˜˜{GOTO}HELP˜ {?}{ESC}{GOTO}HERE˜ /rndHERE˜

This macro is a subroutine that provides the user with a page of help text (at the range name HELP). When the operator reads the information and presses Enter, the macro returns the cell pointer to a range named HERE (its position before the macro executed).

Figure T.49 shows the same macro code after its structure has been improved and documented.

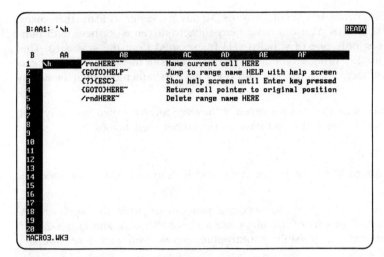

```
B:AA1: '\h                                                READY

    B     AA          AB           AC      AD     AE      AF
1   \h          /rncHERE~~        Name current cell HERE
2               {GOTO}HELP~        Jump to range name HELP with help screen
3               {?}{ESC}           Show help screen until Enter key pressed
4               {GOTO}HERE~        Return cell pointer to original position
5               /rndHERE~          Delete range name HERE
6
7
8
9
10
11
12
13
14
15
16
17
18
19
20
MACRO3.WK3
```

Fig. T.49.
A documented macro.

MACRO PROBLEM #5:

Although your macro seems correct, it starts to beep in the middle of some commands and puts some commands in a label.

EXPLANATION: The macro may look correct, but 1-2-3 is not interpreting the macro in the way you anticipated. Either something is missing, or the macro contains extraneous keystrokes.

SOLUTION: This problem commonly occurs if you forget to include tildes (to indicate Enter) in a macro. You can use one of two methods to find errors.

Press Step (Alt-F2) to put macro execution in single-step mode. When you execute the macro, 1-2-3 executes only one keystroke and then waits for you to press any key. When you press a key, you signal the program to execute the next macro keystroke. As you watch the macro execute in slow motion, you usually can see where the error lies. (With some macros, this single-step approach can be slow.)

Play "computer" and execute the macro manually. First, print the macro; then replay it from the keyboard, doing exactly as the macro indicates, keystroke by keystroke. Unless this problem happens only during macro execution, you will find the error if you follow the script faithfully. If the macro works when you execute it manually, change recalculation to manual and try again.

MACRO PROBLEM #6:

You have written a series of handy macros for your worksheet, but you cannot remember all their names.

EXPLANATION: You can name 26 macros (A to Z) per worksheet file for execution from the keyboard using the Alt key. In addition, you can name any number of macros for execution using the Run (Alt-F3) key.

RELEASE 3

SOLUTION: Use menus to execute macros. Menus are easier to learn than many of the macro keywords. You can have a large macro-driven worksheet with hundreds of macros, only one of which (\M) is executed from the keyboard. This one macro is used to bring up the main menu. A series of hierarchical menus can contain any number of macros, but you don't have to remember their names in advance.

If you use more than five macros, even if they are for your own use only, put them in a menu so that you won't have to remember their names.

MACRO PROBLEM #7:

You wrote a macro that contains an error, and it destroyed your worksheet or file.

EXPLANATION: A macro can do anything you can do from the keyboard. A macro can erase all or part of the file, erase a file on the disk, and quit 1-2-3. If you don't prepare for possible catastrophic errors, you can lose hours—even days—of work.

SOLUTION: Always save all active files before you test a macro. Then, if the macro destroys something, you still have the data on disk. If part of the macro saves or extracts one or more files, make sure that you first save them with different names or copy the files to another disk. Saving a file is futile if the macro erases most of the file in error and then saves the destroyed file with the name of the original file.

In fact, using a macro to save a file automatically is so dangerous that you should save your files manually until you are completely familiar with macros and the advanced macro commands.

MACRO PROBLEM #8:

You have many macros in your file, and you don't want the macros affected when other parts of the file are changed.

EXPLANATION: Many commands affect parts of a worksheet you cannot see when you execute the command. /Worksheet Delete Row or Column or /Worksheet Insert Row or Column can delete macros or insert a line in the middle of a macro or menu. /Worksheet Page and /Data Parse Format-Line Create also insert rows. A one-row output range in a /Data Query erases everything below it.

SOLUTION: Keep your macros in either a separate worksheet or in a separate file. This way the macros are unaffected by the commands used to manipulate the data.

MACRO PROBLEM #9:

Your macros are in the last worksheet of a multiple-worksheet file, but they are still affected when you insert and delete rows and columns.

EXPLANATION: If you have a multiple-worksheet file with data in the same format in each worksheet, you may keep the file in GROUP mode. In GROUP mode, any change to one worksheet changes all the worksheets in the file. Putting the macros in a separate worksheet does not protect the worksheet.

SOLUTION: Keep your macros in a separate file and use /File Open to read the macro file into memory when you need to execute the macros. Or you could reverse the process and use /File Retrieve to read the macro file and then have the AUTOEXEC (\0) macro open the data file. You can execute a macro in any active file, not just in the current file.

MACRO PROBLEM #10:

You have moved your macros into a separate file, but the macros do not operate correctly.

EXPLANATION: When you have multiple active files in memory, you have to be careful about range names, macro names, and the contents of the current file.

If the cell pointer is in the macro file when you execute the macro, the macro tries to execute commands using range names in the macro file. Because you want to execute commands on ranges in your data file, you may get errors. The range names are not defined, or the data does not exist in the macro file.

If the cell pointer is in the data file when you execute the macro and there is a range name in the data file with the same name as the macro, the range name in the data file is executed. Because the macros are not in the data file, either the macro stops on a blank cell, or you get unpredictable results.

These problems are common if you start out with macros and data in one file and later split them into two files.

SOLUTION: You must follow a number of simple rules to execute macros from a separate file.

1. Make sure that the macro file is active and contains the range names for the macros and no other range names.

2. Make sure that the data file is active and contains range names for the data and no other range names.

3. Make sure that there are no other active files with range names that match the names of the macros.

4. Make sure that the cell pointer is in the data file when you execute the macro.

To execute a macro with the Alt-letter key combination, hold down the Alt key and press the letter as you would if the macros were in the current file. To execute a macro using the Run (Alt-F3) key, press Run (Alt-F3). Then, at the list of range names and other active files, select the name of the macro file and then select the name of the macro from the list of range names.

When you execute macros across files, 1-2-3 assumes that a reference to another macro in a macro command such as {BRANCH}, {MENUCALL}, or {DISPATCH} refers to a range name in the macro file, and a reference to a range in a menu command such as /Copy, /Print, or /Data refers to a range in the current file (the file with the cell pointer).

MACRO PROBLEM #11:

You write macro-driven worksheet files for sophisticated 1-2-3 users, and you don't want them to tinker with the macros.

EXPLANATION: Unlike most "programs" such as database management systems, the data and the programs are in the same files. Even if you put all the macros into separate files, the files are still just 1-2-3 worksheet files; they can be changed by anyone who knows 1-2-3 well enough.

SOLUTION: You can protect a file completely with /File Admin Seal File. You then supply a password. Before you seal the file, you want to use /Range Unprotect to unprotect the data input areas. Keep the formulas and macros protected. Then use /Worksheet Global Protection Enable to enable the protection feature. Once the file is sealed with a password, anyone can read the file, update unprotected fields, run macros, and save the file, but they cannot change the protected fields or change the protection settings.

If the macros can delete rows, columns, or worksheets, you probably cannot seal the file because these commands won't work unless you disable protection. But if the macros are in a separate file, you can seal the macro file and leave the data file unsealed.

1-2-3 Command Reference

Worksheet Commands /W

The /Worksheet commands control the display formats, screen organization, protection, and start-up settings for files. If you want to change these settings for only a portion of the worksheet, use the /Range commands. To change settings that affect the entire worksheet or file, however, use the /Worksheet commands shown in the following menu map.

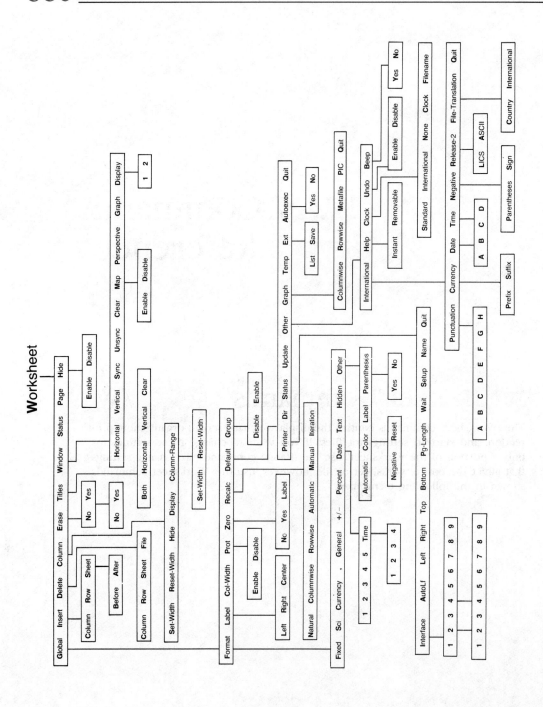

Worksheet Global Format /WGF

Purpose

Defines the display format for numeric values and formulas in the worksheet. The display format for the entire file is formatted if GROUP mode is on.

Formats previously entered with /Range Format are not affected.

Reminders

- Before you use /wgf, decide what your most-used format for numeric data is.

- If you want to format only a portion of the worksheet, use /Range Format instead of /wgf.

Procedures

1. Type /wgf

2. Select one of the following formats:

Menu Item	Description
Fixed	Fixes the number of decimal places displayed. If the setting is 3 decimal places, the number 1.2345, for example, appears as 1.235.
Sci	Displays in scientific notation large or small numbers. In a 2-decimal format, the number 950000, for example, appears as 9.50E+05.
Currency	Displays the default currency symbol (for example, $ or £) and commas. Currency is often used for the first row and the bottom line of financial statements. In a 2-decimal format, 24500.254, for example, appears as $24,500.25.
,	Marks thousands and multiples of thousands. In a 2-decimal format, 24500.254 appears as 24,500.25.
General	Suppresses zeros after the decimal point, uses scientific notation for large or small numbers, and serves as the default decimal display

Menu Item	Description
+/−	Creates horizontal bar graphs or time-duration graphs on computers that do not have graphics. A positive number displays as + symbols; a negative number, as − symbols. The number of symbols equals the integer value of the cell contents. For example, 6.23 appears as + + + + + +.
Percent	Displays a decimal number as a percentage followed by a percent sign (%). In a 2-decimal format, .346 appears as 34.60%.
Date	Displays the date in one of five customary formats. One selection under Date formats the Time display.

1 DD–MMM–YY   12–Jan–51
2 DD–MMM   12–Jan
3 MMM–YY   Jan–51
4 MM/DD/YY   01/12/51
5 MM/DD   01/12

Time:

  1 HH:MM:SS AM/PM   1:04:34 PM
  2 HH:MM AM/PM   1:04 PM
  3 HH:MM:SS   13:04:34
  4 HH:MM   13:04

Menu Item	Description
Text	Evaluates formulas as numbers but displays formulas as text. Numbers in cells appear in General format.
Hidden	Hides cell contents from display and printing but evaluates contents. Use this command to hide confidential notes or variables.
Other	Supplies additional formatting choices:

Automatic

Automatically recognizes and formats entries. Typed dates or times should match the date or time formats shown in the /wgfd menu. Improper formulas and labels beginning with numbers are entered as labels.

Color

Provides two options: **Negative**, which displays negative numbers brighter or in color; and **Reset**, which restores the setting

Label

Automatically enters a label prefix before the numeric values entered in a cell. Existing values remain as numbers. New numeric entries appear as labels.

Parentheses

Provides two options: **Yes**, which puts parentheses around all values; and **No**, which removes parentheses

3. After you select **Fixed**, **Sci**, **Currency**, comma (,), or **Percent**, enter the number of decimal places. 1-2-3 normally truncates trailing zeros, but these appear for the number of decimal places you set.

4. Press Enter.

Important Cues

- Use /**R**ange Format to format only a portion of the worksheet.

- Use **Text** format to display formulas as text while still using the numeric result from the formula.

- If you enter a number too large for the formatted cell, the cell fills with asterisks. To remove them, move the pointer to the cell, select /**W**orksheet Column Set-Width, and press the right-arrow key until the column is wide enough to display the entire number.

- To display non-USA formats with commands, use /**W**orksheet Global **D**efault **O**ther **I**nternational. Type /wgdoi and select one of the following formats:

Menu Item	*Description*
Punctuation	Changes numeric punctuation
Currency	Changes currency symbol
Date	Changes international date formats
Time	Changes international time formats

Cautions

- /wgf rounds displayed numbers to the specified decimal setting, but calculations are performed to 15-decimal precision. To keep apparently wrong values from being displayed, use @ROUND to round formula results so that calculated results match displayed values.

- Other operators may enter percentage values incorrectly if you use the **Percent** format. You should thus include a screen prompt to remind operators to place a percent sign (%) after percentages. 1-2-3 automatically divides the entry by 100.

For more information, see /Range Format, /Worksheet Global Default, and Chapter 5.

Worksheet Global Label /WGL

Purpose

Selects how you want text labels aligned throughout the worksheet. When GROUP mode is on, label alignment is changed for the entire file.

Labels narrower than the cell width can be aligned to the left, right, or center. Labels longer than the cell width are left-aligned. Previously entered labels do not change.

Reminders

- Before you begin building the worksheet, decide how to align the labels. Use /Worksheet Global Label to select left-alignment (the default setting), right-alignment, or center-alignment.

- If you use /wgl after you begin to build the worksheet, existing labels are not affected. Any alignment previously set with /Range Label is not altered by /wgl.

- To change the alignment of labels in a single cell or a range of cells, use /Range Label.

Procedures

1. Type /wgl

2. Select one of the following:

Menu Item	Description
Left	Aligns label with cell's left edge
Right	Aligns label with cell's right edge
Center	Centers label in a cell

3. Type the labels as you want them to appear on the worksheet.

Important Cues

- Align labels in a cell by entering one of the following prefixes before you type the label:

Label Prefix	Function
' (apostrophe)	Aligns label to the left (default)
" (quotation mark)	Aligns label to the right
^ (caret)	Centers label in the cell
\	Repeats character to fill the cell

Note: The backslash (\) label prefix cannot be selected with /wgl.

- The label prefix appears as the first character in the control panel when the cell pointer is positioned on a cell that contains a label. Use /Worksheet Status to show the global label prefix.

- You must enter a label prefix in front of labels that begin with a number or formula symbol. 1-2-3 automatically enters the label prefix if the worksheet is formatted with /Worksheet Global Format Other Automatic or /Range Format Other Automatic. If the worksheet or range is not formatted, you must supply a prefix such as that in one of the following correct examples:

Correct	Incorrect
'2207 Cheyenne Dr.	2207 Cheyenne Dr.
"34-567FB	34-567FB

- To turn a number into a label, position the cell pointer on the number you want to change and press Edit (F2). Then press Home to move the cursor to the beginning of the number; type the label prefix and press Enter. Be careful: if you format numbers as text, formulas evaluate them as zeros.

- Because every line of macro code must be entered as a string, a label prefix must precede text used as macro code. For example, if your macro line begins with the command sequence /ppooc, you must precede the entry with a label prefix, as in '/ppooc; otherwise, the keystrokes in the macro select the command instead of typing macro code.

- Preserve a formula that has an unidentified error by adding a label prefix before the formula. (The /Worksheet Global Format Other Automatic and /Range Format Other Automatic commands also change incorrect formulas to labels.) Consider the following formula:

  +B5*@PMT(B16B12/12,B14*12)

If you enter this formula, 1-2-3 signals an error and enters EDIT mode. (The problem is a missing comma after B16.) If you can't find the error, press Home to move to the beginning of the formula. Type an apostrophe and press Enter. The formula will then be accepted as a text label. You can return to the formula later to look for the error and make the correction. Delete the apostrophe and press Enter after you make the correction.

- Document formulas by temporarily adding a label prefix and then copying the label to another part of the worksheet. To do this procedure, move the cell pointer to the formula and press Edit (F2). Next, press Home to move the cell pointer to the front of the formula; type an apostrophe and press Enter. The formula is changed to text, and you can copy the text formula to a documentation area of your worksheet. Use the Edit, Home, and Del keys to remove the apostrophe from the original formula so that the formula can operate normally.

- To turn a numeric label into a number, use EDIT mode and delete the label prefix.

Caution

Numbers or formulas preceded by a label prefix have the value of zero when evaluated by a numeric formula. In a database query, you must use text searches to search for numbers that have a label prefix.

*For more information, see /**Worksheet Global Format Other Automatic**, /**Range Format Other Automatic**, and Chapter 5.*

Worksheet Global Col-Width /WGC

Purpose

Sets the column width for the entire worksheet; sets the column width for the entire file if GROUP mode is on. Column widths set with /Worksheet Column are not affected.

Reminder

Before you use /wgc, decide the column widths you need for the worksheet, and position the cell pointer so that an average column width is displayed.

Procedures

1. Type /wgc

2. Enter a number for the column width used most frequently; or press the right- or left-arrow key to increase or decrease the column width, respectively.

3. Press Enter.

Important Cues

- Use /Worksheet Column Set-Width to set individual columns so that numbers and labels display correctly. When the column width is too narrow for the value entered, asterisks are displayed in the cell.

- Any global column width can be set to a new width with /Worksheet Global Col-Width. Column widths previously set with /Worksheet Column Set-Width keep their original setting.

- The default column width for all columns is 9 characters. Column width settings can range from 1 to 240 characters.

- You can see the current setting for the global column width by selecting /Worksheet Status.

Caution

If you use a split worksheet and change the column width in one or both windows, settings used in the bottom or right windows are lost when the windows are cleared. 1-2-3 keeps the column widths used in the top window of a horizontal split or the left window of a vertical split.

*For more information, see /**Worksheet Column** and Chapter 4.*

Worksheet Global Prot /WGP

Purpose

Protects the entire worksheet or file from being changed. If GROUP mode is on, the entire file is protected.

Cells previously marked with the **/Range Unprot** command will be unprotected when worksheet protection is on.

Reminder

Before you enable worksheet protection, save time by making sure that your worksheet is complete. After the worksheet is protected, you must disable protection or unprotect a range before you can modify the worksheet.

Procedures

1. Type /wgp

2. Select one of the following options:

Menu Item	Description
Enable	Protects the worksheet. Only cells specified with **/Range Unprot** can be changed.
Disable	Unprotects the worksheet. Any cell can be changed.

Important Cues

- Before or after you protect the entire worksheet, you can use **/Range Unprot** to specify cells that can be changed.

- Protected cells display a PR on the status line. Unprotected cells display a U on the status line.

- While **/Worksheet Global Prot** is enabled, the **/Range Input** commands restrict the cell pointer to cells unprotected by the **/Range Unprot** command. This arrangement makes movement between data-entry cells easier.

Cautions

- Macros that change cell content can change only unprotected cells. When you program macros, include code necessary to enable or disable protection.

- **/Worksheet Erase** is one of the few commands that can be used while **/Worksheet Global Prot** is enabled.

*For more information, see **/Range Unprot**, **/Range Prot**, and Chapter 4.*

Worksheet Global Zero   /WGZ

Purpose

Suppresses zeros in displays and printed reports so that only nonzero numbers appear; suppresses zeros in the entire file when GROUP mode is on. Also enables you to display a label instead of a zero.

When **/Worksheet Global Zero** is in effect, zeros from formulas and typed entries are hidden.

Reminder

Protect hidden zeros in the worksheet by using the /Worksheet Global Prot and /Range Unprot commands. Doing so prevents users new to 1-2-3 from typing over or erasing necessary hidden zero values or formulas.

Procedures

1. Type /wgz

2. Choose one of the following options:

Menu Item	Description
No	Displays as zeros those cells containing a zero or a result of zero
Yes	Displays as blank those cells containing a zero or a result of zero
Label	Displays a custom label that replaces those cells containing a zero or zero result.

3. If you chose Label, enter the label you want displayed. Precede the label with an apostrophe (') for left-alignment or with a caret (^) for right-alignment. The default label alignment is right-alignment.

Important Cues

- The worksheet's default setting is No so that zeros are displayed in normal operation.

- Zeros that continue to display are actually values greater than zero; however, their format displays them rounded to a zero value.

- You cannot suppress zeros in a range of cells by using a Format command.

- Suppressed zeros in formulas and typed entries are still evaluated as zeros by other formulas.

Caution

If zeros are suppressed, you can easily erase or write over portions of the worksheet that appear blank but contain suppressed zeros. To prevent accidental erasures and typeovers, use /Worksheet Global Prot Enable and /Range Unprot.

*For more information, see /**Worksheet Global Prot**, /**Range Prot and Unprot**, and Chapter 4.*

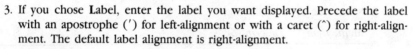

Worksheet Global Recalc /WGR

Purpose

Defines how worksheets recalculate and how many times they calculate.

Reminders

- You may need to use this menu more than once. The first time, use it to set whether calculation is automatic or manual. The second time, use the menu to define how you want calculations done or how many times calculations should be done.

- Recalculation can be set to **Automatic** or **Manual**. Manual recalculation should be used to increase data-entry speed on large worksheets or databases. By selecting either the **Columnwise** or **Rowwise** option, you can have 1-2-3 calculate formulas in a particular order. You also can use /wgr to calculate a formula many times to ensure correct results.

- If you change recalculation to **Columnwise** or **Rowwise**, enter formulas in a specific order so that they will be calculated correctly. 1-2-3's default settings are **Natural** and **Automatic** recalculation. In nearly all cases, you should leave recalculation in **Natural** mode.

Procedures

1. Type /wgr

2. Select one of the following:

Menu Item	Description
Natural	Calculates formulas in the order the results are needed (the normal worksheet setting for the order of recalculation)
Columnwise	Starts at the top of column A and recalculates downward; then moves to column B
Rowwise	Starts at the beginning of row 1 and recalculates to the end; then continues through the following rows
Automatic	Recalculates whenever cell contents change (the normal worksheet setting for when recalculation occurs)
Manual	Recalculates only when you press Calc (F9) or when {CALC} is encountered in a macro. The CALC indicator appears at the bottom of the screen when recalculation is advised.
Iteration	Recalculates the worksheet a specified number of times

3. If you selected **Iteration**, enter a number from 1 to 50. The default setting is 1. Iteration works with **Columnwise** and **Rowwise** recalculations or with **Natural** recalculation when the worksheet contains a circular reference.

4. If you selected **Columnwise** or **Rowwise** recalculation, you may need to repeat Step 1 and select **Iteration** in Step 2. In Step 3, enter the number of recalculations necessary for correct results. **Columnwise** and **Rowwise** recalculations often require multiple calculations in order for all worksheet results to be correct.

Important Cues

- Display the current recalculation setting by selecting /Worksheet Status.

- Columnwise or Rowwise recalculation often requires multiple recalculations. Set the number of automatic recalculations by selecting /wgr and choosing Iteration.

Caution

When you use Manual recalculation, the screen display is not valid when the CALC indicator appears at the bottom of the screen. This indicator means that changes have been made on the worksheet, and you need to press Calc (F9) so that 1-2-3 will recalculate the worksheet to reflect the changes.

*For more information, see /**Worksheet Status** and Chapter 4.*

Worksheet Global Default /WGD

Purpose

Specifies display formats and start-up settings for hardware.

With this command, you can control how 1-2-3 works with the printer; which disk and directory are accessed automatically; which international displays are used; and which type of clock is displayed. The settings can be saved so that each time you start 1-2-3, the specifications go into effect. For temporary changes, see the /File or /Print menu options.

Reminder

Before you set the interface for serial printers, find out the baud rate of your printer. The printer should be set to standard operating-system serial printer settings of 8 bits, no parity, and 1 stop bit (2 stop bits at 110 baud). These printer settings can be set with microswitches (DIP switches in your printer) and are normally preconfigured at the factory.

Procedures

1. Type /wgd

2. Select the setting you want to change:

Menu Item	Description
Printer	Specifies printer settings and connections. Choose from the following options:
	Interface
	Selects parallel or serial port from 9 settings, 1 through 9. The menu displays each of the 9 ports. The initial setting is 1 (Parallel 1).

AutoLF

Tells 1-2-3 whether your printer inserts its own line feed or whether 1-2-3 should insert a line feed. If the printer is printing double-spaces or overlapped printing, choose the opposite setting.

Left

Sets left margin. Default: 4, 0–1000

Right

Sets right margin. Default: 76, 0–1000

Top

Sets top margin. Default: 2, 0–32

Bottom

Sets bottom margin. Default: 2, 0–32

Pg-Length

Sets page length. Default: 66, 1–1000

Wait

Pauses for page insert

Setup

Creates initial printer-control code

Name

Selects from multiple printers

Quit

Returns you to the **Printer** menu

Dir Specifies directory for read or write operations. Press Esc to clear. Type the new directory and press Enter.

Status Displays settings for /Worksheet Global Default

Update Saves to disk the current global defaults for use during the next start-up

Other Provides the following five options:

International

Specifies display settings for **Punctuation**, **Currency**, **Date**, **Time**, **Negative** formats, **Release-2** character sets, and **File-Translation** of international characters

Help

Enables you to choose whether the Help file is immediately accessible from disk (**Instant**) or whether the Help file is on a removable disk (**Removable**)

Clock

Enables you to choose between **Standard** and **International** date and time formats or to have **None** displayed on the screen. **Clock** displays the date and time set by other commands, and **Filename** displays the file name instead of the date and time.

Undo

Offers two options: **Enable**, which enables the Undo feature; and **Disable**, which disables the Undo feature

Beep

Offers two options: **Yes**, which turns the computer's sound on; and **No**, which turns it off

Graph Sets the directions used by 1-2-3 to divide cell ranges into automatic graph ranges. A range may be divided into data sets by column (**Columnwise**) or by row (**Rowwise**). **Graph** also specifies which type of graphic file is saved when you save a graph: Metafile (.CGM) or PIC (picture).

Temp Sets the directory where 1-2-3 saves temporary files used during operation

Ext Provides two options: **List**, which enables you to change the file extensions of files displayed by /File commands; and **Save**, which enables you to change the file extensions under which files are saved

Autoexec Provides two options: **Yes**, which automatically executes autoexecute macros (\0); and **No**, which stops autoexecute macros from executing

Quit Returns you to the worksheet

Important Cue

Changes made with /Worksheet Global Default are good only while 1-2-3 is running. To save the settings so that they load automatically at start-up, select /Worksheet Global Default Update.

For more information, see Chapter 5.

Worksheet Global Group   /WGG

Purpose

While a file is in GROUP mode, transfers formatting changes made on one worksheet to the entire file.

Reminder

Use GROUP mode when you format files containing worksheets that are exact copies of each other.

Procedures

1. Type /wgg

2. Select **Disable** to turn off GROUP, or select **Enable** to turn on GROUP.

Important Cues

- When GROUP is enabled, the GROUP status indicator appears at the bottom of the screen.

- When you are in GROUP mode, the following commands affect all worksheets:

    Of the **/Range** commands: Format, Label, Prot, and Unprot

    Of the **/Worksheet** commands: Column, Delete Column, Delete Row, Insert Column, Insert Row, Page, and Titles

    Of the **/Worksheet Global** commands: Col-Width, Format, Label, Prot, and Zero

For more information, see Chapter 4.

Worksheet Insert   /WIC or /WIR or /WIS
[Column, Row, Sheet]

Purpose

Inserts one or more blank columns or rows in the worksheet or one or more blank worksheets in the file.

Use this command to add space for formulas, data, or text, or to add worksheets to a file to create three-dimensional worksheets.

Reminder

Before you use /wi, do one of the following:

- Place the cell pointer in the column that you want to move to the right when one or more columns are inserted.

- Place the cell pointer in the row that you want to move down when one or more rows are inserted.

- Place the cell pointer in the worksheet that you want to insert a worksheet before or after.

Procedures

1. Type /wi

2. Select one of the following:

Menu Item	Description
Column	Inserts column(s) at the cell pointer; moves the current column right
Row	Inserts row(s) at the cell pointer; moves the current row down
Sheet	Inserts worksheet(s) before or after the current worksheet

3. If you chose Column, move the cell pointer right to highlight one cell for each column you want inserted.
If you chose Row, move the cell pointer down to highlight one cell for each row you want inserted.

If you chose Sheet, select Before or After to indicate whether you want to insert the new worksheets before or after the current worksheet. Indicate how many worksheets you want to insert. The total number of worksheets in memory cannot exceed 256.

Important Cues

- Addresses and ranges adjust automatically to the new addresses created when columns or rows are inserted.

- Check all worksheet areas for composition, lines, and layout that may have changed. Use /Move to reposition labels, data, and formulas.

- Use the /File New command to insert a new blank file in memory rather than insert a blank worksheet in an existing file.

Cautions

- Cell addresses in macros do not adjust automatically. Adjust cell addresses in macros to reflect the inserted column(s) or row(s). Range names in macros will remain correct.

- Make certain that inserted columns and rows do not pass through databases, print ranges, or a column of macro code. Macros will stop execution if they reach a blank cell. Database and data-entry macros may stop or work incorrectly if they encounter unexpected blank columns or rows in the database or data-entry areas.

- Inserting rows and columns uses up conventional memory. Keep this fact in mind when designing large worksheets.

*For more information, see /**Worksheet Delete**, /**File New**, and Chapter 4.*

Worksheet Delete /WDC or /WDR
[Column, Row, Sheet, File] or /WDS or /WDF

Purpose

Deletes one or more columns or rows from the worksheet; deletes one or more worksheets from a file or deletes an active file from memory but not from the disk.

When you use /wd, the entire column, row, worksheet, or file and the information and formatting it contains are deleted from memory.

Reminders

- Before you delete a column or row, use the End and arrow keys to make sure that distant cells in that column or row do not contain needed data or formulas.

- If you may need active files again, save them before deleting them.

- Before you invoke /wd, place the cell pointer on the first column or row to be deleted. Place the cell pointer in the top worksheet or in the file to be deleted.

Procedures

1. Type /wd

2. Select one of the following:

Menu Item	Description
Column	Deletes column(s) at the cell pointer. Remaining columns to the right move left.
Row	Deletes row(s) at the cell pointer. Remaining rows below move up.
Sheet	Deletes worksheet(s) from memory
File	Deletes the active file from memory but does not erase the file from disk

3. Specify a range containing the columns, rows, or worksheets you want deleted. If you want to delete a file, specify the file.

Important Cues

- /Worksheet **D**elete deletes all the data and formulas in the column or row. To erase the contents of cells but leave the blank cells in their location, use /**R**ange **E**rase.

- Formulas, named ranges, and ranges in command prompts are adjusted automatically to the new cell addresses after you delete a column or row.

- Use /**M**ove when you need to reposition a portion of the worksheet and cannot delete a column or row.

Cautions

- Formulas that refer to deleted cells have the value ERR.

- Deleting all cells belonging to a named range leaves the named range in formulas, but it is left as an undefined name. You must redefine the name by using /**R**ange **N**ame.

- Deleting a row that passes through an area containing macros can create errors in the macros. Deleting code in the middle of the macro causes problems, and deleting a blank cell between two macros merges their code.

*For more information, see /**Worksheet Insert**, /**Range Erase**, and Chapter 4.*

Worksheet Column [Set-Width, Reset-Width, Hide, Display, Column-Range]

/WCS, /WCR, /WCH, /WCD, or /WCC

Purpose

Changes the column-display characteristics of one or more columns.

Columns wider than 9 characters are needed to display large numbers, to display dates, and to prevent text from being covered by adjacent cell entries. Narrow column widths are useful for short entries, such as (Y/N), and for organizing the display layout.

Use **H**ide to hide columns you do not want to display or print. Redisplay these columns with the **D**isplay command.

Reminders

- Make certain that changing the width of a column does not destroy the appearance of displays in another portion of the worksheet.

- Move the cell pointer to the widest entry in the column before you use /wcs.

Procedures

1. Type /wc

2. Select one of the following menu items:

Menu Item	Description
Set-Width	Sets a new column width
Reset-Width	Returns to the global width default
Hide	Hides the column(s) from view or from printing
Display	Displays the hidden column(s)
Column-Range	Sets the width of more than one column; provides the following two options:

Set-Width

Sets new column widths

Reset-Width

Returns to the global width default

3. If you chose **Set-Width**, enter the new column width by typing the number of characters or by pressing the left- or right-arrow keys to shrink or expand the column.

   If you chose **Hide** or **Display**, indicate the columns you want changed. When you choose **Display**, hidden columns are displayed.

   If you chose **Column-Range**, then choose **Set-Width** or **Reset-Width**; indicate the columns you want to change, and enter the column width as a number or press the left- or right-arrow key to shrink or expand the column.

Important Cues

- Asterisks appear in a cell whose column is too narrow to display numeric or date information.

- Text entries wider than the cell may be partially covered by text or numeric entries in the cell to the right.

- Use /Worksheet Global Column-Width to set the column width for columns that were not set individually with /Worksheet Column.

- Column width settings from /Worksheet Column override settings from /Worksheet Global Col-Width.

- Use /wch to suppress the printing of unnecessary columns.

- You can use /wch to suppress columns in the current window without affecting the display in other windows. When the windows are cleared, the settings used in the top window of a horizontal split or the left window of a vertical split are kept; the settings used in the bottom or right windows are lost.

- When preparing reports, use /wch to hide the display of unnecessary data and reduce the number of printed columns.

Cautions

- Be sure that other operators who use your worksheet are aware of the hidden columns. Although the values and formulas of hidden columns work properly, the display may be confusing if data appears to be missing.

- When cells are hidden on an unprotected worksheet, ranges copied or moved to the hidden area overwrite existing data.

- Changing a column's width throughout the entire worksheet can alter the appearance of the worksheet in other areas.

For more information, see Chapter 4.

Worksheet Erase   /WE

Purpose

Erases all active worksheets from memory, leaving one blank worksheet on-screen.

Use this command to clear away old work after you have saved it and to start fresh with a blank worksheet.

Reminder

Be sure to save active worksheet(s) before you use /Worksheet Erase.

Procedures

1. Type /we

2. Select one of the following:

Menu Item	Description
No	Cancels the command, leaving all worksheets in memory
Yes	Erases all active worksheets if they have not changed since last being saved. If worksheets have been changed, and the changes have not been saved, a Yes/No prompt appears, asking whether you still want to erase worksheets. Press **Y** to erase; press **N** to keep the worksheets and return to READY mode.

Important Cue

Use /Worksheet Delete to delete individual worksheets from a file.

Caution

Files and worksheets that have been erased from memory without first being saved are lost. Make sure that you save files and worksheets you want to use again.

*For more information, see /**File Save** and Chapter 4.*

Worksheet Titles   /WT

Purpose

Displays row or column headings that might otherwise be scrolled off the screen. When GROUP mode is on, Titles applies to all worksheets in the file.

Reminders

- You can "freeze" cell contents horizontally (in rows), vertically (in columns), or both ways.

- Rows are frozen across the top of the worksheet. Columns are frozen down the left edge.

Procedures

1. If you want column headings at the top of the screen, move the cell pointer so that the column headings you want frozen on-screen occupy the top row of the worksheet.

   If you want row headings along the leftmost edge of the screen, move the cell pointer so that the column containing the leftmost row headings is at the left edge of the screen.

   If you want both row and column headings, move the cell pointer so that the column headings are at the top of the screen and the row headings are in the leftmost column.

2. Move the cell pointer one row below the lowest row to be used as a title, and one column to the right of the column(s) to be used as title(s).

3. Type /wt

4. Select one of the following:

Menu Item	Description
Both	Creates titles from the rows above the cell pointer and from the columns to the left of the cell pointer
Horizontal	Creates titles from the rows above the cell pointer
Vertical	Creates titles from the columns to the left of the cell pointer

Clear   Removes all frozen title areas so that all worksheet areas
             scroll

Important Cues

- To return the worksheet to normal, select the /Worksheet Titles Clear command.

- /Worksheet Titles does not work when the displaying of the titles and the cell pointer is impossible. This situation occurs when there is no room to display Titles rows or columns effectively, as when you use /Worksheet Window Perspective.

- If you have split the worksheet into two windows with /Worksheet Window, each window can have its own titles.

- Press Home to move the cell pointer to the top left corner of the unfrozen area.

- Press GoTo (F5) to move the cell pointer inside the title area. This action creates duplicates of the frozen rows and columns. The double appearance can be confusing.

- The cell pointer can enter title areas when you are entering cell addresses in POINT mode.

- /Worksheet Titles can be useful for displaying protected screen areas when /Range Input is active. Position titles so that they display labels and instructions adjacent to the unprotected input range.

- /Worksheet Titles is especially useful for freezing column headings over a database or an accounting worksheet. You also can freeze rows of text that describe figures in adjacent cells.

For more information, see Chapter 4.

Worksheet Window   /WW

Purpose

Displays your worksheet from many points of view. You can display portions of three worksheets, display two different views of the same worksheet, display part of a worksheet and a graph, or display a maplike overview of the worksheet.

Reminders

- If you want to see many views of the same worksheet, decide whether you want the worksheet split horizontally or vertically. If you want two horizontal windows, move the cell pointer to the top row of what will become the lower window. To produce two vertical windows, move the cell pointer to the column that will become the left edge of the right window. Position the screen so that the cell pointer is at midscreen.

- If you want to display a graph on-screen with the worksheet, use the cell pointer to define the column that divides the worksheet and graph. The left part of the screen will show the worksheet; the right part will show the graph.

Procedures

1. Type /ww

2. Select one of the following:

Menu Item	Description
Horizontal	Splits the worksheet into two horizontal windows at the cell pointer
Vertical	Splits the worksheet into two vertical windows at the cell pointer
Sync	Synchronizes titles so that they move together. Windows are in Sync when they are first opened.
Unsync	Unsynchronizes two windows so that they can move independently of each other. You can then simultaneously view different rows and columns in the worksheet. A window will move only when it contains the cell pointer.
Clear	Removes the inactive window (the one that does not contain the cell pointer)
Map	Switches between the worksheet and a map view of the worksheet. The map view displays labels as "; in formulas or annotated numbers, the map view displays values as # and +. Map provides two options: Enable, which turns the map on; and Disable, which turns the map off.
Perspective	Displays three worksheets stacked so that portions of each are shown
Graph	Displays the graph in the worksheet area to the right of the cell pointer. Changing data changes the graph.
Display	Switches between the two screen-display modes that you selected at installation. Choose 1 for the first mode you installed and 2 for the second mode.

3. Repeat Steps 1 and 2 and select Unsync if you want the windows to move independently of each other. You can then simultaneously view different rows and columns in the worksheet.

Important Cues

- Each window can have different column widths. When /Worksheet Window Clear is selected, the settings used in the top or left window determine the column width for the remaining worksheet.

- Press Ctrl-PgUp or Ctrl-PgDn to move the cell pointer between worksheets.

- Horizontal windows are useful when you work with databases. The criteria range and database column labels can appear in the upper window while the data or extracted data appears in the lower window.

- You can use /Worksheet Window to display messages, instructions, warnings, help text, and so on, without having to leave the worksheet.

Caution

Always clear windows and reposition the screen before you invoke windows in a macro. Macros that split windows may become "confused" if the window configuration differs from what the macros "expect."

For more information, see Chapter 4.

Worksheet Status   /WS

Purpose

Displays the current global settings and hardware options. You also can use /ws to check available memory.

Reminder

The screen displays the status of the following information:

Available Memory

Math Coprocessor

Recalculation (Method, Order, Iterations)

Circular Reference (One cell in the circular error)

Cell Display (Format, Label Prefix, Column Width, Zero Suppression)

Global Protection

You can check the worksheet's status whenever a worksheet is displayed.

Procedures

1. Type /ws

2. Press any key to return to the worksheet.

Important Cues

- The disk-file size of the saved worksheet cannot be calculated from the amount of memory used.

- You can reduce the size of a worksheet by deleting unnecessary worksheets, formulas, labels, and values. Use /**R**ange Format **R**eset to reset the numeric format for unused areas; then save the revised worksheet to a file and retrieve a smaller version.

- The Circular Reference status displays a single cell within a ring of formulas that reference each other. The Circular Reference status shows only one cell address from this ring.

For more information, see Chapter 4.

Worksheet Page   /WP

Purpose

Manually inserts page breaks in printed worksheets. When GROUP mode is on, the page break is inserted in all worksheets in the file.

1-2-3 automatically inserts page breaks when the printing reaches the bottom margin. For some reports, however, you may want page breaks to occur at designated rows. The /**W**orksheet **P**age command indicates to the printer where manually selected page breaks should occur.

Reminders

- If you will need to reuse the worksheet in a form without page breaks, save the worksheet before you insert the page breaks. The /**W**orksheet **P**age command inserts a row and inserts characters in that row, altering your worksheet so that it may be inconvenient for normal use.

- Before you use /wp, move the cell pointer to the leftmost column of the current print range and to the row where you want the page break to occur.

Procedures

1. Type /wp

2. Press Enter.

3. A row is inserted where the page will break, and a double colon (::) appears in the left column.

Important Cues

- Use /**W**orksheet **D**elete **R**ow to delete the row containing a page break.

- /**W**orksheet **P**age overrides the /**P**rint **F**ile **O**ptions **O**ther **U**nformatted command, which normally suppresses page breaks. If you need to print to disk without using page breaks, make sure that you use /**Range Erase** to remove the page-break markers.

Caution

Do not make entries in the row that contains the page-break marker (::). Entries in this row do not print.

For more information, see Chapter 8.

Worksheet Hide   /WH

Purpose

Hides or displays one or more worksheets.

Reminder

Move the cell pointer into the topmost worksheet of the worksheets you want to hide or display.

Procedures

1. Type /wh

2. Select **Enable** to hide worksheets, or select **Disable** to display worksheets.

3. Specify the range containing the worksheets you want to hide or display. Hidden worksheets display with an asterisk (*) next to the worksheet letter.

Important Cues

- You cannot move the cell pointer into a hidden worksheet.

- Data and formulas in a hidden worksheet still work normally.

- Three-dimensional commands, such as @SUM commands, that pass through hidden worksheets evaluate the contents of the hidden worksheets.

- Data can be hidden in other ways. Use /**Worksheet Global Format Hidden** to hide the contents of a worksheet; use /**Range Format Hidden** to hide a range of cells in a visible worksheet; and use /**Worksheet Column Hide** to hide the contents of a column.

Caution

Be careful that you do not delete hidden worksheets when deleting across a range of worksheets.

For more information, see Chapter 4.

Range Commands /R

/Range commands control the display formats, protection, and manipulation of portions of the worksheet. (If you want to affect the entire worksheet, as by inserting an entire column, look at the /Worksheet command menu.)

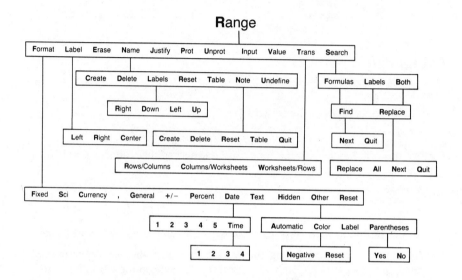

Range Format /RF

Purpose

Prepares cells so that they display with a specific format for both values (numbers) and formula results.

/Range Format formats a cell or range of cells so that numbers appear in a specific format: with fixed decimal places; as currency; with commas only; in scientific notation; or as dates. The Hidden and Text formats affect text in cells. All of these formats affect both screen display and printing.

Reminders

- Use /Worksheet Global Format to format the majority of the worksheet's cells that will contain numeric data. Use /Range Format to reset formats for areas that differ.

- Move the cell pointer to the upper-left corner of the range you want to format.

Procedures

1. Type /rf

2. Select a format from the following menu items:

Menu Item	Description
Fixed	Fixes the number of decimal places displayed
Sci	Displays large or small numbers, using scientific notation
Currency	Displays currency symbols (such as $ or £) and commas
, (comma)	Inserts commas to mark thousands and multiples of thousands
General	Displays values with up to 10 decimals or in scientific notation
+/−	Creates horizontal bar graphs or time-duration graphs on computers that do not have graphics. Each symbol equals one whole number. Positive numbers display as plus (+) symbols; negative numbers, as minus (−) symbols.
Percent	Displays a decimal number as a whole number followed by a percent (%) sign
Date	Displays serial date numbers in the following five formats; provides the Time option, which offers four time formats

1	DD–MMM–YY	12–Jan–51
2	DD–MMM	12–Jan
3	MMM–YY	Jan–51
4	MM/DD/YY	01/12/51
5	MM/DD	01/12

Time:

1	HH:MM:SS AM/PM	1:04:34 PM
2	HH:MM AM/PM	1:04 PM
3	HH:MM:SS	13:04:34
4	HH:MM	13:04

Menu Item	Description
Text	Continues to evaluate formulas as numbers, but displays formulas as text on-screen
Hidden	Hides contents from the display and printing but still evaluates contents
Other	Enables you to choose the following four formatting options:

Automatic

> Automatically formats numbers and dates when they are entered in a cell that has the **General** format

Color

> Provides two options: **Negative**, which displays negative numbers in color; and **Reset**, which turns off color formats

Label

> Formats numeric data and entries as labels, using a label prefix

Parentheses

> Provides two options: **Yes**, which encloses all numbers in parentheses; and **No**, which removes parentheses

Reset

> Returns the format to current /**Worksheet Global** format

3. If 1-2-3 prompts, enter the number of decimal places to be displayed. The full value of a cell—not the value displayed—is used for calculation. (See the first caution.)

4. If you select **Date** or **Time**, also select a format number to indicate how you want the date or time to appear.

5. Specify the range by entering the range address, highlighting the range, or using an assigned range name.

6. Verify that the specified range is correct.

7. Press Enter.

Important Cues

- Use /**Worksheet Global Format** to format new numbers entered throughout the worksheet. Numbers entered in ranges formatted with /**Range Format** will not be affected.

- To apply a format to the same cells in all the file's worksheets, put the file in GROUP mode by using /**Worksheet Global Group**. Then use /**Range Format**.

- Use /**Range Prot** and /**Worksheet Global Prot** to protect cell contents hidden with /**Range Format Hidden** from being accidentally written over.

- /**Range Format Hidden** is the only format that affects labels. All other /**Range Format** commands work on values and numeric formulas.

- Redisplay hidden data with the **Reset** format or any other new format.

- Dates and times are generated from serial date and time numbers created with @DATE, @DATEVALUE, @TIME, @NOW, and @TIMEVALUE.

- If you use a format other than General, asterisks fill the cell when a value is too large to fit the cell's current column width. (In the General format, values that are too large are displayed in scientific notation.)

- Use /Worksheet Global Default Other International to display non-USA formats. Select one of these international format options: Punctuation, Currency, Date, or Time.

- Range formats take precedence over /Worksheet Global formats.

Cautions

- /Range Format rounds only the appearance of the displayed number. The command does not round the number used for calculation. This difference can cause displayed or printed numbers to appear to be incorrect. In some worksheets, such as mortgage tables, results may be significantly different than expected. Enclose numbers, formulas, or cell references in the @ROUND function to ensure that the values in calculations are truly rounded.

- Use the Fixed decimal format to enter percentage data. Use the Percent format to display or print results. The Percent format displays a decimal numeral in percentage form; a decimal numeral such as .23 is displayed as 23%. If the Percent format is used for data entry, most users will see numerals in percentage form (such as 23%) and attempt to enter similar percentages (.24 as 24, for example), producing grossly incorrect entries (such as 2,400%). If the Percent format is used, numeric entries should be followed by a percent sign, as in 24%. The trailing percent sign causes 1-2-3 to divide the value by 100.

*For more information, see /**Worksheet Global Format**, /**Worksheet Global Default**, /**Worksheet Global Group**, and Chapters 5 and 6.*

Range Label   /RL

Purpose

Selects how you want to align text labels in their cells.

Labels narrower than the cell width can be aligned to the left, right, or center. To change how numbers appear on-screen, use either /Range Format or /Worksheet Global Format.

Reminders

- Move the cell pointer to the upper-left corner of the range containing the cells you want to align.

- Use /Worksheet Global Label-Prefix to align labels that have not been aligned with /Range Label.

Procedures

1. Type /rl

2. Select one of these menu items:

Menu Item	Description
Left	Aligns labels with cell's left edge
Right	Aligns labels with cell's right edge
Center	Centers labels in cell

3. Specify the range by entering the range address, highlighting the range, or using an assigned range name. Figure R.1 shows a highlighted range ready to be aligned to the right.

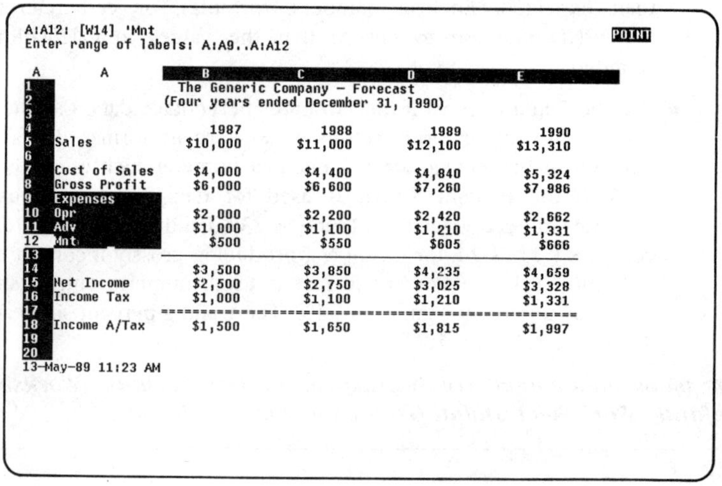

Fig. R.1.
The highlighted range A9..A12 about to be aligned to the right.

```
A:A12: [W14] 'Mnt                                                    POINT
Enter range of labels: A:A9..A:A12

     A        A          B          C          D          E
1                      The Generic Company — Forecast
2                      (Four years ended December 31, 1990)
3
4                          1987       1988       1989       1990
5             Sales       $10,000    $11,000    $12,100    $13,310
6
7             Cost of Sales $4,000    $4,400     $4,840     $5,324
8             Gross Profit  $6,000    $6,600     $7,260     $7,986
9             Expenses
10            Opr          $2,000     $2,200     $2,420     $2,662
11            Adv          $1,000     $1,100     $1,210     $1,331
12            Mnt            $500       $550       $605       $666
13
14                         $3,500     $3,850     $4,235     $4,659
15            Net Income    $2,500     $2,750     $3,025     $3,328
16            Income Tax    $1,000     $1,100     $1,210     $1,331
17            ====================================================
18            Income A/Tax  $1,500     $1,650     $1,815     $1,997
19
20
13-May-89 11:23 AM
```

4. Press Enter.

Important Cues

- If you want the align commands to apply to the same cells throughout a file, put the file in GROUP mode before aligning labels.

- The label prefix appears on the status line (the screen's first line, directly before the cell contents).

- Alignment works only for text smaller than the cell width. Text larger than the cell width is left-aligned. The text that exceeds the cell width "squeezes" out the cell's right edge.

- To align labels in a cell manually, enter one of these label prefixes before typing the label:

Label Prefix	Function
' (apostrophe)	Aligns label to the left
" (quotation mark)	Aligns label to the right
^ (caret)	Centers label in the cell
\ (backslash)	Repeats character to fill a cell*

Note that this prefix cannot be selected from the menu.

- Unmodified worksheets start with labels left-aligned. Use /Worksheet Global Label-Prefix to set the label prefix used by text entries in areas not specified with /Range Label.

- /Range Label does not affect values (numeric cell entries). Values are always right-aligned.

- Labels beginning with numbers or formula symbols require label prefixes. Enter the label prefix before entering the numbers or symbols, or use /Range Format Other Label to create an area where numbers will enter as labels. This process is necessary for such items as addresses, part numbers, Social Security numbers, and phone numbers, as in the following examples:

Correct	Incorrect
'2207 Cheyenne Dr.	2207 Cheyenne Dr.
"34-567FB	34-567FB

- Use a label prefix to preserve formulas that have errors you have not yet identified. For example, if you have a problem with the formula +B5*@PMT(B16B12/12,B14*12), and you don't have time to look for the error (a comma is missing after B16), use an apostrophe label prefix to turn the formula into text. Later, when you have more time, use EDIT mode to remove the apostrophe to change the text back to a formula. Then correct the formula error.

- Document formulas by inserting a label prefix before each formula and copying the formula as a label to your worksheet documentation area. Later, remove the label prefix from the original formula to restore it to its original, operable form.

Cautions

- /Range Label Center does not center labels on the screen or page. You must center the text manually by moving the cell pointer with the text and following these steps:

  1. Enter the text if you have not done so already.

  2. Determine how many leading spaces are necessary to center the text on-screen.

3. Press Edit (F2); then press Home. The cursor moves to the label prefix at the beginning of the text.

4. Move the cell pointer right one character and insert spaces in front of the first character to center it.

5. Press Enter.

- Macro code text must be in the form of labels. If you don't place a label prefix before the macro commands, such as /wglr, your keystrokes select menu items.

- Numbers or formulas preceded by label prefixes have a value of zero when evaluated by a numeric formula. (In Release 2.0, however, a formula [but not a function] that references a label returns an ERR; Release 2.01 eliminates this bug.) In a database query, you must use text searches to search for these numbers that have label prefixes.

For more information, see /Worksheet Global Label-Prefix, /Range Format, and Chapter 5.

Range Erase   /RE

Purpose

Erases the contents of a single cell or range of cells while leaving the cell's format.

Reminders

- If you have any doubts about erasing a range of cells, use /File Save to save the worksheet to a file before erasing the range. If you have memory available for the Undo feature, turn on Undo by using /Worksheet Global Default Other Undo Enable. You then can undo the erase by pressing Alt-F4.

- Move the cell pointer to the upper-left corner of the range to be erased.

Procedures

1. Type /rc

2. Specify the range to be erased by entering the range address, highlighting the range, or using an assigned range name. Figure R.2 shows a highlighted range to be erased.

3. Press Enter.

Important Cues

- To erase protected cells, you must first remove worksheet protection by using /Worksheet Global Protection Disable. You cannot remove protection if the file is sealed.

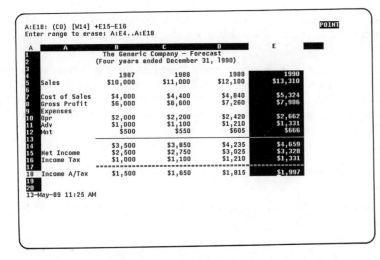

Fig. R.2.
The highlighted range about to be deleted.

- Erasing data or formulas may produce an ERR display in formulas that depend on the erased data or formulas.

- Erasing a range does not change the format, label prefix, or protection status assigned to the cells. Use /Range Format Reset, /Range Prot, or /Range Unprot to change these.

Cautions

- Be careful when using /Worksheet Erase: it erases all active files and worksheets. Remove individual worksheets or files from memory with /Worksheet Delete Sheet or /Worksheet Delete File.

- Be careful not to erase formulas or values hidden with /Worksheet Global Format Hidden or /Range Format Hidden.

For more information, see /Worksheet Delete, /Worksheet Erase, /Worksheet Global Default Other Undo, and Chapter 4.

Range Name   /RN

Purpose

Assigns an alphabetical or alphanumeric name to a cell or a range of cells. (See the caution about alphanumeric range names.)

Instead of column-and-row cell addresses, use range names to make formulas and macros easy to read and understand.

Reminders

- You can use range names instead of cell references to make formulas and macros easier to understand. If you frequently print specific areas of a worksheet or go to specific areas, you can name these locations and use the easily remembered range name when asked for the print range or the GoTo location.

- There are two types of range names: defined and undefined. A *defined* range name refers to a cell or range address and can be used in formulas or command prompts. An *undefined* range name has not been assigned an associated address or range and can be used only in formulas. Formulas that use undefined range names result in ERR.

Procedures

To create a range name that describes a single cell or range of cells, follow these steps:

1. Move the cell pointer to the cell or upper-left corner of the range of cells to be named.

2. Type /rn

3. Select **Create.**

4. When prompted to enter the range name, press Name (F3) to see a full-screen display of names already in use. If the name you want to use is listed, delete it before you create another range by that name. Press Esc to exit from the list.

5. Type a range name of as many as 15 characters. Avoid using symbols other than the underline.

6. Press Enter.

7. To specify the range to be named, enter the range address or highlight the range.

8. Press Enter.

To delete one or more range names, follow these steps:

1. Type /rn

2. Select **Delete** to delete a single range name. Select **Reset** to delete all range names.

3. If you selected **Delete,** then type or highlight the name you want deleted. Press Enter. Formulas containing the range names revert to using cell and range addresses.

To create range names from labels, follow these steps:

1. Move the cell pointer to the upper-left corner of the column or row of labels.

2. Type /rn

3. Select **Labels.**

4. Select one of these menu items:

Menu Item	Description
Right	Uses the labels to name the cell to the right of each label
Down	Uses the labels to name the cell below each label
Left	Uses the labels to name the cell to the left of each label
Up	Uses the labels to name the cell above each label

5. By entering the range address or highlighting the range, specify the range of labels to be used as names. Verify that the range encloses only labels.

6. Press Enter.

To display the addresses of existing range names, follow these steps:

1. Move the cell pointer to a clear area of the worksheet. The table requires two columns and as many rows as there are range names, plus one blank row.

2. Type /rn

3. Select **T**able.

4. Press Enter to create a table of range names and their associated addresses.

To attach or edit notes associated with a range name, follow these steps:

1. Type /rn

2. Choose **N**ote **C**reate.

3. Type the range address or highlight the cells to which you want to attach a note.

4. Press Enter.

5. Type or edit a note of up to 512 characters.

6. Press Enter.

7. Choose **Q**uit to return to the previous menu.

To delete one or more notes associated with range names, follow these steps:

1. Type /rn

2. Choose **N**ote **D**elete to delete one range name note, or **N**ote **R**eset to delete all range name notes.

3. If you chose **N**ote **D**elete, specify the range name whose note you want deleted.

To display a table of notes in the current file, follow these steps:

1. Move to a location where 1-2-3 can enter notes and addresses without destroying needed data. The table is three columns wide and has as many rows as there are names, plus one.

2. Type /rn

3. Choose **N**ote **T**able.

4. Press Enter.

To preserve an existing range name but separate it from its associated address, follow these steps:

1. Type /rn

2. Choose **U**ndefined.

3. Select the name you want undefined.

Important Cues

- Use a range name when you enter a function. Instead of entering a function as @SUM(P53..P65), for example, type it as @SUM(EXPENSES). You do not have to create the name EXPENSES before entering the formulas; however, until the name is created, the SUM formula will return ERR.

- Use range names when you respond to a prompt. For example, when the program requests a print range, provide a range name, as in the following:

   Enter print range: **JULREPORT**

- Undefined range names remain in formulas, although the formulas result in ERR. Use the /**R**ange **N**ame **C**reate or **L**abels command to redefine the name.

- To move the cell pointer rapidly to the upper-left corner of any range, press GoTo (F5) and then enter the range name, or press Name (F3) to display a list of range names. After you have entered the range name or selected a name from the list, press Enter.

- To print a list of range names, use /**R**ange **N**ame **T**able and press Shift-PrtSc after the list appears.

- /**M**ove moves range names with cells if the entire range is included in the block to be moved.

- Macro names are range names; therefore, macros must be named through the use of /rnc or /rnl.

Cautions

- A range name can be alphanumeric (as in SALES87), but avoid creating a range name that looks like a cell reference (for example, AD19). Such a range name does not function correctly in formulas.

- Be sure that you are in the correct file before deleting range names or range name notes.

- Always delete existing range names before re-creating them in a new location. If you don't delete an original range name, formulas that used the original name may be wrong.

- Do not delete columns or rows that form the corner of a named range. Doing so produces an ERR in formulas.

- Moving one or more corners of a range name can redefine the range name. To check the addresses that a range name applies to after a corner has been moved, issue /**R**ange **N**ame **C**reate and select the name in question. The name's range appears on-screen. Press Ctrl-Break or Esc to return to the menu.

- When two named ranges have the same upper-left corner, moving one of the corners moves the address location for both range names. To move a corner of overlapping named ranges, first delete one range name, move the range, and then re-create the deleted range name in its original location.

- /**R**ange **N**ame **T**able does not update itself automatically. If you move, copy, or change range names, you must re-create the range name table.

For more information, see Chapter 4.

Range Justify /RJ

Purpose

Fits text within a desired range by wrapping words to form complete paragraphs.

Use /**R**ange **J**ustify to join and "word wrap" automatically any lines of text in adjacent vertical cells to form a paragraph. /**R**ange **J**ustify redistributes words so that sentences are approximately the same length.

Reminders

- If you are uncertain about the results of /**R**ange **J**ustify, save your worksheet with /**F**ile **S**ave before using /**R**ange **J**ustify.

- Delete any blank cells or values between vertically adjacent cells you want to join. Blank cells or values stop text from justifying.

- Move the cell pointer to the top of the column of text you want justified. Make sure that the cell pointer is in the first cell containing the text. On the status line, you should see the first words of the text from the first row of the column.

- Remember that other cells are moved to reflect the justification unless you specify a range for /rj. In figure R.3, a range has been specified in which the text will be reformatted; this specification keeps the value in B10 from being displaced.

Fig. R.3.
The worksheet
range marked
for justi-
fication.

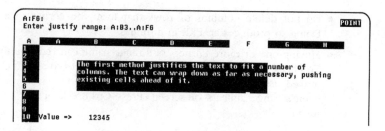

A:F6:
Enter justify range: A:B3..A:F6   POINT

The first method justifies the text to fit a number of
columns. The text can wrap down as far as necessary, pushing
existing cells ahead of it.

Value =>   12345

Procedures

1. Type /rj

2. Highlight the range in which you want the text to be justified. If you choose not to specify a range for the justification, highlight only the first row of the text column.

3. Press Enter, and the text will be justified. If you specified a range, worksheet cells within the highlighted range are justified; cells outside the highlighted range are not moved.

Important Cues

- /**Range J**ustify justifies all contiguous text in a column until justification is stopped by nonlabel cell contents (a blank cell, a formula, or a value).

- Use /**File I**mport to import text from word processors (ASCII text files only). Once in 1-2-3, the text can be justified with /**R**ange **J**ustify to fit the worksheet.

Cautions

- If the specified range is not large enough to hold the justified text, 1-2-3 displays an error message. To solve this problem, enlarge the range or move the text to a new location. If you enlarge the range, you may need to move other cell contents.

- Using /**R**ange **J**ustify on protected cells results in an error. Remove protection with /**W**orksheet **G**lobal **Prot D**isable.

- 1-2-3 is not a word processor. Although /**R**ange **J**ustify wraps words, you are much better off learning the fundamental commands of a word processor than using 1-2-3 for something it was not designed for.

For more information, see /**Move,** /**File Import,** /**Worksheet Page,** *and Chapter 5.*

Range Prot and Range Unprot /RP and /RU

Purpose

/Range Prot enables you to change the identification of worksheet cells from unprotected to protected. /Range Unprot enables you to make changes to cells in a protected worksheet.

Use /Range Unprot and /Worksheet Global Prot (protect) to protect files from accidental changes. /Range Unprot identifies which cells' contents can be changed when /Worksheet Global Prot is enabled. Cells not identified with /Range Unprot cannot be changed when /Worksheet Global Prot is enabled.

Reminder

Move the cell pointer to the upper-left corner of the range you want to identify as unprotected. /Worksheet Global Prot may be enabled or disabled. If the file has been sealed, the seal must be removed with /File Admin Seal Disable before worksheet global protection can be removed.

Procedures

To return an unprotected range to its original, protected identification, follow these steps:

1. Type /r

2. Select Prot.

3. Specify the range by typing the range address, highlighting the range, or using an assigned range name.

4. Press Enter.

To identify a cell or a range of cells as unprotected, follow these steps:

1. Type /r

2. Select Unprot.

3. Specify the range to be identified as unprotected by typing the range address, highlighting the range, or using a range name.

4. Press Enter.

Important Cues

- /Range Prot and /Range Unprot affect data entry only when /Worksheet Global Prot is enabled. The screen display of unprotected contents may be brighter or in a different color, depending on your graphics hardware. (See Chapter 4.)

- Use high-contrast characters in unprotected cells to attract attention to instructions or comments, even when worksheet protection is disabled.

- Use /Range Input to limit cell pointer movement to unprotected cells. Combine /Range Input with the macro {FORM} to create custom data-entry forms.

- Use /Worksheet Status to see whether worksheet protection is enabled or disabled.

Cautions

- When the file is in GROUP mode, identifying a range as unprotected on one worksheet identifies and removes the protection from the same range on all worksheets.

- Macros that make changes to cell contents will not work correctly if /Worksheet Global Prot is enabled and the macro attempts to change protected cells. Prevent this situation by limiting cell pointer movement to unprotected cells or by disabling worksheet protection when the macro starts. Macros should enable worksheet protection before they end.

*For more information, see /**Worksheet Global Protection**, /**Range Input**, /**Worksheet Status**, /**File Admin Seal**, and Chapter 4.*

Range Input   /RI

Purpose

Restricts cell pointer movement to unprotected cells.

/Range Input is an excellent way to create fill-in-the-blank worksheets. Such worksheets prevent inexperienced users from making accidental changes to worksheet labels and formulas.

Reminders

- To use /Range Input effectively, organize your worksheet so that the data-entry cells are together. Include text and examples that show the operator the format and type of data to enter. R.4 shows a worksheet arranged to maximize /Range Input.

Fig. R.4.
Loan
Calculator
worksheet
arranged to
maximize
/Range Input.

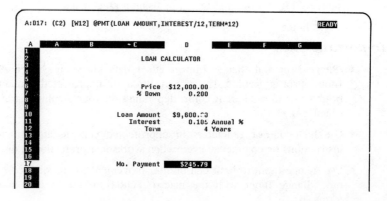

- Before you use /**R**ange **I**nput, use /**R**ange **U**nprot to identify unprotected data-entry cells. /**W**orksheet **G**lobal **P**rot does not have to be enabled.

- Move the cell pointer to one corner of a range that will include the unprotected data-entry cells.

Procedures

1. Type /ri

2. Specify the input range to be displayed. Include a range covering all cells in which you want to enter data. Type the range address, highlight the range, or use a range name.

3. Press Enter. The input range's upper-left corner is moved to the screen's upper-left corner. Cell pointer movements are restricted to unprotected cells in the designated input range.

4. Make data entries, using normal methods. Press Esc or Enter to exit from /**R**ange **I**nput and return to normal cell pointer movement.

Important Cues

- /**R**ange **I**nput restricts your key selections to Esc; Enter; Edit; Help; Home; End; and the left-, right-, up-, and down-arrow keys. Use standard alpha-numeric keys for data entry and editing.

- /**R**ange **I**nput is most valuable when used within macros. Within macros, the command can be used to restrict data entry to one worksheet range for one part of the macro and to another worksheet range for another part of the macro.

*For more information, see /**Range Name**, /**Range Unprot**, and Chapter 4.*

Range Value   /RV

Purpose

Copies formulas to the same or to a new location and replaces the copied formulas with their resulting values.

Reminders

- Check to see that the destination area is large enough to hold the copied values, which will replace existing cell contents.

- Ensure that the source file is calculated. If CALC shows at the bottom of the screen, press Calc (F9) to recalculate the file. If the file is linked to other active files or to files on disk, use /**F**ile **A**dmin **L**ink-**R**efresh to update linked values.

- Move the cell pointer to the upper-left corner of the range containing the formulas.

Procedures

1. Type /rv

2. Specify the source range by typing the range address, highlighting the range, or using a range name.

3. Press Enter.

4. Specify the upper-left corner cell of the destination range by typing a cell address or range name, or by moving the cell pointer to this location.

5. Press Enter. The values appear in the destination range and preserve the numeric formats used in the original formulas.

Important Cues

- /Range Value copies labels and string formulas and converts string (text) formulas to labels.

- Use /Copy to copy formulas without changing them into values.

Cautions

- /Range Value overwrites data in the destination (TO) range. Be sure that the destination range is clear.

- If you make the destination range the same as the source range, formulas in the range are converted to their values. These values, however, overwrite the formulas they came from. The formulas are replaced permanently.

For more information, see /Copy and Chapter 4.

Range Trans /RT

Purpose

Copies formulas from one location and orientation to another location and orientation. Formulas are replaced by their values.

/Range Trans is useful when you want to change data from spreadsheet format (headings on left, data in rows) to database format (headings on top, data in columns), or vice versa. The command also can transpose data from rows and columns on one worksheet to individual rows or columns on multiple worksheets.

Reminders

- Transpose to a clear worksheet or file area(s). The transposed data overwrites any existing data.

- Move the cell pointer to the upper-left corner of the range of cells you want to transpose.

- Ensure that the source file is calculated. If CALC shows at the bottom of the screen, press Calc (F9) to recalculate the file. If the file is linked to other active files or to files on disk, use /File Admin Link-Refresh to update linked values.

Procedures

1. Type /rt

2. Specify the range to be transposed by typing the range address, highlighting the range, or using an assigned range name.

3. Press Enter.

4. When 1-2-3 displays the TO prompt, do one of two things: (1) If you want to transpose rows to columns or columns to rows on a single worksheet, specify the upper-left corner of where you want the transposed data to appear; (2) If you want to transpose data across multiple worksheets, specify the upper-left corner of the three-dimensional range for each copy on each of the multiple worksheets. Move the cell pointer to the upper-left corner of the destination cells where the transposed data will be copied.

5. Press Enter. The data transposes immediately if you are working on a single worksheet.

6. If you are transposing across multiple worksheets, choose one of the following commands:

Menu Item	Description
Rows/Columns	Copies rows to columns or vice versa
Columns/Worksheets	Copies each column to a succeeding worksheet in the TO range
Worksheets/Rows	Copies each row to a succeeding worksheet in the TO range

Figure R.5 shows data in A6..B10 transposed to D6..H7 on a single worksheet.

```
A:D10:                                           READY

A     A       B       C    D    E       F       G       H
1
2
3
4  Original Data            Transposed Data
5  ==================       ==============================================
6        Top   Right              Top   43      32      21    Bottom
7        43    65               Right   65      87      32    Right
8        32    87
9        21    32
10  Bottom    Right
11
12
13
14
15
16
17
18
19
20
```

Fig. R.5.
Data in A6..B10 transposed to D6..H7.

Important Cue

Transposing copies the cell format and protection status from the original cell.

Caution

Using the same upper-left corner for the original and transposed data can result in incorrect data.

*For more information, see /**Range Value** and Chapter 4.*

Range Search /RS

Purpose

Finds or replaces text within a label or formula. The search and replace can be limited to a range.

Use this command to search databases quickly or to find locations on a worksheet. The command also is useful for finding and replacing cell references, functions, and range names in formulas.

Reminders

- Move to the top left corner of the range you want to search.

- /Range Search makes it easy to correct or change formulas that use range names.

- /Range Search does not work with values.

Procedures

1. Type /rs

2. Type the cell addresses or highlight or type a range name to specify the range you want searched.

3. Enter the text string you want to find or replace. You may use either upper- or lowercase text; the /Range Search command is not case-sensitive.

4. Choose one of the following:

Menu Item	Description
Formulas	Searches through formulas
Labels	Searches through labels
Both	Searches through both formulas and labels

5. Choose one of the following:

Menu Item	Description
Find	Finds the item, displays it, and pauses before continuing
Replace	Finds the item; displays it; and requests a continue, replace, or quit action

6. If you chose **Find**, 1-2-3 finds and displays the cell containing the text. You then are prompted to choose one of the following:

Menu Item	Description
Next	Finds the next occurrence
Quit	Stops the search

If you chose **Replace**, 1-2-3 finds and displays the cell containing the text. You then are prompted to choose one of the following:

Menu Item	Description
Replace	Replaces the found text with the replacement text, then finds the next occurrence
All	Replaces all occurrences of found text
Next	Finds the next occurrence without replacing the current text
Quit	Stops the search

Important Cues

- When no more matching text is found, an error message appears at the bottom of the screen. Press Enter or Esc to return to the worksheet.

- Use spaces and label prefixes to prevent finding unwanted text. For example, a search for *and* finds *and* and *Sandwich*. A search for '*and* finds *and* as the first entry in a left-aligned text cell, but not *Sandwich*. A search for (space)*and*(space) finds the phrase *This and that*, but not *Sandwich*.

- Use /Range Search as a quick way to update text information in a database.

Cautions

- Beware of replacing with All. You can easily replace text or formulas you did not want to replace.

- /Range Search neither finds nor replaces values. It cannot be used to update numbers in the worksheet.

For more information, see Chapter 4.

Copy and Move Commands /C and /M

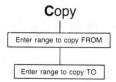

Copy

Enter range to copy FROM

Enter range to copy TO

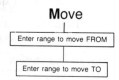

Move

Enter range to move FROM

Enter range to move TO

Copy /C

Purpose

Copies formulas, values, and labels to new locations. The copied data retains its format and its cell-protection status.

The cell addresses in copied formulas either change to reflect the new location or stay fixed, depending on whether you use relative or absolute cell references.

Reminders

- Make sure that the worksheets contain enough blank space to receive the cell or range of cells being copied. Three-dimensional worksheets must have enough room in the TO range to hold the entire three-dimensional duplicate. Copies replace the original contents of cells.

- If the receiving cell address is not close to the cell or range of cells being copied, note the address before entering /Copy, so that you can type the TO address. Pointing across a long distance to the TO address can be tedious.

- Before you issue the /Copy command, move the cell pointer to the upper-left corner of the range you want copied. If you are copying one cell, put the cell pointer on that cell. If you are copying a three-dimensional range, put the cell pointer on the topmost worksheet.

Procedures

1. Type /c

2. The FROM prompt requests the range of the cells to be copied. Enter the range to be copied by typing the range name or range address or by highlighting the range.

3. Press Enter.

4. At the TO prompt, specify on the topmost worksheet the upper-left corner of the area where you want the duplicate to appear. If you want multiple adjacent duplicates, you can specify the top left corner where each duplicate should appear. If you are copying a three-dimensional worksheet, specify only the top left cell on the topmost worksheet.

5. Press Enter.

6. Make sure that the copied formulas produce correct answers. If the answers are not correct, the copy procedure has probably adjusted cell addresses that should have remained fixed.

Important Cues

- /Copy creates duplicates of labels and values. Formulas that use relative cell references are adjusted to the new location; formulas that use absolute cell references remain fixed.

- You can link files by copying formulas that use absolute range names. For example, copying @SUM($EXPENSES) from TRIP.WK3 to another file creates on the receiving worksheet the duplicate formula

@SUM (<<C:\123\DIVISION\TRIP.WK3>>$EXPENSES)

- You can make single or multiple copies, depending on the range you enter at the TO prompt. Enter the ranges as follows:

Original Range FROM	Desired Copies	Duplicate Range TO
One cell	Fill an area	Row, column, or range on one or more worksheets
Rectangular range	One duplicate	Upper-left cell of duplicate, outside original range, on one or more worksheets
Single column	Multiple columns	Adjacent cells across a row, formed from the top cell of each duplicate column, on one or more worksheets
Single row	Multiple rows	Adjacent cells down a column, formed from the left cell in each duplicate row, on one or more worksheets
Three-dimensional rectangular range	One duplicate	Upper-left cell of topmost worksheet of duplicate's range

Cautions

- Overlapping FROM and TO ranges (original and duplicate) can cause formulas to yield incorrect results. To avoid producing incorrect results, move the cell pointer off the original cell before anchoring the TO range with a period.

- If the worksheet to be copied to does not have enough room to receive the copied range, the contents of the existing cells will be covered by the copied data. If there are not enough worksheets to receive a three-dimensional copy, the copy is stopped, and a warning appears at the bottom of the screen. To fix this problem, use /Move to move existing data; use /Worksheet Insert to insert blank columns, rows, or worksheets.

For more information, see /Worksheet Insert Column, /Worksheet Insert Row, /Worksheet Insert Sheet, /Range Value, /Range Name, and Chapter 4.

Move   /M

Purpose

Reorganizes your worksheet by moving blocks of labels, values, or formulas to different locations or worksheets.

Cell references and range names used in formulas stay the same, which means that formula results do not change. You cannot move data across files.

Reminders

- Make sure that you have enough blank space in the receiving worksheets to receive the cell or range of cells being moved. The moved data replaces the original contents of the cell.

- Before you issue the /Move command, position the cell pointer on the top left corner of the range to be moved. If you want to move one cell, place the cell pointer on that cell.

Procedures

1. Type /m

2. The FROM prompt requests the range of the cells to be moved. Highlight a range, or enter one by typing the range name or range address.

3. Press Enter.

4. At the TO prompt, enter the address of the single upper-left corner of the range to which the cells will be moved. Do so by typing the cell address, typing a range name, or highlighting the cell with the cell pointer.

5. Press Enter.

Important Cues

- /Move does not change cell addresses. The range names and cell references in the formula remain the same.

- Use /Copy when you want to create at a new location a duplicate range of cells while keeping the original range intact.

- Range names move with the moved cells if the named area is completely enclosed.

Cautions

- The contents of moved cells replace the contents of existing cells. To make room for moved cells, use /Move to move existing data; use /Worksheet Insert to insert rows, columns, or worksheets to provide additional room for copies.

- You cannot move an original so that the duplicate is beyond the worksheet or file boundaries. Use /Worksheet Insert to insert additional rows, columns, or worksheets.

- Moving the anchor cell and/or the diagonally opposite cell of a named range or formula's range moves the corner(s) of the named range or formula's range to the new location as well. If you have doubts about what is being moved, save the worksheet, delete the old range name, make the move, and then re-create the range name.

- Moving cell contents over the top of the corner in a formula's range creates an ERR in the referencing formula. The formula's range is replaced by ERR, and all dependent formulas show ERR.

- If a formula uses a named range, and cell contents are moved over a corner of the range, then the name remains in the formula. The formula's results, however, display as ERR.

- Be careful when moving a named range that has the same upper-left corner as another range. Moving one range changes the upper-left corner for both named ranges.

For more information, see /**Worksheet Insert**, /**Copy**, /**Range Name**, *and Chapter 4.*

File Commands /F

File commands are used to save and retrieve worksheets, extract a small worksheet from a larger worksheet, combine two worksheets, import ASCII data, and select the drive and directory for storage.

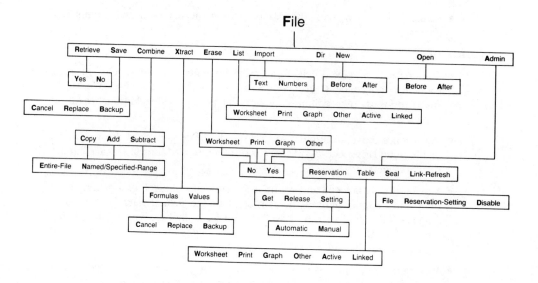

File Retrieve /FR

Purpose

Loads the requested file from disk.

Reminder

Before you retrieve a new file, use /File Save to save the current worksheets in the active file. When a new file is retrieved, it replaces the file currently displayed.

Procedures

1. Type /fr

2. Select the name of the file you want to retrieve, either by typing the name or by using the right- or left-arrow key.

3. Press Enter.

Important Cues

- You can display a listing of file names by pressing Name (F3) in response to the prompt

    Enter name of file to retrieve:

    Use the arrow keys to move to the file name you want, and then press Enter. To return to the menu without making a selection, press Esc three times.

- Retrieve a single file from a different disk drive or directory by typing the drive designation, the path, and the file name, as in the following:

    Enter name of file to retrieve: **C:\123\FORECAST\JUNEV3**

    In this example, the file JUNEV3 is located on drive C in the FORECAST subdirectory of the 123 directory. To clear the previous path, you may need to press Esc twice after the prompt.

- Use the /File Open command to retrieve a file from disk without replacing the active files. If 1-2-3 has too little memory for you to open additional files, remove one or more active files from memory with /Worksheet Delete File. To remove all active files, use /Worksheet Erase.

- Protected worksheets require a password. When you enter a password, be sure to use the same upper- and lowercase letter combination you originally typed.

- If you attempt to retrieve from a network a file that is in use by someone else, 1-2-3 displays a Yes/No menu. Press Y if you want the file without having the reservation. Doing so enables you to use the file, although you cannot save it under the same name. Press N if you do not want to retrieve the file. See /File Admin for more information on file reservations.

- When you start 1-2-3, the worksheet file loads automatically if you save it under the name AUTO123 into the same directory as 123.EXE.

- To change a drive or directory for the current work session, use the /File Dir command.

- Use /Worksheet Global Default Dir to change the directory that 1-2-3 uses on start-up. Use /Worksheet Global Default Update to save the settings to the disk.

- 1-2-3 Release 3 can retrieve Lotus 1-2-3 Release 1A and Symphony files, but they are saved as .WK3 files. Use the Translate utility to convert the .WK3 file back to 1-2-3 Release 1A or Symphony.

Caution

The retrieved file replaces the active files on-screen. Use /File Save to store your current file or worksheet before retrieving a new one.

*For more information, see /**File Admin**, /**File Save**, /**File Combine**, /**Worksheet Global Default Dir**, /**File Dir**, and Chapter 7.*

File Save /FS

Purpose

Saves the active files and their settings.

/**File Save** stores files and worksheets so that they can be retrieved later.

Reminders

- Remember to save frequently to guard against data loss.

- Name files so that they are easy to remember and group together. If you give related files similar names (such as TRENDV1, TRENDV2, and TRENDV3), you can use the wild cards * and ? to copy and erase files.

Procedures

1. Move the cell pointer so that it is in the active worksheet or file you want to save.

2. Type /fs

3. If the file has not been saved before, 1-2-3 supplies a default name and extension, such as FILE0001.WK3. You can enter the file name for the worksheet by using the default name displayed; by highlighting an existing name; by typing a new name; or by entering a new drive designation, path name, and file name.

   If more than one file is active, 1-2-3 displays the message [ALL MODIFIED FILES]. Press Edit (F2) if you want a single file name. You may edit the file name.

4. Press Enter. If the message [ALL MODIFIED FILES] is displayed, all active modified files are saved under their original names.

5. If a file already exists under the name you have selected, choose one of the following:

Menu Item	Description
Cancel	Cancels the save operation
Replace	Replaces an existing file with the current file
Backup	Saves the active file and renames the existing file with the extension .BAK

Important Cues

- Write file names of up to eight characters by using the letters A through Z, the numbers 0 through 9, and the underline character (_) or hyphen (–). Spaces cannot be used.

- If you attempt to save a file, and a file with the same name already exists, you have one of three choices: **Cancel**, **Replace**, and **Backup**. Choosing **Cancel** cancels the operation. Choosing **R**eplace replaces the existing file on disk with the active file you are saving. You will not be able to recover the replaced file. Use **B**ackup if you want to save a copy of the original file.

- Password protection prevents unauthorized access to 1-2-3 worksheets. If you save worksheets with a password, the password must be entered before the file can be retrieved. To save a file with a password, follow these steps:

  1. Move the cell pointer into the active file you want saved.

  2. Type /fs

  3. Type the file name, press the space bar, and press P. (If the message [ALL MODIFIED FILES] appears, press Edit (F2) to see the file name.)

  4. Press Enter.

  5. Type a password of up to 15 characters (no spaces). An asterisk appears in place of each letter. Be sure to remember the upper- and lowercase letter combination. When you retrieve the file, you must enter the password in exactly the same way.

  6. Press Enter.

  7. After the Verify prompt appears, type the password again and press Enter.

- To change a protected file's password, use the Backspace key to erase the Password Protected message displayed when you use /File **S**ave. Then repeat Steps 3 through 7.

- From the list of existing files on disk, you can select a file name to save to. When prompted for a name, press Esc to remove the default file name. Press Name (F3), use the arrow keys to move to the file name you want to replace, and press Enter.

- Save single worksheets from 1-2-3 Release 3 (.WK3) to 1-2-3 Release 2 (.WK1) format by typing the file extension .WK1 after the file name when you save. .WK3 files that contain more than one worksheet or that are sealed cannot be saved to .WK1 format. Remember to save a backup copy in .WK3 format in case features or functions are lost during the conversion.

- Use /File **L**ist to display the size and the date of the existing files.

- If a file is too large to save in its entirety, use /File **X**tract to save portions of it to disk as separate files.

Cautions

- Saving a file under an existing file name replaces the old file. This means that you could accidentally write over files you want to keep. A safer practice is to use the **B**ackup option or to save each copy under a different name and delete old versions later, using /File **E**rase or the operating system's ERASE command.

- After executing /File Save, do not remove your data disk until the light on your disk drive goes off. Pay no attention to the READY indicator. Wait several seconds after the READY indicator has disappeared before you remove the disk. If you remove the disk prematurely, information can be lost.

*For more information, see /**File Dir**, /**File Erase**, /**File Xtract**, and Chapter 7.*

File Combine   /FC

Purpose

Combines values or formulas from a file or worksheet on disk into the current file. Any part of a saved file can be combined with the current file.

Reminders

- Remember that /File Combine can be used three different ways: to copy the contents from the file on disk to the current file; to add values from the file on disk to the current file; and to subtract incoming values from the numeric values in the current file.

- Before starting the /File Combine operation, you must know the cell references or ranges you want from disk and the name of the file on disk.

- The /File Combine operation is easiest if the files on disk contain named ranges for the ranges that will be combined with the current file in memory.

- Use /File Import and /Data Parse to bring ASCII files into the current worksheet and organize them. To send your file to an ASCII text file, use /Print File to print the file to disk.

- The format of the cells coming in from disk takes priority over the formats in the current file. Global formats, range names, and column widths do not change.

Procedures

1. Move the cell pointer to the upper-left corner of the range in which the data will be combined.

2. Type /fc

3. Select one of the following choices:

Menu Item	Description
Copy	Copies incoming cell contents over the cells in the current worksheet. Cells in the current worksheet that correspond to blank incoming cells do not change. Labels and formulas in the current worksheet are replaced.

Menu Item	Description
Add	Adds values from cells in the file worksheet to cells containing blanks or values in the current worksheet. Labels and formulas in the current worksheet are not changed.
Subtract	Subtracts values from cells in the file worksheet from the corresponding blanks or values in the current worksheet. Labels and formulas in the current worksheet are not changed.

4. Select how much of the saved worksheet file you want to use:

Menu Item	Description
Entire-File	Combines the entire file worksheet with the current worksheet. Use when the disk file has been created with /File Xtract and contains only raw data.
Named/ Specified- Range	Combines information from a named range or range address on the disk-based file into the current worksheet. Use when you want to retrieve only part of the information contained in a file on disk.

5. If you select Entire-File, choose a file name from the menu by pressing the right- or left-arrow key, by typing the file name, or by pressing Name (F3) to display a list of file names and using the arrow keys. Press Enter. If you select Named/Specified-Range, you are asked to enter the range name (or the range address) and the file name.

Important Cues

- If you will frequently combine a small portion from a file, first give that portion a range name. Use /Range Name to name the portion on the file and save the file back to disk. You then can use /File Combine and enter the range name as the part you want to combine.

- When creating worksheets, you can save time by using /File Xtract and /File Combine to merge parts of existing worksheets to form the new one.

- Use /fcc to copy sections of a macro file to your worksheet so that you don't have to type the macros on every new worksheet. Keep your favorite macros in one worksheet. You can use /fcc to copy the macro into the new worksheet, but you need to use /Range Name Create or /Range Name Labels to rename the macro on the new worksheet.

- When you use /File Combine Add, cells in the incoming file that contain labels or string formulas are not added.

- Create a macro with /File Combine to consolidate worksheets.

Cautions

- /fcc combines values, labels, and formulas. All cell references, relative and absolute, are adjusted to reflect their new locations on the worksheet.
  Cell references are adjusted according to the upper-left corner of the combined data range (the cell pointer location). Combined formulas adjust for the difference between the cell pointer and cell A1 on the current worksheet.

- Data copied into the current worksheet replaces existing data. Blank cells in the incoming worksheet take on the value of the cells in the current worksheet.

- Range names are not brought to the new worksheet when a file is combined. This arrangement prevents possible conflicts with range names in the current worksheet. After combining files, you must re-create range names with /**Range** Name Create or /**Range** Name Labels.

For more information, see /**Range Name Create**, /**Range Name Labels**, /**File Xtract**, *and Chapter 7.*

File Xtract /FX

Purpose

Saves to disk a portion of the active file as a separate file.

You can save the portion as it appears on the worksheet (with formulas) or save only the results of the formulas.

Reminders

- Extracted ranges that include formulas should include the cells the formulas refer to; otherwise, the formulas will not be correct.

- If you want to create a 1-2-3 Release 2 file, extract only from a range on a single worksheet and from files that are not sealed.

- If the CALC indicator appears at the bottom of the screen, you should calculate the file before extracting values. Press Calc (F9) to do so.

Procedures

1. Position the cursor at the upper-left corner of the range you want to extract.

2. Type /fx

3. Choose one of the following:

Menu Item	Description
Formulas	Saves as a new file both the formulas and cell contents from the current file
Values	Saves as a new file the results from formulas and labels

4. Specify a file name other than that of the current worksheet.

5. Highlight the range of the file to be extracted as a separate file. Enter the range by typing the range address (such as B23..D46), by typing the range name, or by moving the cell pointer to the opposite corner of the range.

6. Press Enter.

7. If the name already exists, choose one of the following:

Menu Item	Description
Cancel	Cancels the extract operation
Replace	Replaces the existing file with the extracted file
Backup	Saves the extracted file and renames the existing file with the extension .BAK

Important Cues

- If you used /fxf to save a portion of a worksheet, the extracted file can function as a normal worksheet.

- To freeze a worksheet so that formulas and results don't change, extract a file with /File Xtract Values. The formulas are replaced with values.

- Use /File Xtract to save memory when a worksheet becomes too large. Separate the worksheet into smaller worksheets that require less memory.

- Increase worksheet execution speed and save memory by breaking large worksheets into smaller ones with /File Xtract Formulas. Link the extracted worksheets so that they still pass data between them (see Chapter 3).

- You can protect an extracted file by using a password. For more information, read about /File Save in the Command Reference.

Caution

Make sure that the extracted worksheet does not use values or formulas outside the extract range.

For more information, see **/File Combine** *and Chapter 7.*

File Erase   /FE

Purpose

Erases 1-2-3 files from disk.

Use /fe to erase unnecessary files from disk so that you have more available disk space. You cannot erase files on disk that are in use with a reservation, as on a network drive. Use /Worksheet Erase or /Worksheet Delete to remove files from memory.

Reminders

- Use the operating system's ERASE or DEL command to remove a large number of files. From within 1-2-3, select the /System command, use ERASE or DEL at the system prompt, and return to 1-2-3 by typing **exit** and pressing Enter.

- Before you use /FE, use /File Directory to specify the drive designation and the directory that contains the file(s) you want to erase.

- You cannot restore an erased file. Before you erase a file, be sure that you do not need it.

Procedures

1. Type /fe

2. Select the type of file you want to erase:

Menu Item	Description
Worksheet	Displays worksheet files with .WK extensions as specified by /wgdel
Print	Displays ASCII text files created with /Print or another program. The file extension must be .PRN.
Graph	Displays files created with /Graph, which end with the extension .PIC or .CGM
Other	Displays all files in the current drive and directory

3. Type the path and the name of the file, or use the arrow keys to highlight the file you want to erase.

4. Press Enter.

5. By selecting **Yes** or **No** from the menu, verify that you do or do not want to erase the file.

Important Cues

- You can erase files from different drives or directories either by specifying the drive designation, path, and file name or by changing the settings with /File Directory.

- Press Name (F3) at Step 3 to see a full-screen listing of files.

For more information, see /File Directory, /File List, and Chapter 7.

File List   /FL

Purpose

Displays all file names of a specific type that are stored on the current drive and directory.

/fl displays the size of the file (in bytes) and the date and time the file was created.

Reminder

Use /File List to select different directories and display the current files.

Procedures

1. Type /fl

2. Select the type of file you want to display:

Menu Item	Description
Worksheet	Displays worksheet files with .WK extensions as specified by /wgdel
Print	Displays ASCII text files created with /Print or another program. The file extension must be .PRN.
Graph	Displays files created with /Graph, which end with the extension .PIC or .CGM
Other	Displays all files in the current drive and directory
Active	Displays all files in memory
Linked	Displays all files linked to the current file

3. Use the arrow keys to highlight individual file names and display their specific information. If the list of file names extends off the screen, use the arrow keys, PgDn, or PgUp to display the file names.

4. Display files from a different directory by moving the cursor to a directory name (such as \BUDGET) and pressing Enter. Move to a parent directory by pressing Backspace.

5. Press Enter to return to the worksheet.

Important Cues

- Use the /File Admin Table command to create a list of file information on the current worksheet. Be sure that you are in a blank part of the worksheet before you create a table; otherwise, data will be erased.

- Use /fl to check your file listing before you use /File Erase. You don't want to erase files that are linked to files you still use.

- 1-2-3 displays the date and time each file was created so that you can find the most recent version of a file. (Date and time values are accurate only if you supply the correct entries at start-up. Date and time values can be reset at the system prompt through the DATE and TIME commands.)

For more information, see /File Erase, /File Directory, and Chapter 7.

File Import   */FI*

Purpose

Brings ASCII text files from other programs into 1-2-3 worksheets.

Many software programs use ASCII files to exchange data with other programs. Most databases, word processors, and spreadsheets have a method of printing ASCII files to disk.

Reminders

- Remember that you can use /File Import two different ways to transfer data into a 1-2-3 worksheet. The first method reads each row of ASCII characters as left-aligned labels in a column; the second method reads into separate cells text enclosed in quotation marks, or numbers surrounded by spaces or separated by commas.

- Be sure that you have enough room on the worksheet to receive the imported data; incoming characters replace the current cell contents. One row in an ASCII file is equal to one row on the worksheet. The number of columns depends on whether the incoming ASCII data is pure text (a single column) or delimited text (multiple columns).

- ASCII files must have the extension .PRN. If you want to import a text file that does not have the .PRN extension, use the operating system's RENAME command to change the extension.

Procedures

1. Before you issue /fi, move the cursor to the upper-left corner of the range in which you want to import data.

2. Type /fi

3. Choose how to import the ASCII file:

Menu Item	Description
Text	Makes each row of characters in the ASCII file a left-aligned label in the worksheet. Labels will be in a single column from the cell pointer down.
Numbers	Enters each row of characters in the ASCII file into a row in the worksheet. Text enclosed in quotation marks is assigned to a cell as a label. Numbers surrounded by a space or separated by commas are assigned to a cell as values. Other characters are ignored.

4. Select or type the name of the ASCII print file. Do not type the .PRN extension.

5. Press Enter.

Important Cues

- 1-2-3 cannot import ASCII files that have more than 8,192 rows. Lines longer than 512 characters wrap to the next worksheet row. If necessary, you can use a word processor to read, modify, and divide the ASCII files into smaller files before saving them to disk as ASCII files.

- Display ASCII files by using the operating system's TYPE command.

- You can print the ASCII file by pressing Ctrl-P before issuing the operating system's TYPE command. To disconnect the printer, press Ctrl-P again when printing is complete.

- You can separate ASCII text files that are not delimited by quotation marks or commas. Use /File Import Text to bring the file into the worksheet. Use /Data Parse to separate the resulting long label into separate cells of data.

Cautions

- Incoming data replaces existing cell contents. If you are unsure of the size of the file you are importing, use the operating system's TYPE command to review the ASCII file.

- Word processing files contain special control codes that 1-2-3 cannot handle. Be sure to save your word processing document as an ASCII file before you try to import it into 1-2-3.

*For more information, see /**Data Parse** and Chapter 7.*

File Dir

/FD

Purpose

Changes the current disk drive or directory for the current work session.

Reminder

Sketching how your directories and subdirectories are arranged on your hard disk makes /fd easier to use. Include the types of files stored in different directories.

Procedures

1. Type /fd

2. If the displayed drive and directory are correct, press Enter. If you want to change the settings, type a new drive letter and directory name; then press Enter.

Important Cues

- Access another drive and directory temporarily by selecting /fr or /fs and pressing Esc twice to clear the current drive and directory from the command line. Then type the drive designator and directory name, including a final backslash (\ ). You then can either type a file name or press Enter to see a list of file names on that drive or directory; move the cursor and press Enter to select a name from the list.

- Access another directory on the same drive by selecting /fr or /fs and pressing the Backspace key as many times as necessary to clear the current directory from the command line. Then type the directory name, including a final backslash (\ ). You then can either type a file name or press Enter to see a list of file names on that drive or directory; move the cursor and press Enter to select a name from the list.

- Display current file names and directories by selecting /File List, choosing Other, and pressing Name (F3). Press Backspace to go to the parent directory.

- You can change 1-2-3's start-up drive and directory by using /Worksheet Global Default Dir to enter a new drive or directory. Save this new setting to the System disk by using /wgdu.

Caution

When specifying drive letters and path names, be sure to enter the correct symbols. The most common mistakes include using a semicolon (;) instead of a colon (:) after the drive designator, using a slash (/) instead of a backslash (\ ) between subdirectory names, and inserting spaces in names.

For more information, see **/Worksheet Global Default Update**, **/File List**, **/File Retrieve**, **/File Save**, *and Chapter 7.*

File New /FN

Purpose

Creates a new blank file on disk and positions a new worksheet on-screen either before or after the current file.

Reminders

- The new file contains one blank worksheet. The cell pointer will appear at A1.

- Current files remain in memory.

- Use the /**File Open** command to open existing files without deleting files currently in memory.

Procedures

1. Move the cell pointer to a file that will be adjacent to the new file's location.

2. Type /fn

3. Choose the location for the new file:

Menu Item	Description
Before	Places the new file before the current file
After	Places the new file after the current file

4. Type a new file name to replace the default name given by 1-2-3.

5. Press Enter.

Important Cue

After entering data in the worksheet, you must use /**File Save** to save the worksheet to disk if you want to use the worksheet later.

*For more information, see /**File Open**, /**File Save**, and Chapter 7.*

File Open /FO

Purpose

Opens a file from disk into memory without removing active files.

You choose whether the file opens before or after the current file. The cell pointer positions itself in the file at the same address that the cell pointer was at when the file was saved.

Reminder

Move to a file and its worksheet that are adjacent to where you want the opened file to appear.

Procedures

1. Type /fo

2. Choose the location for the file to be opened:

Menu Item	Description
Before	Places the new file before the current file
After	Places the new file after the current file

3. Specify the name of the file by typing or highlighting the name with the left- or right-arrow key. Press Name (F3) to see all the names.

Important Cues

- Files saved with a password require a password entered exactly as originally recorded.

- Files under reservation will prompt **Yes** or **No**. Press Y if you want to open the file (you must save it under a different name). Press N if you do not want to open the file.

- Close unneeded files if there is not enough memory to open the files you want.

- Use /File **New** to open a new blank file in memory.

Caution

The opened file controls recalculation and window settings for all active files.

*For more information, see /**File Retrieve**, /**File New**, and Chapter 7.*

File Admin Reservation   */FAR*

Purpose

Controls the reservation status of a file. If more than one person has access to a file in a network, /File Admin Reservation controls how the file is shared.

Reminder

/File Admin Reservation enables you to get or release a file's reservation so that you can make changes to a file and save it under the original file name. You also can change the file setting so that the first person opening or retrieving the file will automatically get the file reservation.

Procedures

1. Type /far

2. Choose one of the following commands:

Menu Item	Description
Get	Gets the file reservation for you after you have opened or retrieved the file and if no one has changed the file on disk since you opened it into memory. The read-only indicator (RO) disappears from screen.
Release	Releases the file reservation so that others can get the reservation. The read-only indicator (RO) appears on-screen.
Setting	Provides two options:

Automatic

Gives the file reservation to the first person to open or retrieve the file

Manual

Requires the user to issue the /farg command to get the reservation

3. If you changed the file setting, use /File Save to save the file and its new setting.

Important Cues

- Use /File Admin Seal to prevent unauthorized users from changing the setting.

- If you requested to get the reservation, but it was not available, a message appears to that effect.

- The /File Save command with the [ALL MODIFIED FILES] prompt saves active files only when you have the reservations for all files. Use the /farg command to get the reservations you need.

Caution

Do not release the reservation until you have saved your changes with /File Save. Releasing the reservation prevents you from making changes to the original file on disk.

*For more information, see /**File Admin Seal** and Chapter 7.*

File Admin Table /FAT

Purpose

Enters a table of files on the worksheet. You select which type of files will be in the table.

Reminder

To set up the table, first find on the worksheet an area that is blank or unneeded. Information in the table will overwrite information in the same worksheet location.

Procedures

1. Move the cell pointer to an area where the table will not destroy needed information.

2. Type /fat

3. Choose one of the following commands:

Menu Item	Description
Worksheet	Enters a table of worksheet files
Print	Enters a table of .PRN files
Graph	Enters a table of .CGM or .PIC graph files
Other	Enters a table of all files
Active	Enters a table of active files
Linked	Enters a table of files linked to the current file

3. If you choose Worksheet, Print, Graph, or Other, press Enter to enter a table for the current directory. If you want a table from another directory, type a different directory and press Enter.

4. Highlight the range where you want the table.

5. Press Enter.

Important Cues

- Use /File List to see file information without creating a table on your worksheet.

- The table will contain as many rows as there are files, plus one. Disk files or linked files use four columns. Active files use seven columns.

- The table columns for disk-based files are in the following order: file name, date, time, and file size. Use the /Range Format command to format the date and time columns so that their entries appear as dates or times.

- The table columns for active files are in the following order: file name, date, time, file size, number of worksheets in the file, modified file attribute, and file reservation attribute. A modified file attribute of 1 means that the file has been modified since you read it into memory; 0 means that the file is unmodified. A file reservation attribute of 1 means that you have the file reservation; 0 means that you do not.

- The /File Admin Table command is an excellent way to read file information into a worksheet so that macros can operate on selected files.

- A table of linked files shows the path name for each linked file, if the path was included in the linking formula.

- The graph or worksheet files are selected for listing by their file extensions. The file extensions selected are set by the /Worksheet Global Default Graph and /Worksheet Global Default Ext List settings.

Caution

Information in the table will overwrite information in the worksheet. If you are unsure how many files will be in a table, limit the length of the table range in Step 4 of the procedure.

*For more information, see /**File Admin Reservation**, /**File List**, and Chapter 7.*

File Admin Seal   /FAS

Purpose

Protects a file's format or its file reservation setting from being changed.

Reminders

- Sealing a file also seals the settings that result from these commands:

/File Admin Reservation-Setting	/Range Name Note
/Graph Name	/Range Prot
/Print Name	/Range Unprot
/Range Format	/Worksheet Column
/Range Label	/Worksheet Global
/Range Name	/Worksheet Hide

- To set up a file for data entry yet protect formulas and macros, use /Range Unprot to mark ranges to receive data; then choose /Worksheet Global Prot to enable worksheet protection. Seal the file to prevent unauthorized changes to the protected ranges.

- The network administrator should use /File Admin Seal Reservation-Setting to prevent unauthorized changes to the file reservation settings.

Procedures

1. Type /fas

2. Choose one of the following commands:

Menu Item	Description
File	Puts a seal on the current file and its reservation setting
Reservation-Setting	Puts a seal only on the reservation setting for the current file

Menu Item	Description
Disable	Removes the seal from the current file and its reservation setting

3. Type a password and press Enter.

4. If you are sealing the file or reservation setting, reenter the password and press Enter.

Important Cue

Ensure that the file is correctly formatted and well tested before putting a seal on it.

Cautions

- Use memorable passwords, but don't make them public. Keep backup copies of passwords with an alternate PC administrator or manager.

- In passwords, an uppercase letter and the corresponding lowercase letter are considered different characters. Remember exactly how you type the password, and always use that form.

For more information, see **/File Admin Reservation Setting**, **/Range Unprot**, **/Range Prot**, **/Worksheet Global Prot**, *and Chapters 4 and 7.*

File Admin Link-Refresh   /FAL

Purpose

Recalculates, in the active files, formulas that depend upon data in other active files or files on disk. Link-Refresh ensures that your worksheet is using current data when all the files are not active or are shared among users.

Procedures

Type /fal

Important Cue

Use the /File List Linked command to see whether other files are linked into the current file.

Caution

If the current file is linked to other files that may have changed, use Link-Refresh before printing or reviewing the final results. If you do not use Link-Refresh, your current file's results may be incorrect.

For more information, see **/File List Linked** *and Chapter 7.*

Print Commands /P

Prints worksheet contents as values or formulas.

Use /pp to send output to the printer; use /pf to send output (as an ASCII file) to disk and control the print queue; use /pe to send a print-encoded file to disk.

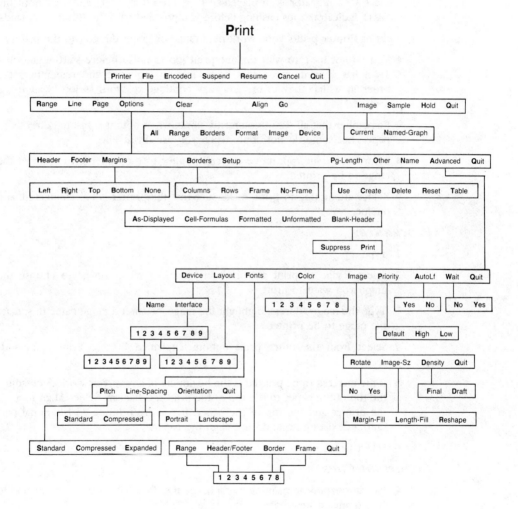

Print Printer */PP*

Purpose

Prints worksheet contents (values or formulas) and graphs to the printer.

Reminders

- Before you print, check the lower-right corner of the screen to see whether the CALC indicator is displayed. If it is, press Calc (F9) and wait until the WAIT indicator stops flashing before you proceed with the /Print commands.

- /Print Printer prints your worksheet range or graph directly to the printer.

- You do not have to wait for one print job to finish before starting another. 1-2-3 has a print queue that keeps jobs in sequence and remembers the order in which they print. You may continue to work as jobs wait to be printed.

- Remember that all /Print commands apply when output is printed directly to paper, but some do not apply when you use /Print File.

- Before you issue /pp, move the cell pointer to the upper-left corner of the range to be printed.

- Before attempting to print, make sure that the printer is on, connected, and on-line.

Procedures

1. Type /pp

2. Select **R**ange to print a worksheet range, or select **I**mage to choose the graph you want to print.

3. Type the range address, highlight the range, or enter a range name to specify the range to be printed.

4. Select from the other print options explained in the /Print commands section.

5. If the material to be printed is the beginning of a report or worksheet, adjust the top of the paper to the top of the print mechanism. Select **A**lign to align the printer and the top of the paper. If you are printing an additional part onto an existing page, do not align the paper.

6. Select **G**o to print.

Important Cues

- For information on printing a graph, see the /Print [**P**, **E**] Image command in the Command Reference.

- You can use 1-2-3's /Print commands to set formats for your reports. Use commands from /Print [**P**, **F**, **E**] Options to control formats for printing.

- Print an ASCII text file to disk by using /**Print File**. Most popular software programs, including word processing and database programs, can import ASCII text files.

Caution

Do not manually adjust paper in the printer once the **Align** command has been given. Use the **Line** or **Page** command to move paper after it is aligned. Moving paper manually misaligns the paper and 1-2-3's line counter, resulting in large blank spaces in your printout.

*For more information, see /**Print File**, /**Print [Printer, File, Encoded] Range**, and Chapter 8.*

Print File   /PF

Purpose

Prints worksheet contents as an ASCII text file to disk.

ASCII text files are a common means of transferring data to and from different software packages.

Reminders

- Before you print the file, check the lower-right corner of the screen to see whether the CALC indicator is displayed. If it is, press Calc (F9) and wait until the WAIT indicator stops flashing before you proceed with the /**Print** commands.

- Before you issue /pf, move the cell pointer to the upper-left corner of the range to be printed.

- You do not have to wait for one print job to finish before you start another. 1-2-3 has a print queue that keeps jobs in sequence and remembers the order in which they print. You may continue to work as jobs wait to be printed.

- Before attempting to print, make sure that the printer is on, connected, and on-line.

Procedures

To create an ASCII file for use in word processing, follow these steps:

1. Type /pf

2. Respond to the following screen prompt:

   Enter name of print file:

   Limit the file name to eight characters (don't use spaces). 1-2-3 automatically gives the file name a .PRN extension.

3. Select **R**ange.

4. Type the range address, highlight the range, or use a range name to specify the range to be printed to disk.

5. Select **O**ptions **M**argins. Set the top, left, and bottom margins to zero; set the right margin to 255.

6. Select **O**ther **U**nformatted to remove headers, footers, and page breaks. (These print options can cause extra work in reformatting when the file is imported by another program.)

7. Select **G**o from the second-level **P**rint menu.

To create an ASCII file to be used with a database program, follow these steps:
1. Reset all numbers and dates to a format understood by the database you are using.

2. Set column widths so that all data is displayed. Note the column position in which each column begins and ends.

3. Type /pf and specify a file name.

4. Select **R**ange.

5. Specify the range to be printed; you may not want to include field names at the top of databases. Specify the range by typing the range address, highlighting the range, or using an assigned range name.

6. Select **O**ptions **M**argins. Set the top, left, and bottom margins to zero; set the right margin to 255.

7. Select **O**ther **U**nformatted to remove headers, footers, and page breaks.

8. Select **G**o from the second-level **P**rint menu.

Important Cues

- 1-2-3 will not print a graph to a .PRN file. To export a graph to a graphics program, save the graph with a picture file format (.PIC) or metafile format (.CGM).

- To add multiple ranges of data to an ASCII text file, stay in the **P**rint menu; continue to choose new ranges and to select **G**o. The additional ranges append to the end of the ASCII text file you named with /**P**rint **F**ile. When you quit the **P**rint menu, all final text ranges are printed to the ASCII file, and the file is closed so that you can no longer append data.

- To see an ASCII text file on-screen, return to the operating system. At the operating-system prompt, type the command TYPE, press the space bar, and type the path name and the name of the ASCII text file you want to review. For example, after the prompt (C>), you could enter

   TYPE C:\123\BUDGET\VARIANCE.PRN

Press Ctrl-S to stop the data from scrolling off the screen. Press the space bar to continue scrolling.

- Before you print the file to disk, make sure that the columns are wide enough to display all the data. If a column is too narrow, values are changed to asterisks, and labels are truncated.

- Refer to your word processor's documentation for instructions on importing ASCII files. Refer to your database's documentation for instructions on importing column-delimited ASCII files.

Caution

Different database programs accept data in different formats; check to see in what form dates are imported and whether the receiving program accepts blank cells. Be sure to prepare your 1-2-3 file accordingly before printing to an ASCII file. As a general rule, remove numeric formats and align labels to the left before you print the data to disk. Because of an error in 1-2-3's method of calculating serial date numbers, dates in General format may be one day different from dates used in your database. If the right margin setting is too low, data may be moved to a following page when the file is printed to disk.

*For more information, see /**Print Printer**, /**Print [Printer, File, Encoded] Range**, and Chapter 8.*

Print Encoded   /PE

Purpose

Prints worksheet contents (values or formulas) and graphs to an encoded file for later printing.

Reminders

- Before you print, check the lower-right corner of the screen to see whether the CALC indicator is displayed. If it is, press Calc (F9) and wait until the WAIT indicator stops flashing before you proceed with the /Print commands.

- Remember that all /Print commands apply when output is printed directly to paper, but some do not apply when you use /Print Encoded.

- Before you issue /pe, move the cell pointer to the upper-left corner of the range to be printed.

- /Print Encoded creates a file on disk that can later be sent to a printer through the operating system's COPY command.

Procedures

1. Type /pe

2. Respond to the screen prompt Enter name of encoded file:. 1-2-3 will automatically add the file extension .ENC.

3. Select **R**ange to print a worksheet range, or select **I**mage to choose the graph you want to print.

4. Type the range address, highlight the range, or enter a range name to specify the range to be printed.

5. Select from the other print options explained in this section.

6. If the material to be printed is the beginning of a report or worksheet, adjust the top of the paper to the top of the print mechanism. Select **A**lign to align the printer and the top of the paper. If you are printing an additional part onto an existing page, do not align the paper.

7. Select **G**o to print.

Important Cues

- For information on printing a graph, see the /Print [P, E] Image command in the Command Reference.

- You can use 1-2-3's print commands to set formats for your reports. Use commands from /Print [P, F, E] Options to control formats for printing.

- Print an ASCII text file to disk by using /Print File. Most popular software programs, including word processing and database programs, can import ASCII text files.

- You can print an encoded file by copying it to the printer at any time, whether or not 1-2-3 is in use. This capability is useful if you need to use a printer that isn't available where your PC is. When you create the .ENC file, ensure that the designated printer is the same type that the file will later be copied to. Once a file has been created, use the COPY command to copy the encoded file to the printer. For example, to copy the FRCST.ENC file in the C:\123 directory to the printer on the first parallel port, use the command

    COPY C:\123\FRCST.ENC/B LPT1

    Do not forget the /B part of the command. PostScript or Apple LaserWriter printers may be connected to a serial port. In this case, use COM1 or COM2 instead of LPT1 or LPT2.

Caution

Do not manually adjust paper in the printer once the Align command has been given. Use the Line or Page command to move paper once it is aligned. Moving paper manually misaligns the paper and 1-2-3's line counter, resulting in large blank spaces in your printout.

For more information, see Chapter 8.

Print Suspend

/PS

Purpose

Suspends (temporarily stops) the printer on the current print job.

1-2-3 may have in a queue more than one print job waiting to be printed. A print queue prints jobs in the "background" as you continue to work with the 1-2-3 worksheet or graph in the "foreground." This arrangement increases your efficiency with the computer.

Reminder

A printer may continue to print for a short time after the Suspend command is issued. The reason is that data has already been sent to and is stored in the printer.

Procedure

Type /ps

Important Cues

- Suspending print jobs in the queue increases the performance of your operations and calculations in 1-2-3.

- Use the **/Print Cancel** command to cancel all print jobs.

*For more information, see **/Print Resume**, **/Print Cancel**, and Chapter 8.*

Print Resume

/PR

Purpose

Resumes printing after the queue has been suspended.

Reminder

Use **Resume** to restart the printer if it is waiting for the next sheet of paper.

Procedure

Type /pr

Caution

Resume clears any printer error messages.

*For more information, see **/Print Printer Options Advanced Wait**, **/Worksheet Global Default Printer Wait**, **/Print Suspend**, and Chapter 8.*

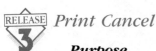

Print Cancel   /PC

Purpose

Cancels the current job in the printer and removes all other print jobs from the queue.

Important Cues

- Some printers contain memory called a *buffer* to store pages about to be printed. If you cancel a job, one or more pages that remain in the printer's buffer may still print. To clear them, turn the printer off, pause, and then turn it back on.

- Canceling print jobs in the queue increases the performance of your operations and calculations in 1-2-3.

- /pc realigns the printer and paper for the next job in the queue.

Procedure

Type /pc

Caution

Printing may not stop when canceled if you are printing to a shared printer on a network. Refer to your network administrator for assistance.

*For more information, see /**Print Suspend** and Chapter 8.*

Print [Printer, File, Encoded]   /PPR or /PFR
Range   or /PER

Purpose

Defines the area of the worksheet to be printed.

Reminders

- Check the lower-right corner of the screen to see whether the CALC indicator is displayed. If it is, press Calc (F9) and wait until the WAIT indicator stops flashing before you proceed with the /Print commands.

- Before you print, move the cell pointer to the upper-left corner of the range to be printed.

Procedures

To define the worksheet area to be printed, follow these steps:

1. Type /pp to print directly to the printer; type /pf to print to disk; or type /pe to print an encoded file that can later be copied to a printer. Specify a file name if one is requested. 1-2-3 adds the appropriate file extension for File or Encoded files.

2. Select **R**ange.

3. Type the range address, highlight the range, or enter an assigned range name to specify the range to be printed. You can enter a single range, multiple ranges, or a named graph. The following table shows sample entries:

Range Type	Example	Description
Single range	B12..R56 or MONTH_RPT	One range per print job
Multiple range	B12..R56;MONTH_ RPT	Multiple ranges within a single print job. You separate ranges with a semicolon (;).
Named graph	*BDGTGRF or B12..R56;*BDGTGRF	Graph or graph and worksheet in a single print job. Precede the named graph with an asterisk (*).

4. Verify that the range is correct and press Enter.

Important Cues

- /**P**rint [**P, F, E**] **R**ange "remembers" the last print range used, which means that you can reprint the specified worksheet portion without reentering the range. You also can edit existing print ranges.

- Hidden columns within a print range do not print.

- To display the current print range, select **R**ange from the second-level **P**rint menu. The status line displays the current range address, and the specified range is highlighted on the screen.

- To display each corner of the range, press the period key (**.**). Each time you press the period key, the next corner is displayed.

- Use /**P**rint [**P, F, E**] **O**ptions **B**orders to print headings at the top or side of every printed page. Use this technique, for example, when you want to print database field names at the top of every page.

- Use /**W**orksheet **P**age to insert mandatory page breaks in a range.

- After a range has been printed, 1-2-3 does not advance the paper to the top of the next page. Instead, 1-2-3 waits for you to print another range. To advance the paper, use the **P**age command in the second-level **P**rint menu.

- If the print range is wider than the distance between the left and right margins, the remaining characters are printed on the following page (if printed to paper) or in the rows below the data (if printed to disk).

Caution

If you want long text labels to print, ensure that they are completely within the highlighted range. Highlighting only the cell containing text does not print text that extends beyond the cell.

For more information, see /Worksheet Page, /Print Printer, /Print File, and Chapter 8.

Print [Printer, File, Encoded] Line   /PPL or /PFL or /PEL

Purpose

Inserts blank lines. Use this command to put spaces between ranges on the same paper or between graphs and print ranges.

Reminder

/Print File Line puts a blank line on paper or in the .ENC or .PRN file.

Procedures

1. Type /pp or /pf or /pe

2. Select Line to advance the paper one line or to insert a blank line in a file. Repeat the keystroke (or press Enter) as many times as are necessary to advance the paper to the desired position.

Important Cue

Use this command to insert a blank line between printed ranges. You can get paper out of alignment with 1-2-3's internal line count if you change the position of paper in a printer manually (either by turning the platen knob or by pressing the printer's line feed button). Blank lines in the middle of your printed output can signify that the printer and 1-2-3 are out of alignment. To realign the paper and reset 1-2-3, turn off the printer and roll the paper until the top of a page is aligned with the print head. Then turn on the printer again and use /Print Printer Align to reset 1-2-3.

Print [Printer, File, Encoded] Page   /PPP or /PFP or /PEP

Purpose

Ejects the page in the printer or marks the end of the current page in an .ENC or .PRN file. Paper alignment is maintained.

Reminders

- All /Print commands apply when output is printed directly to paper, but some do not apply when output is directed to disk.

- Use /Worksheet Page to create a page break in a worksheet. When you print the worksheet, a new page will begin at the page break.

Procedures

1. Type /pp or /pf or /pe

2. Select Page to advance to the next page and print the footer at the bottom of the page.

Important Cue

If the top of the paper is not in line with the print head when the paper is advanced, manually move the paper into position and reset 1-2-3 with /Print Printer Align.

Cautions

- The length of the printed page may not match the length of the paper. Check the paper-length settings with /Print [P, F, E] Options Pg-Length. This problem also occurs when the page-length setting does not match the number-of-lines-per-inch setting.

- The paper in the printer can get out of alignment if you manually advance the paper to the top of the next page. This misalignment causes printing over the paper serration and blanks in the middle of the page. To realign the paper and reset 1-2-3, turn off the printer and roll the paper until the top of a page is aligned with the print head. Then turn on the printer again and use /Print Printer Align to reset 1-2-3.

Print [Printer, File, Encoded] Options Header

/PPOH or /PFOH or /PEOH

Purpose

Prints a header below the top margin on each page. Use the Header option to print page numbers and dates in the heading. Two blank lines are inserted after the header.

Reminders

- Use /Print [P, F, E] Options Borders to print column headings above data.

- A header uses the three lines below the top margin.

Procedures

1. Type /pp or /pf or /pe

2. Select **H**eader.

3. Type a header as wide as the margin and paper width allow. The header can be up to 512 characters wide.

4. Press Enter.

Important Cues

- The date and page number can be printed automatically in a header. Enter an at sign (@) where you want the date to appear; enter a pound sign (#) where you want the page number. The # causes page numbering to begin with 1 and increase by 1 sequentially. Page numbering restarts at 1 whenever you issue an **A**lign command.

- Break the header into as many as three centered segments by entering a vertical bar (|) between segments. For example, to print at page 21 a three-segment header that uses the computer's internal date of June 30, 1989, enter the following:

  @|Hill and Dale XeriLandscaping|Page #

  The header appears as:

  30-Jun-89   Hill and Dale XeriLandscaping   Page 21

- To start page numbers at a specific number, use a ## (double-pound sign) followed by the starting number—for example, ##10 to start the page numbering at 10.

- Create a header from cell contents by typing a backslash (\) in the header, followed by the cell reference that contains header information. Typing \B12, for example, creates a header out of the information in B12. This capability cannot be used in combination with other header data, and the cell contents will only left-align in the header.

- Use /Print [**P**, **F**, **E**] **O**ptions **B**orders **R**ows to select worksheet rows that will be printed above the data on each page. The **B**orders command is especially useful for printing database column headings above the data on each page.

Caution

Headers longer than margin settings print on the following page.

For more information, see /Print [Printer, File, Encoded] Options Margins, /Print [Printer, File, Encoded] Options Borders, /Print [Printer, File, Encoded] Options Setup, and Chapter 8.

Print [Printer, File, Encoded]   */PPOF or /PFOF*
Options Footer   *or /PEOF*

Purpose

Prints a footer above the bottom margin of each page.

Reminders

- Use /Print [**P, F, E**] **O**ptions **F**ooter to print, for example, a title, department heading, or identifier. Footers can be used to print page numbers and dates automatically.

- Footers reduce the size of the printed area by three rows.

Procedures

1. Type /pp or /pf or /pe

2. Select **F**ooter.

3. You can type a footer that is as wide as the margin and paper width allow. The footer can be up to 512 characters wide. Characters exceeding the margin width print on another page.

4. Press Enter.

Important Cues

- Use the same cues as reported in **O**ptions **H**eaders for creating footers that insert the date, page numbers, or data contained in cells.

- Footers occupy one line. Two blank lines are left between a footer and the body copy. The footer prints on the line above the bottom margin.

*For more information, see /**Print [Printer, File, Encoded] Options Header**, /**Print [Printer, File, Encoded] Options Margins**, /**Print [Printer, File, Encoded] Options Borders**, and /**Print [Printer, File, Encoded] Options Setup**.*

Print [Printer, File, Encoded]   */PPOM or /PFOM*
Options Margins   *or /PEOM*

Purpose

Changes the left, right, top, and bottom margins from the default margin settings.

Reminder

If you are not sure how margins align on the paper, turn the printer off and on to reposition the print head to the zero position. Adjust the paper so that the left paper edge and the top of the paper align with the print head. Choose the **Align** command from the second-level **Print** menu. Now print a sample worksheet and check alignment.

Procedures

1. Type /pp or /pf or /pe

2. Select **Margins**. Specify margins from these options:

Menu Item	Description
Left	Sets 0 to 1,000 characters
Right	Sets greater than the left margin but not larger than 1,000
Top	Sets 0 to 240 lines
Bottom	Sets 0 to 240 lines
None	Sets the left, top, and bottom margins to 0 and the right margin to 100

Important Cues

- Most nonproportional fonts print at 10 characters per horizontal inch and 6 lines per vertical inch. Standard 8 1/2-by-11-inch paper is 85 characters wide and 66 lines long.

- You do not have to change margin settings if you use 1-2-3 commands to change between different character print modes. For example, if the print settings were for normal 10-pitch characters and then you select **Options Advanced Layout Pitch Compressed**, the margins automatically compensate for the smaller characters.

- The size of a graph can be determined by the margins. Be sure that you set at least a right margin when printing graphs.

- When you want to print to disk, remember that you should set the left margin to 0 and the right margin to 255. These settings remove blank spaces on the left side of each row. Setting the right margin to 255 ensures that the maximum number of characters per row will be printed to disk.

- Before printing to disk, select **None** for margins and **/Print File Options Other Unformatted** to remove page breaks, headers, and footers. Page breaks, headers, and footers will confuse data transfer to a database. If you are importing the file to a word processor, use the word processor to insert margins, page breaks, headers, and footers.

Caution

If the line length is too short for the characters in a printed line, the additional characters are printed on the following page. To get a full-width print, use a condensed print setup string.

For more information, see /Print File and /Print [Printer, File, Encoded] Options Setup, and Chapter 8.

Print [Printer, File, Encoded]   */PPOB or /PFOB*
Options Borders   *or /PEOB*

Purpose

Prints row or column headings from the worksheet on every page of the printout.

Use row borders to print database field names as headings at the top of each page. Use column borders to print worksheet labels at the left of each page.

When specifying your print range, do not include the rows or columns containing the borders. Doing so causes the row or column borders to print twice, once from the print range and again from **Options Borders**.

Reminders

- Before you issue /ppob or /pfob, move the cell pointer to the leftmost column of headings or to the top row of headings on the worksheet that you want repeated.

- The Borders command does not print borders around ranges or graphs.

Procedures

1. Type /ppob or /pfob or /peob

2. Select from these menu items:

Menu Item	Description
Columns	Prints the selected columns at the left side of each page
Rows	Prints the selected rows at the top of each page
Frame	Prints the row and column frame around the top and left of the printed range
No-Frame	Removes the frame

3. If necessary, press Esc to remove the current range. Move the cell pointer to the top row of the rows you want to use as a border or to the leftmost column you want to use. Press the period key (.) to anchor the first corner of the border. Then move the cell pointer, highlighting down for more rows or to the right for more columns.

4. Press Enter.

Important Cue

Including borders is useful when you want to print multiple pages. If you want to print sections of a wide worksheet, you can further condense the columns by using /Worksheet Column Hide to hide blank or unnecessary columns.

Cautions

- If you include in the print range the rows or columns specified as borders, the rows or columns will be printed twice.

- When you use /Print [P, F, E] Options Borders Columns or Rows, the cell pointer's current location becomes a border automatically. To clear the border selection, use /Print [P, F, E] Clear Borders.

Print [Printer, Encoded]   */PPOS or /PEOS*
 Options Setup

Purpose

Controls from within 1-2-3 the printing features offered by some printers.

The command gives you printing features controllable at the printer and not available through the /Print [P, E] Options Advanced commands. Such features may include underlining or strike-through.

Before using setup strings, check the /Print [Printer, Encoded] Options Advanced commands to see whether an equivalent command is available.

Reminders

- Your printer manual contains lists of printer setup codes (also known as *printer control codes* or *escape codes*). These codes may be shown two ways: as a decimal ASCII number representing a keyboard character, or as the Escape key (Esc) followed by a character.

- 1-2-3 setup strings include decimal number codes (entered as three-digit numbers), preceded by a backslash (\). For example, the EPSON printer control code for condensed print is 15. The 1-2-3 setup string is \015.

- Some codes start with the Esc character, followed by other characters. Because the Esc character cannot be typed in the setup string, the ASCII decimal number for Esc (27) is used instead. For example, the EPSON printer code for emphasized print is

    Esc "E"

    In the 1-2-3 setup string, enter Esc "E" as \027E.

- Some printers retain previous control codes. Before sending a new code to the printer, clear the previous codes by turning your printer off and then on. You also can send the printer a reset code (\027@ for EPSON-compatible printers). Put the reset code in front of the new code you send. For example, the 1-2-3 printer setup string that resets previous codes and switches to emphasized printing mode is

\027@\027E

Procedures

1. Type /ppos or /peos

2. Enter the setup string. If a setup string has already been entered, press Esc to clear the string. Each string must begin with a backslash (\). Upper- or lowercase letters must be typed as shown in your printer's manual.

3. Press Enter.

Important Cues

- Setup strings can be up to 512 characters long.

- You cannot combine some character sets or print modes. Your printer manual may list combinations that will work for your printer.

- Do not combine setup strings with the Advanced menu commands. The result can be unpredictable.

- Use embedded setup strings in the print range to change printing features by row. Move the cell pointer to the leftmost cell in the print range row where you want the printing to change. Insert a row with /Worksheet Insert Row. Type two vertical bars (Shift-\), and then type the appropriate setup string. Note that only one vertical bar displays. This setup string applies to all following rows. The row containing the double vertical bars does not print.

- When reading setup strings from the printer manual, don't confuse zero (0) with the letter O, or one (1) with the letter l.

- If you get the same several nonsense characters at the top of every printed page, you probably have those nonsense characters in your setup string.

Caution

Some printers retain the most recent printer control code. Clear the last code by turning off the printer for approximately five seconds or by preceding each setup string with the printer reset code. The reset code for EPSON-compatible printers is \027@.

For more information, see /Print [Printer, Encoded] Sample, /Print [Printer, Encoded] Options Advanced Fonts, /Print [Printer, Encoded] Options Advanced Layout, and Chapter 8.

Print [Printer, File, Encoded] Options Pg-Length

/PPOP or /PFOP
or /PEOP

Purpose

Specifies the number of lines per page by using a standard 6 lines per inch of page height.

Reminders

- Setting the lines per inch with a setup string creates an incorrect number of lines per page from this command. This command assumes 6 lines per inch.

- Determine the printing area available for body copy by taking the page height at 6 lines per inch and subtracting the top and bottom margins. Also subtract 3 lines for each header and footer.

Procedures

1. Type /ppop or /pfop or /peop

2. Enter the number of lines per page if that number is different from the number shown. The page length can be 1 to 1,000 lines.

3. Press Enter.

Important Cue

Most printers print 6 lines per inch unless the ratio is changed with a setup string (printer control code). At 6 lines per inch, 11-inch paper has 66 lines, and 14-inch paper has 84 lines.

For more information, see **/Print [Printer, File, Encoded] Options Margins**, **/Print [Printer, Encoded] Options Setup**, *and Chapter 8.*

Print [Printer, File, Encoded] Options Other

/PPOO or /PFOO
or /PEOO

Purpose

Selects the form and formatting in which cells print. Worksheet contents can be printed as displayed on-screen or as formulas. You can print either option with or without formatting features.

Reminders

- As-Displayed (the default setting) is used with Formatted for printing reports and data.

- Use Cell-Formulas with Formatted to show formulas and cell contents. (Cell-Formulas often is used for documentation.)

- To print to disk the data to be used in a word processor or database, choose **As-Displayed** with **Unformatted**. If you are printing to disk (creating an ASCII file to export to a word processor or database), set the left, top, and bottom margins to 0 and the right margin to 255.

Procedures

1. Type /ppoo or /pfoo or /peoo

2. Select the type of print from these options:

Menu Item	Description
As-Displayed	Prints the range as displayed on-screen. This is the default setting.
Cell-Formulas	Prints the formula, label, or value contents of each cell on one line of the printout. Contents match information that appears in the control panel: address, protection status, cell format, formula or value, and annotation.
Formatted	Prints with page breaks, headers, and footers. This default setting is normally used for printing to paper.
Unformatted	Prints without page breaks, headers, or footers. This setting is normally used for printing to disk.
Blank-Header	Removes the three blank lines at the top and bottom of each page if you don't use a header or footer. **Suppress** prevents the header and footer from printing. **Print** enables the header and footer to print.

3. Select **Quit** to exit from **Options**.

Important Cues

- Use **Cell-Formulas** to print documentation that shows the formulas and cell settings used to create the worksheet. Figure P.1 shows an example of cell listings printed with **Cell-Formulas**.

- In a **Cell-Formulas** listing may appear codes that indicate cell contents and formatting. *P* indicates a protected cell; *U* indicates an unprotected cell. Other codes, such as *F2* for "fixed to 2 decimal places," are compatible with control panel codes for different formats.

- Document your worksheets by using the **Cell-Formulas** command to print a copy of all formulas. Use /**Range Name Table** to create a table of range names and addresses.

P.1.
A sample cell listing printed with Cell-Formulas.

```
A:B1:   [W11]   '   The Generic Company - Forecast
A:B2:   [W11]   '(Four years ended December 31, 1990)
A:B4:   [W11]   +B23
A:C4:   [W14]   +B4+1
A:D4:   [W14]   +C4+1
A:E4:   [W14]   +D4+1
A:A5:   [W14]   'Sales
A:B5:   (C0)    [W11]   +B24
A:C5:   (C0)    [W14]   +B5+(B5*C25)
A:D5:   (C0)    [W14]   +C5+(C5*D25)
A:E5:   (C0)    [W14]   +D5+(D5*E25)
A:A7:   [W14]   'Cost of Sales
A:B7:   (C0)    [W11]   +B5*$B$26
A:C7:   (C0)    [W14]   +C5*$B$26
A:D7:   (C0)    [W14]   +D5*$B$26
A:E7:   (C0)    [W14]   +E5*$B$26
A:A8:   [W14]   'Gross Profit
A:B8:   (C0)    [W11]   +B5-B7
A:C8:   (C0)    [W14]   +C5-C7
```

- Usually you should select Unformatted for printing to disk. Headers, footers, and page breaks can be added more easily with a word processor than with 1-2-3. Also, use Unformatted on files to be imported to databases. Databases expect ASCII-file data in a consistent order, and headers and footers can disrupt that order.

For more information, see /Print [Printer, File, Encoded] Options Margins and Chapter 8.

Print [Printer, File, Encoded] Options Name

/PPON or /PFON or /PEON

Purpose

You can assign names to print settings you use frequently. These commands help you manage the library of print setting names you create.

Reminder

To ensure that the settings are what you want, do a test print before assigning names.

Procedures

To change print settings to the settings you have previously given a name, do the following:

1. Type /ppo or /pfo or /peo

2. Select **Name Use**.

3. Select the name of the setting you want to print with.

To name a print setting, do the following:

1. Type /ppo or /pfo or /peo

2. Select **Name Create**.

3. Type for the settings a name of 15 characters or fewer. Do not use a double less-than sign (<<). Using an existing name replaces the previous settings for that name with the current settings.

To change settings assigned to an existing name, do the following:

1. Type /ppo or /pfo or /peo

2. Select **Name Use**.

3. Select the name you want to modify.

4. Change settings by using /**Print** commands.

5. Type /pponc or /pfonc or /peonc, as though you were going to create the same name.

6. Select the same name.

To delete a print setting name, do the following:

1. Type /ppo or /pfo or /peo

2. Select **Name Delete**.

3. Select the name you want to delete.

To delete all print setting names in the file, do the following:

1. Make sure that the cell pointer is in the file from which you want to delete names.

2. Type /ppo or /pfo or /peo

3. Select **Name Reset**.

To create a table on the current worksheet containing a list of all the print setting names in the current file, do the following:

1. Move the cell pointer to a blank area in the worksheet that is one column wide and as many rows long as there are print setting names.

2. Type /ppo or /pfo or /peo

3. Select **Name Table**.

4. Press Enter.

Important Cue

If you switch between print settings frequently, write or record a keyboard macro that implements the change to the named settings most frequently used.

Caution

Ensure that you are in the correct file before assigning, deleting, or resetting print names.

For more information, see Chapter 8.

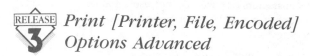 *Print [Printer, File, Encoded]*   */PPOA or /PFOA*
Options Advanced   *or /PEOA*

Purpose

Enables you to use the full printing capabilities of your printer to enhance printing and graphs.

Features accessed through the Advanced option include these:

Feature	Description
AutoLF	Switches between the printer supplying line feeds and 1-2-3 supplying line feeds
Color	Prints color text, if your printer can print color
Device	Changes between printers and printer interfaces that you chose during installation
Fonts	Selects from as many as eight fonts for use with text
Image Density	Selects whether to print graphs in low density or high density
Image Image-Sz	Selects the size and shape of a printed graph
Image Rotate	Rotates a graph on the printed page
Layout Line-Spacing	Selects standard or compressed spacing between lines
Layout Orientation	Selects printing in portrait (vertical) or landscape (horizontal) mode
Layout Pitch	Selects spacing between characters
Priority	Selects the order of printing
Wait	Waits for a page before resuming printing

Reminders

- To see the capabilities of your printer, use the **/Print [P, E] Sample** command to print a sample page.
- Printers that cannot print graphs will print an equivalent area of blank space.

Procedures

1. Type /ppoa or /pfoa or /peoa

2. Select one of the following commands:

Menu Item	Description
Device	Selects the printer you want to print to. Device offers the following two options:

Name

Enables you to select the printer you want

Interface

Enables you to select the interface for this printer. Nine different printer ports are available on the menu.

Layout	Selects printer characteristics that affect character and line spacing. These characteristics may vary with your printer. Layout offers the following four options:

Pitch

Provides three options: Standard, which is approximately 10 cpi; Compressed, which is approximately 17 cpi; and Expanded, which is approximately 5 cpi

Line-Spacing

Provides two options: Standard, which is approximately 6 lines per inch; and Compressed, which is approximately 8 lines per inch

Orientation

Provides two options: Portrait, which designates vertical orientation on the page; and Landscape, which designates sideways or horizontal orientation on the page

Quit

Returns you to the Advanced menu

Fonts	Selects different typefaces and styles for a print range. Fonts offers the following five options:

Range

Enables you first to highlight the worksheet range you want to change, then select from fonts 1 through 8

Menu Item	Description

Header/Footer

Enables you to select from fonts 1 through 8 for both the header and footer

Border

Enables you to select from fonts 1 through 8 for the border

Frame

Enables you to select from fonts 1 through 8 for the frame

Quit

Returns you to the Advanced menu

Color

Enables you to select the color you want to print text in. All text prints in the same color. Select a color from 1 to 8.

Image

Selects the quality, size, and orientation of printed graphs. Image offers the following four options:

Rotate

Provides two options: Yes, which indicates that you want the graph rotated; and No, which indicates that you want to keep the graph oriented with the text

Image-Sz

Sets the size and shape of the graph through three options: Margin-Fill, which creates the largest graph in the width entered; Length-Fill, which creates the largest graph in the length you enter; and Reshape, which creates a graph in the dimensions you enter. Length- and Margin-Fill preserve proportions.

Density

Provides two options: Final, for high-quality graphs; and Draft, for less-dark graphs

Quit

Returns you to the Advanced menu

Priority

Selects the priority for the current print job with respect to other jobs. Priority provides three options: Default, which prints the current job after high-priority and other default jobs but ahead of low-priority jobs; High, which prints the current job ahead of default and

Menu Item	Description
	low-priority jobs; and **Low**, which prints the current job after all other jobs.
AutoLf	Selects when the chosen printer uses a line-feed setting different from the default printer's. Select **Yes** if your printer inserts a line feed; select **No** if you want 1-2-3 to insert the line feed. If your printer overlaps lines or prints double-spaced, choose the opposite setting.
Wait	Suspends printing after ejecting a page so that you can insert a new page. After inserting a page, use /**Print Resume** to continue. Choose **No** if you want continuous printing; choose **Yes** if you want to pause between pages.
Quit	Displays the **Options** menu

Important Cues

- If you select COM1 or COM2 as the printer interface, you must use the operating system's MODE command to configure this printer port.

- 1-2-3 remembers the printer and interface used with the file if you save the file after printing.

- Change the margin settings and page length when you change the layout orientation.

- Use /**Print Printer Sample** to see which fonts correspond to fonts 1 through 8. You cannot see the fonts on-screen. The position of characters on-screen may not represent the position of characters when printed.

- On some printers, printing graphs in **Draft** may be faster.

Cautions

- Not all printers are capable of using advanced features. Use **Sample** to see a page printed with the full capabilities of your printer.

- Fonts of different sizes or proportional fonts may print narrower or wider than shown on-screen. Use different column widths to vary the printed position of different cells until columns print correctly. You also can change the width of the print range to vary the amount of text printed.

*For more information, see /**Print Printer Sample** and Chapter 8 for a description and illustration of available fonts.*

Print [Printer, File, Encoded] Clear

/PPC or /PFC or /PEC

Purpose

Clears some or all print settings and options.

Reminders

- Cleared formats return to default settings.

- This option is the only way to clear borders after they have been set.

Procedures

1. Type /ppc or /pfc or /pec

2. Choose one of the following:

Menu Item	Description
All	Clears all print options and resets all formats and setup strings to their defaults
Range	Clears the print range
Borders	Clears the borders and frame
Format	Resets the margins, page length, layout, fonts, colors, setup strings, and graph settings to the default setting
Image	Clears the name of the graph to be printed
Device	Resets the printer name and interface to the default setting

Important Cue

Use the /ppc, /pfc, and /pec commands in macros to cancel earlier print settings or to reestablish default settings you have specified. For example, use the /Worksheet Global Default Printer menu to create as default settings the settings you use most often for margins, the page length, and the setup string. Be sure to use /Worksheet Global Default Update to update the configuration file to make these settings the default settings for future sessions. Then when you place a /Print Printer Clear All command at the beginning of a macro (or use the command interactively), the default settings you specify will be entered automatically.

Caution

In 1-2-3, print parameters remain in effect until you give different instructions. If you want to provide a new set of parameters, use /Print Printer Clear All to ensure that you are starting from the default parameters.

Print [Printer, File, Encoded]   /PPG or /PFG
Go   or /PEG

Purpose

Executes the /Print command, sending the print data in the range to the printer and file.

Reminders

- Before printing for the first time, align the top of the paper with the print head and choose the Align command from the second-level Print menu.

- Use the /Print [P, F, E] Range command to specify the range to print.

Procedure

Type /ppg or /pfg or /peg

Important Cue

Printing to a file will not be complete until you quit all print menus.

Caution

Use the Page command to eject pages and keep the printer aligned. If you manually eject pages, realign the paper and print head and choose /Print [P, F, E] Align.

For more information, see **/Print [Printer, File, Encoded]** *Align and Chapter 8.*

Print [Printer, File, Encoded]   /PPA or /PFA
Align   or /PEA

Purpose

Aligns 1-2-3's internal line counter with the physical page in the printer. Failure to use Align can cause blank gaps in the middle of printed documents.

Reminder

Use this command only after you have manually aligned the print head with the top of a sheet of printer paper. Use Align before printing for the first time or when printing to a printer that other operators have used.

Procedures

1. Position the printer paper so that the top of a page is aligned with the print head.

2. Type /pp or /pf or /pe

3. Select Align to synchronize 1-2-3 with the printer.

Cautions

- Printed pages may have gaps (blank lines) if you do not use this command.
- Align resets the page counter to 1 so that the page number automatically starts over at 1 after each Align command.

Print [Printer, Encoded] Image   /PPI or /PEI

Purpose

Selects the graph you want to print. The graph can be the current graph or any named graph.

Reminders

- If you want more than one graph associated with a file, use /Graph Name to name each of the graphs. You then can use these names when printing.
- Ensure that the cell pointer is in the file that contains the graph(s) you want to print.

Procedures

1. Type /pp or /pf or /pe
2. Select **Image**.
3. Select one of the following menu items:

Menu Item	Description
Current	Selects the current graph as the graph to be printed
Named-Graph	Selects a named graph from the current file as the graph to be printed

4. If you selected **Named-Graph**, specify the name of the graph you want to print.
5. Select **Options Advanced Image** to format how the image will appear on the page.
6. Select **Align** if you need to start the graph at the top of a page.
7. Select **Go** to print.

Important Cues

- Select **Page** from the second-level **Print** menu to eject a graph from the printer. Do not manually roll the paper from the printer.
- If you do not use the **Options Advanced Image Image-Sz** command to change the graph's printed size, the graph will be the maximum size so that it fits within the left and right margins.

- Printers that cannot print a graph print a blank space of equivalent size.

- You can print a graph by entering the graph's name in the print range. When prompted for a print range, type an asterisk immediately followed by the graph's name, such as

  *BDGT.PIC

- Use **Line** to insert blank lines between graphs and worksheets on the printed page.

- A graph will not be divided by a page break. The graph will print on the next page.

Caution

1-2-3 may not not have enough memory available to print the graph when requested. To make more memory available, save files and then delete them from memory. Use **/Print Resume** to resume printing of the graph. The graph and worksheet do not have to be active to print, because the printing information was stored during the first print request.

Print Printer Sample

/PPS

Purpose

Prints a sample page from the printer, using current settings and showing the capabilities of your printer.

Reminders

- A sample includes four sections:

  1. Print settings

  2. Sample worksheet

  3. Printer capabilities showing

     a. Fonts 1 through 8

     b. Colors 1 through 8

     c. Compressed and expanded pitch

     d. standard and compressed line spacing

  4. Sample graph and graph text, using current settings

- Before printing, ensure that your printer is on, that the paper is aligned, and that the printer is on-line.

Procedures

1. Set the print settings that will be in effect when you use this sample to improve a worksheet or graph.

2. Type /pp or /pf or /pe

3. Select Sample.

4. Select Align, then Go.

Important Cues

- Because you cannot see on-screen how a font, color, or pitch will appear when printed, save a copy of the sample printout for each printer you have and for each variation in printer settings. These samples will help you decide which Advanced settings to use to improve printing appearance.

- If your printer does not support graphics, a blank space appears in the sample where the graphic would have been.

- The data in the sample is preset. You cannot change the data or the graph.

Caution

The sample will change depending on the current print settings.

Print [Printer, File, Encoded] Hold

/PPH or /PFH or /PEH

Purpose

Enables you to change a print job on the fly while the job is still open.

Reminder

You can return to 1-2-3 and make changes such as the following:

- Correcting a worksheet that is in the print queue or currently printing

- Opening additional worksheets

- Using /Print Resume to continue printing after the printer has stopped because of an error or for additional paper

Procedures

To leave a print job, do the following:

1. Type /pp or /pf or /pe

2. Select Hold.

To take the print job off hold, do one of the following:

- Return to the main Print menu and complete the job

- Select /Print Cancel
- Select a different printer or printer interface
- Select a different type of printing (**Printer**, **File**, or **Encoded**)

Caution

If you attempt to end 1-2-3 with a print job still on hold, you will be asked whether you want it completed. You can choose to complete it or to end 1-2-3.

Print [Printer, File, Encoded] Quit

/PPQ or /PFQ or /PEQ

Purpose

Closes the print job so that it will complete correctly; returns to READY mode.

Reminder

To properly finish a print job, quit the **Print** menu by using **Quit**, Esc, or Ctrl-Break.

Procedure

Type /ppq or /pfq or /peq

For more information, see Chapter 8.

Graph Commands /G

/Graph commands control the graph's appearance and specify worksheet ranges to be used as graph data.

Store multiple graphs with **/Graph Name** and display them at a later time. You can print either the current graph or a named graph. To send graphs to another program, use **/Graph Save** to create a .PIC or .CGM file.

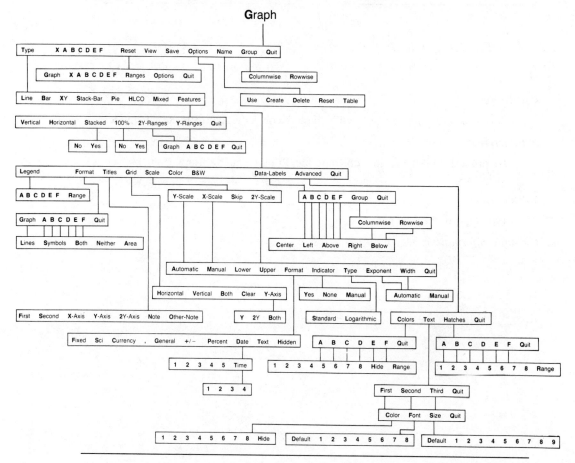

Graph Type /GT

Purpose

Selects from among the 1-2-3 graph types: **Line**; **Bar**; **XY**; **Stack-Bar**; **Pie**; **HLCO**, or high-low-close-open (stock market); and **Mixed** (bar and line). Each type of graph is best suited for displaying and analyzing a specific type of data.

Reminders

- Before you can create a graph, you must have created a worksheet that has the same number of cells in each x- and y-axis range, similar to the one in figure G.1. Each *y* data item must be in the same range position as the corresponding *x* value. Figure G.2 shows the bar graph produced from the worksheet displayed in figure G.1. (The legends and titles were added separately.)

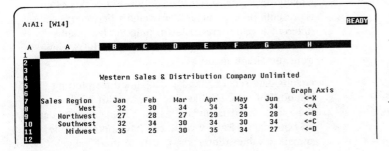

Fig. G.1.
Worksheet with the same number of cells in each x- and y-axis range.

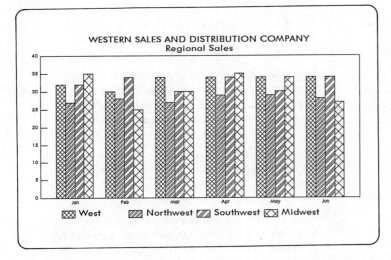

Fig. G.2.
Bar graph produced from the worksheet in fig. G.1.

- Except for pie graphs, graphs can have on the y-axis as many as six different series of data. The **Graph** menu choices **A** through **F** are used to highlight the data series. The pie graph accepts data from only the A range.

Procedures

1. Type /gt

2. Select the type of graph from the following options:

Menu Item	Description
Line	Usually depicts a continuous series of data. The change frequently occurs over time. Enter an x-axis label, such as months, in the X-selection range from the Graph menu. Line graphs can be altered to appear as area graphs.
Bar	Usually displays discrete data series. The x-axis often represents time. Comparative weights between different *y* values are easier to judge in bar graphs than in line charts. Enter x-axis labels in the X range from the Graph menu.
XY	Graphs data sets of *x* and *y* data; good for plotting "clouds" of data. (Unlike line graphs with labels on the x-axis and data on the y-axis, XY graphs have data on both axes.) Each *x* value can have between one and six *y* values. Enter x-axis data in the X range of the Graph menu.
Stack-Bar	Shows how proportions change within the whole. Enter x-axis labels in the X range from the Graph menu. A bar can have as many as six portions.
Pie	Shows how the whole is divided into component portions. Use only the A range to contain the values of each portion. The X range is used to label the pie wedges. 1-2-3 automatically calculates each portion's percentage from the A values.
HLCO	Tracks items that vary over time. High-low-close-open graphs are most commonly used in the stock market to show the price at which a stock opens and closes and its high and low during the day.
Mixed	Contains both bar and line graphs, and is therefore useful for relating trends in two distinct measurable quantities. If the scales for items vary significantly, you can add a second y-axis (2Y-Axis) that has a different scale. Mixed graphs can have up to three bars and three lines.
Features	Varies the original graph type. Features provides these options: **Vertical** Moves the x-axis to the bottom of the graph (default)

Menu Item	Description

Horizontal

Moves the x-axis to the left side. The y-axis runs across the top, and the 2Y-axis runs across the bottom.

Stacked

Works with line, bar, XY, and mixed graphs containing two or more data sets. **No** plots values separately (default); **Yes** stacks values.

100%

Changes data values to a percentage of 100. **No** graphs the actual value; **Yes** graphs as percentages of whole.

2Y-Ranges

Creates a second y-axis and specifies each data range. Choose **Graph** to assign all data ranges to the 2Y-axis. Choose **A** through **F** to specify individual data ranges on the 2Y-axis.

Y-Ranges

Enables you to move 2Y-ranges back to the y-axis. **Y** Ranges offers the same options as **2Y-Ranges**.

Quit

Displays the main **Graph** menu

3. After you make your selection, the **Graph** menu reappears.

4. If you have already highlighted the X range and ranges A through F to indicate the data to graph, select View. If you are beginning the graph, see **/Graph X A B C D E F** in this section.

Important Cues

- With 1-2-3, you can build graphs interactively. After selecting /Graph Type and at least one x- and y-axis range, select View to see the graph as it is currently defined.

- When you save the worksheet to disk, you also save the most recently specified graph type and other graph settings.

- You can shade a pie graph's wedges with eight different shadings. You can even extract wedges from the pie. Use the B range to define the shade of a pie graph wedge and to extract the wedge from the pie. (To learn how to shade the pie graph, see /Graph **X A B C D E F** in this section.)

For more information, see **/Graph** *X A B C D E F and Chapter 9.*

Graph X A B C D E F   */GX, /GA through /GF*

Purpose

Specifies the worksheet ranges containing x-axis and y-axis data or labels.

Reminders

- The x-axis is the graph's horizontal (bottom) axis. The y-axis is the graph's vertical (left) axis. The labels or data assigned to the x-axis and the six possible sets of y-axis data (A through F) must have the same number of cells. To ensure that the x-axis and y-axis have an equal number of elements, place all the labels and data on adjacent rows. Figure G.3 shows the x- and y-axis labels and data in rows. Notice that some of the *y* values are blank but that each range has an equal number of elements.

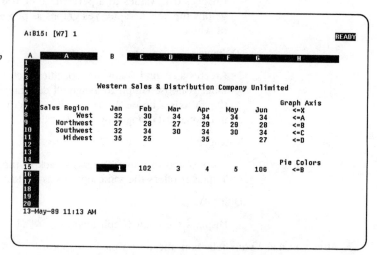

Fig. G.3.
Worksheet with some blank y values but an equal number of elements.

- Pie graph ranges are different from those of other graph types. Pie graphs use only the A range for data. (The B range contains code numbers to control shading and the extraction of wedges from the pie. The C range controls the removal of percentage labels on wedges.)

Procedures

1. Type /g

2. From the following options, select the ranges for x- or y-axis data or labels to be entered:

Menu Item	Description
X	Enters x-axis label range. These are labels such as Jan, Feb, Mar, and so on. Creates labels for pie graph wedges and line, bar, and stacked-bar graphs (x-axis data range for XY graphs). The X range in figure G.3 is B7..G7.
A	Enters first y-axis data range, the only data range used by a pie graph. The A range in figure G.3 is B8..G8.
B	Enters second y-axis data range; enters pie graph shading values and extraction codes. (For more information, see this section's "Important Cues.") The B range in figure G.3 is B9..G9.
C	Enters third y-axis data range; enters pie graph control over percentage labels
D to **F**	Enters fourth through sixth data ranges

3. Indicate the data range by entering the range address, entering a range name, or highlighting the range.
4. Press Enter.

Important Cues

- If your graph data is in adjacent rows or columns like those in figure G.3, you may be able to save time by using /Graph **G**roup.

- To ease the task of keeping track of graph data and labels, put the data and labels in labeled rows (see fig. G.3).

- You do not need to change the **G**raph menu settings when you change or update the data in the ranges. /Graph remembers all the settings.

- Use /Graph **R**eset **G**raph to clear all graph settings. Use /Graph **R**eset [**X** through **F**] to clear individual ranges and their associated settings.

- 1-2-3 automatically updates graphs when you input new data in the worksheet (for new data or labels in the x- and y-axis ranges). Once you have set the graphs with the /Graph commands, you can view new graphs from the worksheet by pressing Graph (F10). If the computer beeps and no graph appears, you have not defined that graph, or your computer does not have graphics capability.

- Pie graphs do not use the x- and y-axis title options, grids, or scales.

- Pie graphs are limited because they often have too many elements in the A range, a situation that causes wedges to be small and labels to overlap. The A range is the only data range needed for pie graphs. Enter wedge labels in the X range, as you would for line graphs.

- Use the B range to enter the numbers from 1 to 14 that control the color or black-and-white patterns in each wedge. Add 100 to a shading code to extract one or more wedges from the pie. Enter a negative number in the B range to hide a wedge. To hide the percentage label for a wedge, enter a zero in the C range for that cell while leaving other cells in the C range blank.

Caution

If your graph has missing data or if the y values do not match the corresponding x positions, check to ensure that the x- and y-axis ranges have the same number of elements. The values in the y ranges (A through F) graph the corresponding x-range cells.

*For more information, see /**Graph Type** and Chapter 9.*

Graph Reset   /GR

Purpose

Cancels all or some of a graph's settings so that you can either create a new graph or exclude from a new graph one or more data ranges from the old graph.

Reminder

The **Graph** option of this command (see "Procedures") enables you to reset all graph parameters quickly.

Procedures

1. Type /gr

2. Choose one of the following:

Menu Item	Description
Graph	Resets all graph parameters but does not alter a graph named with /**Graph Name Create**. Use this option if you want to exclude all preceding graph parameters from the new graph.
X	Resets the X range and removes the labels (but not on XY graphs)
A through **F**	Resets a designated range and corresponding labels so that these are not displayed in the new graph
Ranges	Resets all data ranges and all data labels
Options	Resets all settings defined by /**Graph Options**
Quit	Returns you to the **Graph** menu

Important Cues

- Use /**Graph** **T**ype to change the type of graph.

- The **Reset** command enables you to remove unwanted features from a graph quickly so that you can update it.

- Create templates of graphs that can be used with different sets of data by defining a graph, then removing its data ranges with **Reset**. Respecify the data ranges to create a new graph with the same format.

Caution

If you delete too much from a graph, use /**File Open** to retrieve the original file containing the original graph settings.

For more information, see Chapter 9.

Graph View   /GV

Purpose

Displays a graph on-screen.

Reminders

- What is displayed depends on the system hardware and the system configuration.

- On a nongraphics screen, no graph displays.

- If your system has a graphics card and either a monochrome display or a color monitor, you can see a graph instead of the worksheet on the screen after you select **View**. You must select /**Graph Options Color** to see the graph in color.

Procedures

1. Select **View** from the /**Graph** menu when you are ready to see the graph you have created. The graph must be defined before you can view it.

2. Press any key to return to the **Graph** menu.

3. Select **Quit** to return to the worksheet and READY mode.

Important Cues

- You can use /**Graph View** to redraw the graph, but an easier way is to press Graph (F10) while you are in READY mode. Graph (F10) is the equivalent of /**Graph View**, but the function key enables you to view a graph after making a change in the worksheet. You can use Graph (F10) without having to return to the **Graph** menu. (Graph [F10] does not function while the **Graph** menu is visible.) If your system doesn't have two monitors and graphics cards for each, you can use Graph (F10) to toggle back and forth between the worksheet and the graph. You can therefore use Graph (F10) to do rapid "what if" analysis with graphics.

- If you want to see a portion of the worksheet at the same time that you see the graph, use /Worksheet Window Graph to split the screen between the worksheet and graph.

- If you want to create a series of graphs and view the series, you must use /Graph Name to name each graph.

- If the screen is blank after you select View, make certain that you have defined the graph adequately, that your system has graphics capability, and that 1-2-3 was installed for your particular graphics device(s). Press any key to return to the Graph menu. Then select Quit to return to the worksheet.

*For more information, see /**Worksheet Window Graph** and Chapter 9.*

Graph Save   /GS

Purpose

Saves the graph so that it can be printed with a different program.

/Graph Save saves a graph file that cannot be viewed or retrieved from within 1-2-3. This file can be used by graphics programs to improve the quality of 1-2-3 graphs.

Use /Graph Name Create and /File Save to save the graph's settings with the worksheet so that you can view multiple graphs.

Reminders

- Select View or press Graph (F10) to review the graph. Ensure that the graph has the correct scaling, labels, and titles.

- Check the screen's lower-right corner for a CALC indicator. If CALC appears and the worksheet is still visible, press Calc (F9) to update all worksheet values before you save the graph.

- If you need to return to this graph later, use /Graph Name Create to save the graph settings; then use /File Save to save the worksheet to disk.

- The graph saved to a file is the current graph that displays on the screen.

Procedures

1. Type /g

2. Select Save.

3. Enter a new file name, or use the right- or left-arrow key to highlight a name already on the menu bar.

4. Press Enter.

Important Cues

- Saved graphs can have either .PIC or .CGM file extensions. Other software programs may use either a .PIC or a .CGM file format.

- Use the /Worksheet Global Default Graph command to change the default file type and extension for graphs saved to disk. In Step 3, you can type the file extension you want—either .PIC or .CGM—to override the default file format.

Caution

If you need to save graph settings and the worksheet's graph display, name the graph with /**Graph Name Create** and then use /**File Save** to save the worksheet and graph together. /**Graph Save** saves information used only to transfer the graph to another program. Files saved with /**Graph Save** cannot be edited from the worksheet.

*For more information, see /**Graph Name**, /**File Save**, and Chapter 7.*

Graph Options Legend /GOL

Purpose

Legends indicate which line, bar, or point belongs to a specific y-axis data range.

Y-axis data is entered in ranges A, B, C, D, E, and F. Legend titles for each range also are assigned by A, B, C, D, E, and F. Figure G.4 shows a legend at the bottom of the bar graph, relating shading patterns to the division names West, Northwest, Southwest, and Midwest.

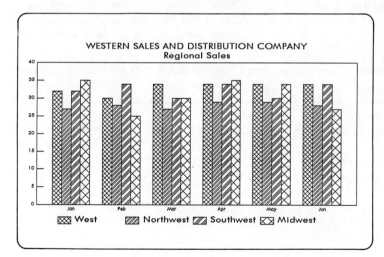

Fig. G.4. Legends relating shading patterns to division names.

Reminder

As you create a graph, write on paper a list of the legend titles you want to associate with each data range (ranges A through F). If you have already created the graph, you can reenter the A-through-F data ranges to see the associated legend ranges. To reenter these legends, follow the steps outlined in the following section.

Procedures

1. Type /go

2. Select **Legend**.

3. Select one of the following:

Menu Item	Description
A to **F**	Creates a legend for y-axis range
Range	Assigns a legend to all ranges

4. If you chose **A** through **F**, enter the text for the legend. If you chose **Range**, specify the range containing the legends.

Important Cues

- 1-2-3 displays the legend along the bottom of the graph.

- 1-2-3 may cut a legend short if there is not enough room or if the legend exceeds the graph's frame. If this happens, reenter a shorter legend.

- Create changeable legends by entering the text for a legend in cells. When /Graph Options Legend requests the legend title, you can enter a backslash (\) and the cell address or range name of a cell that holds the text.

Caution

If you relocate a graph by using /Move, /Worksheet Insert, or /Worksheet Delete, 1-2-3 will not adjust cell addresses that have been used to create legends. Create your graphs by using range names to describe data and legend ranges to prevent this problem.

*For more information, see /**Range Name**, /**Graph X A B C D E F**, and Chapters 4 and 9.*

Graph Options Format   */GOF*

Purpose

Selects the symbols and lines that identify and connect data points.

Some line and XY graphs present information better if the data is linked with data points or if the data is represented by a series of data points linked with a solid line. Use /Graph Options Format to select the type of data points used for each data range (symbols, lines, or both).

Reminders

- Time-related data is usually best represented by a continuous series of related data. Trends and slopes are more obvious when they are represented with lines rather than a cluster of data points.

- Data-point clusters representing multiple readings around different x-axis values are likely candidates for symbols instead of lines. Symbols better reflect groupings. The symbol for each y-axis range is unique so that you can keep data separated.

Procedures

1. Type /gof

2. Select the data ranges to be formatted:

Menu Item	Description
Graph	Selects a format for the entire graph
A to **F**	Selects a format for y-axis data points

3. Select the data point type:

Menu Item	Description
Lines	Connects data points with a line
Symbols	Encloses each data point in a symbol. Different ranges have different symbols. Symbols is most commonly used with XY graphs.
Both	Connects data points with a line and marks the data point
Neither	Selects neither lines nor symbols. Use /Graph Options Data-Labels to "float" labels or data within the graph.
Area	Fills the space between the line and the line or axis directly below

Important Cues

- Figure G.5 is an illustrative worksheet, and figure G.6 shows the corresponding line graph. The A and D data ranges, West and Midwest, are each plotted with a line. The B and C data ranges, Northwest and Southwest, are each plotted with a particular symbol.

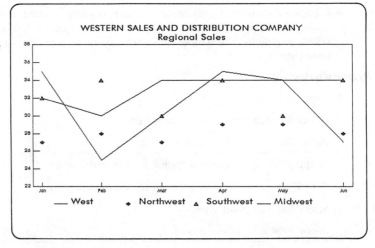

Fig. G.5.
Sample worksheet for the line graph.

Fig. G.6.
A and C ranges plotted with lines, and B and D ranges plotted with symbols.

- Use the /Graph Options Advanced Colors A-F command to set the colors for a set of data.

- Use /Graph Options Advanced Colors A-F Hide to hide a set of data.

- If you are plotting a regression analysis trend line (/Data Regression), set the data points as symbols only and the regression's calculated *y* values as a line. This arrangement highlights the trend as a straight line through a swarm of data points.

Caution

If your XY line graphs are a confusing jumble of crossed lines, you must sort the data in x-axis order by arranging each *x,y* data pair in ascending, or descending, x-axis order within the worksheet range. Be sure to sort the y-axis data with the corresponding x-axis data.

*For more information, see /**Graph Options Advanced Text**, /**Graph Options Advanced Hatches**, and Chapter 9.*

Graph Options Titles   /GOT

Purpose

Adds headings to the graph and to each axis.

To increase the reader's understanding, use x- and y-axis titles.

Reminder

You must know the measurement units used in the x-axis and y-axis. 1-2-3 automatically scales graphs to fit accordingly and displays the scaling factor (for example, thousands) along each axis.

Procedures

1. Type /got

2. Select the title to be entered from the following options:

Menu Item	Description
First	Specifies the top heading of a graph
Second	Specifies a second heading of a graph
X-Axis	Specifies a title below the x-axis
Y-Axis	Specifies a title to the left of the y-axis
2Y-Axis	Specifies a title for the second y-axis
Note	Specifies the first graph note at the lower-left corner
Other-Note	Specifies the second graph note at the lower-left corner

3. Type a title or enter the cell address of a cell containing a title. Use cell contents for a title by entering first a backslash (\) and then the cell address. If a title already exists, press Esc to cancel the title, or press Enter to accept it.

4. Press Enter.

Caution

You can lose titles and headings contained in cell addresses if you move the cells with /**Move**, /**Worksheet Insert**, or /**Worksheet Delete**. Using range names instead of cell addresses solves this problem.

*For more information, see /**Graph Options Data-Labels**, /**Graph Options Scale**, and Chapter 9.*

Graph Options Grid   */GOG*

Purpose

Overlays a grid on a graph to enhance readability. The grid lines can be horizontal, vertical, or both.

Reminders

- Before you add a grid, create a graph to view.
- Grid lines cannot be used with pie graphs.

Procedures

1. Type /gog

2. Select the type of grid from the following options:

Menu Item	Description
Horizontal	Draws horizontal grid lines over the current graph from each major y-axis division
Vertical	Draws vertical grid lines over the current graph from each major x-axis division
Both	Draws both horizontal and vertical grid lines
Clear	Removes all grid lines
Y-axis	Selects whether you want the grid lines to align with tick points on the **Y** axis, the **2Y** axis, or **B**oth.

Important Cues

- Select grid lines that run in a direction that will enhance the presentation of data.

- Use grid lines sparingly. Inappropriate grid lines can make some line and XY graphs confusing.

- Use **/Graph Options Scale** to change the graph's scale, thereby changing the number of grid lines shown on the graph. Note that although this technique changes the number of grid lines, it also magnifies or reduces the graph's proportion.

- Some data-point graphs are more accurate if you use data labels. Use **/Graph Options Data-Labels** to create data labels that display precise numbers next to the point on the graph.

*For more information, see **/Graph Options Scale**, **/Graph Options Data-Labels**, and Chapter 9.*

Graph Options Scale   */GOS*

Purpose

Varies the scale along either y-axis. The x-axis scale can be varied on XY graphs.

Options within this command include the following:

- Making changes manually to the upper- or lower-axis end points.

- Choosing formats for numeric display. (Options are identical to those in /Worksheet Global Format or /Range Format.)

- Improving display of overlapping x-axis labels by skipping every specified occurrence, such as every second or third label.

Use /Graph Options Scale to change the axes' end points manually, thereby expanding or contracting the graph scale. Changing the end points expands or contracts the visible portion of the graph.

Use /Graph Options Scale to format numbers and dates that appear on the axes. These formats are the same as /Range Format options.

Reminder

First create and view the graph. Notice which portions of the graph you want to view and which beginning and ending numbers you should use for the new X-scale or Y-scale. Also notice whether the x-axis labels overlap or seem crowded. You can thin the x-axis tick marks by using /Graph Options Scale Skip.

Procedures

1. Type /gos

2. Select from the following options the axis or skip frequency to be changed:

Menu Item	Description
Y-Scale	Changes the y-axis scale or format
X-Scale	Changes the x-axis scale or format
Skip	Changes the frequency with which x-axis indicators display
2Y-Scale	Changes the 2Y-axis scale or format

3. If you select **Y**-Scale, **X**-Scale, or 2Y-Scale, choose from the following:

Menu Item	Description
Automatic	Automatically scales the graph to fill the screen; default (normal) selection
Manual	Overrides automatic scaling with scaling you have selected. Other menu options are available from this selection.
Lower	Enters the lowest number for axis. Values are rounded.
Upper	Enters the highest number for axis. Values are rounded.
Format	Selects the formatting type and decimal display from the following ten options (see /Range Format for descriptions of these options):

Fixed	+/−
Sci	Percent
Currency	Date
,	Text
General	Hidden

Menu Item	Description
Indicator	Displays or suppresses the magnitude indicator (thousands, millions, and so on) that appears between the scale and axis titles. Select Yes to have 1-2-3 display its automatically calculated scaling factor; select No to suppress the display. Select Manual to be prompted for a display that you type.
Type	Displays the scale, using either Standard (a linear scale) or Logarithmic (a logarithmic scale)
Exponent	Defines the order of magnitude (factor of 10) for numbers on the scale. Select Automatic to have 1-2-3 calculate a scaling factor; select Manual if you want to enter your own scaling factor.
Width	Defines how many characters will display for each number on the scale. The width of 0 is used as a unit of measure. Select Automatic if you want 1-2-3 to set the maximum width; select Manual and enter a number from 1 to 50 to set your own width.
Quit	Leaves this menu and returns to the Options menu

4. If you choose Skip, you must enter a number to indicate the intervals at which the x-axis scale tick marks will appear. If you enter the number 25, for example, then the 1st, 26th, and 51st range entries will appear. X-axis tick-mark spacing cannot be controlled from the menu.

Important Cues

- Selecting a scale inside the minimum and maximum data points creates a graph that magnifies an area within the data.

- If data points have grossly different magnitudes, you may not be able to see all the data; some ranges will be too large for the graph, and others will be too small. Scale down values on the y-axis by entering a larger exponent. An exponent of 3, for example, means that numbers on the y-axis are divided by 10 to the third power (1,000).

*For more information, see /**Graph Options Grid** and Chapter 9.*

Graph Options Color/B&W   /GOC or /GOB

Purpose

Defines the color 1-2-3 will try to use to display graphs on your monitor.

If you have a monochrome display, use /gob; if you have a color display, use /goc.

Reminder

If you have a monochrome monitor, you should use /gob. If you need to print to a color printer, however, you must change to /goc. Color monitors set to /goc will automatically print black and white on printers that are capable of only black and white.

Procedures

To set the color option, do the following:

Type /goc

To set the B&W option, do the following:

Type /gob

Important Cues

- To set color text, use the /Graph Options Advanced Text Color command.

- To set color shading, use the /Graph Options Advanced Colors command.

*For more information, see /**Graph Options Advanced** commands and Chapter 9*

Graph Options Data-Labels /GOD

Purpose

Labels graph points from data contained in cells.

Graph labels can be numeric values that enhance the graph's accuracy, or text labels that describe specific graph points. The labels for graph points come from worksheet ranges.

Reminders

- First create the graph. Then view the graph and note future label locations that correspond to data they represent. Figure G.7 shows three ranges: the X range, the A range, and A-range labels.

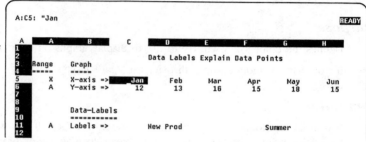

Fig. G.7.
X and A ranges used to plan the A-range labels.

- Enter labels in an order corresponding to the order of the data-entry points they describe.

- Figure G.8 shows the resulting graph with labels over data points. Note that you do not have to enter a label for every data point.

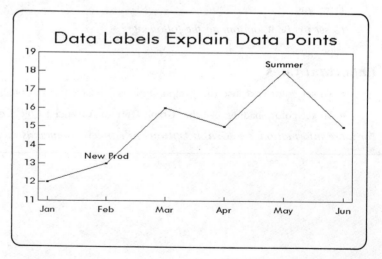

Fig. G.8.
The resulting graph with labels over data points.

Procedures

1. Type /god

2. From the following options, select the data range you want to label:

Menu Item	Description
A through F	Enters the range to be labeled
Group	Enters at one time all the ranges that will have labels. The commands Columnwise and Rowwise will appear. Select Columnwise if data sets are in a column; select Rowwise if data sets run across a row.
Quit	Returns you to the worksheet

3. Specify the range containing the labels. This range should be the same size as the range you selected for A through F. If you are grouping data ranges, the range selected here must be the same size as all the data ranges combined.

4. From the following options, select the data label location relative to the corresponding data points. (Note that in fig. G.8, the Above option has been selected.)

Menu Item	Description
Center	Centers a label on a data point
Left	Aligns a label left of a data point
Above	Aligns a label above a data point
Right	Aligns a label right of a data point
Below	Aligns a label below a data point

6. Choose Quit or return to Step 2 to enter more data labels.

Important Cues

- Data labels can be formulas, values, or labels.

- Lines can have labels that are centered, left, right, above, or below. Bars can have labels that are above or below. If you choose a different option, the label appears above the bar. Pie graphs cannot have labels.

- Position "floating" labels that can be moved anywhere within the graph area by creating a set of labels that are assigned to invisible data points. To create floating labels, follow these steps:

  1. Set up two ranges that have the same number of cell locations and data points on the graph.

  2. In one range, enter floating labels in the left-to-right order in which you want them to appear in the graph.

3. In the other range, enter the elevation of the y-axis labels. If the floating labels are to be positioned exactly where you want them, the cells in the elevation and label ranges must parallel actual data points in the x-axis and y-axis.

4. Use /Graph **F** to enter the elevations for the F data range.

5. Use /Graph Options **Data-Labels F** to specify the label range, and press Enter.

6. Select **Center** to center the labels on the data points.

7. To keep the F range data from plotting, Use /Graph Options Format **F Neither** (invisible).

*For more information, see /**Graph Options Titles**, /**Graph Options Scale**, and Chapter 9.*

Graph Options Advanced Colors   */GOAC*

Purpose

Selects the colors used by data ranges A through F. /Graph Options Advanced Colors also can be used to hide data ranges.

Reminders

- /Graph Options Advanced Colors affects both the displayed and printed graph.

- Assign colors by choosing a number from 1 to 8. To see the color corresponding to each number, create a dummy bar graph and assign a different color to each bar. Test printer colors by using /Print Printer Sample to print the sample printout.

- You do not have to use the Advanced Colors settings to create color graphs. 1-2-3 defaults to the colors 2, 3, 4, 5, 6, and 7 for the respective data ranges A through F.

Procedures

1. Type /goac

2. Select the data range you want to change—A through F.

3. From the following options, select the appearance of that data range:

Menu Item	Description
1–8	Colors 1 through 8 are set for the entire data range, A through F
Hide	Hides this data range

Menu Item	Description
Range	Specifies colors for specific data items within the range A through F. Colors are entered as numbers, 1 through 14, in a range the same size as the range they are assigned to.

4. If you selected **R**ange, specify the range containing the colors.

Important Cues

- Setting colors by choosing a number from 1 to 8 sets a color for the entire data range. For example, all of the B data range will have color 3. The **R**ange method of setting colors enables you to set a specific color for each data item within a data range. For example, within the C data range, the first data item will be color 4, the second data item will be color 6, and so on.

- The size of the range containing **R**ange colors should be the same size as the data range it will color. Put the color numbers in the same relative cell location as the data item they will color. Enter a negative number in a color range to hide a data item.

- Use formulas in the color range to assign colors based on data meeting certain criteria.

- The first color in a color range defines the color of the legend.

- Use /Graph Options Advanced **T**ext to set text colors in a graph.

*For more information, see /**Graph Options Advanced Text**, /**Graph Options Advanced Hatches**, and Chapter 9.*

Graph Options Advanced Text and Text [First, Second, Third] [Color, Font, Size]

/GOAT, /GOATFC, /GOATSC, /GOATTC, /GOATFF, /GOATSF, /GOATTF, /GOATFS, /GOATSS, or /GOATTS

Purpose

Changes the font, size, and color for graph text.

Reminders

- /Graph Options Advanced **T**ext affects both the displayed and printed graph.

- Text on a graph is grouped into three types. The first group contains the first line of the graph title. The second group contains the second line of the graph title, as well as axes titles and legend titles. The third group contains other text on the graph.

- You must use /Graph Options Colors to set the graph display to color if you want to print color text on a color printer.

Procedures

1. Type /goa

2. Select Text.

3. Select the group of text you want to change: First, Second, or Third.

4. Select Color.

5. Select the color for the group of text you want to change. The choices are 1 through 8 or Hide.

6. Select Font.

7. Select the font you want for the group of text. The fonts are 1 through 8 or Default.

8. Select Size.

9. Select the size of font you want for the group of text. Sizes are 1 through 9 or Default.

Important Cues

- You can select Color, Font, and Size in any order.

- Text colors vary among monitors. To see a sample of which printer colors are available, print the sample output by using /Print Printer Sample.

Cautions

- The display does not show how the printed graph will appear. Only three font sizes display on-screen. Printed font sizes vary among printers. Use /Print Printer Sample to print a sample output on your printer to see which font sizes are available.

- 1-2-3 may reduce font sizes automatically to keep text on-screen. If the text cannot be reduced enough, it is cut off.

For more information, see /Graph Options Advanced Color, /Graph Options Hatches, and Chapters 8 and 9.

Graph Options Advanced Hatches   /GOAH

Purpose

Changes the hatching (shading) for each data range in a graph.

Reminder

/Graph Options Advanced Hatches affects both the displayed and printed graph.

Procedures

1. Type /goah

2. Specify the range you want to hatch, A through F.

3. Select the hatch pattern from the following options:

Menu Item	Description
1–8	Uses the hatch pattern corresponding to this number
Range	Specifies hatch patterns for specific data items within the range A–F. Hatches are entered as numbers, 1 through 14, in a range the same size as the range they are assigned to. Numbers 1 through 8 are hatches; numbers 9 through 14 are gray scales.

4. If you are using /Range, specify the range containing the hatch values.

Important Cues

- The hatch patterns vary depending on the printer. To test the patterns your printer uses, print a test pattern with /Print Printer Sample.

- Use negative numbers in the hatch range to hide the corresponding data item.

- Use formulas within a hatch range to calculate a hatch pattern based on specific criteria. The first number in a hatch range determines the legend pattern for that data range.

- You can color and hatch at the same time by combining /Graph Options Advanced Hatches with /Graph Options Advanced Colors.

- Adding 100 to a hatch range for pie graphs pulls out that wedge of the pie.

For more information, see /Graph Options Advanced Text, /Graph Options Advanced Color, and Chapter 9.

Graph Name   /GN

Purpose

Stores graph settings for later use with the same worksheet.

Because 1-2-3 enables only one graph to be active at a time, use /Graph Name to name graphs and store their settings with the corresponding worksheets. To reproduce a stored graph, recall the graph and graph settings by name.

Reminders

- Before you can name a graph, you must create one that you can view.

- If you want to name a graph, make sure that it is the active graph.

- Before creating a table of graph names, make sure that you are in the file that contains the graphs you want to name.

Procedures

1. Type /gn

2. From these options, select the activity to name the file:

Menu Item	Description
Use	Retrieves previous graph settings with a saved graph name
Create	Creates for the active graph a name of up to 15 characters. Make sure that no graph currently has the same name.
Delete	Removes the settings and name for the graph name chosen from the menu. Be sure that you have the correct name; you are not given the option to cancel.
Reset	Erases all graph names and their settings
Table	Creates a table of graph names, types, and the first line of the graph title for names in the current file

3. If you are switching to a new graph, creating a name, or deleting or resetting names, specify the name. If you are creating a table of graph names, specify the location for the graph.

Important Cues

- Using /Graph Name is the only way to store and recall graphs for later use with the same worksheet. /Graph Save saves graphs as .PIC or .CGM files for use with graphic enhancement programs.

- The graph table overwrites existing cell contents.

- The graph table has three columns and as many rows as there are names.

- Graphs recalled by /Graph Name Use reflect changed data within the graph ranges.

- Create a slide-show effect by naming several graphs and recalling them in succession with a macro that controls /Graph Name Use.

Cautions

- You can recall graphs in later work sessions only if you have first saved the graph settings with /Graph Name Create and then saved the worksheet with /File Save. Even in the same work session, you cannot return to a previous graph unless you have saved the graph settings with /Graph Name Create.

- Respect the power of /Graph Name Reset. It deletes not only all graph names in the current worksheet but also all graph parameters. The graph has no "Yes/No" confirmation step; once you press R for Reset, all graphs are gone.

*For more information, see /**Print [Printer, Encoded] Image**, /**File Save**, /**File Retrieve**, and Chapters 7 and 9.*

Graph Group /*GG*

Purpose

Quickly selects the data ranges for a graph, X and A through F, when data is in adjacent rows and columns are in consecutive order.

Designing worksheets with the /Graph Group command in mind can save you time later.

Reminder

In figure G.1, the /Graph Group range is B7..G11. /Graph Group automatically defines row 7 in this range as the X data range, row 8 as the A data range, row 9 as the B data range, and so on.

Procedures

1. Type /gg

2. Specify the range containing X and A–F data values. The rows or columns must be adjacent and in the order X, A, B, C, and so on.

3. Select Columnwise if the data ranges are in columns; select Rowwise if the data ranges are in rows.

Important Cues

- /Graph Group assigns data ranges in the order X, A, B, and so on. Rows or columns that exceed the seven data ranges are ignored.

- Selecting a range for /Graph Group that contains blank rows or columns produces a graph containing blanks. For example, a rowwise group containing a blank row creates a bar graph with a missing set of bars.

*For more information, see /**Graph X, A, B, C, D, E, F**, and Chapter 9 .*

Data Commands /D

/Data commands work on data tables and enable you to perform three functions: database selection and maintenance, data analysis, and data manipulation. One of the most used /Data commands is Query. You use Query commands to rapidly find, update, extract, or delete information from within a large collection of data. You also use /Data commands to perform many different types of data manipulation, such as sorting, filling ranges with numbers, and parsing imported data.

Data Fill /DF

Purpose

Fills a specified range with a series of equally incremented numbers, dates, times, or percentages.

Use /Data Fill to create date or numeric rows or columns, headings for depreciation tables, sensitivity analyses, data tables, or databases.

Reminder

Before you issue /Data Fill, move the cell pointer to the upper-left corner of the range you want to fill.

Procedures

1. Type /df

2. Specify the range to be filled: type the address (such as B23..D46), type a range name, or highlight the range.

3. When a Start value is requested, enter the starting number, date, or time in the filled range, and then press Enter. You can also reference a cell or range that results in a value. Use a number or time format that 1-2-3 recognizes. (The default value is 0.)

4. When a Step value is requested, type the positive or negative number by which you want the value to be incremented. Date or time Step values can use special units described in this entry's "Important Cues." (The default value is 1.)

5. Enter a Stop value. You can use a date or time in any date or time format except Short International (D5). If the step is negative, make sure that the Stop value is less than the Start value. /Data Fill fills the cells in the range column-by-column from top to bottom and from left to right until the Stop value is encountered or the range is full. (The default value is 8191.)

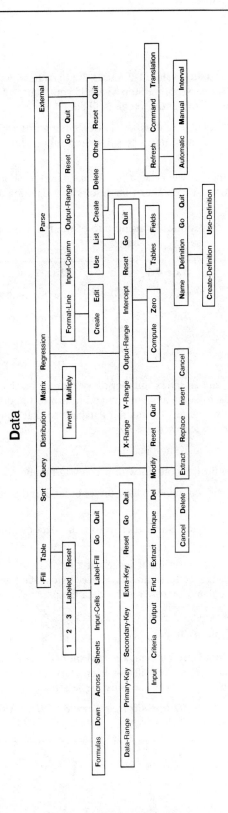

Important Cues

- If you do not supply a Stop value, 1-2-3 uses the default, which may give you results you don't want. Supply a Stop value if you want 1-2-3 to stop at a particular value before the entire range is filled.

- Use /Data Fill to fill a range of numbers in descending order. Enter a positive or negative Start value and enter a negative Step value. The Stop value must be less than the Start value.

- Enter dates and times in valid date/time formats except Short International (D5). Entering a MMM-YY combination results in a date for the first of that month.

- Enter date or time Step values by using one of the following formats:

To increment	Enter	Example
Days	# or #d	2 or 2d for two days
Weeks	#w	2w for two weeks
Months	#m	2m for two months
Quarters	#q	2q for two quarters
Years	#y	2y for two years

- Use /Data Fill to create an index numbering system for database entries. You can then sort the database on any column and return to the original order by sorting on the index column. To index a database so that you can return to the original sort order, follow these steps:

1. Insert a column through the data.

2. Use /Data Fill to fill the column with ascending numbers.

3. Sort the data by any column. Include the column of index numbers in the sort range.

4. To return to the original sort order, resort the data on the column containing the index numbers.

- Use data tables to change the input values in a formula so that you can see how the output changes. If the input values vary by constant amounts, use /df to create an input column or row for the data table.

Cautions

- Numbers generated by /Data Fill cover previous entries in the cell.

- If the Stop value is not large enough, a partial fill occurs. If the Stop value is smaller than the Start value, /df will not even start. Remember that if your increment is negative, the Stop value must be less than the Start value.

*For more information, see /**Data Table**, /**Range Format Other Automatic**, and Chapter 10.*

Data Table 1   /DT1

Purpose

Generates a table composed of one varying input value and the result from multiple formulas.

/Data Table 1 is useful for generating "what if" models that show the results of changing a single variable.

Reminders

- /Data Table 1 is used to show how changes in one variable affect the output from one or more formulas.

- Formulas in /dt1 can include @ functions.

- To change two variables in a single formula, use /Data Table 2.

- Before executing /dt1, enter data and formulas as though you are solving for a single solution (see cells B4..C8 in fig. D.1).

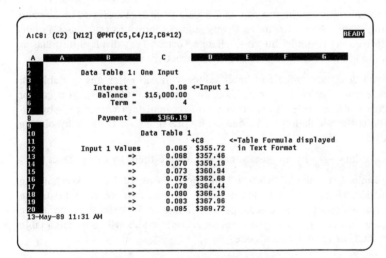

Fig. D.1.
/Data Table 1:
Solving with
single inputs.

- In the leftmost column of the table, enter the numbers or text that will be used as the replacement for the first variable (Input 1). In the second blank cell in the top row of the data table, type the address of the cell containing the formula. Enter additional formulas to the right on the same row. The upper-left corner of the /Data Table 1 area (C11 in fig. D.1) remains blank.

- Display the cell addresses of the formulas at the top of the table by using /Range Format Text. You may need to widen the columns if you want to see entire formulas.

Procedures

1. Type /dt1

2. Enter the table range so that it includes the Input 1 values or text in the leftmost column and the formulas in the top row. If a range has been previously specified, press Esc and define the range: type the address, type a range name, or highlight the range.

3. Enter the address for Input 1 by moving the cell pointer to the cell in which the first input values will be substituted. In figure D.1, the values from C12 to C20 will be substituted into C4.

4. 1-2-3 then substitutes an Input 1 value into the designated cell and recalculates each formula at the top of the data table. After each substitution, the results are displayed in the data table. In figure D.1, the variable input for interest (.080) produces a monthly payment of $366.19. With /Data Table **1**, you can see how "sensitive" the monthly payments are to variations in the interest rate.

Important Cues

- Make the formulas in the top row of the data table area easier to understand by using /**R**ange **N**ame **C**reate to change address locations (such as C4) into descriptive text (such as Interest). /**R**ange **F**ormat **T**ext displays formulas as text although the formulas still execute correctly.

- After you designate range and input values, you can enter new variables in the table and recalculate a new table by pressing Table (F8). You cannot recalculate a data table the same way you recalculate a worksheet—by setting **G**lobal **R**ecalculation to **A**utomatic, by pressing Calc (F9), or by placing {CALC} in a macro.

- If input values vary by a constant amount, create them by using /**D**ata **F**ill.

- /**D**ata **T**able **1**, combined with @D functions, is useful for cross-tabulating information from a data table. For example, suppose that you have a database of checks with amount and account code. Using an @DSUM function as the data table formula and an input range of account codes will generate a table of the total for each account code.

Cautions

- The data table will cover existing information in cells.

- Press the Table key (F8) to repeat the most recent /**D**ata **T**able command so that you update the table after worksheet changes.

For more information, see /**Data Fill** *and Chapter 10.*

Data Table 2 /DT2

Purpose

Generates a table composed of two varying input values and their effect on a single formula.

/Data Table 2 is useful for generating "what if" models that show the results of changing two variables.

Reminders

- Formulas in /Data Table 2 can include @ functions.

- If you have to change a single input and see its result on many formulas, use /Data Table 1.

- Before executing /Data Table 2, enter data and formulas as though you were solving for a single solution (see cells B4..C8 in fig. D.2).

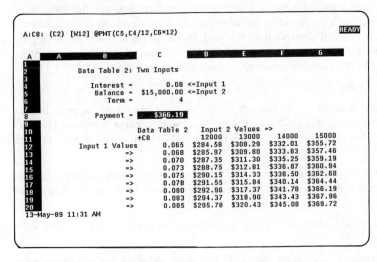

Fig. D.2.
/Data Table 2:
Solving with
two inputs and
a single
formula.

- In the leftmost column of the table, enter the numbers or text that will be used by the first variable, Input 1 (C12..C20 in fig. D.2). In the top row of the table, enter the numbers or text to be used by the second variable, Input 2 (D11..G11). In the blank cell (C11) in the upper-left corner of the table, type the address of the cell containing the formula (+C8).

- Make the cell address in the upper-left corner of the table visible with /Range Format Text. You may need to widen the columns if you want to see all of the formula.

Procedures

1. Type /dt2

2. Enter the table range so that it includes the Input 1 values in the leftmost column, and the Input 2 values as the top row. If a range has been previously specified, press Esc and define the range: type the address, type an assigned range name, or highlight the range.

3. Enter the address for Input 1 (C4) by moving the cell pointer to the cell in which the first input values will be substituted. In figure D.2, the values from C12 to C20 will be substituted in C4 as the interest amount. Press Enter.

4. Enter the address for Input 2 (C5) by moving the cell pointer to the cell in which the second input values will be substituted. In the example, the values from D11 to G11 will be substituted in C5 as the principal amount. Press Enter.

5. 1-2-3 then substitutes Input 1 and Input 2 and recalculates the formula in C8. After each combination of substitutions, the formula in C8 calculates a new answer and displays it in the grid. In the example, the variable inputs for interest (.075) and balance ($13,000) produce a monthly payment of $314.33. The monthly payment formula (C8) is referenced in cell C11.

Important Cues

- Make the formula in the top left corner of the table range easier to understand by using /**Range Name Create** to change address locations (C4) to descriptive text (Interest). Make the formula visible with /**Range Format Text**.

- After you designate range and input values, you can change input values in the input column and row, and recalculate a new table by pressing Table (F8).

- If input values will be an evenly spaced series of numbers, create them with /**Data Fill**.

- /**Data Table 2**, combined with @D functions, is useful for cross-tabulating information from a database table.

*For more information, see /**Data Fill** and Chapter 10.*

Data Table 3 /*DT3*

Purpose

Generates a three-dimensional table that shows how a single formula's results change when three input variables change.

/Data Table 3 is useful for generating "what if" models that show the results of changing three variables.

Reminders

- Formulas in /Data Table 3 can include @ functions.

- If you have to change a single input and see its effect on many formulas, use /Data Table 1. If you have to change two variables and see the effect on a single formula, use /Data Table 2.

- Before executing /Data Table 3, enter data and formulas as though you were solving for a single solution. Make sure that you get the correct result for a single solution before attempting a table. Figure D.3 shows a table created with /Data Table 3 that solves the @PMT formula in cell B2 for varying principal, interest, and term. The input variables are in cells B4, B5, and B6. The formula, instead of its results, appears in cell B2 because the cell was formatted as /Range Format Text.

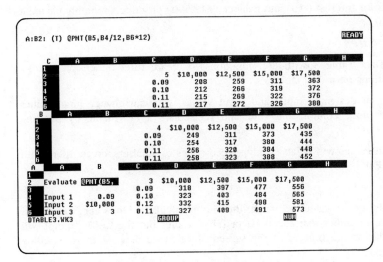

Fig. D.3.
/Data Table 3:
Solving with
three inputs.

- The table appears in worksheet A in the range C2..G6. In the leftmost column of the table, enter the numbers or text that will be used by the first variable, Input 1 (C3..C6 in fig. D.3). In the top row of the table, enter the numbers or text to be used by the second variable, Input 2 (D2..FG). At the top left corner of the table range, enter the third variable, Input 3 (C2). Use the /Copy command to copy the table range (C2..G6) to additional worksheets behind it. Replace Input 3 at the top left of the table range on each worksheet with each value you want tested for Input 3.

- Make the formula being evaluated, cell B2 in figure D.3, visible by using the /Range Format Text command. The formula is evaluated even though you can see the formula itself and not its result.

Procedures

1. Type /dt3

2. Enter the table range so that it includes the Input 1 values in the leftmost column, the Input 2 values as the top row, and the Input 3 value at the top left corner. Press Ctrl-PgDn to extend the range to additional worksheets at lower levels.

3. Enter the address for the formula cell (cell B2 in fig. D.3).

4. Enter the address for Input 1 (B4).

5. Enter the address for Input 2 (B5).

6. Enter the address for Input 3 (B6).

7. 1-2-3 then substitutes values from the table range into Input 1, Input 2, and Input 3 and recalculates the formula in B2. The result of that calculation is put in the table at the appropriate location. In the example, the variable inputs for Interest (.10) and Balance ($12,500) produce a monthly payment of $403.

Important Cues

- Use /Data Table 3 with @D functions to create three-dimensional cross-tabulations on a data table.

- After you designate range and input values, you can change input values in the input column and row, and recalculate a new table by pressing Table (F8).

- If input values will be an evenly spaced series of numbers, create them with /Data Fill.

Caution

Tables do not recalculate when the file recalculates. In some cases, you can enter a number that affects /Data Table results, but the CALC prompt will not display at the bottom of the screen. Recalculate data tables by pressing Table (F8).

*For more information, see /**Data Table 1**, /**Data Table 2**, /**Data Table Labeled**, and Chapter 10.*

Data Table Labeled   /DTL

Purpose

/Data Table Labeled is a flexible but more complex method of creating tables that test one or more input changes on one or more formulas.

Reminders

- Practice creating /Data Table **1**, **2**, or **3** before using /Data Table Labeled. Although a labeled data table is more flexible and allows greater analysis, such a table is more complex to create. Figure D.4 shows a table created with /Data Table Labeled.

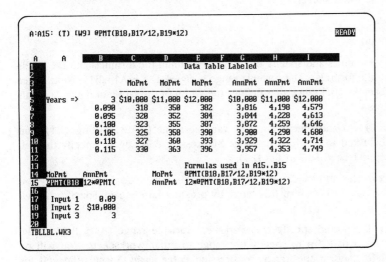

Fig. D.4.
/Data Table
Labeled:
Solving with
multiple inputs
and formulas.

- The labeled data table is in the range A:B3..B:I11. It is on two worksheets, uses three input variables, and produces a table showing the results of two formulas.

- Before building a table, solve a single-solution problem for each formula from which you want results. In figure D.4, cell A15 uses @PMT to calculate a monthly payment by using the input cells in B17..B19. Similarly, cell B15 calculates the total annual payments for the input cells in B17..B19. Both cells have been formatted with /Range Format Text so that you can read the formulas. (The formulas are repeated in cells E14 and E15.)

- Notice that A14 and B14 contain labels describing the formulas being calculated in the table. (This is the origin of the name of the command: /Data Table Labeled.)

- The formula labels from A14 and B14 must be copied to the top row of the /Data Table Labeled range—row 3. For example, MoPmt is in cells C3..E3. This tells the /Data Table Labeled command in which columns the results from MoPmt calculations should be placed. Similarly, AnnPmt is copied into cells G3..I3 so that the /Data Table Labeled command will know where to put results from the AnnPmt formula.

- Row 4 and column F demonstrate that the table can contain text or blank areas that can make the table more readable.

- Variables for Input 1 are put in the range B6..B11. Variables for Input 2 are put in the range C5..E5 and again in G5..I5. Input 3 is in cell A:B5.
- You build three-dimensional tables by copying this framework to other worksheets. Use the Copy command and Ctrl-PgUp to copy the table's framework into worksheets behind. Enter different Input 3 values, such as years 4, 5, and so on, in these sheets.

Procedures

1. Type /dtl

2. Select Formulas and specify the range containing the formulas and the labels above the formulas. The formula range in figure D.4 is A14..B15. Next, enter the formula label range that defines the width of the table. In figure D.4, this range is C3..I3.

3. Select Down and specify the row variable range (B6..B11 in fig. D.4). You will be asked to confirm the range by pressing Enter again. Specify the cell for Input 1 (cell B17 in fig. D.4).

4. Select Across and specify the column variable range (C5..I5 in fig. D.4). You will be asked to confirm this range by pressing Enter again. Specify the cell for Input 2 (cell B18 in fig. D.4).

5. Select Sheets and specify the worksheet variable range (A:B5..B:B5 in fig. D.4). Use Ctrl-PgUp to specify the range to other worksheets. You will be asked to confirm this range by pressing Enter again. Specify the cell for Input 3 (cell B19 in fig. D.4).

6. Select Input-Cells if you want to review or change any of the variable ranges and their corresponding input cells.

7. Select Go to calculate and fill the table.

Important Cues

- You can leave blank or text-filled rows or columns in the /Data Table Labeled range to make the table easier to read.
- The formula labels at the top of the /Data Table Labeled range must match the labels above each formula. Use the Copy command to create exact duplicates of the formula labels.
- The /Data Table Labeled command is flexible but complex. Refer to Chapter 10 for more examples and information on creating three-dimensional tables and tables that use more than three variables.

Caution

Plan your table arrangement and formulas before starting to build a labeled data table. Follow the steps in this entry's "Reminders" section to build the layout of your table before beginning the procedures to calculate the table.

*For more information, see /**Data Table 1**, /**Data Table 2**, /**Data Table 3**, /**Data Fill**, and Chapter 10.*

Data Sort   /DS

Purpose

Sorts the database in ascending or descending order, according to the entries in one or two columns.

Reminders

- Sorting can be done on one or more fields (columns). The first sort field is called the Primary-Key; the second is the Secondary-Key. Additional sorting using keys 3 through 253 is done with Extra-Key. All keys can be sorted in ascending or descending order.

- Save a copy of the worksheet with /**File Save** before sorting. Save to a different name to preserve your original file.

- If you want to return after sorting to records (rows) that are in a specific order after sorting, insert a column and use /Data Fill to fill it with index numbers. Re-sort on the index numbers to return to the original order. This procedure is described in more detail in the /Data Fill entry.

Procedures

1. Type /ds

2. Highlight the data range to be sorted. It must include every field (column) in the database but does not have to include every record (row). Only records in the specified range will be sorted, however. Do not include the field labels at the top of the database, or the labels will be sorted with the data. Enter the range: type the address, type a range name, or highlight the range. Press Enter.

3. Move the cell pointer to the column of the database that will be the Primary-Key; then press Enter.

4. Specify ascending or descending order by entering **A** or **D**.

5. Select Secondary-Key if you want duplicate copies of the Primary-Key sorted. Move the cell pointer to the column of the database that will be the Secondary-Key, and then press Enter.

6. Specify ascending or descending order by selecting **A** or **D**.

7. Select Extra-Key if you want to sort on additional keys. Enter the number of the extra key, from 3 to 253. Enter a cell address in the column this key will sort on.

8. Specify ascending or descending order by selecting **A** or **D**.

9. Repeat Steps 7 and 8 to sort on additional keys.

10. Select **G**o.

Important Cues

- Sorting occurs within each worksheet. If you select a three-dimensional sort range, data is sorted within each worksheet, but not across worksheets.

- Select **Q**uit to return to READY mode at any time. Select **R**eset to clear previous settings.

- Sort settings are saved with the worksheet.

- During the Install process, you can change the order in which 1-2-3 sorts characters. The three sort precedences are ASCII, Numbers First, and Numbers Last. In ASCII and Numbers First formats, cell contents are sorted as follows:

    Blank spaces
    Special characters (!, #, $)
    Numeric characters
    Alpha characters
    Special compose characters

- In ASCII, uppercase letters are sorted before lowercase; in Numbers First, the case of characters is ignored. Numbers Last is similar to Numbers First except that numeric data is sorted after alpha characters.

Cautions

- If you sort a database without including the full width of records, the sorted portion will be split from the nonsorted portion. Putting the records back together may be nearly impossible. If you saved the worksheet before sorting, you can retrieve the original file.

- Do not include blank rows or the data labels at the top of the database when you highlight the **D**ata-Range. Blank rows sort to the top or bottom of the database in ascending or descending order, and the data labels are sorted into the body of the database.

- Formulas in a sorted database may not be accurate because sorting switches rows to new locations. If the addresses do not use absolute and relative addressing correctly, the formulas in sorted records will change. As a rule, use a relative address in a formula when the address refers to a cell in the same row. If the address refers to a cell outside the database, use an absolute address.

*For more information, see /**Data Fill** and Chapter 10.*

Data Query Input   /DQI

Purpose

Specifies a range of data records to be searched.

The records can be within a worksheet's data table or within an external table. You can specify more than one data table.

Reminders

- You must indicate an input range before you use the Find, Extract, Unique, or Del command from the Data Query menu.

- The input range can be the entire database or a part of it.

- The input range must include the field names.

Procedures

1. Type /dqi

2. At the Enter Input range: prompt, specify the range of data records you want searched. Either type the range address or move the cell pointer to highlight the range. Be sure to include in the range the field names at the top of the range and portions of the records that may be off the screen.

3. To specify more than one data table, use an argument separator—a comma (,), period (.), or semicolon (;)—to separate the input ranges. Press Enter after specifying all the databases.

Caution

Redefine the input range if you add one or more rows to the bottom of the range, add one or more columns before or after the range, or delete the first column or the last row or column of the range. A defined input range will be adjusted automatically if you insert or delete rows or columns within the range.

*For more information, see /**Data Query Output**, /**Data Query Criteria**, /**Data Query Find**, /**Data Query Extract**, and Chapter 10.*

Data Query Criteria   /DQC

Purpose

Specifies the worksheet range containing the criteria that define what records are to be found.

Reminders

- You must indicate a criteria range before you use the Find, Extract, Unique, or Del options of the /Data Query command.

- You do not need to include in the criteria and output ranges all the field names in the database. If you do include all the field names, however, you won't have to alter the criteria range to apply a criterion to a new field.

- The first row of the criteria range must contain field names that exactly match the field names of the database. Use the /Copy command to copy field names from input ranges to ensure that criteria and input range field names exactly match.

- The row below the first row of the criteria range contains the search criteria.

- You can use more than one criteria for a search.

- More than one row can contain criteria, but no row in the criteria range should be blank.

- Criteria can be numbers, labels, or formulas. Numbers and labels must be positioned directly below the field name to which they correspond.

- Criteria labels can contain wild-card characters. An asterisk (*) stands for any group of characters; a question mark (?) represents a single character.

- A tilde (~) before a label excludes that label from a search.

- Criteria can contain logical operators (<, <=, >, >=, <>).

- You can use #AND#, #NOT#, or #OR# to create compound logical formulas as criteria.

- Criteria on the same row of the criteria range are treated as if they were linked by #AND# for every condition to be met. Criteria on separate rows are treated as if they were linked by #OR# for any condition to be met.

Procedures

1. Type /dqc

2. At the Enter Criterion range: prompt, specify or highlight the range that contains field names and criteria. The range should contain at least two rows: the first row for field names from the top row of the database you want searched, and the second row for the criteria you specify. Allow two or more rows for criteria if you use them to specify #OR# conditions.

Important Cues

- Use wild cards in the criteria if you are unsure of spelling or want to find data that may have been misspelled. 1-2-3 will search only for exact matches for the characters in the criteria range.

- You can place the criteria range in the data-entry portion of the worksheet and use a split screen to view the criteria and output ranges simultaneously.

Cautions

- Including a blank row in the criteria range causes all records to be found, retrieved, or deleted with Query commands.

- If you alter the number of rows in a defined criteria range, you need to redefine the range to reflect the change.

For more information, see **/Data Query Input**, **/Data Query Find**, **/Data Query Extract**, *and Chapter 10.*

Data Query Output   /DQO

Purpose

Assigns a location to which found records can be copied by the Extract or Unique commands.

Reminders

- You must indicate an output range before you use the Extract and Unique options of the /Data Query command. The Find and Del options do not use an output range.

- Locate the output range so that there is nothing below its columns. Locate the output range so that it will not overlap the input or criteria ranges.

- You can limit the output range by specifying the size of the (multiple-row) range. Or you can ensure that the output range is unlimited in size if you specify the range as the single row of field names. That way, the results of the search can be listed in the unlimited area below the field names.

- If the input range includes multiple databases with the same field names, precede field names in the output range with the database name, such as DBONE.AMOUNT and DBTWO.AMOUNT.

- The first row of the output range must contain field names that match the field names of the input and criteria ranges, but the field names in the output range can be in any order, and the label prefixes and the case of the letters can be different.

Procedures

1. Type /dqo

2. At the Enter Output range: prompt, specify or highlight the output field names. If you want a limited number of extracted records, include as many rows in the output range as you want extracted rows.

Cautions

- If you specify the row of field names as a single-row output range and use /Data Query Extract, matching records will be listed below the output range. Any information in the cells in the row-and-column path from directly below the output range through the bottom of the worksheet, however, will be erased. If you want to preserve any information in those cells, specify the output range as a multiple-row range. That way, cells below the last row of the output range will not be affected by any results of a search.

*For more information, see /**Data Query Input**, /**Data Query Criteria**, /**Data Query Extract**, /**Data Query Unique**, and Chapter 10.*

Data Query Find   /DQF

Purpose

Finds records in the database that meet conditions you have set in the criteria range.

Reminders

- /Data Query Find moves the cell pointer to the first cell of the first record that meets the condition. By pressing the up arrow or down arrow, you can display previous or succeeding records that meet the criteria. Using /dqf can be the best way to access a record in a database quickly.

- /Data Query Find works only with a single input range or external database.

- You must define the input range, external database (if one is used), and criteria range before using /Data Query Find. Enter a criterion that specifies the type of records you want in the criteria range.

Procedures

1. Type /dqf

2. The cell pointer highlights the first record that meets the criteria. You hear a beep if no record in the input range meets the criteria. Figure D.5 shows a found record that matches the criteria.

Fig. D.5.
Found record that matches criteria.

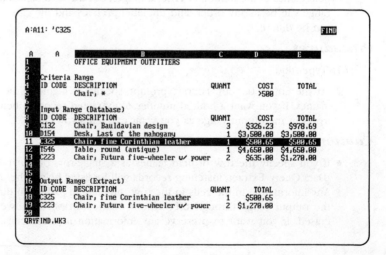

3. Press the up- or down-arrow key to move to the next record that meets the criteria. Pressing the Home key or the End key finds in the database the first or last record that meets the criteria.

4. You can edit contents within a record by moving the cell pointer right or left with the arrow keys. When the cell pointer highlights the cell you want to edit, press the Edit (F2) key and edit the cell contents. Press Enter when you have finished editing.

5. Return to the **Data Query** menu by pressing Enter or Esc when you are not in EDIT mode.

Important Cues

● After you have entered the /Data Query commands and ranges, you can repeat the operation simply by changing the criteria and pressing the Query (F7) key.

● /Data Query Find remembers the last input and criteria range used from the **Query** menu. You do not have to enter the input and criteria range if they are the same as those used by the previous database command. Check the current ranges by selecting **I**nput or **C**riteria; then press Enter to accept the range, or Esc to clear the old range so that you can specify a new one.

● Use wild cards (* or ?) in the criteria if you are unsure of the spelling or if you want to find data that may have been misspelled. 1-2-3 will find only exact matches for the characters in the criteria range.

● Before you delete records with /Data Query Del, use /Data Query Find to display the records that will be deleted.

Cautions

● If /Data Query Find will not find a record, use /**R**ange Erase to erase old criteria from the criteria range. A space character may have been used to "erase" a field in the criteria range. If so, /Data Query Find looks for a space in the database, a process resulting in no found records.

● If /Data Query Find finds all records, use the /Data Query Criteria command to check the size of the criteria range. Do not include blank rows in the criteria range; if you do, these commands find all records.

*For more information, see /**Data Query Input**, /**Data Query Criteria**, and Chapter 10.*

Data Query Extract   /DQE

Purpose

Copies to the output range of the worksheet those records that meet conditions set in the criteria.

Reminders

- /Data Query Extract extracts copies of information from the input range that matches specific criteria found in the criteria range (see fig. D.6, row 17).

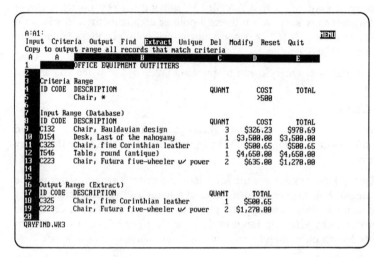

*Fig. D.6.
Extracted data
in an output
range.*

- You must define a 1-2-3 database complete with input, output, and criteria ranges. The output range must have field names entered exactly as they appear at the top of each database column.

- Choose an output range in a blank area of the worksheet. You can limit the output range to a specified number of rows, or you can give the output range an unlimited number of rows.

Procedure

Type /dqe

Important Cues

- Records that match the criteria range are copied to the output range. If there is not enough room in the output range, 1-2-3 beeps, and an error message appears.

- After entering new criteria in the criteria range, press the Query (F7) key to repeat the most recent query.

- /Data Query Extract remembers the last input, criteria, and output ranges used from the Query menu. You do not have to enter the ranges if they are the same as the previous ranges. Check the current ranges by selecting Input, Criteria, or Output; then press Enter to accept the ranges, or Esc to clear the old range so that you can specify a new one.

- Output ranges that are external ranges format and arrange extracted information according to the external database driver. Refer to your database driver documentation to learn more about this feature.

- Select the **Reset** command to clear all range settings.
- /**Data Query Unique** works the same way as /**Data Query Extract**, but /**Data Query Unique** extracts only unique records that meet the criteria.

Caution

If you select only the field names as the output range, you are given an unlimited amount of rows for the extracted report, but existing contents below the output field names are erased.

*For more information, see /**Data Query Find**, /**Data Query Unique**, /**Data External**, and Chapter 10.*

Data Query Unique   /DQU

Purpose

Copies to the output range of the worksheet unique records that meet conditions set in the criteria.

Records are sorted after being copied.

Reminders

- /**Data Query Unique** extracts copies of information from the input range that matches specific criteria found in the criteria range.
- You must define the input, output, and criteria ranges before using /**Data Query Unique**.

Procedure

Type /dqu

Important Cues

- Nonduplicate records that match the criteria range will be copied to the output range. If there is not enough room in the output range, 1-2-3 beeps, and an error message appears.
- Only field names in the output range are used to test whether a record has a duplicate. A single copy of all duplicates appears in the output range.
- To extract all records from the database, both duplicate and unique, use /**Data Query Extract**.
- After entering new criteria in the criteria range or copying new headings into the output range, press the Query (F7) key to repeat the most recent query.
- /**Data Query Unique** remembers the last input, criteria, and output ranges used from the Query menu. You do not have to enter the ranges if they are the same as the previous ranges. Check the current ranges by selecting

Input, Criteria, or Output; then press Enter to accept the ranges, or Esc to clear the old range so that you can specify a new one.

- Select **Reset** to clear all range settings.

- /Data Query **Unique** sorts the extracted records by the leftmost field.

Cautions

- As with other /Data Query commands, the field names in the criteria range must match the field names in the database.

- If you select only the field names as the output range, you are given an unlimited number of rows for the extracted report, but existing contents below the output field names will be erased.

*For more information, see **/Data Query Input**, **/Data Query Output**, **/Data Query Criteria**, **/Data Query Find**, **/Data Query Extract**, **/Data External**, and Chapter 10.*

Data Query Del   /DQD

Purpose

Removes from the input range any records that meet conditions in the criteria range.

Reminders

- Use /Data Query **Del** to "clean up" your database; remove records that are not current or that have been extracted to another worksheet.

- You must define a 1-2-3 database complete with input and criteria ranges.

- Create a backup file before using /dqd. If data is incorrectly deleted, a copy of the worksheet will be intact.

- Before deleting, use the /Data Query **Find** command to test that your criteria is accurate.

- To check which records will be deleted, select /Data Query **Find** after you have entered the input and criteria ranges. Use the up- and down-arrow keys to display the records that meet the criteria.

- Another method of checking the records marked for deletion is to use /Data Query **Extract** to make a copy of the records. Check this copy against the records you want to delete.

Procedures

1. Type /dqd

2. You will be asked whether you want to delete the records. Select **Cancel** to stop the command and not delete records. Select **Del** to remove the records from the input range.

3. Save the worksheet under a new file name by using /File Save. Do not save the worksheet under the same file name. Doing so will replace the original database with the database from which records have been deleted.

Important Cues

- After entering new criteria, press the Query (F7) key to repeat the most recent query.

- Create a "rolling" database that stores only current records and removes old records to archive files. Use /Data Query Extract to extract old records from the file; save them to another worksheet by using /File Xtract. Then use /Data Query Del to remove the old records from the database file.

Cautions

- As with other /Data Query commands, the field labels in the criteria range must match the field labels in the database. The labels can appear in a different order, but the spelling and cases must match. The easiest and safest method of creating criteria labels is to use /Copy.

- You can inadvertently delete more than you want with /Data Query Del, particularly if a row in the criteria range is empty when you execute /dqd. Make sure that your criteria range is set up correctly before you use this command.

For more information, see **/Data Query Find**, **/Data Query Extract**, **/Worksheet Delete Row**, **/Range Erase**, *and Chapter 10.*

Data Query Modify

Purpose

Inserts or replaces records in the input range with records from the output range.

Use this command to select a group of records, edit them, and then reinsert them into the database.

Reminder

Before using the Extract and Replace commands, you must have correct input, output, and criteria ranges.

Procedures

1. Type /dqm

2. Select one of the following items:

Menu Item	Description
Extract	Copies into the output range records that match the criteria
Replace	Replaces records in the input range (1-2-3 database or external database) with the corresponding records from the Modify Extract range
Insert	Adds new records to the bottom of the original input range
Cancel	Cancels the command without replacing records in the input range

3. If you choose **Extract**, you can modify the records in the output range. Start with Step 1 and choose **Replace** or **Insert** to update the input range when you are finished. Choose **Cancel** if you do not want to modify the input range.

Cautions

- The **Replace** command can replace a formula in the input range with a value from the output range. Be careful not to accidentally change formulas to values in your database.

- Do not use the /**Data Query Extract** command if you want to modify records and replace them. The /**Data Query Modify Replace** or **Insert** commands work only with data extracted by /**Data Query Modify Extract**.

- Do not insert or delete rows or sort records in the output range while using /**Data Query Modify**. Doing so reorganizes the records. 1-2-3 will not be able to recognize and restore them to their correct locations.

For more information, see /**Data External**, /**Data Query Extract**, /**Data Query Input**, /**Data Query Output**, *and Chapter 10.*

Data Distribution   /DD

Purpose

Creates a frequency distribution showing how often specific data occurs in a database.

For example, using data from a local consumer survey, you can have /**Data Distribution** determine how income is distributed. After you set up income brackets as a bin, /dd will show how many people's incomes fall within each bin. Figure D.7 shows an example of this type of distribution. The contents of column E (text values) were entered manually.

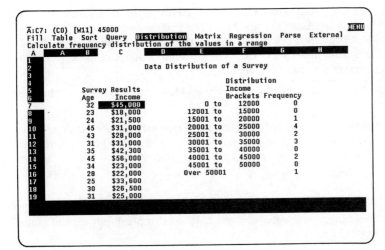

Fig. D.7.
Example of
/Data
Distribution.

Reminders

- /Data Distribution works only on numeric values.

- Data must be arranged in a *value range*: a column, row, or rectangular range.

- You must move the cell pointer to a worksheet portion that has two adjacent blank columns. In the left column, enter the highest value for each entry in the bin range. Enter these bin values in ascending order.

Procedures

1. Type /dd

2. Enter the value range, which contains the data being analyzed. The value range in figure D.7 is C7..C19.

3. Enter the bin range: type the range address, type a preset range name, or highlight the range. The bin range in figure D.7 is F7..F15.

4. The frequency distribution appears in the column to the right of the bin range. In figure D.7, the distribution appears in G7..G16. Note that the frequency column extends one row beyond the bin range. The last frequency value is the number of values that are greater than the last bin value.

Important Cues

- Use /Data Fill to create a bin range with evenly distributed bins.

- You can find distribution patterns of subgroups in your database by first using /Data Query Extract to create a select database. Use /Data Distribution to find distribution in the subgroup.

- You can make data distribution tables easier to read by including a text column at the left of the bin range.

- Use @DCOUNT with /Data Table **1** to determine the data distribution for text in a database. Enter the text being counted down the left column of the data table. The input cell is the cell in the criteria range into which you would manually insert text. The @DCOUNT function should be placed in the top row of the data table area.

- Use the /Graph commands to create bar and line graphs that display the data distributions.

- Use @DCOUNT if you need to count items that match more than one criterion. (/Data Distribution uses the bin as the only criterion.) Insert criteria in the criteria range by using /Data Table **1** or /Data Table **2**.

Cautions

- Text labels and blanks are evaluated as zero in the value's range.

- /Data Distribution overwrites any cell contents that previously existed in the frequency column.

*For more information, see /**Data Table 1**, /**Data Table 2**, /**Data Table 3**, /**Data Table Labeled**, /**Data Fill**, and Chapter 10.*

Data Matrix   /DM

Purpose

Multiplies column-and-row matrices of cells. Inverts columns and rows in square matrices.

Reminder

/Data Matrix, a specialized mathematical command, enables you to solve simultaneous linear equations. You also can do array math or array manipulations.

Procedures

To invert a matrix, follow these steps:

1. Type /dm

2. Choose Invert. You can invert a nonsingular square matrix of up to 80 rows and columns.

3. Enter the range address or range name of the range you want to invert.

4. Type or highlight an output range to hold the inverted solution matrix. You can indicate or point to only the upper-left corner of the output range. You can locate the output range anywhere on the worksheet, including on top of the matrix you are inverting.

5. Press Enter.

To multiply matrices, follow these steps:

1. Type /dm

2. Choose Multiply. You can multiply two rectangular matrices together in accordance with the rules of matrix algebra.

3. Enter the range address or range name of the first range to multiply. The number of columns of the first range must equal the number of rows of the second range. Again, the maximum size of the matrix is 80 rows by 80 columns.

4. Enter the range address or range name of the second range to multiply.

5. Enter an output range to hold the multiplied solution matrix. You can type or point to only the upper-left corner of the output range, and then press Enter. The resulting matrix has the same number of rows as the first matrix, and the same number of columns as the second.

Caution

The output matrix overwrites existing cell contents.

For more information, see Chapter 10.

Data Regression   /DR

Purpose

Finds trends in data by using multiple linear regression techniques.

Data regression calculates the "best straight line" relating dependent values to independent values.

Reminders

- /Data Regression measures the dependency of dependent values to independent. The measure of this dependency is displayed as R Squared. The closer R Squared is to one, the greater the dependency.

- A completed regression analysis produces the constant and X coefficients so that you can predict new values of Y from a given X. The following equation calculates Y values:

    Y = Constant + Coeff. of X1*X1 + Coeff. of X2*X2 + Coeff. of X3*X3 + .l.l.

- If there is a single X for each Y, the formula is the familiar formula for a straight line:

    Y = Constant + Coeff. of X1*X1

- The *Constant* term is the location where the best-fit line intersects the y-axis.

- The output area must be at least nine rows in length and two columns wider than the number of sets of X values (no less than four columns wide).

Procedures

1. Type /dr

2. Select **X-Range**; then specify the range containing up to 75 independent variables. The values must be in adjacent columns.

3. Select **Y-Range**; then specify the range containing a single column of dependent variables. This single column must have the same number of rows as the **X-Range**.

4. Select **Intercept** and choose one of the following:

Menu Item	Description
Compute	Calculates the best-fit equation. The y-axis intercept finds its own value.
Zero	Calculates the best-fit equation but forces the equation to cross the y-axis at zero when all X values are zero

5. Select **Output-Range** and enter the cell address of the upper-left corner of the output range.

6. Select **Go**.

Important Cues

- You can enter a row of coefficient labels between the Degrees of Freedom row and the X Coefficient(s) rows that will not be overwritten by the output range.

- To create a best-fit straight line from the results of /Data Regression, execute /dr, sort the original X and Y data in ascending order by using X data as the primary sort field (so that the graph will plot correctly), and then enter the following formula in the top cell of the calculated Y column:

  Ycalc = Xvalue * Coeff. of X1 + Constant

  Copy this formula down a column to produce all the calculated Y values for each real X value. Use the /Graph commands to generate an XY graph where the X range for the graph is the real X value. The A graph range is the original Y data, and the B graph range is the calculated Y data.

Caution

/Data Regression produces the warning Cannot Invert Matrix if one set of X values is proportional to another set of X values. They are proportional when one set of X values can be multiplied by a constant to produce the second set of X values.

For more information, see /Graph commands and Chapter 10.

Data Parse   /DP

Purpose

Separates the long labels resulting from /File Import into discrete text and numeric cell entries.

The separated text and numbers are placed in individual cells in a row.

Reminders

- Import the data with /File Import Text. Each row of text from the file appears in a single cell. Rows of text appear down a single column.

- The long label resulting from /File Import Text may appear to be entries in more than one cell; however, the long label is located in the single cell at the far left.

- If the file you are importing includes numbers surrounded by spaces and text within quotation marks, use /File Import Numbers. This command automatically separates numbers and text in quotation marks into separate cells.

- Find in the worksheet a clear area to which the parsed data can be copied, and then note the cell addresses of the corners. Move the cell pointer to the first cell in the column you want to parse.

- /Data Parse separates the long label by using the rules displayed in the format line. You can edit the format line if you want the data to be separated in a different way.

Procedures

1. Move the cell pointer to the first cell in the row where you want to begin parsing.

2. Type /dp

3. Select Format-Line.

4. Select Create. A format line is inserted at the cell pointer, and the row of data moves down. This format line shows 1-2-3's "best guess" at how the data in the cell pointer should be separated.

5. You may need to edit the format line if a parsed area is not wide enough to include all the data in a field or if a field is not the correct type. If you want to change the format line, select Edit from the Format-Line menu. Edit the format line and press Enter.

6. If the imported data is in different formats, such as an uneven number of items or a mixture of field names and numbers, you will need to create additional format lines. Enter these lines at the row where the data format changed. Create additional format lines by selecting Quit and repeating the procedure.

7. Select Input-Column.

8. Specify the column containing the format line and the data it will format. Do not highlight the columns to the right that appear to contain data but do not.

9. Select **Output-Range**.

10. Move the cell pointer to the upper-left corner of the range to receive the parsed data, and press Enter.

11. Select **Go**.

Important Cues

- Figure D.8 shows two format lines generated automatically by 1-2-3. The first format line is for the field names; the second is for the data. The initial format lines will separate inventory items that have a blank in the name. The asterisk (*) followed by an L shows where 1-2-3 "thinks" that a new field should begin.

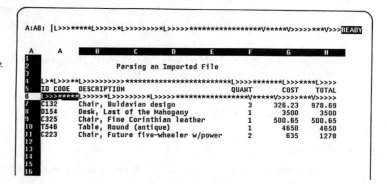

Fig. D.8.
Format lines
for /Data Parse.

- Use symbols to indicate the first character of a label (L), value (V), date (D), or time (T). You also can choose to skip a character (S), specify additional characters of the same type (>), or add a blank space (*) if the data is longer than the > symbols indicate.

- Editing keys can be used on the format line to change the parsing rules. In addition, you can use the up- and down-arrow, PgDn, and PgUp keys to scroll the information on-screen. Use this method to see whether the format line has assigned enough space for each piece of data being parsed.

Caution

The output range should be blank. Parsed data covers any information previously in the output range.

*For more information, see /**File Import** and Chapter 10.*

Data External Use /DEU

Purpose

Links 1-2-3 database capabilities to a table in an external database created by another program.

Reminder

A link must be made to an external table and that table assigned a range name before the table's information can be used by 1-2-3.

Procedures

1. Type /deu

2. Select the name of the database driver to use. Use SAMPLE if you want to use the dBASE III driver that comes with 1-2-3.

3. Enter or specify the path containing the external table you want to use.

4. Specify the table you want to use. Use EMPFILE to use the sample dBASE file that comes with 1-2-3.

5. Specify a range name to be assigned to the table you have selected. The range name can be up to 15 characters in length.

Important Cues

- The range name assigned in Step 5 can be used with @D functions to analyze the contents of external tables.

- Issuing the External Reset command breaks the link between the range name created in Step 5 and the external table.

Caution

/Data External commands work only if you have an external database driver designed for your external database. 1-2-3 comes with a dBASE III driver.

For more information, see /Data External Table, /Data External List, /Data External Reset, and Chapter 10.

Data External List /DEL

Purpose

Lists the tables and fields in an external database.

These lists can then be used with /Data Query commands to create criteria and output ranges used to extract information from a table in an external database.

Reminder

Before you use /Data External List, you must create a link to a table in an external database by using the /Data External Use command.

Procedures

1. Move to a blank area of the worksheet.

2. Type /del

3. Select **F**ields to extract the field names used in the external table.

4. Specify the name of the external table and location where you want the field names copied.

5. Select **Q**uit to return to the worksheet.

6. Use the /**R**ange **T**rans command to convert the column of field names into a row of field headings. Use these field headings as the top row for the /**D**ata **Q**uery Criteria range.

7. Copy the field names from the top of the criteria range to the top of where you want the output range. Use the /**D**ata **Q**uery **O**utput command to name the output range.

8. Enter a criterion in the criteria range.

9. Select /**D**ata **Q**uery **E**xtract to extract information from the external table into the output range in the worksheet.

Important Cue

If you are unfamiliar with entering criteria or extracting information, practice with a small worksheet database before using an external database.

Caution

A range name must be assigned to the table in the external database before you use this command. Use the /**D**ata **E**xternal **U**se command to create that range.

*For more information, see /**Data Query Criteria**, /**Data Query Extract**, /**Data Query Output**, /**Data External Use**, and Chapter 10.*

Data External Create   /DEC

Purpose

Creates the structure for a new table in an external database, using 1-2-3 to create the external table.

The new table will contain only field names.

Reminders

- Before you can define a new table in an external database, you must define its structure. The table structure is defined through the use of six columns with one row for each field name. The column and its contents appear in the following:

Column	Contents
1	Field names as they will appear in the external table
2	Data types as defined by the external database driver
3	Field widths for fields containing labels. Numeric fields may or may not need a width.
4	Column label for the field. The column label is a synonym for the field name and makes the field name easier to read because some such names are abbreviations.
5	Field descriptions that help users and programmers recognize the contents of the field
6	Creation strings used by the external database driver to specify the field in the table

For more detailed information on table definitions, check the documentation for your database driver.

- Use the /Data External List Fields command to find the definition of tables in a similar external database.

- If a database structure similar to the one you want already exists, select /Data External Create Definition Create-Definition. Specify the table or 1-2-3 database that will act as the model, and specify a location for the table definition. You can edit this definition and use it to create a new table definition.

Procedures

1. Type /de

2. Select Create Name to connect to the external database and assign a name to the table. Specify the database driver you want to use. Then enter a range name of up to 15 characters and press Enter. You may enter a table creation string. If you do not have a table creation string, press Enter.

3. Select Definition Use-Definition and specify the range containing the six-column table definition. Include all rows for the fields you want in the table.

4. Select Go.

Important Cues

- Use /Data Query Modify to add information to the new table from an Output range on the worksheet.

- Some databases will require a user name, ID, or password. Type each as requested and press Enter. See the network or database administrator if you are unable to access data.

Caution

/Data External Create Name must be used to name the database you are creating before it can be used with any /Data Query or @D functions.

For more information, see /Data Query Modify, /Data External Use, /Range Name, and Chapter 10.

Data External [Delete, Reset]   /DED or /DER

Purpose

/Data External Delete deletes a table from an external database; /Data External Reset breaks the link to a table in an external database.

Reminder

/Data External Delete can be used even if a link has not been established to an external table by means of the /Data External Use command.

Procedures

To delete a table in an external database, follow these steps:

1. Type /de

2. Select **Delete**.

3. Specify the name of the external database.

4. Specify the name of the table in the external database.

5. Select **Yes** to delete the table or **No** to keep the table.

To break the link to a table in an external database, but preserve the table on disk, follow these steps:

1. Type /dr

2. Select **Reset**.

3. Specify the range name of the link you want to break.

Important Cue

If a single table was in use only when you reset the table, the database driver is removed from memory.

Caution

Either the database administrator or database driver can prevent you from deleting tables in an external database.

*For more information, see /**Data External Use**, /**Data External List**, and Chapter 10.*

Data External Other /DEO

Purpose

Sends commands directly to an external database to control the database, update worksheet **Q**uery or **T**able functions, or translate data by using foreign-character sets.

Reminders

- A link to a table in an external database with the /Data External Use command must be created before you use /Data External Other.

- Commands used in /Data External Other **C**ommand are external database commands and are not related to 1-2-3 commands. Some database drivers may not allow the use of **O**ther **C**ommand.

Procedures

To update the worksheet for changes that may have occurred in the database, follow these steps:

1. Type /de

2. Select **O**ther **R**efresh.

3. Choose one of the following items:

Menu Item	Description
Automatic	Updates the worksheet's data from the external database and recalculates the worksheet with the time interval you specify with the **R**efresh **I**nterval command.
Interval	Sets the frequency with which updates occur. Enter the number of seconds from 0 to 36000 (one hour). The default is 1 second.
Manual	Stops /Data Query and /Data Table commands and worksheet recalculations from automatically updating.

To send commands to an external database, follow these steps:

1. Type /de

2. Select **O**ther **C**ommand.

3. Specify the database driver.

4. Specify the name of the external database.

5. Enter a command or the cell address containing a command as a label. These commands will be shown in your database driver documentation or in the database documentation.

To translate character sets used by an external database, follow these steps:

1. Type /de

2. Select **O**ther **T**ranslation.

3. Specify the name of the database driver.

4. Specify the name of the table you want translated.

5. Specify the name of a character set.

Important Cue

The /**D**ata **R**efresh **I**nterval resets with every work session unless you save it with /**W**orksheet **G**lobal **D**efault **U**pdate.

*For more information, see /**Data External** commands and Chapter 10.*

System and Quit Commands   /S and /Q

System   */S*

Purpose

Leaves the current worksheet, exits from 1-2-3 temporarily so that you can run operating-system commands, and enables you to return to 1-2-3 and the worksheet.

Reminders

- Be certain that the programs you run from within 1-2-3 can fit in your computer's available memory. Do not load or run memory-resident programs while at the system level.

- If you want to run an external operating-system command, be sure that the command is available on your disk drive or is on the path for a hard disk system.

Procedures

1. Type /s

2. Type the internal operating-system commands or program names that you want to run.

3. When you have finished running a program, return to the operating system.

4. Return to 1-2-3 from the operating-system prompt by typing **exit**.

Important Cue

For a complete discussion of the various operating-system commands, see *Using PC DOS*, 3rd Edition; *MS-DOS User's Guide*, 3rd Edition; or *Using OS/2*, all published by Que Corporation.

For more information, see Chapter 2.

Quit   */Q*

Purpose

Leaves 1-2-3 for the current work session and returns to the operating system.

Reminder

Make sure that you have saved the current worksheet and graph before exiting from 1-2-3. If print jobs are pending and you want them completed, do not quit.

Procedures

1. Type /q

2. Press Y to quit 1-2-3 and return to the operating system. Press N to return to 1-2-3 and the current worksheet.

3. If you made changes to the worksheet, press Y to quit without saving. Press N to return to the worksheet.

4. If you started 1-2-3 from the Access System menu, you will be returned to it. From the Access System menu, choose Exit to leave 1-2-3. If you started 1-2-3 by typing **123**, you will be returned to the operating system.

Important Cue

Use COPY or DISKCOPY to create a backup of important files. To guard against data loss, be sure to make backup copies regularly and keep a weekly archival backup copy at a separate location. In most cases, your computer can be replaced, but your data and worksheets cannot.

Caution

Worksheets not saved with /File Save or /File Xtract are lost when you exit from 1-2-3. Changes to existing worksheets or graphs will not be recorded unless the worksheet has been saved with /File Save.

*For more information, see /**File Save**, /**File Xtract**, and Chapter 2.*

A

Installing 1-2-3 Release 3

Installing 1-2-3 Release 3 is much easier than installing previous releases of 1-2-3. An Install program makes installation almost automatic; once you start the program, you simply follow the on-screen instructions. Note that you must install Release 3 on a hard disk. The Install program is designed for this type of installation. You cannot run Release 3 from a floppy disk.

The Install program begins by creating a subdirectory on your hard disk. Then the program copies the program files to the new subdirectory. The program also asks you to select the type of video display you have, as well as the type of printer. Before you install Release 3, verify the brand and model of your printer. The program can detect the type of video display you use.

You need about 15 or 20 minutes to complete the installation. When you are ready to begin, turn on your computer and follow the instructions in this appendix.

Checking DOS Configuration

If you are configuring 1-2-3 to run under DOS, you must complete one preliminary step before you install Release 3. You must make sure that DOS is configured adequately to run 1-2-3. To do so, check your CONFIG.SYS file for the FILES statement. CONFIG.SYS is found on your start-up hard disk in the root directory. Type the following command to see the contents of CONFIG.SYS (assuming that drive C is your start-up hard disk):

TYPE C:\CONFIG.SYS

The screen will display something like the following:

```
FILES=25
BUFFERS=20
DEVICE=C:\BIN\ANSI.SYS
```

The FILES statement tells DOS how many files can be open at once. The minimum number of files you should have is 20 (FILES=20). If you do not have a FILES statement or if the number of files is less than 20, you must change your CONFIG.SYS file. You can edit CONFIG.SYS with any text editor, such as EDLIN, or with a word processor that can save files as ASCII unformatted text.

If you modify your CONFIG.SYS file, be sure to restart your computer. A change in CONFIG.SYS does not modify DOS until you reload DOS. Restart your computer with the Ctrl-Alt-Del sequence.

OS/2 users do not need to check their configuration. While DOS has a specific ceiling for the number of files that it manages, OS/2 does not have this restriction.

Using the Install Program

1-2-3 Release 3 comes with 4 high-density 5 1/4-inch or 7 double-density 3 1/2-inch high-capacity disks. Release 3 is also available on 14 double-density 3 1/2-inch disks to users who are upgrading from a previous version of 1-2-3. The disks are labeled as follows:

5 1/4-inch high-density (1.2M)	Install disk, Drivers disk, 1-2-3 System disk, and Font disk
5 1/4-inch double-density (360K)	Install disk, Utility disk 1, Utility disk 2, Utility disk 3, Translate disk, 1-2-3 System disk 1 (DOS), 1-2-3 System disk 2 (DOS), Drivers disk 1, Drivers disk 2, Font disk 1, and Font disk 2
3 1/2-inch double-density (720K)	Install disk, Translate disk, 1-2-3 System disk (DOS), 1-2-3 System disk (OS/2), Drivers disk 1, Drivers disk 2, and Font disk

After installation is complete, be sure to make backup copies of the original disks and store the originals in a safe place.

Starting the Install Program

To install 1-2-3, place the Install disk in drive A. If you are using OS/2, start the DOS-mode session. From this point, OS/2 and DOS installation operate the same.

Switch to drive A by typing **A:** and pressing Enter. At the DOS or OS/2 DOS-mode A > prompt, type **install** and press Enter.

You first see 1-2-3's welcome screen (see fig. A.1). Read the information on-screen, and then press Enter to continue the installation and register your disks.

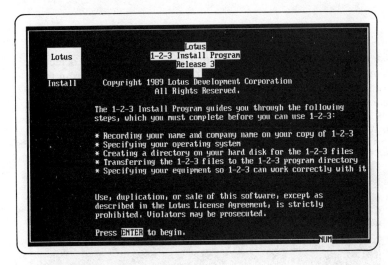

Fig. A.1.
The installation welcome screen.

Registering Your Original Disks

To make your disks usable, you must *register* them by entering and saving your name and company name on the Install disk. When you see the screen shown in figure A.2, type your name and press Enter, and then type your company name. Be sure that you have typed the information correctly. If everything is correct, press Ins (the Insert key) to continue.

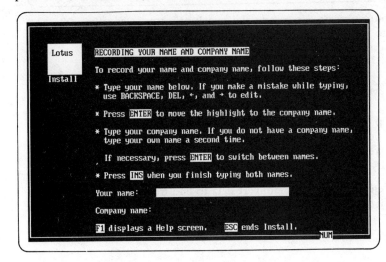

Fig. A.2.
The registration screen.

The Install program then asks whether you want to record what you typed on the disk. Choose **Yes** and press Enter. Your typed information is recorded, and your copy of 1-2-3 is now registered. Your name and company name, along with a serial number, will appear every time you start 1-2-3.

Selecting Your Operating System

After you register your disks, the next screen that appears asks you to select the operating system under which you want to run 1-2-3. As you can see from figure A.3, you can run Release 3 under DOS, OS/2, or both DOS and OS/2. Type the number that corresponds to your selection and press Enter. For example, to run 1-2-3 with DOS only, type **2** and press Enter. (Note: If you are installing 5 1/4-inch double-density disks, you won't see the screen shown in fig. A.3.)

Fig. A.3.
The screen for selecting your operating system.

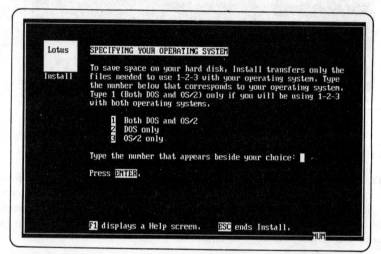

Notice that you can press Esc to exit the Install program at any time. You also can press F1 to receive help. The help screens provide an explanation of each screen you encounter as you install 1-2-3.

Choosing Files To Copy

In the next step of the installation procedure, you can choose to copy the Translate files (see fig. A.4). Translate is a program that converts outside data files, such as those created by Symphony and dBASE, as well as data file formats, such as DCA and DIF, to 1-2-3 and vice versa.

Translate is useful if you plan to convert data to and from 1-2-3 and other programs. To copy the Translate files during the installation, press Y and then press Enter.

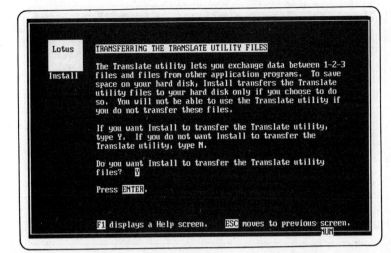

Fig. A.4.
The screen for copying the Translate files.

Creating a Directory for the 1-2-3 Files

The next screen allows you to choose the hard disk on which you install 1-2-3 (see fig. A.5). Most often, you install programs on drive C. If you want to install 1-2-3 on drive C, press Enter. If you want to install 1-2-3 on a different drive, type the letter of the drive—for example, **D**—and press Enter.

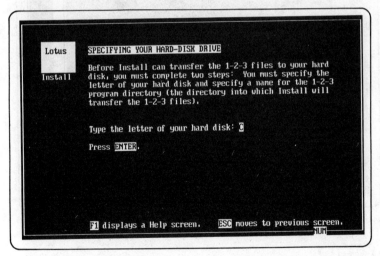

Fig. A.5.
The drive being specified.

After you choose the drive, you are prompted for the name of the directory to which to copy the 1-2-3 files. The default directory name is \123R3 (see fig. A.6). You can type another name if you want. Press Enter to continue.

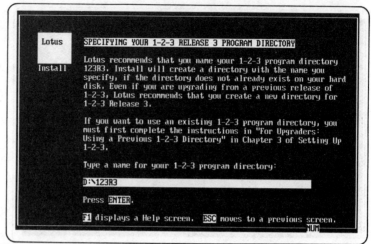

Fig. A.6.
The directory
being specified.

If the directory does not exist, the Install program creates it. First, the Install program asks you to confirm that the directory should be created, as shown in figure A.7. If you want to change the name, press Enter to accept the N default. Or press Y and then press Enter to confirm that the directory should be created.

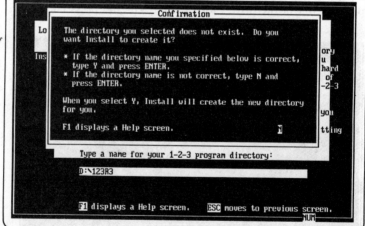

Fig. A.7.
The creation of
the directory
being
confirmed.

Copying Files

After you name the drive and directory, the Install program begins copying files to the hard disk. The program copies files first from the Install disk. After copying the files, the program prompts you to place the next disk in drive A. Which disk comes next depends on which disks you are using to install 1-2-3. You are prompted for the following disks in the order listed here:

5 1/4-inch high-density (1.2M)	Drivers disk, 1-2-3 System disk
5 1/4-inch double-density (360K)	Utility disk 1, Utility disk 2, Utility disk 3, Translate disk, 1-2-3 System disk 1, 1-2-3 System disk 2
3 1/2-inch double-density (720K)	Translate disk, Drivers disk 1, 1-2-3 System disk

Note: The Translate disk is necessary only if you answered Yes that you wanted to copy the Translate files. The 1-2-3 System disks are for either DOS or OS/2, depending on your choice during installation. If you chose to install 1-2-3 for both DOS and OS/2, then the 1-2-3 System disks for DOS are requested first, followed by the 1-2-3 System disks for OS/2.

Remove the Install disk from drive A, insert the next disk in the required order, and press Enter to continue. The program copies files from that disk to the hard disk. Continue placing the appropriate disks in the drive as you are prompted.

Configuring 1-2-3 for Your Computer

After the program copies files from the System disk, the second part of the installation begins (see fig. A.8). The first screen that appears provides information about making selections in this part of the installation. Press Enter to continue to the Main menu (see fig. A.9).

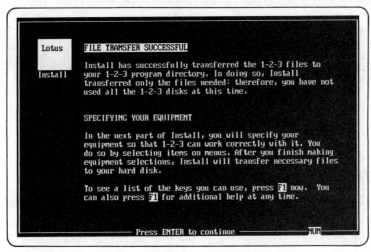

Fig. A.8.
The second part of the installation process being started.

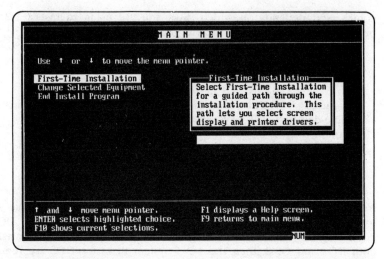

Fig. A.9.
The Main
menu.

In the Main menu, the first option, First-Time Installation, is highlighted. To make a different selection, press the up- or down-arrow keys to highlight the correct selection, and then press Enter. Because you are installing 1-2-3 for the first time, simply press Enter.

Note: After you install 1-2-3 to your hard disk, you can change your configuration. For example, if you purchase a new printer, you need to add the printer to 1-2-3's configuration. In this case, you choose Change Selected Equipment from this menu. See the section "Changing 1-2-3's Configuration" later in this appendix.

Next, the program displays what it detects as the type of video display. Figure A.10 shows the screen that appears when the program has detected a Video Graphics Array. Note this information and press Enter. When the Screen Selection menu appears, choose the type of display detected (see fig. A.11).

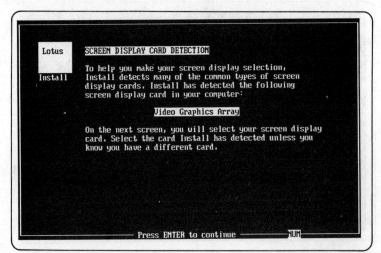

Fig. A.10.
The screen
display being
detected.

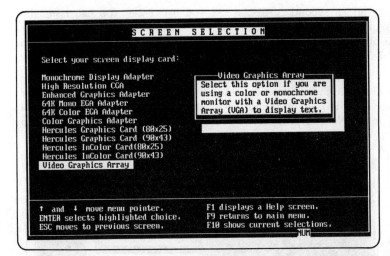

Fig. A.11.
The screen
display being
selected.

Often, a video display has more than one mode or way of displaying information on-screen. After you select your display, the program displays the available modes. Figure A.12 shows the modes for a VGA. If your video display offers more than one mode, choose the one that best suits your needs. The selected mode in this case displays 25 lines with 80 characters per line in color. After 1-2-3 is installed, you can change this selection.

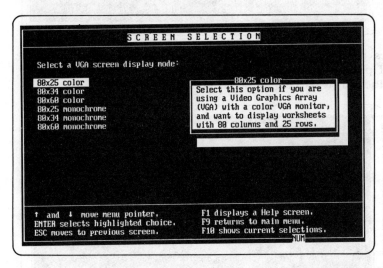

Fig. A.12.
The video
display modes.

If your video display does not offer different modes for displaying information on-screen, you will not see the screen in figure A.12. Instead, the Install program records the display you chose and moves on to installing a printer.

In some cases, you may have more than one video display card in your computer or you may want to install more than one video mode. 1-2-3 lets you install a primary display and a secondary display. As you use 1-2-3, you can issue the /Worksheet Window Display command and choose to activate the primary or secondary display driver. For now, install just one display. See the section "Installing 1-2-3 for Two Displays" for instructions on adding a secondary display.

You next select a printer. First, you are asked whether you want to use a printer with 1-2-3 (see fig. A.13). If you do not have a printer or do not want to install a printer now, select No and press Enter to continue. Otherwise, press Enter to select Yes.

Fig. A.13.
A printer being installed.

Choosing **Yes** displays a Printer Selection menu (see fig. A.14). Highlight the brand of printer you have and press Enter. Notice that in figure A.14, HP (Hewlett-Packard) is selected as the brand of printer.

Fig. A.14.
The brand of printer being selected.

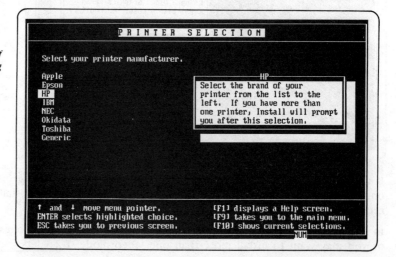

After you select the brand of printer, you next select the model. In figure A.15, for example, the HP LaserJet II with Added Memory is the selected model. When you select the correct model, press Enter.

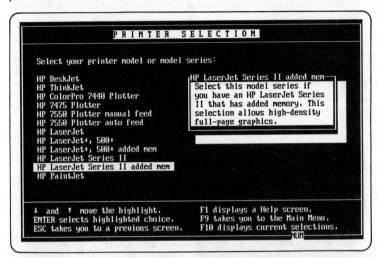

Fig. A.15. The printer model being selected.

If your printer supports font cartridges (most laser printers and a few dot-matrix printers allow you to add fonts), you can choose which font cartridge you will be using with 1-2-3. For the HP LaserJet II with Added Memory, the font cartridge selected is the 92286Z Microsoft 1A cartridge (see fig. A.16). Select the cartridge you want and press Enter. If, however, your printer does not support font cartridges, your printer information is recorded and you will not see this screen. Install continues normally.

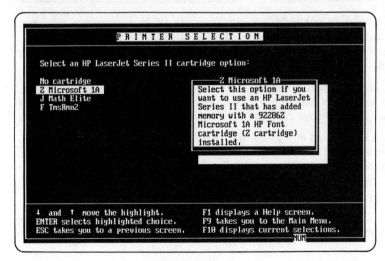

Fig. A.16. The font cartridge being selected.

After you install your printer, you are asked whether you want to install another printer. Answering **Yes** returns you to the Printer Selection menu. Here you follow the same procedure to select another printer. If you have only one printer or if you do not want to install another printer at this time, press Enter to answer No—the default answer.

After you make your video and printer selections, the program prompts you to name your driver configuration file or DCF (see fig. A.17). The DCF contains all the information from your responses to questions about your display type and printer. At the prompt that appears, you can answer **No**, and the program automatically will name the file 123.DCF. Or you can answer **Yes** and name the file something else.

Fig. A.17.
The driver configuration file (DCF) being named.

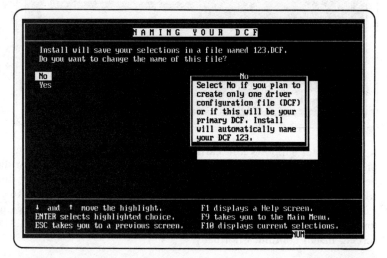

To use a DCF other than 123.DCF, you supply the DCF's name when you start 1-2-3. For example, if you create a DCF called 60LINE.DCF, when you start 1-2-3, you type **123 60LINE** and press Enter. If you use the default name, you don't have to specify the DCF when you start 1-2-3.

For the first-time installation, choose **No** and press Enter to accept the default name. In the section "Changing 1-2-3's Configuration," the benefits of having more than one DCF on your disk, each with its own name, are explained.

The Install program copies files to the hard disk to complete the installation. The copied files differ, based on your selection of video display and printer. However, you may be asked to type the disk drive that contains the 1-2-3 disk. Type **A**, for example, and press Enter.

The Install program asks you to insert disks for copying files based on your configuration of 1-2-3. Again, the disks requested depend on what type of disks you are using to install the program. The disks are requested in the following order:

5 1/4-inch high-density (1.2M)	Install disk, Drivers disk, Font disk
5 1/4-inch double-density (360K)	Drivers disk 1, Drivers disk 2, Font disk 1, Font disk 2
3 1/2-inch double-density (720K)	Drivers disk 1, Drivers disk 2, Font disk

When all files have been copied to the hard disk and no errors have occurred, a screen appears which states that the installation was successful (see fig. A.18). Press Enter to continue to the Exit menu (see fig. A.19).

From the Exit menu, select **Yes** to end the installation procedure. If you want to make additional changes to your configuration or if you decide to add other DCFs (so that you can start 1-2-3 in different configurations), select **No** and press Enter.

Changing 1-2-3's Configuration

In some cases, you may need to change 1-2-3's configuration. For example, if you purchase a new printer or a new video display, you must reconfigure 1-2-3 for that printer or video display. Also, if you want to create additional DCFs, you need to start the Install program again.

After you install 1-2-3 on your hard disk, you can start and run the Install program easily. First, make the directory that contains 1-2-3 the current directory.

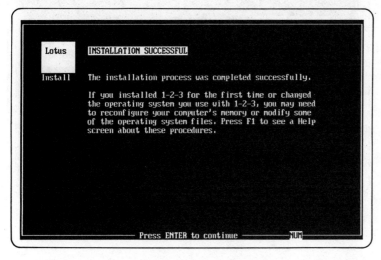

Fig. A.18.
A successful installation.

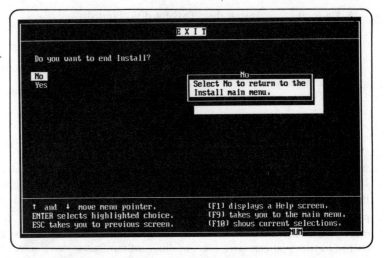

Fig. A.19.
The Exit menu.

For example, if the directory is C:\123R3, type the following command from a
C› prompt and press Enter:

CD \123R3

Next, type **install** and press Enter. A welcome screen appears, just as it did when
you installed 1-2-3 for the first time. Press Enter to continue to the Main menu.
This time, choose Change Selected Equipment. The Change Selected Equipment
menu appears as shown in figure A.20.

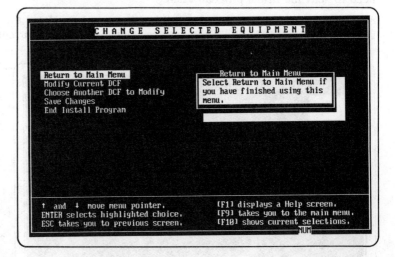

Fig. A.20.
*The Change
Selected
Equipment
menu.*

The menu selections have the following actions:

Return to Main Menu	Returns to the Main menu
Modify Current DCF	Allows you to change the configuration of the current DCF (normally 123.DCF)
Choose Another DCF to Modify	Allows you to choose a different DCF to place in memory for changing
Save Changes	Saves any modifications to the current DCF to the disk
End Install Program	Exits the Install program

If you purchase a new printer or video display, you need to modify the current DCF. To do so, you select Modify Current DCF. The Modify Current DCF menu appears (see fig. A.21). Here, you can change the selected display, printer, or country. Press F10 to display a screen that shows the current configuration.

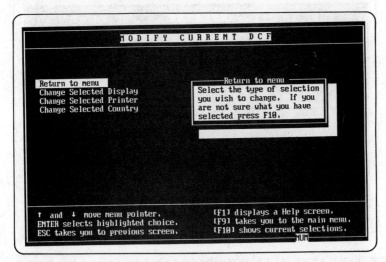

Fig. A.21.
The Modify
Current DCF
menu.

The selections for display and printer are similar to the ones available when you first installed 1-2-3. However, before you can choose a new display or printer, you must delete your previous selection.

For example, to change the video display mode, select Change Selected Display. Notice that on the Display screen, the Video Graphics Array selection has a 1 in front of it (see fig. A.22). The 1 indicates that this item is currently selected. With Video Graphics Array highlighted, press Enter. Notice that 80X25 color also has a 1 in front of it (see fig. A.23).

To select a new mode—for example, 80×60 color (60 lines, 80 characters per line, in color)—you first must "unselect" 80×25 in color. Highlight 80×25

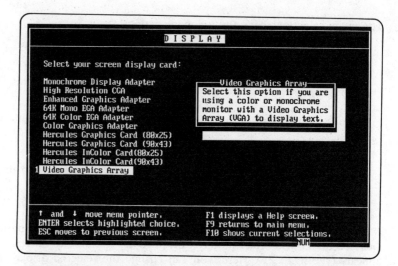

Fig. A.22.
The current
display.

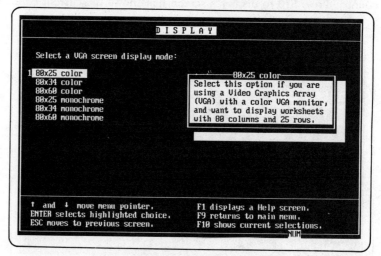

Fig. A.23.
The current
display mode.

color (or your display's variant) and press the space bar. Notice that the 1 disappears. Use the down-arrow key to highlight 80×60 color and press the space bar. The 1 appears in front of 80×60 color (see fig. A.24). Press Enter to return to the Modify Current DCF screen.

Next, choose Return to Menu; this selection returns you to the Change Selected Equipment menu. Select Save Changes. You are prompted to name this DCF. Because the current file, 123.DCF, contains the video mode selection for 25 lines and 80 characters per line and you now have selected 60 lines and 80 characters per line, you may want to change the name of your DCF. Assigning a new name gives you the ability to start 1-2-3 in either video mode. Using the right-arrow key, move your cursor past C:\123R3\ and delete 123. Type **60LINE**, as shown

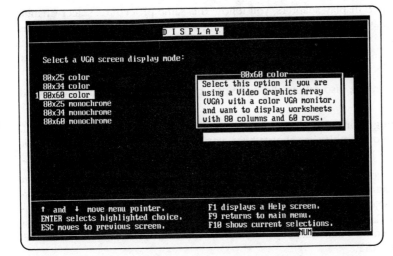

Fig. A.24.
The display mode being changed.

in figure A.25, and press Enter. The file 60LINE.DCF is created in the \123R3 directory.

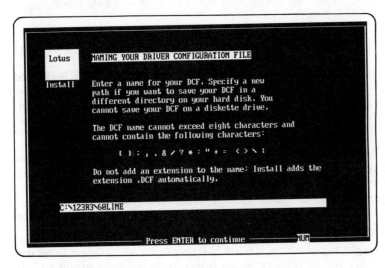

Fig. A.25.
The DCF being named.

As you save your DCF, be prepared to insert the Drivers disk(s) and then the Font disk(s), if requested. Depending on the changes you made to the configuration, the Install program may have to read files from these disks. You are prompted for the drive, and then you are prompted to place one of the disks in the drive.

Finally, a screen appears which states that the installation was completed successfully. Press Enter to return to the Change Selected Equipment screen.

To change video display adapters, you follow this same procedure: select Change Selected Display, highlight the current adapter, and press Del. If your adapter has video modes, press the space bar to toggle off the mode, and then press Esc. Highlight the correct video adapter and press Enter. The new video adapter selection is the current selection.

To change printers, also follow the same procedure, but select Change Selected Printer.

Note: Creating more than one driver configuration file (DCF) can be useful. While only two examples are shown here, you will, no doubt, find other uses for multiple DCFs.

Suppose that you install 1-2-3 with the Country selection Numbers First, so that information starting with a number will be sorted to the beginning of your information. However, you also would like to sort the same information with the setting Numbers Last. You can create a second DCF that contains the Numbers Last setting. You could name that DCF NULAST.DCF. To start 1-2-3 with this DCF, type **123 NULAST**.

Another use for more than one DCF has already been shown. If your video display has more than two display modes, you can create more than one DCF. Each DCF, then, would contain the information needed for each display mode.

Installing 1-2-3 for Two Display Drivers

Perhaps your computer has two video displays, or your video display is capable of displaying information in more than one mode. 1-2-3's /Worksheet Window Display command allows you to switch between two video drivers. While configuring 1-2-3 with the Install program, simply choose the two video drivers you want.

For example, for your initial installation, you installed 1-2-3 for a Monochrome monitor. But you also have in your computer a Color/Graphics Adapter (CGA) with a color monitor you would like to use with 1-2-3. Select Modify Current DCF, and then select Change Selected Display. Highlight Color Graphics Adapter and press Enter. When you press F10 to display your current selections, your screen will look similar to figure A.26.

As another example, suppose that you initially installed a VGA display using the mode 80×25 color as your primary display driver. Now you want to add 80×60 color as a secondary display driver. Select Modify Current DCF, and then select Change Selected Display. Highlight Video Graphics Array and press Enter. Using the down-arrow key, highlight the 80×60 color selection and press the space bar. Your screen will look like the one shown in figure A.27. Press Enter to accept the selections.

You may use any combination of compatible display adapters and modes. However, you are limited to two. Creating multiple DCFs will give you the capability to use different combinations of video display adapters and modes.

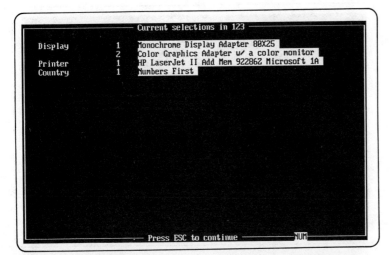

Fig. A.26.
The current
DCFs listed.

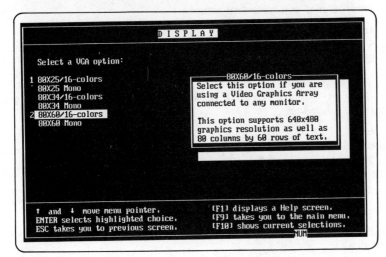

Fig. A.27.
The current
display driver
after
modification.

Changing the Selected Country

You use Change Selected Country to change the sorting order that 1-2-3 uses. Notice that three options are available when you select Change Selected Country (see fig. A.28).

The selections are as follows:

Numbers First — Numbers are sorted before letters

Numbers Last — Letters are sorted before numbers

ASCII — Characters are sorted according to the ASCII table

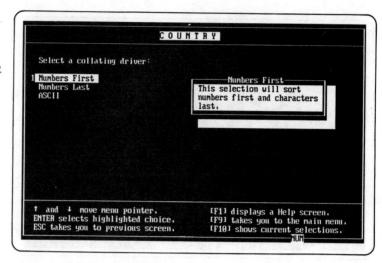

Fig. A.28.
A sort order
being selected.

Suppose, for example, that you have four entries:

123 Main Street
Adams Rib Plaza
4 Market Place
ADAMS RIB PLAZA

With the Numbers First option selected, sorting the four entries in ascending order results in the following:

123 Main Street
4 Market Place
Adams Rib Plaza
ADAMS RIB PLAZA

With the same preceding entries, the Numbers Last selection sorts the entries as in the following:

Adams Rib Plaza
ADAMS RIB PLAZA
123 Main Street
4 Market Place

In an ASCII table, each character is assigned a numeric value. Numbers have lower numeric values than letters. Uppercase letters have a lower numeric value than lowercase letters. Therefore, sorting the entries again in ASCII order results in the following order:

123 Main Street
4 Market Place
ADAMS RIB PLAZA
Adams Rib Plaza

These three options give you greater flexibility in sorting data.

Choosing Another DCF

In some cases, you may need to modify a DCF other than the one currently in memory. For example, if you have purchased a new video display, you need to update all DCFs in order to use it. To update the DCFs, start the Install program, and from the Change Selected Equipment screen, select Choose Another DCF to Modify. The screen shown in figure A.29 is displayed. Type the name of the DCF you want to modify and press Enter. The DCF is loaded into memory, and you return to the Change Selected Equipment screen. From this screen, select Modify Current DCF and make changes to the file as described previously in this chapter.

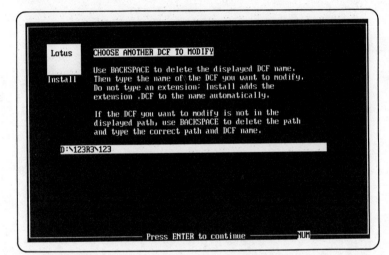

Fig. A.29.
Another DCF to modify being chosen.

Summary

You will find that installing 1-2-3 is a simple process. The Install program handles the installation automatically. You need only make selections and follow on-screen instructions.

After you install the program, you can make changes easily. The capability to store your configuration in a separate file and create more than one configuration file is handy. Not only can you easily modify 1-2-3, but you can customize 1-2-3 in several different ways, choosing the customization you want when you start 1-2-3.

Compose Sequences for the Lotus Multibyte Character Set

The Lotus Multibyte Character Set (LMBCS) includes characters you may not find on your keyboard. These special characters include monetary symbols, mathematical symbols and operator signs, and diacritical marks.

To enter a character that is not on your keyboard, you press the Compose key (Alt-F1) and then a series of keystrokes that Lotus calls a *compose sequence*. To create some characters, you can use one of several compose sequences. For example, to enter the British pound sign (£), you press compose (Alt-F1) and then type **L=** or **I=**. Depending on your hardware, some LMBCS characters may not display on your monitor or print from your printer. If a character does not display on your screen, print a sample range to see whether the character is available from your printer.

The table that follows lists the special characters with their LMBCS codes, a description of each character, and the compose sequence(s) used to create each character.

If you use some characters frequently, you can easily create macros to perform the compose sequences for you. You then can store the macros in your macro library and access them as you need them. (See Chapter 11 to learn how to create macros and macro libraries.)

LMBCS characters also can be generated using the @CHAR function. For example, @CHAR(156) enters the British pound symbol (£) into the worksheet. See Chapter 6 for a complete discussion of the @CHAR function.

845

Group 0

This section defines the Group 0 LMBCS characters.

NOTE: Codes 1 through 31 are not LMBCS codes. Using @CHAR with the numbers 1 through 31 will produce the characters for LMBCS codes 256 through 287, listed in the Group 1 table.

LMBCS code	Compose sequence	Description	Character
32		Space	Space
33		Exclamation point	!
34		Double quotes	"
35	+ +	Pound sign	#
36		Dollar sign	$
37		Percent	%
38		Ampersand	&
39		Close single quote	'
40		Open parenthesis	(
41		Close parenthesis	)
42		Asterisk	*
43		Plus sign	+
44		Comma	,
45		Minus sign	−
46		Period	.
47		Slash	/
48		Zero	0
49		One	1
50		Two	2
51		Three	3
52		Four	4
53		Five	5
54		Six	6
55		Seven	7
56		Eight	8
57		Nine	9
58		Colon	:
59		Semicolon	;
60		Less than	<
61		Equal sign	=
62		Greater than	>
63		Question mark	?
64	aa or AA	At sign	@
65		A, uppercase	A
66		B, uppercase	B
67		C, uppercase	C
68		D, uppercase	D
69		E, uppercase	E
70		F, uppercase	F
71		G, uppercase	G
72		H, uppercase	H
73		I, uppercase	I
74		J, uppercase	J
75		K, uppercase	K
76		L, uppercase	L
77		M, uppercase	M
78		N, uppercase	N

LMBCS code	Compose sequence	Description	Character
79		O, uppercase	O
80		P, uppercase	P
81		Q, uppercase	Q
82		R, uppercase	R
83		S, uppercase	S
84		T, uppercase	T
85		U, uppercase	U
86		V, uppercase	V
87		W, uppercase	W
88		X, uppercase	X
89		Y, uppercase	Y
90		Z, uppercase	Z
91	((	Open bracket	[
92	//	Backslash	\
93	))	Close bracket	]
94	v v	Caret	^
95		Underscore	_
96		Open single quote	`
97		a, lowercase	a
98		b, lowercase	b
99		c, lowercase	c
100		d, lowercase	d
101		e, lowercase	e
102		f, lowercase	f
103		g, lowercase	g
104		h, lowercase	h
105		i, lowercase	i
106		j, lowercase	j
107		k, lowercase	k
108		l, lowercase	l
109		m, lowercase	m
110		n, lowercase	n
111		o, lowercase	o
112		p, lowercase	p
113		q, lowercase	q
114		r, lowercase	r
115		s, lowercase	s
116		t, lowercase	t
117		u, lowercase	u
118		v, lowercase	v
119		w, lowercase	w
120		x, lowercase	x
121		y, lowercase	y
122		z, lowercase	z
123	(-	Open brace	{
124	^ /	Bar		
125	)-	Close brace	}
126	- -	Tilde	~
127		Delete	⌂
128	C,	C cedilla, uppercase	Ç
129	u"	u umlaut, lowercase	ü
130	e'	e acute, lowercase	é
131	a^	a circumflex, lowercase	â
132	a"	a umlaut, lowercase	ä
133	a`	a grave, lowercase	à

LMBCS code	Compose sequence	Description	Character
134	a*	a ring, lowercase	å
135	c,	c cedilla, lowercase	ç
136	e^	e circumflex, lowercase	ê
137	e"	e umlaut, lowercase	ë
138	e`	e grave, lowercase	è
139	i"	i umlaut, lowercase	ï
140	î	i circumflex, lowercase	î
141	i`	i grave, lowercase	ì
142	A"	A umlaut, uppercase	Ä
143	A*	a ring, uppercase	Å
144	E'	E acute, uppercase	É
145	ae	ae diphthong, lowercase	æ
146	AE	AE diphthong, uppercase	Æ
147	o^	o circumflex, lowercase	ô
148	o"	o umlaut, lowercase	ö
149	o`	o grave, lowercase	ò
150	u^	u circumflex, lowercase	û
151	u`	u grave, lowercase	ù
152	y"	y umlaut, lowercase	ÿ
153	O"	O umlaut, uppercase	Ö
154	U"	U umlaut, uppercase	Ü
155	o/	o slash, lowercase	ø
156	L = l = L- or l-	British pound sterling symbol	£
157	O/	O slash, uppercase	Ø
158	xx or XX	Multiplication sign	×
159	f f	Guilder	ƒ
160	a'	a acute, lowercase	á
161	i'	i acute, lowercase	í
162	o'	o acute, lowercase	ó
163	u'	u acute, lowercase	ú
164	n~	n tilde, lowercase	ñ
165	N~	N tilde, uppercase	Ñ
166	a _ or A _	Feminine ordinal indicator	ª
167	o _ or O _	Masculine ordinal indicator	º
168	??	Question mark, inverted	¿
169	RO ro R0 or r0	Registered trademark symbol	®
170	-]	End of line symbol/Logical NOT	¬
171	1 2	One half	½
172	1 4	One quarter	¼
173	!!	Exclamation point, inverted	¡
174	‹ ‹	Left angle quotes	«
175	› ›	Right angle quotes	»
176		Solid fill character, light	
177		Solid fill character, medium	
178		Solid fill character, heavy	
179		Center vertical box bar	
180		Right box side	
181	A'	A acute, uppercase	Á
182	A^	A circumflex, uppercase	Â
183	A`	A grave, uppercase	À
184	CO co C0 or c0	Copyright symbol	©
185		Right box side, double	
186		Center vertical box bar, double	
187		Upper right box corner, double	
188		Lower right box corner, double	
189	cl c/ Cl or c/	Cent sign	¢

LMBCS code	Compose sequence	Description	Character
190	Y = y = Y- or y-	Yen sign	¥
191		Upper right box corner	⌐
192		Lower left box corner	L
193		Lower box side	⊥
194		Upper box side	⊤
195		Left box side	├
196		Center horizontal box bar	─
197		Center box intersection	┼
198	a~	a tilde, lowercase	ã
199	A~	A tilde, uppercase	Ã
200		Lower left box corner, double	╙
201		Upper left box corner, double	╓
202		Lower box side, double	╨
203		Upper box side, double	╥
204		Left box side, double	╟
205		Center horizontal box bar, double	═
206		Center box intersection, double	╫
207	XO xo X0 or x0	International currency sign	
208	d-	Icelandic eth, lowercase	
209	D-	Icelandic eth, uppercase	
210	Ê	E circumflex, uppercase	Ê
211	E"	E umlaut, uppercase	Ë
212	E'	E grave, uppercase	È
213	i‹space›	i without dot (lowercase)	ı
214	I'	I acute, uppercase	Í
215	Î	I circumflex, uppercase	Î
216	I"	I umlaut, uppercase	Ï
217		Lower right box corner	
218		Upper left box corner	
219		Solid fill character	■
220		Solid fill character, lower half	▬
221	/‹space›	Vertical line, broken	¦
222	I'	I grave, uppercase	Ì
223		Solid fill character, upper half	▀
224	O'	O acute, uppercase	Ó
225	ss	German sharp (lowercase)	
226	Ô	O circumflex, uppercase	Ô
227	O'	O grave, uppercase	Ò
228	o~	o tilde, lowercase	õ
229	O~	O tilde, uppercase	Õ
230	/u	Greek mu, lowercase	µ
231	p-	Icelandic thorn, lowercase	
232	P-	Icelandic thorn, uppercase	
233	U'	U acute, uppercase	Ú
234	Û	U circumflex, uppercase	Û
235	U'	U grave, uppercase	Ù
236	y'	y acute, lowercase	ý
237	Y'	Y acute, uppercase	Ý
238	ˆ	Overline character	‾
239		Acute accent	´
240	- =	Hyphenation symbol	-
241	+ −	Plus or minus sign	±
242	- - or = =	Double underscore	=
243	3 4	Three quarters sign	¾
244		Paragraph symbol	¶
245		Section symbol	§

LMBCS code	Compose sequence	Description	Character
246	:-	Division sign	÷
247	, ,	Cedilla accent	,
248	0	Degree symbol	°
249		Umlaut accent	¨
250	^	Center dot	·
251	^1	One superscript	1
252	^3	Three superscript	3
253	^2	Two superscript	2
254		Square bullet	■
255		Null	

Group 1

This section defines the Group 1 LMBCS characters.

LMBCS code	Key code	Compose sequence	Description	Character
256	(000)		Null	
257	(001)		Smiling face	☺
258	(002)		Smiling face, reversed	■
259	(003)		Heart suit symbol	♥
260	(004)		Diamond suit symbol	♦
261	(005)		Club suit symbol	♣
262	(006)		Spade suit symbol	♠
263	(007)		Bullet	●
264	(008)		Bullet, reversed	◘
265	(009)		Open circle	○
266	(010)		Open circle, reversed	◙
267	(011)		Male symbol	♂
268	(012)		Female symbol	♀
269	(013)		Musical note	♪
270	(014)		Double musical note	♫
271	(015)		Sun symbol	
272	(016)		Forward arrow indicator	►
273	(017)		Back arrow indicator	◄
274	(018)		Up-down arrow	↕
275	(019)		Double exclamation points	‼
276	(020)	!p or !P	Paragraph symbol	¶
277	(021)	SO so S0 or s0	Section symbol	§
278	(022)		Solid horizontal rectangle	▬
279	(023)		Up-down arrow, perpendicular	↨
280	(024)		Up arrow	↑
281	(025)		Down arrow	↓
282	(026)		Right arrow	→
283	(027)	mg	Left arrow	←
284	(028)		Right angle symbol	∟
285	(029)		Left-right symbol	↔
286	(030)	ba	Solid triangle	▲
287	(031)	ea	Solid triangle inverted	▼
288	(032)	"‹space›	Umlaut accent, uppercase	¨
289	(033)	~‹space›	Tilde accent, uppercase	~
290	(034)		Ring accent, uppercase	°
291	(035)	^‹space›	Circumflex accent, uppercase	^
292	(036)	`‹space›	Grave accent, uppercase	`
293	(037)	'‹space›	Acute accent, uppercase	´

LMBCS code	Key code	Compose sequence	Description	Character
294	(038)	" ∧	High double quotes, opening	"
295	(039)		High single quote, straight	'
296	(040)		Ellipsis	...
297	(041)		En mark	–
298	(042)		Em mark	—
299	(043)		Null	
300	(044)		Null	
301	(045)		Null	
302	(046)		Left angle parenthesis	<
303	(047)		Right angle parenthesis	>
304	(048)	‹space›"	Umlaut accent, lowercase	¨
305	(049)	‹space›~	Tilde accent, lowercase	~
306	(050)		Ring accent, lowercase	°
307	(051)	‹space›^	Circumflex accent, lowercase	^
308	(052)	‹space›`	Grave accent, lowercase	`
309	(053)	‹space›'	Acute accent, lowercase	´
310	(054)	"∨	Low double quotes, closing	„
311	(055)		Low single quote, closing	‚
312	(056)		High double quotes, closing	"
313	(057)		Underscore, heavy	▬
314	(058)		Null	
315	(059)		Null	
316	(060)		Null	
317	(061)		Null	
318	(062)		Null	
319	(063)		Null	
320	(064)	OE	OE ligature, uppercase	Œ
321	(065)	oe	oe ligature, lowercase	œ
322	(066)	Y"	Y umlaut, uppercase	Ÿ
323	(067)		Null	
324	(068)		Null	
325	(069)		Null	
326	(070)		Left box side, double joins single	╞
327	(071)		Left box side, single joins double	╟
328	(072)		Solid fill character, left half	▌
329	(073)		Solid fill character, right half	▐
330	(074)		Null	
331	(075)		Null	
332	(076)		Null	
333	(077)		Null	
334	(078)		Null	
335	(079)		Null	
336	(080)		Lower box side, double joins single	╨
337	(081)		Upper box side, single joins double	╤
338	(082)		Upper box side, double joins single	╥
339	(083)		Lower single left double box corner	╙
340	(084)		Lower double left single box corner	╘
341	(085)		Upper double left single box corner	╒
342	(086)		Upper single left double box corner	╓
343	(087)		Center box intersection, vertical double	╫
344	(088)		Center box intersection, horizontal double	╪
345	(089)		Right box side, double joins single	╡
346	(090)		Right box side, single joins double	╢
347	(091)		Upper single right double box corner	╖
348	(092)		Upper double right single box corner	╕

LMBCS code	Key code	Compose sequence	Description	Character
349	(093)		Lower single right double box corner	╜
350	(094)		Lower double right single box corner	╛
351	(095)		Lower box side, single joins double	╧
352	(096)	ij	ij ligature, lowercase	ij
353	(097)	IJ	IJ ligature, uppercase	IJ
354	(098)	fi	fi ligature, lowercase	fi
355	(099)	fl	fl ligature, lowercase	fl
356	(100)	'n	n comma, lowercase	'n
357	(101)	l.	l bullet, lowercase	l·
358	(102)	L.	L bullet, uppercase	L·
359	(103)		Null	
360	(104)		Null	
361	(105)		Null	
362	(106)		Null	
363	(107)		Null	
364	(108)		Null	
365	(109)		Null	
366	(110)		Null	
367	(111)		Null	
368	(112)		Single dagger symbol	†
369	(113)		Double dagger symbol	‡
370	(114)		Null	
371	(115)		Null	
372	(116)		Null	
373	(117)		Null	
374	(118)	TM Tm or tm	Trademark symbol	™
375	(119)	lr	Liter symbol	.r
376	(120)		Null	
377	(121)		Null	
378	(122)		Null	
379	(123)		Null	
380	(124)	KR Kr or kr	Krone sign	Kr
381	(125)	-[	Start of line symbol	⌐
382	(126)	LI Li or li	Lira sign	
383	(127)	PT Pt or pt	Peseta sign	Pt

NOTE: LMBCS codes 384 through 511 duplicate LMBCS codes 128 through 255, for use with code groups of other countries. Refer to LMBCS codes 128 through 255 in the Group 0 table for a list of these characters.

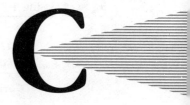

Summary of
Release 3 Features

Normally, the way to determine how different a new release of a program is from the previous release is by the release number. For example, when Lotus Development Corporation made some minor repairs to 1-2-3 Release 2, they called the new release 1-2-3 Release 2.01. The addition of the .01 signified that there were changes, but they were very minor.

Release 3.0 of 1-2-3 is a .99 increment. This increment means that the changes were significant. Actually, however, the enhancements and new features to 1-2-3 warrant an even larger number. No doubt, if you were a user of 2.01, you will be extremely delighted with the enhancements and new features in Release 3.

In this appendix, you will find a list of enhancements and new features. They are laid out in table format, with one column indicating that the feature was in Release 2 and the other column indicating that the feature is new in Release 3. If a check mark appears in both the Release 2 column and the Release 3 column, then the feature is an enhancement. If, however, a check mark appears only in the Release 3 column, then the feature is new with Release 3. Along with each enhancement, you will find the keystrokes needed to activate it, if keystrokes are applicable.

The changes and enhancements are presented in the following order: /Worksheet, /Range, /File, /Print, /Graph, /Data, @ functions, advanced macro commands, macro keywords, installation, screen appearance, keyboard control, memory usage, and networking.

Enhancement or New Feature	Release 2	Release 3
/Worksheet		
Hide or redisplay worksheets—/wh.		✔
Insert a new worksheet in the file—/wis.		✔
Delete a worksheet from the current file or delete a file from memory—/wds or /wdf.		✔
Use GROUP mode to affect all worksheets in a file when changing the cell format, label prefix, column width, protection, and zero suppression—/wgg.		✔
Store negative numbers in a different color/ intensity or in parentheses—/wgfoc.	✔	✔
Store all entries automatically as labels—/wgfol.		✔
Format a cell according to the appearance of the entry—/wgfoa.		✔
Suppress the display of any cell containing a zero—/wgzy.	✔	✔
Replace a 0 cell entry with a label—/wgzl.		✔
Set up translation for importing ASCII files— /wgdoif.		✔
Replace the clock at the lower-left of the screen with a file name—/wgdocf.		✔
Shut off 1-2-3's beep—/wgdob.		✔
Determine data ranges by row or column for automatic graphs; set the file type for saving a graph—/wgdg.		✔
Choose a directory for temporary files and default file extensions—/wgdt or /wgde.		✔
Enable or disable autoexecute macros—/wgda.		✔
Change the width of a range of columns—/wcc.		✔
Erase all worksheets from memory, closing all files—/we.	✔	✔
Display a map of the worksheet, showing where numbers, annotated numbers, formulas, and labels reside—/wwm.		✔

Enhancement or New Feature	Release 2	Release 3
Display three consecutive worksheets on-screen—/wwp.		✔
Display a graph on the screen with a worksheet—/wwg.		✔
Switch between two video display drivers—/wwd1 or /wwd2.		✔
Display the worksheet's status; defaults—/ws.	✔	✔
/Range		
Store negative numbers in a different color/intensity or in parentheses—/rfoc.	✔	✔
Store all entries automatically as labels—/rfol.		✔
Format a cell according to the appearance of the entry—/rfoa.		✔
Attach a note to a range name—/rnnc.		✔
Create a table of range names, addresses, and notes—/rnnt.		✔
Remove a range name's address but leave the range name in use—/rnu.		✔
Transpose cells, columns for rows—/rt.	✔	✔
Search a range for a string in a formula, label, or both; optionally replace a search string with another string—/rs.		✔
Specify a range in two noncontiguous areas or across worksheets.		✔
/File		
Open a new file in memory—/fn.		✔
Open an existing file in memory—/fo.		✔
Protect files from being overwritten when 1-2-3 is used on a Local Area Network (LAN)—/far.	✔	✔
Seal a file with a password, protecting changes to the file—/fas.	✔	✔
/Print		
Capture data and printer setup codes in a file—/pe.	✔	✔

Enhancement or New Feature	Release 2	Release 3
Pause, resume, and cancel printing—/ps, /pr, or /pc.		✔
Print row and column letters and numbers—/p[p,f,e]obf.		✔
Suppress blank lines at the top and bottom of the page if there is no header or footer—/p[p,f,e]oob.		✔
Save print settings with a name—/p[p,f,e]on.		✔
Change the pitch, line-spacing, and orientation of the print job—/p[p,e]oal.	✔	✔
Change the font of the range, header/footer, border, and frame for the current print job—/p[p,e]oaf.	✔	✔
Specify how 1-2-3 should manage background printing—/ppoap.		✔
Choose a graph to print without leaving 1-2-3—/p[p,e]i.		✔
Print a sample document displaying line-spacing, fonts, graph capabilities, and other formatting elements—/pps.		✔
Return to READY mode while a print job is still open—/p[p,f,e]h.		✔
/Graph		
Create an HLCO (High-Low-Close-Open) graph or mix lines and bars on a graph—/gth or /gtm.		✔
Display graphs on-screen with the x-axis positioned vertically or horizontally—/gtfv or /gtfh.		✔
Stack data ranges so that all types of graphs may display data in stacked form—/gtfs.		✔
Display data ranges as a percentage of the total—/gtf1.		✔
Using a second y-axis, assign each data range to either the first or second y-axis—/gtf2 or /gtfy.		✔

Enhancement or New Feature	Release 2	Release 3
Fill in the area between lines in a line, XY, mixed, or HLCO graph to make an area graph—/gof*data range*a.		✔
Add two lines of notes to a graph—/gotn or /goto.		✔
Select colors or hatching patterns for data ranges—/goac or /goah.	✔	✔
Select the color, font, and size of a graph's titles—/goat[f,s,t][c,f,s].	✔	✔
Create a table in the current file of named graphs—/gnt.		✔
Set all graph ranges at once with data either columnwise or rowwise—/gg*range*[c,r].		✔
View a graph by pressing F10 when the cell pointer is in a range of numbers—F10.	✔	✔

/Data

Enhancement or New Feature	Release 2	Release 3
Create a three-dimensional data table—/dt3.		✔
Create a data table (using any number of variables and formulas) that does not have to be in a contiguous ranges—/dtl.		✔
Specify more than two sort keys—/dse.		✔
Query on more than one database at a time—/dql*range;range*.		✔
Update extracted records, and then replace them or insert them as new records—/dqm[e,r,i].		✔
Use a database created by a database management program such as dBASE III as the input range for database queries and calculations—/de.		✔

@ Functions

Enhancement or New Feature	Release 2	Release 3
Create a cell address that is relative, absolute, or mixed, based on values given—@COORD(worksheet,column,row,absolute).		✔
Return a label or value from a field in the input range, based on the criteria range—@DGET(input,field,criteria).		✔

Enhancement or New Feature	Release 2	Release 3
Use a function provided by an external database management program— @DQUERY(external function,argument1,arg2,...).		✔
Return a sample standard deviation of values from a database, based on the criteria range—@DSTDS(input,field,criteria).		✔
Return the number of days between two dates, based on a 360-day year— @D360(date1,date2).		✔
Return a sample variance of values from a database, based on the criteria range—@DVARS(input,field,criteria).		✔
Locate a value in a range at a specified column-, row-, and worksheet-offset— @INDEX(range,column-offset,row-offset,[worksheet-offset]).	✔	✔
Return one of 11 pieces of information about your system—@INFO(attribute).		✔
Determine whether or not a string is a defined range name—@ISRANGE(string).		✔
Determine the number of worksheets in a given range—@SHEETS(range).		✔
Return a sample standard deviation from a list of values—@STDS(list).		✔
Return a value that is the sum of the products of corresponding cells in two or more ranges of the same size— @SUMPRODUCT(range1,range2,...).		✔
Return the integer portion of the day/time value from the computer's clock—@TODAY.	✔	✔
Return a sample variance from a list of values—@VARS(list).		✔
Use the double-declining balance method to return the depreciation allowance of an asset for a specific time period or to calculate for other rates. Optionally, you can make the calculation never use the ongoing straight-line depreciation calculation— @VDB(cost,salvage,life,[period][,percent]).		✔

Enhancement or New Feature	*Release 2*	*Release 3*
Advanced Macro Commands		
Copy data from a range to the bottom of another range—{APPENDBELOW}.		✔
Copy data from a range to the right of another range—{APPENDRIGHT}.		✔
Pause a macro for entry in the unprotected cells of a form that you create—{FORM}.		✔
Shut off and restore the worksheet borders—{FRAMEOFF} and {FRAMEON}.		✔
Display and eliminate a graph on the screen—{GRAPHON} and {GRAPHOFF}.		✔
Change the mode indicator to display a label up to the width of the screen—{INDICATE}.	✔	✔
Shut off display in the control panel; clear the control panel and status line—{PANELOFF}.	✔	✔
Call the operating system while 1-2-3 remains in memory—{SYSTEM}.		✔
Macro Keywords		
Issue a Ctrl-Break—{BREAK}.		✔
Clear the default label from the edit line—{CLEARENTRY} or {CE}.		✔
Display the menu to use LEAF applications—{EXTEND}.		✔
Turn on the FILE indicator for cell pointer movement between files—{FILE}.		✔
Move the cell pointer to worksheet A, cell A1—{FIRSTCELL} or {FC}.		✔
Move the cell pointer to the first active file—{FIRSTFILE} or {FF}.		✔
Activate help—{HELP}.		✔
Move the cell pointer to the last cell that contains data in the current file—{LASTCELL} or {LC}.		✔
Move the cell pointer to the last active file—{LASTFILE} or {LF}.		✔

Enhancement or New Feature	Release 2	Release 3
Move the cell pointer to the next active file—{NEXTFILE} or {NF}.		✔
Move the cell pointer to the next worksheet in the current file—{NEXTSHEET} or {NS}.		✔
Move the cell pointer to the previous active file—{PREVFILE} or {PF}.		✔
Move the cell pointer to the previous worksheet in the current file—{PREVSHEET} or {PS}.		✔
Move the cell pointer up, down, left, or right—{U}, {D}, {L}, or {R}.	✔	✔
Make a small worksheet that is not the full size of the screen become the full size of the screen or return to a partial screen—{ZOOM}.		✔

Installation

Register your copy of 1-2-3 once, and then make backup copies of the disks.	✔	✔
Use the automatic installation program to copy files from the 1-2-3 disks to your hard disk.		✔
Install two video display types, and then switch between the two types while running 1-2-3.		✔

Screen Appearance

The worksheet letter is displayed in the upper-left corner of the border.		✔
The cell pointer's location is visibly shown by changes in colors or border highlighting.		✔
Choose to display either the current file name or date and time in the lower-left corner of the screen.		✔

Keyboard Control

Start a LEAF application—Alt-F7, Alt-F8, and Alt-F9.	✔	✔
Display the menu to use LEAF applications —Alt-F10.	✔	✔

Enhancement or New Feature	*Release 2*	*Release 3*
Jump to a cell in the current worksheet, a different worksheet, or a different active file—F5.	✔	✔
Display a list of @ functions, range names, macro commands, file names, and names of tables in an external database when a listing is possible—F3.	✔	✔
Use keystrokes from the record buffer or turn on STEP mode for macro execution—Alt-F2.	✔	✔
Make a small worksheet that is not the full size of the screen become the full size of the screen or return to a partial screen—{ZOOM}.		✔
Move the cell pointer to the next worksheet, stopping at the intersection between a blank cell and one that contains data—End Ctrl-PgUp.		✔
Move the cell pointer to the previous worksheet, stopping at the intersection between a blank cell and one that contains data—End Ctrl-PgDn.		✔
Move the cell pointer to worksheet A, cell A1 in the current file—Ctrl-Home.	✔	✔
Move the cell pointer to the last cell you highlighted in the first active file—Ctrl-End Home.		✔
Move the cell pointer to the last cell that contains data in the current file—End Ctrl-Home.		✔
Move the cell pointer to the last cell you highlighted in the last active file—Ctrl-End End.		✔
Move the cell pointer to the last cell you highlighted in the next active file—Ctrl-End Ctrl-PgUp.		✔
Move the cell pointer to the next worksheet—Ctrl-PgUp.		✔
Move the cell pointer to the last cell you highlighted in the previous active file—Ctrl-End Ctrl-PgDn.		✔

Enhancement or New Feature	Release 2	Release 3
Move the cell pointer to the previous worksheet—Ctrl-PgDn.		✔
Memory Usage		
Use up to 15M of extended memory with DOS or OS/2.		✔
Use up to 32M of LIM 4.0 or 8M of LIM 3.2 expanded memory with DOS.	✔	✔
Networking		
Share data files on a LAN.	✔	✔
After a file is read from a LAN, that file is protected from updating by multiple users at the same time.		✔
Protect files with a password.	✔	✔

Index

1-2-3 advanced macro commands
see also advanced macro commands
{?}, 544-545
{APPENDBELOW}, 570, 575-576
{APPENDRIGHT}, 570, 576
{BEEP}, 577-578
{BLANK}, 570, 574-575
{BRANCH}, 539, 552-554, 613
{BREAKOFF}, 552, 560-561
{BREAKON}, 552, 561
{CALC}, 509, 670, 790
{CLOSE}, 585, 587-588
{CONTENTS}, 126, 174, 570, 572-574
{DEFINE}, 552, 563-565
{DISPATCH}, 552, 562-563
{FILESIZE}, 585, 591
{FORBREAK}, 567, 569-570
{FORM}, 125, 544, 550-551, 699
{FOR}, 567, 569-570
{FRAMEOFF}, 577, 580
{FRAMEON}, 577, 580
{GETLABEL}, 544, 546-547
{GETNUMBER}, 544, 547-548
{GETPOS}, 585, 591
{GET}, 544-546
{GRAPHOFF}, 577, 582
{GRAPHON}, 577, 581-582
{IF}, 567-569
{INDICATE}, 577, 582
{LET}, 570-571
{LOOK}, 544, 548-549
{MENUBRANCH}, 539, 552, 554-555
{MENUCALL}, 552, 556-557
{ONERROR}, 552, 558-560
{OPEN}, 584-587
{PANELOFF}, 577-579
{PANELON}, 577-578
{PUT}, 570, 572
{QUIT}, 552, 558
{READLN}, 585, 588-589
{READ}, 585, 588
{RECALC}, 577, 583-584, 603, 653
{RECALCCOL}, 577, 583-584, 653
{RESTART}, 552, 565-566
{RETURN}, 552, 557-558
{SETPOS}, 585, 590-591
{SYSTEM}, 552, 566-567
{WAIT}, 552, 562
{WINDOWSOFF}, 577, 579-580

{WINDOWSON}, 577, 580
{WRITELN}, 585
{WRITE}, 585, 589-590
1-2-3 commands
see also commands
/Copy, 22, 99, 136-145, 579, 584, 604, 616, 625, 658, 706-708, 793, 800
/Data, 81, 101, 412, 414, 658, 786-820, 857
/Data Distribution, 488-489, 808-810
/Data External, 26-27, 290, 414, 499-511
/Data External Create, 504, 816-818
/Data External Create Definition Create-Definition, 505, 649, 817
/Data External Create Go, 507
/Data External Create Name, 505, 818
/Data External Create Quit, 507
/Data External Delete, 508, 818
/Data External List, 503, 815-816
/Data External List Fields, 504-505, 507, 817
/Data External List Tables, 503
/Data External Other, 503, 507, 819-820
/Data External Other Control, 483, 509-510
/Data External Other Refresh, 508-509
/Data External Other Refresh Interval, 509
/Data External Other Translate, 510
/Data External Reset, 503, 511, 818
/Data External Use, 427, 501, 503, 650, 815-816, 818-819
/Data Fill, 242, 484-487, 571, 621, 786, 788, 792, 794, 797
/Data Matrix, 26, 494, 810
/Data Matrix Multiply, 494
/Data Parse, 286, 495-499, 627, 714, 721, 813-814
/Data Parse Format-Line Create, 656
/Data Query, 106, 172, 414, 427-437, 479, 499, 509-510, 645, 648, 650, 656, 815, 818-819
/Data Query Criteria, 645-646, 799-801, 803, 816
/Data Query Del, 447-448, 803, 806-807
/Data Query Extract, 106, 419, 433, 440, 449, 502, 648, 650-651, 801, 803-809, 816
/Data Query Find, 25, 648, 802-803, 806
/Data Query Input, 106, 429, 449, 646, 799
/Data Query Modify, 435-436, 503, 807-808, 817
/Data Query Modify Extract, 436, 650-651, 808
/Data Query Modify Insert, 436-437
/Data Query Modify Replace, 436, 650-651, 808

/Data Query Output, 433, 801-802, 816
/Data Query Unique, 25, 446-447, 449, 458, 805-806
/Data Refresh Interval, 820
/Data Regression, 26, 489-493, 772, 811-812
/Data Sort, 420, 422-426, 484-485, 797-798
/Data Sort Data-Range, 420
/Data Sort Primary-Key, 103
/Data Table, 26, 172, 413, 451-452, 484, 509, 610, 819
/Data Table 1, 453-456, 789-791, 793, 795, 810
/Data Table 2, 456-458, 789, 791-793, 795, 810
/Data Table 3, 462, 466, 792-795
/Data Table Labeled, 466-468, 472, 476-479, 794-796
/Data Table Labeled Formulas, 474
/Delete, 616
/File, 23, 710-728, 855
/File Admin Link-Refresh, 86, 291, 701, 703, 728
/File Admin Reservation, 724-725
/File Admin Reservation Get, 291
/File Admin Reservation Release, 291
/File Admin Reservation-Setting, 727
/File Admin Reservation-Setting Manual, 291
/File Admin Seal, 617, 725, 727-728
/File Admin Seal Disable, 128, 699
/File Admin Seal File, 128, 173, 658
/File Admin Table, 285, 720, 725-727
/File Combine, 276-277, 282, 495, 714-716
/File Combine Add, 280-281, 614, 626, 715
/File Combine Add Named/Specified-Range, 280
/File Combine Copy, 277-279, 625-626
/File Combine Subtract, 280-281
/File Dir, 265, 269, 386. 624, 711, 718-719, 722
/File Erase, 261, 284, 713, 718-720
/File Import, 257, 286, 495, 584, 698, 714, 720-721, 813
/File Import Numbers, 287, 626, 813
/File Import Text, 286, 627, 721, 813
/File List, 261, 269, 285, 713, 719-720, 722, 726
/File List Linked, 728
/File New, 83, 270, 608, 675, 723-724
/File New After, 270
/File Open, 83, 268, 282, 289, 543, 608, 657, 711, 723-724, 767
/File Retrieve, 263, 268-269, 282, 289, 291, 495, 624-625, 657, 710-711
/File Save, 94-95, 113, 265, 282-283, 291, 321, 420, 448, 614, 617, 692, 697, 710-714, 717, 723, 725, 768-769, 784, 797, 807
/File Xtract, 271-272, 282, 432, 560, 713, 715-717, 807
/File Xtract Formulas, 274-275, 717

/File Xtract Values, 272, 615, 717
/Global Protection Enabled, 173
/Go Print, 526
/Graph, 81, 101, 760-785, 812, 856-857
/Graph Group, 24, 357-358, 765, 785
/Graph Name, 386, 727, 756, 783-784
/Graph Name Create, 391, 402, 635, 644, 766, 768-769, 784
/Graph Name Reset, 784
/Graph Name Use, 393, 635, 784
/Graph Options, 766
/Graph Options Advanced Colors, 777, 780-781, 783
/Graph Options Advanced Colors A Range, 380
/Graph Options Advanced Colors A-F, 772
/Graph Options Advanced Colors A-F Hide, 772
/Graph Options Advanced Hatches, 636, 641, 643, 782-783
/Graph Options Advanced Hatches A Range, 381, 396
/Graph Options Advanced Text, 781-782
/Graph Options Advanced Text Color, 777
/Graph Options Advanced Text First Color, 781-782
/Graph Options Advanced Text First Font, 781-782
/Graph Options Advanced Text First Size, 781-782
/Graph Options Advanced Text Second Color, 781-782
/Graph Options Advanced Text Second Font, 781-782
/Graph Options Advanced Text Second Size, 781-782
/Graph Options Advanced Text Third Color, 781-782
/Graph Options Advanced Text Third Font, 781-782
/Graph Options Advanced Text Third Size, 781-782
/Graph Options B&W, 402, 643
/Graph Options Color, 401, 767
/Graph Options Color/B&W, 777
/Graph Options Data-Labels, 362, 774, 778-780
/Graph Options Format, 362-363, 366, 370-371, 772
/Graph Options Format F Neither, 780
/Graph Options Grid, 367, 774
/Graph Options Grid Clear, 370
/Graph Options Grid Horizontal, 368
/Graph Options Legend, 769-770
/Graph Options Scale, 368, 371, 774-777
/Graph Options Scale Format, 370
/Graph Options Scale Skip, 369, 639, 775
/Graph Options Scale Y-Scale Exponent Manual, 638

/Graph Options Scale Y-Scale Indicator, 638
/Graph Options Scale Y-Scale Manual, 641
/Graph Options Scale Y-Scale Type Logarithmic, 640
/Graph Options Titles, 360, 773
/Graph Reset, 387, 765-767
/Graph Reset B Quit, 392
/Graph Reset Graph, 387, 389, 393, 765
/Graph Reset Range, 355
/Graph Save, 385-386, 768-769, 784
/Graph Type, 355, 760-763, 767
/Graph Type Bar, 356, 377
/Graph Type Features, 374
/Graph Type XY, 397
/Graph View, 355, 383, 401, 767-768
/Graph X A B C D E F, 764-766
/Move, 22, 99, 132-136, 584, 604, 616, 675, 677, 708-709, 770, 773
/Page, 630
/Print, 27, 81, 101, 297, 614, 658, 729-759, 855-856
/Print Cancel, 342-343, 633, 735-736
/Print Encoded, 401, 597, 633, 733-734
/Print Encoded Align, 755-756
/Print Encoded Clear, 754
/Print Encoded Go, 755
/Print Encoded Hold, 758-759
/Print Encoded Image, 756-757
/Print Encoded Line, 738
/Print Encoded Options Advanced, 750-753
/Print Encoded Options Advanced Device Name, 633
/Print Encoded Options Borders, 743-744
/Print Encoded Options Footer, 741
/Print Encoded Options Header, 739-740
/Print Encoded Options Margins, 741-742
/Print Encoded Options Name, 748-750
/Print Encoded Options Name Use, 633
/Print Encoded Options Other, 746-748
/Print Encoded Options Pg-Length, 746
/Print Encoded Options Setup, 744-745
/Print Encoded Page, 738-739
/Print Encoded Quit, 759
/Print Encoded Range, 736-738
/Print File, 323, 344, 584, 589, 633, 730-734
/Print File Align, 755-756
/Print File Clear, 754
/Print File Go, 755
/Print File Hold, 758-759
/Print File Image, 756-757
/Print File Line, 738
/Print File Options Advanced, 750-753
/Print File Options Borders, 743-744
/Print File Options Footer, 741
/Print File Options Header, 739-740
/Print File Options Margins, 741-742

/Print File Options Name, 748-750
/Print File Options Other, 746-748
/Print File Options Other Unformatted, 684, 742
/Print File Options Pg-Length, 746
/Print File Options Setup, 744-745
/Print File Page, 738-739
/Print File Quit, 759
/Print File Range, 736-738
/Print Name, 727
/Print Printer, 309, 318, 325, 401, 730-731
/Print Printer Align, 343, 738-739, 755-756
/Print Printer Clear, 343, 754
/Print Printer Clear All, 629, 754
/Print Printer Clear Borders, 325
/Print Printer Go, 755
/Print Printer Hold, 342, 758-759
/Print Printer Image, 756-757
/Print Printer Image Current Go Quit, 404
/Print Printer Image Named-Graph, 404
/Print Printer Line, 341, 343, 738
/Print Printer Options Advanced, 750-753
/Print Printer Options Advanced Device, 340
/Print Printer Options Advanced Device Interface, 598
/Print Printer Options Advanced Device Name, 401, 598, 633
/Print Printer Options Advanced Image Density Draft, 643
/Print Printer Options Advanced Image Density Final, 643
/Print Printer Options Advanced Image Image-Sz, 644
/Print Printer Options Advanced Image Image-Sz Margin-Fill, 643
/Print Printer Options Advanced Image Image-Sz Reshape, 404
/Print Printer Options Advanced Layout Line-Spacing, 632
/Print Printer Options Advanced Layout Orientation Landscape, 629
/Print Printer Options Advanced Layout Pitch, 632
/Print Printer Options Advanced Priority, 341
/Print Printer Options Advanced Wait Yes, 343
/Print Printer Options Borders, 743-744
/Print Printer Options Footer, 741
/Print Printer Options Header, 739-740
/Print Printer Options Margins, 741-742
/Print Printer Options Name, 748-750
/Print Printer Options Name Create, 629
/Print Printer Options Name Use, 629, 633
/Print Printer Options Other, 746-748
/Print Printer Options Other Blank-Header Suppress, 630
/Print Printer Options Other Formatted, 344

/Print Printer Options Pg-Length, 746

/Print Printer Options Setup, 525, 744-745

/Print Printer Page, 341, 403, 738-739

/Print Printer Quit, 759

/Print Printer Range, 102, 332, 406, 526, 644, 736-738

/Print Printer Sample, 382, 753, 757-758, 780, 782-783

/Print Printer Sample Go, 402

/Print Resume, 342-343, 633, 735, 757-758

/Print Sample, 329

/Print Suspend, 342-343, 735

/Print [P,E], 730

/Print [P,E] Image, 734

/Print [P,E] Options Advanced, 329, 744

/Print [P,E] Options Advanced AutoLf, 340

/Print [P,E] Options Advanced Fonts, 333

/Print [P,E] Options Advanced Layout, 329, 336

/Print [P,E] Options Advanced Layout Orientation Landscape, 403

/Print [P,E] Options Name, 339

/Print [P,E] Options Setup, 335

/Print [P,E] Range, 336

/Print [P,E] Sample, 750

/Print [P,F,E], 322, 730

/Print [P,F,E] Clear Borders, 744

/Print [P,F,E] Options, 734

/Print [P,F,E] Options Borders, 737, 739

/Print [P,F,E] Options Borders Columns, 325, 744

/Print [P,F,E] Options Borders Frame, 328

/Print [P,F,E] Options Borders Rows, 740, 744

/Print [P,F,E] Options Footer, 741

/Print [P,F,E] Options Other, 323-324

/Print [P,F,E] Options Other Blank-Header Suppress, 303

/Print [P,F,E] Options Other Unformatted, 329

/Print [P,F,E] Options Pg-Length, 739

/Print [P,F,E] Range, 737

/Quit, 35-36, 38-39, 94, 151, 263, 291, 821-822

/Range, 20-21, 99, 686-783, 855

/Range Erase, 21, 91, 97, 99, 110, 136, 280-281, 434, 534, 574, 677, 685, 692-693, 803

/Range Format, 79, 158, 161, 164, 169, 171, 173, 191, 239, 324, 417, 498, 573, 661, 686-689, 726-727, 775-776

/Range Format +/-, 166

/Range Format Automatic, 599

/Range Format Currency, 165

/Range Format Date, 167, 169, 239, 627

/Range Format Date Time, 167, 170-171, 242-243

/Range Format Fixed, 159, 163

/Range Format General, 163

/Range Format Hidden, 125, 173, 320, 462, 685, 688, 693

/Range Format Label, 599

/Range Format Other Automatic, 174, 176, 487, 665-666

/Range Format Other Color Negative, 177

/Range Format Other Color Reset, 177

/Range Format Other Label, 174, 691

/Range Format Other Parentheses, 176-177

/Range Format Percent, 165

/Range Format Reset, 125, 161, 320, 684, 693

/Range Format Sci, 166

/Range Format Text, 439, 462, 789-793, 795

/Range Input, 124-125, 550, 584, 668, 681, 699-701

/Range Justify, 180, 697-698

/Range Label, 178-179, 664-665, 689-692, 727

/Range Label Center, 691

/Range Name, 289, 677, 693-697, 715, 727

/Range Name Create, 104, 449, 515, 526, 652, 696-697, 715-716, 790, 792

/Range Name Delete, 105

/Range Name Labels, 104-105, 715-716

/Range Name Labels Right, 104, 517, 523, 530, 555, 564

/Range Name Note, 534-535, 727

/Range Name Note Create, 105

/Range Name Note Table, 105, 612

/Range Name Reset, 105

/Range Name Table, 696-697, 747

/Range Prot, 23, 123, 173, 688, 693, 699-700, 727

/Range Search, 99, 101, 148-150, 704-705

/Range Trans, 148, 491, 650, 702-704, 816

/Range Unprot, 123, 668-669, 693, 699-701, 727

/Range Unprotect, 550, 617, 658

/Range Value, 145-147, 434, 576, 610, 614, 701-702

/System, 151, 624, 634, 718, 821

/Window Graph, 643

/Worksheet, 21, 90, 93, 659-685, 854-855

/Worksheet Column, 667, 727

/Worksheet Column Column-Range, 677-679

/Worksheet Column Column-Range Reset-Width, 109

/Worksheet Column Column-Range Set-Width, 109

/Worksheet Column Display, 319, 631, 677-679

/Worksheet Column Hide, 126, 319, 631, 677-679, 685, 744

/Worksheet Column Reset-Width, 109, 677-679

/Worksheet Column Set-Width, 109, 228, 417, 663, 667, 677-679

/Worksheet Column Set-Width 14, 516

/Worksheet Delete, 605, 679, 718, 770, 773
/Worksheet Delete Column, 419, 656, 676-677
/Worksheet Delete File, 83, 112, 263, 284, 291, 610, 633, 676-677, 693, 711
/Worksheet Delete Row, 110, 313, 419, 447, 608, 656, 676-677, 684
/Worksheet Delete Sheet, 83, 112, 676-677, 693
/Worksheet Erase, 263, 270, 291, 668, 679-680, 693, 711, 718
/Worksheet Erase Yes, 113, 633
/Worksheet Global, 342, 727
/Worksheet Global Col-width, 20, 109, 228, 667, 678
/Worksheet Global Default, 93, 154, 300, 671-673
/Worksheet Global Default Autoexec, 523, 526, 543
/Worksheet Global Default Dir, 265, 624, 711, 722
/Worksheet Global Default Ext List, 264, 284, 727
/Worksheet Global Default Ext Save, 264
/Worksheet Global Default Graph, 355, 385, 727, 769
/Worksheet Global Default Graph Columnwise, 356
/Worksheet Global Default Graph PIC, 284
/Worksheet Global Default Other Beep, 155
/Worksheet Global Default Other International, 177, 663, 689
/Worksheet Global Default Other International Currency, 164, 176
/Worksheet Global Default Other International Date, 168, 240
/Worksheet Global Default Other International Negative Parentheses, 164
/Worksheet Global Default Other International Negative Sign, 164
/Worksheet Global Default Other International Punctuation, 187
/Worksheet Global Default Other International Time, 170, 244
/Worksheet Global Default Other Undo Disable, 80
/Worksheet Global Default Other Undo Enable, 80, 82, 692
/Worksheet Global Default Printer, 301-302, 305, 312, 321, 754
/Worksheet Global Default Printer AutoLf, 340
/Worksheet Global Default Printer Interface, 598
/Worksheet Global Default Printer Name, 598
/Worksheet Global Default Printer Setup, 335
/Worksheet Global Default Printer Wait Yes, 343

/Worksheet Global Default Status, 155, 401
/Worksheet Global Default Update, 80, 155, 177, 264-265, 305, 509, 673, 711, 754, 820
/Worksheet Global Format, 79, 160-161, 661-664, 686, 688-689, 775
/Worksheet Global Format Currency, 528
/Worksheet Global Format Date, 167
/Worksheet Global Format Date Time, 167
/Worksheet Global Format Hidden, 685, 693
/Worksheet Global Format Other Automatic, 665-666
/Worksheet Global Format Other Color Negative, 338
/Worksheet Global Format Other Parentheses, 176
/Worksheet Global Group, 20, 109, 161, 674, 688
/Worksheet Global Group Disable, 473
/Worksheet Global Group Enable, 83, 111, 472
/Worksheet Global Label, 664-666
/Worksheet Global Label-Prefix, 690-691
/Worksheet Global Prot, 23, 124, 667-669, 688, 699-701, 727
/Worksheet Global Prot Disable, 692, 698
/Worksheet Global Prot Enable, 123-124, 617, 658, 669
/Worksheet Global Recalc, 509, 669-671
/Worksheet Global Recalc Iteration, 132
/Worksheet Global Recalc Manual, 130, 527, 614
/Worksheet Global Width, 618
/Worksheet Global Zero, 182, 668-669
/Worksheet Global Zero Label, 182
/Worksheet Hide, 685, 727
/Worksheet Hide Enable, 126
/Worksheet Insert, 708-709, 770, 773
/Worksheet Insert Column, 24, 114, 419, 656, 674-676
/Worksheet Insert Row, 24, 114, 418, 656, 674-676, 745
/Worksheet Insert Sheet, 83, 114, 618, 674-676
/Worksheet Insert Sheet After, 460, 527
/Worksheet Insert Sheet After 1, 472
/Worksheet Page, 313, 628, 632, 656, 684-685, 737, 739
/Worksheet Status, 130, 132, 155, 601, 609, 665, 667, 671, 683-684, 700
/Worksheet Titles, 120, 457, 680-681
/Worksheet Titles Both, 121
/Worksheet Titles Clear, 122, 681
/Worksheet Titles Horizontal, 122
/Worksheet Titles Vertical, 122
/Worksheet Window, 681-683
/Worksheet Window Clear, 118, 683
/Worksheet Window Display, 92, 832
/Worksheet Window Display Primary, 116

/Worksheet Window Display Secondary, 116
/Worksheet Window Graph, 119, 384, 768
/Worksheet Window Horizontal, 116
/Worksheet Window Perspective, 83, 118, 460, 681
/Worksheet Window Sync, 117
/Worksheet Window Unsync, 117, 616
/Worksheet Window Vertical, 116
1-2-3 functions
see also functions
@@, 225-226
@ABS, 188-189
@ACOS, 194-196
@ASIN, 194-196
@ATAN, 194-196
@ATAN2, 194-196
@AVG, 197-198, 450
@CELL, 225, 227-228, 602
@CELLPOINTER, 225, 227-228
@CHAR, 246, 258-259, 845-846
@CHOOSE, 225, 229-230
@CLEAN, 246, 257
@CODE, 246, 259
@COLS, 225, 230-231
@COORD, 225, 229
@COS, 194-195
@COUNT, 197-199, 450
@CTERM, 204, 213-214
@D360, 237-238
@DATE, 237-239, 486, 689
@DATEVALUE, 237, 239-240, 627, 689
@DAVG, 479
@DAY, 237, 240-241
@DCOUNT, 479, 810
@DDB, 205, 215
@DGET, 479, 482-483
@DMAX, 455, 479
@DMIN, 479
@DQUERY, 479, 483
@DSTD, 479
@DSTDS, 479, 482
@DSUM, 455, 458, 466, 479, 790
@DVAR, 479
@DVARS, 482
@ERR, 225, 231-232
@EXACT, 245, 251-252
@EXP, 188, 193
@FALSE, 217, 221
@FIND, 245, 247-249
@FV, 204, 211-212
@HLOOKUP, 225, 232-234
@HOUR, 237, 244
@IF, 217-220, 600, 621
@INDEX, 226, 234-235
@INFO, 226, 235-236, 609
@INT, 188-190

@IRR, 204-207
@ISERR, 217, 220-221
@ISNA, 217, 220-221
@ISNUMBER, 222-225
@ISRANGE, 217, 221-222
@ISSTRING, 217, 222-225
@LEFT, 245, 250
@LENGTH, 245, 251
@LN, 188, 193
@LOG, 188, 193
@LOWER, 245, 253
@MAX, 197, 199-200, 450
@MID, 245, 248-250
@MIN, 197, 199-200, 450
@MINUTE, 237, 244
@MOD, 189-190
@MONTH, 237, 240-241
@N, 246, 255
@NA, 226, 231-232, 618
@NOW, 237, 241, 689
@NPV, 204, 209-210
@PI, 194
@PMT, 204, 208, 454, 457, 460-461, 473, 793
@PROPER, 246, 253
@PV, 204, 211
@RAND, 189, 191-192
@RATE, 204, 207
@REPEAT, 246, 253-254
@REPLACE, 245, 250-251
@RIGHT, 245, 250
@ROUND, 158, 189-191, 602, 620-621
@ROWS, 226, 230-231
@S, 246, 255, 607, 622-623
@SECOND, 237, 244
@SHEETS, 226, 230-231
@SIN, 194-195
@SLN, 205, 214
@SQRT, 189, 192
@STD, 197, 200-201
@STDS, 197, 200-201
@STRING, 246, 256, 622
@SUM, 21-22, 132, 134, 136, 197, 201-202, 450, 601, 606, 696, 707
@SUMPRODUCT, 197
@SYD, 205, 215-216
@TAN, 194-195
@TERM, 204, 212-213
@TIME, 237, 242-243, 689
@TIMEVALUE, 237, 243-244, 689
@TODAY, 237, 241
@TRIM, 246, 254
@TRUE, 217, 221
@UPPER, 245, 253
@VALUE, 246, 256-257
@VAR, 197, 202-203
@VARS, 197, 202-203

@VDB, 205, 216-217
@VLOOKUP, 226, 232-234
@YEAR, 237, 240-241
{ macro keyword, 517
} macro keyword, 517
~ macro keyword, 517-518
#AND# operator, 76, 219, 445, 646
#NOT# operator, 76, 219, 445-446, 645-646
#OR# operator, 76, 219, 445, 646
+/- format, 166-167
/ macro keyword, 517
/ [slash] (start command from READY mode) key, 43
\123R3 subdirectory, 34
1-2-3
    changing configuration, 835-840
        selected country, 841-842
    command menu, 35
    Command Reference, 659-822
    configuring, 829-835
    exiting, 35-36, 821-822
        from 1-2-3 Access System, 38-39
    Install program, 824-826
    installing, 823-843, 860
    multiuser environment, 290-291
    operating systems required, 29-31
    overview, 11-32
    Release 1A, 40
    Release 2, 40
    Release 2.01, 40
    Release 3, 853-862
    starting
        1-2-3 Access System, 36-39
        operating system, 34-36
    transferring files with other programs, 37-40
    tutorial, 54-55
1-2-3 (1-2-3 Access System) command, 38
1-2-3 Access System
    command menu, 38
    exiting from 1-2-3, 38-39
    starting 1-2-3 from, 36-39
123.DCF file, 597
123R3.BAT file, 34
360 day years, 238
:STRING suffix, 571
:VALUE suffix, 571
< (less than) operator, 438
< macro keyword, 517
< [less than sign] (start command from READY mode) key, 43
<= (less than or equal to) operator, 438
<> (not equal to) operator, 438
= (equal to) operator, 438
> (greater than) operator, 438
>= (greater than or equal to) operator, 438
? advanced macro command, 544-545

@ function, 225-226

A

Abs (F4) key, 44, 79, 139-140, 144-145, 613
ABS function, 188-189
ABS macro keyword, 519
absolute cell
    addressing, 78-79, 139-140
        problems, 613
    references, 605, 647
absolute value, 189
Access System see 1-2-3 Access System
accounting functions, 203-17
ACOS function, 194-96
Addin (Alt-F10) key, 45
addition (+) operator, 74
addresses
    cell, 68, 78-79
        absolute, 139-140
        relative, 138-139
    range
        pointing to, 96
        typing, 96
    saving on stack, 565
advanced macro commands, 28-29, 536-592, 859
    see also 1-2-3 advanced macro commands
    arguments, 542
    controlling programs, 551-567
    data input, 544-551
    programs, 542-543
    syntax, 541-542
Advanced menu, 382
ALL MODIFIED FILES message, 283
alphanumeric keyboard, 42-43
Alt (change function of key) key, 42
Alt-letter macro, 520
    will not work: Macro Problem #1, 652
ampersand (&) concatenation operator, 76, 246, 622
AND condition, criteria ranges, 440-441
annuity
    future value, 211-212
    present value, 211
apostrophe (') in labels, 70, 599
App1 (Alt-F7) key, 44
APP1 macro keyword, 519
App2 (Alt-F8) key, 45
APP2 macro keyword, 519
App3 (Alt-F9) key, 45
APP3 macro keyword, 519
APP4 macro keyword, 519
APPENDBELOW advanced macro command, 570, 575-576
APPENDRIGHT advanced macro command, 570, 576
arccosine, 195-196

arcsine, 195-196

arctangent, 195-196

arguments, 18

    advanced macro commands, 542

    associating with subroutines, 563-565

    functions, 187-188

    maximum and minimum values, 199-200

arithmetic mean, 198

arithmetic operators *see* operators

ASCII files, 344

    imported files are scrambled: File Problem #6, 626-627

ASIN function, 194-196

asterisk (*) wild-card character, 269, 438, 712

ATAN function, 194-196

ATAN2 function, 194-196

attributes of cells, 227-228

AUTOEXEC.BAT file, 610

Automatic format, 174-176

automatic

    macros, 522-523

    recalculation, 129

    retrieving files, 270

    specifying data ranges, 354-358

AVG function, 197-198, 450

B

background

    grid for graphs, 367-368

    printing, 342

    recalculation, 129-130

Backspace (erase or cancel) key, 43, 102

BACKSPACE macro keyword, 517

BAK file extension, 22, 95, 263, 617, 625, 712, 717

bar graphs, 353, 388-391, 762

bars, separating in graphs: Graphing Problem #3, 636

basic commands, 89-152

batch files, 34-35, 38

BEEP advanced macro command, 577-578

beeping on error, 155

BIGLEFT macro keyword, 518

BIGRIGHT macro keyword, 518

BLANK advanced macro command, 536, 570, 574-575

blank headers in reports, 323

borders, printing, 325

BRANCH advanced macro command, 539, 552-554, 613

Break (cancel and return to READY mode) key, 45

BREAK macro keyword, 518

BREAKOFF advanced macro command, 552, 560-561

BREAKON advanced macro command, 552, 561

BS macro keyword, 517

buffers, 736

C

Calc (F9) key, 44, 130, 147, 176, 228, 276, 281, 579, 602, 670, 701, 703, 716, 730-731, 733, 736, 768, 790

CALC advanced macro command, 509, 519, 670, 790

CALC indicator, 51, 130, 614

call-table, 550

cancel

    graph settings, 766-767

    printing, 736

        printer doesn't stop: Printing Problem #15, 633-634

    subroutine, 565-566

Cancel/Replace menu, 386

CAP status indicator, 51

Caps Lock (uppercase letters) key, 42

CD (DOS) command, 34, 37-38, 624, 836

CE macro keyword, 517, 525

cell address, 47, 68, 229

    macros refer to wrong addresses: Macro Problem #2, 652

    pass program control to, 552-554

    relative, 625-626

    wrong after copying formulas: Addressing Problem #1, 613

CELL function, 225, 227-228, 602

cell pointer, 16, 46, 62-69

    move to field and will not stay: Data Management Problem #7, 648

    restricted to unprotected cells, 124-125, 700-701

cell references

    absolute, 605, 647

    formulas pointing to, 77

    relative, 605, 647

CELLPOINTER function, 225, 227-228

cells

    absolute addressing, 78-79

    adding notes, 79

    addressing, 78-79

    aligning labels, 689-692

    cell pointer restricted to unprotected, 700-701

    changing formats, 79

    checking

        aspect, 222-225

        attributes, 227-228

    contents, 156, 158

    copying, 22

        contents, 137-138, 140-142

    counting entries, 198-199

    current, 58

determine formula in hidden cell, 126
display, 156-158
    as blank, 173
erasing, 21
    contents, 692-693
    range, 91, 574-575
form and formatting for printing, 746-748
formatting, 153-183
free, 98-99
input, 468
jump directly to, 68
moving contents, 22, 132-133
multiply column-and-row matrices, 810-811
printing contents, 323-324
protecting, 123-124
referencing indirectly, 226
relative addressing, 78-79
repeating strings within, 253-254
restricting cell pointer to unprotected, 124-125
CGM file extension, 22, 264, 385, 673, 718-719,
    726, 732, 769
CHAR function, 246, 258-259, 845-846
character set, translate for database, 510
characters
    displaying LMBCS, 258-259
    removing nonprintable from strings, 257
CHOOSE function, 225, 229-230
CIRC indicator, 51, 130
circular references, 155
    iteration, 130-132
    problems, 600-603
CLEAN function, 246, 257
CLEARENTRY macro keyword, 517, 525
clock indicator, 52
CLOSE advanced macro command, 585, 587-588
closing files, 587-588
CMD status indicator, 51
CODE function, 246, 259
codes, computing LMBCS, 259
color
    graphs, 378-380, 777, 780-781
    printing reports, 338
    viewing graphs, 384
Color format, 177
COLS function, 225, 230-231
columns, 656-657
    changing defaults, 516
    converting to rows, 148
    deleting, 109-111, 676-677
    displaying/hiding, 677-679
        headings, 680-681
    erasing, 109
    excluding while printing multiple ranges, 319
    hiding, 126
    inserting, 114-115, 674-676
    label, 506

lining up on decimal point, 163
printing
    borders, 325-327
    headings on every page, 743-744
variable range, 468
width, 20, 108-109, 667
    problems, 618
worksheet columns default width: Column
    Width Problem #1, 618
comma format, 163-164
command language see advanced macro commands
    and 1-2-3 advanced macro commands
command menu, 20-22
Command Reference, 659-822
commands
    see also 1-2-3 commands
    1-2-3 Access System
        1-2-3, 38
        Exit, 38
        Install, 38-39
        Translate, 38-40
    advanced macro, 28-29, 537-592, 859
    basic, 89-152
    controlling external database, 819-820
    data manipulation, 570-576
    database, 24-27
    decision-making, 567-570
    display on control panel, 578
    DOS
        CD, 34, 37-38, 624, 836
        COPY, 34, 38, 298, 597, 733
        COPY CON, 34, 38
        DEL, 284, 718
        DIR, 624
        ERASE, 284, 713, 718
        MODE, 753
        TREE, 624
        TYPE, 721, 732
    executing named in programs, 566-567
    file manipulation, 584-591
    fundamental, 89-152
    Install, 39
    invisible, 539
    macro won't execute: Macro Problem #5, 655
    multiple worksheet, 20
    program enhancement, 577-584
    prohibit display on control panel, 578
    range, 21-22
    repeating with macros, 516-517
    run operating-system, 821
    selecting from menus, 90-94
    send to database management program,
        509-510
    Translate, 282
    troubleshooting, 611-619
    worksheet, 21

Compose (Alt-F1) key, 44, 258
compose sequences, Lotus Multibyte Character Set
    (LMBCS), 845-852
compound
    growth rate, 207
    term of investments, 213-214
concatenating strings, 75-76
conditional tests, 217
    trapping errors, 220-221
CONFIG.SYS file, 823-824
configuring 1-2-3, 829-840
consolidation worksheets, 106
CONTENTS advanced macro command, 126, 174,
    570, 572-574
    numeric format codes, 574
control panel, 47-48, 578
    display commands, 578
convergence, 131
COORD function, 225, 229
COPY (DOS) command, 34, 38, 298, 597, 733
Copy command, 22, 99, 136-145, 579, 584, 604,
    616, 625, 658, 706-708, 793, 800
COPY CON (DOS) command, 34, 38
copying
    cells, 22
    contents
        of cell, 137-138, 140-142
        of ranges, 142-143
    data, 706-708
    files, 828-829
    formulas, 701-704
        absolute addressing, 139-140
        relative addressing, 138-139
    mixed addressing, 143-145
    with range names, 145
    records to location, 801-802
    source range to destination range, 575-576
COS function, 194-195
cosine, 195
COUNT function, 197-199, 450
country, changing selected, 841-842
criteria ranges, 172
    AND condition, 440-441
    complicated, 437-446
    formulas in, 438-440
    join formula in, 448-449, 451
    multiple, 440-441
    OR condition, 442-444
    records that meet conditions, 802-803
    searching records, 429-432
    wild cards, 438
cross-tabulated data table, 454-458, 477-479
    three-dimensional, 463-466
CTERM function, 204, 213-214
Ctrl (change function of key) key, 42, 91
Currency format, 164-165

current
    cell, 58
    printer settings, 300-301
cursor, 63
    anchoring, 529
    movement keys, 43-46
custom mode indicator, 582

D

D macro keyword, 517
D360 function, 237-238
data
    copying, 706-708
    destruction problem, 616-617
    displaying with fixed number of decimal places,
        163-164
    entering in database, 416-418
        problems, 599-600
    erasing from template to use template again:
        Template Problem #1, 617
    extracting from file to create another file,
        716-717
    filling ranges, 786, 788
    finding, 148-150
    formatting, 153
        for graphs, 366-367
        imported, 813-814
    frequency distribution, 808-810
    hiding, 122-123, 125-127
    including dollar sign ($), 164
    input
        labels, 546
        numeric, 547-548
    linking, 17
    loading from other programs, 495-499
    managing, 411-511
        troubleshooting, 645-651
    manipulation commands, 570-576
    missing from worksheet: Template Problem #2,
        617-618
    moving, 708-709
    parsing, 495-499, 813-814
    printing one screen, 305, 308
    protecting, 122-125
    replacing, 148-150
    retrieving from specified locations, 234-235
    sending to printer, 755
    trends, 811-812
Data commands, 81, 101, 412, 414, 658, 786-820,
    857
Data Distribution command, 488-489, 808-810
Data External command, 26-27, 290, 414, 499-511
Data External Create command, 504, 816-818
Data External Create Definition Create-Definition
    command, 505, 649, 817
Data External Create Go command, 507

Data External Create Name command, 505, 818
Data External Create Quit command, 507
Data External Delete command, 508, 818
Data External List command, 503, 815-816
Data External List Fields command, 504-505, 507, 817
Data External List Tables command, 503
Data External Other command, 503, 507, 819-820
Data External Other Control command, 483, 509-510
Data External Other Refresh command, 508-509
Data External Other Refresh Interval command, 509
Data External Other Translate command, 510
Data External Reset command, 503, 511, 818
Data External Use command, 427, 501, 503, 650, 815-816, 818-819
Data Fill command, 484-487, 571, 621, 786, 788, 792, 794, 797
data legend on graphs, 365
Data Matrix command, 26, 494, 810-811
Data Matrix Multiply command, 494
Data Parse command, 286, 495-499, 627, 714, 721, 813-814
Data Parse Format-Line Create command, 656
Data Query command, 106, 172, 414, 427-437, 479, 499, 509-510, 645, 648, 650, 656, 815, 818-819
Data Query Criteria command, 645-646, 799-801, 803, 816
Data Query Del command, 447-448, 803, 806-807
Data Query Extract command, 106, 419, 433, 440, 449, 502, 648, 650-651, 801, 803, 804-809, 816
Data Query Find command, 25, 648, 802-803, 806
Data Query Input command, 106, 429, 449, 646, 799
Data Query Modify command, 435-436, 503, 807-808, 817
Data Query Modify Extract command, 436, 650-651, 808
Data Query Modify Insert command, 436-437
Data Query Modify Replace command, 436, 650-651, 808
Data Query Output command, 433, 801-802, 816
Data Query Unique command, 25, 446-447, 449, 458, 805-806
data ranges
    hiding for graphs, 780-781
    selecting for graphs, 785
    specifying
        automatically, 354-358
        for graphs, 353-358
        manually, 353-354
Data Refresh Interval command, 820

Data Regression command, 26, 489-493, 772, 811-812
Data Sort command, 420, 422-426, 484-485, 797-798
Data Sort Data Range command, 420
Data Sort Primary-Key command, 103
Data Table command, 26, 172, 413, 451-452, 484, 509, 610, 819
Data Table 1 command, 453-456, 789-791, 793, 795, 810
Data Table 2 command, 456-458, 789, 791-793, 795, 810
Data Table 3 command, 462, 466, 792-795
Data Table Labeled command, 466-468, 472, 476-479, 794-796
Data Table Labeled Formulas command, 474
data tables, 413, 451-479
    cross-tabulated, 454-458, 477-479
    input
        cell, 453
        value, 453
    labeled, 466-479, 794-796
    range, 452
    results area, 453
    three-dimensional cross-tabulated, 463-466
    type 1, 453-456, 789-790
    type 2, 456-458, 791-792
    type 3, 458-466, 792-794
    variable, 452
database, 411-511
    adding new fields, 419
    blank row inserted while printing: Printing Problem #10, 632
    cannot create: Data Management Problem #8, 649
    column label, 506
    commands, 24-27
        controlling external, 819-820
    creating external tables, 504-507, 816-818
    data tables see data tables
    deleting
        fields, 419
        external tables, 508
    disconnecting external, 511
    driver, 501
    duplicating external tables, 505
    entering data, 416-418
    external, 499-511
    fields, 412
        creation string, 507
        description, 507
    filling ranges, 484-488
    forgetting field names: Data Management Problem #10, 650
    frequency distributions, 488-489

functions, 24-25, 479-483
inserting and deleting records, 418-419
joining multiple, 448-451
key fields, 412
link 1-2-3 to external database, 815
listing external database tables and fields, 503-504, 815-816
loading data from other programs, 495-499
management, 24-27
modifying, 418
multiple-regression analysis, 489-493
names and output range do not match: Data Management Problem #5, 648
querying, 427
records, 412
    searching for records, 427-448
required output, 415-416
send commands to management program, 509-510
simultaneous linear equations, 494
sorting records, 420-426, 797-798
table, 413
    creation string, 501
    definition, 501, 505
    name, 501
transferring, 290
translate character set, 510
updating worksheet, 508-509
date
    and time functions, 19
    converting serial numbers to, 240-241
    defaults, 167
    filling ranges, 486-488
    finding current, 241
    strings changing to serial numbers, 239-240
    unrecognizable format: File Problem #7, 627
    values converting to serial numbers, 238-239
Date Fill command, 242
Date format, 167-172
DATE function, 237-239, 486, 689
Date menu, 167
DATEVALUE function, 237, 239-240, 627, 689
DAVG function, 479
DAY function, 237, 240-241
dBASE II, 39-40, 495
dBASE III, 39-40, 290, 495, 649-650
dBASE III Plus, 39-40, 495
DCOUNT function, 479, 810
DDB function, 205, 215
decimal point, lining columns up, 163
defaults
    changing, 93, 155
        column, 516
        margins, 741-742
    date, 167
    line graph, 358-359

new worksheet, 162-163
print settings, 300-305
worksheet global, 154-155
DEFINE advanced macro command, 552, 563-565
Del (delete/reverse selection) key, 45
DEL (DOS) command, 284, 718
DEL macro keyword, 518
Delete command, 616
deleting
    files, 112-113
    records, 418-419
    rows and columns, 109-111
    specified records, 447-448
    table from external database, 818
    worksheets, 109, 112-113
dependent variable, 397
depreciation
    double-declining balance, 215
    straight-line, 214
    sum-of-the-years'-digits, 215-216
    variable-declining balance, 216-217
DESQView, 610
destination cell, store contents of source cell, 572-573
DGET function, 479, 482-483
DIF file format, 39-40, 495
DIR (DOS) command, 624
directories
    changing, 265, 722
    creating, 827-828
    finding which directory file is in: File Problem #2, 624
disconnecting external databases, 511
disk drive, 722
Disk drive not ready error message, 586
Disk full error message, 267
disks
    loading files from, 710-711
    registering, 825-826
    retrieving files from, 268-269
DISPATCH advanced macro command, 552-563
display
    appearance, 860
    drivers, installing for two, 840
    formats, 671-673
displaying
    columns, 677-679
    graphs, 581-582, 767-768
    numbers only, 162-163
    worksheets, 685
        changing format, 115-116
        from different views, 681-683
        frame, 580
        multiple, 61-62
DisplayWrite, 39-40
division (/) operator, 74

DMAX function, 455, 479
DMIN function, 479
documenting macro, 534-535, 654
    comments in worksheets, 535
    descriptive names, 534-535
    printout of macro, 535
dollar sign ($)
    absolute addressing, 139-140
    including in data, 164
DOS
    checking configuration, 823-824
    operating system, 826
double-declining balance depreciation, 215
DOWN macro keyword, 517
DQUERY function, 479, 483
driver control (DCF) file, 597-598, 843
DSTD function, 479
DSTDS function, 479, 482
DSUM function, 455, 458, 466, 479, 790
DVAR function, 479
DVARS function, 482

E

Edit (F2) key, 24, 44, 80-81, 140, 176, 284, 432, 533, 692, 712-713, 803
edit line, clear of data, 525
EDIT macro keyword, 518
EDIT mode, 49, 63, 70, 77-78, 80-81, 176, 533, 599-600
    clear edit line of data, 525
editing
    data in worksheet, 79-81
    keys, 81
    records, 807-808
ELSE clause, 569
ENC file extension, 22, 264, 298, 344, 733-734, 738
encoded file, 298
End key, 65-68, 97
END macro keyword, 518
END status indicator, 51, 65-67
enhanced keyboard, 40, 43
Enter [Tilde (~)] key, 515
equal (=) operator, 76
ERASE (DOS) command, 284, 713, 718
Erase command, 528
erasing
    cells, 21, 91, 692-693
    files, 284, 718-719
    ranges, 91, 110, 692-693
    rows and columns, 109
    worksheets, 109, 679-680
ERR problems, 604-608
    combining numbers and strings: Function
        Problem #3, 621-622

deletion in worksheet, formulas change to ERR:
    ERR Problem #2, 605-606
formulas change to ERR: ERR Problem #1,
    604-605
range name no longer valid: Range Name
    Problem #1, 611-612
saving file causes formula ERR in other files:
    ERR Problem #4, 607-608
string formulas ERR after cell or range erasure:
    ERR Problem #3, 606-607
unable to insert row in worksheet: ERR
    Problem #5, 608
ERR function, 225, 231-232
error messages, 52
    ALL MODIFIED FILES, 283
    Disk drive not ready, 586
    Disk full, 267
    File not found, 587
    Invalid use of MENU macro command, 554
    output range full: Data Management Problem
        #6, 648
    PASSWORD PROTECTED, 282-283
    Too many records for Output range, 648
    when trying to extract records: Data
        Management Problem #3, 646-647
ERROR mode, 52
errors
    beeping on, 155
    checking for, 221
    macros, 533-534
    trapping, 220-221, 231-232
Esc (cancel) key, 45, 91, 102
ESC macro keyword, 518
EXACT function, 245, 251-252
exclude-keys, 550
Exit (1-2-3 Access System) command, 38
exiting 1-2-3, 35-36, 821-822
EXP function, 188, 193
exponent, 166
exponentiation (^) operator, 74
EXTEND macro keyword, 519
external databases, 499-511
extra-key sorting, 423-424
extracting
    data, 271-276
    unique records, 446-447

F

FALSE function, 217, 221
FC macro keyword, 518
Features menu, 376-377
FF macro keyword, 518
fields, 412
    adding new to database, 419
    creation string, 507
    deleting from database, 419

description, 507
key, 412, 448, 451
names, 413, 417
    forgetting: Data Management Problem #10,
        650
    string functions used on: Function Problem #4,
        622-623
File commands, 23, 710-728, 855
File Admin Link-Refresh command, 86, 291, 701,
    703, 728
File Admin Reservation command, 724-725
File Admin Reservation Get command, 291
File Admin Reservation Release command, 291
File Admin Reservation Setting Manual command,
    291
File Admin Reservation-Setting command, 727
File Admin Seal command, 617, 725, 727-728
File Admin Seal Disable command, 128, 699
File Admin Seal File command, 128, 173, 658
File Admin Table command, 285, 720, 725-727
File Combine Add command, 280-281, 614, 626,
    715
File Combine Add Named/Specified-Range
    command, 280
File Combine command, 276-277, 282, 495,
    714-716
File Combine Copy command, 277-279, 625-626
File Combine Subtract command, 280-281
File Dir command, 265, 269, 386, 624, 711,
    718-719, 722
FILE END macro keyword, 518
File Erase command, 261, 284, 713, 718-720
file extensions
    .BAK, 22, 95, 263, 617, 625, 712, 717
    .CGM, 22, 264, 385, 673, 718-719, 726, 732,
        769
    .ENC, 22, 264, 298, 344, 733-734, 738
    .DIF, 39-40, 495
    .PIC, 22, 264, 385, 673, 718-719, 726, 732, 769
    .PRN, 22, 264, 286, 298, 344, 718-720, 726,
        731-732, 738
    .WK1, 22, 40, 264, 713
    .WK3, 22, 263, 711, 713
    .WKS, 264
    .WR1, 264
    .WRK, 264
file formats
    metafile, 385
    picture (PIC), 385
    RTF/DCA, 39-40
FILE HOME macro keyword, 518
File Import command, 257, 286, 495, 584, 698,
    714, 720-721, 813
File Import Numbers command, 287, 626, 813
File Import Text command, 286, 627, 721, 813

File List command, 261, 269, 285, 713, 719-720,
    722, 726
File List Linked command, 728
FILE macro keyword, 518
File menu, 261-262
File New command, 83, 270, 608, 675, 723-724
File New After command, 270
File not found message, 587
FILE NS macro keyword, 518
File Open command, 83, 268, 282, 289, 543, 608,
    657, 711, 723-724, 767
FILE PS macro keyword, 518
File Retrieve command, 263, 268-269, 282, 289,
    291, 495, 624-625, 657, 710-711
File Save command, 94-95, 113, 265, 282-283,
    291, 321, 420, 448, 614, 617, 692, 697,
    710-714, 717, 723, 725, 768-769, 784, 797,
    807
FILE status indicator, 51
File Xtract command, 271-272, 282, 432, 560,
    713, 715-717, 807
File Xtract Formulas command, 274-275, 717
File Xtract Values command, 272, 615, 717
files, 46, 58-62
    123.DCF, 597
    123R3.BAT, 34
    ASCII text, 344
    AUTOEXEC.BAT, 610
    automatically retrieving, 270
    backup copies, 625
    cannot find backup copy: File Problem #4, 625
    changing all worksheets in, 111
    changing while protecting macros:
        Macro Problem #8, 656
        Macro Problem #9, 656-657
    clearing all from memory, 113
    closing, 587-588
    combining, 714-716
    CONFIG.SYS, 823-824
    copied formulas meaningless: File Problem #5,
        625-626
    copying, 828-829
        during installation, 826
    dates are unrecognizable format: File Problem
        #7, 627
    deleting, 112-113, 676-677
    destroyed by macro: Macro Problem #7, 656
    directory for, 827-828
    driver control (DCF), 597-598, 843
    encoded, 298
    erasing, 284, 718-719
    extracting
        and combining data, 271-281
        portion to create another file, 716-717
    finding files: File Problem #1, 624

finding which directory file is in: File Problem
    #2, 624
imported ASCII files are scrambled: File
    Problem #6, 626-627
importing, 720-721
    delimited files, 287
    text files, 286
indicator, 52
linking, 60, 86-87
listing names, 284-286, 719-720
loading from disk, 710-711
LOTUS.BAT, 38
making mistakes in: File Problem #3, 625
managing, 22-24, 261-292
    in memory, 262-263
manipulation commands, 584-591
new blank, 723
naming, 263-264
nonsharable, 290
opening, 584-587, 723-724
opening new in memory, 270
out of memory: Memory Problem #1, 609-610
pointer, 590-591
print image, 597
protecting, 23, 727-728
    passwords, 282-283
read from, 588-589
record size of, 591
renaming, 617
reservations for, 291
retrieving
    from disk, 268-269
    from subdirectories, 269-270
    with wild cards, 269
saving, 94-95, 265-267, 712-714
    causes formula ERR in other files: ERR
        Problem #4, 607-608
    under different names, 625
    with passwords, 129
sealing, 128, 727-728
sharing, 724-725
tables of, 284-286, 725-727
text, 298
transferring, 286-290
    between other programs and 1-2-3, 37-40
    early releases of 1-2-3 and Symphony, 289
Translate, 826
troubleshooting, 624-627
write string to, 589-590
FILES mode, 49
FILESIZE advanced macro command, 585, 591
filling ranges, 484-488
financial functions, 19, 203-217
FIND function, 245, 247-249
FIND mode, 49, 431-432
FIRSTCELL macro keyword, 518

FIRSTFILE macro keyword, 518
Fixed format, 163
fonts, selecting for printing reports, 333-335
footers, 321-322
    printing on each page, 741
FOR advanced macro command, 567, 569-570
FORBREAK advanced macro command, 567,
    569-570
FORM advanced macro command, 125, 544,
    550-551, 699
formats
    +/-, 166-167
    Automatic, 174-176
    changing for cells, 79
    Color, 177
    comma, 163-164
    Currency, 164-165
    Date and Time, 167-172
    display of cell contents, 157
    Fixed, 163
    General, 162-163
    Hidden, 173-174
    International, 177-178
    Label, 174
    Parentheses, 176
    Percent, 165
    range, 156-183
    Scientific, 166
    Text, 172-173
    transferring changes to other worksheets, 674
formatting
    cells, 153-183
    current worksheet, 161
    data, 153
    output for reports, 323
    ranges, 686-689
formulas, 17
    after copying formula, addresses are wrong:
        Addressing Problem #1, 613
    change to ERR: ERR Problem #1, 604-605
    CIRC indicator appears after entry, formula
        does not refer to itself: Circular Reference
        Problem #2, 601-602
    CIRC indicator appears after entry: Circular
        Reference Problem #1, 600-601
    converting to values, 145-147
    copied are meaningless in file: File Problem #5,
        625-626
    copying, 701-704
        absolute addressing, 139-140
        relative addressing, 138-139
    correcting errors in, 77-78
    criteria ranges, 438-440
    deletion in worksheet changes formula to ERR:
        ERR Problem #2, 605-606
    determine in hidden cell, 126

display format in worksheet, 661-664
don't work in range names: Range Name
    Problem #2, 612-613
entering
    invalid, 176
    multiple worksheets, 85-86
    worksheets, 73-78
erasing and defaulting to EDIT mode: Data-
    Entry Problem #2, 599-600
extracting from worksheet, 274-275
filling ranges, 486
label range, 467-468
linking worksheets, 86-88
logical, 73, 76
modifying, 150
numeric, 73-75
pointing to cell references, 77
range, 467
recalculation problems: Circular Reference
    Problem #3, 602-603
string, 73, 75-76
    searches, 444-445
four-quadrant, 195-196
frame borders, printing, 328
FRAMEOFF advanced macro command, 577, 580
FRAMEON advanced macro command, 577, 580
free cell, 98-99
frequency distribution, 488-489, 808-810
function keys, 43-45
    see also keys
functions, 18-20, 185-260, 857-858
    see also 1-2-3 functions
    arguments, 18, 187-188
    database, 24-25, 479-483
    date and time, 19, 237-245
    entering, 186-188
    equal numbers test as unequal: Function
        Problem #2, 620-621
    filling ranges, 486
    financial and accounting, 19, 203-217
    ISNUMBER, 217
    LMBCS (Lotus Multibyte Character Set),
        258-259
    logarithmic, 192-193
    logical, 19, 217-225
    mathematical, 18, 188-192
    rounding errors: Function Problem #1, 620
    special, 19, 225-236
    statistical, 18, 197-203
    string, 20, 245-257
        used on fields: Function Problem #4,
        622-623
    SUMPRODUCT, 202
    trigonometric, 194-196
    troubleshooting, 620-623

future value of annuity, 211-212
FV function, 204, 211-212

G

General format, 162-163
GET advanced macro command, 544-546
GETLABEL advanced macro command, 544-547
GETNUMBER advanced macro command, 544,
    547-548
GETPOS advanced macro command, 585, 591
Global Protection Enabled command, 173
global
    display settings, 683-684
    worksheet formats, 156-158
Go Print command, 526
GoTo (F5) key, 44, 68, 84-86, 103, 122, 524
GOTO macro keyword, 519, 524
Graph (F10) key, 24, 44, 356, 383, 386, 401, 643,
    765, 767-768
Graph commands, 81, 101, 760-785, 812, 856-857
Graph Group command, 24, 357-358, 765, 785
GRAPH macro keyword, 519
Graph menu, 350, 371, 378-383, 387, 393,
    396-397
Graph Name command, 386, 727, 756, 783-784
Graph Name Create command, 391, 402, 635, 644,
    766, 768-769, 784
Graph Name Reset command, 784
Graph Name Use command, 393, 635, 784
Graph Options command, 766
Graph Options Advanced Colors A Range
    command, 380
Graph Options Advanced Colors A-F command,
    772
Graph Options Advanced Colors A-F Hide
    command, 772
Graph Options Advanced Colors command, 777,
    780-781, 783
Graph Options Advanced Hatches command, 636,
    641, 643, 782-783
Graph Options Advanced Hatches A Range
    command, 381, 396
Graph Options Advanced Text command, 781-782
Graph Options Advanced Text Color command,
    777
Graph Options Advanced Text First Color
    command, 781-782
Graph Options Advanced Text First Font
    command, 781-782
Graph Options Advanced Text First Size command,
    781-782
Graph Options Advanced Text Second Color
    command, 781-782
Graph Options Advanced Text Second Font
    command, 781-782

Graph Options Advanced Text Second Size command, 781-782

Graph Options Advanced Text Third Color command, 781-782

Graph Options Advanced Text Third Font command, 781-782

Graph Options Advanced Text Third Size command, 781-782

Graph Options B&W command, 402, 643

Graph Options Color command, 401, 767

Graph Options Color/B&W command, 777

Graph Options Data-Labels command, 362, 774, 778-780

Graph Options Format command, 362-363, 366, 370, 771-772

Graph Options Format F Neither command, 780

Graph Options Grid command, 367, 774

Graph Options Grid Clear command, 370

Graph Options Grid Horizontal command, 368

Graph Options Legend command, 769-770

Graph Options Scale command, 368, 371, 774-777

Graph Options Scale Format command, 370

Graph Options Scale Skip command, 369, 639, 775

Graph Options Scale Y-Scale Exponent Manual command, 638

Graph Options Scale Y-Scale Indicator command, 638

Graph Options Scale Y-Scale Manual command, 641

Graph Options Scale Y-Scale Type Logarithmic command, 640

Graph Options Titles command, 360, 773

Graph Reset command, 387, 765-767

Graph Reset B Quit command, 392

Graph Reset Graph command, 387, 389, 393, 765

Graph Reset Range command, 355

Graph Save command, 385-386, 768-769, 784

Graph Type command, 355, 760-763, 767

Graph Type Bar command, 356, 377

Graph Type Features command, 374

Graph Type XY command, 397

Graph View command, 355, 383, 401, 767-768

Graph X A B C D E F command, 764-766

GRAPHOFF advanced macro command, 577, 582

GRAPHON advanced macro command, 577, 581-582

graphs, 23, 347-408

    adding

        grid, 774

        headings to graph and axes, 773

        labels

            and numbers, 360-365

            below x-axis, 364

        legends, 769-770

        second y-axis, 374-375

    advanced options, 378-383

altering default display, 366-374

axis

    number format, 370-374

    scale indicator, 371

    type, 371-372

background grid, 367-368

bad hatching patterns: Graphing Problem #2, 635-636

bar, 353, 388-391, 762

cancel settings, 766-767

changing

    appearance of printed, 402

    font, size, and color for text, 781-782

    options and viewing graph: Graphing Problem #8, 642-643

colors, 378-380

confusing multiple-value graph: Graphing Problem #7, 641-642

data legend, 365

default line, 358-359

defining color, 777

density of printed, 403

display, 581-582, 767-768

    in worksheet, 119

enhancing appearance, 359-365

finding error after lengthy printing: Graphing Problem #9, 643

format for data, 366-367

hardware requirements, 348

hatches, 380-381, 782-783

hiding data ranges, 780-781

HLCO (high-low-close-open), 354, 388, 399-400, 762

in reports, 405-407

label points of data, 778-780

line, 353, 366-367, 388-389, 762

mixed, 354, 388, 393, 762

modifying axis, 368-370

name and store settings, 783-784

numbers scrunched along X-axis: Graphing Problem #6, 639-640

out of memory while printing: Printing Problem #14, 633

pie, 354, 388, 393-396, 762

print to encoded file for later printing, 733-734

printing, 27-28, 347-348, 400-405, 730-731

    bar graph without hatching: Graphing Problem #10, 643

    customized, 404

    text and graphs on same page: Graphing Problem #11, 644

    with default settings, 404

    with text, 339

ranges selection slow: Graphing Problem #1, 635

resetting current, 387

saving, 385-386, 768-769
     print settings, 404-405
scale number
     exponent, 372-373
     width, 374
scatter plot, 396
selecting
     color, 780-781
     data range, 785
     for printing, 756-757
     symbols and lines, 771-772
     type, 352-354, 760-763
selection of graph ranges slow: Graphing
     Problem #1, 635
separating bars: Graphing Problem #3, 636
settings, 385-386, 581-582
shading, 782-783
simple, 350-351
sizing printed, 402-403
software requirements, 348
specifying data range, 353-358
stacked-bar, 354, 388, 391-393, 762
symbols, 366-367
text, 381-383
troubleshooting, 635-644
turn off display, 582
types, 387-400
vary scale on y-axis, 775-777
viewing, 383-384, 767-768
     from worksheet, 383
     in color, 384
     in windows, 384, 643
worksheet ranges for x-axis and y-axis, 764-766
wrong automatic notation on y-axis: Graphing
     Problem #4, 636-638
x-axis labels overlap: Graphing Problem #5,
     638-639
XY, 353, 388, 396-399, 762
greater than (>) operator, 76
greater than or equal to (> =) operator, 76
grids, add to graph, 774
GROUP mode, 109, 111, 114, 124, 161, 182,
     472-473, 618, 656
GROUP status indicator, 51

H

hardware
     options, display, 683-684
     requirements, 16, 29, 30-32
          graphs, 348
     start-up settings, 671-673
hatches for graphs, 380-381, 782-783
headers
     printing on each page, 739-740
     reports, 321-322
headings, adding to graph and axes, 773

help, 52-55
     1-2-3 tutorial, 54-55
     on-screen, 53-54
Help (F1) key, 44, 52-54
Help Index screen, 53
HELP macro keyword, 518
HELP mode, 49
Hidden format, 173-174
hiding
     columns, 126, 677-679
     data in worksheets, 122-127
     worksheets, 126-127, 685
highlighting ranges, 97-101
HLCO (high-low-close-open) graph, 354, 388,
     399-400, 762
HLOOKUP function, 225, 232-234
HOME macro keyword, 519
horizontal
     bar chart, 166
     page breaks, 311-313
HOUR function, 237, 244

I

IF advanced macro command, 567-569
IF function, 217-220, 600-621
importing
     delimited files, 287
     files, 720-721
     formatting data, 813-814
     text files, 286
include-keys, 550
independent variable, 397
INDEX function, 226, 234-235
INDICATE advanced macro command, 577, 582
indicators *see* status indicators
indirect program branching, 562-563
INFO function, 226, 235-236, 609
input
     cell, 453, 468
     data with advanced macro commands, 544-551
     range
          remove records in criteria range, 806-807
          record search, 429
     value, 453
Ins (overtype/insert mode) key, 46, 825
INS macro keyword, 519
inserting
     records, 418-419
     rows and columns, 114-115
     worksheets, 114-115
Install (1-2-3 Access System) command, 38-39
Install program, 37, 39, 154, 824-826, 828
installing 1-2-3, 823-860
     copying files, 826
     problems, 597-598
     two display drivers, 840

INT function, 188-190
integers, 189-190
internal rate of return, 205-207
International formats, 177-178
International menu, 154
Invalid use of MENU macro command error message, 554
investments, terms, 212-213
invisible commands, 539
IRR function, 204-207
ISERR function, 217, 220-221
ISNA function, 217, 220-221
ISNUMBER function, 217, 222-225
ISRANGE function, 217, 221-222
ISSTRING function, 217, 222-225
iteration, 130-132

J

join formula in criteria range, 448-451
joining multiple databases, 448-451
jump directly to cell, 68
justifying text, 179-181

K

key field, 412, 448, 451
keyboards, 40-43
    alphanumeric, 42-43
    control, 860-862
    enhanced, 40, 43
    macros, 28-29
    numeric keypad, 43-46
keys
    . [period] (range address or POINT mode), 43
    / [slash] (start command from READY mode), 43
    < [less than sign] (start command from READY mode), 43
    Alt (change function of key), 42
    Alt-F1 (Compose), 44, 258
    Alt-F2 (Record), 44, 527-528, 531-533, 543, 655
    Alt-F3 (Run), 44, 519-521, 526-527, 543, 652, 655, 657
    Alt-F4 (Undo), 44, 80, 94, 134, 232
    Alt-F6 (Zoom), 44, 118
    Alt-F7 (App1), 44
    Alt-F8 (App2), 45
    Alt-F9 (App3), 45
    Alt-F10 (Addin), 45
    Backspace (erase or cancel), 43, 102
    Break (cancel and return to READY mode), 45
    Caps Lock (uppercase letters), 42
    Ctrl (change function of key), 42
    Ctrl-Break, 91
    cursor-movement, 43-46

Del (delete/reverse selection), 45
    editing, 81
    End, 65-68, 97
    Esc (cancel), 45, 91, 102
    F1 (Help), 44, 52-54
    F2 (Edit), 24, 44, 80-81, 140, 176, 284, 432, 533, 692, 712-713, 803
    F3 (Name), 44, 103, 110, 113, 268, 502, 521, 524, 652, 711, 713, 715, 722, 724
    F4 (Abs), 44, 79, 139-140, 144-145, 613
    F5 (GoTo), 44, 68, 84-86, 103, 122, 524
    F6 (Window), 44, 118-119
    F7 (Query), 44, 440-441, 648, 807
    F8 (Table), 44, 790, 794
    F9 (Calc), 44, 130, 147, 176, 228, 276, 281, 579, 602, 670, 701, 703, 716, 730-731, 733, 736, 768, 790
    F10 (Graph), 24, 44, 356, 383, 386, 401, 643, 765, 767-768
    function, 43-45
    Ins (overtype/insert mode), 46, 825
    moving around the worksheet, 64-65
    multiple worksheet movement, 84
    Num Lock (cursor-movement/numbers), 46
    Pause (pause actions), 46
    period (.), 98-101
    Scroll Lock (scroll window), 46-65
    Shift (change character produced), 42
    Shift-PrtSc (print one screen), 305, 308
    Shift-Tab (cell pointer one screen left), 42
    slash (/), 35
    sort, 420
    special, 45-46
    Tab (cell pointer one screen right), 42
    Tilde (~) [Enter], 515
keystrokes
    place in target cell, 545-546
    repeating in macros with Playback, 531
keywords in macros, 517-519, 859-860

L

L macro keyword, 517
Label format, 174
LABEL mode, 49, 63
label-fill characters, 468
labeled data tables, 466-479, 794-796
    column-variable range, 468
    formatting results, 470
    formula range, 467
    formula-label range, 467-468
    label-fill characters, 468
    more than three variables, 476-477
    positioning results, 468-470
    row-variable range, 468
    worksheet-variable range, 468
labeled data variables, input cells, 468

labels, 413, 546
    adding to graphs, 360-365
        below x-axis, 364
    aligning in cells, 689-692
    apostrophe (') in, 70, 599
    changing prefixes, 178-179
    points of data in graphs, 778-780
    entering in worksheets, 69-71
    text alignment in worksheet, 664-666
    typing and returning to EDIT mode: Data-Entry
        Problem #1, 599
Landscape mode, 332
LASTCELL macro keyword, 518
LASTFILE macro keyword, 518
LC macro keyword, 518
LEFT function, 245, 250
LEFT macro keyword, 517
legends, adding to graphs, 769-770
LENGTH function, 245, 251
less than (<) operator, 76
less than or equal to (< =) operator, 76
LET advanced macro command, 570-571
LF macro keyword, 518
line graphs, 353, 388-389, 762
linear equations, 494
lines in graphs, 366-367, 771-772
linking
    data, 17
    files, 60, 86-87
listing
    all specified records, 432-437
    files, 284-286
    names of files, 719-720
    selecting item from, 229-230
LMBCS (Lotus Multibyte Character Set)
    compose sequences, 845-852
    functions, 258-259
LN function, 188, 193
loan payments, calculating, 459-462
locking titles, 119-122
LOG function, 188, 193
logarithmic functions, 192-193
logical
    formulas, 73, 76
        operators, 76
    functions, 19, 217-225
LOOK advanced macro command, 544, 548-549
looping, controlling in programs, 569-570
Lotus 1-2-3 Release 3 see 1-2-3
LOTUS.BAT file, 38
LOWER function, 245, 253

M

macro commands see advanced macro commands
macro keywords, 517-519, 859-860
    /, 517

<, 517
repetition factor, 524-525
{ABS}, 519
{APP1}, 519
{APP2}, 519
{APP3}, 519
{APP4}, 519
{BACKSPACE}, 517
{BIGLEFT}, 518
{BIGRIGHT}, 518
{BREAK}, 518
{BS}, 517
{CALC}, 519
{CE}, 517, 525
{CLEARENTRY}, 517, 525
{D}, 517
{DEL}, 518
{DOWN}, 517
{EDIT}, 518
{END}, 518
{ESC}, 518
{EXTEND}, 519
{FC}, 518
{FF}, 518
{FILE}, 518
{FILE}{END}, 518
{FILE}{HOME}, 518
{FILE}{NS}, 518
{FILE}{PS}, 518
{FIRSTCELL}, 518
{FIRSTFILE}, 518
{GOTO}, 519, 524
{GRAPH}, 519
{HELP}, 518
{HOME}, 519
{INS}, 519
{L}, 517
{LASTCELL}, 518
{LASTFILE}, 518
{LC}, 518
{LEFT}, 517
{LF}, 518
{MENU}, 517
{NAME}, 519, 524
{NEXTFILE}, 518
{NEXTSHEET}, 518
{NF}, 518
{NS}, 518
{PF}, 518
{PGDN}, 519
{PGUP}, 519
{PREFILE}, 518
{PRVSHEET}, 518
{PS}, 518
{QUERY}, 519
{R}, 517

{RIGHT}, 517
{TABLE}, 519
{U}, 517
{UP}, 517
{WINDOW}, 519
{ZOOM}, 519
{{}, 517
{}}, 517
{~}, 517-518
macros, 513-592
    add another worksheet, 527
    Alt-key will not work: Macro Problem #1, 652
    Alt-letter, 520
    apostrophe (') in, 523
    automatic, 522-523
    blank row inserted while printing: Printing
        Problem #10, 632
    can't remember how it works: Macro Problem
        #4, 653-654
    checking range name, 652
    define printer setup strings, 525-526
    descriptive names for, 521-522
    destroyed worksheet or file: Macro Problem
        #7, 656
    documenting, 534-535, 654
        comments in worksheets, 535
        descriptive names, 534-535
        printout of macro, 535
    don't work in range names: Range Name
        Problem #2, 612-613
    entering text with, 515-516
    errors in, 533-534
    interrupt for data input, 550-551
    keyboard, 28-29
    keystrokes repeating with Playback, 531
    move to separate file and will not operate:
        Macro Problem #10, 657-658
    library, 525-527
    naming, 516, 519-522
    never works properly: Macro Problem #3, 653
    planning layout of, 524-525
    printing
        macro won't work after printing another
            report: Printing Problem #2, 628-629
        reports, 526
    protecting from change
        by user: Macro Problem #11, 658
        to file:
            Macro Problem #8, 656
            Macro Problem #9, 656-657
    recalculate worksheet, 526-527
    recording, 527-531
    refer to wrong addresses: Macro Problem #2,
        652
    remembering name: Macro Problem #6,
        655-656
    repeating commands, 516-517
    repetition factor, 530
    running, 519-520, 522
    testing, 527-533
    troubleshooting, 652-658
    won't execute commands: Macro Problem #5,
        655
    writing, 514-516
mantissa, 166
Manuscript, 39-40
margins
    changing, 741-742
    setting for printing reports, 328-329
mathematical functions, 18, 188-192
matrix algebra, 202
MAX function, 197, 199-200, 450
maximum values of arguments, 199-200
mean, 198, 480-481
MEM status indicator, 51
memory
    checking on available, 155
    clearing all files, 113
    display available, 683-684
    managing files, 262-263
    management problems, 609-610
    opening new file, 270
    out of memory: Memory Problem #1, 609-610
    requirements, 30
    usage, 862
MENU macro keyword, 517
MENU mode, 49, 63, 90
MENUBRANCH advanced macro command, 539,
    552, 554-555
MENUCALL advanced macro command, 552,
    556-557
menus
    1-2-3 Access System command, 38
    1-2-3 command, 20-22, 35
    Advanced, 382
    Cancel/Replace, 386
    Date, 167
    execute as subroutine for program, 556-557
    Features, 376-377
    File, 261-262
    Graph, 350, 371, 378-383, 387, 393-397
    International, 154
    Options, 360, 366
    Options Advanced, 334
    Parse, 497
    pointer, 63
    Print, 295-297, 298-300, 401, 525, 732
    Printer Options, 525
    Record, 528
    selecting
        commands from, 90-94
        items for programs, 554-555

Time, 170
Worksheet Window, 384
messages see error messages
metafile file format, 385
MID function, 245, 248-250
MIN function, 197, 199-200, 450
MINUTE function, 237, 244
mixed
    addressing, copying, 143-145
    graphs, 354, 388, 393, 762
MOD function, 189-190
MODE (DOS) command, 753
mode indicators, 48-50
    custom, 582
    reset, 582
modes
    EDIT, 49, 63, 70, 77-78, 80-81, 176, 525, 533,
        599-600
    ERROR, 52
    FILES, 49
    FIND, 49, 431-432
    GROUP, 109, 111, 114, 124, 161, 182,
        472-473, 618, 656
    HELP, 49
    LABEL, 49, 63
    Landscape, 332
    MENU, 49, 63, 90
    NAMES, 49
    POINT, 43, 50, 63, 77, 79, 87, 96, 99, 126-127,
        309, 357, 462, 522, 529
    Portrait, 332
    READY, 43, 48, 50, 63, 81-82, 90-91, 309, 401,
        431, 550
    RECALC, 653
    STAT, 50
    STEP, 527, 532-533, 543
    VALUE, 50, 63, 70
    WAIT, 50
modifying
    database, 418
    formulas, 150
    graph axes, 368-370
    records, 435-437, 807-808
modulus, 190
MONTH function, 237, 240-241
Move command, 22, 99, 132-136, 584, 604, 616,
    675, 677, 708-709, 770, 773
moving
    around worksheets, 62-68, 83-86
    between windows, 118-119
    cell entries, 22
    contents of
        cells, 132-133
        ranges, 133-137
    data, 708-709
Multiplan, 39

multiple
    criteria ranges, 440-441
    linear regression, 811-812
    regressions, 26
        analysis, 489-493
    worksheets, 59-62, 82-88
        commands, 20
        display, 61-62
        entering formulas, 85-86
        key movement, 84
        moving around, 83-86
        ranges, 106-107
multiplication (*) operator, 74
multiply column-and-row matrices of cells,
    810-811
multiuser environment, 290-291

N

N function, 246, 255
NA function, 226, 231-232
NA macro, 618
Name (F3) key, 44, 103, 110, 113, 268, 502, 521,
    524, 652, 711, 713, 715, 722, 724
NAME macro keyword, 519, 524
NAMES mode, 49
naming
    fields, 413, 417
    files, 263-264, 625
    graphs, 783-784
    macros, 516, 519-522
    print settings, 339-340, 748-750
    ranges, 21-22, 102-105, 693-697
natural
    logarithms, 193
    order of recalculation, 130
negative (-) operator, 74
negative numbers, displaying with minus sign or
    parentheses, 164
net present value, 209-210
networking, 290-862
NEXTFILE macro keyword, 518
NEXTSHEET macro keyword, 518
NF macro keyword, 518
nonsharable files, 290
not equal (<>) operator, 76
notes, appending to range names, 105
NOW function, 237, 241, 689
NPV function, 204, 209-210
NS macro keyword, 518
null string, 255, 607
Num Lock (cursor-movement/numbers) key, 46
NUM status indicator, 51
numbers
    adding to graphs, 360-361
    displaying, 162-163, 166
    enclosing in parentheses, 176

entering
    invalid, 176
    in worksheets, 71-73
equal numbers test as unequal: Function
    Problem #2, 620-621
ERR combining with strings: Function Problem
    #3, 621-622
filling ranges, 484-485
format for graph axis, 370-374
random, 191-192
rounding, 190-191
    errors: Function Problem #1, 620
numeric
    data input, 547-548
    format codes, CONTENTS advanced macro
        command, 574
    formulas, 73-75
        displaying, 172
        operators, 74-75
    keypad, 43-46
    values, 567-568
        display format in worksheet, 661-664

O

on-screen help, 53-54
one-key sorting, 420-421
ONERROR advanced macro command, 552,
    558-560
OPEN advanced macro command, 584-587
operating system
    accessing, 151
    OS/2, 29-31, 610
    required to run 1-2-3, 29-31
    run commands, 821
    selecting, 826
    starting 1-2-3 from, 34-36
operators, 17
    #AND#, 76, 219, 646
    #NOT#, 76, 219, 645-46
    #OR#, 76, 219, 646
    < (less than), 438
    <= (less than or equal to), 438
    <> (not equal to), 438
    = (equal to), 438
    > (greater than), 438
    >= (greater than or equal to), 438
    addition (+), 74
    ampersand (&) concatenation, 246, 622
    division (/), 74
    equal (=), 76
    exponentiation (^), 74
    greater than (>), 76
    greater than or equal to (>=), 76
    less than (<), 76
    less than or equal to (<=), 76
    logical formulas, 76

multiplication (*), 74
negative (-), 74
not equal (<>), 76
numeric formulas, 74-75
positive (+), 74
string formulas, 75-76
subtraction (-), 74
optimal recalculation, 129
Options Advanced menu, 334
Options menu, 360, 366
OR condition, criteria ranges, 442-444
OS/2 operating system, 29-31, 610, 826
output
    devices, multiple driver configuration (DCF)
        files: Installation Problem #2, 597-598
    range
        and database names do not match: Data
            Management Problem #5, 648
        copying records to, 803-806
        defining for records, 432-433
        filling and getting error message: Data
            Management Problem #6, 648
    required from database, 415-416
OVR status indicator, 51

P

page breaks, 628
    characters, 631-632
    horizontal, 311-313
    vertical, 313-316
    worksheets, 684-685
Page command, 630
pages
    automatically breaking for printing, 631
    blank between printed pages: Printing Problem
        #5, 630
    end of page, 738-739
    layout default options, 302-303
    number of lines per, 746
    setting length for printing reports, 328-329
PANELOFF advanced macro command, 577-579
PANELON advanced macro command, 577-578
Parentheses format, 176
Parse menu, 497
parsing data, 495-499, 813-814
PASSWORD PROTECTED message, 282-283
passwords, 128
    protecting files, 282-283
    saving files, 129
path, 265
Pause (pause actions) key, 46
pausing programs, 562
Percent format, 165
percentages, displaying, 165
period (.) key, 98-101
PF macro keyword, 518

PGDN macro keyword, 519
PGUP macro keyword, 519
PI function, 194
PIC file extension, 22, 264, 385, 673, 718-719, 726, 732, 769
pie graph, 354, 388, 393-396, 762
pitch, 632
plotters, multiple driver configuration (DCF) files: Installation Problem #2, 597-598
PMT function, 204, 208, 454, 457, 460-461, 473, 793
POINT mode, 43, 50, 63, 77, 79, 87, 96, 99, 126-127, 309, 357, 462, 522, 529
Portrait mode, 332
positive (+) operator, 74
PREFILE macro keyword, 518
present value of annuity, 211
preventing stopping programs before completion, 560-561
PRVSHEET macro keyword, 518
primary-key sorting, 420, 422
print buffer, 736
Print Cancel command, 342-343, 633, 735-736
Print commands, 27, 81, 101, 297, 614, 658, 729-759, 855-856
Print Encoded command, 401, 597, 633, 733-734
Print Encoded Align command, 755-756
Print Encoded Clear command, 754
Print Encoded Go command, 755
Print Encoded Hold command, 758-759
Print Encoded Image command, 756-757
Print Encoded Line command, 738
Print Encoded Options Advanced command, 750-753
Print Encoded Options Advanced Device Name command, 633
Print Encoded Options Borders command, 743-744
Print Encoded Options Footer command, 741
Print Encoded Options Header command, 739-740
Print Encoded Options Margins command, 741-742
Print Encoded Options Name command, 748-750
Print Encoded Options Name Use command, 633
Print Encoded Options Other command, 746-748
Print Encoded Options Pg-Length command, 746
Print Encoded Options Setup command, 744-745
Print Encoded Page command, 738-739
Print Encoded Quit command, 759
Print Encoded Range command, 736-738
Print File command, 323, 344, 584, 589, 633, 730-734
Print File Align command, 755-756
Print File Clear command, 754
Print File Go command, 755
Print File Hold command, 758-759

Print File Image command, 756-757
Print File Line command, 738
Print File Options Advanced command, 750-753
Print File Options Borders command, 743-744
Print File Options Footer command, 741
Print File Options Header command, 739-740
Print File Options Margins command, 741-742
Print File Options Name command, 748-750
Print File Options Other command, 746-748
Print File Options Other Unformatted command, 684, 742
Print File Options Pg-Length command, 746
Print File Options Setup command, 744-745
Print File Page command, 738-739
Print File Quit command, 759
Print File Range command, 736-738
print image file, 597
  won't reproduce:
      Printing Problem #12, 633
      Printing Problem #13, 633
Print menu, 295-300, 401, 525, 732
Print Name command, 727
Print Printer command, 309, 318, 325, 401
Print Printer Align command, 343, 738-739, 755-756
Print Printer Clear command, 343, 754
Print Printer Clear All command, 629, 754
Print Printer Clear Borders command, 325
Print Printer Go command, 755
Print Printer Hold command, 342, 758-759
Print Printer Image command, 756-757
Print Printer Image Current Go Quit command, 404
Print Printer Image Named-Graph command, 404
Print Printer Line command, 341, 343, 738
Print Printer Options Advanced command, 750-753
Print Printer Options Advanced Device command, 340
Print Printer Options Advanced Device Interface command, 598
Print Printer Options Advanced Device Name command, 401, 598, 633
Print Printer Options Advanced Image Density Draft command, 643
Print Printer Options Advanced Image Density Final command, 643
Print Printer Options Advanced Image Image-Sz command, 644
Print Printer Options Advanced Image Image-Sz Margin-Fill command, 643
Print Printer Options Advanced Image Image-Sz Reshape command, 404
Print Printer Options Advanced Layout Line-Spacing command, 632

Print Printer Options Advanced Layout Orientation Landscape command, 629
Print Printer Options Advanced Layout Pitch command, 632
Print Printer Options Advanced Priority command, 341
Print Printer Options Advanced Wait Yes command, 343
Print Printer Options Borders command, 743-744
Print Printer Options Footer command, 741
Print Printer Options Header command, 739-740
Print Printer Options Margins command, 741-742
Print Printer Options Name command, 748-750
Print Printer Options Name Create command, 629
Print Printer Options Name Use command, 629, 633
Print Printer Options Other command, 746-748
Print Printer Options Other Blank-Header Suppress command, 630
Print Printer Options Other Formatted command, 344
Print Printer Options Pg-Length command, 746
Print Printer Options Setup command, 525, 744-745
Print Printer Page command, 341, 403, 738-739
Print Printer Quit command, 759
Print Printer Range command, 102, 332, 406, 526, 644, 736-738
Print Printer Sample command, 382, 753, 757-758, 780, 782-783
Print Printer Sample Go command, 402
print ranges
    adjusting, 629-630
    multiple ranges: Printing Problem #8, 631
    skip data: Printing Problem #6, 630, 631
    specifying different: Printing Problem #1, 628
Print Resume command, 342-343, 633, 735, 757-758
Print Sample command, 329
print settings
    changing, 301-302
    clearing, 754
    default, 300-305
    naming, 748-750
        and saving, 339-340
    saving, 629
print spooler, 634
Print Suspend command, 342-343, 735
Print [P,E] command, 730
Print [P,E] Image command, 734
Print [P,E] Options Advanced AutoLf command, 340
Print [P,E] Options Advanced command, 329, 744
Print [P,E] Options Advanced Fonts command, 333
Print [P,E] Options Advanced Layout command, 329, 336

Print [P,E] Options Advanced Layout Orientation Landscape command, 403
Print [P,E] Options Name command, 339
Print [P,E] Options Setup command, 335
Print [P,E] Range command, 336
Print [P,E] Sample command, 750
Print [P,F,E] command, 322, 730
Print [P,F,E] Clear Borders command, 744
Print [P,F,E] Options command, 734
Print [P,F,E] Options Borders command, 737, 739
Print [P,F,E] Options Borders Columns command, 325, 744
Print [P,F,E] Options Borders Frame command, 328
Print [P,F,E] Options Borders Rows command, 740, 744
Print [P,F,E] Options Footer command, 741
Print [P,F,E] Options Other command, 323-324
Print [P,F,E] Options Other Blank-Header Suppress command, 303
Print [P,F,E] Options Other Unformatted command, 329
Print [P,F,E] Options Pg-Length command, 739
Print [P,F,E] Range command, 737
printer, 298
    align 1-2-3 line counter with, 755-756
    buffer, 633-634
    choosing, 340
    clearing options, 343-344
    control features, 744-745
    controlling paper movement, 340-341
    current settings, 300-301
    eject page, 738-739
    multiple driver configuration (DCF) files: Installation Problem #2, 597-598
    pausing, 342-343
    print sample page, 757-758
    put on hold, 758-759
    requirements, 31-32
    send data to, 755
    setup string, 335-338
    stopping, 343
    using all capabilities, 750-753
    won't print landscape mode: Printing Problem #3, 629
Printer Options menu, 525
printing
    automatically breaking pages, 631
    background, 342
    bar graph without hatching: Graphing Problem #10, 643
    blank
        pages between printed pages: Printing Problem #5, 630
        row inserted through macro or database: Printing Problem #10, 632

borders, 325-328
    columns and rows, 325-327
    frame borders, 328
canceling, 736
    and printer doesn't stop: Printing Problem
        #15, 633-634
cell contents, 323-324
close print job, 759
compressed print wraps to next line: Printing
    Problem #11, 632
control printer features, 744-745
define worksheet area to be printed, 736-738
end of page, 738-739
footers on each page, 741
form and formatting of cells, 746-748
graphs, 27-28, 347-348, 400-405
    and finding error: Graphing Problem #9,
        643
    changing appearance, 402
    customized, 404
    density, 403
    rotating graph, 403
    saving settings, 404-405
    sizing graph, 402-403
    with default settings, 404
headers on each page, 739-740
holding print job, 342
information gets separated: Printing Problem
    #9, 631-632
insert blank lines, 738
macro won't work after printing another
    report: Printing Problem #2, 628-629
multiple ranges, 316-320
    excluding columns and rows, 318-319
    hiding
        portions, 318-320
        ranges, 320
numbering multiple copies of reports: Printing
    Problem #7, 631
one screen of data, 305, 308
out of memory while printing graph: Printing
    Problem #14, 633
pause, 735
print image file won't reproduce:
    Printing Problem #12, 633
    Printing Problem #13, 633
printer won't print landscape mode: Printing
    Problem #3, 629
reports, 27-28, 295-345
    changing
        line spacing, 332
        pitch settings, 330
    color, 338
    enhancing layout, 329
    macro, 526
    margins, 328-329

multiple-page, 309-316
one page or less, 308-309
page
    length, 328-329
    orientation, 332
    runs off the page: Printing Problem #4,
        629-630
    selecting fonts, 333-335
resume after pausing, 735
row and column headings on every page,
    743-744
sample page from printer, 757-758
select graph, 756-757
setting priorities, 341-342
skip data in print range: Printing Problem #6,
    630-631
specifying print ranges:
    Printing Problem #1, 628
    Printing Problem #8, 631
temporarily stop, 735
text and graphs, 339
    on same page: Graphing Problem #11, 644
troubleshooting, 628-634
using all printer's capabilities, 750-753
worksheet
    worksheets as ASCII text file, 731-733
    contents and graphs, 730-731
        to encoded file for later printing,
            733-734
PRN file extension, 22, 264, 286, 298, 344,
    718-720, 726, 731-732, 738
programs
    advanced macro command, 542-543
    controlling
        looping, 569-570
        with advanced macro commands, 551-567
    dBASE II, 39-40, 495
    dBASE III, 39-40, 290, 495, 649-650
    dBASE III Plus, 39-40, 495
    DESQView, 610
    DisplayWrite, 39-40
    enhancement commands, 577-584
    evaluate numeric and string values, 567-568
    executing
        menu as subroutine, 556-557
        named commands in, 566-567
    indirect branching, 562-563
    Install, 37, 39, 154, 824-826, 828
    Manuscript, 39-40
    Multiplan, 39
    pass control to cell address, 552-554
    pausing, 562
        while information is entered, 544-545
    prevent stopping before completion, 560-561
    return from subroutine to program, 557-558
    selecting items from menus, 554-555

sidestepping system errors, 558-560
stopping before completion, 561
terminate unconditionally, 558
Translate, 37, 39-40
Windows, 610
PROPER function, 246, 253
protecting
cells, 123-124
data in worksheets, 122-125
files and worksheets, 23
ranges, 699-700
worksheets, 667-668
PS macro keyword, 518
PUT advanced macro command, 570, 572
PV function, 204, 211

Q

Query (F7) key, 44, 440-441, 648, 807
QUERY macro keyword, 519
question mark (?) wild-card character, 269, 438, 712
QUIT advanced macro command, 552, 558
Quit command, 35-36, 38-39, 94, 151, 263, 291, 821-822

R

R macro keyword, 517
RAND function, 189, 191-192
random numbers, 191-192
Range command, 20-21, 99, 686-705, 793, 855
Range Erase command, 21, 91, 97, 99, 110, 136, 280-281, 434, 534, 574, 677, 685, 692-693, 803
Range Format command, 79, 158, 161, 164, 169, 171, 173, 191, 239, 324, 417, 498, 573, 661, 686-689, 726-727, 775-776
Range Format +/- command, 166
Range Format Automatic command, 599
Range Format Currency command, 165
Range Format Date command, 167, 169, 239, 627
Range Format Date Time command, 167, 170-171, 242-243
Range Format Fixed command, 159, 163
Range Format General command, 163
Range Format Hidden command, 125, 173, 320, 462, 688, 693
Range Format Label command, 599
Range Format Other Automatic command, 174, 176, 487, 665-666
Range Format Other Color Negative command, 177
Range Format Other Color Reset command, 177
Range Format Other Label command, 174, 691
Range Format Other Parentheses command, 176-177
Range Format Percent command, 165

Range Format Reset command, 125, 161, 320, 684, 693
Range Format Sci command, 166
Range Format Text command, 439, 462, 789-793, 795
Range Input command, 124-125, 550, 584, 668, 681, 699-701
Range Justify command, 180, 697-698
Range Label command, 178-179, 664-665, 689-692, 727
Range Label Center command, 691
Range Name command, 289, 677, 693-697, 715, 727
Range Name Create command, 104, 449, 515, 526, 652, 696-697, 715- 716, 790, 792
Range Name Delete command, 105
Range Name Labels command, 104-105, 715-716
Range Name Labels Right command, 104, 517, 523, 530, 555, 564
Range Name Note command, 534-535, 727
Range Name Note Create command, 105
Range Name Note Table command, 105, 612
Range Name Reset command, 105
Range Name Table command, 696-697, 747
Range Prot command, 23, 123, 173, 688, 693, 699-700, 727
Range Search command, 99, 101, 148-150, 704-705
Range Trans command, 148, 491, 650, 702-704, 816
Range Unprot command, 123, 550, 617, 658, 668-669, 693, 699-701, 727
Range Value command, 145-147, 434, 576, 610, 614, 701-702
ranges, 20-22, 95-107
all records selected despite criteria range: Data Management Problem #1, 645
column-variable, 468
copying
contents of, 140-143
source to destination, 575-576
erasing, 110, 692-693
cells in, 91
filling, 484-488
with data, 786-788
with dates or times, 486-488
with formulas and functions, 486
with numbers, 484-485
finding dimensions of, 230-231
formats, 156-183, 686-689
formula, 467
formula-label, 467-468
hiding while printing multiple ranges, 320
highlighting, 97-101
moving contents, 133-137
multiple worksheets, 106-107

names, 21-22, 68, 102-105, 693-697
   appending notes, 105
   checking for, 221-222
   copying with, 145
   macros and formulas don't work: Range
      Name Problem #2, 612-613
   no longer valid: Range Name Problem #1,
      611-612
   problems, 611-613
   table, 105
no records selected despite criteria range: Data
   Management Problem #2, 645-646
pointing to address, 96
printing multiple, 316-320
protecting/unprotecting, 699-700
records to be searched, 799
remembered, 101-102
row-variable, 468
search criteria for records, 799-801
three-dimensional, 106
typing address, 96
value, 809
worksheet-variable, 468
wrapping text to fit, 697-698
RATE function, 204, 207
READ advanced macro command, 585, 588
READLN advanced macro command, 585, 588-589
READY mode, 43, 48, 50, 63, 81-82, 90-91, 309,
   401, 431, 550
RECALC advanced macro command, 577, 583-584,
   603, 653
RECALC mode, 653
RECALCCOL advanced macro command, 577,
   583-584, 653
recalculate worksheet, 583-584, 669-671
recalculation, 129-132
   automatic, 129
   background, 129-130
   circular references, 130-132
   incorrect values: Recalculation Problem #2,
      615
   natural order, 130
   optimal, 129
   problems, 614-615
      circular references: Circular Reference
         Problem #3, 602-603
   recalculation time extended: Recalculation
      Problem #1, 614
Record (Alt-F2) key, 44, 527-528, 531-533, 543
Record menu, 528
recording macros, 527-531
records, 412
   adding out of order to dBASE III: Data
      Management Problem #9, 649-650
   all records
      but first record selected: Data Management
         Problem #4, 647

despite criteria range: Data Management
   Problem #1, 645
buffer, 527
copying to output range, 803-806
criteria range of search, 429-432
defining output range, 432-433
deleting specified, 447-448
editing, 807-808
error message when trying to extract: Data
   Management Problem #3, 646-647
extracting
   and modifying, then getting error when
      replacing: Data Managment Problem
      #11, 650
   unique, 446-447
input range of search, 429
inserting and deleting, 418-419
listing all specified, 432-437
location to copy found records, 801-802
meet conditions in criteria range, 802-803
modifying, 435-437, 807-808
none selected despite criteria range: Data
   Management Problem #2, 645-646
only record selected: Data Management
   Problem #4, 647
range contains search criteria, 799-801
remove from input range records in criteria
   range, 806-807
returning to presort order, 426
searching for, 427-448
   minimum requirements, 428
sorting, 420-426
specifying range to be searched, 799
referencing cells, indirectly, 226
regression, multiple-linear, 811-812
relative cell addressing, 78-79, 138-139, 625-626
   problems, 613
   references, 605-647
remainder, 190
renaming files, 617
REPEAT function, 246, 253-254
repetition factor, 530
   macro keywords, 524-525
REPLACE function, 245, 250-251
replacing
   data, 148-150
   text, 704-705
reports
   blank headers, 323
   designing, 321-329
   enhancing, 329-335
   headers and footers, 321-322
   including graphs, 405-407
   number multiple copies: Printing Problem #7,
      631
   printing, 27-28, 295-345

macro, 526
    multiple-page, 309-316
    one page or less, 308-309
    runs off the page: Printing Problem #4,
       629-630
  unformatted or formatted output, 323
RESTART advanced macro command, 552,
  565-566
results area, 453
RETURN advanced macro command, 552, 557-558
RIGHT function, 245, 250
RIGHT macro keyword, 517
Range Format Hidden command, 685
RO status indicator, 51
rotating printed graphs, 403
ROUND function, 158, 189-191, 602, 620-621
rounding numbers, 190-191
rows, 656-657
  converting to columns, 148
  deleting, 109-111, 676-677
  display headings, 680-681
  erasing, 109
  excluding while printing multiple ranges,
    318-319
  inserting, 114-115, 674-676
  printing
    borders, 325-327
    headings on every page, 743-744
  unable to insert in worksheet: ERR Problem
    #5, 608
  variable range, 468
ROWS function, 226, 230-231
RTF/DCA file format, 39-40
Run (Alt-F3) key, 44, 519-521, 526-527, 543, 652,
  655, 657

S

S function, 246, 255, 607, 622-623
saving
  files, 94-95, 265-267, 712-714
    under different names, 625
    with passwords, 129
  graphs, 385-386, 768-769
  print settings, 339-340, 629
scale
  indicator for graph axis, 371
  number
    exponent for graphs, 372-373
    width for graphs, 374
scatter plot graphs, 396
Scientific format, 166
screens
  display, 46-50
  freezing
    lower part of display, 579-580
    titles, 119-122

Help Index, 53
  splitting display, 116-118
  unfreeze lower part of display, 580
Scroll Lock (scroll window) key, 46, 65
SCROLL status indicator, 52, 65
scrolling
  multiple windows simultaneously: Split Screen
    Problem #1, 615-616
  synchronized, 117
sealing files, 128, 727-728
searching database for records, 427-448
SECOND function, 237, 244
secondary-key sorting, 422
semicolon (;), adding notes to cells, 79
serial numbers, converting
  date strings to, 239-240
  date values to, 238-239
  time values, 242-243
  to dates, 240-241
  to time values, 244
serial values, converting time strings to, 243-244
SETPOS advanced macro command, 585, 590-591
setup string
  compressed print wraps to next line: Printing
    Problem #11, 632
  printer, 335-338
sharing files, 724-725
SHEETS function, 226, 230-231
Shift (change character produced) key, 42
Shift-PrtSc (print one screen) keys, 305, 308
Shift-Tab (cell pointer one screen left) keys, 42
simultaneous equations, 26
SIN function, 194-195
sine, 195
slash (/) key, 35
SLN function, 205, 214
software requirements, 16
  graphs, 348
sorting
  database, 797-798
  extra-key, 423-424
  keys, 420
  one-key, 420-421
  order, 424-426
  primary-key, 420-422
  records, 420-426
  secondary-key, 422
  two-key, 422
source cell store contents in destination cell,
  572-573
special
  functions, 19, 225-236
  keys, 45-46
  operators for searching database
    #AND#, 445
    #NOT#, 445-446

#OR#, 445
splitting screen, 116-118
    problems, 615-616
SQRT function, 189, 192
square root, 192
stacked-bar graphs, 354, 388, 391-393, 762
stacking, 565
standard deviation, 200-201, 480-481
STAT mode, 50
statistical functions, 18, 197-203
status indicators, 50-52
    CALC, 51, 130, 614
    CAP, 51
    CIRC, 51, 130
    CMD, 51
    END, 51, 65-67
    FILE, 51
    GROUP, 51
    MEM, 51
    NUM, 51
    OVR, 51
    RO, 51
    SCROLL, 52, 65
    SST, 52
    STEP, 52
    ZOOM, 52, 118
STD function, 197, 200-201
STDS function, 197, 200-201
Step (Alt-F2) key, 655
STEP mode, 527, 532-533, 543
STEP status indicator, 52
stopping programs before completion, 561
straight-line depreciation, 214
STRING function, 246, 256, 622
strings, 245
    comparing, 251-252
    computing length, 251
    concatenating, 75-76
    converting
        case of strings, 253
        to values, 256-257
        values to, 256
    combining with numbers, then getting ERR:
        Function Problem #3, 621-622
    extracting
        from left and right, 250
        one from another, 248-250
    formulas, 73, 75-76
        displaying, 172
        ERR after cell or range erasure: ERR
            Problem #3, 606-607
        operators, 75-76
    functions, 20, 245-257
    locating one within another, 247-249
    null, 607
    place in target cell, 570-571

removing
    blank spaces, 254
    nonprintable characters, 257
repeating within cells, 253-254
replacing string within a string, 250-251
searching with formulas, 444-445
testing for, 255
values, 567-568
subdirectories, 265, 624
    retrieving files from, 269-270
    \123R3, 34
subroutines, 556-557
    associating arguments, 563-565
    cancel, 557-558, 565-566
substringing, 248
subtraction (-) operator, 74
suffixes
    :STRING, 571
    :VALUE, 571
SUM function, 21-22, 132, 134, 136, 197, 201-202,
    450, 601, 606, 696, 707
sum-of-the-years'-digits depreciation, 215-216
SUMPRODUCT function, 197, 202
SYD function, 205, 215-216
symbols in graphs, 366-367, 771-772
synchronized scrolling, 117
syntax, advanced macro commands, 541-542
system
    configuration, DOS, 823-824
    errors, sidestepping in programs, 558-560
    hangs at blank screen: Installation Problem #1,
        597
    information, current session, 235-236
SYSTEM advanced macro command, 552, 566-567
System command, 151, 624, 634, 718, 821

T

Tab (cell pointer one screen right) key, 42
Table (F8) key, 44, 790, 794
TABLE macro keyword, 519
tables
    break link from external database, 818
    creating in external database, 504-507, 816-818
    creation string, 501
    definition, 501, 505
    deleting from external database, 508, 818
    duplicating from external database, 505
    files, 284-286, 725-727
    listing from external database, 503-504
    looking up entries, 232-234
    name in external database, 501
TAN function, 194-195
tangent, 195
target cell
    keystroke in, 545-546
    values in, 570-572

templates
    erasing data to use template again: Template
        Problem #1, 617
    problems, 617-618
TERM function, 204, 212-213
term of investment, 212-213
terminate program unconditionally, 558
testing macros, 527-533
text
    change font, size, and color for graphs, 781-782
    entering with macro, 515-516
    file, 298
    find or replace, 704-705
    in graphs, 381-383
    justifying, 179-181
    printing with graphs, 339
    wrapping to fit in range, 697-698
Text format, 172-173
THEN clause, 568
three-dimensional ranges, 106
tilde (~) wild-card character, 438
time
    converting
        serial numbers to values, 244
        strings to serial values, 243-244
        values to serial numbers, 242-243
    filling ranges, 486-488
    finding current, 241
    fractions, 170
    functions, 237-245
Time Format, 167-172
TIME function, 237, 242-243, 689
Time menu, 170
TIMEVALUE function, 237, 243-244, 689
titles
    freezing on-screen, 119-122
    locking, 119-122
TODAY function, 237, 241
tones, producing from computer, 577-578
Too many records for Output range error message,
    648
totaling values, 201-202
transferring
    databases, 290
    files, 286-290
Translate (1-2-3 Access System) command, 38-40,
    282, 826
Translate program, 37, 39-40, 288-289
trapping errors, 231-232
TREE (DOS) command, 624
trigonometric functions, 194-196
TRIM function, 246-254
troubleshooting, 595-658
    circular references, 600-603
    column width problems, 618
    command problems, 611-619

data
    destruction problem, 616-617
    entry problems, 599-600
    management, 645-651
    ERR problems, 604-608
    file operations, 624-627
    function problems, 620-623
    graphing, 635-644
    installation problems, 597-598
    macros, 652-658
    memory management problems, 609-610
    printing, 628-634
    range name problems, 611-613
    recalculation problems, 614-615
    relative and absolute cell addressing problems,
        613
    split screen problems, 615-616
    template problems, 617-618
    worksheet problems, 599-608
TRUE function, 217, 221
two-key sorting, 422
TYPE (DOS) command, 721, 732
type 1 data table, 453-456, 789-790
type 2 data table, 456-458, 791-792
type 3 data table, 458-466, 792-794
type-ahead buffer, 548-549

U

U macro keyword, 517
Undo (Alt-F4) key, 44, 80-82, 94, 134, 232
UP macro keyword, 517
UPPER function, 245, 253

V

VALUE function, 246, 256-257
VALUE mode, 50, 63, 70
values
    converting
        strings to, 256-257
        to strings, 256
    extracting from worksheet, 276
    formulas converting to, 145-147
    incorrect after recalculation: Recalculation
        Problem #2, 615
    place in target cell, 570-572
    range, 809
    relationships between, 489
    testing for, 255
    totaling, 201-202
VAR function, 197, 202-203
variable-declining balance depreciation, 216-217
variables, 452
    dependent, 397
    independent, 397
    using more than three, 476-477
variance, 202-203, 480-481

VARS function, 197, 202-203
VDB function, 205, 216-217
vertical page breaks, 313, 315-316
video display requirements, 31
viewing
    graphs, 383-384
    worksheets, 115-119
VLOOKUP function, 226, 232-234

W

WAIT advanced macro command, 552, 562
WAIT mode, 50
what-if analysis, 17-18, 26, 793
wild-card characters
    asterisk (*), 269, 438, 712
    criteria ranges, 438
    question mark (?), 269, 438, 712
    retrieving files with, 269
    tilde (~), 438
Window (F6) key, 44, 118-119
Window Graph command, 643
WINDOW macro keyword, 519
windows, 610
    moving between, 118-119
    multiple windows scroll simultaneously: Split
        Screen Problem #1, 615-616
    viewing graphs, 384, 643
    zooming, 118-119
WINDOWSOFF advanced macro command, 577,
    579-580
WINDOWSON advanced macro command, 577,
    580
WK1 file extension, 22, 40, 264, 713
WK3 file extension, 22, 263, 711, 713
WKS file extension, 264
worksheet, 15, 58-88
    add another worksheet macro, 527
    basics, 57-88
    changing
        all in file, 111
        display format, 115-116
    columns are default width: Column Width
        Problem #1, 618
    consolidation, 106
    data missing: Template Problem #2, 617-618
    default for new, 162-163
    defining area to be printed, 736-738
    deleting, 109, 112-113, 676-677
        columns, rows, 676-677
    destroyed by macro: Macro Problem #7, 656
    destroying parts of: Data Destruction Problem
        #1, 616-617
    displaying
        different views, 681-683
        formats and hardware start-up settings,
            671-673

    for numeric values and formulas,
        661-664
    frame, 580
    global settings, 683-684
    graph in, 119
    hardware options, 683-684
    row and column headings, 680-681
    editing data, 79-81
    entering
        data, 68-79
        formulas, 73-78
        labels, 69-71
        numbers, 71-73
    erasing, 109, 679-680
        range of cells, 574-575
    extracting
        formulas, 274-275
        values, 276
    file with formulas, 86
    formatting current, 161
    frame display suppressed, 580
    global formats, 156-158
    hiding/displaying, 126-127, 685
        data, 122-127
    inserting, 114-115
    inserting blank row, blank column, or blank
        worksheet, 674-676
    linking with formulas, 87-88
    moving around, 62-68
    multiple, 59-62, 82-88
    page breaks, 684-685
    print
        as ASCII text file, 731-733
        contents, 730-731
        to encoded file for later printing, 733-734
    problems, 599-608
    protecting, 23, 667-668
        data, 122-125
    recalculating, 583-584, 669-671
        macro, 526-527
    setting
        column width, 667
        global defaults, 154-155
    suppress zeros, 668-669
    text label alignment, 664-666
    transferring format changes to other
        worksheets, 674
    Undo feature, 80-82
    updating database, 508-509
    variable range, 468
    viewing, 115-119
        graphs, 383
Worksheet commands, 21, 90, 93, 659-685,
    854-855
Worksheet Column command, 667, 727

Worksheet Column Column-Range command, 677-679

Worksheet Column Column-Range Reset-Width command, 109

Worksheet Column Column-Range Set Width command, 109

Worksheet Column Display command, 319, 631, 677-679

Worksheet Column Hide command, 126, 319, 631, 677-679, 685, 744

Worksheet Column Reset-Width command, 109, 677-679

Worksheet Column Set-Width command, 109, 228, 417, 663, 667, 677-679

Worksheet Column Set-Width 14 command, 516

Worksheet Delete command, 605, 679, 718, 770, 773

Worksheet Delete Column command, 419, 656, 676-677

Worksheet Delete File command, 83, 112, 263, 284, 291, 610, 633, 676-677, 693, 711

Worksheet Delete Row command, 110, 313, 419, 447, 608, 656, 676-677, 684

Worksheet Delete Sheet command, 83, 112, 676-677, 693

Worksheet Erase command, 263, 270, 291, 668, 679-680, 693, 711, 718

Worksheet Erase Yes command, 113, 633

Worksheet Global command, 342, 727

Worksheet Global Column-Width command, 20, 109, 228, 667, 678

Worksheet Global Default command, 93, 154, 300, 671-673

Worksheet Global Default Autoexec command, 523, 526, 543

Worksheet Global Default Dir command, 265, 624, 711, 722

Worksheet Global Default Ext List command, 264, 284, 727

Worksheet Global Default Ext Save command, 264

Worksheet Global Default Graph command, 355, 385, 727, 769

Worksheet Global Default Graph Columnwise command, 356

Worksheet Global Default Graph PIC command, 284

Worksheet Global Default Other Beep command, 155

Worksheet Global Default Other International command, 177, 663, 689

Worksheet Global Default Other International Currency command, 164, 176

Worksheet Global Default Other International Date command, 168, 240

Worksheet Global Default Other International Negative Parentheses command, 164

Worksheet Global Default Other International Negative Sign command, 164

Worksheet Global Default Other International Punctuation command, 187

Worksheet Global Default Other International Time command, 170, 244

Worksheet Global Default Other Undo Disable command, 80

Worksheet Global Default Other Undo Enable command, 80, 82, 692

Worksheet Global Default Printer command, 301-302, 305, 312, 321, 754

Worksheet Global Default Printer AutoLf command, 340

Worksheet Global Default Printer Interface command, 598

Worksheet Global Default Printer Name command, 598

Worksheet Global Default Printer Setup command, 335

Worksheet Global Default Printer Wait Yes command, 343

Worksheet Global Default Status command, 155, 401

Worksheet Global Default Update command, 80, 155, 177, 264-265, 305, 509, 673, 711, 754, 820

Worksheet Global Format command, 79, 160-161, 661-664, 686, 688-689, 775

Worksheet Global Format Currency command, 528

Worksheet Global Format Date command, 167

Worksheet Global Format Date Time command, 167

Worksheet Global Format Hidden command, 685, 693

Worksheet Global Format Other Automatic command, 665-666

Worksheet Global Format Other Color Negative command, 338

Worksheet Global Format Other Parentheses command, 176

Worksheet Global Group command, 20, 109, 161, 674, 688

Worksheet Global Group Disable command, 473

Worksheet Global Group Enable command, 83, 111, 472

Worksheet Global Label command, 664-666

Worksheet Global Label-Prefix command, 690-691

Worksheet Global Prot command, 23, 124, 667-669, 688, 699-701, 727

Worksheet Global Prot Disable command, 692, 698

Worksheet Global Prot Enable command, 123-124, 617, 658, 669
Worksheet Global Recalc command, 509, 669-671
Worksheet Global Recalc Iteration command, 132
Worksheet Global Recalc Manual command, 130, 527, 614
Worksheet Global Width command, 618
Worksheet Global Zero command, 182, 668-669
Worksheet Global Zero Label command, 182
Worksheet Hide command, 685, 727
Worksheet Hide Enable command, 126
Worksheet Insert command, 708-709, 770, 773
Worksheet Insert Column command, 24, 114, 419, 656, 674-676
Worksheet Insert Row command, 24, 114, 418, 656, 674-676, 745
Worksheet Insert Sheet command, 83, 114, 618, 674-676
Worksheet Insert Sheet After command, 460, 527
Worksheet Insert Sheet After 1 command, 472
Worksheet Page command, 313, 628, 632, 656, 684-685, 737, 739
Worksheet Status command, 130, 132, 155, 601, 609, 665, 667, 671, 683-684, 700
Worksheet Titles command, 120, 457, 680-681
Worksheet Titles Both command, 121
Worksheet Titles Clear command, 122, 681
Worksheet Titles Horizontal command, 122
Worksheet Titles Vertical command, 122
Worksheet Window command, 384, 681-683
Worksheet Window Clear command, 118, 683
Worksheet Window Display command, 92, 832
Worksheet Window Display Primary command, 116
Worksheet Window Display Secondary command, 116
Worksheet Window Graph command, 119, 384, 768
Worksheet Window Horizontal command, 116

Worksheet Window Perspective command, 83, 118, 460, 681
Worksheet Window Sync command, 117
Worksheet Window Unsync command, 117, 616
Worksheet Window Vertical command, 116
WR1 file extension, 264
WRITE advanced macro command, 585, 589-590
write string to file, 589-590
WRITELN advanced macro command, 585
WRK file extension, 264

X-Y-Z

x-axis, 348, 349
  labels overlap: Graphing Problem #5, 638-639
  numbers scrunched: Graphing Problem #6, 639-640
  specify range for graph, 764-766
/xc command, 540
/xg command, 540
/xi command, 540
/xl command, 540, 547
/xm command, 540
/xn command, 540, 548
/xq command, 540
/xr command, 540
XY graph, 353, 388, 396-399, 762
y-axis, 348-349
  adding second to graph, 374-375
  specify range for graph, 764-766
  vary scale of graph, 775-777
  wrong automatic notation: Graphing Problem #4, 636-638
YEAR function, 237, 240-241
years, 360 day, 238
zeros, suppressing display, 182, 668-669
Zoom (Alt-F6) key, 44, 118
ZOOM macro keyword, 519
ZOOM status indicator, 52, 118
zooming windows, 118-119

More Computer Knowledge from Que

SELECT QUE BOOKS TO INCREASE
YOUR PERSONAL COMPUTER PRODUCTIVITY

Upgrading to
1-2-3 Release 3

Developed by
Que Corporation

An excellent introduction to new Release 3, this informative text smoothes your transition from Release 2.01 with helpful techniques and troubleshooting tips. *Upgrading to 1-2-3 Release 3* has the answers to all your upgrading questions!

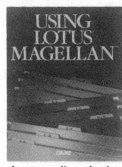

Using Lotus Magellan

David Gobel

The ultimate book on Lotus' new file management software! Covers Magellan's file viewing capability and shows how to edit and print files, organize data, index files, use "fuzzy searching," work with macros, and set up Magellan for network use.

Upgrading and
Repairing PCs

by Scott Mueller

A comprehensive resource to personal computer upgrade, repair, maintenance, and troubleshooting. All types of IBM computers—from the original PC to the new PS/2 models—are covered, as are major IBM compatibles. You will learn about the components inside your computers, as well as how to use this information to troubleshoot problems and make informed decisions about upgrading.

dBASE IV Handbook,
3rd Edition

by George T. Chou, Ph.D.

Learn dBASE IV quickly with Que's new *dBASE IV Handbook*, 3rd Edition! dBASE expert George Chou leads you step-by-step from basic database concepts to advanced dBASE features, using a series of Quick Start tutorials. Experienced dBASE users will appreciate the extensive information on the new features of dBASE IV, including the new user interface, the query-by-example mode, and the SQL module. Complete with comprehensive command and function reference sections, *dBASE IV Handbook*, 3rd Edition, is an exhaustive guide to dBASE IV!

BUSINESS REPLY MAIL
First Class Permit No. 9918   Indianapolis, IN

Postage will be paid by addressee

11711 N. College
Carmel, IN 46032

NO POSTAGE
NECESSARY
IF MAILED
IN THE
UNITED STATES

BUSINESS REPLY MAIL
First Class Permit No. 9918   Indianapolis, IN

Postage will be paid by addressee

11711 N. College
Carmel, IN 46032

Here's a tiny sample of the kinds of articles you'll read in every issue of *Absolute Reference*:

Discover the incredible power of macros— shortcuts for hundreds of applications and subroutines.

- A macro for formatting text
- Monitoring preset database conditions with a macro
- Three ways to design macro menus
- Building macros with string formulas
- Having fun with the marching macro
- Using the ROWs macro
- Generating a macro for tracking elapsed time

New applications and new solutions—every issue gives you novel ways to harness 1-2-3 and Symphony

- Creating customized menus for your spreadsheets
- How to use criteria to unlock your spreadsheet program's data management power
- Using spreadsheets to monitor investments
- Improving profits with more effective sales forecasts
- An easy way to calculate year-to-date performance
- Using /**D**ata **F**ill to streamline counting and range filling

Extend your uses—and your command— of spreadsheets

- Printing spreadsheets sideways can help sell your ideas
- How to add goal-seeking capabilities to your spreadsheet

- Hiding columns to create custom worksheet printouts
- Lay out your spreadsheet for optimum memory management
- Toward an "intelligent" spreadsheet
- A quick way to erase extraneous zeros

Techniques for avoiding pitfalls and repairing th damage when disaster occurs

- Preventing and trapping errors in your worksheet
- How to create an auditable spreadsheet
- Pinpointing specific errors in your spreadsheets
- Ways to avoid failing formulas
- Catching common debugging and data-entry errors
- Detecting data-entry errors
- Protecting worksheets from accidental (or deliberate) destruction
- Avoiding disaster with the /**S**ystem command

Objective product reviews—we accept *no advertising*, so you can trust our editors' outspoken opinions

- Metro Desktop Manager
- Freelance Plus
- Informix

- 4Word, InWord, Write-in
- Spreadsheet Analyst
- 101 macros for 1-2-3

Mail this card today!